ISBN 978-0-282-43973-6
PIBN 10851831

1 MONTH OF
FREE
READING

at

www.ForgottenBooks.com

By purchasing this book you are eligible for one month membership to ForgottenBooks.com, giving you unlimited access to our entire collection of over 1,000,000 titles via our web site and mobile apps.

To claim your free month visit: www.forgottenbooks.com/free851831

English
Français
Deutsche
Italiano
Español
Português

www.forgottenbooks.com

Mythology Photography **Fiction**
Fishing Christianity **Art** Cooking
Essays Buddhism Freemasonry
Medicine **Biology** Music **Ancient
Egypt** Evolution Carpentry Physics
Dance Geology **Mathematics** Fitness
Shakespeare **Folklore** Yoga Marketing
Confidence Immortality Biographies
Poetry **Psychology** Witchcraft
Electronics Chemistry History **Law**
Accounting **Philosophy** Anthropology
Alchemy Drama Quantum Mechanics
Atheism Sexual Health **Ancient History**
Entrepreneurship Languages Sport
Paleontology Needlework Islam
Metaphysics Investment Archaeology
Parenting Statistics Criminology
Motivational

SYSTEM

OF

PHRENOLOGY

BY

GEORGE COMBE.

RES NON VERBA QUÆSO.

THE ONLY COMPLETE AMERICAN EDITION, BEING FROM THE FOURTH

AND LAST (REVISED AND ENLARGED) EDINBURGH EDITION.

WITH UPWARD OF ONE HUNDRED ENGRAVINGS.

NEW YORK:

WILLIAM H. COLYER,

No. 5 Hague-street.

BOSTON:

LEWIS & SAMPSON.

1843.

PREFACE

TO THE SECOND EDITION.

THE following are the circumstances which led to the publication of the present work:

My first information concerning the system of Drs. Gall and Spurzheim was derived from No. 49 of the Edinburgh Review. Led away by the boldness of that piece of criticism, I regarded the doctrines as contemptibly absurd, and their authors as the most disingenuous of men. In 1816, however, shortly after the publication of the Review, my friend Mr. Brownlee invited me to attend a private dissection of a recent brain, to be performed in his house by Dr Spurzheim. The subject was not altogether new, as I had previously attended a course of demonstrative lectures on Anatomy by Dr. Barclay. Dr. Spurzheim exhibited the structure of the brain to all present, (among whom were several gentlemen of the medical profession,) and contrasted it with the bold averments of the reviewer. The result was a complete conviction in the minds of the observers, that the assertions of the reviewer were refuted by physical demonstration.

The faith placed in the Review being thus shaken, I attended the next course of Dr. Spurzheim's lectures, for the purpose of hearing from himself a correct account of his doctrines. The lectures satisfied me that the system was widely different from the representations given of it by the reviewer, and that, if true, it would prove highly important; but the evidence was not conclusive. I therefore appealed to Nature by observation; and at last arrived at complete conviction of the truth of Phrenology.

In 1818 the Editor of the "Literary and Statistical Magazine for Scotland" invited me to a free discussion of the merits of the system in his work, and I was induced to offer him some essays on the subject. The notice which these attracted led to their publication in 1819, in a separate volume, under the title of "Essays on Phrenology." A second edition of these Essays has since been called for, and the present volume is offered in compliance with that demand. In the present work I have adopted the title of "A System of Phrenology," on account of the wider scope and closer connexion of its parts; but pretend to no novelty in principle, and to no rivalry with the great founders of the science.

The controversial portions of the first edition are here almost entirely omitted. As the opponents have quitted the field, these appeared no longer necessary, and their place is supplied by what I trust will be found more interesting matter. Some readers may think that retributive justice required the continued republication of the attacks of the opponents, that the public mind, when properly enlightened, might express a just disapprobation of the conduct of those who so egregiously misled it: but Phrenology teaches us forbearance; and, besides, it will be misfortune enough to the individuals who have distinguished themselves in the work of misrepresentation, to have their names handed down to posterity as the enemies of the greatest and most important discovery ever communicated to mankind.

In this work the talents of several living characters are adverted to, and compared with the developement of their mental organs—which is a new feature in philosophical discussion, and might, without explanation, appear to some readers to be improper: but I have founded such observations on the *printed works and published busts or casts* of the individuals alluded to; and both of these being public property, there appeared no impropriety in adverting to them. In instances in which reference is made to the cerebral developement of persons whose busts or casts are not published, I have ascertained that the observations will not give offence.

1825.

ADVERTISEMENT TO THE FOURTH EDITION.

THE cause of Phrenology continues prosperously to advance, and I hail with pleasure the increase of its advocates. Since the third edition of this work was printed, Dr. Vimont, of Paris, Dr. Caldwell, of Lexington, and Mr. Macnish, of Glasgow, have contributed valuable additions to the philosophy or literature of the science. During the same interval the present work has been reprinted in America, and very ably translated into German by Dr. Hirschfeld, of Bremen; while the "Elements of Phrenology" have been translated into French by Dr. Fossati. The study of the science thus appears to increase in all the enlightened countries of the globe.

Large additions have been made to the present edition; improved cuts have been used; and, in treating of topics of interest, I have added references to other phrenological works in which they are discussed or illustrated, so as to render this edition an index, as far as possible, to the general literature of the science. The appendix contains Testimonials in favour of the truth of Phrenology, and of its utility in the classification and treatment of criminals, presented in February, 1836, by Sir George S. Mackenzie, one of the earliest and most zealous advocates of the science, to Lord Glenelg, Secretary for the Colonies. His lordship transmitted the documents to Lord John Russell, Secretary for the Home Department, who promised to Sir George S. Mackenzie to bestow on them due consideration.

Dr. Spurzheim, in the American edition of his "Phrenology," published at Boston in 1832, has adopted a new arrangement of the organs, different from any which he had previously followed. It will be impossible, however, to arrive at a perfect classification and numeration of the organs until the whole of them shall have been discovered, and the primitive or elementary faculties shall have been ascertained. Any order, therefore, adopted in the meantime, must be to some extent arbitrary. Dr. Spurzheim has shown this to be the case by the frequent alterations which he has made in the numeration of the organs, without having added any corresponding discoveries to the science. The difficulties attending a correct classification are stated in the Appendix, No. II., and for the present I retain the order followed in the third edition of this work as a matter of convenience.

EDINBURGH, 31*st October*, 1836.

CONTENTS.

1*

LIST OF FIGURES.[*]

[*] The figures marked (1) are copied from engraved portraits, &c , in general circulation; the others, with the exception of those marked (2), are drawn from skulls, or casts from nature, in the collection of the Phrenological Society. These figures of skulls and casts are drawn as nearly as possible on the same scale, the dimensions being reduced to one-fifth of those of the real subjects, except in the case of the figures on pages 80 and 82.

The measurements in the Tables on pp. 94 and 436 are taken by inserting the point of the leg of a pair of callipers into the hole of the ear, and bringing the point of the other leg to the centre of the situation of the organ on the skull. The distance noted in the tables is the length of a straight line extending from one of these points to the other. In reducing the skulls to a flat surface in the drawings, the measurements could not be made to correspond exactly with those given in the tables, because the lines represented are different The approximation, however, is as great as possible, and one principle is followed in all the drawings, so that relatively to each other they are correct.

SYSTEM

OF

PHRENOLOGY.

INTRODUCTION.

PHRENOLOGY (derived from the Greek words φρην, mind and λογος, discourse) professes to be a system of Philosophy of the Human Mind, founded on the physiology of the brain. It was first offered to public consideration on the continent of Europe in 1796, but in Britain was almost unheard of till the year 1815. It has met with strenuous support from some individuals, and determined opposition from others ; while the great body of the public remain uninstructed as to its merits. On this account it may be useful to present, in an introductory form, 1st, A short notice of the reception which other discoveries have met with on their first announcement ; 2dly, A brief outline of the principles involved in Phrenology ; 3dly, An inquiry into the presumptions for and against these principles, founded on the known phenomena of human nature ; and, 4thly, An historical sketch of the discovery of the organs of the mind.

I shall follow this course, not with a view of convincing the reader that Phrenology is true, (because nothing short of patient study and extensive personal observation can produce this conviction,) but for the purpose of presenting him with motives to prosecute the investigation for his own satisfaction.

First, then—one great obstacle to the reception of a discovery is the difficulty which men experience in at once parting with old notions which have been instilled into their minds from infancy, and become the stock of their understandings. Phrenology has encountered this impediment, but not in a greater degree than other discoveries which have preceded it. Mr. Locke, in speaking of the common reception of new truths, says : " Who ever, by the most cogent arguments, will be prevailed with to disrobe himself at once of all his old opinions and pretences to knowledge and learning, which with hard study he hath all his time been labouring for, and turn himself out stark naked in quest afresh of new notions ? All the arguments that can be used will be as little able to prevail as the wind did with the traveller to part with his cloak, which he held only the faster."*

Professor Playfair, in his historical notice of discoveries in physical science, published in the Supplement to the Encyclopædia Britannica, observes, that " in every society there are some who think themselves interested to maintain things in the condition wherein they have found them. The considerations are indeed sufficiently obvious, which, in the moral and political world, tend to produce this effect, and to give a stability to human institutions, often so little proportionate to their real value or to their general utility. Even in matters purely intellectual, and in which

* Locke On the Human Understanding, b. iv., c. 20, sect. 11.

the abstract truths of arithmetic and geometry seem alone concerned, the prejudices, the selfishness, or the vanity of those who pursue them, not unfrequently combine to resist improvement, and often engage no inconsiderable degree of talent in drawing back, instead of pushing forward, the machine of science. The introduction of methods entirely new must often change the relative place of the men engaged in scientific pursuits, and must oblige many, after descending from the stations they formerly occupied, to take a lower position in the scale of intellectual improvement. The enmity of such men, if they be not animated by a spirit of real candour and the love of truth, is likely to be directed against methods by which their vanity is mortified and their importance lessened."*
› Every age has afforded proofs of the justness of these observations. "The disciples of the various philosophical schools of Greece inveighed against each other, and made reciprocal accusations of impiety and perjury. The people, in their turn, detested the philosophers, and accused those who investigated the causes of things of presumptuously invading the rights of the Divinity. Pythagoras was driven from Athens, and Anaxagoras was imprisoned, on account of their novel opinions. Democritus was treated as insane by the Abderites for his attempts to find out the cause of madness by dissections; and Socrates, for having demonstrated the unity of God, was forced to drink the juice of hemlock."†

But let us attend in particular to the reception of the three greatest discoveries that have adorned the annals of philosophy, and mark the spirit with which they were hailed.

Mr. Playfair, speaking of the treatment of Galileo, says : " Galileo was twice brought before the Inquisition. The first time, a council of seven cardinals pronounced a sentence which, for the sake of those disposed to believe that power can subdue truth, ought never to be forgotten, viz : That to maintain the sun to be immoveable, and without local motion, in the centre of the world, is an absurd proposition, false in philosophy, heretical in religion, and contrary to the testimony of Scripture; and it is equally absurd and false in philosophy to assert that the earth is not immoveable in the centre of the world, and, considered theologically, equally erroneous and heretical." The following extract from Galileo's Dialogue on the Copernican System of Astronomy, shows, in a very interesting manner, how completely its reception was analogous to that of Phrenology :

" Being very young, and having scarcely finished my course of philosophy, which I left off as being set upon other employments, there chanced to come into those parts a certain foreigner of Rostoch, whose name, as I remember, was Christianus Urstitius, a follower of Copernicus, who, in an academy, gave two or three lectures upon this point, to whom many flocked as auditors ; but I, thinking they went more for the novelty of the subject than otherwise, did not go to hear him : for I had concluded with myself that that opinion could be no other than a solemn madness ; and questioning some of those who had been there, I perceived they all made a jest thereof, except one, who told me that the business was not altogether to be laughed at : and because the man was reputed by me to be very intelligent and wary, I repented that I was not there, and began from that time forward, as oft as I met with any one of the Copernican persuasion, to demand of them if they had been always of the same judgment. Of as many as I examined, I found not so much as one who told me that he had been a long time of the contrary opinion, but to have changed it for this, as convinced by the strength of the reasons proving the same ;

* Part ii., p. 27.
† Dr. Spurzheim's *Philosophical Principles of Phrenology* London, 1825 p. 96.

and afterward questioning them one by one, to see whether they were well possessed of the reasons of the other side, I found them all to be very ready and perfect in them, so that I could not truly say that they took this opinion out of ignorance, vanity, or to show the acuteness of their wits. On the contrary, of as many of the Peripatetics and Ptolemeans as I have asked (and out of curiosity I have talked with many) what pains they had taken in the book of Copernicus, I found very few that had so much as superficially perused it, but of those who I thought had understood the same, not one : and, moreover, I have inquired among the followers of the Peripatetic doctrine if ever any of them had held the contrary opinion, and likewise found none that had. Whereupon, considering that there was no man who followed the opinion of Copernicus that had not been first on the contrary side, and that was not very well acquainted with the reasons of Aristotle and Ptolemy, and, on the contrary, there was not one of the followers of Ptolemy that had ever been of the judgment of Copernicus, and had left that to embrace this of Aristotle ;—considering, I say, these things, I began to think that one who leaveth an opinion imbued with his milk and followed by very many, to take up another, owned by very few and denied by all the schools, and that really seems a great paradox, must needs have been moved, not to say forced, by more powerful reasons. For this cause I became very curious to dive, as they say, into the bottom of this business."

Mr. Hume, the historian, mentions the fact that Harvey was treated with great contumely on account of his discovery of the circulation of the blood, and in consequence lost his practice. An eloquent writer in the 94th Number of the Edinburgh Review, when adverting to the treatment of Harvey, observes, that " the discoverer of the circulation of the blood— a discovery which, if measured by its consequences on physiology and medicine, was the greatest ever made since physic was cultivated—suffers no diminution of his reputation in our day, from the incredulity with which his doctrine was received by some, the effrontery with which it was claimed by others, or the knavery with which it was attributed to former physiologists by those who could not deny and would not praise it. The very names of these envious and dishonest enemies of Harvey are scarcely remembered ; and the honour of this great discovery now rests, beyond all dispute, with the great philosopher who made it." This shows that Harvey, in his day, was treated exactly as Dr. Gall has been in ours ; and if Phrenology be true, these or similar terms may one day be applied by posterity to him and his present opponents.

Again, Professor Playfair, speaking of the discovery of the composition of light by Sir Isaac Newton, says : " Though the discovery now communicated had everything to recommend it which can arise from what is great, new, and singular ; though it was not a theory nor system of opinions, but the generalization of facts made known by experiments ; and though it was brought forward in a most simple and unpretending form ; a host of enemies appeared, each eager to obtain the unfortunate pre-eminence of being the first to attack conclusions which the unanimous voice of posterity was to confirm." (P. 56.) " Among them, one of the first was Father Pardies, who wrote against the experiments, and what he was pleased to call the Hypothesis of Newton. A satisfactory and calm reply convinced him of his mistake, which he had the candour very readily to acknowledge. A countryman of his, Mariotte, was more difficult to be reconciled, and though very conversant with experiment, appears never to have succeeded in repeating the experiments of Newton." An account of the hostility with which Newton's discoveries were received by his contemporaries, will be found in his *Life* by Brewster, p. 171.

Here, then, we see that persecution, condemnation, and ridicule awaited

Galileo, Harvey, and Newton, for announcing three great scientific discoveries. In mental philosophy the conduct of mankind has been similar.

Aristotle and Descartes "may be quoted, to show the good and bad fortune of new doctrines. The ancient antagonists of Aristotle caused his books to be burned; but in the time of Francis I. the writings of Ramus against Aristotle were similarly treated, his adversaries were declared heretics, and, under pain of being sent to the galleys. philosophers were prohibited from combating his opinions. At the present day the philosophy of Aristotle is no longer spoken of. Descartes was persecuted for teaching the doctrine of innate ideas; he was accused of atheism, though he had written on the existence of God; and his books were burned by order of the University of Paris. Shortly afterward, however, the same learned body adopted the doctrine of innate ideas; and when Locke and Condillac attacked it, the cry of materialism and fatalism was turned against them. Thus the same opinions have been considered at one time as dangerous because they were new, and at another as useful because they were ancient. What is to be inferred from this, but that man deserves to be pitied; that. the opinions of contemporaries on the truth or falsehood, and the good or bad consequences, of a new doctrine, are always to be suspected; and that the only object of an author ought to be to point out the truth."*

To these extracts many more might be added of a similar nature; but enough has been said to demonstrate that, by the ordinary practice of mankind, great discoveries are treated with hostility, and their authors with hatred and contempt, or at least with neglect, by the generation to whom they are originally published.

If, therefore, Phrenology be a discovery at all, and especially if it be also important, it must of necessity come into collision, on the most weighty topics, with the opinions of men hitherto venerated as authorities in physiology and the philosophy of mind; and, according to the custom of the world, nothing but opposition, ridicule, and abuse could be expected on its first announcement. If we are to profit, however, by the lessons of history, we ought, after surveying these mortifying examples of human weakness and wickedness, to dismiss from our minds every prejudice against the subject before us, founded on its hostile reception by men of established reputation of the present day. He who does not perceive that, if Phrenology shall prove to be true, posterity will regard the contumelies heaped by the philosophers of this generation on its founders as another dark speck in the history of scientific discovery—and who does not feel anxious to avoid all participation in this ungenerous treatment—has reaped no moral improvement from the records of intolerance which we have now contemplated : but every enlightened individual will say, Let us dismiss prejudice, and calmly listen to evidence and reason; let us not encounter even the chance of adding our names to the melancholy list of the enemies of mankind, by refusing, on the strength of mere prejudice, to be instructed in the new doctrines submitted to our consideration; let us inquire, examine, and decide.

. These, I trust, are the sentiments of the reader; and on the faith of their being so, I shall proceed, in the second place, to state very briefly the principles of Phrenology.

It is a notion inculcated—often indirectly, no doubt, but not less strongly —by highly-venerated teachers of intellectual philosophy, that we are acquainted with Mind and Body as two distinct and separate entities. The anatomist treats of the body, and the logician and moral philosopher of the mind, as if they were separate subjects of investigation, either not at all, or only in a remote and unimportant degree, connected with each other.

* Dr. Spurzheim's *Philosophical Principles of Phrenology*, p. 97.

In common society, too, men speak of the dispositions and faculties of the mind, without thinking of their close connexion with the body.

But the human mind, as it exists in this world, cannot, *by itself*, become an object of philosophical investigation. Placed in a material world, it cannot act or be acted upon, but through the medium of an organic apparatus. The soul sparkling in the eye of beauty transmits its sweet influence to a kindred spirit only through the filaments of an optic nerve; and even the bursts of eloquence which flow from the lips of the impassioned orator when mind appears to transfuse itself almost directly into mind emanate from, and are transmitted to, corporeal beings, through a voluminous apparatus of organs. If we trace the mind's progress from the cradle to the grave, every appearance which it presents reminds us of this important truth. In earliest life the mental powers are feeble as the body; but when manhood comes, they glow with energy and expand with power; till at last the chill of age makes the limbs totter and the fancy's fires decay.

Nay, not only the great stages of our infancy, vigour, and decline, but the experience of every hour, reminds us of our alliance with the dust. The lowering clouds and stormy sky depress the spirits and enerve the mind;—after short and stated intervals of toil, our wearied faculties demand repose in sleep;—famine or disease is capable of levelling the proudest energies with the earth;—and even the finest portion of our compound being, the Mind itself, apparently becomes diseased, and, leaving nature's course, flies to self-destruction to escape from wo.

These phenomena must be referred to the organs with which, in this life, the mind is connected: but if the organs exert so great an effect over the mental manifestations, no system of philosophy is entitled to consideration, which neglects their influence and treats the thinking principle as a disembodied spirit. The phrenologist, therefore, regards man as he exists in this world; and desires to investigate the laws which regulate the connexion between the mind and its organs, but without attempting to discover the essence of either, or the manner in which they are united.

The popular notion, that we are acquainted with mind unconnected with matter, is, therefore, founded on an illusion. In point of fact, we do not in this life know mind as one entity, and body as another; but we are acquainted only with the compound existence of mind and body. A few remarks will place this doctrine in its proper light.

In the first place, we are not *conscious* of the existence and functions of the organs by which the mind operates in this life, and, in consequence, many acts appear to us to be purely mental, which experiment and observation prove incontestibly to depend on corporeal organs. For example, in stretching out or withdrawing the arm, we are conscious of an act of the will, and of the consequent movement of the arm, but not of the existence of the apparatus by means of which our volition is carried into execution. Experiment and observation, however, demonstrate the existence of bones of the arm curiously articulated and adapted to motion; of muscles endowed with powers of contraction; and of three sets of nervous fibres all running in one sheath—one communicating feeling, a second exciting motion, and a third conveying to the mind information of the state of the muscles, when in action; all which organs, except the nerve of feeling, must combine and act harmoniously before the arm can be moved and regulated by the will. All that a person uninstructed in anatomy knows, is, that he wills the motion, and that it takes place; the whole act appears to him to be purely mental, and only the arm, or thing moved, is conceived to be corporeal. Nevertheless, it is positively established by anatomical and physiological researches that this conclusion is erroneous—that the act is not purely mental, but is accomplished by the instrumentality of the various organs now enumerated. In like manner, every act of vision involves a certain state of the optic nerve, and every act of hearing a certain state of the tympanum ; yet of the existence and functions of these organs we obtain, by means of consciousness, no knowledge whatever.

Now, I go one step farther in the same path, and state, that every act of the will, every flight of imagination, every glow of affection, and every effort of the understanding, in this life, is performed by means of cerebral organs unknown to us through consciousness, but the existence of which is capable of being demonstrated by experiment and observation ; in other words, that *the brain is the organ of the mind*—the material condition without which no mental act is possible in the present world. The greatest physiologists admit this proposition without hesitation. The celebrated Dr. Cullen, of Edinburgh, states, that " the part of our body more immediately connected with the mind, and therefore more especially concerned in every affection of the intellectual functions, is the common origin of the nerves ; which I shall, in what follows, speak of under the appellation of the Brain." Again, the same author says : " We *cannot doubt* that the operations of our intellect *always* depend upon certain motions taking place in the brain." The late Dr. James Gregory, when speaking of memory, imagination, and judgment, observes, that " Although at first sight these faculties appear to be so purely mental as to have no connexion with the body, yet certain diseases which obstruct them prove that a certain state of the brain is necessary to their proper exercise, and that the brain is the primary organ of the internal powers." The great physiologist of Germany, Blumenbach, says : " That the mind is closely connected with the brain, as the material condition of mental phenomena, is demonstrated by our consciousness, and by the mental disturbances which ensue upon affections of the brain."* According to Magendie, a celebrated French physiologist, " the brain is the material instrument of thought : this is proved by a multitude of experiments and facts."

" I readily concur," says Mr. Abernethy, " in the proposition, that the brain of animals ought to be regarded as the organization by which the percipient principle becomes variously affected. First, because, in the senses of sight, hearing, &c., I see distinct organs for the production of each perception. Secondly, because the brain is larger and more complicated in proportion as the variety of the affections of the percipient principle is increased. Thirdly, because disease and injuries disturb and annul particular faculties and affections without impairing others. And, fourthly, because it seems more reasonable to me to suppose that whatever is perceptive may be variously affected by means of vital actions transmitted through a diversity of organization, than to suppose that such variety depends upon original differences in the nature of the percipient principle."

" If the mental processes," asks Mr. Lawrence, " be not the function of the brain, what is its office ? In animals which possess only a small part of the human cerebral structure, sensation exists, and in many cases is more acute than in man. What employment shall we find for all that man possesses over and above this portion—for the large and prodigiously-developed human hemisphere ? Are we to believe that these serve only to round the figure of the organ, or to fill the cranium ?"† And in another place he says : " In conformity with the views already explained respecting the mental part of our being, I refer the varieties of moral feeling, and of capacity for knowledge and reflection, to those diversities

* Elliotson's translation of Blumenbach's *Physiology*, 4th edit., p. 196
† *Lectures on Physiology*, &c., Lect. 4.

of cerebral organization which are indicated by, and correspond to, the differences in the shape of the skull."*

Dr. Mason Good, speaking of intellect, sensation, and muscular motion, says : " All these diversities of vital energy are now well known to be dependent on the organ of the brain, as the instrument of the intellectual powers, and the source of the sensific and motory ; though, from the close connexion and synchronous action of various other organs with the brain, and especially the thoracic and abdominal viscera, such diversities were often referred to several of the latter in earlier ages, and before anatomy had traced them satisfactorily to the brain as their fountain-head. And of so high an antiquity is this erroneous hypothesis, that it has not only spread itself through every climate on the globe, but still keeps a hold on the colloquial language of every people ; and hence the heart, the liver, the spleen, the reins, and the bowels generally are, among all nations, regarded, either literally or figuratively, as so many seats of mental faculties or moral feeling. . . . The study of anatomy, however, has corrected the loose and confused ideas of mankind upon this subject; and while it distinctly shows us that many of the organs popularly referred to as the seat of sensation, do, and must, from the peculiarity of their nervous connexion with the brain, necessarily participate in the feelings and faculties thus generally ascribed to them, it also demonstrates that the primary source of these attributes, the quarter in which they originate, or which chiefly influences them, is the brain itself."†

Dr. Neil Arnott, in his *Elements of Physics*, writes thus : " The laws of mind which man can discover by reason, are not laws of independent mind, but of mind in connexion with body, and influenced by the bodily condition. It has been believed by many that the nature of mind separate from body, is to be at once all-knowing and intelligent. But mind connected with body can only acquire knowledge slowly, through the bodily organs of sense, and more or less perfectly according as these organs and the central brain are perfect. A human being born blind and deaf, and therefore remaining dumb, as in the noted case of the boy Mitchell, grows up closely to resemble an automaton ; and an originally mis-shapen or deficient brain causes idiocy for life. Childhood, maturity, dotage, which have such differences of bodily powers, have corresponding differences of mental faculty : and as no two bodies, so no two minds, in their external manifestation, are quite alike. Fever, or a blow on the head, will change the most gifted individual into a maniac, causing the lips of virgin innocence to utter the most revolting obscenity, and those of pure religion to speak the most horrible blasphemy : and most cases of madness and eccentricity can now be traced to a peculiar state of the brain." (Introduction, p. xxiii.) Let it be observed that most of these authors are nowise inclined to support Phrenology.‡

The fact that the mental phenomena of which we are conscious are the result of mind and brain acting together, is farther established by the effects of swooning, of compression of the brain, and of sleep. In profound sleep consciousness is entirely suspended : this fact is explicable on the principle of the organ of the mind being then in a state of repose ; but it is altogether inconsistent with the idea of the immaterial principle, or the mind itself, being capable of acting independently of the brain—for if this were the case, thinking should never be interrupted by any material cause. In a swoon, blood is rapidly withdrawn from the brain, and consciousness is for the moment obliterated. So also, where part of the brain

* *Lectures on Physiology*, sect. ii., ch. 8.

† Good's *Study of Medicine*, 2d edit., iv. 3, 4.   ‡ Additional authorities are cited by Mr. Wildsmith in his excellent *Inquiry concerning the Relative Connexion which subsists between the Mind and the Brain.* London, 1828.

has been laid bare by an injury inflicted on the skull, it has been found that consciousness could be suspended at the pleasure of the surgeon, by merely pressing on the brain with his fingers, and that it could be restored by withdrawing the pressure. A few such cases may be cited :

M. Richerand had a patient whose brain was exposed in consequence of disease of the skull. One day, in washing off the purulent matter, he chanced to press with more than usual force ; and instantly the patient, who, the moment before, had answered his questions with perfect correctness, stopped short in the middle of a sentence, and became altogether insensible. As the pressure gave her no pain, it was repeated thrice, and always with the same result. She uniformly recovered her faculties the moment the pressure was taken off. M. Richerand mentions also the case of an individual who was trepanned for a fracture of the skull, and whose faculties and consciousness became weak in proportion as the pus so accumulated under the dressings as to occasion pressure of the brain.* A man at the battle of Waterloo had a small portion of his skull beaten in upon the brain, and became quite unconscious and almost lifeless ; but Mr. Cooper having raised up the depressed portion of bone, the patient immediately arose, dressed himself, became perfectly rational, and recovered rapidly.† Professor Chapman, of Philadelphia, mentions in his Lectures, that he saw an individual with his skull perforated and the brain exposed, who used to submit himself to the same experiment of pressure as that performed on Richerand's patient, and who was exhibited by the late Professor Westar to his class. The man's intellect and moral faculties disappeared when pressure was applied to the brain : they were literally "held under the thumb," and could be restored at pleasure to their full activity.‡ . A still more remarkable case is that of a person named Jones, recorded by Sir Astley Cooper. This man was deprived of consciousness, by being wounded in the head while on board a vessel in the Mediterranean. In this state of insensibility he remained for several months at Gibraltar, whence he was transmitted to Deptford, and subsequently to St. Thomas's Hospital, London. Mr. Cline, the surgeon, found a portion of the skull depressed, trepanned him, and removed the depressed part of the bone. Three hours after this operation he sat up in bed, sensation and volition returned, and in four days he was able to get up and converse. The last circumstance he remembered was the capture of a prize in the Mediterranean thirteen months before. A young man at Hartford, in the United States of America, was rendered insensible by a fall, and had every appearance of being in a dying condition. Dr. Brigham removed more than a gill of clotted blood from beneath the skull ; upon which "the man immediately spoke, soon recovered his mind entirely, and is now, six weeks after the accident, in good health both as to mind and body."§

Pinel relates a case which strikingly illustrates the connexion of the mind with the brain. "A man," says he, "engaged in a mechanical employment, and afterward confined in the Bicêtre, experiences at irregular intervals fits of madness characterized by the following symptoms : At first there is a sensation of burning heat in the abdominal viscera, with intense thirst, and a strong constipation ; the heat gradually extends to the breast, neck, and face—producing a flush of the complexion ; on reaching the temples, it becomes still greater, and is accompanied by very strong

---

* *Nouveaux Elémens de Physiologie*, 7th edit., ii. 195–6.
† Hennen's *Principles of Military Surgery.*
‡ *Principles of Medicine*, by Samuel Jackson, M.D.
§ *Remarks on the Influence of Mental Cultivation, &c., upon Health.* By Amariah Brigham, M.D , 2d edit., p. 23. Boston, U. S., 1833. Several of the cases in the text have already been collected by this very intelligent writer.

and frequent pulsations in the temporal arteries, which seem as if about to burst : finally, the nervous affectation arrives at the brain ; the patient is then seized with an irresistible propensity to shed blood ; and if there be a sharp instrument within reach, he is apt to sacrifice to his fury the first person who presents himself."* The same writer speaks of another insane patient, whose manners were remarkably mild and reserved during his lucid intervals, but whose character was totally altered by the periodical morbid excitement of his brain ; for, says Pinel, " on the return of the paroxysm, *particularly when marked by a certain redness of the face, excessive heat in the head,* and a violent thirst, his walk is precipitate, his look is full of audacity, and he experiences the most violent inclination to provoke those who approach him, and to fight with them furiously."†
Dr. Richy has recorded the case of a Madagascar negro, who had an attack of intensely destructive delirium, in consequence of a wound on the head near the lower part of the left parietal bone. When recovering he was calmer and less blood-thirsty ; but an overpressure of his bandage on the wound brought back his furious paroxysms.‡

That the brain is the organ of the mind, is strongly confirmed by the phenomena observed when it is exposed to view, in consequence of the removal of a part of the skull. Sir Astley Cooper mentions the case of a young gentleman who was brought to him after losing a portion of his skull just above the eyebrow. " On examining the head," says Sir Astley, " I distinctly saw the pulsation of the brain ; it was regular and slow ; but, at this time, he was agitated by some opposition to his wishes, and directly the blood was sent with increased force to the brain, and the pulsation became frequent and violent. If, therefore," continues Sir Astley, " you omit to keep the mind free from agitation, your other means (in the treatment of injuries of the brain) will be unavailing."§

In a case of a similar description, which fell under the notice of Blumenbach, that physiologist observed the brain to sink whenever the patient was asleep, and to swell again with blood the moment he awoke.‖

A third case is reported by Dr. Pierquin, as having been observed by him in one of the hospitals of Montpelier, in the year 1821. The patient was a female, who had lost a large portion of her scalp, skull, and dura mater, so that a corresponding portion of the brain was subject to inspection. When she was in a dreamless sleep, her brain was motionless, and lay within the cranium. When her sleep was imperfect, and she was agitated by dreams, her brain moved and protruded without the cranium, forming cerebral hernia In vivid dreams, reported as such by herself, the protrusion was considerable ; and when she was perfectly awake, especially if engaged in active thought or sprightly conversation, it was still greater.¶ A writer in the *Medico-Chirurgical Review,* after alluding to this case, mentions that many years ago he had " frequent opportunities of witnessing similar phenomena in a robust young man, who lost a considerable portion of his skull by an accident which had almost proved mortal. When excited by pain, fear, or anger, his brain protruded greatly, so as sometimes to disturb the dressings, which were necessarily applied loosely ; and it throbbed tumultuously, in accordance with the arterial pulsations."**

The cause of these appearances obviously was, that the brain, like the muscles and other organs of the body, is more copiously supplied with blood when in a state of activity than while at rest ; and that when the

* Pinel, *sur l'Aliénation Mentale,* p. 157, § 160.
† *Op. Cit.,* p. 101, § 116.
‡ *Journal de la Société Phrénologique de Paris,* No. 2, p. 171.
§ Sir A. Cooper's *Lectures on Surgery,* by Tyrrel, i. 279.
‖ Elliotson's *Blumenbach,* 4th edit , p. 283.
¶ *Annals of Phrenology,* No. 1. Boston, U. S., Oct. 1833, p. 37.
** *Medico-Chirurgical Review,* No. 46, p. 366, Oct. 1835.

cerebral bloodvessels were filled, the volume of the brain was augmented, and the protrusion above noticed took place.*

Even in the *Edinburgh Review*, where the dependence of the mind upon the brain was formerly held to be exceedingly questionable,† the doctrine is now admitted in all its latitude. " Almost from the first casual inspection of animal bodies," says a writer in No. 94, " the brain was regarded as an organ of primary dignity, and, more particularly in the human subject, the seat of thought and feeling, the centre of all sensation, the messenger of intellect, the presiding organ of the bodily frame." " All this superiority (of man over the brutes,) all these faculties which elevate and dignify him, this reasoning power, this moral sense, these capacities of happiness, these high aspiring hopes, are *felt*, and *enjoyed*, and *manifested*, by means of his superior nervous system. Its injury weakens, its imperfection limits, its destruction (humanly speaking) ends them."

Besides referring to these facts and authorities, I may remark, that consciousness localizes the mind in the head, and gives us a full conviction that it is situated there ; but consciousness does not reveal what substance is in the interior of the skull. It does not tell whether the mind occupies an airy dome, a richly-furnished mansion, one apartment, or many ; or in what state or condition it resides in its appointed place. It is only on opening the head that we discover that the skull encloses the brain ; and then, by an act of the understanding, we infer that the mind must have been connected with it in its operations.

It is worthy of observation also, that the popular notions of the independence of the mind on the body are modern, and the offspring of philosophical theories that have sprung up chiefly since the days of Locke. In Shakspeare, and our older writers, the brain is frequently used as implying the mental functions ; and, even in the present day, the language of the vulgar, which is less affected by philosophical theories than that of polite scholars, is more in accordance with nature. A stupid person is vulgarly called a numb-skull, a thick-head ; or said to be addle-pated, badly furnished in the upper-story ; while a clever person is said to be strong-headed or long-headed, to have plenty of brains ; a madman is called wrong in the head, touched in the noddle, &c. When a catarrh chiefly affects the head, we complain of stupidity, because we have such a cold in the head."‡

The principle which I have so much insisted on, that we are not conscious of the existence and functions of the organs by which the mind acts, explains the source of the metaphysical notion which has affected modern language, that we know the mind as an entity by itself. The acts which really result from the combined action of the mind and its organs appear, previously to anatomical and pathological investigation, to be produced by the mind exclusively ; and hence have arisen the neglect and contempt with which the organs have been treated, and the ridicule cast upon those who have endeavoured to speak of them as important in the philosophy of mind. After the explanations given above, the reader will appreciate the real value of the following statement by Lord Jeffrey, in his strictures on the second edition of this work, in the 88th number of the *Edinburgh Review*. His words are : " The truth, we do not scruple to say it, is, that there is not the smallest reason for supposing that the mind ever operates through the agency of any material organs, except in its perception of material objects, or in the spontaneous movements of the body which it inhabits." And, " There is not the least reason to suppose that any of our faculties, but those which connect us with external objects, or direct the movements of our bodies, act

---

* Additional evidence that the brain is the organ of the mind will be found in the Appendix, No. 1.
† See No. 48, Article 10 ; also No. 88, cited below.
‡ Elliotson's *Blumenbach*, p. 66.

by material organs at all :" that is to say, feeling, fancy, and reflection are acts so purely mental, that they have no connexion with organization.

Long before Lord Jeffrey penned these sentences, however, Dr Thomas Brown had written, even in the *Edinburgh Review*, that "Memory, imagination, and judgment may be all set to sleep by a few grains of a very common and simple drug ;" and Dr. Cullen, Blumenbach, Dr. Gregory, Magendie, and in short all physiological authors of eminence, had published positive statements that the mental faculties are connected with the brain.

Lord Brougham also, in his *Discourse of Natural Theology*, argues in favour of the mind's independence of matter in this life, and adduces in support of his position the phenomena of dreaming, and the allegation that "unless some unusual and violent accident interferes, such as a serious illness or a fatal contusion, the ordinary course of life presents the mind and the body running courses widely different, and in great part of the time in opposite directions." (P. 120.) Dugald Stewart has furnished an apposite answer to this remark. "In the case of old men," says he, "it is generally found that a decline of the faculties keeps pace with the decay of bodily health and vigour. The few exceptions that occur to the universality of this fact only prove that there are some diseases fatal to life, which do not injure those parts of the body with which the intellectual operations are more immediately connected."[*] Lord Brougham, moreover, is glaringly inconsistent with himself. He first maintains that the mind is wholly independent of the body, and then admits that " a serious illness " is capable of impairing its power. Yet how, on his hypothesis, should it be affectable by this any more than by the slightest disease ?

It is a popular opinion, that in pulmonary consumption, and other lingering diseases attended with waste of the body, the mind nevertheless continues to act with entire vigour up to the very day or hour of dissolution. This notion, if true, would militate against the doctrine of the mind being affected by the state of the organs ; but it is really unfounded. There is a difference between derangement of an organ and mere weakness in its functions. In pulmonary consumption the lungs alone are disorganized ;—the brain and other organs, remaining entire in their structure, are sound although weakened in their functions. The mind in such patients, therefore, does not become disordered ; but its vigour is unquestionably impaired. In the case of the patient's legs, the bones and muscles, remaining entire, he can walk : in health, however, he could have accomplished a journey of many miles without fatigue, whereas he cannot in disease do more than move across his bedroom. It might certainly be said that he could *walk* to the last, but it could not with truth be maintained that his power of perambulation was as great at his death as in health ; and so it is with the brain and the mind.

What, then, does the proposition that the brain is the organ of the mind imply ? Let us take the case of the eye as somewhat analogous. If the eye be the organ of vision, it will be conceded, first, That sight cannot be enjoyed without its instrumentality ; secondly, That every act of vision must be accompanied by a corresponding state of the organ, and, *vice versa*, that every change of condition in the organ must influence sight ; and, thirdly, That the perfection of vision will be in relation to the perfection of the organ. In like manner, if the brain be the organ of the mind, it will follow that the mind does not act in this life independently of its organ—and hence, that every emotion and judgment of which we are conscious is the result of the mind and its organ acting together ; secondly, that every mental affection must be accompanied by a corresponding state of the organ, and, *vice versa*, every state of the organ must be attended by a certain condition of the mind ; and, thirdly, that the perfection of the manifestations of the mind will bear a relation

[*] *Outlines of Moral Philosophy*, p. 233.

to the perfection of its organ. These propositions appear to be incontrovertible, and to follow as necessary consequences from the simple fact that the mind acts by means of organs. But if they be well founded, how important a study does that of the organs of the mind become ! It is the study of the mind itself, in the only condition in which it is known to us ; and the very fact that in past ages the mind has been studied without reference to organization, accounts for the melancholy truth, that, independently of Phrenology, no mental philosophy suited to practical purposes exists.

Holding it, then, as established by the evidence of the most esteemed physiologists, and also by observation, that the brain is the organ of the mind, and that the state of the brain influences that of the mental powers, the next question which presents itself is, Whether the mind in *every act* employs the *whole* brain as one organ, or whether separate mental faculties are connected with distinct portions of the brain as their respective organs ! The following considerations may enable us to solve this question :

1*st*, In all ascertained instances, different functions are never performed by the same organ, but the reverse ; each function has an organ for itself : the stomach, for instance, digests food, the liver secretes bile, the heart propels the blood, the eyes see, the ears hear, the tongue tastes, and the nose smells. Nay, on analysing these examples, it is found that wherever the function is compound, each element of it is performed by means of a distinct organ : thus, to accomplish the lingual duties, there is one nerve whose office is to move the tongue, another nerve whose duty it is to communicate the ordinary sense of feeling to the tongue, and a third nerve which conveys the sensation of taste. A similar combination of nerves takes place in the hands, arms, and other parts of the body which contain voluntary muscles : one nerve gives motion, another bestows feeling, while a third conveys to the mind a knowledge of the state of the muscle ; and, except in the case of the tongue, all these nerves are blended in one common sheath.

In the economy of the human frame, there is no ascertained example of one nerve performing two functions, such as feeling and communicating motion, or seeing and hearing, or tasting and smelling. The spinal marrow consists of three double columns . the anterior column of each lateral division is for motion, the posterior for sensation, and the middle for respiration. In the case of the brain, therefore, analogy would lead us to expect, that if reasoning be an act essentially different from loving or hating, there will be one organ for reasoning, another for loving, and a third for hating.

2*dly*,[*] It is an undisputed truth, that the various mental powers of man appear in succession; and, as a general rule, that the reflecting or reasoning faculties are those which arrive latest at perfection. In the child, the emotions of fear and of love appear before that of veneration ; and the capacity of observing the existence and qualities of external objects arrives much sooner at maturity than that of abstract reasoning. Daily observation shows that the brain undergoes a corresponding change ; whereas we have no evidence that the immaterial principle varies in its powers from year to year. If every faculty of the mind be connected with the whole brain, this successive developement of mental powers is utterly at variance with what we should expect *a priori ;* because, if the general organ is fitted for manifesting with success one mental faculty, it ought to be equally so for manifesting all. On the contrary, observation shows that different parts of the brain are really developed at different periods of life, corresponding with the successive evolution of the faculties. In infancy, according to Chaussier, the cerebellum forms

----

* Most of the following arguments are taken from Dr. Andrew Combe's Observations on Dr. Barclay's Objections to Phrenology, published in the *Transactions of the Phrenological Society*, (Edinburgh, 1824,) page 412.

one-fifteenth of the encephalic mass, and, in adult age, from one-sixth to one-eighth; its size being thus in strict accordance with the energy of the sexual propensity, of which it is the organ. In childhood the middle part of the forehead generally predominates; in later life the upper lateral parts become more prominent—which facts also are in strict accordance with the periods of unfolding of the observing and reasoning powers.

3dly, Genius is almost always partial, which it ought not to be if the organ of the mind were single. A genius for poetry, for mechanics, for drawing, for music, or for mathematics, sometimes appears at a very early age in individuals who, in regard to all other pursuits, are mere ordinary men, and who, with every effort, can never attain to anything above mediocrity.

4thly, The phenomena of dreaming are at variance with the supposition of the mind manifesting all its faculties by means of a single organ; while they are quite consistent with, and explicable by, that of a plurality of organs. In dreaming the mind experiences numerous vivid emotions—such as fear, anger, and affection—arising, succeeding one another, and departing, without control from the intellectual powers; or it is filled with a thousand varied conceptions, sometimes connected and rational, but more frequently disjointed and absurd, and all differing widely from the waking operations of the mind, in wanting consistency and sense. These phenomena harmonize remarkably with the doctrine of a variety of faculties and organs, some of which, being active, communicate those disordered ideas and feelings that constitute a dream, while the repose of others permits the disordered action which characterizes the pictures formed by the fancy in sleep.

Were the organ of mind single, it is clear that all the faculties should be asleep or awake to the same extent at the same time; or, in other words, that no such thing as dreaming could take place.

5thly, The admitted phenomena of partial idiocy and partial insanity are so plainly and strongly in contradiction with the notion of a single organ of mind, that Pinel himself, no friend to Phrenology, asks if they can be reconciled to such a conception.

Partial idiocy is that state in which an individual manifests one or several powers of the mind with an ordinary degree of energy, while he is deprived to a greater or less extent of the power of manifesting all the others. Pinel, Haslam, Rush, Esquirol, and, in short, every writer on insanity, speaks of the partial developement of certain mental powers in idiots; and Rush, in particular, alludes not only to the powers of intellect, but also to the partial possession of the moral faculties. Some idiots, he observes, are as remarkable for correct moral feelings as some great geniuses are for the reverse. Foderé, in his *Traité du Goitre et de la Crétinisme*, thus speaks, p. 133: "It is remarked, that, by an *inexplicable singularity*, some of these individuals, (cretins,) endowed with so weak minds, are born with a particular talent for copying paintings, for rhyming, or for music. I have known several who taught themselves to play passably on the organ and harpsichord; others who understood, without ever having had a master, the repairing of watches and the construction of some pieces of mechanism." He adds, that these powers could not be attributed to the intellect, "for these individuals not only could not read books which treated of the principles of mechanics, but *ils etaient deroutés lo-squ'on en parlait, et ne se perfectionnaient jamais.*" It must be observed also, that these unfortunate individuals differ very much in the kind as well as quantity of mental power possessed. One, for example, is all kindness and good nature, another quarrelsome and mischievous, or one has a lively perception of harmony in music, while another has none. An instance is given by Pinel of an idiot girl who manifested a most wonderful propensity to *imitate* whatever she heard or saw, but who displayed

4

no intellectual faculty in a perceptible degree, and never attached an idea to any sound she uttered. Dr. Rush particularizes one man who was remarkable for his religious feelings, although exceedingly deficient in the other moral sentiments and in understanding; and, among the cretins, many are to be found who scarcely manifest any other faculty of the mind except Amativeness.

It ought farther to be observed, that the characteristic features of each particular case are strictly permanent. The idiot, who to-day manifests the faculty of Tune, or the feeling of Benevolence, of Veneration, or of Self-Esteem, will not to-morrow, nor in a year, exhibit a different kind of predominant manifestations. Were deficiency of the brain as a *single* organ the cause of idiocy, these phenomena ought *not* to appear; for, being able to manifest one faculty, it ought, according to the circumstances in which the individual is placed, to be equally able to manifest all others whose activity may be required, and thus the character of the idiocy ought to change with every passing event—which it never does. Fodéré calls these facts " inexplicable singularities ;" and no doubt, on his theory, they truly are so. To the phrenologist, however, they offer no difficulty ; for they are in perfect harmony with *his* views. The difference in the *kind* of powers manifested in cases of partial idiocy—between the capacity for mechanics, for instance, and the sentiment of Veneration, Self-Esteem, or Benevolence—is as great as between the sensations excited by a sound and an odour. To infer, therefore, that one organ serves for the manifestation of all these faculties, is really much the same, in point of logic, as to suppose all the external senses to have only one organic apparatus, in spite of the fact of many individuals being blind who are not deaf, or deaf and not blind.

Partial insanity, or that state in which one or more faculties of the mind are deranged, while the integrity of the remainder is unaffected, is known by the name of monomania, and appears equally with the former to exclude the possibility of one organ manifesting all the mental faculties, for the argument constantly recurs, that if the organ be sufficiently sound to manifest one faculty in its perfect state, it ought to be equally capable of manifesting all—which, however, is known to be in direct opposition to fact. On this subject I shall confine myself to the statement of a single instance, merely in illustration.

Of *folie raisonnante* Pinel thus speaks : " Hospitals for the insane are never without some example of mania marked by acts of extravagance, or even of fury, with a kind of judgment preserved in all its integrity, if we judge of it by the conversation : the lunatic gives the most just and precise answers to the questions of the curious ; no incoherance of ideas is discernible ; he reads and writes letters as if his understanding were perfectly sound ; and yet, by a singular contrast, he tears in pieces his clothes and bed-covers, and always finds some plausible reason to justify his wandering and his fury. This sort of mania is so far from rare, that the vulgar name of *folie raisonnante* has been given to it."—P. 98. Here, again, the difficulty recurs of reconciling such facts with the idea of one organ executing all the functions of the mind. How comes that organ to be able to manifest, in a sound state, several but *not all* the faculties ?

6thly, Besides the phenomena of idiocy and insanity, there is another class of facts (to which, however, I shall only allude) equally at variance with the supposition of a single organ of mind, viz , partial injuries of the brain, which are said to have occurred without injury to the mental faculties. I merely observe, that if every part of the brain is concerned in every mental act, it appears strange that all the processes of thought should be manifested with *equal success* when a great part of the brain is injured or destroyed, as when its whole structure is sound and entire.

If the fact were really as here stated, the brain would form an exception to the general laws of organic structure ; for although a part of the lungs may be sufficient to maintain respiration, or a part of the stomach to execute digestion, in such a way as to support life, there is no instance in which these functions have been as successfully performed by impaired organs as they would have been by lungs and a stomach in their natural state of health and activity. The phrenologists are reduced to no strait to reconcile the occurrence of such cases with their system ; for as soon as the principle of a plurality of organs is acknowledged, the facts admit of an easy and satisfactory explanation.

7thly, Daily experience may satisfy us that the mind manifests a plurality of faculties by a plurality of organs. An individual receives an affront, in a venerable assembly, and the following mental states may present themselves simultaneously : He feels anger : yet he feels awe or respect for the persons present ; he uses reflection and restrains his wrath. These states of mind may continue to coexist for hours. A single organ could not serve to give consciousness of indignation, to feel awe, and to practise restraint, all at the same moment ; but this is quite practicable by a plurality of organs Indeed we are able at the same moment to manifest opposite emotions in our actions, if we employ different instruments in doing so. A man may wound another deliberately with a dagger, and at the same instant speak peace to him and smile in his face. An artist may execute a drawing, and at the same instant sing a song. If one cannot compose poetry and calculate logarithms at the same moment, it is because some of the organs required in the one operation are necessary also in the other ; and the same organs cannot perform two duties at once.

From the preceding considerations it appears, that any theory founded upon the notion that the brain is a single organ, is uniformly at variance with all that is ascertained to be fact in the philosophy of mind ; and that, on the other hand, the principle of a plurality of organs, while it satisfactorily explains *most* of these facts, is consistent with *all* of them. Its truth is thus almost demonstrated, not by far-fetched nor pretended facts which few can verify, but by facts which daily " obtrude themselves upon the notice of the senses." This principle, indeed, bears on the face of it so much greater a degree of probability than the opposite one, that it has long since forced itself on the minds of many inquirers. " The brain is a very complicated organ," says Bonnet, " or rather an assemblage of very different organs ;"[*] Tissot contends that every perception has different fibres ;[†] and Haller and Van Swieten were of opinion that the internal senses occupy, in the brain, organs as distinct as the nerves of the external senses.[‡] Cabanis entertained a similar notion ;[§] and so did Prochaska. Cuvier says, that " certain parts of the brain in all classes of animals are large or small, according to certain qualities of the animals ;"[||] and the same eminent author admits that Gall's doctrine of the functions of the brain is nowise contradictory to the general principles of physiology.[¶] Soemmering trusts that we shall one day find the particular seats of the different orders of ideas. "' Let the timid, therefore, take courage," says Dr. Georget, " and after the example of such high authorities, fear not to commit the unpardonable crime of innovation, of passing for cranioscopists, in admitting the plurality of the faculties and the mental organs of the brain, or at least in daring to examine the subject."[**] Foderé himself, a very zealous opponent of Phrenology, after recapitulating a great many reasons similar to those given above, which had been

* *Palingénésie*, i. 334. ·   † *Œuvres*, iii. 33.   ‡ Van Swieten, i. 454.
§ *Rapports du Physique et du Moral de l'Homme*, 2de edit., i. 233–4.
|| *Anatomie Comparée*, tom. ii.
¶ *Rapport Historique sur les Progrès des Sciences Naturelles*, &c., p. 193.
** *Physiologie du Système Nerveux*, i. 126.

employed by philosophers antecedent to Drs. Gall and Spurzheim, for
believing in a plurality of mental organs, is constrained to admit, that
"this kind of reasoning has been employed by the greater number of
anatomists, from the time of Galen down to our own day, and even by the
great Haller, who experienced a necessity for assigning a function to each
department of the brain." Pinel also, (in the article *Manie* in the *En-
cyclopedie Méthodique*,) after relating some cases of partial insanity, asks
whether all this collection of facts can be reconciled with the opinion of
a single faculty and a single organ of the understanding? Even in the
Edinburgh Review, (No. XCIV.,) Sir Charles Bell is commended for "at-
tacking the common opinion, that a separate sensation and volition are
conveyed by the same nerves," and for asserting "the different functions
of different parts of the cerebrum and cerebellum."

It is not surprising, therefore, that reflecting men were early led to
imagine that particular mental powers must be connected with particular
parts of the brain; and accordingly, before the eighteenth century, when
modern metaphysics sprang up, we find traces of this opinion common,
not only among eminent anatomists and physiologists, but among authors
on human nature in general. Burton, in his *Anatomy of Melancholy*,
published in 1621, says : "Inner senses are three in number, so called
because they be within the brain-pan, as common sense, phantasie, and
memory :" of common sense, he says, that "the fore part of the brain is
his organ or seat ;" of phantasie or imagination, which some call æstima-
tive or cogitative, that his "organ is the middle cell of the brain ;" and
of memory, that "his seat and organ is the back part of the brain." This
was the account of the faculties given by Aristotle, and repeated, with
little variation, by the writers of the middle ages. In the thirteenth century a head, divided into regions according to these opinions, was designed
by Albert the Great, Bishop of Ratisbon; and another was published by
Petrus Montagnana, in 1491.* One published at Venice, in 1562, by
Ludovico Dolci, in a work upon strengthening and preserving the memory, is here represented :

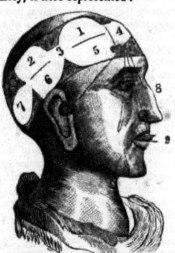

REFERENCES TO FIGURE.

1 Fantasia.

2 Cogitativa.

3 Vermis.

4 Sensus Communis.

5 Imagina.

6 Æstimativa.

7 Memorativa.

8 Olfactus.

9 Gustus.

In the British Museum is a chart of the universe and the elements of

* Gall, *Sur les Fonctions du Cerveau*, 8vo., Paris, 1822-1825, ii. 354-5.
This work is a reprint of the physiological portion of the *Anatomie et Phy-
siologie du Système Nerveux*, 4to., partly by Gall and Spurzheim, and partly by
Gall alone.

all sciences, in which a large head so delineated is conspicuous. It was published at Rome so late as 1632.*

If, then, so many physiologists and others have been led to believe in a plurality of mental organs, by a perception of the contradiction and inconsistency existing between the phenomena and the supposition of the whole brain being the single organ of the mind, I cannot err much in saying, that the latter notion, far from being self-evident, appears so improbable—as to require even stronger facts to prove it than the opposite view; and that the presumptions are all in favour of a plurality of mental faculties manifesting themselves by means of a plurality of organs.

I have now endeavoured to show, first, That the ridicule, opposition, and abuse with which Phrenology was treated at its first announcement, and its continued rejection by men of established reputation, whose opinions it contradicts, afford no presumption that it is untrue, for many great discoveries have met with a similar fate :—Secondly, That we are really unacquainted with the mind, as an entity distinct from the body, and that it is owing to the mind not being conscious of its organs that metaphysicians have supposed their feelings and intellectual perceptions to be emanations of pure spirit, whereas they are the results of mind and its organs acting in combination :—Thirdly, That the greatest anatomists and physiologists admit the brain to be the organ of the mind, and common feelings localizes thought in the head, although it does not inform us what substance occupies the interior of the skull ; farther, that the very idea of the mind having an organ, implies that every mental act is accompanied with an affection of the organ, and vice versa, so that the true philosophy of the mind cannot be discovered without taking the influence of the organs into account at every step :—And, fourthly, That the analogy of the nerves of feeling and motion, of the five senses, and of other parts of the body, all of which perform distinct functions by separate organs—also the successive appearance of the faculties in youth, and the phenomena of partial genius, of dreaming, of partial insanity, of monomania, and of partial injuries of the brain—furnish presumptive evidence that the mind manifests a plurality of faculties by means of a variety of organs, and exclude the supposition of a single power operating by a single organ. The next inquiry, therefore, naturally is, What effect does the condition of the organs produce on the state of the mind? Is it indifferent whether the organs be large or small—well or ill constituted—in health or in disease ?

I submit the following facts to prove that in other departments of organized nature size in an organ, other conditions being the same, is a measure of power in its function ; i. e., that small size indicates little power, and large size much power, when all other circumstances are alike :†

In our infancy we have all been delighted with the fable of the old man who showed his sons a bundle of rods, and pointed out to them how easy it was to snap one asunder, and how difficult to break the whole. The principle involved in this simple story pervades all material substances ; for example, a muscle is composed of a number of fleshy fibres, and hence it follows that each muscle will be strong in proportion to the number of fibres which enter into its composition. If nerves be composed of parts, a nerve which is composed of twenty parts must be more vigorous than one which consists of only one. To render this principle universally true, however, one condition must be observed—namely, that all the parts compared with each other, or with the whole, shall be of the same quality :

* Elliotson's Blumenbach, p. 205.
† This subject is fully treated of by Dr. Andrew Combe in an Essay on the Influence of Organic Size on Energy of Function, particularly as applied to the Organs of the external Senses and Brain, in the Phrenological Journal, vol. iv. p. 161.

for example, if the old man in the fable had presented ten twigs of wood tied up in a bundle, and desired his sons to observe how much more difficult it was to break ten than to sever one ; and if his sons, in refutation of this assertion, had presented him with a rod of iron of the same thickness as one twig, and said that it was as difficult to break that iron rod, although single, as his whole bundle of twigs, although tenfold, the answer would have been obvious, that the things compared differed in kind and quality, and that if he took ten' *iron* rods, and tried to break them, the difficulty would be as great compared with that of severing one, as the task of breaking ten twigs of wood compared with that of breaking one. In like manner, nerves, muscles, brain, and all other parts of the body, may be sound, or they may be diseased ; they may be of a fine structure or a coarse structure : they may be old or young ; they may be almost dissolved by the burning heat of a tropical sun, or nearly frozen under the influence of an arctic winter ; and it would be altogether irrational to expect the influence of size to stand forth as a fixed energy overruling all these circumstances, and producing effects constantly equal. The strength of iron itself, and adamantine rock, depends on temperature ; for either will melt with a certain degree of heat, and at a still higher point they will be dissipated into vapour. The true principle, then, is, that—constitution, health, and outward circumstances being the same—a large muscle, or large nerve, composed of numerous fibres, will act with more force than a small one comprehending few.

In tracing the influence of this law in animated beings, however, we cannot consistently compare one species with another ; because in such comparisons other conditions besides size are not the same. Man, the beaver, and the bee, for example, all construct, yet the bee's organ of Constructiveness must be very minute ; and if we compare the imperceptible organ in it with the relative organ in man or the beaver, it may plausibly be argued, that man and the beaver do not excel the bee in art, in proportion to the excess of size in their organs of Constructiveness. But this is an incorrect method of reasoning. The structure of every species of animals is modified to suit its own condition of life. The ox has four stomachs, and the horse only one ; yet both digest the same kind of food. The proper mode of proceeding is to compare, in different individuals of *the same species*, size of particular organs with strength of particular functions, (health, age, exercise, and constitution being alike,) and then size will be found correctly to indicate power.[*] The more nearly any two species resemble each other, the fitter they become for being profitably compared in their structure and functions ; and hence a reflected light of analogy may be obtained in regard to the laws of the human economy, by studying that of the more perfect of the lower animals. Still, however, we derive only presumptive evidence from this source, and positive proof can be obtained only by direct observations on man himself. This last evidence alone is admitted by phrenologists as sufficient, and on it exclusively their science rests..

In the following observations on the influence of size in the organs upon the power of function in different species of animals, I intend merely to illustrate in a popular manner an abstract point of doctrine, and not to prove it by rigid evidence : for that evidence I confine myself to direct observations on the human species alone :

It will scarcely be disputed, that the strength of the bones is always, other circumstances being equal, proportioned to their size. So certain is this, that when nature requires to give strength to a bone in a bird, and, at the same time, to avoid increasing the weight of the animal, the bone

---

[*] See *Phrenological Journal*, vol. ix., p. 515.

'a made of large diameter, but hollow in the middle; and, on mechanical principles, the increase of volume adds to its strength. That the law of size holds in regard to the bloodvessels and heart, is self-evident to every one who knows that a tube of three inches diameter will transmit more water than a tube of only one inch. And the same may be said in regard to the lungs, liver, kidneys, and every other part. If a liver with a surface of ten square inches can secrete four ounces of bile, it is perfectly manifest that one having a surface of twenty square inches will be able, all other things being equal, to secrete a quantity greater in proportion to its greater size. If this law did not hold true, what would be the advantage of large and capacious lungs over small and confined? There could be none.

Speaking generally, there are two classes of nerves distributed over the body, those of motion and those of sensation or feeling. In motion, the muscle is the essential or chief apparatus, and the nerve is required only to communicate to it the impulse of the will; but in sensation the reverse is the case—the nerve itself is the chief instrument, and the part on which it is ramified is merely a medium for putting it into relation with the specific qualities which it is destined to recognise.

To illustrate in a general way the effect of size in regard to these nerves, the following cases may be adduced; they are stated on the authority of Desmoulins, a celebrated French physiologist, when no other name is given: The horse and ox have much greater muscular power, and much less intensity of sensation, in their limbs than man; and, in conformity with the principle now under discussion, the nerves of motion going to the four limbs in the horse and ox are at least one-third more numerous than the nerves of sensation going to the same parts—whereas in man, the nerves of motion going to the legs and arms are a fifth or a sixth part less than the nerves of sensation distributed on the same parts. In like manner, in birds and reptiles which have scaly skins and limited touch, but vigorous powers of motion, the nerves of sensation are few and small, and the nerves of motion numerous and large. Farther, wherever nature has given a higher degree of sensation or touch to any particular part than to the other parts of an animal, there the nerve of sensation is invariably increased; for example, the single nerve of feeling ramified on the tactile extremity of the proboscis of the elephant exceeds in size the united volume of all the muscular nerves of that organ. Some species of monkeys possess great sensibility in the tail, and some species of bats have great sensibility in their wings; and in these parts the nerves of sensation are increased in size in proportion to the increase of functional power. Birds require to rise in the air, which is a medium much lighter than their own bodies. To have enlarged the size of their muscles would have added to their weight, and increased their difficulty in rising. Nature, to avoid this disadvantage, has bestowed on them large nerves of motion, which infuse a very powerful stimulus into the muscles, and increase their power of flying. Fishes live in water, which has almost the same specific gravity with their bodies. To them Nature has given large muscles, in order to increase their locomotive powers; and in them the nerves of motion are less. In these instances Nature curiously adds to the power of motion by increasing the size of that part of the locomotive apparatus which may be enlarged most conveniently for the animal; but either the muscle or the nerve must be enlarged, otherwise there is no increase of power.

In regard to the external senses, it is proper to observe that each is composed, first, of an instrument or medium on which the impression is made—the eye for example; and, secondly, of a nerve to conduct that impression to the brain. The same law of size holds in regard to these organs of the senses : a large eye will collect more rays of light, a large ear more vibrations of sound, and large nostrils more odorous particles, than the same organs if small. This is so obvious, that it scarcely requires proof ; yet, as Lord Jeffrey has ridiculed the idea, I may mention that Monro, Blumenbach, Soemmering, Cuvier, Magendie, Georget, and a whole host of other physiologists, support it. Blumenbach, when treating of smell, says : " While animals of the most acute smell have the nasal organs most extensively evolved, precisely the same holds in regard to some barbarous nations. For instance, in the head of a North American Indian (represented in one of his plates) the internal nostrils are of an extraordinary size," &c. And again : " The nearest to these in point of magnitude are the internal nostrils of the Ethiopians, from among whom I have eight heads, very different from each other, but each possessing a nasal organ much larger than that described by Soemmering. These anatomical observations accord with the accounts given by most respectable travellers, concerning the wonderful acuteness of smell possessed by those savages." In like manner, Dr. Monro primus—no mean authority —in treating, in his Comparative Anatomy, of the large organ of smell in the dog, says : " The sensibility (of smell) seems to be increased in proportion to the surface ; and this will also be found to take place in all the other senses." The same author states, " that the external ear in different quadrupeds is differently framed, but always calculated to the creature's manner of life ; thus, hares, and such other animals as are daily exposed to insults from beasts of prey, have large ears directed backward, their eyes warning them of danger before."

These observations apply to the external portion of the organs of sense, but the inner parts or nerves are not less subject to the same law of size. Georget, an esteemed physiological writer, in treating of the nerves, affirms, that " The volume of these organs bears a uniform relation, in all the different animals, to the extent and force of the sensations and movements over which they preside. Thus, the nerve of smell in the dog is larger than the five nerves of the external senses in man." The nerve of smell is small in man and in the monkey tribe ; scarcely, if at all, perceptible in the dolphin ; large in the dog and the horse ; and altogether enormous in the whale and the skate, in which it actually exceeds in diameter the spinal marrow itself. In the mole it is of extraordinary size, while the optic nerve is very small. In the eagle the reverse is observed, the optic nerve being very large, and the olfactory small. Most of the quadrupeds excel man in the acuteness of their hearing, and accordingly it is a fact, that the auditory nerve in the sheep, the cow, the horse, &c., greatly exceeds the size of the same nerve in man. In some birds of prey, which are known to possess great sensibility of taste, the palate is found to be very copiously supplied with nervous filaments.

But the organ of sight affords a most interesting example of the influence of size. The office of the eyeball is to collect the rays of light. A large eye, therefore, will take in more rays of light, or, in other words, command a greater sphere of vision, than a small one. But to give intensity or power to vision, the optic nerve also is necessary. Now, the ox placed upon the surface of the earth is of a heavy structure and ill fitted for motion, but he has a large eyeball, which enables him to take in a large field of vision without turning ; yet, as he does not require very keen vision to see his provender, on which he almost treads, the optic nerve is not large in proportion to the eyeball. The eagle, on the other hand, by ascending to a great height in the air, enjoys a wide field of vision from its mere physical position. It looks down from a point over an extensive surface. It has no need, therefore, of a large eyeball to increase artificially its field of vision, and accordingly the ball of its eye is compara-

tively small; but it requires, from that height, to discern its prey upon
the surface of the earth—and not only is the distance great, but the prey
often resembles in colour the ground on which it rests. To the eagle,
therefore, great intensity of vision is necessary. Accordingly, in it the
optic nerve is increased to an enormous extent. Instead of forming a
single membrane only lining the inner surface of the posterior chamber
of the eye, as in man and animals which do not require extraordinary
vision—and consequently only equalling in extent the sphere of the eye to
which it belongs—the retina or expansion of the nerve of vision in these
quick-sighted birds of prey is found to be composed of a great number of
folds, each hanging loose into the eye, and augmenting, in a wonderful
degree, not only the extent of nervous surface, but the mass of nervous
matter, and giving rise to that intensity of vision which distinguishes the
eagle, falcon, hawk, and similar animals. In the case of the senses, then,
we plainly see, that when Nature designs to increase their power, she
effects her purpose by augmenting the size of their organs.

Let us now attend to the brain. Were I to affirm that difference of
size in the brain produces no effect on the vigour of its functions—or that
a small brain, in perfect health and of a sound constitution, is equal in
functional power and efficiency to a large one in similar condition—would
the reader, after the evidence which has been laid before him of the
influence of size in increasing the power of function in other parts of the
body, be disposed to credit the assertion? He would have the utmost
difficulty in believing it, and would say that, if such were the fact, the brain
must form an exception to a law which appears general over organized
nature; and yet the phrenologists have been assailed with vituperation
for maintaining that the brain does not form an exception to this general
law, but that in it also vigour of function is in proportion to size, other
conditions being alike. I shall proceed to state some direct evidence in
proof of this fact; but the reader is requested to observe that I am here
expounding only general principles in an introductory discourse. The
conditions and modifications under which these principles ought to be
applied in practice will be stated in a subsequent chapter.

First, The brain of a child is small, and its mind weak, compared with
the brain and mental faculties of an adult.

Secondly, Small size in the brain is an invariable cause of idiocy. Phrenologists have in vain called upon their opponents to produce a single
instance of the mind being manifested vigorously by a very small brain.
Dr. Gall has laid it down as a fact to which there is no exception, that
where the brain is so small that the horizontal circumference of the head
does not exceed thirteen or fourteen inches, idiocy is the invariable consequence. "Complete intelligence," he remarks, "is absolutely impossible with so small a brain; in such cases idiocy, more or less complete,
invariably occurs, and to this rule no exception—either has been, or ever
will be, found."* To the same effect, Dr. Spurzheim, in his work on
Insanity, says: "We are very well aware that a great number of facts
repeated under various circumstances are necessary before we can draw a
general conclusion; but with respect to idiotism from birth, we have made
such a number of observations in various countries, that we have no hesitation in affirming that a too small brain is unfit for the manifestation of
the mind. I beg to remark, that I do not say that idiotism is the attribute
of a too small brain only; idiotism may be the result of different causes,
one of which is a too small brain. We are convinced from observation,
that the laws of nature are constant; and if we continually observe that
the same phenomenon takes place under the same circumstances, we
consider our conclusion as certain, till experience shows the contrary.

* *Sur les Functions du Cerveau,* ii. 330.

No one, then, has the right to maintain that an inference is too hastily drawn because he has not made a sufficient number of observations. It is his duty to show facts which prove the contrary, if he intend to deny the inference." In the *Journal of the Phrenological Society of Paris* for April, 1835, Dr. Voisin reports observations made upon the idiots under his care at the Parisian Hospital of Incurables, in order to verify the assertion of Gall in the passage just quoted; and mentions that he found it substantiated by every one of his cases. In the lowest class of idiots, where the intellectual manifestations were null, the horizontal circumference, taken a little higher than the orbit, varied from eleven to thirteen inches, while the distance from the root of the nose backward over the top of the head to the occipital spine was only between eight and nine inches. When the size varied from fourteen to seventeen inches of horizontal measurement, and eleven or twelve in the other direction, glimpses of feelings and random intellectual perceptions were observable, but without any power of attention or fixity of ideas. Lastly, when the first measurement extended to eighteen or nineteen inches, although the head was still small, the intellectual manifestations were regular enough, but deficient in intensity. In a full-sized head, the first measurement is equal to twenty-two inches, and the second to about fourteen inches. So large was the head of Spurzheim, that even on the *skull* these two measurements amount to twenty-two and one quarter and thirteen and six-tenths inches respectively. Those who deny the influence of size of the brain on the manifestations of the mind, should reconcile these facts with their own views before they denounce Phrenology as at variance with nature, and maintain that, so far as vigour of mind is concerned, it is indifferent whether the head be large or small.

Even Pinel, who will not be suspected of any desire to favour Phrenology, admits, that "it appears that idiocy from birth always accompanies an original defect of the brain, that it cannot undergo any sort of change, and that its duration is the same with that of the physical cause from which it arises."[*] Dr. Gall has represented, in the Atlas of his quarto work, (Plates 18, 19, and 20,) three very small heads of idiots; and similar engravings are given by Pinel. A striking case of idiocy in conjunction with a diminutive brain, will be found in the 42d number of *The Phrenological Journal.*[†] An engraving of the head is here subjoined, in contrast with a sketch of that of the celebrated Hindoo reformer Rammohun Roy.

IDIOT, aged 20.   RAMMOHUN ROY.

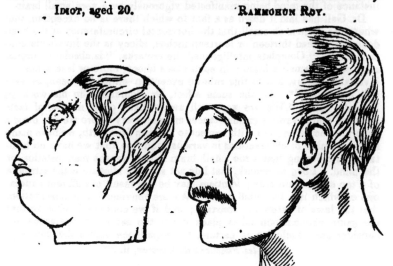

Dr. Ellioteon mentions a cast of the head of a male idiot, aged eighteen years, which he received from Dr, Formby, of Liverpool, and subsequently presented to the London Phrenological Society.: It is only 16 inches in circumference, and 7½ inches from ear to ear over the vertex. The cerebrum weighed only 1 lb. 7½ oz., and the cerebellum but 4 ounces.*

Deficiency of size in the brain is not, however, the only cause of idiocy. A brain may be large and diseased, and mental imbecility may arise from the disease; but, as above shown, although disease be absent, if the size be very deficient, idiocy is invariable.

Thirdly, Men who have been remarkable, not for mere cleverness, but for great force of character, such as Napoleon Bonaparte, Franklin, and Burns, have had heads of unusual magnitude.

Fourthly, It is an ascertained fact, that nations in whom the Brain is large, possess so great a mental superiority over those in whom that organ is small, that they conquer and oppress them at pleasure. The Hindoo brain, for example, is considerably smaller than the European, and it is well known that a few thousands of Europeans have subdued and keep in subjection millions of Hindoos. The brain of the aboriginal American also is smaller than the European, and the same result has been exem-, plified in that quarter of the world.'

Lastly, The influence of size is now admitted by the most eminent phy siologists. "The volume of the brain," says Magendie, "is generally in direct proportion to the capacity of the mind. We ought not to suppose, however, that every man having a large head is necessarily a person of superior intelligence; for there are many causes of an augmentation of the volume of the head besides the size of the brain; but it is rarely found that a man distinguished by his mental faculties has not a large head. The only way of estimating the volume of the brain, in a living person, is, to measure the dimensions of the skull; every other means, even that proposed by Camper, is uncertain."† The following passage, which occurs in the 94th number of the *Edinburgh Review*, also implies, not only that different parts of the nervous system, including the brain, have different functions, but that an increase of volume in the brain is marked by some addition to, or *amplification* of, the powers of the animal. "It is in the nervous system alone that we can trace a gradual progress in the provision for the subordination of one (animal) to another, and of all to man; and are enabled to associate every faculty which gives superiority with some addition to the nervous mass, even from the smallest indications of sensation and will, up to the highest degree of sensibility, judgment, and expression. The brain is observed progressively to be improved in its structure, and, with reference to the spinal marrow and nerves, augmented in volume more and more, until we reach the human brain, each addition being marked by some addition to, or amplification of, the powers of the animal—until in man we behold it possessing some parts of which animals are destitute, and wanting none which theirs possess."

There is, here, then, pretty strong evidence and authority for the assertion, that the brain does not form an exce tion to the eneral law o nature the

† *Compendium of Physiology*, Milligan's Translation, p. 104, edit. 1826.

‡ It is certified by hatters, that the lower classes of the community, who are distinguished for muscular vigour much more than mental capacity, require a smaller size of hat than those classes whose occupations are chiefly mental, and in whom vigour of mind surpasses that of body. But the phrenologist does not compare *intellectual* power with the size of brain in general; and, besides, the hat does not indicate the size of the whole head. The reader will find details on this point in the *Phrenological Journal*, iv. 539, and v. 213.

The circumstances which modify the effects of size come next to be considered. These are constitution, health, exercise, excitement from without, and, in some cases, the mutual influence of the organs.

The question naturally presents itself, Do we possess any index to constitutional qualities of brain? The temperaments indicate them to a certain extent. There are four temperaments, accompanied with different degrees of activity in the brain—the Lymphatic, the Sanguine, the Bilious, and the Nervous. The temperaments are supposed to depend upon the constitution of particular systems of the body; the brain and nerves being predominantly active from constitutional causes, seem to produce the nervous temperament; the lungs, heart, and bloodvessels being constitutionally predominant, to give rise to the sanguine; the muscular and fibrous systems to the bilious; and the glands and assimilating organs to the lymphatic.

The different temperaments are indicated by external signs, which are open to observation. The first, or *lymphatic*, is distinguishable by a round form of the body, softness of the muscular system, repletion of the cellular tissue, fair hair, and a pale skin. It is accompanied by languid vital actions, with weakness, and slowness in the circulation. The brain, as part of the system, is also slow, languid, and feeble in its action, and the mental manifestations are proportionally weak.

The second, or *sanguine*, temperament is indicated by well-defined forms, moderate plumpness of person, tolerable firmness of flesh, light hair inclining to chestnut, blue eyes, and fair complexion, with ruddiness of countenance. It is marked by great activity of the bloodvessels, fondness for exercise, and an animated countenance. The brain partakes of the general state, and is active.

The *bilious* temperament is recognised by black hair, dark skin, moderate fulness and much firmness of flesh, with harshly expressed outline of the person. The functions partake of great energy of action, which extends to the brain; and the countenance, in consequence, shows strong, marked, and decided features.

The *nervous* temperament is recognised by fine thin hair, thin skin, small thin muscles, quickness in muscular motion, paleness of countenance, and often delicate health. The whole nervous system, including the brain, is predominantly active, and the mental manifestations are proportionally vivacious.

It is thus clearly admitted, that constitution or quality of brain greatly modifies the effects of size upon the mind: but let us attend to the consequences. As a general rule, all the parts of the same brain have the same constitution, and if size be a measure of power, then in each head the large organs will be more powerful that the small ones? This enables us to judge of the strong and the weak points in each head. But if we compare two separate brains, we must recollect that the size of the two may be equal, and that nevertheless the one, from possessing the finest texture and most vigorous constitution, may be exceedingly active, while the other, from being inferior in quality, may be naturally inert. The uence may be, that the better const   maller, brain will st the mind with the   ··· ··   ize is, nev
                                                  rasting the manifestations of a
        . . .   arge brain, possessing the same configuration, and equally well constituted; the power or energy will then be found superior in the latter. This illustrates what is meant by other natural conditions being equal: As the temperaments are distinguishable by the countenance and the general make of the body, and as the brain partakes of the general constitution, we possess a valuable, though not all-sufficient, index to its natural qualities.. I repeat that these remarks apply only to the case of

LYMPHATIC.   **SANGUINE.**

BILIOUS.   **NERVOUS.**

comparing one brain with another. The same brain has in general the same constitution, and on the principle that size is a measure of power, the largest organs in each individual will be naturally the most vigorous. If the temperament be lymphatic, all the organs will act slowly, but the largest will be most powerful and most active, on account of their superior size. If the temperament be active, all will be active, but the largest will take the lead. It is on this account that a student of Phrenology, in search of evidence, should not compare the same organ in different brains, without attending very strictly to the temperament.

Of the causes of the temperaments various theories have been formed, but none hitherto propounded can be regarded as satisfactory. But, as is well remarked by a writer in *The Phrenological Journal*, "it is with the *effects* of the temperaments, more than their *causes*, that we are concerned —and happily the former are less obscure than the latter. When an individual is characterized by softness of flesh, fairness of the skin, flaxen hair, plumpness of figure, a weak slow pulse, and a loutish inanimate expression, physiologists agree in describing him as a person of a lymphatic temperament ; and whatever be the *cause* of these appearances, we know from experience that they are *indications* of great languor of the bodily and mental functions. *Cæteris paribus*, temperament seems to affect equally every part of the body ; so that if the muscles be naturally active and energetic, we may expect also activity and energy of the brain ; and if one set of muscles be active, the like vivacity may be looked for in the others. This principle is practically recognised by William Cobbett, who, whatever may be his merits or demerits as a politician, is certainly a shrewd observer and describer of real life. In his Letter to a Lover he discusses the question, ' Who is to tell whether a girl will make an industrious woman ? How is the purblind lover especially to be able to ascertain whether she, whose smiles, and dimples, and bewitching lips have half bereft him of his senses ; how is he to be able to judge, from anything that he can see, whether the beloved object will be industrious or lazy ? Why, it is very difficult,' he answers : ' There are, however, certain outward signs, which, if attended to with care, will serve as pretty sure guides. And, first, if you find the *tongue* lazy, you may be nearly certain that the hands and feet are the same. By laziness of the tongue I do not mean *silence ;* I do not mean an *absence of talk*, for that is, in most case, very good ; but I mean a *slow* and *soft utterance ;* a sort of *sighing out* of the words, instead of *speaking* them ; a sort of letting the sounds fall out, as if the party were sick at stomach. The pronunciation of an industrious person is generally *quick* and *distinct*, and the voice, if not strong, *firm* at least. Not masculine ; as feminine as possible : not a creak nor a bawl, but a, quick, distinct, and sound voice.' ' Another mark of industry is a *quick step*, and a somewhat heavy tread, showing that the foot comes down with a hearty good will.' ' I do not like, and I never liked, your sauntering, soft-stepping girls, who move as if they were perfectly indifferent as to the result.'* We are disposed to think that Cobbett's homely advice will prove sound in all cases where the nervous and muscular systems are equally developed, equally healthy, and equally accustomed to exercise. But if the head be large and the muscles small, the individual will be much more inclined to mental than to muscular activity ; and, on the other hand, if he have large muscles and a small brain, the activity derived from a sanguine or bilious temperament will have a tendency to expend itself in exercise or labour of the body. The reason of this is, that the largest organs have, *cæteris paribus*, the greatest tendency to act ; their activity is productive of the greatest pleasure ; hence they are more frequently exercised than the smaller organs ; and

* Cobbett's *Advice to Young Men*, Letter III, sect. 102-5

thus the energy and activity of the former are made to predominate still more than they did originally, over those of the latter" "The remarks now offered in reference to the comparative efficiency of the muscular and cerebral functions are equally applicable to the cerebral organs, considered in relation to each other. Where two organs are alike in developement and cultivation, a nervous or sanguine temperament will render them equally active; but where one is more fully developed than the other, it will excel the latter both in power and in activity. In another brain of the same size and form, but with a lymphatic temperament, a similar predominance of the power and activity of one organ over those of the other will be found; but the absolute power and activity of both will be less than in the other case supposed. Temperament, therefore, besides influencing the *activity* of the organs, affects their *power* also, to a greater extent than some phrenologists seem inclined to allow."[*]

Farther, the brain must possess a healthy constitution, and that degree of activity which is the usual accompaniment of health. Now, the brain, like other parts of the body, may be affected with certain diseases which do not diminish nor increase its magnitude, but yet impair its functions. The phrenologist ascertains the health by inquiry. In cases of disease, great size may be present, and very imperfect manifestations appear; or the brain may be attacked with other diseases, such as inflammation, or any of those particular affections whose nature is unknown, but to which the name of mania is given in nosology, and which greatly exalt its action; and then very forcible manifestations may proceed from a brain comparatively small: but it is no less true, that, when a larger brain is excited to the same degree by the same causes, the manifestations are still more energetic, in proportion to the superiority of size. These cases, therefore, form no valid objection to Phrenology; for the phrenologist ascertains, by previous inquiry, that the brain is in a state of health. If it is not, he makes the necessary limitations in drawing his conclusions.

The effects of exercise in adding to the mental power are universally known, and ought never to be overlooked by the phrenologist. "The brain, being an organized part, is subject, in so far as regards its exercise, to precisely the same laws as the other organs of the body. If it be doomed to inactivity, its health decays, and the mental operations and feelings, as a necessary consequence, become dull, feeble, and slow. If it be duly exercised, after regular intervals of repose, the mind acquires

---

[*] *Phrenological Journal*, vol. ix., p. 116--118. See also pp. 54, 267. Engravings illustrative of the Temperaments will be found in Dr. Spurzheim's *Phrenology in Connexion with the Study of Physiognomy*, London, 1826, Pl. I. As the error is still very common, that phrenologists consider the power of an organ to depend on its size alone, I subjoin several passages on this subject, extracted from phrenological works. Dr. Gall, in the first volume of his treatise *Sur les Fonctions du Cerveau*, says: "L'énergie des fonctions des organes ne dépende pas seulement de leur développement, *mais aussi de leur excitabilité*."—(P. 196.) "Les fonctions des sens dont les organes sont plus considérables, plus sains, et plus développés, ou qui ont reçu une irritation plus forte, sont, par cela même, plus vives. La même phénomène se reproduit dans les facultés de l'âme; les organes de ces facultés agissent avec plus d'énergie, s'ils sont *plus irrités* ou plus développés."—(P. 306.) And Dr. Spurzheim, in his work on Physiognomy, above referred to, states that "it is important, in a physiological point of view, to take into account *the peculiar constitution or temperament* of individuals, not as the cause of determinate faculties, but *as influencing the energy* with which the special functions of the several organs are manifested."—(P. 15.) "The energy and excellence of the brain," says Dr. Caldwell, "depend on its size, configuration, *and tone*—its extensity *and intensity*.—(*Elements of Phrenology*. Lexington, Ky., 1824, p. 38.) See farther on the temperaments, *The Phrenological Journal*, viii., 293, 369, 447, 509, 564, 595.

readiness and strength; and, lastly, if it be overtasked, either in the force or duration of its activity, its functions become impaired, and irritability and disease take the place of health and vigour."* The other influences which modify size will be considered afterward.

Let us turn our attention to the point of the argument at which we are now arrived. We have seen that the brain is the organ of the mind; that it is not a single organ, but that the analogy of all the other organs, the successive developement of the faculties, with the phenomena of partial genius, partial insanity, monomania, dreaming, and partial injuries of the brain, indicate that it is a congeries of organs manifesting a plurality of faculties; and that, in the cases of the bones, muscles, nerves of motion, nerves of sensation, and nerves of the five senses, size has an influence on power of function: and from the analogy of these organs, as well as from direct facts and physiological authorities, we have come to the same conclusion regarding the brain—that vigour of function, other circumstances besides magnitude being equal, is in proportion to the size of the organ. From these premises it follows, as a necessary consequence, that, with respect to the manifestation of the mental faculties, it will not be indifferent in what direction the brain is most or least developed: for example, if different parts of the brain possess different functions, and if the strength of function be in proportion to the size of the part, the vigour of the faculties connected with the forehead, whatever these may be, will be greater where the frontal region predominates in size than where the predominance is in the posterior portion; and differences will occur also in cases of preponderance in the superior or inferior regions. In short, it is obvious that two brains may be composed of exactly the same number of cubic inches of cerebral matter, and yet serve to manifest two minds totally different from each other in the kind of disposition or capacity by which they are characterised; so that the form of the head is an object of attention to the phrenologist, not less interesting and important than its size. This fact shows clearly the absurdity of assuming the size of a hat as an accurate indication of the magnitude of its wearer's head; for although there may be considerable length and breadth, yet, if the height be deficient, the brain may be of very ordinary size.

Here we have a representation of the skull of Dr. Spurzheim, and of the

DR. SPURZHEIM.

skull of a native of New Holland; both taken from casts in the collection of the Phrenological Society. The difference in the forehead is very conspicuous. If the part of the brain lying in that region have any function connected with intellect, and if size be a measure of power, the two beings should form a strong contrast of power and weakness in that department. And, accordingly, the case is so. Dr. Spurzheim has left in his phrenological works an imperishable record of moral and intellectual greatness; while Sir Walter Scott describes the other as follows: "The natives of New Holland are, even at present, in the very lowest scale of humanity, and ignorant of every art which can add

* The Principles of Physiology applied to the Preservation of Health and to the Improvement of Physical and Mental Education. By Andrew Combe, M.D. 3d edit., p. 277.

NATIVE OF NEW HOLLAND.

comfort or decency to human life. These unfortunate savages use no clothes, construct no cabins nor huts, and are ignorant even of the manner of chasing animals or catching fish, unless such of the latter as are left by the tide, or which are found on the rocks; they feed upon the most disgusting substances, snakes, worms, maggots, and whatever trash falls in their way. They know, indeed, how to kindle a fire; in that respect only they have stepped beyond the deepest ignorance to which man can be subjected; but they have not learned how to boil water; and when they see Europeans perform this ordinary operation, they have been known to run away in great terror."

We have now arrived, by a fair and legitimate induction, at strong presumptive evidence in favour of the general principles of Phrenology—namely, that the brain is the organ of the mind; that different parts of it are connected with different faculties; and that the size of the organ exerts an influence on the power of manifestation. Here, then, the inquiry presents itself, What faculties and what parts of the brain are mutually connected? This is the grand question remaining to be solved, in order to render our knowledge of the functions of the brain and the organs of the mind precise and practically useful. Let us inquire what progress the metaphysician and anatomist have made in elucidating this point. It is of importance to take a view of the past efforts of philosophers on this subject, that we may be able correctly to appreciate both what remains to be done, and how far Phrenology affords the means of accomplishing it.

The mind has been studied, by one set of philosophers, with too little reference to the body; and the laws of thought have been expounded with as much neglect of organization as if we had already "shuffled off this mortal coil." From this erroneous practice of many distinguished authors, such as Locke, Hume, Reid, Stewart, and Brown, a prejudice has arisen against the physiology of man, as if the mind were degraded by contemplating it in connexion with matter; but man is the work of the Creator of the world, and no part of his constitution can be unworthy of regard and admiration. The whole phenomena of life are the result of mind and body joined, each modifying each; and how can we explain a result without attending to all the causes which combine toward its production? In the words of Dr. John Gregory, "It has been the misfortune of most of those who have studied the philosophy of the human mind, that they have been little acquainted with the structure of the human body and the laws of the animal economy; and yet the mind and body are so intimately connected, and have such a mutual influence on one another, that the constitution of either, examined apart, can never be thoroughly understood. For the same reason, it has been an unspeakable loss to physicians, that they have been so generally inattentive to the peculiar laws of the mind and their influence on the body."* Even Mr. Dugald Stewart admits, that "among the different articles connected with the natural history of the human species," the laws of union between the "mind and body, and the mutual influence they have on one another," are subjects of one of the most important inquiries that ever "engaged

* *Comparative View of the State and Faculties of Man with those of the Animal World*, 3d edit., London, 1766, p. 5.

he attention of mankind, and almost equally necessary in the sciences of morals and of medicine."*

Another set of philosophers, in avoiding Scylla, have thought it necessary to dash into Charybdis, and, teaching that the mind is nought but a combination of matter, have endeavoured to explain its functions by supposed mechanical motions in its parts: but, as we shall hereafter see, this course of proceeding is equally erroneous with the other.

In surveying the phenomena of mind, we are struck by the variety of faculties with which it appears to be endowed. Philosophers and the vulgar equally admit it to be possessed of different powers. Thus it is by one faculty that it reasons, by another that it fears, and by a third that it discriminates between right and wrong.

If, however, we inquire what progress has hitherto been made by metaphysicians in ascertaining the primitive mental powers, and in rendering the philosophy of man interesting and practically useful to persons of ordinary understanding, we shall find a deficiency that is truly deplorable. From the days of Aristotle to the present time, the most powerful intellects have been directed, with the most persevering industry, to this department of science; and system after system has flourished, fallen, and been forgotten, in rapid and melancholy succession. To confine our attention to modern times : Dr. Reid overturned the philosophy of Locke and Hume ; Mr. Stewart, while he illustrated Reid, yet differed from him in many important particulars ; and, recently, Dr. Thomas Brown has attacked, with powerful eloquence and philosophical profundity, the fabric of Stewart, which already totters to its fall. The very existence of the most common and familiar faculties of the mind is debated among these philosophers. Mr. Stewart maintains Attention to be a faculty, but this is denied by Dr. Brown. Others, again, state Imagination to be a primitive power of the mind, while Mr. Stewart informs us, that " what we call the power of Imagination is *not the gift of nature*, but the result of acquired habits, aided by favourable circumstances."† Common observation informs us, that a taste for music and a genius for poetry and painting are gifts of nature, bestowed only on a few ; but Mr. Stewart, by dint of his philosophy, has discovered that these powers, and also a genius for mathematics, " are gradually formed by particular habits of study or of business."‡ On the other hand, he treats of Perception, Conception, and Memory as original powers ; while Dr. Thomas Brown denies their title to that appellation. Reid, Stewart, and Brown admit the existence of moral emotions ; but Hobbes, Mandeville, Paley, and many others, resolve the sentiment of right and wrong into a regard to our own good, perceptions of utility, and obedience to the laws or to the Divine command. Thus, after the lapse and labour of more than two thousand years, philosophers are not yet agreed concerning the existence of many of the most important principles of action, and intellectual powers of man. While the philosophy of mind shall remain in this uncertain condition, it will be impossible to give to morals and natural religion a scientific foundation ; and, until these shall assume the stableness and precision of sciences— education, political economy, and legislation must continue defective in their principles and application. If, therefore, Phrenology could introduce into the philosophy of mind even a portion of the certainty and precision which attend physical investigations, it would confer no small benefit on this interesting department of science ; and that it is fully competent to do so, shall be made apparent after we have attended to a few preliminary points requiring consideration.

In the next place, supposing the number and nature of the primitive

* Stewart's *Preliminary Dissertation, Supp. Encyc. Brit.*, Part ii., pp. 199, 200.
† *Elements*, chap. 7, sect. 1.   ‡ *Outlines*, p. 16.

faculties to be ascertained, it is to be remarked, that, in actual life, they are successively developed. The infant feels anger, fear, attachment, before it is alive to the sublime or the beautiful; and it observes occurrences long before it reasons. A correct theory of mind ought to unfold principles to which these facts also may be referred.

Farther—even after the full maturity of age is attained, how *different the degrees* in which we are endowed with the various mental powers! Admitting each individual to possess all the faculties which constitute the human mind, in what a variety of degrees of relative strength do they appear in different persons! In one, the love of glory is the feeling which surpasses all; another is deaf to the voice of censure, and callous to the accents of applause. The soul of one melts with softest pity at a tale of wo; while the eye of another never shed a sympathetic tear. One individual spends his life in an ardent chase of wealth, which he stops not to enjoy; another scatters in wasteful prodigality the substance of his sires, and perishes in want from a mere incapacity to retain. One vast intellect, like Newton's, fathoms the profundities of science; while the mind of another can scarcely grope its way through the daily occurrences of life. The towering imagination of a Shakspeare or a Milton soars beyond the boundaries of sublunary space; while the sterile fancy of a clown sees no glory in the heavens and no loveliness on earth.

A system of mental philosophy, therefore, pretending to be true, ought not only to unfold the simple elements of thought and of feeling, but to enable us to discover *in what proportions* they are combined in different individuals. In chemical science, one combination of elementary ingredients produces a medicine of sovereign virtue in removing pain; another combination of the same materials, but differing in their relative proportions, brings forth a mortal poison. In human nature, also, one combination of faculties may produce the midnight murderer and thief—another a Franklin, a Howard, or a Fry, glowing with charity to man.

If, however, we search the works of those philosophers who have hitherto written on the mind, for rules by which to discriminate the effects produced upon the character and conduct of individuals by different combinations of the mental powers, what information do we receive? Instead of light upon this interesting subject, we find only disputes whether such differences exist in nature, or are the result of education and other adventitious circumstances; many maintaining the one opinion, while some few advocate the other. This department of the philosophy of man, in short, is a perfect waste. Mr. Stewart was aware equally of its importance and of its forlorn condition. The varieties of intellectual character among men, says he, present another very interesting object of study, which, "considering its practical utility, has not yet excited, so much as might have been expected, the curiosity of our countrymen."[*] The reason appears sufficiently obvious: the common modes of studying man afforded no clew to the discovery desired.

In thus surveying the philosophy of man, as at present exhibited to us in the writings of philosophers, we perceive, *first*, That no account is given of the influence of the material organs on the mental powers; and that the progress of the mind from youth to age, and the phenomena of sleep, dreaming, idiocy, and insanity, are left unexplained or unaccounted for by any principles admitted in their systems: *secondly*, That the existence and functions of some of the most important primitive faculties are still in dispute: and, *thirdly*, That no light whatever has been thrown on the nature and effects of combinations of the primitive powers, in different degrees of relative proportion. It is with great truth, therefore, that Monsieur De Bonald, quoted by Mr. Stewart, observes, that "diversity of

* *Dissertation, Supp. Encyc. Brit.*, Part. ii., p. 198.

doctrine has increased from age to age, with the number of masters, and with the progress of knowledge ; and Europe, which af present possesses libraries filled with philosophical works, and which reckons up almost as many philosophers as writers ; poor in the midst of so much riches, and uncertain, with the aid of all its guides, which road it should follow ; Europe, the centre and focus of all the lights of the world, has yet its *philosophy* only in expectation."

While philosophers have been thus unsuccessfully engaged in the study of mental science, human nature has been investigated by another set of observers—moralists, poets, and divines. These have looked upon the page of life merely to observe the characters there exhibited, with the view of tracing them anew in their own compositions ; and certainly they have executed their design with great felicity and truth. In the pages of Shakspeare, Addison, Johnson, Tillotson, and Scott, we have tho lineaments of mind traced with a perfect tact, and exhibited with matchless beauty and effect. But these authors had no systematic object in view, and aimed not at founding their observations on principles which might render them subservient to the practical purposes of life. Hence, although in their compositions we find ample and admirable materials for the elucidation of a true system of the philosophy of man, yet, without other aids than those which they supply, we cannot arrive at fundamental principles sufficient to guide us in our intercourse with the world. The charge against their representations of human nature is, not that they are incorrect, but that they are too general to be useful. They draw striking pictures of good men and of bad men, but do not enable us to discover, previously to experience, whether any particular individual with whom we may wish to connect our fortunes, belongs to the one class or to the other—a matter of extreme importance, because, in the course of gaining experience, we encounter the risk of suffering the greatest calamities. In short, poets and novelists describe men as they do the weather : in their pages they make the storm to rage with terrific energy, or the sun to shine with the softest radiance, but do not enable us to discover whether, to-morrow, the elements will war, or the zephyrs play ; and, without this power, we cannot put to sea with the certainty of favouring gales, nor stay in port without the risk of losing winds that would have wafted us to the wished-for shore. Phrenology, therefore, if a true system of human nature, ought not only to present to the popular reader a key of philosophy which shall enable him to unlock the stores of intellectual wealth contained in the volumes of our most gifted authors, but likewise to render their representations of human character practically useful, by enabling him to discover the natural qualities of living individuals previously to experience of their conduct, and thus to appreciate their tendencies before becoming the victim of their incapacity or passions.

The causes of the failure of the metaphysician are easily recognised. He studied the mind chiefly by reflecting on his own consciousness ; he turned his attention inward, observed the phenomena of his own faculties, and recorded these as metaphysical science. 'But the mind is not conscious of organs at all ; we are not informed by it of the existence of muscles, nerves of motion, nerves of taste, nerves of smell, an auditory apparatus, optic nerves, nor any mental organs whatever. All that consciousness reveals is, that the mind inhabits the head ; but it does not inform us what material substances the head contains : hence it was impossible for the metaphysician to discover the organs of the mind by his method of philosophizing, and no metaphysical philosopher pretends to have discovered them. The imperfection of this mode of investigation accounts for the contradictory representation of the human mind given by different metaphysicians. Suppose an individual with a brain like that of a New Hollander, to turn philosopher; he would never, by reflecting on his own consciousness, find an instinctive sentiment of justice, and, therefore, he would exclude it from his system. On the other hand, another philosopher, constituted like Dr. Spurzheim, would feel it strongly, and give it a prominent place.

When we turn our attention to the works of physiologists, we discover the most ceaseless, but fruitless, endeavours to ascertain and determine the parts of the body with which the several mental powers are most closely connected. Some of them have dissected the brain, in the hope of discovering in its texture an indication of the functions which it performs in relation to the mind; but success has not hitherto crowned their efforts. When we examine, with the most scrupulous minuteness, the form, colour, and texture of the brain, no sentiment can be perceived slumbering in its fibres, nor half-formed ideas starting from its folds. It appears to the eye only as a mass of curiously convoluted matter; and the understanding declares its incapacity to penetrate the purposes of its parts. In fact, we cannot, by merely dissecting any organ of the body whatever, discover its functions. Anatomists for many centuries dissected the nerves of motion and feeling, and saw nothing in their structure that indicated the difference of their functions; and, at this moment, if the nerves of taste and of hearing were presented together on the table, we might look at them for ages without discovering traces of separate functions in their structure. Simple dissection of the brain, therefore, could not lead to the discovery of the functions of its different parts.[*]

Thus, the obstacles which have hitherto opposed the attainment of this information have been numerous and formidable. The imagination, however, has been called in, to afford the knowledge which philosophy withheld, and theories have been invented to supply the place of principles founded on facts and legitimate induction. Some physiologists, while they locate the understanding in the brain, derive the affections and passions from various abdominal and thoracic viscera, ganglia, and nerves. But the fallacy of this notion is apparent from a variety of circumstances. In the first place, there is a presumption against it in the fact, that the heart, liver, and intestines have well-known functions entirely different from those so ascribed to them; and it is contrary to the established principles of physiology to suppose that a muscular organ like the heart is at once a machine for propelling the blood and the organ of courage or love—or that the liver, which secretes bile, and the bowels, which are organs of nutrition, are at the same time respectively the organs of anger and compassion. These emotions being mental phenomena, it is presumable that they ought to be referred, like the analogous phenomena of intellect, to the nervous system. Secondly, no relation is found to subsist between the size of these viscera and the mental qualities ascribed to them: cowardly men have not small hearts, nor do we find the liver more ample in angry men than in mild and pacific. Thirdly, disease of the brain influences the affective faculties not less than the intellectual; while the abdominal and thoracic viscera, on the other hand, may be in a morbid state without any corresponding change of the faculties ascribed to them. Fourthly, why do not children, in whom these viscera are well developed even at birth, manifest all the passions in their earliest years? Fifthly, many idiots, almost or wholly

* The proposition that the structure of an organ does not reveal its function is to be understood with reference, not to mechanical functions, but only to vital. Harvey was led to discover the function of the heart and bloodvessels, by observing in them certain valves capable of permitting the blood to flow in one direction, but not in the opposite. So true it is, however, that vital functions are not revealed by dissection, that physiologists have not even yet been able to determine the purpose of the spleen.

destitute of some of the affections, have nevertheless a complete developement of the thoracic and abdominal viscera. Sixthly, it is very
improbable that animals of different species, having the viscera alike,
should manifest opposite affections—that the heart, for example, should
be the organ of fear in the sheep and of courage in the dog.[*] Lastly,
and above all, observation proves that the affective faculties are stronger
or weaker, according as certain parts of the brain are more or less developed ; a fact which will be demonstrated when we come to treat of them
in detail. Those who argue that, because fear and anger cause palpitation of the heart, the latter must be the organ of these passions. do, in
reality (according to the remark of Dr. Mason Good, quoted above, p. 12)
mistake an effect for its cause. By means of the nerves the thoracic and
abdominal viscera are intimately connected with the brain, and a very
close sympathy exists between them. Excitement and disease of the
brain; therefore, often produce marked effects upon the viscera ; and in
like manner diseases of the stomach and liver have a very obvious influence on the brain. Excitement even of the intellectual faculties is not
unfrequently found to affect the viscera : thus it is recorded of Malebranche, that he was seized with lively palpitations of the heart when
reading the *Treatise on Man* of Descartes ; and Tissot, in his work on
the Diseases of Literary and Sedentary Persons, refers to many cases
where overexertion of the intellect occasioned the same diseases of the
viscera as those produced by too great violence of the passions. So, also,
vomiting is sometimes occasioned by wounds of the brain ; but the brain
is not, therefore, the seat of vomiting. On the other hand, nervous affections, equally with those of the viscera, result from great activity of the
passions, in the various forms of palsy, convulsions, madness, and epi-
lepsy. Grief, as every one is aware, makes us shed tears ; fear produces
a sensation of cold in the skin, and causes the legs to totter ; and indi-
gestion frequently occasions toothache : but are we thence to infer that
the lachrymal glands are the organs of grief, the teeth the seat of indi-
gestion, and the skin or legs the organs of fear ? In short, to use the
words of Adelon, who has adopted all the arguments of Gall, " les objections se présentent en foule contre toute cette doctrine."[†] Even Dr.
Prichard, who has no other seat for the passions, abandons the claim of
the thoracic and abdominal viscera as utterly hopeless—on the ground,
among others, " that the same emotion will display its effect on different
organs in different individuals. Fear or terror will occasion in one person fainting or palpitation of the heart ; in another, it affects the liver or
intestinal canal ; but the particular effect would probably be uniform and
unvaried if the mental emotion were dependent on some particular ganglion of the great sympathetic nerve (which was the idea of Bichât.) The
vagueness of popular language on this subject is sufficient to prove that
the physical effects of the emotions are very various. The Greeks
referred most of the passions to the liver, spleen, and diaphragm ; the
Hebrews, to the bowels and reins ; the moderns refer them almost solely
to the heart. The diversity of these phenomena, which vary according
to the peculiarities of constitution, proves that they are secondary effects
produced by the emotions through sympathy on the functions of the
viscera, those organs being most affected which in each individual have
the greatest irritability or susceptibility of impressions."[‡]

* Gall, ii., 93-97.—I do not reckon the sixth argument as of much value ;
for an organ apparently the same may have different functions in different
species of animals. See this subject adverted to in the *Phrenological Journal*, ix., 514.
† Adelon, *Physiologie de l'Homme*, 2d. édit., i., 160.
‡ Prichard's *Review of the Doctrine of a Vital Principle*, &c., p. 179. In a

Another class of physiologists have compared the size of the brain of man with that of the brains of the lower animals, contrasting at the same time their mental powers ; and have been led to the conclusion that it is the organ of the mind, and that its superior developement in man indicates his mental superiority over the brutes : but those philosophers have not succeeded in determining the functions of the *different parts* of this organ, and have not been able, in any important degree, to connect their discoveries with the philosophy of mind. Camper, in order to measure the extent of the brain, and, as he imagined, the corresponding energy of the intellectual faculties, drew a vertical line, touching the upper lip and the most prominent part of the forehead ; and also a horizontal line, crossing the former, and touching the tips of the upper front teeth and the external opening of the ear, or at least corresponding to these points in its direction : and he thought that man and brutes have more understanding, the more the upper and inner angle formed by the two lines, or that including the upper jaw, nose, &c., is obtuse ; and, on the contrary, that they are more stupid, the more this " facial angle " is acute. But this way of measuring the intellectual faculties is not more correct than that previously mentioned. ' The facial angle applies only to the middle parts of the brain situated in the forehead, and is inapplicable to all the lateral and posterior parts ; hence it could, even if there were no other objection, indicate only those faculties whose organs constitute the middle of the forehead. Besides, in many negroes the jaw-bones are extremely prominent and the facial angle acute ; while their foreheads are, in fact, largely developed and their intellectual faculties powerful—although, by Camper's rule, they ought to be inferior to many stupid Europeans, whose foreheads are deficient, but whose jaws recede. Hence, the facial angle cannot serve as a means of measuring the moral sentiments and intellectual faculties.[*]

Some physiologists, as Sœmmering and Cuvier, have compared the size of the brain in general with the size of the face ; and, according to them, animals are stupid as the face is large in proportion to the brain. But that this rule is not infallible, is easily proved ; because Leo, Montaigne, Leibnitz, Haller, and Mirabeau had large faces and very considerable brains. Bossuet, Voltaire, and Kant had, on the contrary, small faces and also large brains.[†]

The cerebral parts have likewise been compared with each other, in order to ascertain their functions ; as, the brain with the cerebellum, the brain with the medulla oblongata, with the nerves, &c. : but these modes also have led to no satisfactory results.

The elder writers, such as Aristotle and his followers, who assigned different faculties to different parts of the brain, proceeded on fancy, or on notions of supposed suitableness of the place in the head to the nature of the power ; and their views have been entirely abandoned both by physiologists and by metaphysicians. In short, it is well known that, before Gall's discovery, no theory of the functions of the brain was admitted and taught as certain science, such as the doctrine of the circulation of the blood, and the functions of the muscles, nerves, and bones.[‡]

subsequent sentence this author displays no small degree of ignorance, real or affected, of the facts collected and observed by other physiologists. " Later writers," says he, " have abandoned the notion of Bichat, and have refused the passions to the brain. But this supposition is *equally gratuitous, and supported by no proof /*" P. 180.

[*] Spurzheim's *Phrenology*, p. 58–60.   [†] *Ibid.* p. 61.

[‡] An inclination has occasionally been evinced to detract from the honour due to Dr. Gall, by affirming that many previous writers taught the plurality of cerebral organs. In answer to such assertions I quote the following remarks from a late number of *The Medico-Chirurgical Review :* " No great discovery was probably ever made instanter. Conjectures long precede

Dr. Roget, an opponent of Phrenology, freely confesses that "the brain is still as incomprehensible in its functions, as it is subtile and complex in its anatomy ;"* and the writer in the 94th number of *The Edinburgh Review*, says : " Even within our own time, although many great anatomists had devoted themselves almost exclusively to describing the brain, this organ used to be demonstrated by the greater number of teachers in a manner which, however invariable, was assuredly not particularly useful. It was so mechanically cut down upon, indeed, as to constitute a sort of exhibition connected with nothing. The teacher and the pupil were equally dissatisfied with the performance, and the former probably the most ; the latter soon gave up the painful attempt to draw any kind of deductions from what he witnessed, and disposed of the difficulty as he best could, when he had to render an account of what he had seen. Up to this day, our memory is pained by the recollection of the barbarous names and regular sections of what was then the dullest part of anatomical study ; which, although often repeated, left no trace but of its obscurity or its absurdity   Here an oval space of a white colour, and there a line of gray or curve of red, were displayed ; here a cineritious, there a medullary mass ; here a portion white without and gray within, there a portion white within and gray without ; here a gland-pituitary, there a gland like grains of sand ; here a ventricle, there a cul-de-sac ; with endless fibres, and lines, and globules, and simple marks, with appellations no less fanciful than devoid of meaning."

" The anatomist dissected, and toiled on in this unpromising territory, and entangled himself more in proportion to his unwillingness to be defeated ; and he succeeded, no doubt, in making out a clear display of all these complicated parts, which few, however, could remember, and fewer still could comprehend.   Then came the physiologist in still greater perplexity, and drew his conclusions, and assigned offices to the multiplied portions and ramifications of nervous substance, by arbitrary conjecture for the most part, and often with manifest inconsistency.   Although the brain was generally allowed to be the organ of the intellectual faculties, it was supposed to give out from particular portions of the mass, but quite indifferently, nerves of sensation, general and specific, nerves of motion, and proofs, in most instances,   The real and effective discoverer, we imagine, is he who fixes the attention of the world on, and *proves* the discovery, by bringing it into complete operation.   If Harvey, or some other person, had not *demonstrated* the circulation of the blood, all the hints and suppositions of his predecessors, from Hippocrates downward, would have gone for nothing. Of what use was the *actual knowledge* of vaccination, possessed by the Gloucestershire farmers, till Jenner fixed the attention of the profession on it, and proved its efficacy in preventing variola ?   Great numbers of Harvey's contemporaries denied the truth of the discovery—and afterward, when the world acknowledged the truth of it; they attempted to prove that the circulation was known to many others before he was born.   This has ever been the case, and arises from the envy and jealousy which men feel toward each other, while living, and rivals."—(No. 43, p. 31, January, 1835.)   If the plurality of the cerebral organs was *known* before the time of Gall, how was it possible for a physiologist like Dr. Cullen to pen the following sentences ?   " Although we cannot doubt that the operations of our intellect always depend upon certain motions taking place in the brain, yet these motions have never been the objects of our senses, *nor have we been able to perceive that any particular part of the brain has more concern in the operations of our intellect than any other*. Neither have we attained any knowledge of *what share the several parts of the brain have in that operation ;* and, therefore, in this situation of our science, it must be a very difficult matter to discover those states of the brain that may give occasion to the various states of our intellectual functions." (*Practice of Physic*, vol. i., sect. 1539.)   See also Dr. T. Brown's *Lectures*, i., 420.

* *Supplement to Encyc. Brit.*, article " Cranioscopy."

nerves of volition; the single, double, or multipled origin of nerves, which
had not escaped notice, not being supposed to be connected with these
separate offices.

"Such, so vague, so obscure, so inexact, so unsatisfactory, was the kind
of knowledge communicated to the student, until a very recent period;
and the impression left by it was that of confused and unintelligible profusion in the distribution of nerves, of intricacy without meaning, of an
expenditure of resources without a parallel in the other works of nature."
(Pages 447, 448.)

Unless, then, Dr. Gall could boast of some other method of investigation
than those of the ordinary physiologist and metaphysician, he could offer
no legitimate pretensions to the solution of the question, What parts of
the brain, and what mental faculties, are connected? By great good fortune, however, he was led to adopt a different and superior mode of inquiry; and this leads me to state shortly a few particulars of the history
of the science which is now to be expounded.

Dr. Francis Joseph Gall, a physician of Vienna, afterward resident
in Paris,† was the founder of the system. From an early age he was
given to observation, and was struck with the fact, that each of his brothers
and sisters, companions in play, and schoolfellows, was distinguished from
other individuals by some peculiarity of talent or disposition. Some of
his schoolmates were characterized by the beauty of their penmanship,
some by their success in arithmetic, and others by their talent for acquiring
a knowledge of natural history or languages.. The compositions of one
were remarkable for elegance; the style of another was stiff and dry;
while a third connected his reasonings in the closest manner, and clothed
his argument in the most forcible language. Their dispositions were
equally different; and this diversity appeared also to determine the direction of their partialities and aversions. Not a few of them manifested a
capacity for employments which they were not taught: they cut figures
in wood, or delineated them on paper; some devoted their leisure to
painting, or the culture of a garden; while their comrades abandoned
themselves to noisy games, or traversed the woods to gather flowers, seek
for bird-nests, or catch butterflies In this manner each individual presented a character peculiar to himself; and Gall observed, that the individual who in one year had displayed selfish or knavish dispositions, never
became in the next a good and faithful friend.

The scholars with whom Gall had the greatest difficulty in competing,
were those who learned by heart with great facility; and such individuals
frequently gained from him, by their repetitions, the places which he had
obtained by the merit of his original compositions.

Some years afterward, having changed his place of residence, he still
met individuals endowed with an equally great talent for learning to
repeat. He then observed that his schoolfellows so gifted possessed
prominent eyes, and recollected that his rivals in the first school had been
distinguished by the same peculiarity. When he entered the university
he directed his attention, from the first, to the students whose eyes were
of this description, and found that they all excelled in getting rapidly by
heart, and giving correct recitations, although many of them were by no
means distinguished in point of general talent. This fact was recognised
also by the other students in the classes; and although the connexion
between talent and external sign was not at this time established upon
such complete evidence as is requisite for a philosophical conclusion, Gall
could not believe that the coincidence of the two circumstances was entirely accidental. From this period, therefore, he suspected that they

† Born at Tiefenbrun, near Pforzheim, in Suabia, on 9th March, 1757; died
at Paris, 22d August, 1828.

stood in an important relation to each other. After much reflection, he conceived that if memory for words was indicated by an external sign, the same might be the case with the other intellectual powers ; and, thereafter, all individuals distinguished by any remarkable faculty became the objects of his attention. By degrees he conceived himself to have found external characteristics which indicated a decided disposition for painting, music, and the mechanical arts. He became acquainted also with some individuals remarkable for the determination of their character, and he observed a particular part of their heads to be very largely developed : this fact first suggested to him the idea of looking to the head for signs of the dispositions or affective powers. But, in making these observations, he never conceived for a moment that the skull was the cause of the different talents, as has been erroneously represented : from the first, he referred the influence, whatever it was, to the brain.

In following out, by observations, the principle which accident had thus suggested, he for some time encountered difficulties of the greatest magnitude. Hitherto he had been altogether ignorant of the opinions of physiologists touching the brain, and of metaphysicians respecting the mental faculties. He had simply observed nature. When, however, he began to enlarge his knowledge of books, he found the most extraordinary conflict of opinions everywhere prevailing ; and this, for the moment, made him hesitate about the correctness of his own observations. He found that the affections and passions had, by almost general consent, been consigned to the thoracic and abdominal viscera ; and that, while Pythagoras, Aristotle, Plato, Galen, Haller, and some other physiologists, placed the sentient soul or intellectual faculties in the brain, Van Helmont placed it in the stomach, Descartes and his followers in the pineal gland, and Drelincourt and others in the cerebellum.

He found also that a great number of philosophers and physiologists asserted that all men are born with equal mental faculties ; and that the differences observable among them are owing either to education or to the accidental circumstances in which they are placed. If differences were accidental, he inferred, there could be no natural signs of predominating faculties ; and, consequently, the project of learning, by observation, to distinguish the functions of the different portions of the brain must be hopeless. This difficulty he combated by the reflection, that his brothers, sisters, and schoolfellows had all received very nearly the same education, but that he had still observed each of them unfolding a distinct character, over which circumstances appeared to exert only a limited control ; and farther, that not unfrequently those whose education had been conducted with the greatest care, and on whom the labours of teachers had been most assiduously bestowed, remained far behind their companions in attainments. "Often," says he, " we were accused of want of will, or deficiency in zeal ; but many of us could not, even with the most ardent desire, followed out by the most obstinate efforts, attain, in some pursuits, even to mediocrity ; while in some other points some of us surpassed our schoolfellows without an effort, and almost, it might be said, without perceiving it ourselves. But, in point of fact, our masters did not appear to attach much faith to the system which taught equality of mental faculties ; for they thought themselves entitled to exact more from one scholar, and less from another. They spoke frequently of natural gifts, or of the gifts of God, and consoled their pupils in the words of the Gospel, by assuring them that each would be required to render an account only in proportion to the gifts which he had received."*

Being convinced by these facts that there is a natural and constitutional diversity of talents and dispositions, he encountered in books still another

* *Sur les Fonctions du Cerveau,* Preface ; and tome v., p. 12.

6

obstacle to his success in determining the external signs of the mental powers. He found that, instead of faculties for languages, drawing, music, distinguishing places, and mechanical arts, corresponding to the different talents which he had observed in his schoolfellows, the metaphysicians spoke only of general powers, such as perception, conception, memory, imagination, and judgment; and when he endeavoured to discover external signs in the head, corresponding to these general faculties, and to determine the correctness of the physiological doctrines taught by the authors already mentioned regarding the seat of the mind, he found perplexities without end, and difficulties insurmountable.

Abandoning, therefore, every theory and preconceived opinion, Dr. Gall gave himself up entirely to the observation of nature. Being a friend to Dr. Nord, physician to a Lunatic Asylum in Vienna, he had opportunities, of which he availed himself, of making observations on the insane. He visited prisons and resorted to schools; he was introduced to the courts of princes, to colleges, and to seats of justice; and wherever he heard of an individual distinguished in any particular way, either by remarkable endowment or deficiency, he observed and studied the developement of his head. In this manner, by an almost imperceptible induction, he at last conceived himself warranted in believing that particular mental powers are indicated by particular configurations of the head.

Hitherto he had resorted only to physiognomical indications, as a means of discovering the functions of the brain. On reflection, however, he was convinced that physiology is imperfect when separated from anatomy. Having observed a woman of fifty-four years of age, who had been afflicted with hydrocephalus from her youth, and who, with a body a little shrunk, possessed a mind as active and intelligent as that of other individuals of her class, Dr. Gall declared his conviction, that the structure of the brain must be different from what was generally conceived—a remark which Tulpius also had made, on observing a hydrocephalic patient who manifested the mental faculties. He therefore felt the necessity of making anatomical researches into the structure of the brain.

In every instance where an individual whose head he had observed while alive happened to die, he requested permission to examine the brain, and frequently was allowed to do so; and he found, as a general fact, that, on removal of the skull, the brain, covered by the dura mater, presented a form corresponding to that which the skull had exhibited in life.

The successive steps by which Dr. Gall proceeded in his discoveries are particularly deserving of attention. He did not, as many have imagined, first dissect the brain, and pretend, by that means, to discover the seats of the mental powers; neither did he, as others have conceived, first map out the skull into various compartments, and assign a faculty to each, according as his imagination led him to conceive the place appropriate to the power. On the contrary, he first observed a concomitance between particular talents and dispositions, and particular forms of the head; he next ascertained, by removal of the skull, that the figure and size of the brain are indicated by external appearances; and it was only after these facts had been determined, that the brain was minutely dissected, and light thrown upon its structure.

At Vienna, in 1796, Dr. Gall, for the first time, delivered lectures on his system.

In 1800 Dr. JOHN GASPAR SPURZHEIM* began the study of Phrenology under him, having in that year assisted, for the first time, as one of his lectures. In 1804 he was associated with him in his labours; and, subsequently to that period, not only added many valuable discoveries to those

* Born at Longuich, near Treves, on the Moselle, 31st December, 1776; died at Boston, United States, on 10th November, 1832.

of Dr. Gall in the anatomy and physiology of the brain, but principally contributed to form the truths brought to light by their respective observations, into a beautiful and interesting system of mental philosophy. In Britain we are indebted chiefly to his personal exertions and printed works for a knowledge of the science.

In the beginning of his inquiries, Dr. Gall neither did nor could foresee the results to which they would lead, or the relation which each successive fact, as it was discovered, would bear to the whole truths which time and experience might bring into view. Having established any circumstance, he boldly affirmed its reality, without regard to anything but truth. Perceiving, for instance, that the intensity of the desire for property bore a relation to the size of one part of the brain, he announced this fact by itself, and called the part the organ of Theft, because he found it prominent in thieves. When he had discovered that the propensity to conceal was in connexion with another part of the brain, he announced this fact also as an isolated truth, and named the part the organ of Cunning, because he found it very large in sly and fraudulent criminals. In a similar way, when he had discovered the connexion between the sentiment of Benevolence and another portion of the cerebral mass, he called the part the organ of Benevolence; and so on in regard to the other organs. This proceeding has nothing in common with the formation of an hypothesis; and, so far from a disposition to invent a theory being conspicuous, there appears, in the disjointed items of information which Dr. Gall at first presented to the public, a want of even an ordinary regard for systematic arrangement. His only object seems to have been to furnish a candid and uncoloured statement of the facts in nature which he had observed; leaving their value to be ascertained by time and farther investigation.

As soon, however, as observation had brought to light a great body of facts, and the functions of the organs had been contemplated with a philosophical eye, a system of mental philosophy appeared to emanate almost spontaneously from the previous chaos.

Although, when the process of discovery had proceeded a certain length, the facts were found to be connected by relations, yet, at first, it was impossible to perceive their relationship. Hence, the doctrines appeared as a mere rude and undigested mass, of rather unseemly materials; the public mirth was, not unnaturally, excited by the display of organs of Theft, Quarrelsomeness, and Cunning, as they were then named; and a degree of obloquy was brought upon the science, from which it is only now recovering. At this stage the doctrines were merely a species of physiognomy, and the apparent results were neither very prominent nor very inviting. When, however, the study had been pursued for years, and the torch of philosophy had been applied to the facts discovered by observation, its real nature as the science of the human mind, and its beautiful consistency and high utility, became apparent, and its character and name changed as it advanced. For, as Middleton has finely remarked, no truth "can possibly hurt or obstruct the good effect of any other truth whatsoever: for they all partake of one common essence, and necessarily coincide with each other; and, like the drops of rain which fall separately into the river, mix themselves at once with the stream, and strengthen the general current."*

Having now unfolded the principles and method of investigation of Phrenology, I solicit the attention of the reader to one question. We have heard much of antiphrenologists; and I would ask, What does the term antiphrenologist mean? Does it mean a person who, like Lord Brougham or Lord Jeffrey, denies that the mind in feeling and reflecting uses organs at all? To such I reply, that they ought to call themselves

* Middleton's *Life of Cicero*, Preface.

antiphysiologists; because, as already mentioned, every physiological writer of eminence in Europe maintains, that the brain is the organ of the mind, and that injuries of it impair the mental faculties. Or does antiphrenologist mean one who admits the brain to be the organ of the mind, but contends that the whole of it is essential to every mental act? Then I request of him to reconcile with his theory the phenomena of dreaming, partial genius, partial idiocy, partial insanity, partial lesion of mental functions arising from partial injuries of the brain, and the successive developement of the mental powers in youth. If antiphrenologist means a person who admits the mind to manifest a plurality of faculties by a plurality of organs, but denies that phrenologists have ascertained any of them, I ask him, Whether he disputes the three grand propositions, first, That dissection alone does not reveal functions; second, That reflection on consciousness does not reveal organs; and, third, That mental manifestations may be compared with developement of brain? If he denies these principles, he is beyond the reach of reason; while, if he admits them, I would ask him to state what forms of brain, and what mental manifestations, he has found concomitant in his observations? because, until he shall make such a statement, his denial of the correctness of the observations of others is entitled to no consideration. But an antiphrenologist furnished with counter-facts has never yet appeared. The word, in its common signification, seems to indicate only an individual who, like the Ptolemeans in the time of Galileo, is pleased to deny that phrenologists are right, without knowing either their principles or their facts, or having any pretensions to advance the cause of truth by propounding sounder data or correcter observations of his own.

GENERAL VIEW OF THE FUNCTIONS OF THE SPINAL MARROW AND NERVES.

Before entering on the discussion of the cerebral organs, it may be useful to give a brief account of Sir Charles Bell's discoveries of the functions of the Nerves. Dr. Spurzheim, and many authors before him, very early published the conjecture, that there must be different nerves for sensibility and for motion, because one of the powers is occasionally impaired, while the other remains entire. Sir C. Bell has furnished demonstrative evidence of this being actually the fact. He has also given due prominence to the philosophical principle so urgently insisted on by phrenologists, That, in all departments of the animal economy, each organ performs only one function; and that wherever complex functions appear, complex organs may be safely predicated, even anterior to the possibility of demonstrating them. The present section is derived from Sir C. Bell's *Anatomy and Physiology of the Human Body*, vol. ii., 7th edition, 1829; and, in as far as possible, I have adhered to his own expressions. My object is to introduce general readers to a knowledge of his discoveries, which form parts of an extensive System of Anatomy, or of Philosophical Transactions, or of other professional publications, which they seldom peruse. I shall omit all details necessary only for medical students, as Sir C. Bell's work is the proper source of instruction for them. Even the general reader will probably resort to Sir C. Bell's pages, after being informed of their interesting contents; he will find them clear, instructive, and most ably supported by evidence. Any errors or inaccuracies in the following condensed abstract are chargeable against myself; for although in general I have followed the author's own expressions, the arrangement is greatly altered, and occasionally sentences of my own are introduced:

A nerve, says Sir Charles, is a firm white cord, composed of nervous matter and cellular substance. The nervous matter exists in distinct threads, which are bound together by the cellular membrane. They may be likened to a bundle of hairs or threads, enclosed in a sheath composed of the finest membrane.

The figure represents a nerve greatly magnified, for the sake of illustration, and consisting of distinct filaments. A, the nerve, enveloped in its membranous sheath ; B, one of the threads dissected out. The nerves vary in thickness from the diameter of a small thread to that of a whip-cord. They are dispersed through the body, and extend to every part which enjoys sensibility or motion, or which has a concatenated action with another part.

The matter of a nerve in health and in the full exercise of its influence, is of an opaque white hue ; it is soft and pulpy, between fluid and solid, and drops from the probe. When putrid, it acquires a green colour ; when dried, it is transparent. Corrosive sublimate and muriate of soda harden it ; alkalis dissolve it. Each fibril of a nerve is convoluted, and runs not in a straight line, but zigzag, like a thread drawn from a worsted stocking, which has by its form acquired elasticity that it would not otherwise have possessed. By want of use the matter of a nerve is either not secreted in due proportion, or changes its appearance ; for the nerve then acquires a degree of transparency.

There is no evidence that any fluid or spirit circulates in the nerves ; nor is there any that the nervous fibrils are tubes.

Nerves are supplied with arteries and veins, and their dependence on the supply of blood is proved by the fact, that, if a limb be deprived of blood, the nerves lose their powers, and sensibility is lost. If a nerve be partially compressed, so as to interrupt the free entrance of the blood into it, both the power over the muscles and the reception of sensation through it are interrupted ; and when the blood is admitted again, painful tingling accompanies the change. It is not the compression of the tubes of a nerve, but the obstruction of its bloodvessels, which produces the loss of power consequent on tying it. The brain, the nerves of the eye and the ear, the nerves of sense and motion, are all affected by changes in the circulation ; and each organ, according to its natural function, is *variously* influenced by the *same* cause—the rushing of blood into it, or the privation of its proper quantity.

A nerve consists of distinct filaments ; but there is nothing perceptible in these filaments to distinguish them from each other. One filament serves for the purpose of sensation ; another for muscular motion ; a third for combining the muscles when in the act of respiration. But the subserviency of any of all these filaments to its proper office must be discovered by following it out, and observing its relations, and especially its origin in the brain and spinal marrow. In their substance there is nothing particular. They all seem equally to contain a soft pulpy matter, enveloped in cellular membrane, and so surrounded with a tube of this membrane as to present a continuous track of pulpy nervous matter, from the nearest extremity in the brain to the extremity which ends in a muscle or in the skin.

The key to the system will be found in the simple proposition, that each filament or track of nervous matter has its peculiar endowment, independently of the others which are bound up along with it ; and that it continues to have the same endowment throughout its whole length.   There is no interchange of powers between the different filaments; but a minute filament of one kind may be found accompanying a filament of a different kind, each giving a particular power to the part in which it is ultimately distributed.

Some nerves give sensibility ; but there are others, as perfectly and delicately constituted, which possess no sensibility whatever.   Sensibility results from the particular part of the brain which is affected by the nerve. If the eyeball is pressed, the outward integuments feel pain ; but the retina gives no pain—only rings of light or fire appear before the eye.   In the operation of couching the cataract, the needle must pierce the retina ; the effect, however, is not pain, but to produce, as it were, a spark of fire ; and so an impression on the nerve of hearing, the papillæ of taste, or the organ of any sense except feeling, does not produce pain.   The sensation excited has its character determined by the part of the brain to which the nerve is related at its root.   But there are nerves which have no relation to outward impression.   There are nerves purely for governing the muscular frame : these being constituted for conveying the mandate of the will, do not stand related to an organ of sense in the brain ; hence no sensibility and no pain will be produced by them.   Each of these may be said to be a nerve of exquisite feeling in one sense ; that is, it may be a cord which unites two organs in intimate sympathies, so as to cause them to act in unison ; yet, being bruised or injured, it will give rise to no perception of any kind, because it does not stand related to a part of the brain whose office it is to produce either the general impression of pain, or heat, or cold, or vision, or hearing : it is not the office of that part of the brain to which it is related to produce perception at all.

At the conflux of the nervous filaments small reddish tumours appear, which are named GANGLIONS—(See D, in fig., p. 67.)   A ganglion resembles in form the circular swellings which appear on the stalk of a straw or of a cane ; but ganglions do not rise at regular intervals on the nerves like these swellings.   Ganglions are laid in a regular succession in the whole length of the body, and, in the vertebral animals, form a regular series down each side of the spinal marrow ; the nerve of communication among them is the great sympathetic nerve.   There are other ganglions seated in the head, neck, and cavities of the chest and belly, which are very irregular in their situation and form.

The colour of the ganglions differs from that of the nerves ; it is redder, which is owing to the greater number of bloodvessels : they consist of the same matter with the brain.

Wherever we trace nerves of motion, we find that, before entering the muscles, they interchange branches, and form an intricate mass of nerves, which is termed a PLEXUS.   A plexus is intricate in proportion to the number of muscles to be supplied, and the variety of combinations into which they enter.   The filaments of nerves which go to the skin, and have the simple function of sensation, regularly diverge to their destination without forming a plexus.   From the fin of a fish to the arm of a man, the plexus increases in complexity in proportion to the variety or extent of motions to be performed in the extremity.   It is by the interchange of filaments that combination among the muscles is formed.

Different columns of nervous matter combine to form the SPINAL MARROW, (AB, p. 67.)   Each lateral portion of the spinal marrow consists of three tracks or columns ; one for voluntary motion, one for sensation, and one for the act of respiration.   So that the spinal marrow comprehends in all six rods, intimately bound together, but distinct in office ; and the capital of this compound column is the *medulla oblongata.*

The anterior column of each lateral division of the spinal marrow is for motion; the posterior column is for sensation; and the middle one is for respiration. The former two extend up into the brain, and are dispersed or lost in it; for their functions stand related to the sensorium: but the last stops short in the medulla oblongata, being in function independent of reason, and capable of its office independently of the brain, or when separated from it.

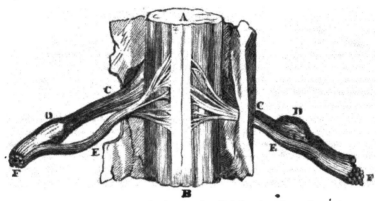

A B the spinal marrow seen in front; the division into lateral portions appearing at the line A B. The nervous cord C arises from the posterior lateral division, and gives sensibility. The swelling D is its ganglion. The nervous cord E arises from the anterior lateral division, and gives motion. It has no ganglion. These two cords combine at F, and proceed under one sheath to their destination.

Sir C. Bell struck a rabbit behind the ear, so as to deprive it of sensibility by the concussion, and then exposed the spinal marrow. On irritating the posterior roots of the nerve, he could perceive no motion consequent in any part of the muscular frame; but on irritating the anterior roots of the nerve, at each touch of the forceps there was a corresponding motion of the muscles to which the nerve was distributed. These experiments satisfied him that the different roots, and different columns from which those roots arose, were devoted to distinct offices, and that the notions drawn from the anatomy were correct.

He also performed certain interesting experiments on the fifth pair of nerves, which originates from the brain. In his Plate I. he represents this nerve rising from two roots, one of them coming from the crus cerebri, corresponding to the anterior column of the spinal marrow; and the other from the crus cerebelli, corresponding to the posterior column of the spinal marrow. There is a ganglion on the latter branch, and none on the former; which circumstance also is in exact correspondence with the nerves rising from the spinal marrow. The two branches combine at a short distance from their origin, and are universally distributed to the head and face. Sir C. Bell conceived that this nerve is the uppermost of those nerves which confer motion and bestow sensibility. To confirm this opinion, he cut across the posterior branch, or that which has a ganglion, on the face of an ass, and it was found that the sensibility of the parts to which it was distributed was entirely destroyed. Again, he exposed the anterior branch of the fifth pair at its root, in an ass, the moment the animal was killed; and, on irritating the nerve, the muscles of the jaw acted, and the jaw was closed with a snap. On dividing the root of the nerve in a living animal, the jaw fell relaxed. Thus its functions were no longer matter of doubt: it was at once a muscular nerve and a nerve of sensibility. And thus the opinion was confirmed, that the fifth nerve was to the head what the spinal nerves were to the other parts of the body.

The muscles have two nerves, which fact had not been noticed previously to Sir C. Bell's investigations, because they are commonly bound up together: but whenever the nerves, as about the head, go in a separate course, we find that there is a sensitive nerve and a motor nerve distributed to the muscular fibres; and we have reason to conclude that those branches of the spinal nerves which go to the muscles, consist of a motor and a sensitive filament. The nerve of touch or feeling, ramified on the skin, is distinct from both.

It was formerly supposed that the office of a muscular-nerve is only to carry out the mandate of the will and to excite the muscle to action. But this betrays a very inaccurate knowledge of the action of the muscular system; for before the muscular system can be controlled under the influence of the will, there must be a consciousness or knowledge of the condition of the muscle.

When we admit that the various conditions of the muscle must be estimated or perceived, in order to be under the due control of the will, the natural question arises, Is that nerve which carries out the mandate of the will, capable of conveying, at the same moment, an impression retrograde to the course of that influence, which, obviously, is going from the brain toward the muscle? If we had no facts of anatomy to proceed upon, still reason would declare to us, that the same filament of a nerve could not convey a motion, of whatever nature that motion may be, whether vibration or motion of spirits, in opposite directions, at the same moment of time.

Sir C. Bell has found that, to the full operation of the muscular power, two distinct nervous filaments are necessary, and that a circle is established between the sensorium and the muscle; that one filament or simple nerve carries the influence of the will toward the muscle, which nerve has no power to convey an impression backward to the brain; and that another nerve connects the muscle with the brain, and, acting as a sentient nerve, conveys the impression of the condition of the muscle to the mind—but has no operation in a direction outward from the brain toward the muscle, and does not, therefore, excite the muscle, however irritated.

There are four nerves coming out of a track or column of the spinal marrow, from which neither the nerves of sensation nor those of common voluntary motion take their departure. Experiment proves that these nerves excite motions connected with the act of respiration.

Under the class of respiratory motions we have to distinguish two kinds; first, the involuntary or instinctive; and, secondly, those which accompany an act of volition. We are unconscious of that state of alternation of activity and rest which characterizes the instinctive act of breathing in sleep; and this condition of activity of the respiratory organs, we know by experiment, is independent of the brain. But, on the other hand, we see that the act of respiration is sometimes an act of volition, intended to accomplish some other operation, as that of smelling or speaking. Sir C. Bell apprehends that it is this compound operation of the organs of breathing which introduces a certain degree of complexity into the system of respiratory nerves. A concurrence of the nerves of distinct systems will be found necessary to actions, which, at first sight, appear to be very simple.

If we cut that division of the fifth nerve which goes to the lips of an ass, we deprive the lips of sensibility; so that, when the animal presses the lips to the ground, and against the oats lying there, it does not feel them; and, consequently, there is no effort made to gather them. If, on the other hand, we cut the seventh nerve, where it goes to the lips, the-animal feels the oats, but it can make no effort to gather them, the power of muscular motion being cut off by the division of the nerve. Thus we perceive that, in feeding, just as in gathering anything with the hand, the feeling directs the effort ; and two properties of the nervous system are necessary to a very simple action.

After the investigation of the regular system of nerves of sensation and voluntary motion, the question that had so long occupied Sir C. Bell, viz., What is the explanation of the excessive intricacy of the nerves of the face, jaws, throat, and breast? became of easy solution. These nerves are agents of distinct powers, and they combine the muscles in subserviency to different functions.

As animals rise in the scale of being, new organs are bestowed upon them ; and, as new organs and new functions are superadded to the original constitution of the frame, new nerves are given also, with new sensibili ties and new powers of activity.

Sir C. Bell remarks, that we understand the use of all the intricate nerves of the body, with the exception of the sixth nerve, which stands connected with another system of nerves altogether, namely, the system hitherto called the Sympathetic, or sometimes the Ganglionic System of Nerves ; and of this system we know so little, that it cannot be matter of surprise if we reason ignorantly of the connexion of the sixth with it.

PRINCIPLES

OF

PHRENOLOGY.

In the Introduction I have shown that the brain is admitted by physi ologists in general to be the organ of the mind ; but that two obstacles have impeded the discovery of the uses of its particular parts. In the first place, *dissection* alone does not reveal the vital *functions* of any organ : no person, by dissecting the optic nerve, could predicate that its office is to minister to vision ; or, by dissecting the tongue, could discover that it is the organ of taste. Anatomists, therefore, could not, by the mere prac tice of their art, discover the functions of the different portions of the brain. Secondly, the mind is unconscious of acting by means of organs ; and hence the material instruments, by means of which, in this life, it performs its operations and communicates with the external world, cannot be dis covered by reflection on consciousness.

The phrenologist compares developement of brain with manifestations of mental power, for the purpose of discovering the functions of the brain and the organs of the mind. This course is adopted, in consequence of the accidental discovery made by Dr. Gall, that certain mental powers are vigorously manifested when certain portions of the brain are large, and *vice versa*, as detailed in the Introduction. It is free from the objections attending the anatomical and metaphysical modes of research, and is conformable to the principles of the inductive philosophy.

No inquiry is instituted into the substance or essence of the mind, nor into the question, Whether does the mind fashion the organs, or do the organs determine the constitution of the mind? If dissection of organs does not reveal their functions, and if reflection on consciousness fails to disclose the nature of the mind's connexion with matter, no means remain of arriving at philosophical conclusions on these points; and speculative reasoning concerning them, although it may amuse the fancy, cannot instruct the understanding. Mr. Stewart justly observes, " that the metaphysical opinions which we may happen to have formed concerning the *nature* either of body or of mind, and the efficient causes by which their phenomena are produced, have no necessary connexion with our inquiries concerning the laws according to which the phenomena take place." " Whether, for example, the *cause* of gravitation be material or immaterial, is a point about which two Newtonians may differ, while they agree perfectly in their physical opinions. It is sufficient if both admit the general fact, that bodies tend to approach each other, with a force varying with their mutual distance, according to a certain law. In like manner, in the study of the human mind, the conclusions to which we are led by a careful examination of the phenomena it exhibits, have no necessary connexion with our opinions concerning its *nature* and *essence*."[*] The object of Phrenology is, to discover the faculties of the human mind, the organs by means of which they are manifested, and the influence of the organs on the manifestations. It does not enable us to predict actions.

A mental organ is a material instrument, by means of which the mind in this life manifests a particular power. Dr. Gall's discovery leads us to view the brain as a congeries of such organs, and, in the Introduction, reasons have been assigned for regarding this proposition as sufficiently probable to justify an inquiry into the direct evidence by which it is supported. For the purpose of comparing mental faculties with cerebral developement, it is necessary to show, 1*st*, that the mental qualities of individuals can be discovered; and, 2*dly*, that the size of different parts of the brain can be ascertained during life.

Let us consider, therefore, in the first place, whether it be possible *to discriminate mental dispositions and talents*. In regard to the Feelings, men familiar with human life and conduct have observed, that one individual is strongly addicted to covetousness—another to cruelty—another to benevolence—another to pride—another to vanity; and they are accustomed to regard these dispositions as natural, uniform, and permanent. They have never believed that a man, by an effort of the will, can totally change his nature, nor that the true character is so little manifested, that a person may be prone to benevolence to-day, who yesterday was addicted to avarice; that one who is now sinking in the lowest abasement of self-humiliation in his own eyes, may to-morrow become conceited, confident, and proud; or that to-day an individual may be deaf to the voice of censure or of fame, who yesterday was tremblingly alive to every breath that was blown upon his character. Nay, they have even regarded these dispositions as independent of one another, and separable; for they have often found that the possession of one was not accompanied by the presence of the whole. Hence, in addressing any individual, they have been in the custom of modifying their conduct according to their previous knowledge of his dispositions or genius, obtained by observing his actions. To the covetous man they address one motive; to the benevolent another ; to the proud a third : and to the vain a fourth. When they wish to move such individuals to act, they speak to the first, *of his personal interest* ; to the second, *of the pleasure of doing good* ; to the third, *of the necessity of preserving his own dignity* ; and to the fourth, *of the great praise* that will attend the performance of the action recommended.

As to intellectual endowments, a person who has heard, for the most fleeting momont, the bursts of melody which flow from the throat of Catalani, cannot be deceived as to the fact of her possessing a great endowment of the faculty of Tune ; he who has listened but for a few minutes to the splendid eloquence of Chalmers, can have no doubt that he is gifted with Ideality ; and he who has studied the writings of Dr. Thomas Brown, cannot hesitate as to his having manifested profound discriminative and analytic talent. In surveying the wonderful performances of some individuals in mechanics, poetry, mathematics, painting, and sculpture, it is equally impossible to doubt the existence of mental powers, conferring capacities for excelling in these different branches of science and art. It is equally easy to find individuals in whom the same powers are as indubitably deficient. Hence the difficulties of determining the existence of particular intellectual talents, and their degrees of strength, are not insurmountable ; especially if extreme cases be sought for—and these, as the *instantia ostentiva*, ought to be first resorted to. Men of observation have acted on these principles without hesitation, and without injury to themselves. They have not designed for the orchestra the individual whom they found incapable of distinguishing between a rude noise and a melodious sound, on the notion that " a genius for *music* " might be " acquired by habits of study or of business."* They do not place in difficult situations, requiring great penetration and much sagacity, individuals who cannot trace consequences beyond the stretch of three ideas ; nor do they conceive that a man who has no intellectual capacity to-day, may become a genius to-morrow, or in ten years hence, by an effort of the will. They, no doubt, have observed, that the faculties are developed in succession ; that the child is not in possession of the powers of the full-grown man ; and that hence a boy may be dull at ten, who may turn out a genius at twenty years of age, when his powers are fully unfolded by time. But they do not imagine that *every* boy may be made a genius by " habits of study or of business ;" nor do they believe that, after the faculties are fully developed, any individual may, if he chooses, become great in a department of philosophy or science for which he had previously no natural capacity. They have observed that cultivation strengthens powers in themselves vigorous ; but they have not found that education can render eminently energetic dispositions or capacities which nature has created feeble. They would laugh at any one who should attempt to convert an idiot into a well-informed philosopher. On the other hand, they have remarked, that, where Nature has bestowed a powerful disposition or capacity of a particular kind, it holds the predominant sway in the character during life, notwithstanding every effort to eradicate or subdue it. They have noticed, too, that, where Nature has conferred, in an eminent degree, the faculties which constitute genius, the individual manifests his native superiority in spite of great obstacles arising from circumstances or situation. The lives of poets, painters, and artists, in every age, bear witness to the truth of this observation.

An individual, it is true, may do particular actions, or even for a time follow a line of conduct, the same in external appearance, from *different* internal motives. But few men can pass their whole lives in disguise, or acquire the art of *acting* in the business and enjoyments of life, so

* Dugald Stewart.

habitually and so skilfully as not to allow their true characters to appear to those who are placed in a favourable situation for observing them : or, if their be persons who do possess this power of dissimulation, it forms the predominant feature in their mental constitution ; and, as will afterward be shown, it is indicated by a particular form of organization.   But, farther, let it be observed, that it is only in so far as the *propensities* and *sentiments* of our nature are concerned, that the display of pretended qualities is possible, even in a single case.   In regard to every act which depends on the knowing and reflecting faculties, this is absolutely impracticable.   No man can either write logical discourses, or trace profoundly an abstract principle, who has *not* powerful reflecting faculties.   No one can compose exquisite music, who has *not* the faculty of Tune strong, nor write exquisite poetry, who has *not* a powerful sentiment of Ideality.   When, therefore, we perceive, even with the most transient glance, the performance of such acts, we have evidence, insuperable and irresistible, of the existence of the faculties which produce them.

These opinions have been entertained by persons conversant with society, not in consequence of logical deduction nor metaphysical investigations, but from the observation of plain facts presented to the cognizance of their understandings.   Medical men are in a situation peculiarly favourable for studying even the most hidden traits of human character.   The physician, as Dr. Gall remarks, has daily opportunities of knowing the most secret affairs and most intimate relations of families ; and it is not easy for the man who is in the agonies of disease, or struggling with death, to veil his true character from him.   Besides, with how many private matters are physicians confidentially made acquainted ! for who would not make a friend and adviser of the man to whose care he intrusts the safety of himself and his family ?   It is to such a friend, as one who knows and can sympathize with the failings of humanity, that men unfold the secret recesses of their souls.   Gall and Spurzheim were physicians.

For these reasons I venture to conclude that the first point is established in favour of Phrenology—namely, that it is possible, by accurate, patient, and continued observation of actions, to discover the true dispositions and capacities which individuals possess.   As this philosophy is founded on a comparison of the manifestations of these faculties with developement of the brain, we now proceed to consider the *second* question, Whether it be possible, in general, to discover *the true form of the brain* by observing the figure of the head ?

OF THE BRAIN, CEREBELLUM, AND SKULL.

THE anatomy of the brain is minutely described by Drs. Gall and Spurzheim, in their anatomical and physiological work.[*]   It is not indispensably necessary, although highly advantageous, to become acquainted with it in order to be a practical phrenologist.   A brief description of its general appearance will suffice to convey an idea of it to the non-medical reader.   The proper subjects for observation are healthy individuals not beyond the middle period of life.

The brain, stripped of its outer covering, the *dura mater,* is represented in figures 1 and 2.   These figures, (which are copied from Dr. Spurzheim's plates,) and the accompanying descriptions, are not intended for anatomical purposes ; their sole object is to convey some conception of the appearance of the brain to readers who have no opportunity of seeing it in nature.

[*] *Anatomie et Physiologie du Système Nerveux,* &c., tom. i.   Also Spurzheim's *Anatomy of the Brain,* &c.   London, 1826.

Fig. 1. Upper Surface of the Brain.

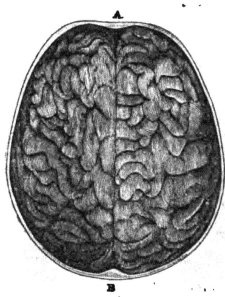

Fig. 1 represents the upper surface of the brain, stripped of membrane; the skull, through the middle part of which a horizontal section is made, surrounds it. The front is at A; and the line A B is the division between two halves or hemispheres. A strong membrane called the falciform process of the *dura mater*, represented on page 80, descends into it, and forms the partition. It goes down only about two-thirds of the depth; below which the two hemispheres are joined together by fibres which cross, forming what is called the *corpus callosum*. Sir Charles Bell observes, that " whatever we observe on one side has a corresponding part on the other ; and an exact resemblance and symmetry* is preserved in all the lateral divisions of the brain. And so, if we take the proof of anatomy, we must admit that, as the nerves are double, and the organs of sense double, so is the brain double, and every sensation conveyed to the brain is conveyed to the two lateral parts, and the operations performed must be done in both lateral portions at the same moment."† The waving lines in the figure are the convolutions, the furrows between which descend from half an inch to an inch in depth. When water collects in the internal parts, the convolutions are unfolded, and the brain presents a uniform surface of great extent. The parts seen in this figure are all composed externally of cineritious substance, to be afterward noticed.

Fig. 2 represents the base of the brain, as it appears when taken out of the skull ; the forehead being represented uppermost. Anatomists, for the sake of giving precision to their descriptions, divide the brain into three lobes, called the anterior, middle, and posterior. The parts before a vertical plane passing through the dotted line E E, are called the anterior lobe ; those between E E and F F, the middle lobe ; and those behind F F, the posterior lobe. The convolutions before E E lie chiefly on the bones which form the roofs of the sockets of the eyeballs. The two lobes of the cerebellum (which is distinct from, but connected with, the brain) are marked A A. Its surface presents convolutions, differing, however, in size and appearance from those observed in the brain. The thick cord or root C springing from the base of the brain, is named the *medulla oblongata*, or oblong portion of the spinal marrow, which is continued downward, and fills the cavity of the spine or backbone. At one time the brain

---

* This statement of Sir Charles Bell is not rigidly correct. There is a general correspondence between the parts on the opposite sides of the brain, but not " an exact symmetry " in the strict sense of these words. The approximation to symmetry is about as great as between the bloodvessels in the right and left arms.

† *Anatomy*, ii., 381. An ingenious paper by Mr. Hewett C. Watson, on the probable object of the duplicity of the brain, will be found in *The Phrenological Journal*, vol ix., No. 47.

has been regarded as proceeding from, and at another as giving rise to, the spinal marrow; but, in reality, the two are merely connected, and neither grows from the other. The false analogy of a stem growing from a root has led to this abuse of language.

The small round filaments or cords seen to proceed from the sides of the medulla oblongata, and from near the base of the brain, are various *nerves* of sensation and motion, some of them going to the organs of sense, and others to the skin and muscles of the face, head, and other more distant parts. The long flat-looking nerve *a a*, lying on the surface of the anterior lobe, is the *olfactory*, or nerve of smell, going to the nose. The round thick nerve 4 4, near the roots of the former, is the *optic*, or nerve of vision, going to the eye. That marked *b* is the motor nerve which supplies the muscles of the eyeball. A little farther back the

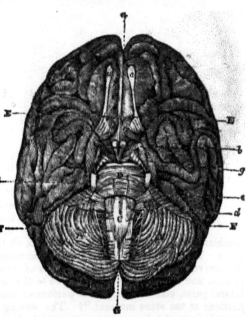

Fig. 2. UNDER SURFACE OF THE BRAIN.

fifth pair *c* is seen to issue apparently from the arch D, called *pons Varolii*, or *bridge of Varolius*. It is a large compound nerve, and divides into three branches, which are ramified on almost all the parts connected with the head and face, and the upper and under jaw. It is a nerve of both sensation and motion, and one branch of it ramified on the tongue is the nerve of taste. Other branches supply and give sensibility to the teeth, glands, and skin. The seventh or *auditory* nerve *e* is distributed on the internal ear, and serves for hearing. The eighth or *pneumogastric* nerve *d* sends filaments to the windpipe, lungs, heart, and stomach, and is one of great importance in the production of the voice and respiration. It also influences the action of the heart and the process of digestion.

The brain is a mass of soft matter, not homogeneous, but presenting different appearances. Part of it is white in colour, and fibrous or striated in texture. This is generally named *medullary substance*, and is found almost exclusively in the interior.

In figure 3 is represented a perpendicular section of the interior of the brain, not far from the mesial plane, proceeding from the convolutions at the top to the medulla oblongata at the base. The darkest portions in the cut are the external surface of the convolutions, and the other parts are seen in section. S is the cerebellum. The lightest and radiated parts are the medullary or fibrous substance. The *medulla oblongata* is marked *b c e e*, the part *b* being its *annular protuberance*, or the *pons Varolii*. At *e e* is one of the *corpora restiformia;* and at *c* one of the *corpora pyramidalia*. From *g*, which is one of the *crura cerebri*, the cerebral fibres, which have passed from *c* under the *pons Varolii*, proceed toward the convolutions, as seen at 34, 35, 37, 38, 11. In figs. 1 and 2, and also in

FIG. 3. SECTION OF THE SKULL AND BRAIN.

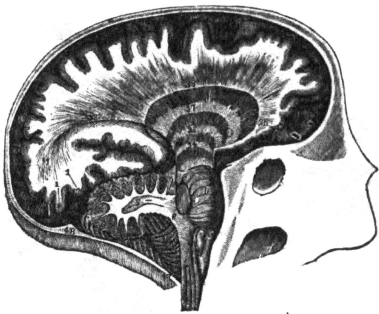

the dark folds in fig. 3, the *cineritious* substance is seen. This substance is of a gray colour, and has no fibrous appearance. It is called cineritious, from the similarity of its hue to that of ashes; and sometimes cortical, because it covers the brain as bark covers a tree. It forms the outer part of the brain. The cineritious substance does not blend gradually with the white medullary matter, but, on the contrary, the line of distinction is abrupt, as shown in fig. 3. The cineritious matter seems to have a greater proportion of blood circulating in it than the medullary. There is no fat nor adipose substance within the skull, although it is found in every other part of the body.

The external or cineritious substance of the brain is arranged, as we have seen, in convolutions or folds. The convolutions appear intended for the purpose of increasing the superficial extent of the brain, without enlarging its absolute size; an arrangement analogous to that employed in the eye of the eagle and falcon, in which the retina does not form a simple concave surface, as in man and quadrupeds, but is presented in folds to the rays of light, whereby the intensity of vision is increased in proportion to the extent of nervous surface exposed to their influence. The rolling up of the substance of the brain in folds in a similar manner strongly indicates that extent of surface is highly important in reference to its functions. In some of the inferior animals there are no convolutions; as we ascend in the scale of beings, they generally seem to increase; "and in man, above all other animals, are the convolutions numerous, and the *sulci* (or furrows) deep, and, consequently, the cineritious mass great, and its extension of surface far beyond that of all other creatures."*

The weight of the brain is very different in different individuals. According to Meckel, it weighs in the newly-born infant about ten ounces. Its consistence is then soft and pulpy, and no trace of fibres is seen; but gradually the fibrous appearance becomes more and more obvious as the individual approaches manhood. The period when the developement

* Bell's *Anatomy*, ii., 386.

and texture of the brain are at maturity varies in different persons; it is seldom before the age of twenty, and sometimes, according to Dr. Gall, so late as forty.* During the period of maturity no cerebral change is observable: but on the approach of old age the brain, like other parts of the body, begins to diminish; the convolutions lose their plumpness, and, as they are now shrivelled, flaccid, and less closely packed together than formerly, the anfractuosities or furrows between them become enlarged.

he weight of the adult brain, including the cerebellum, &c., is generally bout three pounds five ounces and a half;† but sometimes it is much eavier: that of Cuvier, for instance, weighed three pounds ten ounces our drachms and a half.‡

The cineritious matter is extended over all the upper and lateral, and over part of the inferior, surfaces of the brain: the white or medullary matter lies within it, and in some places in intimate combination with it. Medullary fibres run from the convolutions of the brain upon one side to the convolutions on the other: by these fibres (which, collected, form the *corpus callosum*, and the anterior and posterior commissures) the two hemispheres, and of course the organs of each side, are brought into communication and co-operation. "Unless," says Sir Charles Bell, "the cineritious masses were important organs, why should there be commissures or nerves forming a distinct system, arising and terminating in nothing? But if we take them as commissures, i. e., bonds of union between the corresponding sides of the great organ of the mind, we at once perceive how careful Nature is to unite the two lateral organs together, and out of two organs to make ONE MORE PERFECT."§

It is an important question, what particular functions the medullary matter and the cineritious matter respectively perform in the manifestation of the mind. The opinion is becoming prevalent, that the cineritious matter is essentially the organ of the mind, and that the fibrous medullary matter is an apparatus of communication, by means of which the different mental organs are brought into co-operation, and also enabled to influence the other portions of the body. Drs. Gall and Spurzheim attached great importance to the convolutions, and considered the depth, size, and number of them to have a great effect on the intensity of the mental manifestations; but it does not appear that they regarded the cineritious substance as exclusively the organ of the mind. "Dr. Gall and I," says Spurzheim, "suppose that each nervous apparatus is composed of the two peculiar substances, the pulpy and the fibrous, and that both are necessary to produce an instrument adequate to perform a particular function."‖

The organs, including their supposed apparatus of communication, extend from the surface of the brain to the medulla oblongata: each organ has been likened to a cone, of which the apex lies in the medulla ob-

* *Sur les Fonctions du Cerveau*, i.; 192 Dr. Vimont says, that in man the developement of the skull "is only completed from twenty-five to thirty." *Treatise on Human and Comparative Phrenology*, i., 166.

† Meckel, *Anatomie*, traduite par Jourdan et Breschet, ii., 619, 632, 682.

‡ *Journal de la Société Phrénologique de Paris*, tom. ii., No. v. The *post-mortem* examination of Cuvier's brain took place on 15th May, 1832, in presence of MM. Orfila, Duméril, Dupuytren, Allard, Bieu, Valenciennes, Laurillard, Rousseau, Andralnevru, and Bérard. It was ascertained that the superiority of size occurred almost exclusively in the cerebral lobes, particularly their anterior and superior parts; the cerebellum, &c., exhibiting no unusual developement. It was stated by M. Bérard to Dr. Foissac, the writer in the *Journal*, that none of the gentlemen present at the dissection remembered to have seen so complicated a brain, convolutions so numerous and compact, or such deep anfractuosities—"un cerveau aussi plissé, des circonvolutions aussi nombreuses et aussi pressées, des anfractuosités si profondes."

§ *Anatomy*, loc. cit.   ‖ *Anatomy of the Brain*, p. 10.

length and the base in the surface of the brain. In proportion to the diameter of the organ at the inner surface of the skull, is the thickness or number of the fibres contained in it. This is proved by the constant relation between the size of the anterior lobe of the brain, devoted to intellect, and that of the corpora pyramidalia, (c, fig. 3, p. 75,) from which, as roots, an uninterrupted line of fibres can be traced, expanding at length into the convolutions of the anterior lobe ; as also by the relation between the thickness of the posterior bundle of the *crus cerebri* (g, fig. 3, p. 75) and the size of the posterior and middle lobes of the brain. But I introduce the similitude of a cone merely as a popular illustration, and not as a technical description of the appearance of the organs ; for they are not separable into definite figures, such as this comparison, if literally understood, might seem to imply.

The opinion of Drs. Gall and Spurzheim, that the convolutions are of great importance in reference to the power of the mental faculties, is entertained by physiologists in general.

It is long since it was remarked by Scemmering, that, in the earlier months of human existence, there is yet no trace of that complicated and convoluted arrangement of the cerebral surface which is so striking in the adult brain. According to this eminent anatomist, it is only about the sixth or seventh month of gestation that the convolutions begin to appear. From this period they go on increasing in number and size, with a decreasing rapidity, even to the age of puberty. To this progressive growth of the convolutions we have a well-marked counterpart in the gradual developement of the mental powers, from the state of almost absolute nullity in which they exist in the fœtus during the greater part of its intra-uterine life, to the expanded mind of the adult.

Analogous to this concomitance of developement of the mind and cerebral surface in man, in the different stages of his life, a diminution or increase of intelligence in the lower animals is said by some physiologists to accompany any subtraction from, or addition to, the number and depth of the convolutions of their brains. The old objection to Phrenology, that some animals with large brains have less intelligence than others which have small ones, might, even if the comparison of the brains of different species were strictly allowable, be sufficiently answered, not only by referring to the fact of the parts of the brain which are developed not being the same in both, but also by opposing to it the statement of Desmoulins and Magendie,[*] that, in numerous examinations of the brains of almost every genus of the mammalia, they found a nearly constant relation between the extent of surface presented by the brain in each genus, and the amount of intelligence displayed by it. Where differences occur in one of these points, differences are stated to be usually found in the other, not only between different genera, but between different species, of the same genus, and also between different individuals of the same species.

Professor Tiedemann of Heidelberg, in his work on the Brains of Apes and of some other animals, has accurately delineated and described the progressive diminution and final disappearance of the folds of the brain in the mammalia, from the apes down to the rodentia ; and, according to Desmoulins, (p. 602,) this progression corresponds exactly with the diminution of intelligence. The most striking difference exists between the apes of the old world and those of the new. Many of the former are capable of being trained and employed for useful purposes, while the latter are incapable of instruction, and scarcely exceed squirrels in the degree of their intelligence. This corresponds with the state of the convolutions. In some dogs, especially those employed in hunting, the convolutions are scarcely less numerous and deep than in the higher tribes of apes ; while

* *Anatomie des Systèmes Nerveux des Animaux vertebrés*, p. 620.

7*

in the less intelligent species, and in wolves, they exist in a much inferior degree of developement. Every one must have been struck by the great difference as to docility observable between dogs and cats ; an equally striking difference is found in the appearances presented by the somber and depth of the convolutions of their brains—a difference so great, that Desmoulins estimates the convolutions of the dog to exceed by six or eight times those of the cat. The paucity of convolutions found in the cat prevails throughout the entire genus to which it belongs. That genus, Felis, which includes the cat, lion, tiger, panther, and other animals of a similar nature, is likewise remarkable for the uniformity observed in the number and arrangement of the convolutions in the different species ; and in no genus are the species more distinguished for similarity of disposition, for through none do the faculties of Secretiveness and Destructiveness prevail in so extreme a degree of strength.

It must also have struck every observer, that differences of mental character are met with to a much greater extent, and with much greater frequency, among men. than among the individuals of any species of the lower animals. It is rare, for instance, to find one sheep differing much from its companions, or one cow from another. This must, therefore, be regarded as a circumstance affording a presumption in favour of the idea that varieties of disposition depend on varieties occurring in the convolutions ; since, as has been observed by various physiologists,* the brains of men vary, with respect to the number and depth of their convolutions, in a far greater degree than those of any other species.

It has been remarked, that, in most idiots, the number and depth of the convolutions are less than usual, on at least one side of the brain. In chronic insanity, too, the convolutions are found more or less effaced, and separated from each other by the thickening and infiltration of the laminæ of the pia mater occupying the furrows of the brain. In these cases, likewise, as well as in individuals of congenital imbecility, the thickness of the cineritious substance of the convolutions has been found greatly diminished ; while in acute mania, on the other hand, it has been found of the usual thickness, and highly injected with blood. In old age the convolutions shrink.

The greater part of the brain is destitute of sensibility : it may be pierced or cut without the patient being aware; from any feeling of pain, that it is suffering injury. Sir Charles Bell mentions, that he " had his finger deep in the anterior lobes of the brain, when the patient, being at the same time acutely sensible, and capable of expressing himself, complained only of the integument." So far from thinking the parts of the brain which are insensible to be parts inferior in function, (as every part has its use,) Sir Charles Bell states, that, even from this, he should be led to imagine that they have a higher office, namely, that they are more allied to intellectual operations. The wide difference of function between a part destined to receive impressions, and a part which is the seat of thought, is in accordance with the presence of sensibility in some parts of the brain, and its absence in others.

The brain receives an unusually large supply of blood, in comparison with the rest of the body. According to Haller, the quantity is one-fifth of the entire amount which leaves the heart ; Monro, however, estimates it at one-tenth.

Each side of the brain, and also the cerebellum, are supplied with separate arteries conveying the blood to them ; but the sinuses, or canals by means of which the blood is returned to the heart, are common to them all.

The CEREBELLUM is composed of the same kind of nervous matter with

* Vicq d'Azyr, *Mém. de Paris*, 1783, p. 512 ; cited by Meckel, *Anatomie, &c.*, vol. ii., p. 646. See also Wenzel, *De penitiori Structura Cerebri*, p. 23, and Mayo's *Physiology*.

the brain, and presents both cineritious and medullary substances; but it differs from it in form and internal arrangement. In fig. 3, p. 75, it is seen partly in section (between 8 and 48) and partly with its natural external appearance (1.) The cerebellum is separated from the brain by a strong membrane called the *tentorium :* in animals which leap, as the cat and tiger, the separation is produced by a thin plate of bone.* Its fibres, however, originate in that part of the *medulla oblongata* called the *corpora restiformia,* from which also the organs of several propensities arise; so that the brain and cerebellum, although separated by the tentorium, are both connected with the *medulla oblongata,* and through it with each other.

The MEDULLA OBLONGATA is sometimes spoken of as one of the three great divisions of the brain. It is, in fact, the part from which the fibrous matter of the brain and cerebellum proceeds; and it forms, as it were, the capital of the column of the spinal marrow.

OF THE INTEGUMENTS OF THE BRAIN.

THE brain is formed before the bones which invest it. The ossification of the skull is a gradual process. The brain already formed is invested with strong membranes, and between the coats of the outer membrane the ossification commences, which process is not completed until the ninth year. During life the brain is embraced in its whole peripheral extent by a very thin transparent and delicate membrane called the *pia mater,* which sinks down into its furrows, and serves to convey the bloodvessels to its different parts. Immediately above the *pia mater* are two layers of a still thinner membrane, resembling in its tenuity a spider's web, and thence named the *tunica arachnoidea.* It covers the surface of the brain uniformly, without passing into its folds. A fluid secretion takes place from the opposed surfaces of this membrane, by which they are lubricated and prevented from adhering to each other. The *dura mater* is a thin, but strong, opaque membrane, lining and strongly adhering to the inner surface of the skull, and which embraces the outer surface of the brain above the membrane last-mentioned. When in health it does not possess sensibility, and has been pricked without causing pain. The brain, enclosed in these membranes, fills exactly the interior of the skull; so that a cast, in plaster, of the interior of the skull is a *fac simile* of the brain, covered by the *dura mater.* Between the two layers of the arachnoid membrane a very small quantity of fluid is said to exist, but not exceeding a line in thickness. This fluid does not, in any degree that can be distinguished by the hand or eye, cause the form of the interior of the skull to differ from the form of the exterior of the brain.

The skull is not an adamantine barrier, confining the brain within specific boundaries; but a strong, yet changeable, covering, shielding it, and accommodating itself to its size while in the progress of its growth.† At birth it is small; it increases as the brain increases, and alters its shape with every change of the cerebral form; it stops in developement when the brain has attained its full size, and diminishes when the size of the brain suffers diminution, as happens in old age or disease.‡ A process of ab-

* Richerand conceives the purpose of this arrangement to be the prevention of cerebral concussion in leaping: but Dr. Vimont objects to this view, on the ground that many animals accustomed to take great leaps, such as the squirrel and monkey, have not an osseous tentorium; while, on the other hand, a bony plate occurs in some animals whose movements are slow and heavy, such as the badger. Vimont's *Treatise on Human and Comparative Phrenology,* i., 63.
† On the admirable fitness of the skull to protect the brain, see *The Phrenological Journal,* viii., 332.
‡ Cases of diminution of the skull will be found in *The Phrenological Journal,* ix., 468–470.

sorption and deposition goes continually on in its substance; so that, if the brain presses from within, the renovating particles arrange themselves according to this pressure, and thus the figure of the skull and of the brain in general correspond. In cases of water in the head, the skull sometimes extends itself, by this process, to an enormous size.

The skull is composed of nine bones. These are—two *frontal* bones, which compose the forehead, and generally soon unite into one, though in some adults they continue double ; two *parietal* bones, forming the greater part of the upper and lateral regions of the skull; two *temporal*, around the ears ; one *sphenoid*, in the anterior part of the basilar region ; one *occipital*, in the back and under part of the skull, immediately above the neck ; and one *ethmoidal*, at the base behind the nose. The lines of junction of these bones are termed sutures, and form, in most parts, a sort of dovetailing. The principal sutures are the *sagittal*, separating the two parietal bones at the middle of the top of the head ; the *coronal*, which divides the frontal from the parietal bones ; the *lambdoidal*, between the occipital bone and the two parietals, and deriving its name from its resemblance to the Greek letter lambda (Λ) ; the *frontal*, dividing the two frontal bones when they are not conjoined ; and the *temporal*, named also the *squamous*, from its scaly appearance, dividing the temporal bones from the parietal, and to some extent from the sphenoid and occipital.

The annexed figure represents a skull with the two sides cut away, down nearly to the level of the eyebrow, leaving a narrow ridge in the

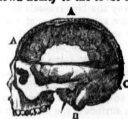

middle of the top standing. AAA is the edge of the skull, resembling an arch. It is here represented thicker than it is in nature, in order to show the diploë. Most parts of the skull consist of two plates, called the outer and inner tables, having between them a spongy substance, like cells in a marrow-bone, called the diploë. The substance hanging down from the arch of the skull, having delicate lines traced on it, like the sap-vessels in leaves, is the membrane which separates the two halves of the brain. It is a continuation of the dura mater, and is called the falciform process, from its resemblance to a scythe. It is well supplied with bloodvessels; and a large portion of the blood returning from the brain to the heart, goes up these vessels into a canal formed by the membrane all along the line of its attachment to the skull. The course of the blood through the canal is from the front backward, and then downward. The two hemispheres of the brain are completely separated, as far as this membrane is seen to extend downward in the cut. At the lower edge of it an open space appears : the commissure, or collection of fibres which unite the two sides, named the *corpus callosum*, goes through that space. The cerebellum lies at B C, in a part of the skull not opened. The membrane, on reaching the point C, spreads out to the right and left, and runs forward, so as to separate the cerebellum from the brain ; the latter lying above, and the former below it. B is the mastoid process, or bone to which the sterno-mastoid muscle is attached. It lies immediately behind the opening of the ear, and is not connected with the brain.

As the diploë, except in the parts mentioned below, is almost equally thick, it follows that the two tables of the skull are nearly parallel to each other. This is seen in the section represented in fig. 3, p. 75.[*] The internal, indeed, bears some slight impressions of bloodvessels, glands, &c., which do not appear externally ; but these are so small as not to interfere with phrenological observations. The departure from perfect parallelism,

[*] See Dr. Caldwell on the parallelism of the tables, *Phren. Journ.*, ix., 222.

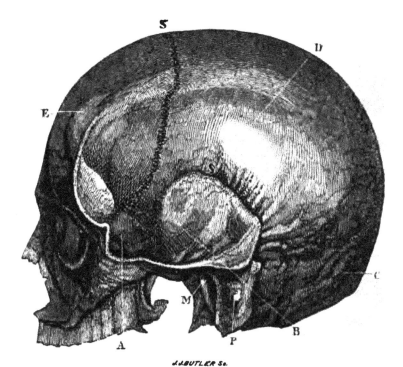

J.J.BUTLER Sc.

A. Basilar or Sphenoid Bone. Small portion reaching the surface at the side.

B. Temporal Bone.

C. Occipital Bone.

D. Parietal Bone.

E. Frontal Bone.

M. Meatus Auditorius Externus, or external opening of the ear.

P. Mastoid process of the Temporal Bone, which serves to give attachment to the Sterno-mastoid muscle.

SS. Sutures, or serrated edges by which the different bones are joined together.

where it occurs, is limited to a line, one-tenth or one-eighth of an inch, according to the age and health of the individual. The difference in developement, between a large and a small organ of the propensities and some of the sentiments amounts to an inch and upward; and to a quarter of an inch in the organs of intellect, which are naturally smaller than the others.*

The squamous portion of the temporal bones is much thinner than the other parts of the skull. But as this is the case in all heads indiscriminately, it is not a source of error to the phrenologist. Every skull, moreover, is thick at the ridges of the frontal bone and the transverse ridge of the occipital, (48, fig. 3, p. 75,) and very thin at the super-orbitar plates of the frontal bone, forming the roof of the sockets of the eyes—and also in the middle of the occipital fossæ. Dr. Gall states that sometimes the skulls of very stupid people are unusually thick;† and Dr. Vimont has frequently observed the same thing to occur in persons of an athletic constitution.‡ In savages the skull is often thick.

The integuments which cover the skull on the outside, indisputably lie close upon its surface, and are so uniform in their thickness as to exhibit, with sufficient accuracy, its true figure. The temples and occiput are the only parts where the integuments are thicker than at the others, and the phrenologist attends to this fact in making his observations. Thus there is no obstacle in general to the discovery of the figure of the brain, by observations on the form of the skull or head.

This doctrine has been frequently disputed by opponents of Phrenology; but many anatomists have taught it. Magendie, in his *Compendium of Physiology*, says, that "the only way of estimating the *volume of the brain* in a living person is, to *measure the dimensions of the skull*; every other means, even that proposed by Camper, is uncertain."§

Sir Charles Bell also observes, "that the bones of the head are moulded to the brain, and the peculiar shapes of the bones of the head are determined by the original peculiarity in the shape of the brain."‖ Dr. Gordon likewise, in the 49th number of *The Edinburgh Review*, has the following words: "But we will acquiesce implicitly for the present in the proposition, (familiar to physiologists long before the age of Gall and Spurzheim,) that there is, in most instances, a general correspondence between the size of the cranium and the quantity of cerebrum; that large heads usually contain large brains, and small heads small brains."—(P. 246.)

There are, however, cases in which it is not possible to discover the form of the brain by examining the skull. These are instances of disease and old age. In disease the skull may be enlarged or diminished in volume by other causes than changes of the brain; and in old age the inner table of the skull sometimes sinks, while the outer table preserves its original size: in such cases the true developement of the brain cannot be accurately inferred from the appearances of the head.**

* "Jamais je n' al prétendu distinguer des modifications peu prononcées des formes du crâne, ou de légères nuances du caractère."—Gall, iii., 41.
† Tome iii., p. 43. ‡ Vol. i., p. 285.
§ Milligan's Translation, p. 104.
‖ Bell's *Anatomy*, ii., 390. Sir C. Bell adds, in a foot-note, "Certainly the skull is adapted to the form of the brain; but there is a deeper question, which our craniologists have forgotten—Is the brain constituted in shape with a reference to the future form of the head?"—It is difficult to see the importance of this question. Not only is the skull, at every period before the decline of life, adapted to the form of the brain, but it increases in size when the brain enlarges, and decreases when the brain diminishes. The reader will find an answer to Sir Charles Bell's objections in *The Phrenological Journal*, viii., 333.
** According to Dr. Gall, the skulls of aged people are generally thicker, lighter, and more spongy than those of young men and adults: but Dr. Vi-

There are parts at the base of the brain, in the middle and posterior regions, the size of which cannot be discovered during life, and whose functions in consequence are still unknown. From analogy, and from some pathological facts, they are supposed to be the organs of the sensations of Hunger and Thirst, Heat and Cold, and some other mental affections for which cerebral organs have not been discovered; but demonstrative evidence to this effect being wanting, the conjecture is stated merely to incite to farther investigation.

The sutures interrupt the absolute parallelism of the tables; but their situation is known, and only one of them, the lamb-doidal, where it passes over the organ of Concentrativeness, presents any difficulty to the student. In some individuals it presents a bony projection at that part; which may be mistaken for a large developement of Concentrativeness; but the bone is generally sharp and angular, whereas the developement presented by the organ when large is full and round. The sagittal and frontal sutures, which run longitudinally from the back part of the crown of the head forward and downward, sometimes so low as the top of the nose, occasionally present a narrow prominent ridge, which is sometimes mistaken for developement of the organs of Benevolence, Veneration, Firmness, and Self-Esteem. It may, however, be easily distinguished, by its narrowness and isolation, from the full broad swell of cerebral developement. In anatomy projecting bony points are called processes. The mastoid process of the temporal bone, (B in figure, p. 80,) which is a small knob immediately behind the ear, serving for the attachment of a muscle, is sometimes mistaken for the indication of large Combativeness. It is, however, merely a bony prominence, which is found in every head, and does not indicate developement of brain at all. Another process, called by anatomists the spinous process of the transverse ridge of the occipital bone, requires to be known. Phrenologists generally name it shortly the Occipital Spine, and its situation is indicated by C in the figure, p. 80.

There is one part of the skull where the external configuration does not always indicate exactly the size of the subjacent parts of the brain, and upon which objections have been raised. At the part of the frontal bone immediately above the top of the nose, a divergence from parallelism is sometimes produced by the existence of a small cavity called the *frontal sinus*.

The frontal sinus is the dark hole seen in the annexed cut, above the nose. Its size in one individual is shown; it is sometimes larger and sometimes smaller than that which is here represented. It is formed between the two tables of the bone, either by the external table swelling out a little without being followed by the internal, and presenting an appearance like that of a blister on a biscuit, or by the internal table sinking in without being followed by the external; and hence, as the outer surface does not indicate the precise degree of developement of brain beneath, it has been argued by some individuals that the existence of a frontal sinus is an insuperable objection to Phrenology in general, because it throws so much uncertainty in the way of our observations as commont thinks that farther observations are necessary to determine whether this is the most frequent appearance.—(Gall, iii., 50.; Vimont, i., 288.) Sometimes, in extreme old age, portions of the outer table and diploë are absorbed and not renewed, so that the skull becomes, in various parts, very thin and transparent. There is such a skull in the collection of the Phrenological Society, and Dr. Gall possessed several specimens.—(Gall, iii., 53; and *Phren. Jour.*, vii., 28.) That the skull becomes thin in old age by absorption is maintained also in a work called *Anatomia Senilis*, published in 1799. According to Tenon, the skull loses two-fifths of its weight in old age.—*Memoirs of the French Institute* for the year 6.)

pletely to destroy their value. Other opponents, however, more rationally confine their objection to those organs only over which the sinus extends. The first objection is manifestly untenable. Even granting the sinus to be an insuperable obstacle in the way of ascertaining the developement of the organs over which it is situated, it is plain that, in ordinary cases, it interferes with only a few, viz., Form, Size, Weight, Individuality, and Locality ; and that the whole external appearances of the other thirty or thirty-one organs are left as unaltered as if no frontal sinus existed at all. It would be quite as logical to speak of a snow-storm in Norway obstructing the highway from Edinburgh to London, as of a small sinus at the top of the nose concealing the developement of Benevolence, Firmness, or Veneration on the crown of the head.

To enable the reader to form a correct estimate of the value of the objection as applicable to the individual organs particularly referred to, I subjoin a few observations. In the *first* place, Below the age of twelve or fourteen the sinus, if it exists at all, rarely extends so high as the base of the frontal lobe of the brain ; *secondly*, In adult age it frequently occurs to the extent above admitted ;* and, *thirdly*, In old age, and in diseases such as chronic idiocy and insanity, it is often of very great extent, owing to 'the brain diminishing in size, and the inner table of the skull following it, while the outer remains stationary. The first cases present no objection, for in them the sinus does not exist so high as to interfere with the observation of the size of the organs ; the third are instances of disease, which are uniformly excluded in phrenological observations ; and thus our attention is limited solely to the cases forming the second class. In regard to them the objection is, that large developement of brain and large frontal sinus present so nearly the same appearance that we cannot accurately distinguish them, and that, therefore, our observations must be inconclusive.

To this the following answer is given : 1st, We must distinguish between the possibility of *discovering the function* of an organ and of applying this discovery practically in *all* cases, so as to be able, in every instance, to predicate the exact degree in which every particular mental power is present in each individual. The sinus does not, in general, extend so high as the brain until after the ages of twelve or fourteen, before which time Individuality is most conspicuously active in the mind. If, then, in children, in whom no sinus exists, that mental power is observed to be strong when the part of the head is large, and weak when it is small, we *ascertain the function*, whatever may subsequently embarrass us. If in after-life the sinus comes to exist, this throws a certain impediment in the way of the practical application of our knowledge ; and, accordingly, phrenologists admit a difficulty in determining the exact degree of developement of the organs lying immediately above the top of the nose, except in extreme instances, in which even the sinus itself will form but a fraction of the difference between great developement and deficiency. In the next place, the objection applies only to one set of cases. If there be a hollow or depression in the external surface of the skull at the situation of the organs in question, and the sinus be absent, then the organ must

* This may seem at variance with a statement given in the first edition of this work, on the authority of a friend in Paris, who, in the course of many months' dissections, had never found a frontal sinus except in old age and in disease. In sawing open the skull for anatomical purposes, the section is almost always made horizontally through the middle of the forehead, or over the organs of Tune, Time, and Eventuality ; in all the cases alluded to by the gentleman in Paris, this line was followed, and as the sinus rarely extends so high up, he could not, and did not, meet with it. On examining vertical sections, however, for the purpose of seeing the sinus, he has since frequently found it to the extent mentioned in the text.

necessarily be deficient in proportion to the depression. If, with such an external appearance, the sinus be present—which is not generally the case, but which, for the sake of argument, I shall suppose—then it must be formed by the inner table receding more than the outer table : hence a greater deficiency of the organs will actually exist than what is externally indicated ; and, of course, the deficiency of mental power. will be *at least equal* to that which is indicated by the exterior of the head. In cases of this kind, therefore, the sinus forms no objection. Thus the only instances in which it can occasion embarrassment are those where it causes a swelling outward of the parts of the skull in question, when there is no corresponding developement of brain within. Now, if, in all cases in youth, when no sinus exists, and in all cases in mature age in which a depression is found, the mental power is ascertained to correspond with the external developement ; and if, in certain cases in adult age, an external indication appears to which the mental power does not correspond, what conclusion ought to be drawn according to the rules of a correct logic ? Not that the functions of the parts are uncertain—because they have been ascertained in cases not liable to impediment or objection ; but only that, in the particular cases in mature age in which the external developement is large and the corresponding power absent, *there must be a frontal sinus*.

Finally, by practice in observing, it is possible, in general, to distinguish between external appearances produced by a frontal sinus, and those indicating a large developement of organs. In the *first* instance the elevations are more abrupt and ridgy ; in the *second*, they present a rounder swell, and follow the direction of the organs as delineated on the busts.

If, then, men in general manifest their natural capacities in their actions ; and if, in healthy individuals, not beyond the middle period of life, the form of the brain may be discovered by observing the figure of the head, it follows that the true faculties and the true cerebral developement may be compared in living subjects ; and on these grounds the proposition is established, that the phrenological mode of philosophizing is competent to enable us to attain the results sought for.

PRACTICAL APPLICATION OF THE PRINCIPLES OF PHRENOLOGY.

It has already been mentioned, that there are two hemispheres of the brain, corresponding in form and functions. There are, therefore, two organs for each mental power, one in each hemisphere. Each organ, including its supposed apparatus of communication, extends from the *medulla oblongata*, or top of the spinal marrow, to the surface of the brain or cerebellum ; and every person not an idiot has all the organs in a greater or less degree. Such of the organs as are situated immediately on the sides of the middle line separating the hemispheres, are included in one space on the busts and plates. To avoid circumlocution, the expression "organ" of a faculty will be used, but both organs will be thereby meant.

The brain is not divided by lines corresponding to those delineated on the busts ; but the forms produced on the skull by its different parts, when extremely large or small, resemble those there represented—though it is not to be understood that the angles of the compartments are ever seen on the head.* Each part is inferred to be a separate organ, because its size, *cæteris paribus*, bears a regular proportion to the energy of a particular mental faculty.

* In Dr Gall's plates, the organs are, in many instances, represented apart from each other, and all of them bounded entirely by curved lines, without angels. See his Atlas, Plates 98, 99, and 100.

As size, *cæteris paribus*, is a measure of power,* the first object ought to be to distinguish the size of the brain generally, so as to judge whether it be large enough to admit of manifestations of ordinary vigour; for, as we have already seen, (p. 45,) if it be too small, idiocy is the invariable consequence. The second object should be to ascertain the relative proportions of the different parts, so as to determine the direction in which the power is greatest.

It is proper to begin with observation of the more palpable differences in size, and particularly to attend to the relative proportions of the different lobes. The size of the anterior lobe is the measure of intellect. In the brain it is easily distinguished, and in the living head it is indicated by the portion lying before Constructiveness and Benevolence. Sometimes the lower part of the frontal lobe, connected with the perceptive faculties, is the largest, and this is indicated by the space before Constructiveness extending farthest forward at the base; sometimes the upper part, connected with the reflecting powers, is the most amply developed, in which case the projection is greatest in the upper region; and sometimes both are equally developed. The student is particularly requested to resort invariably to this mode of estimating the size of the anterior lobe, as the best for avoiding mistakes. In some individuals the forehead is tolerably perpendicular, so that, seen in front, and judged of without attending to longitudinal depth, it appears to be largely developed; whereas, when viewed in the way now pointed out, it is seen to be extremely shallow. In other words, the mass is not large, and the intellectual manifestations will be proportionately feeble.

Besides the projection of the forehead, its vertical and lateral dimensions require to be attended to; a remark which applies to all the organs individually—each having, of course, like other objects, the three dimensions of length, breadth, and thickness.

The posterior lobe is devoted chiefly to the animal propensities. In the brain its size is easily distinguished; and in the living head a perpendicular line may be drawn through the mastoid process, and all behind will belong to the posterior lobe. Wherever this and the basilar region are large, the animal feelings will be strong, and *vice versa.*

The coronal region of the brain is the seat of the moral sentiments;

Fig. 1. HARE.

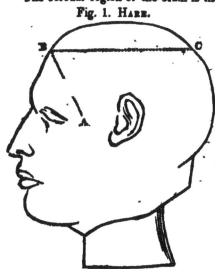

and its size may be estimated by the extent of elevation and expansion of the head above the organs of Causality in the forehead and of Cautiousness in the middle of the parietal bones. When the whole region of the brain rising above these organs is shallow and narrow, the moral feelings will be weakly manifested; when high and expanded, they will be vigorously displayed.

Fig. 1 represents the head of William Hare, the associate of Burke in the murder of sixteen individuals in Edinburgh, for the purpose of selling their bodies for dissection.†

* See Introduction, p. 42, *et seq.*   † *Phrenological Journal*, v., 549.

Fig. 2 represents that of Melancthon, the highly intellectual, moral, religious, and accomplished associate of Luther in effecting the Reformation in Germany.* All that lies before the line A B, in fig. 1, is the anterior lobe, comprising the organs of the intellectual faculties. The space above the horizontal line B C marks the region of the moral sentiments. The space from A backward, below B C, indicates the region of the propensities.

Fig. 2. MELANCTHON.

Fig. 3 represents the head of Gesche Margarethe Gottfried, who was executed at Bremen, in 1828, for poisoning, in cold blood, during a succession of years, both her parents, her three children, her first and second husbands, and about six other individuals.†

The line A B commences at the organ of Causality B, and passes through the middle of Cautiousness 12. These points are in general sufficiently distinguishable on the skull, and the line can easily be traced. The convolutions lying above the line A B must have been shallow and small, compared with those below, which are devoted to the animal propensities.

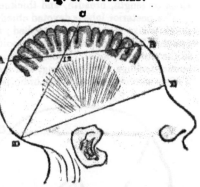

Fig. 3. GOTTFRIED.

Fig. 4 is a sketch of the head of a negro called Eustache,‡ who was as much distinguished for high morality and practical benevolence as Gottfried was for deficiency of these qualities. During the massacre of the whites by the negroes in St. Domingo, Eustache, while in the capacity of a slave, saved, by his address, courage, and devotion, the lives of his master and upward of 400 other whites, at the daily risk of his own safety. The line A B is drawn from Causality B, through Cautiousness 12; and the great size of the convolutions of the moral sentiments may be judged of from the space lying between that line and the top of the head C.

Both of the sketches are drawn from busts, and the convolutions are filled in suppositively for the sake of illustration. The depth of the con-

* Spurzheim's *Phrenology in Connexion with the Study of Physiognomy*, p. 160.
† This woman's history will be found in *The Phrenological Journal*, vol. vii., p. 560.
‡ *Phrenological Journal*, vol. ix., p. 134.

Fig. 4. EUSTACHE.

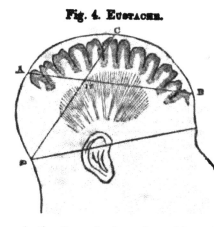

-volutions, in both cuts, is greater than in nature, that the contrast may be rendered the more perceptible. It will be kept in mind that I am here merely teaching rules for observing heads, and not proving particular facts. The spaces, however, between the line A B and the top of the head are accurately drawn to a scale. Mr. Abram Cox has suggested, that the size of the convolutions which constitute the organs of Self-Esteem, Love of Approbation, Concentrativeness, Adhesiveness, and Philoprogenitiveness, may be estimated by their projection beyond a base formed by a plane passing through the centres of the two organs of Cautiousness and the spinous process of the occipital bone. He was led to this conclusion by a minute examination of a great number of the skulls in the collection of the Phrenological Society. A section of this plane is represented by the lines C D, in figs. 2 and 3.

To determine the size of the convolutions lying in the lateral regions of the head, Mr. Cox proposes to imagine two vertical planes passing through the organs of Causality in each hemisphere, and directly backward, till each meets the outer border of the point of insertion of the trapezius muscle at the back of the neck. The more the lateral convolutions project beyond these planes, the larger do the organs in the sides of the head appear to be—namely, Combativeness, Destructiveness, Secretiveness, Cautiousness, Acquisitiveness, and Constructiveness; also to some extent Tune,. Ideality, Wit, and Number.

Fig. 5. CINGALESE.   Fig. 6. GOTTFRIED

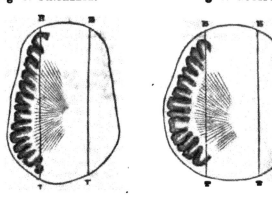

Fig. 5 represents a horizontal section of the skull of a Cingalese, the lines B T being sections of the planes above described. Fig. 6 represents the same section of the skull of Gottfried, the female poisoner already referred to. The lateral expansion of the head beyond the lines B T, in fig. 6, forms a striking contrast with the size of the same regions in fig. 5. The Cingalese are a tribe in Ceylon, and in disposition are remarkably mild and pacific.*

Mr. Cox suggests farther, that the size of the convolutions lying at the

* See description of their character in *The Phrenological Journal*, vii., 634.

base of the brain may be estimated by their projection below a plane passing through the superciliary ridges and the occipital spine, (D E, fig. 3, and D, fig. 4,) and by observing the distance at which the opening of the ear, the mastoid process, and other points of the base of the skull lie below that plane.

So many instances have occurred in which I have verified the accuracy of the inferences drawn from the projection of the brain. beyond these planes, that I recommend this mode of observation as useful in practice. In the course of my lectures, I have frequently pointed out the difference, in different individuals, in the position of the opening of the ear in relation to the level of the eye, as one indication of the size of the organ of Destructiveness, and of the basilar convolutions situated inward from it toward the mesial line. The lower the ear descends, the larger are the inferior convolutions of the middle lobe, which occupy the middle fossæ of the skull. Individuals in whom the opening of the ear stands nearly on a level with the eye, are in general little prone to violence of temper. Dr. G. M. Paterson mentions incidentally, in his paper " On the Phrenology of Hindostan,"* that the situation of the ears is high in the Hindoos, while, at the same time, their skulls, over the organ of Destructiveness, are " either quite flat, or indicate a slight degree of concavity."

I have multiplied observations to so great an extent in regard to the above-described methods of estimating the size of the anterior lobe and the coronal region of the brain, that I regard them as altogether worthy of reliance. The observations on the planes suggested by Mr. Abram Cox, however, are still too limited to authorize me to state these as certain guides. They are open to the verification of every observer. I particularly recommend to students of Phrenology who have opportunities of dissecting the brains of individuals whose dispositions are known, to run straight wires through the brain before removing it from the skull, in the directions of the lines represented in the figures.; then to make sections, passing through the course of the wires ;. and to observe and report to what extent the convolutions develope themselves externally from the planes so formed.

By observing the proportions of the different regions, it will be discovered, that in some instances the anterior lobe bears a large and in others a small proportion to the rest of the head ; in some cases the coronal region is large in proportion to the base, while in others it is small. Great differences also in projection beyond the line running from Causality to the trapezius will be discovered. The busts of the Reverend Mr M., Pallet, Steventon, and Sir Edward Parry may be contrasted with this view. A head that is very broad in proportion to its height, indicates a mind in which the animal propensities are the ruling springs of action. The Roman emperor, Vitellius, a monster of vice, is represented with such a head.

After becoming familiar with the general size and configuration of heads, the student may proceed to the *observation of individual organs ;* and, in studying them, the real dimensions, including length, breadth, and thickness, and not the mere prominence of each organ, should be looked for.

The length of an organ, including its supposed apparatus of communication, is ascertained by the distance from the *medulla oblongata* to the peripheral surface. A line passing through the head from one ear to the other, would nearly touch the *medulla oblongata*. and hence the external opening of the ear is assumed as a convenient point from which to estimate length. The breadth of an organ is judged of by its peripheral expansion ; for it is a general law of physiology, that the breadth of an organ throughout its whole course bears a relation to its expansion at the surface : the optic and olfactory nerves are examples in point.

* *Transactions of the Phrenological Society,* (Edin., 1824,) p. 443.

VITELLIUS.

It has been objected that the breadth of the organs cannot be ascertained, because the boundaries of them are not sufficiently determinate. In answer I observe, that although the boundaries of the different organs cannot be determined with mathematical precision, like those of a triangle, a square, or rhomboid, yet, in a single case, an accurate observer may make a very near approximation to the truth ; and, in a great multitude of cases, the very doctrine of chances, and of the compensation of errors, must satisfy any one that these boundaries may be defined with sufficient precision for all practical purposes. Even in the exact sciences themselves an approximate solution is frequently all that is attainable ; and if the opponents would only make themselves masters of the binomial theorem, or pay a little attention to the expansion of infinite series, they would not persist in calling for a degree of accuracy which is impossible, or in neglecting an important element in a calculation because it is involved in a certain liability to error within very narrow limits. The absurdity of the reason assigned for this omission is rendered still more apparent by the case of the prismatic spectrum, which I conceive to be exactly in point. Now, what is it that this beautiful phenomenon displays ? The seven primary colours, arranged in a peculiar order, and glowing with an almost painful intensity. But each of these colours occupies a certain space in relation to the whole, the boundaries of which it may be impossible for the hand or eye to trace with geometrical precision, although the relative space in question has, nevertheless, been made the subject of measurement, and a very close approximation obtained from the mean of a vast number of trials. According to the principle followed by some antiphrenologists, however, *breadth* should be altogether neglected, on the ground that the boundaries of the respective colours are " purely ideal ;" as if a mathematical line were not the most perfect idealism or

8*

abstraction which the mind of man can possibly form. This idealism or abstraction, however, has no more to do with those approximations which may be obtained practically by repeated trials, than the mathematical definition of a line with a metallic rod ; and it is a mere quibble to pretend, for example, that we ought not to measure the length of the rod, because it may not correspond with the definition of the line. Upon the strange principle which some opponents have adopted, they must be prepared to maintain, that the boundaries of a hill or hillock are purely *ideal*, and depend in *every* instance on the *fancy* of the measurer.* The science of geology affords another illustration. The leading rocks bear so many characteristic marks of distinction, that no ordinary observer can mistake them ; yet particular specimens graduate so much into each other, that the most skilful observers will sometimes err, and believe basalt to be claystone, or gneiss to be granite. In teaching this science, however, the leading features of the rocks are found sufficient to guide the student to knowledge of the principles, and his own sagacity, improved by experience, enables him in due time to deal successfully with the intricacies and difficulties of the study. The same rule ought to be followed in cultivating Phrenology.†

The *whole* organs in a head should be examined, and their relative proportions noted.‡ Errors may be committed at first ; but without practice there will be no expertness. Practice, with at least an average endowment of the organs of Form, Size, Individuality, and Locality, is necessary to qualify a person to make observations with success. Individuals whose heads are very narrow between the eyes, and little developed at the top of the nose, where these organs are placed, experience great difficulty in distinguishing the situations and minute shades in the proportions of different organs. If one organ be much developed, and the neighbouring organs very little, the developed organ will present an elevation or protuberance ; but if the neighbouring organs be developed in proportion, no protuberance can be perceived, and the surface is smooth. The student should learn from books, plates, and casts, or personal instruction, (and the last is by far the best,) to distinguish the *form* of each organ, and its *appearance* when developed in different proportions to the others, because there are slight modifications in the position of them in each head.

The phrenological bust shows the situations of the organs, and their proportions, only in one head ; and it is impossible by it to communicate more information.§ The different appearances in all the varieties of re-

* *Caledonian Mercury*, 11th June, 1829.

† See additional illustrations in *The Phrenological Journal*, viii., 640.

‡ "There are many convolutions," says Dr. Spurzheim, "in the middle line between the two hemispheres of the brain, and others at the basis and between the anterior and middle lobes, which do not appear on the surface ; but it seems to me that a great part, at least, of every organ does present itself there, and farther, that all the parts of each organ are equally developed, so that, though a portion only appear, the state of the whole may be inferred. The whole cerebellum reaches not the skull, yet its function may be determined from the part which does. The cerebral parts situated in the middle line between the hemispheres, seem proportionate to the superincumbent convolutions.; at least I have always observed a proportion, in the vertical direction, between them."—*Phrenology*, p. 116.

"The cerebral parts situated around and behind the orbit also require some care and experience on the part of the phrenologist, to be judged of accurately. Their developement is discoverable from the position of the eyeball, and from the figure of the superciliary ridge. According as the eyeball is prominent or hidden in the orbit, depressed or pushed sideward, inward, or outward, we may judge of the developement of the organs situated around and behind it."—*Ibid.* Particular directions for observing the parts there situated will be given when treating of the individual organs.

§ Attempts have been made by opponents to represent certain changes in

lative size must be discovered by inspecting a *number* of heads.; and especially by contrasting instances of extreme developement with others of extreme deficiency. No adequate idea of the foundation of the science can be formed until this is done. In cases of extreme size of single organs, a close approximation to the *form* delineated on the bust (leaving angles out of view) is distinctly perceived.

The question will perhaps occur—If the relative proportions of the organs differ in each individual, and if the phrenological bust represents only their *most common proportions*, how are their boundaries to be distinguished in any particular living head? The answer is, By their *forms* and *appearances*. Each organ has a form, appearance, and situation, which it is possible, by practice, to distinguish in the living head, otherwise Phrenology cannot have any foundation.

When one organ is very largely developed, it encroaches on the space usually occupied by the neighbouring organs, the situations of which are thereby slightly altered. When this occurs, it may be distinguished by the numbering and marking of the organs in busts recently published, as " a Revolution in Phrenology." A brief explanation will place this matter in its true light. The phrenological bust sold in the shops is an *artificial* head, the utility of which depends on the degree in which the delineation of the organs on it approaches to the appearances *most generally* presented by the organs in nature. The first bust sold in this country exhibited the organs as they would be found in a particular head not very common in this country, the bust having been imported from the continent, and national heads being modified as much as national features. On the 1st of October, 1824, a new bust was published in Edinburgh, in which the delineation exhibited more accurately the appearances and relative proportions of the organs in this country. Subsequent observations showed that this bust might be brought still more closely to resemble the most common proportions of the organs in Britain; and, on the 1st of April, 1829, certain modifications were made on it accordingly. The nature of this operation may be explained by a simple illustration. Suppose that, in 1819, an artist had modelled a bust resembling, as closely as his skill could reach, the face most commonly met with in Scotland, and that, to save the trouble of referring to the different features by name, he had attached numbers to them, beginning at the chin, and calling it No 1, and so on up to the brow, which we may suppose to be No. 33—in this bust he would necessarily give certain proportions to the eyes, nose, cheek, mouth, and chin. But suppose he were to continue his observations for five years, it is quite conceivable he might come to be of opinion that, by making the nose a little shorter, the mouth a little wider, the cheeks a little broader, and the chin a little sharper, he could bring the artificial face nearer to the *most general* form of the Scottish countenance ; and that he might arrange the *numbers* of the features with greater philosophical accuracy : and suppose he were to publish a new edition of his bust with these modifications of the features, and with the numeration changed so that the mouth should be No. 1, the chin No. 5, and the brow No. 35, what should we think of a critic who should announce these alterations as " a revolution." in human physiognomy, and assert that, because the numbers were changed, the nose had obliterated the eyes and the chin had extinguished the mouth? This is what the opponents have done in regard to the new phrenological bust. In the modifications which have been made on it, the essential forms and relative situations of all the organs have been preserved, and there is no instance of the organ of Benevolence being turned into that of Veneration, or Veneration into Hope, any more than, in the supposed new modelled face, the nose would be converted into the eyes, or the eyes into the mouth.

In regard to the numeration, again, the changes are exactly analogous to those which are before supposed to take place in regard to the features : the organ of Ideality formerly was numbered 16, and now it is numbered 19; but the organ and function are nothing different on this account. Dr. Spurzheim adopted a new order of numbering, from enlarged observation of the anatomical relation of the organs, and his improvements have been adopted in Edinburgh and Dublin.

the greatest prominence being near the centre of the large organ, and the swelling extending over a portion only of the other. In these cases the *shape* should be attended to; for the form of the organ is then easily recognised, and is a sure indication of the particular one which is largely developed. The observer should learn, by inspecting a skull, to distinguish the mastoid process behind the ear, as also bony excrescences sometimes formed by the sutures, and several bony prominences which occur in every head, from elevations produced by developement of brain.

In observing the *appearance* of individual organs, it is proper to begin with the largest, and select extreme cases. The mask of Mr. Joseph Hume may be contrasted with that of Dr. Chalmers for Ideality; the organ being much larger in the latter than in the former. The casts of the skulls of Burns and Haggart may be compared at the same part; the difference being equally conspicuous. The cast of the Reverend Mr. M. may be contrasted with that of Dempsey, in the region of Love of Approbation; the former having this organ large, and the latter small. Self-Esteem in the latter, being exceedingly large, may be compared with the same organ in the skull of Dr. Hette, in whom Love of Approbation is much larger than Self-Esteem. Destructiveness in Bellingham may be compared with the same organ in the skulls of the Hindoos; the latter people being in general tender of life. Firmness large, and Conscientiousness deficient, in King Robert Bruce, may be compared with the same organs reversed in the cast of the head of a lady, (Mrs. H.,) which is sold as illustrative of these organs. The object of making these contrasts is, to obtain an idea of the different *appearances* presented by organs, when very large and very small.

The terms used by the Edinburgh phrenologists to denote the gradations of size in the different organs, in an increasing ratio, are,

Very small	Moderate	Rather large
Small	Rather full	Large
Rather small	Full	Very large.

Sir John Ross has suggested, that numerals may be applied with advantage to the notation of developement. He uses decimals; but these appear unnecessarily minute. The end in view may be attained by such a scale as the following:

1.	8 Rather small	15.
2. Idiocy	9.	16. Rather large
3.	10. Moderate	17.
4. Very small	11.	18. Large
5.	12. Rather full	19.
6. Small	13.	20. Very large.
7.	14. Full	

The intermediate figures denote intermediate degrees of size, for which we have no names. The advantage of adopting numerals is, that, the values of the extremes being known, we can judge accurately of the dimensions denoted by the intermediate numbers; whereas it is difficult to apprehend precisely the degrees of magnitude indicated by the terms small, full, large, &c., unless we have seen them applied by the individual who uses them. These divisions have been objected to as too minute; but by those who have long practiced Phrenology, this is not found to be the case. It has even been said that it is *impossible* to distinguish the existence of several of the organs in consequence of their minute size. This objection is obviously absurd. Artisans find it possible not only to distinguish the links in the chain attached to the mainspring of a watch, but to fabricate them; engravers distinguish the minutest lines which they employ to produce shade in pictures; and printers discriminate at a glance the smallest types used in their art;—compared with which objects the smallest phrenological organ is of gigantic size. There is, however, difficulty in distinguishing the size and relative proportions of the minuter organs. But practice has an astonishing effect in giving acuteness to the perception of differences in the appearance of these as well as of other objects. A schoolboy or labourer will confound manuscripts of very different aspects, while the copyist of ten years' standing finds no difficulty in ascribing each of a hundred pages, written by as many individuals, to its appropriate writer. When there is a question of forgery in a court of law, the judge remits to an engraver to report whether or not the signature is genuine, because it is known that the familiarity of engravers with the minute forms of written characters enables them to discriminate points of identity and difference which would escape the notice of ordinary observers. How frequently, moreover, do strangers mistake one member of a family for another, although the real difference of features is so obvious to the remaining brothers and sisters that they are puzzled to discover any resemblance whatever! How easily does the experienced physician distinguish two diseases, by the similarity of whose symptoms a novice would be at once misled! And with what facility does a skilful painter discriminate a copy from an original! It was only after a continued and attentive study of Raphael's pictures that Sir Joshua Reynolds was able to perceive their excellencies. "Nor does painting," he adds, "in this respect differ from other arts. A just poetical taste and the acquisition of a nice discriminative musical ear are equally the work of time. Even the eye, however perfect in itself, is often unable to distinguish between the brilliancy of two diamonds: the experienced jeweller will be amazed at this blindness, though his own powers of discrimination were acquired by slow and scarcely perceptible degrees." The American Indians are able, from long and constant practice, to "discern the footsteps of a wild beast, which escape every other eye, and can follow them with certainty through the pathless forest."* Lord Kames remarks, that "those who live in the world, and in good company, are quick-sighted with respect to every defect or irregularity in behaviour: the very slightest singularity in motion, in speech, or in dress, which to a peasant would be invisible, escapes not their observation. The most minute differences in the human countenance, so minute as to be far beyond the reach of words, are distinctly perceived by the plainest person; while, at the same time, the generality have very little discernment in the faces of other animals, to which they are less accustomed. Sheep, for example, appear to have all the same face, except to the shepherd, who knows every individual in his flock as he does his relations and neighbours."† So it is with Phrenology. The student is often at first unable to perceive differences which, after a few months, become palpably manifest to him, and at the former obscurity of which he is not a little surprised. The following anecdote, related by Dr. Gall,‡ is in point: The physician of the House of Correction, at Grætz, in Stiria, sent him a box filled with skulls. In unpacking them, he was so much struck with the extreme breadth of one of them at the anterior region of the temples, that he exclaimed, "Mon Dieu, quel crâne de voleur!" Yet the physician had been unable to discover the organ of Acquisitiveness in that skull. His letter to Dr. Gall, sent with the box, was found to contain this information: "The skull marked —— is that of N——, an incorrigible thief."

With respect to the practical employment of the scale above described, it is proper to remark, that as each phrenologist attaches to the terms small, moderate, full, &c., shades of meaning perfectly known only to

* Robertson's *Hist. of Amer.*, B. iv.
† *Elements of Criticism*, London edit., 1805, ii., 400.
‡ *Sur les Fonctions du Cerveau*, iv., 240.

himself and those accustomed to observe heads along with him, the separate statements of the developement of a particular head, by two phrenologists, are not likely to correspond entirely with each other. It ought to be kept in mind, also, that these terms indicate only the relative proportions of the organs to each other in the same head; but as the different organs may bear the same proportions in a small and in a large head, the terms mentioned do not enable the reader to discover whether the head treated of be in its general magnitude small, moderate, or large. To supply this information, measurement by callipers is resorted to; but this is used not to indicate the dimensions of particular organs, for which purpose they are not adapted, but merely to designate the *general size* of the head.

The following are a few measurements from nature, taken promiscuously from many more in my possession:

Table of Measurements by Callipers.

Males between twenty-five and fifty.	From Occipital Spine to Individuality.	From Occipital Spine to Ear.	From Ear to Individuality.	From Ear to Firmness.	From Destructiveness to Destructiveness.	From Cautiousness to Cautiousness.	From Ideality to Ideality.
1.	7 1/8	4 3/8	4 1/8	5 1/2	5 1/4	5 1/4	5 3/8
2.	6 7/8	3 7/8	4 1/2	5 1/2	5 1/8	5 1/4	4 3/8
3.	8 1/4	4 7/8	5 1/8	6 1/8	6 1/8	6	5 7/8
4.	7 7/8	4	5	5 1/2	6	5 1/4	5 1/4
5.	8	4 7/8	5 1/4	6 1/4	6 3/8	6	5 1/4
6.	8	4 3/8	4 1/2	5 1/2	5 3/8	5 3/8	5 3/8
7.	7 1/2	4 1/4	4 3/8	5 1/4	6 1/8	5 7/8	6 1/8
8.	7 1/8	4 1/2	4 1/2	5 3/8	5 1/8	5 1/8	5 3/8
9.	7 1/8	4 3/8	4 7/8	6	5 3/8	5 3/8	5 1/8
10.	8 1/4	5	5 3/8	5 7/8	6 1/4	5 1/8	5 1/4
11.	7 1/2	4 3/8	5	5 3/8	5 1/8	5 1/4	4 3/8
12.	7 3/8	4 3/8	5	6	5 3/8	5 3/8	4 1/4
13.	7 3/8	4 1/2	4 1/2	5 1/2	5 3/8	5 1/4	5 3/8
14.	7 1/8	3 7/8	4 1/4	5 3/8	6 1/2	5 3/8	5
15.	7 3/8	4 1/4	4 7/8	6 3/8	6	6	5
16.	7 3/8	4 3/8	5 3/8	6	6 1/4	5 3/8	5 3/8
17.	7 1/2	4 1/2	5 3/8	6 1/2	6 3/8	6 1/4	5 1/2
18.	7 3/8	4 1/4	5	5 1/4	5 3/8	5 3/8	4 7/8
19.	8	4 1/2	5 1/2	6 1/4	6	6	4 1/4
20.	7	4 7/8	4 3/8	5 1/2	5 1/2	5 1/4	4 3/8
	151 5/8	86 3/8	99 1/2	118 1/2	119 3/8	113 7/8	103 3/8
Total divided by 20 gives average.	7 1/2	4 3/8	4 19/20	5 18/20	5 16/20	5 14/20	5 3/20

These measurements are taken above the muscular integuments, and show the sizes of the different heads in the directions specified; but I repeat that they are not given as indicative of the dimensions of any particular organs. The callipers are not suited for giving this latter information, for they do not measure length from the medulla oblongata, or projection beyond the planes mentioned above; neither do they indicate breadth: all of which dimensions must be attended to in estimating the size of individual organs. The average of these twenty heads is probably higher than that of the natives of Britain generally, because there are several large heads among them, and none small.

It ought to be kept constantly in view, in the practical application of Phrenology, that it is the size of each organ in proportion to the others in *the head of the individual observed*, and not their *absolute size*, or their size in reference to any standard head, that determines the predominance in him of particular talents or dispositions.* Thus, in the head of Bellingham *Destructiveness* is very large, and the organs of the moral sentiments and intellect are small in proportion; and according to the rule, that, *cæteris paribus*, size determines energy, Bellingham's most powerful tendencies are inferred to have been toward cruelty and rage. In several Hindoo skulls in the Phrenological Society's collection, the organ of Destructiveness is small in proportion to the others, and we conclude that the tendency of such individuals would be weakest toward the foregoing passions. But in the head of Gordon, the murderer of a pedlar boy, the absolute size of Destructiveness is less than in the head of Dr. Spurzheim; yet Dr. S. was an amiable philosopher and Gordon an atrocious murderer. This illustrates the rule, that we ought not to judge by *absolute* size. In Gordon the organs of the moral sentiments and intellectual faculties are small in proportion to that of Destructiveness, which is the largest in the brain; while in Spurzheim the moral and intellectual organs are large in proportion to Destructiveness. On the foregoing principles, the most powerful manifestations of Spurzheim's mind ought to have been in the department of sentiment and intellect, and those of Gordon's mind in Destructiveness and other animal passions; and their actual dispositions corresponded. Still the dispositions of Spurzheim were affected by the large size of this organ. It communicated a warmth and vehemence of temper, which are found only when it is large, although the higher powers restrained it from abuse. Dr. Spurzheim said to me: "I am too angry to answer that attack just now; I shall wait six months;"—and he did so, and then wrote calmly like a philosopher.

It is one object to prove Phrenology to be true, and another to teach a beginner how to observe organs. For the first purpose, we do not in general compare an organ in one head with the same organ in another; because it is the predominance of particular organs in the *same head* that gives ascendency to particular faculties in the individuals; and, therefore, *in proving Phrenology*, we usually compare the different organs of the same head. But in learning to observe, it is useful to contrast the same organ in different heads, in order to become familiar with its appearance in different sizes and combinations.

With this view, it is proper to begin with the larger organs; and two persons of opposite dispositions in the particular points to be compared, ought to be placed in juxtaposition, and their heads observed. Thus, if we take the organ of Cautiousness, we should examine its developement in those whom we know to be remarkable for timidity, doubt, and hesitation; and we should contrast its appearance with that which it presents in individuals remarkable for precipitancy, and into whose minds doubt or fear rarely enters: or a person who is passionately fond of children may be compared, in regard to the organ of Philoprogenitiveness, with another who regards them as an intolerable annoyance. No error is more to be avoided than beginning with the observation of the smaller organs, and examining these without a contrast.

An objection is frequently stated, that persons having large heads have "little wit," while others with small heads are "very clever." The phrenologist never compares intellectual ability with size of the brain in general; for a fundamental principle of the science is, that different parts of the brain have different functions, and that hence the *same absolute quantity* of brain, if consisting of intellectual organs, may be connected with the highest genius—while, if consisting of the animal organs, lying in the basilar and occipital regions of the head, it may indicate the most

<hr>

* See *Phren. Journ.*, viii., 642.

fearful energy of the lower propensities. The brains of the Caribs seem to be equal in absolute size to those of average Europeans ; but the chief developement of the former is in the animal organs, while the latter are far superior in the organs of moral sentiment and intellect : and no phrenologist would expect the one people to be equal in intelligence and morality to the other, merely because their brains are equal in absolute magnitude. The proper test is to take two heads, in sound health, and similar in temperament, age, and exercise, in each of which the several organs are similar in their proportions, but the one of which is large and the other small ; and then, if the preponderance of power of manifestation be not in favour of the first, Phrenology must be abandoned as destitute of foundation.

In comparing the brains of the lower animals with the human brain, the phrenologist looks solely for the reflected light of analogy to guide him in his researches, and never founds a direct argument in favour of the functions of the different parts of the human brain upon any facts observed in regard to the lower animals ; and the reason is, that such different genera of animals are too dissimilar in constitution and external circumstances, to authorize him to draw positive results from comparing them. Many philosophers, being convinced that the brain is the organ of mind, and having observed that the human brain is larger than that of the majority of tame animals, as the horse, dog, and ox, have attributed the mental superiority of man to the superiority in absolute size of his brain ; but the phrenologist does not acknowledge this conclusion as in accordance with the principles of his science. The brain in one of the lower creatures may be very large, and, nevertheless, if it be composed of parts appropriated to the exercise of muscular energy or the manifestation of animal propensities, its possessor may be far inferior in understanding or sagacity to another animal, having a smaller brain, but composed chiefly of parts destined to manifest intellectual power.[*] Whales and elephants have a brain larger than that of man, and yet their sagacity is not equal to his ; but nobody has shown that the parts destined to manifest intellect are larger in these animals than in man ; and hence the superior intelligence of the human species is no departure from the general analogy of nature. I repeat, however, that it is improper to expect accurate results of any kind from a comparison of the brains of different species of animals.

In like manner, the brains of the monkey and the dog are smaller than those of the ox, hog, and ass, and yet the former approach nearer to man in regard to their intellectual faculties. To apply the principles of Phrenology to them, it would be necessary to ascertain, first, that the brain, in structure, constitution, and temperament, is precisely similar in the different species compared (which it is not) ; [†] then to discover what parts manifest intellect, and what propensity, in each species ; and, lastly, to compare the power of manifesting each faculty with the size of its appropriate organ. If size were found not to be a measure of power, then the rule under discussion would fail in that species ; but even this would not authorize us to conclude that it did not hold good in regard to man ; for human Phrenology is founded, not on analogy, but on positive observations. Some persons are pleased to affirm that the brains of the lower animals consist of the same parts as the human brain, only on a smaller scale ; but this is highly erroneous. If the student will procure brains of the sheep, dog, fox, calf, horse, or hog, and compare them with

---

[*] Spurzheim's *Phrenology*, sect. iii, ch. 2, p. 54.

[†] This subject is fully and ably discussed in *The Annals of Phrenology*, vol. ii., pp. 38–49 ; and in Dr. Caldwell's *Phrenology Vindicated*, (Lexington, Ky., 1835,) pp. 62–73.

the human brain, or with the case of it sold in the shops, he will find a variety of parts.wanting in the animals, especially the convolutions which form the organs of the moral sentiments and the reflecting faculties.*

In commencing the study of Phrenology, as of any science, it is of great importance to have a definite object in view. If the student desire to find the truth, he will consider first the general principles, developed in the introduction to the present work, and the presumptions for and against them, arising from admitted facts in mental philosophy and physiology. He will next proceed to make observations in nature, qualifying himself by previous instruction in the forms, situations, appearances, and functions of the organs.

The chief circumstances which modify the effects of size are constitution, health, and exercise ; and the student ought never to omit the consideration of these, for they are highly important. They have already been considered on pages 48–51, to which I refer. In addition to what is there stated, I observe, that the temperaments rarely occur simple in any individual, two or more being generally combined. The bilious and nervous temperament is a common combination, which gives strength and activity ; the lymphatic and nervous is also common, and produces sensitive delicacy of mind, conjoined with indolence The nervous and sanguine, combined, give extreme vivacity, but without corresponding vigour. Dr. Thomas, of Paris, has published a theory of the temperaments to the following effect :. When the digestive organs filling the abdominal cavity are large, and the lungs and brain small, the individual is lymphatic ; he is fond of feeding, and averse to mental and muscular exertion. When the heart and lungs are large, and the brain and abdomen small, the individual is sanguine ; blood abounds and is propelled with vigour ; he is, therefore, fond of muscular exercise, but averse to thought. When the brain is large, and the abdominal and thoracic viscera small, great mental energy is the consequence. These proportions may be combined in great varieties, and modified results will ensue.†

In some individuals the brain seems to be of a finer texture than in others ; and there is then a delicacy and *fineness* of manifestation, which is one ingredient in genius. A harmonious combination of organs gives *justness* and soundness of perception, but there is a quality of fineness distinguishable from this. Byron possessed this quality in a high degree.

If, in each of two individuals, the organs of propensity, sentiment, and intellect are equally balanced, the general conduct of one may be vicious, and that of another moral and religious. In such a case it will be found that the circumstances of the former have been well calculated to rouse and invigorate the animal propensities and allow the moral sentiments to lie dormant, while the circumstances of the other have been directly the reverse. The *native power* may be equal in the propensities and sentiments ; but the circumstances have given an acquired ascendency to the class of feelings most strenuously cultivated.

Suppose that two individuals possess an organization exactly similar, but that one is highly educated, and the other left entirely to the impulses of nature—the former will manifest his faculties with higher *energy* than the latter ; and hence it is argued, that size is not in all cases a measure of power.

Here, however, the requisite of *cæteris paribus* does not hold. An important condition is altered, and the phrenologist uniformly allows for

* See *Phren. Journ.*, ix., 514.

† The views of Dr. Thomas are more fully explained in *The Phrenological Journal*, iv., 438, 604 ; and in Dr. Caldwell's *Essay on Temperament*, Lexington, Kentucky, 1831. Dr. Thomas's own work is entitled. *Physiologie des Temperamens ou Constitutions, &c.* Paris, 1826.

the effects of education, before drawing positive conclusions.* It may
be supposed that, if exercise thus increases power, it is impossible to draw
the line of distinction between energy derived from this cause, and that
which proceeds from size of the organs ; and that hence the real effects
of size can never be determined. The answer to this objection is, that
education may cause the faculties to manifest themselves with the highest
degree of energy *which the size of the organs will permit*, but that size
fixes a limit which education cannot surpass. Dennis, we may presume,
received some improvement from education, but it did not render him
equal to Pope, much less to Shakspeare or Milton ; therefore, if we take
two individuals whose brains are equally healthy, but whose organs differ
in size, and educate them alike, the advantages in power and attainment
will be greater, in proportion to the size, in him who has the larger brain.
Thus the objection ends in this—that if we compare brains in opposite
conditions, we may be led into error—which is granted ; but this is not
in opposition to the doctrine, that, *cæteris paribus*, power is in proportion
to size. Finally—extreme deficiency in size produces, as we have seen,
incapacity for education, as in idiots ; while extreme developement, if
healthy, as in Shakspeare, Franklin, Burns, Ferguson, and Mozart, anticipates its effects, in so far that the individuals educate themselves.

In saying, then, that, *cæteris paribus*, size is a measure of power, phrenologists demand no concessions which are not made to physiologists in
general ; among whom, in this as in other instances, they rank themselves.

There is a great distinction between *power* and *activity* of mind ; and
it is important to keep this difference in view. *Power*, strictly speaking,
is the *capability* of thinking, feeling, or perceiving, however small in
amount that capability may be ; and in this sense it is synonymous with
faculty : action is the *exercise of power* ; while *activity* denotes *the quickness*, great or small, *with which the action is performed*, and also the degree
of *proneness to act*. The distinction between power, action, and activity
of the mental faculties, is widely recognised by describers of human nature.
Thus Cowper says of the more violent affective faculties of man :

> " His passions, like the watery stores that sleep
> Beneath the smiling surface of the deep,
> Wait but the lashes of a wintry storm,
> To frown, and roar, and shake his feeble form."—*Hope.*

Again :

> " In every heart
> Are sown the sparks that kindle fiery war ;
> Occasion needs but fan them, and they blaze."
>   *The Task*, B. 5.

Dr. Thomas Brown, in like manner, speaks of *latent propensities*—that
is to say, powers not in action. " Vice already formed," says he, " is
almost beyond our power ; it is only in the state of latent propensity that
we can with much reason expect to overcome it by the moral motives
which we are capable of presenting ;" and he alludes to the great extent
of knowledge of human nature requisite to enable us " to distinguish this
propensity before it has expanded itself, and even before it is known to
the very mind in which it exists, and to tame those passions which are
never to rage."† In Crabbe's *Tales of the Hall*, a character is thus
described :

> " He seemed without a passion to proceed,
> Or one whose passions no correction need ;
> Yet some believed those passions only slept,
> And were in bounds by early habit kept."

* *Trans. of the Phren. Soc.*, p. 308.
† *Lectures*, vol. i., p. 60. See also Dr. Blair's Sermon on the Character of
Hazael, *Sermons*, vol. ii

"Nature," says. Lord Bacon, "will be buried a great time, and yet revive upon the occasion or temptation ; like as it was with Æsop's damsel, turned from a cat to a woman, who sat very demurely at the board's end till a mouse ran before her." In short, it is plain that we may have the *capability* of feeling an emotion—as anger, fear, or pity—and that yet this power may be inactive, insomuch that, at any particular time, these emotions may be totally absent from the mind ; and it is no less plain that we may have the *capability* of seeing, tasting, calculating, reasoning, and composing music, without actually performing these operations.

It is equally easy to distinguish *activity* from *action* and *power*. When power is exercised, the action may be performed with very different degrees of rapidity. Two individuals may each be solving a problem in arithmetic ; but one may do so with far greater quickness than the other— in other words, his faculty of Number may be more easily brought into action. He who solves abstruse problems slowly, manifests much power with little activity ; while he who can quickly solve easy problems, and them alone, has much activity with little power. The man who calculates difficult problems with great speed, manifests in a high degree both power and activity of the faculty of Number.

As commonly employed, the word *power* is synonymous with *strength*, or *much power*, instead of denoting mere *capacity, whether much or little, to act* ; while, by *activity*, is usually understood *much quickness of action and great proneness to act*. As it is desirable, however, to avoid every chance of ambiguity, I shall employ the words *power* and *activity* in the sense first before explained ; and to *high* degrees of power I shall apply the terms *energy, intensity, strength*, or *vigour*—while to great activity I shall apply the terms *vivacity, agility, rapidity*, or *quickness*.

In physics strength is quite distinguishable from quickness. The balance-wheel of a watch moves with much rapidity, but so slight is its impetus that a hair would suffice to stop it ; the beam of a steam-engine progresses slowly and massively through space, but its energy is prodigiously great.

In muscular action these qualities are recognised with equal facility as different. The greyhound bounds over hill and dale with animated agility ; but a slight obstacle would counterbalance his momentum, and arrest his progress. The elephant, on the other hand, rolls slowly and heavily along ; but the impetus of his motion would sweep away an impediment sufficient to resist fifty greyhounds at the summit of their speed.

In mental manifestations (considered apart from organization) the distinction between energy and vivacity is equally palpable. On the stage Mrs. Siddons and Mr. John Kemble were remarkable for the solemn deliberation of their manner, both in declamation and in action, and yet they were splendidly gifted with energy. They carried captive at once the sympathies and the understanding of the audience, and made every man feel his faculties expanding, and his whole mind becoming greater under the influence of their power. Other performers, again, are remarkable for agility of action and elocution, who, nevertheless, are felt to be feeble and ineffective in rousing an audience to emotion. *Vivacity* is their distinguishing attribute, with an absence of *vigour*. At the bar, in the pulpit, and in the senate, the same distinction prevails. Many members of the learned professions display great fluency of elocution and felicity of illustration, surprising us with the quickness of their parts, who, nevertheless, are felt to be neither impressive nor profound. They exhibit acuteness without depth, and ingenuity without comprehensiveness of understanding. This also proceeds from vivacity with little energy. There are other public speakers, again, who open heavily in debate—their faculties acting slowly, but deeply, like the first heave of a mountain-wave. Their words fall like minute-guns upon the ear, and to the superficial they appear about to terminate ere they have begun their efforts. But even their first accent is one of power—it rouses and arrests attention; their very pauses are expressive, and indicate gathering energy to be imbodied in the sentence that is to come. When fairly animated, they are impetuous as the torrent, brilliant as the lightning's beam, and overwhelm and take possession of feebler minds, impressing them irresistibly with a feeling of gigantic power

The distinction between vivacity and energy is well illustrated by Cowper, in one of his letters. "The mind and body," says he, "have in this respect a striking resemblance of each other. In childhood they are both nimble, but not strong; they can skip and frisk about with wonderful agility, but hard labour spoils them both. In maturer years they become less active, but more vigorous, more capable of fixed application, and can make themselves sport with that which a little earlier would have affected them with intolerable fatigue." Dr. Charlton also, in his *Brief Discourse concerning the different Wits of Men*, has admirably described two characters, in one of which strength is displayed without vivacity, and in the other vivacity without strength: the latter he calls the man of "nimble wit;" the former the man of "slow but sure wit."[*] In this respect the French character may be contrasted with the Scotch.

As a general rule, the largest organs in each head have naturally the greatest, and the smallest the least, tendency to act, and to perform their functions with rapidity.

The temperaments also indicate the amount of this tendency. The nervous is the most vivacious, next the sanguine, then the bilious, while the lymphatic is characterized by proneness to inaction.

In a lymphatic brain great size may be present, and few manifestations occur through sluggishness; but if a strong external stimulus be presented, energy often appears. If the brain be very small, no degree of stimulus, either external or internal, will cause great power to be manifested.

A certain combination of organs—namely, Combativeness, Destructiveness, Hope, Firmness, Acquisitiveness, and Love of Approbation, all large—is favourable to general vivacity of mind; and another combination —namely, Combativeness, Destructiveness, Hope, Firmness, and Acquisitiveness, small or moderate, with Veneration and Benevolence large— is frequently attended with sluggishness of the mental character: but the activity of the whole brain is constitutionally greater in some individuals than in others, as already explained. It may even happen that, in the same individual, one organ is naturally more active than another, without reference to size; just as the optic nerve is sometimes more irritable than the auditory: but this is by no means a common occurrence. Exercise greatly increases activity as well as power; and hence arise the benefits of education. Dr. Spurzheim thinks that "long fibres produce more activity, and thick fibres more intensity."

The doctrine, that size is a measure of power, is not to be held as implying that much power is the only, or even the most, valuable quality which a mind in all circumstances can possess. To drag artillery over a mountain, or a ponderous wagon through the streets of London, we would prefer an elephant, or a horse of great size and muscular power; while, for graceful motion, agility, and nimbleness, we would select an Arabian palfrey. In like manner, to lead men in gigantic and difficult enterprises—to command by native greatness, in perilous times, when law

* Dr. Charlton was physician to Charles II., and his work was published in 1675. The passages referred to will be found in *The Phrenological Journal*, vol. vii., p. 599.

is trampled under foot—to call forth the energies of a people, and direct them against a tyrant at home, or an alliance of tyrants abroad—to stamp the impress of a single mind upon a nation—to infuse strength into thoughts, and depth into feelings, which shall command the homage of enlightened men in every age—in short, to be a Bruce, Bonaparte, Luther, Knox, Demosthenes, Shakspeare, Milton, or Cromwell—a large brain is indispensably requisite : but to display skill, enterprise, and fidelity in the various professions of civil life—to cultivate, with success, the less arduous branches of philosophy—to excel in acuteness, taste, and felicity of expression—to acquire extensive erudition and refined manners—a brain of a moderate size is perhaps more suitable than one that is very large ; for wherever the energy is intense, it is rare that delicacy, refinement, and taste are present in an equal degree.   Individuals possessing moderate-sized brains easily find their proper sphere, and enjoy in it scope for all their energy.   In ordinary circumstances they distinguish themselves ; but they sink when difficulties accumulate around them.   Persons with large brains, on the other hand, do not readily attain their appropriate place : common occurrences do not rouse or call them forth ; and, while unknown, they are not trusted with great undertakings.   Often, therefore, such men pine and die in obscurity.   When, however, they attain their proper element, they are conscious of greatness, and glory in the expansion of their powers.   Their mental energies rise in proportion to the obstacles to be surmounted, and blaze forth in all the magnificence of self-sustaining energetic genius, on occasions when feebler minds would sink in despair.*

The term *faculty* is used to denote a particular power of feeling, thinking, or perceiving, connected with a particular part of the brain.   Phrenologists consider man by himself, and also compare him with other creatures. When the lower animals manifest the same propensities and intellectual operations as those displayed by man, the faculties which produce them are held to be common to both.   A faculty is admitted as primitive,

1.   Which exists in one kind of animal, and not in another ;

2.   Which varies in the two sexes of the same species ;

3.   Which is not proportionate to the other faculties of the same individual ;

4.   Which does not manifest itself simultaneously with the other faculties ; that is, which appears or disappears earlier or later in life than other faculties ;

5.   Which may act or rest singly ;

6.   Which is propagated in a distinct manner from parents to children ; and,

7.   Which may singly preserve its proper state of health or disease.†

As phrenological observation establishes the existence of a plurality of mental faculties, each connected with a particular part of the brain, the question occurs, Is the mind simple, or is it an aggregate of separate powers ?‡   It is extremely difficult to give a satisfactory answer to this inquiry.   Looking at the facts presented to us by observation, the most obvious inference seems to be, that the mind consists of an aggregate of powers, and that one of them supplies the feeling of Personal Identity, or the *I* of consciousness, to which, as their substratum, all the other feelings and capacities bear reference.   This view of personal identity is strongly supported by some of the phenomena of madness ; for patients are sometimes insane in this feeling, and in no other faculty of the mind. Such individuals lose all consciousness of their past and proper personality, and imagine themselves different persons altogether ; while, with the exception of this erroneous impression, they feel and think correctly.

---

* See remarks on the character of Cromwell, in *The Phrenological Journal*, iii., 482.

† Spurzheim's *Phrenology*, p. 126.

‡ See *Phren. Journ.* vol. i., p. 205.

Under the head of Memory, in a subsequent part of this work, an abstract will be found of a case of divided personality, occurring through disease, reported by Dr. Dyce, of Aberdeen, to Dr. Henry Dewar, and by him published in the *Transactions of the Royal Society of Edinburgh*. A similar case is stated in *The Medical Repository*, communicated by Dr. Mitchell to the Rev. Dr. Nott, dated January, 1816. " When I was employed," says he, " early in December, 1815, with several other gentlemen, in doing the duty of a visiter to the United States Military Academy, at West Point, a very extraordinary case of double consciousness in a woman was related to me by one of the professors. Major Ellicott, who so worthily occupies the mathematical chair in that seminary, vouched for the correctness of the following narrative, the subject of which is related to him by blood, and an inhabitant of one of the western counties of Pennsylvania :—Miss R——— possessed,. naturally, a very good constitution, and arrived at adult age without having it impaired by disease. She possessed an excellent capacity, and enjoyed fair opportunities to acquire knowledge. Besides the domestic arts and social attainments, she had improved her mind by reading and conversation, and was well versed in penmanship. Her memory was capacious, and stored with a copious stock of ideas. Unexpectedly, and without any forewarning, she fell into a profound sleep, which continued several hours beyond the ordinary term. . On waking, she was discovered to have lost every trait of acquired knowledge. Her memory was *tabula rasa*—all vestiges, both of words and things, were obliterated and gone. It was found necessary for her to learn everything again. She even acquired, by new efforts, the art of spelling, reading, writing, and calculating, and gradually became acquainted with the persons and objects around, like a being for the first time brought into the world. In these exercises she made considerable proficiency. But, after a few months, another fit of somnolency invaded her. On rousing from it, she found herself restored to the state she was in before the first paroxysm ; but was wholly ignorant of every event and occurrence that had befallen her afterward. The former condition of her existence she now calls the Old State, and the latter the New State; and she is as unconscious of her double character as two distinct persons are of their respective natures. For example, in her old state she possesses all her original knowledge ; in her new state only what she acquired since. If a gentleman or lady be introduced to her in the old state, and *vice versa*, (and so of all other matters,) to know them satisfactorily she must learn them in both states. In the old state she possesses fine powers of penmanship; while in the new she writes a poor awkward hand, having not had time or means to become expert. During four years and upward, she has undergone periodical transitions from one of these states to the other. The alterations are always consequent upon a long and sound sleep. Both the lady and her family are now capable of conducting the affair without embarrassment. By simply knowing whether she is in the old or new state, they regulate the intercourse, and govern themselves accordingly. A history of her curious case is drawing up by the Rev. Timothy Aldin, of Meadville." I often saw a clergyman of the church of Scotland, who, having become insane, believed himself Napoleon Bonaparte, and, under this conviction, felt the most poignant remorse for having commanded the massacre at Jaffa, and occasioned the death of so many brave men in war. Such cases as the foregoing have led some persons to the inference, that the feeling of personal identity is a primitive mental affection, connected with a particular organ, and hence liable separately to disease. This view corresponds with the apprehension of mankind in general ; for popular language is framed on the principle of the *I* of consciousness being distinct from the other mental affections. We speak of *evil thoughts* intruding themselves into our mind; and of our having strong desires which we forbear to indulge. In such expressions the our and we seem to mean the principle of personal identity; and the evil thoughts and desires appear to be regarded as affections of that principle, originating in sources distinct from it, and different from one another.

The more general opinion of philosophers is, that the mind is a simple and indivisible substance, and that the several faculties are merely different states of it. Such is the light in which the subject is viewed by Dr. Gall. " In my opinion," says he, " there exists but one single principle, which sees, feels, tastes, hears, touches, thinks, and wills. But in order that this principle may become capable of perceiving light and sound—of feeling, tasting, and touching—and of manifesting the different kinds of thought and propensity—it requires the aid of various material instruments, without which the exercise of all these faculties would be impossible."†

This view is espoused also by my excellent friend, the Rev. Dr. David Welsh, Professor of Church History in the University of Edinburgh, who successfully shows that it is consistent with the phrenological doctrine of a plurality of organs. " The leading doctrine of Phrenology," says he, " is, that different portions or organs of the brain are connected with the primitive feelings of the mind. The truth of this position can obviously be ascertained only by observation. But taking it for granted that it is true, it may be asked how it can be reconciled with the great principle to which so frequent reference has been made, that the powers, thoughts, and feelings of the mind are not different from the mind, but merely the mind itself existing in different states ?

" It requires but little reflection to be satisfied that the introduction of cerebral organs does not in any degree affect Dr. Brown's leading principle. The cerebral organs are not the mind—nor is any state of these organs the mind. The mind we believe to be a simple and indivisible substance. And the only difference that the doctrines of Phrenology introduce in regard to Dr. Brown's principle is, that, instead of the feelings and thoughts being merely the relations of the simple substance mind to its own former states or to external objects, they are the relations of the simple substance mind to certain portions of the encephalon.

" In looking upon any object—as snow—we have the notion of a certain colour. Now, the notion is not in the snow, but in the mind. That is, the notion of colour is the mind existing in a certain relation to an external object. But it is allowed on all hands, that there is an intervening step between the snow and the mind: there is an affection of the optic nerve. The notion of colour, then, is the mind existing in a certain relation to the optic nerve. It will be conceded that this does not alter the question as to the simplicity of the mind. And if this is conceded, it is abundantly obvious that another step in the process might be conceived without taking away from the simplicity of the immaterial part, and that, instead of an affection of the optic nerve being the immediate antecedent of the notion of colour, it might be a particular portion of the encephalon. As the notion of colour, upon this supposition, is a relation of the mind to the organ of colour, it follows that, if that organ were changed in any respect, the state of the mind would also be changed. Thus, if it were larger, or of a finer structure, or more active, the perception of colour would be more delicate, or quick, or pleasing. The same remarks might be extended to all the organs. Where the organ of Causality is large, as in the case of Dr. Brown himself, then there will be a tendency to reason ; which tendency is a state of the mind in relation to a material organ, which state would have been different had the organ been different.

" A multitude of organs may all be affecting the mind at the same instant, and in that case a variety of feelings will be experienced. But still the mind is simple, and it is only its relations to these different organs that are complex.

"When we say, then, that when we have any power, as, for example, of reasoning, we are not to suppose that the power is different from the mind. There is a material organ which is separate from the mind, but the perception of relation is a state wholly mental. One state of the organ may give the perception of relation, another the desire to perceive or discover it; but the perception and desire are both attributes, not of matter, but of mind. The effect of the organ being large or small, active or inactive, in different individuals, or upon the same individual at different times, is the subject to which I alluded in the chapter on Cause and Effect, as that which Dr. Brown had not considered."[*]

Dr. Caldwell, again, argues strongly in favour of the singleness of the power of the mind. "We do not believe," says he, "that, in a *separate* or *insulated* capacity, the mind either does or can possess a number of distinct faculties, but that it is *as single in its power* as it is *in its substance.* It is a quickening and operative principle, essential to all the mental faculties, but does not by any means *possess them itself.* It is no more made up of *parts*, in relation to *power*, than in relation to *substance.* In both respects it is *one and indivisible.*

"To advocate a proposition the opposite of this is, to contend that the mind, like the body, is *compound.* To be *single* in essence and *multiplex* in power, implies a contradiction. Conformably to the present arrangement of creation, we consider such a case *impossible* In support of a belief the reverse of this, no evidence presents itself, either *primitive* or *analogical.* On the contrary, all attainable evidence is against it.

"We can conceive of but one possible way in which the human *mind, single* in its essence, can be tributary to the existence of a *multiplicity* of faculties. That is, by being united to a *system* of organs, instead of a *single* one, and serving as the spring of action to the whole. In this case the multiplicity of the organs, each different in structure from the other, although acting from the same principle and impulse, will secure, in the result, the requisite variety. For every organ must necessarily act in a manner corresponding with its specific structure.

"We cannot, therefore, withhold an expression of our deliberate belief, that the doctrine of the perfect *unity* of the human mind, both in *substance* and *power*, constitutes, most certainly, that foundation of the science of Phrenology that nothing can shake; and which the progress of time and improvements in knowledge will only render more stable and secure. For if it be true that the mind, as a *unit*, possesses but unity of power, it follows, of necessity, that the multiplicity of power manifested in the functions of the mental faculties must arise from a *multiplex* system of cerebral organs, acting in conjunction with the mind."[†]

It is not necessary, in studying Phrenology, to decide which of these views is the correct interpretation of nature; because the effects of the organs on the mind are the same, whichever of them be adopted. If the mind consists of *an aggregate of powers*, then each acts by means of a particular organ, and is manifested with a degree of energy varying with its size. Viewed as *one simple substance*, capable of existing in a variety of states, it enters into each state by means of a separate organ: when the organs are spontaneouly *active*, they induce their relative states; without their influence, these cannot take place: when they are large,

* Welsh's *Life of Dr. Thomas Brown*, p. 521.
† Preliminary Discourse in answer to Lord Jeffrey's Criticism on Phrenology in the 88th No. of the *Edinburgh Review*, prefixed to Dr. Caldwell's *Elements of Phrenology*, 2d edit., p. 16.

the states are excited vigorously; when they are small, these exist feebly.
The reader may therefore adopt whichever theory appears to himself preferable. Without meaning to deny that the latter view appears to me the
more plausible, I shall, in the following pages, treat of the faculties as
distinct mental powers, connected with separate organs; because, by
doing so, I shall be able to bring out the doctrine more simply and lumi-
nously, than by considering them as merely particular states of the general
power—the Mind : and this language, moreover, is correct even on what
seems to be the true hypothesis ; because, according to this view, when
the organ of Causality, for example, is largely possessed, the individual
is capable of reasoning logically and acutely—of which mental act he is
incapable when that organ is greatly deficient. The word *faculty* or
power, therefore, is used to express the quality possessed in the one case,
and not in the other, and which is legitimately designated and universally
recognised by either of these terms.

"It has occurred to me," continues Dr. Welsh, " that another difficulty
of a metaphysical nature may suggest itself in regard to the principles of
Phrenology. It may be asked, What is the soul when deprived of the
cerebral organs? But the system of Dr. Brown affords us no more light
upon this point than the system of Dr. Gall. Indeed, a passage which
I have quoted from his Lectures shows that he considered that these who
engaged in such inquiries were ignorant of the limits of our faculties. It
is only experience that can teach us in what state the soul exists when
separated from the body. And in this sense the precept of the poet holds
equally in a scientific and in a religious point of view,

' Wait the great teacher Death, and God adore.' "

DIVISION OF THE FACULTIES.

Dr. Spurzheim divides the faculties into two orders, Feelings and
Intellect, or *affective* and *intellectual* faculties. The feelings are subdivided by him into two genera, denominated Propensities and Sentiments. He applies the name *propensities* to indicate internal impulses,
which invite only to certain actions ; and *sentiments* to designate other
feelings, not limited to inclination alone, but which have an emotion of a
peculiar kind superadded. Acquisitiveness, for example, is a mere
impulse to acquire ; Veneration gives a tendency to worship, accompanied
by a particular emotion, which latter quality is the reason of its being
denominated a sentiment.

The second order of faculties makes us acquainted with objects which
exist, and their qualities and relations ; they are called intellectual.
These are subdivided by Dr. Spurzheim into four genera. The first
includes the external senses and voluntary motion ; the second those
internal powers which perceive existence, or make man and animals
acquainted with external objects and their physical qualities ; and the
third the powers which perceive the relations of external objects. These
three genera are named *perceptive faculties*. The fourth genus comprises
the faculties which act on all the other powers—which compare, judge,
and discriminate : these are named *reflective* faculties.

The names of the faculties employed in this work are, with few exceptions, those suggested by Dr. Spurzheim. To designate *propensity*, he
adds to a root or fundamental word the termination *ive*, as indicating *the
quality of producing ;* the termination *ness* denotes the abstract state,
as Destructiveness. The termination *ous* characterizes a *sentiment*, as
cautious, conscientious. To these is added *ness*, to express the abstract
quality, as Cautiousness, Conscientiousness. The names of the *intel-*

lectual faculties are easily understood, and do not here require any particular explanation.

Considerable difficulty attends the arrangement of the faculties and organs. In the first and second editions of this work they were arranged and numbered according to the order adopted in Dr. Spurzheim's *Physiognomical System*, published in 1815. The principle of that arrangement was, as far as possible, philosophical. The organs common to man and the lower animals were treated of first, beginning with the lowest, and ascending. Next come the organs of the sentiments peculiar to man; and, lastly, the organs of intellect. Since 1815, the great divisions of this classification have been retained, but repeated alterations have been made by Dr. Spurzheim in the arrangement of the details. It appears impossible to arrive at a correct classification until all the organs, and also the primitive faculty or ultimate function of each, shall be definitely ascertained, which is not at present the case. Till this end shall be accomplished, every interim arrangement will be in danger of being overturned by subsequent discoveries. In the meantime, however, for the sake of uniformity, I shall adopt the arrangement followed by Dr. Spurzheim in the third edition of his *Phrenology*, published in 1825.* During his visit to Edinburgh, in 1828, he demonstrated the anatomy of the brain, and traced out the connexion between the organs in a manner so clear and satisfactory, that the basis of his arrangement appeared founded in nature. Dr. Gall seems not to have adopted any philosophical principle of classification; but it is proper that his names and order should be known. I shall, therefore, add a table of these to the present work.†

In the case of many of the organs, observations have been made to such an extent, that the functions are held to be *ascertained*; and in regard to others, where the observations have been fewer, the functions are stated as *probable*. There is no difference of opinion among phrenologists in regard to the kind of manifestations which accompany the organs set down as established; their differences touch only the result of the metaphysical analysis of the feelings and intellectual powers, and the order of their arrangement.

I shall notice briefly the history of the discovery of each organ, and state a few cases in illustration of its function: but the reader is respectfully informed, that I do not pretend to bring forward the evidence on which Phrenology is founded. I beg leave to refer those readers who are fond of perusing cases, to Dr. Gall's work, in six volumes, entitled *Sur les Fonctions du Cerveau, &c.*; to Dr. Spurzheim's work, *Phrenology;* to the *Transactions of the Phrenological Society*; to *The Phrenological Journal and Miscellany*; and to the *Journal de la Société Phrénologique de Paris*. Those persons who desire philosophical conviction are requested to resort directly to *nature*, which is always within their reach; for WELL-GROUNDED CONVICTION CAN BE OBTAINED ONLY BY PERSONAL OBSERVATION.

NATURAL LANGUAGE OF THE FACULTIES

DRS. GALL and Spurzheim have investigated the laws which determine the natural language of the individual faculties, and their exposition of them is highly interesting and instructive.‡ The leading principle is, that the motions are always in the direction of the seat of the organs. Self-Esteem, for instance, produces an attitude in which the head and

---

* See Objections to Dr. Spurzheim's classification of the faculties, in the Appendix, No. II.   † Appendix, No. III.
‡ See Gall, *Sur les Fonctions du Cerveau*, v., 440, and Spurzheim's *Physiognomical System*, London, 1815, p. 398.

body are held high, and reclining backward; Firmness gives erectness and stiffness to the person; Cautiousness carries the head backward and to the side, Veneration upward and forward, and so on. Each organ, when *predominantly powerful and active*, produces these motions and attitudes. It also gives a peculiar expression to the voice and features: thus Destructiveness communicates to the voice a hard ringing quality, and to the countenance a dark harsh expression; while Love of Approbation gives a flattering and pleasing tone to the voice, and gracious smiles to the face. The modes of expression attached to each faculty, being natural, are universal, and are understood in all countries and all ages. They are the foundations of pantomime, and also of expression in painting and sculpture. The knowledge of them renders Physiognomy scientific; without this knowledge, it is a mere empirical art, leading as often to erroneous as to sound conclusions.

Order I.—FEELINGS.

Genus I.—PROPENSITIES.

The faculties falling under this genus do not form ideas nor procure knowledge; their sole function is, to produce a propensity of a specific kind. These faculties are common to man with the lower animals.

I.—AMATIVENESS.

The cerebellum (A A, fig. 2, p. 74) is the organ of this propensity,[*] and is situated between the mastoid process on each side and the projecting point in the middle of the transverse ridge of the occipital bone. The size is indicated during life by the thickness of the neck at these parts, or between the ears, and by the extension of the inferior surface of the occipital bone backward. In some individuals the lobes of the cerebellum descend or droop, increasing the downward convexity of the occipital bone, rather than increasing its expansion between the ears. In such cases the projection may be felt by the hand, if pressed firmly on the neck. The subjoined cuts show the appearances presented by the living head when the organ is moderate and large.

There is nearly half an inch of space between the cerebellum and the commencement of the posterior lobe of the brain, at the insertion of the tentorium.

The tentorium is a strong membrane, which separates the cerebellum from the brain; in animals which leap, as the cat and tiger, the separation is produced by a thin plate of bone.[†] The cerebellum is, however, connected with the brain; for its fibres originate in the *corpora restiformia*, from which also the organs of other animal propensities arise. Certain fibres originating in that source, after passing through the optic *thalami*, expand into the organs of Philoprogenitiveness, Adhesiveness, Combative-

---

[*] Partes genitales, sive testes hominibus et fœminis uterus, propensionem ad venerem excitare nequeunt. Nam in pueris veneris stimulus seminis secretioni sæpè antecedit. Plures eunuchi, quanquam testibus privati, hanc inclinationem conservant. Sunt etiam fœminæ quæ sine utero natæ, hunc stimulum manifestant. Hinc quidam ex doctrinæ nostræ inimicis, harum rerum minimè inscii, seminis præsentiam in sanguine contendunt, et hanc causam sufficientem existimant. Attamen argumenta hujus generis verâ physiologiâ longè absunt, et vix citatione digna videntur. Nonnulli etiam hujus inclinationis causam in liquore prostatico quærunt; sed in senibus aliquandò fluidi prostatici secretio, sine ullâ veneris inclinatione, copiosissima est.—Spurzheim's *Phrenology*, p. 128.　　　　　† See Note on p. 79.

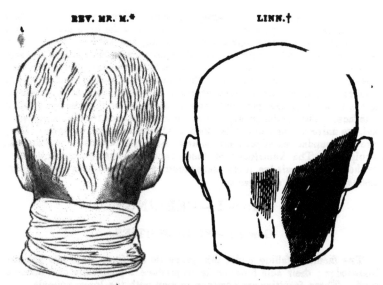

ness, Destructiveness, &c.   The nerves of sight (4 4, fig. 2, p. 74) can
be traced into the *nates*, lying very near the same parts ; while the nerves
of hearing (*e*, same figure) spring from the medullary streaks on the surface of the fourth ventricle, lying immediately under the cerebellum.
These arrangements of structure correspond with the facts, that the eyes,
express more powerfully than the other senses the passion of love ; that
abuses of the amative propensity produce blindness and deafness ; and
that this feeling subsequently excites Adhesiveness, Combativeness, and
Destructiveness into vivid action—rendering attachment irresistibly strong,
and inspiring even females, who, in ordinary circumstances, are timid and
retiring. with courage and determination when under its influence.   The
cerebellum consists of three portions, a central and two lateral.   The central is in direct communication with the *corpora restiformia*, and the two
lateral portions are brought into communication with each other by the
pons Varolii.   (See figs. 2 and 3, pp. 74, 75.)
     Dr. Gall was led to the discovery of the function of this organ in the
following manner : He was physician to a widow of irreproachable character, who was seized with nervous affections, to which succeeded severe
nymphomania.   In the violence of a paroxysm he supported her head, and
was struck with the great size and heat of the neck.   She stated that heat
and tension of these parts always preceded a paroxysm.   He followed
out, by numerous observations, the idea, suggested by this occurrence,
of connexion between the amative propensity and the cerebellum, and he
soon established the point to his own satisfaction.
     This faculty gives rise to the sexual feeling.   In newly-born children
the cerebellum is the least developed of all the cerebral parts.   At this
period the upper and posterior parts of the neck, corresponding to the
cerebellum, appears attached almost to the middle of the base of the skull.
The weight of the cerebellum is then to that of the brain as one to thirteen,
fifteen, or twenty.   In adults it is as one to six, seven, or eight.   The
cerebellum enlarges much at puberty, and attains its full size between the
ages of eighteen and twenty-six.   The neck then appears greatly more
expanded behind.   In general, the cerebellum is less in females than in

males. In old age it frequently diminishes. There is no constant proportion between the brain and it in all individuals; just as there is no invariable proportion between this feeling and the other powers of the mind. Sometimes the cerebellum is largely developed before the age of puberty. This was the case in a child of three years of age, in a boy of five, and in one of twelve; and they all manifested the feeling strongly. In the cast of the skull of Dr. Hette, sold in the shops, the developement is small, and the feeling corresponded.* In the cast of the skull of a convict who died at Chatham, J. L., it is very large, and there was a proportionate vigour of the propensity.† In the casts of Mitchell and Dean it is very large, and the manifestations were in proportion. Farther evidence of the functions of this organ will be found in Dr. Gall's work, *Sur les Fonctions du Cerveau*, tome iii., pp. 225–414; and several cases are mentioned in the following works: *Journal of Pathological Observations kept at the Hospital of the Ecole de Médécine*, No. 108, 15th July, 1817, case of Jean Michel Brigand; *Journal of the Hôtel Dieu*, case of Florat, 19th March, 1819, and of a woman, 11th November, 1818; Wepferus, *Historiæ apoplecticorum*, edit. 1724, page 487; *Philosophical Transactions*, No. 228, case by Dr. Tyson; *Mémoires de Chirurgie Militaire, et Campagnes*, by Baron Larrey, vol. ii., p. 150, vol. iii., p. 262; Serres *On Apoplexy*; Richérand's *Elements of Phisiology*, pp. 379, 380, Kerrison's translation; Dr. Spurzheim's *Phrenology*, p. 130; *The Phrenological Journal*, vol. v., pp. 98, 311, 636; vii., 29; viii., 377, 529; ix., 188, 383, 525; Dr. Andrew Combe's *Observations on Mental Derangement*, p. 161; and *The London Medical and Surgical Journal*, 21st June and 23d August, 1834, vol. v., p. 649, and vol. vi., p 125. Dr. Caldwell has given, in *The Annals of Phrenology*, No. I., pp. 80–84, a summary of the principal reasons for considering the cerebellum to be the organ of Amativeness.

"It is impossible," says Dr. Spurzheim, "to unite a greater number of proofs in demonstration of any natural truth, than may be presented to determine the function of the cerebellum;" and in this I agree with him. Those who have not read Dr. Gall's section on this organ, can form no adequate conception of the force of the evidence which he has collected.‡

M. Flourens, by whom certain experiments were performed on the lower animals, chiefly by inflicting injuries on their cerebella, contends that these experiments show that the cerebellum serves for the regulation of muscular motion. "On removing the cerebellum," says he, "the animal loses the power of executing combined movements." Magendie performed similar experiments on the cerebellum, and found that they occasioned only an *irresistible tendency in the animal to run, walk, or swim backward.* He made experiments also on the *corpora striata* and *tubercula quadrigemina*, with the following results: When one part of these were cut, the animal *rolled*; when another, it *went forward, and extended its head and extremities*; when another, it *bent all these*: so that, according to this mode of determining the cerebral functions, these parts of the brain possess an equal claim with the cerebellum to be regarded as the regulators of motion. The fact is, that all parts of the nervous system are so intimately connected, that the infliction of injury on one deranges others, and hence is not the way to determine the functions of any, even its least important parts. This is now admitted by all sound physiologists; among others Sir Charles Bell.§

* See *Phren. Journ.*, vi., 600.   † Ib., iv., 258.
‡ The nature of the subject prevents me from inserting the details of Dr. Gall's section on this organ. I have translated it, however, and printed it uniformly with his work; and it may be obtained separately by medical students and others who wish to pursue the investigation.
§ See *The Phrenological Journal*, ix., 123.

The great size of the cerebellum, however—the circumstance of its lateral portions not bearing the same relation to the middle part in all animals—and also the results of some late experiments, have suggested the notion that it may not be a single organ, but that, although Amativeness is unquestionably connected with the largest portion of it, other functions may be connected with the other parts. This seems not improbable; but as we have no direct evidence in proof of the fact, or in illustration of the nature of these supposed functions, it is unnecessary to do more than announce the proposition as one worthy of investigation.* In Magendie's *Journal de Physiologie*, for June, 1831, however, a case is reported, in which the cerebellum was found, on dissection, to be wanting, having apparently been destroyed by disease. Yet the patient enjoyed to the last the power of executing combined movements, and performed none of the evolutions described above as the result of Magendie's experiment.†

Mr. Scott, in an excellent essay on the influence of this propensity on the higher sentiments and intellect,‡ observes, that it has been regarded by some individuals as almost synonymous with pollution, and the notion has been entertained that it cannot be even approached without defilement. This mistake has arisen from attention being directed too exclusively to the *abuses* of the propensity. Like everything that forms part of the system of nature, it bears the stamp of wisdom and excellence in itself, although liable to abuse. It exerts a quiet, but effectual, influence in the general intercourse between the sexes, giving rise in each to a sort of kindly interest in all that concerns the other. This disposition to mutual kindness between the sexes does not arise from Benevolence or Adhesiveness, nor any other sentiment or propensity, alone; because, if such were its exclusive sources, it would be equally displayed in the intercourse of the individuals of each sex among themselves, which it is not. "In this quiet and unobtrusive state of the feeling," says Mr. Scott, "there is nothing in the last gross or offensive to the most sensitive delicacy. So far the contrary, that the want of some feeling of this sort is regarded, wherever it appears, as a very palpable defect, and a most unamiable trait in the character. It softens all the proud, irascible, and antisocial principles of our nature, in everything which regards that sex which is the object of it; and it increases the activity and force of all the kindly and benevolent affections. This explains many facts which appear in the mutual regards of the sexes toward each other. Men are, generally speaking, more generous and kind, more benevolent and charitable, toward women, than they are to men, or than women are to one another." This faculty also inspires the poet and dramatist in compositions on the passion of love; and it exerts a very powerful influence over human conduct. Dr. Spurzheim observes, that individuals in whom the organ is very large, ought not to be dedicated to the profession of religion in countries where chastity for life is required of the clergy. The organ is more prone to activity in warm than in cold climates. When very large, however, its function is powerfully manifested even in

* See *The Phrenological Journal*, vii., 440.

† The case alluded to, that of a girl named Labrosse, who was addicted to amative abuse, is reported likewise in *Ferussac's Bulletin* for October, 1831, and has been proclaimed by the enemies of Phrenology to be utterly subversive of the science. Dr. Caldwell, however, has well shown, in the *Annals of Phrenology*, No. I., p. 76, (quoted in *The Phrenological Journal*, vol. ix., p. 226,) that such a conclusion is altogether unwarranted. Although the cerebellum was found, on dissection, to be almost obliterated, the appearances were such as to indicate plainly that the obliteration was recent, and had been caused by inflammatory excitement of the organ—an excitement perfectly in harmony with the manifestations referred to.

‡ *Phrenological Journal*, ii., 392.

the frozen regions. The Greenlanders and other tribes of Esquimaux, for example, are remarkable for the strength of the feeling; and their skulls, of which the Phrenological Society possesses twelve specimens, indicate a corresponding developement of the cerebellum.[*]

The abuses of this propensity are the sources of innumerable evils in life; and, as the organ and feeling exist, and produce an influence on the character, independently of external communication, Dr. Spurzheim suggests the propriety of instructing young persons in the consequences of its improper indulgence, as preferable to keeping them in "a state of ignorance that may provoke a fatal curiosity, compromising in the end their own and their descendants' bodily and mental constitution."

The organ is established.

2. PHILOPROGENITIVENESS.

THE attachment of the inferior animals to their young has often been the subject of admiration. In them it is attributed to instinct. Instinct means an original propensity, impelling the animal endowed with it to act in a certain way, without intention or purpose. Is the attachment of human beings to their young the consequence of a similar innate feeling, or is it the result of reason, or a modification of benevolence or of other feelings? That it does not spring from reflection is abundantly evident. Reason only investigates causes and effects, and decides on a comparison of facts. The mother, while she smiles with ineffable joy on her tender offspring, does not argue herself into the delightful emotion. The excitement is instantaneous; the object requires only to be presented to her eye or imagination, and the whole impetus of parental love stirs the mind. Hence a distinct feeling is obviously the basis of the affection. It is not a modification of any other sentiment, but an original propensity; for, on going into society, we find that the love of children bears no perceptible proportion to any other faculty of the mind. If it depended on Benevolence, no selfish individual could be ardently attached to offspring; and yet the opposite is frequently the fact. If it were a modification of mere self-love, as some have supposed, then parental affection should be weak in proportion as generosity is strong; but this theory also is contradicted by experience. Neither do we find love of young bear a definite relation to intellectual endowment. Sometimes a woman of limited understanding loves her children ardently; occasionally another equally weak is indifferent toward them. Some highly intellectual women add maternal affection to their other virtues; while others, not less acute in understanding, look on offspring as a burden. There are, therefore, the strongest reasons for holding the love of young to be a primitive tendency of the mind; and phrenological observations coincide with this conclusion.

The organ is situated immediately above the middle part of the cerebellum, and corresponds to the protuberance of the occiput. Dr. Gall gives the following account of its discovery: In the course of his observations he had remarked, that, in the human race, the upper part of the occiput is in general more prominent in the female skull than in the male; and he inferred, that the part of the brain beneath must be the organ of some feeling which is stronger in women than in men. But the question presented itself, What is this quality? During several years various conjectures occurred to him, which he successively adopted and rejected; and he frequently stated to his pupils the embarrassment he felt upon the subject. He remarked at last, that, in this particular point, the skulls of monkeys bore a singular resemblance to those of women—and con-

[*] See *Essay on the Character and Cerebral Developement of the Esquimaux*, by Mr. Robert Cox, *Phren. Journ.*, viii., 296-7.

cluded, that the cerebral part placed immediately under the prominence, was probably the organ of some quality or faculty for which the monkey tribes and women were distinguished in a remarkable degree. He was led the more to entertain this idea, because, from the discoveries he had already made in this region, he was aware that there was no reason to look there for the seat of any superior intellectual or moral faculty. He repeatedly revolved in his mind all the feelings manifested by the monkey tribe, so far as known to him. At last, in one of those favourable moments when a lucky thought sometimes does more to elicit truth than years of labour and reflection, it suddenly occurred to him, in the midst of a lecture, that one of the most remarkable characteristics of monkeys is an extreme ardour of affection for their young. This quality has been noticed in them by the most distinguished naturalists; and persons who have resided in countries where monkeys are common have also observed it, and remarked that it leads them to bestow caresses even on the young of the human species, especially negro children, when these happen to fall in their way. The thought flashed upon his mind that this might be the feeling or quality of which he was in search. Impatient to put this conclusion to the test, by a comparison of all the male with the female skulls of animals in his extensive collection, he begged his hearers to go away, and leave him to his researches; and, on making the examination, he found that in fact there existed the same difference between the male and female skull among the lower animals in general, which he had observed between the male and the female skull in the human species. This seemed a confirmation of the idea that the faculty of which this cerebral part is the organ, is affection for young—which, he had already remarked, was possessed in a greater degree by the females of the animal tribes than by the males. The inference appeared to him more plausible from the circumstance that this organ is placed in close vicinity to that of the instinct of propagation. Many subsequent observations established the conclusion.[*]

The faculty produces the innate love of young and delight in children.

The feeling is beautifully represented in the following lines of Lord Byron:

> ADAH.   Where were then the joys,
> The mother's joys of watching, nourishing,
> And loving him? Soft! He awakes. Sweet Enoch!
>   (*She goes to the child.*)
> Oh Cain! Look on him; see how full of life,
> Of strength, of bloom, of beauty, and of joy.
> How like to me—how like to thee, when gentle,
> For *then* we are *all* alike: is't not so, Cain?
> Mother, and Sire, and Son, our features are
> Reflected in each other.
> Look! how he laughs, and stretches out his arms,
> And opens wide his blue eyes upon thine,
> To hail his father; while his little form
> Flutters as wing'd with joy. Talk not of pain!
> The childless cherubs well might envy thee
> The pleasures of a parent! Bless him, Cain,
> As yet he hath no words to thank thee, but
> His heart will, and thine own too.
>   *Cain, Act* III. *Scene* I.

The organ may be verified in the easiest manner by any person who chooses to observe nature. It is one of the most conspicuous and easily distinguished in the head, particularly in the human species; and the

---

[*] Gall, *Sur le Fonctions du Cerveau*, vol. iii., p. 415.—*Phren. Journ.*, vol ii., p. 23.

manifestations may be recognised with equal facility. Those who possess the feeling in a strong degree, show it in every word and look when children are concerned ; and these, again, by a reciprocal tact, or, as it is expressed by the author of Waverley, by a kind of "free-masonry," discover at once persons with whom they may be familiar, and use all manner of freedoms. It is common, when such an individual appears among them, to see him welcomed with a shout of delight. Other individuals, again, feel the most marked indifference toward children, and are unable to conceal it when betrayed into their company. Romping disconcerts them, and, having no sympathy with children's pranks and prattle, they look on them as the greatest annoyances. The same novelist justly remarks, that, when such persons make advances to children for the purpose of recommending themselves to the parents, the awkwardness of their attempts is intuitively recognised by the children, and they fail in attracting attention.` On examining the heads of two persons thus differently constituted, a large developement of this organ will be discovered in the one, which will not be found in the other

It is a remarkable ordination of nature, that the direction of this feeling bears a reference to the weakness and helplessness of its objects, rather than to any other of their physical or moral qualities. The mother doats with fondest delight on her infant in the first months of its existence, when it presents fewest attractions to other individuals ; and her solicitude and affection are bestowed longest and most intensely on the feeblest member of her family. On this principle, the youngest is the reigning favourite, unless there be some sickly being of maturer age ; who then shares with it the maternal sympathies. The primitive function of the faculty seems to be to inspire with an interest in the helplessness of childhood ; but it gives also a softness of manner in treating the feeble and the delicate even in advanced life, and persons in whom this organ is large in combination with Benevolence are better fitted for the duties of a sick-chamber than those in whom Philoprogenitiveness is small. The natural language of the faculty is soft, tender, and endearing. It is essential to a successful teacher of children. Individuals in whom the organ is deficient, have little sympathy with the feeling of the youthful mind, and their tones and manner of communicating instruction repel, instead of engaging, the affections of the scholar. This is the cause why some persons, whose manner, in intercourse with their equals, is unexceptionable, are nevertheless greatly disliked as teachers ; and children are generally in the right in their antipathies, although their parents and guardians, judging by their own feelings, imagine them actuated altogether by caprice.

It has been remarked by Mr. Scott, that the fondness which unmarried females, or married ladies who have no children, sometimes lavish "on animals, generally of the smaller and more delicate kind, whom they nurse and pamper with a degree of devotedness and affection which can be compared only to that of a mother for her children," probably has its origin in this faculty. The feeling seems the same, its objects only being different ; and, instead of overwhelming such individuals with ridicule, they deserve our forbearance at least, if not respect, as "they are merely following the bent of a strong natural propensity, implanted in them for the wisest purposes, and which, in more favourable circumstances, would have rendered them affectionate mothers, and excellent mistresses of families."*

This propensity furnishes the spirit of lullabies, and inspires the poet and dramatist in many of their representations. Wordsworth manifests it strongly, and some of the faults of his manner are clearly attributable to an excess of its influence. It characterizes the Lake school of poetry in general.

* *Phrenological Journal*, vol. ii., pp. 499, 500.

The feeling produced by this faculty is so intense and delightful, that none is more liable to abuse. When too energetic, and not regulated by judgment, it leads to pampering and spoiling children, to irrational anxieties regarding them, and sometimes to the most extravagant conceit of their supposed excellencies. When misapplied, it defeats the object of its institution ; for, instead of conducting to the protection and happiness of children, it renders them nighly miserable. When the organ is deficient, indifference and regardlessness about offspring are the consequences. Children are then felt as a heavy burden ; they are abandoned to the care of menials, or altogether neglected, and left to encounter the perils and distresses incident to tender age, without solace or protection. Instances have been known (such as the case of the Countess of Macclesfield, mother of the poet Savage) of mothers who conceived an unaccountable and seemingly causeless hatred against their own offspring, and who persecuted them with relentless severity. Dr. Gall knew, at Vienna, a lady who loved her husband tenderly, and who managed the concerns of her household with intelligence and activity, but who sent from home, as soon as they saw the light, all the nine children to whom she successively gave birth, and for years never asked to see them. She was somewhat ashamed of this indifference, and could not account for it to herself. To quiet her conscience, she insisted upon her husband seeing them every day, and taking charge of their education. From deficiency of the organ also, combined with other feelings in a strong degree, probably arises the cruelty of such barbarous mothers as Isabel of Bavaria, of whom history relates that she stifled all the sentiments of affection due to her children.

Among twenty-nine infanticides, whose heads Drs. Gall and Spurzheim had occasion to examine, the organ of Philoprogenitiveness was very feebly developed in twenty-five. Dr. Gall has oftener than once made the remark, that it is not this defect in developement alone which determines a mother to child-murder ; but that individuals deficient in this respect yield sooner than others to those unfavourable circumstances which lead to the crime, because they are not endowed with that profound feeling which, in the heart of a good mother, will rise victorious over every such temptation. In selecting a nurse or child's maid, the phrenologist will be directed by the developement of this organ. This application of the science, when mentioned to those who have not studied the subject, generally excites a smile ; and certainly, if the size of the part of the brain in question were no indication of instinctive affection for children, no test for qualification could be more justly deserving of ridicule than the one now recommended : but, on the other hand, if the organ be an unerring index of this disposition, (which it is, otherwise all we are now considering is a delusion,) no weakness can be greater than that which would fear to appeal to it, because it might provoke a smile in those who are ignorant that nature has established the function.

The head of the male has generally a broader and rounder appearance, and that of the female a longer and narrower, when contrasted with each other.* This partly arises from the organ of Philoprogenitiveness being more developed in the female head, and causing the occiput to project. The portion of brain placed in the occiput is greater in women than in men, though the entire female brain is smaller than that of the male. This difference is observable in the foetal skull of the two sexes, and is conspicuous in boys and girls. The manifestations even in the earliest period of life correspond ; for the girl shows attachment to dolls and infants, while the boy is addicted to romping and athletic sports. A curious practical example of the difference in this feeling between males and females

* See Spurzheim's *Phrenology in Connexion with the Study of Physiognomy*, plate XII.

In general, occurs in Morier's Travels in Persia. "The surgeons of the Embassy," says he, "endeavoured to introduce vaccination among the Persians, and their efforts at first were very successful; but on a sudden its progress was checked by the government itself. Several of the king's Ferashes were placed at the gate of the ambassador's hotel, nominally as a mark of attention to his excellency, but really to stop all women from going to our surgeons. They said that, if the people wanted their children to be vaccinated, the *fathers*, and not the *mothers*, were to take them to the surgeons, by which means the eagerness for vaccination was stopped; for we soon discovered that the *males* did not feel one-half the same anxiety for their offspring as the *women*."*

There are, nevertheless, exceptions to this general rule. Sometimes the occipital part of the brain is little developed in a woman, and has acquired a very large size in a man. In such cases the dispositions correspond with the developement. Dr. Gall conjectures, that, in these instances, the woman will be found to resemble her father, and the man his mother, unless this peculiar conformation be hereditary in the family. There are men thus organized who have a particular affection for children, and in whom the organs of Amativeness and Adhesiveness are small—who bear the loss of an affectionate wife with a resignation which appears very philosophic, while the death of an infant plunges them into a deep and lasting grief. The want of children is with such men a constant source of uneasiness, and often this circumstance causes them to treat with unkindness a partner exceedingly estimable in all other respects.

Dr. Gall observes, that we find this organ more developed in some nations than in others. It is generally large in negroes; and infanticide is a crime almost unknown among that variety of the human species. Persons well acquainted with their character assure us that they never heard of such a crime committed by a black. The organ is commonly well developed even in male negroes; and we find that negro men often consent to take charge of children.

Dr. Murray Paterson states that the Hindoos, both male and female, are highly endowed with this feeling; it is manifested by them, he says, " in their predilection for domestic quiet; in the happiness they seem to feel when surrounded by their children; in the spirit of their lullabies; and in their frequent and ardent embraces."† Out of twelve Hindoo skulls originally in the possession of the Phrenological Society, eleven have this organ largely developed, and only one moderately so; and many crania subsequently added show the same configuration. In the skulls of the Ceylonese also, Philoprogenitiveness is equally great. In some of the older descriptions of Ceylon, the exposure of children is said to be common in the island; but this is now ascertained to be at variance with truth. The feeling is manifested very strongly in both sexes.‡

The feeling in question, so necessary for the preservation and continuance of the species, is found strong in the most savage tribes. The organ is decidedly large even in the casts of the skulls of the Caribs, unquestionably the most unfavourably organized, in other respects, of all the races of which we possess any knowledge. Out of six casts of Carib skulls in the Phrenological Society's collection, two have the organ very large, three have it large, and the remaining one rather full. This tribe appears, from the cerebral developement, and the accounts of travellers and historians with regard to their manners and character, to be endued with the most brutal ferocity, almost totally unregulated by either benevolence or

* Second Journey through Persia, p. 191.
† Trans. of the Phren. Soc., p. 441. See also The Phrenological Journal, viii., 529.
‡ See Phren. Journ., vii., 639.

intellect; and, unless they possessed an instinctive propensity
prompting them to take care of
their children, they would soon
become extinct, without the intervention of famine, pestilence,
or an exterminating enemy. A satisfactory answer is here afforded
to those cavillers who object that
there is no necessity for such a
propensity as this, as the feeling
of Benevolence alone would be
sufficient to prompt parents to

CARIB.

bestow the requisite care on their offspring. We have only to point to the
Caribs, and ask, What reliance could be placed on the benevolence of such
beings! And yet they show attachment to their young, and submit to the
inconveniences of rearing them, amid all the toils, privations, and hard-
ships that abound in savage life. The Esquimaux furnish another pointed
illustration of the same fact. In most of the specimens of their skulls in
the Phrenological Society's collection, this organ is very prominently developed, being in only one instance out of twelve below "rather large," and

ESQUIMAUX.

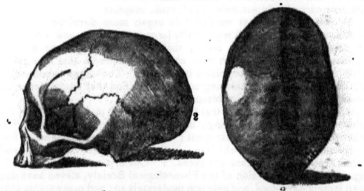

in five "very larger." Blümenbach, moreover, remarks an "occiput pro-
tuberans" in an Esquimaux skull from Labrador, of which he gives a
representation in his *Third Decade*, plate 24.* His next plate contains
an engraving of another Esquimaux skull, in which the same feature is
observable; and he notices the like conformation in the crania of two
Greenlanders from the Danish colony of Godhavn, represented in his 36th
and 37th plates. In accordance with this configuration, and in spite of
the laziness and selfishness of the Esquimaux, their love of children is
uncommonly powerful. "The affection of parents for their children," says
Captain Parry, "was frequently displayed by these people, not only in the
mere passive indulgence and abstinence from corporeal punishment, for
which the Esquimaux have before been remarked, but by a thousand playful endearments also, such as parents and nurses practise in our own
country. *Nothing, indeed, can well exceed the kindness with which they
treat their children;* and this trait in their character deserves to be the
more insisted on, because it is in reality the only very amiable one which
they possess." It is farther mentioned, that "the custom of adoption is

* J. F. *Blumenbachii Decas Tertia Collectionis sua Craniorum diversarum
Gentium Illustrata.* Gottingæ, 1795, p. 9.

carried on to very great lengths among these people."* The testimony
of Captain Lyon is equally strong : " Nothing," he says, " can be more
delightful than the fondness which parents show to their little ones during
infancy. The mothers carry them naked on their backs until they are
stout and able walkers, and their whole time and attention are occupied
in nursing and feeding them. The fathers make little toys, play with,
and are constantly giving them whatever assistance lies in their power.
A child is never corrected nor scolded, but has its own way in everything."†
The same author relates, that, when he sent a supply of food to a party
of starved natives whose "hunger was quite voracious," " the grown
people first supplied all the children, and afterward divided the remainder
in equal portions among themselves."‡   Crantz describes the same trait
in the inhabitants of the eastern coast of Greenland. " The Greenlanders," says he, " love their children excessively. The mothers suckle them
wherever they go, and whatever they are about, in a conveniency made
in their dress between their shoulders. They suckle them till they are
three or four years old, and longer, because their country affords nothing
to make proper food for a tender infant."§ And, in another place, this
traveller, after mentioning that " you will scarce find a Greenlander do
good to another without the mercenary hope of some speedy retribution,"
informs us that, " on the other hand, there are traces of a stronger love
between parents and children, and of the many passions arising from it,
than there are in other nations. A mother cannot suffer her child to be
out of her sight, and many a mother has drowned herself because her
child hath been drowned."· The contrast between this ardour of parental
affection and want of general benevolence seems to have made a forcible
impression on Crantz, and has led him to throw out a conjecture—the
soundness of which is demonstrated by Phrenology—that the phenomenon
can be accounted for only by supposing the existence of two independent
faculties : For he adds—" But just so it is with the irrational creatures ;
they are insensible to the pleasure or pain of other animals, but their love
and concern for their young is so much the stronger. This would almost
lead one to think that the Greenlanders act more from the instinct and
movements which the irrational animals have in common with mankind,
than from human reason."‖ Captain Ross found the same strong attachment to children among the Arctic Highlanders, at the northern extremity
of Baffin's Bay. He asked two of them whether they would allow one
of their sons to go with him ; to which, says he, " they answered, they
would not ; nor could either of them be tempted with any presents to
consent to part with a child."¶
   This, like the other cerebral organs, is liable to disease, and derangement in the manifestations of the propensity is the consequence. Sometimes the most painful anxiety is felt about children, without any adequate
external cause, and this arises from involuntary activity of the organ.
   Dr. Andrew Combe attended a woman while labouring under a temporary alienation of mind, whose constant exclamations during three days,
which the fit lasted, were about her children—she imagined that they

* *Journals of Parry's First, Second, and Third Voyages.* 12mo. London,
1828, vol. v., pp. 273, 277.
   † *Private Journal.* London, 1824, pp. 355-6.
   ‡ Ib., p. 138.
   § *History of Greenland; translated from the High Dutch.* London, 1767, vol.
i., p. 162. See also Egede's *Description of Greenland.* London. 1745. p. 146.
   ‖ *History of Greenland,* i., 189.
   ¶ Ross's *Voyage,* London. 1819, p. 134. See *Essay* on the Character and
Cerebral Developement of the Esquimaux, by Mr. Robert Cox. *Phren. Journ.*
viii., 294-6.

were in distress, murdered, carried away; exposed to every calamity. On recovery, she complained of having had a 'pain in the hind part of her head during the attack, pointing to the situation of Philoprogenitiveness ; but she had no other recollection of what had passed. She was altogether unacquainted with Phrenology.

Dr. Gall mentions a case of a woman in the great hospital at Vienna, who was seized with a very peculiar kind of madness—maintaining that she was about to be delivered of six children. He was led, by his previous observations, to conjecture that this hallucination was owing partly to a great developement, and partly to over-excitement, of the organ of Philoprogenitiveness. The patient died, and he mentions that the developement of this organ in her head was quite extraordinary. The posterior lobes of the brain not only overhung the cerebellum more than is usual in females, but were rounded and voluminous in a very remarkable degree. At Paris, Dr. Gall attended a young lady of perfect modesty, who laboured under mental disease. She lived in the best society, and went to Vienna accompanied by some most respectable friends. She had hardly arrived, when she ran to all her acquaintances, and announced to them, with the most lively joy and in the openest manner, that she was pregnant. The circumstances of this declaration, and the known character of the lady, were sufficient to lead her friends to conclude her to be insane. In a short time her joy gave place to anguish of mind, and to a mournful and invincible taciturnity. Soon afterward she died of consumption. In her, also, this organ was extremely developed ; and during her life she had been remarkable for her love of children. In the lunatic hospital, at Amsterdam, Drs. Gall and Spurzheim saw a female patient who spoke of nothing but of being with child, though no such thing was the case. Her head was small, and the organ of Philoprogenitiveness alone was very largely developed. In another hospital for lunatics they saw a man who maintained that he was with child of twins. They announced that he ought to have this organ large, and, on examining his head, found it to be so. These cases of the diseased state of the organ add to the already numerous proofs that this is an original and special propensity. -

Dr. Gall states, that he examined, with all the attention in his power, the skulls of birds from the smallest up to the greatest, and of mammiferous animals from the shrew-mouse to the elephant, and found throughout that, in the females, the cerebral part which corresponds to the organ of Philoprogenitiveness in the human species, is more developed than in the males. He says, that if there had been presented to him, in water, the fresh brains of two adult animals of any species, one male and the other female, he could have distinguished the two sexes. In the male the cerebellum is larger and the posterior lobes of the brain are smaller. In the female, on the contrary, the cerebellum is smaller, and the posterior lobes, which include the convolutions connected with this faculty, are larger and longer. When these two organs are distinctly marked on the cranium, the two sexes may be distinguished by the simple inspection of the skull. In those species where the sexes differ very much in their regard for their young, the crania differ sometimes so much in their form, that they have been placed in collections as belonging to different varieties of the same species, though in fact they belonged to individuals of the same variety, but of different sexes.

Dr. Gall adduces innumerable facts in support of this proposition; but as these can hardly be made intelligible without the assistance of plates, I must refer those who wish to pursue this inquiry to his work, to that of Dr. Vimont, and to observations in nature. In pursuing it, the utmost patience and attention are necessary, in order to avoid mistakes. The differences will be found uniformly greatest in those species of which the males pay no regard to their young; but it requires a practised eye and great attention to discern the difference in classes of which both the male and female bestow care on their offspring. There is, however, a marked difference in this respect even in females of the same species. Every cottager knows, and can distinguish in her poultry-yard, particular female fowls, ducks, geese, and turkeys, which cover their eggs and bring up their young ones with the greatest care; while there are others which spoil their nests, and neglect or abandon their young. On comparing the heads of the animals which shew these opposite qualities, a decided difference will be found at the organ of Philoprogenitiveness. Those, therefore, who wish to form collections with this view, should know not only the natural history of the species, but the peculiar disposition of the individuals selected.

With regard to the name of this faculty, Dr. Spurzheim observes : "As the English language possesses no single word that indicates love of off-spring, I have employed two Greek roots, which, in conjunction, define accurately the primitive propensity. The title that results is long ; but I could not say Philogenitiveness, because that would indicate the love of producing offspring. As, however, progeny is synonymous with offspring, and philoprogeny means love of offspring, I adopt the term *Philoprogenitiveness* for the faculty producing the love of offspring." Even this term, however, seems liable to objection ; inasmuch as it represents the faculty as bearing relation exclusively to the offspring of its individual possessor, and this whether they be young or adult. Now, although it is highly probable that the feeling acts in parents toward their *grown* children ; yet, on the other hand, there cannot be a doubt that children in general, though not the person's own, are objects in which it takes an interest. *Love of young*, therefore, seems a more appropriate designation than *Love of offspring*. It is difficult to coin an English term to express the former idea : but the German word *Jungenliebe*, employed by Dr. Gall, seems unexceptionable. Almost all metaphysical writers admit the love of young as an instinctive propensity of the human mind. Phrenological observation has discovered the organ, and the effects of its different degrees of developement, and also of its healthy and diseased states, on the manifestations of the feeling ; and to this extent adds to the stock of general knowledge. The following cuts represent the organ large and small :

ROBERT BURNS.

PERUVIAN.

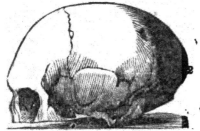

It is proper to bear in mind that these, and all other contrasts, are given in this work not so much to prove Phrenology to be true, as to represent the appearances of the organs in different degrees of developement.— Established.

3. CONCENTRATIVENESS.

THIS organ is situated immediately above Philoprogenitiveness, and below Self-Esteem. A bony excrescence of the suture sometimes presents itself at this part, which may be mistaken for the organ of Concentrativeness; but the former is much narrower and more pointed than the elevation caused by the latter when it is large. A cerebral convolution in each hemisphere runs along the top of the corpus callosum, from the organs of Concentrativeness and Self-Esteem to the intellectual organs in the frontal lobe. It is in connexion with several other organs of the propensities and sentiments; but it appears to me that the posterior end is in Concentrativeness and Self-Esteem, and the anterior end in the anterior lobe.

Observation proves that this is a distinct organ, because it is sometimes found large when the organs of Philoprogenitiveness and Self-Esteem lying below and above it are small, and sometimes small when these are large. Dr. Gall did not discover its function. Dr. Spurzheim observed it to be large in those animals and persons who seemed attached to particular places. "I consider," says he, "in animals, the cerebral part immediately above the organ of Philoprogenitiveness as the organ of the instinct that prompts them to select a peculiar dwelling, and call it the organ of Inhabitiveness. It is known that cats are more attached to places, and dogs to persons. The former remain in the house which is sold, while the latter follows his master. My attention has been, and is still, directed to such individuals of the human kind as show a particular disposition in regard to their dwelling-place. I have many facts in confirmation. I saw a clergyman in Manchester, known to his friends as particularly attached to his dwelling-place, so that he should be unhappy if obliged to sleep elsewhere. I examined his head in company of several gentlemen, some of whom were opponents, but every one was obliged to admit, that the spot of the head where No. 3 is situated was warmer than the rest of the head. I merely asked what part was the warmest, and all agreed at the same place. Some nations are extremely attached to their country, while others are readily induced to migrate. Some tribes of the American Indians and Tartars wander about without fixed habitations, while other savages have a settled home. Mountaineers are commonly much attached to their native soil, and those of them who visit capitals or foreign countries, seem chiefly led by the hope of gaining money enough to return home and buy a little property, even though the land should be dearer there than elsewhere. I therefore invite the phrenologists who have an opportunity of visiting various nations particularly fond of their country, to examine the developement of the organ marked No. 3, and situated immediately above Philoprogenitiveness. Some persons think that Inhabitiveness may give the delight to see foreign countries, and to travel, but it is quite the reverse; the former delight depends on Locality. Those who have Inhabitiveness large and Locality small, do not like to leave home; those who have both organs large, like to travel, but to return home and to settle at last. In all civilized nations some individuals have a great predilection for residing in the country. If professional pursuits oblige them to live in town, their endeavour is to collect a fortune as speedily as possible, that they may indulge their leading propensity. I have examined the heads of several individuals of this description, and found the parts in question much developed."[*] The function, however, is stated by Dr. Spurzheim as not yet fully settled. From a number of observations, the faculty appears to me to have a more extensive sphere of action than that which he is disposed to assign to it.

Some persons can detain their feelings and ideas in their minds, giving them the quality of continuity; while others cannot do this: the minds of the latter may be compared to the surface of a mirror, on which each feeling and thought appears like the shadow of a moving object, making a momentary impression, and passing away. They experience great diffi-

[*] *Phrenology*, last edition, (Boston, U. S., 1832,) p. 167.

culty in detaining their emotions and ideas, so as to examine and compare them; and, in consequence, are little capable of taking systematic views of any subject, and of concentrating their powers to bear on one point. I have observed this organ to be large in the former and small in the latter.

It is difficult to describe in words the manner of a man's mind; but the difference in manifestation is so great between those in whom this organ is small and those in whom it is large, that, if once comprehended, it will always be recognised. In conversing with some individuals, we find them fall naturally into a connected train of thinking; either dwelling on a subject which interests them, till they have placed it clearly before the mind, or passing naturally and gracefully to a connected topic. Such persons uniformly have this organ large. We meet with others who, in similar circumstances, never pursue one idea for two consecutive seconds, but shift from topic to topic without regard to natural connexion, and leave no distinct impression on the mind of the listener: this happens even with individuals in whom reflection is not deficient; but the organ in question is in such persons uniformly small. I have met a military officer, with Locality and Concentrativeness both large, who declared that he liked the stirring and diffuse life of a soldier, while engaged in active operations; but that when the army halted he was equally pleased, and found equal facility in concentrating his mind to reading, writing, or business, and was not annoyed by that dissipation of intellect of which many of his brother-officers complained. On the other hand, a gentleman bred to the profession of the law, who has this organ rather deficient, declares that the effort of concentrated thinking is to him painful, though he has excellent Comparison, Causality, and Language.

The question occurs, What is the primitive feeling which gives rise to these phenomena? The first idea that led me to the conclusion, that it is the tendency to concentrate the mind within itself, and to direct its powers in a combined effort to one object, was suggested by a lady, who had remarked this quality in individuals in whom the organ was large. The Rev. Dr. Welsh, and Dr. Hoppe of Copenhagen, having been informed of this view, unknown to each other communicated to me the inference, that the faculty gives a tendency to dwell in a place, or on feelings and ideas, for a length of time, till all, or the majority, of the other faculties are satisfied in regard to them. Both of these phrenologists acquiesce in the manifestations being such as I have described them, when the organ is large or small. I regard the function of the faculty to be to give continuity to impressions, be they feelings or ideas. The power of giving continuity to emotion and intellectual conception was a striking feature in the minds of the late Mr. John Kemble and Mrs. Siddons. During long and solemn pauses in their declamation, their audience saw the mental state prolonged over the whole interval, which added to the depth and the intensity of the effect produced. The organ in question seems to me to form one indispensable element in this mental character. I am unable to give any more specific definition of the function, and admit that the determination of it is attended with great difficulty. An excellent letter on the subject appeared in *The Phrenological Journal*, vol iii., p. 193, from the pen of an anonymous author, which contains many valuable remarks on the ultimate principle of the faculty, and I avail myself of it with pleasure. The following are extracts:

"'If we consider the human mind,' says Mr. Hume in his Dissertation on the Passions, 'we shall observe that, with regard to the passions, it is not like a wind-instrument of music, which, in running over all the notes, immediately loses the sound when the breath ceases; but rather resembles a string instrument, where, after each stroke, the vibrations still retain some sound, which gradually and insensibly decays.' From this he infers

that, when an object which occasions a variety of emotions is presented
to the mind, each impulse will not produce a clear and distinct note of
passion, but the one passion will always be mixed and confounded with
the other. In his observations on the laws of the suggesting principle,
Dr. Thomas Brown remarks the same fact of permanence or coexistence
as taking place in our mental conceptions in general, when associated
with the interest of any mental emotion. ' I look. at a volume on my
table,' says he ; ' it recalls to me the friend from whom I received it—the
remembrance of him suggests to me the conception of his family—of an
evening which I spent with them—and of various subjects of our conversation. Yet the conception of my friend may continue, mingled indeed
with various conceptions, as they rise successively, but still coexisting
with them.'* Dr. Brown proceeds, with the felicity and ingenuity which
so generally distinguish his writings, to explain how this coexistence of
ideas gives us the capacity of prosecuting with steadiness a mental design
or plan of thought. His words cannot be abridged without doing injustice
to his meaning. ' When we sit down,' he says, ' to study a particular
subject, we must have a certain conception, though probably a dim and
shadowy one, of the subject itself. To study it, however, is not to have
that conception alone, but to have successively various conceptions, its
relations to which we endeavour to trace. The conception of our particular subject must, in the very first stage of our progress, suggest some
other conception. But this second suggestion, if it alone were present,
having various relations of its own, as well as its relation to the subject
which suggested it, would probably excite a third conception, which had
no reference to the original subject—and this third a fourth—and thus a
whole series, all equally unrelated to the subject which we wish to study.
It would hence seem impossible to think of the same subject even for a single minute. Yet we know that the fact is very different, and that we often
occupy whole hours in this manner, without any remarkable deviation
from our original design. Innumerable conceptions, indeed, arise during
this time, but all more or less intimately related to the subject, by the
continued conception of which they have every appearance of being suggested ; and if it be allowed that the conception of a particular subject
both suggests trains of conceptions and continues to exist together with
the conceptions which it has suggested, everything for which I contend
in the present case is implied in the admission.'

"I apprehend," says the writer in the Journal, " that this principle
suggests the true metaphysical theory. If we conceive that the simple
function of this faculty is to give duration or fixity to whatever conceptions or emotions occupy the mind, the various operations ascribed to
Concentrativeness will flow from that function as from an elementary
principle. In Mr. Combe's work lately published,* the ' primitive feeling,'
which gives rise to the phenomena of Concentrativeness, is said to be
' the tendency to concentrate the mind within itself, and to direct its powers in a combined effort to one object.' This, however, may be considered
rather as a description of the operation of the power, than a statement of
the primary element to which its phenomena may be traced. If we attend
to what passes in our minds when we endeavour to concentrate our thoughts
upon a subject, we shall find that we do not attempt any direct coercion
on our different faculties, but simply endeavour to seize upon the object
of thought, and keep it steadily before the mind. We are all occasionally
conscious of ineffectual efforts of attention ; if we examine what we do
on such occasions, we shall find that it consists in an attempt to think of
some subject which is, for the moment, less attractive than some other
objects which are the causes of distraction. An effective concentration

* Lectures, vol ii., p. 303.   † System of Phrenology, 1825.

of the faculties takes place only when the original leading conceptions are of themselves powerful and permanent; and the concentration will be found, consequently, to be most perfect when there is least effort to produce it. We are sensible of this on occasions which may be either painful or pleasant; when a subject, associated with strong emotion, has taken possession of the mind; and when we find ourselves incapable of banishing from our thoughts, even though very desirous of doing so, the train of conceptions which has so strongly concentrated our powers upon itself, and continues to keep them in a state of sustained and perhaps distressing activity. We speak of our minds having the command of our ideas. This may be correct enough in popular language; but, philosophically speaking, our ideas command our minds. And even in those cases which appear most·like exceptions to this principle, it will be found, on examination, that it is merely one class of ideas assuming the predominance over another. When we voluntarily change our train of thought, or endeavour to concentrate our minds upon a subject, the process is one in which, under an impression of the necessity or expediency of attaining to the particular subject, we pass from the train of irrelevant ideas, and endeavour to reach, by the aid of our associations, the subject which we wish to study. Almost every individual is capable of this single effort, and he may repeat it again. But that uninterrupted sustaining of the attention so given, which constitutes Concentrativeness, depends on a quality distinct from efforts of attention—a quality most strongly marked where least effort is necessary —and that is simply the property which this mental power possesses of giving continuance to thoughts and feelings when they have sprung up in the mind. This property appears to exist in different degrees in different minds; to which, of course, the diversity in the manifestations of Concentrativeness, with which we are so often presented, is to be mainly attributed.

"It is not difficult to see in what way this property of permanence operates·in producing the various peculiarities of a concentrative turn of mind. It is a law of thought which all systems of mental philosophy recognise, although they may explain it differently, that a conception or feeling, when present to the mind, naturally acts in calling up other conceptions and feelings of the same class. Ideas of Causality call forth other ideas of Causality; emotions of Benevolence or Destructiveness are followed by trains of conceptions associated by sympathy with the previous mental state. If, then, one predominating conception or feeling be held before the mind by the force of a strong Concentrativeness, the mental action just described will of necessity be greatly enhanced. The secondary conceptions will react upon the original, increasing the intensity of thought and feeling, and adding to the excitement of the mind. A more extensive range of ideas, all bearing the same kindred character, will thus be brought into view; and, while the intellect, seizing from a distance the point to be pursued, arranges its materials on such a plan as is best adapted to attain it, it is at the same time prepared for executing the design with greater strength of conception, or, as the nature of the subject may require, with a tone of more powerful emotion. The effect of this concentration naturally extends to the active·powers in cases where their cooperation is necessary; the associated volitions flow more readily along with the mental train, and participate in the harmony of all the other faculties.

"In perfect consistency with this view, we find that any circumstance which gives permanence to an emotion independently of Concentrativeness, produces the same effect. The continued presence of a cause of provocation will excite Destructiveness to a greater excess of passion. Large Cautiousness, along with deficient Hope, will give a permanent tinge to all the mental feelings; and, when excited by disease, may so completely fill the mind with their gloomy suggestions, as to render it inaccessible to every idea of a brighter complexion. Every sentiment, whatever its character may be, casts its own peculiar light over the mental prospects; and the objects beheld reflect that light alone to the mind, whether it be the splendour of our more bright and joyous feelings, or the fiercer glow of the destructive passions, or the sombre illumination of a more melancholy mood.

"It occurs to me that the amount of this power, in the composition of intellectual character, has not been fully estimated by phrenologists. Independently of Phrenology altogether, the varieties of mental constitution cannot, I think, be satisfactorily accounted for, but by supposing that Concentrativeness is an original element of mind, varying in force in different individuals. In connecting this power with the cerebral organ, phrenologists have proceeded upon experience; and so far as my limited observation has gone, I have been gratified by the remarkable coincidences which it has presented between fact and this part of the system. The following remarks have been suggested by observation, and are not merely speculative; but, at the same time, they are submitted to be set aside or confirmed as to their phrenological accuracy by the more extensive observations of our veteran phrenologists:

"What is the result of extreme defect in this organ I have had no opportunity of knowing. Deficiency, in the more ordinary degrees, discovers itself in different ways, according to its combination with other faculties. In some individuals it produces an indisposition to settle into any regular plan of life; or, if this has been controlled by circumstances and other faculties, there may still be seen a want of method, forethought, and continuity in the various concerns of intercourse or business. The individual does not appear like one driving constantly toward a particular object; his mind takes its direction from shifting circumstances; and, if other faculties conspire, he may be characterized by a sort of careless facility or vivacity of disposition. Should these appearances be restrained by large Cautiousness and Firmness, while the reflecting organs at the same time are full, the manifestations of the deficiency will be considerably different. There may be a propensity to reason, and possibly to deal in abstract speculation; while the individual will exhibit, in his attempts at argument, a degree of cloudiness and ambiguity of conception, which evidently results from an incapacity of holding up distinctly before his mental vision the subject of thought.

"We occasionally find persons with large reflecting organs, whom we are surprised to observe little given to sustained reasoning or philosophical speculation. The writer has noticed some such, with Causality and Wit both large, while he has had reason either to know or to suspect that the organ of Concentrativeness was considerably deficient. The intellectual perceptions of such appeared to be strong and rapid, and possessed the momentary brilliancy imparted by Ideality, or the energy derived from a large Combativeness. But the mental action was never sustained; the energy ceased when its impression had just been felt by the auditor; and the decisions of Causality and Wit were never prolonged into a train of connected argument. They came to their conclusions by judgments, and not by ratiocination. Whatever could be seen at a glance or two, they perceived, and often with much perspicacity and originality; but they failed in everything requiring the investigation of abstract principles or logical deduction. They excelled in whatever admitted of succession and variety of remark, but were unsuccessful where a single point was to be kept in view and carried by argument. They were better orators than writers, and more powerful still in conversation than in prolonged oratory. It might be that they argued well in conversational controversy; but this was because the successive replies of the debate broke the reasoning into steps, if I may say so, and always presented a new point for immediate judgment. All this appears to be the natural consequence of a deficient Concentrativeness. We must observe, however, that such a mind, when its faculties are under the influence of strong excitement, may exhibit a degree of unity and sustainedness of thought beyond what is usual to it at other moments; but this would prove nothing against an actual deficiency in Concentrativeness. All possess the quality in some degree, and, of course, on occasions of greater excitement, its power will be augmented. And still it may be said, that, if great Concentrativeness were placed in the same circumstances, its manifestations would be still more remarkable.

"Full or large Concentrativeness gives rise to other descriptions of intellectual character. We may occasionally observe a class of persons who, with the intellectual organs rather poorly developed, are, notwithstanding, great dabblers in argument. They are a species of Lilliputian gladiators, who are perpetually skirmishing and hair-splitting with all about them in behalf of certain favourite opinions, to the merits of which few, alas! are sensible but themselves. This is the extreme case, but various modifications of it will be found. The probability is, that in all such the organ of Concentrativeness is full; it may be seen, indeed, in the natural language of their looks and gestures: along with this, Causality will be discovered to be relatively the largest of their intellectual organs, although absolutely small. Their reasonings are distinguished by two qualities. The first of these is a deficiency of strength and breadth in the conceptions which compose them; so that their track is something like the lines of navigators' courses in the charts, remarkable for nothing but its continuousness. The second is, that they take no comprehensive survey of the general principles which bear upon a question; but having the power of seeing and dissecting that which is immediately before them, they work onward by the help of certain little formulæ, now right, and now wrong, till they strike upon some palpable absurdity, some contradiction to more general principles or more extensive analogies. When such individuals are compared with persons of the former class, who have large Causality, and yet do not reason, an apparent contradiction is presented to the phrenological account of Causality, as a faculty which disposes to metaphysics, and 'gives the perception of logical consequences in argument.' The contradiction vanishes when we connect two powers together as necessary to reasoning. The Causality of every one whose mind is sound, is capable of perceiving the relation between a cause and its effect, or between simple premises and a conclusion. If Concentrativeness be added, which gives the power of keeping the subject of thought steadily before the mind, there will be a capacity for pursuing such a connected series of judgments as constitutes reasoning. In mathematical reasoning, where every term has a definite extension, the above power will be sufficient for forming sound conclusions. But, in the investigation of moral subjects, there is required a comprehensive conception of the various relations of each term or principle employed in our deductions; and this appears to be the property of a large Causality in conjunction with the knowing organs; the former giving a powerful memory for relations previously discovered, and the latter supplying the materials on which the decisions of Causality are founded. In both of these, such reasoners as we speak of are deficient; and hence their speculations want the elements both of strength and comprehensiveness of thought.

"When full Concentrativeness is joined to large Causality and Individuality, the power of philosophy and reasoning appears in its greatest perfection. The mind is at once possessed of large intellectual resources, and is capable of making the most of them by its power of collecting its

11*

conceptions into a strong mental picture, and conveying them with the full force of a sustained representation to the minds of others. The effects of a large Causality are just the reverse of those we attributed to a small. The intellectual picture is enlarged in its dimensions, is more completely filled up with related conceptions, and has its lines more strongly drawn ; and, along with this, there is a more comprehensive view of the multiplied connexions which the subject of thought has with other remoter truths."*

The styles of Tacitus and Grattan appear to me highly characterized by Concentrativeness, while that of Dugald Stewart is so only in a moderate degree. The quality is much more conspicuous in the poetry of Thomas Campbell and Crabbe than in that of Sir Walter Scott. The organ was not large in the head of Scott. It seems to have been recognised by the late Dr. Thomas Brown, who names it a "comprehensive energy," and it abounds in his own writings.

It has been objected, that concentration of style is, in many instances, the result of labour and condensation ; and in this I agree : but before an author will bestow pains in communicating this quality to his compositions, he must have a relish for it himself; and this, according to my notion, is inspired by the organ in question. The object of his exertions is, to bring his style up to a state which pleases his own faculties ; and if the organ be small, he will not find pleasure in concentration either of feeling or of thought, and be incapable of producing it.

It has been said, that Individuality and Eventuality, when large, produce the effects here attributed to Concentrativeness; but I am acquainted with a literary gentleman in whom these organs are large and Concentrativeness deficient, and who manifests great knowledge of facts and details, combined with deficiency in the power of keeping them continuously before his own mind, so as to discover their relative bearings and applications. On the other hand, I am acquainted with a philosophical author, who possesses large Concentrativeness with deficient Eventuality ; and who complains of experiencing great difficulty in acquiring knowledge of details, who requires to write down instantly the results of his reading and observations, and whose knowledge exists in his portfolio more than in his brain—but who, in reproducing his knowledge as an author, labours incessantly till he has discovered its natural relations, and gives it forth in the most concentrated and systematic form. When Comparison and Causality are large in combination with large Concentrativeness, there is a tendency to systematize knowledge : when the latter is deficient this is not so much felt ; and I regard one element in a systematic mind to be the power of giving continuousness to feelings and ideas, thereby enabling the intellect to contemplate the relations subsisting among them.

According to this account of the faculty, an individual may have great liking for a particular pursuit—Botany, for example, or Phrenology—if he possess the combination of faculties which takes pleasure in it ; and he may pursue it with ardour, and nevertheless be deficient in Concentrativeness. I know such persons, but all of them make efforts collect knowledge, or communicate ideas, without taking a comprehensive and concentrated view of the objects and relations about which they treat.

Dr. Spurzheim, however, objects to my ideas, and states that his experience is in contradiction to them. Facts alone must determine between us. At the same time, there appears to be nothing in the notion of Dr. Spurzheim concerning Inhabitiveness inconsistent with the more extensive views now taken of the nature of this faculty.

It has been objected by him, that "Concentrativeness cannot possible be a primitive faculty, since it can neither act alone nor appear diseased

* *Phren. Journ.*, iii., 193. On the subject of Concentrativeness see also i., 245 ; v., 235 ; viii., 61, 226, 400, 440, 564.

singly ; and since its very existence only becomes apparent by the presence of other powers directed to one object." There are various faculties which very seldom act alone : thus, Firmness usually acts along with
other powers—we persevere in passion, in love, in hate, in ambition, or
in study; but cannot well persevere in mere abstract perseverance :
Cautiousness causes us to fear ; but we generally fear something which
depends on other faculties, and rarely experience abstract fear itself.
Concentrativeness, therefore, is not singular in not acting alone. I have
no doubt of the *possibility* of its acting by itself, although, from the rare-
ness of its doing so, and the obscurity in which the ultimate function is
involved, I cannot specify the effect which it then produces.

As to disease of Concentrativeness, this organ appears to suffer in those
lunatics whose attention is immoveably fixed on some internal impression,
and who remain absorbed in silent and profound meditation, insensible
alike to the threats and caresses of those around them, and to the effects
of external objects. They differ from ordinary monomaniacs in this, that
the latter, with certain unsound feelings or intellectual perceptions, or
with unsound associations on the presentment of certain external objects,
can still direct their attention to other feelings or ideas, and concerning
them can hold rational conversation. The state now attributed to diseased Concentrativeness must be distinguished also from one for which
it has been sometimes mistaken, namely, *dementis*, approaching to idiocy,
in which a fixed look and silent calmness appear, not from internal meditation, but from utter insensibility to stimuli. In disease of Concentrativeness the patient possesses intense consciousness, and, when cured, is
able to give an account of all that passed in his mind during the malady ;
in *dementia* the period of the disease forms a blank in existence, the
individual recollecting nothing. Dr. A. Combe, to whom I owe these
observations, states, that he has heard Esquirol, in his lectures at the
Salpétrière, speak of cases such as those now described ; and he himself
has seen examples which proved the accuracy of his account of them,
although, owing to the function not having been discovered at the time,
he did not observe the condition of this particular organ. I am acquainted
with a gentleman in whom the organ is large, and who, while labouring
under a nervous affection, in which Cautiousness and Conscientiousness
were diseased, experienced a feeling as if the power of concentrating his
mind were about to leave him, and who used vigorous efforts to preserve
it. He directed his attention to an object, frequently a spire at the end
of a long street, and resolutely maintained it immoveably fixed there for a
considerable length of time, excluding all other ideas from his mind.
The consequence was, that, in his then weak state, a diseased fixity of mind
ensued, in which feelings and ideas stood, as it were, bound up and immoveable, and thereafter a state in which every impression and emotion
was fleeting and fickle like images in water. He was then unacquainted
with Phrenology, but knows it now, and expresses his belief that the
circumstances detailed were probably referable to a diseased affection of
the organ in question.

Dr. Spurzheim objects farther, that " no one, in concentrating his mind
and directing his powers to one object, exhibits gestures and emotions
indicating activity in the back part of the head ; the whole of the natural
language shows that concentration takes place in the forehead." With
the greatest deference to Dr. Spurzheim's superior skill and accuracy, I
take the liberty of stating, that, so far as my own observation goes, those
persons who really possess the power of concentration, while preparing
to make a powerful and combined exertion of all their powers, naturally
draw the head and body backward in the line of this organ. The author
of Waverley describes this as the attitude of concentrated internal think-

ing. Preachers and advocates in whom it is large, while speaking with animation, move the head in the line of Concentrativeness and Individuality, or straight backward and straight forward. When Combativeness predominates over Concentrativeness in a pleader, he draws his head backward and to the side, in the line of Combativeness, and advances it in a corresponding direction.

" The organ," continues Dr. Spurzheim, " is also commonly larger in women than in men, and I leave every one to decide upon the sex which supports the more close and vigorous attention." In Scotland, and I may almost say in England, although my observations there have been less extensive, this is not the case ; the developement being in general larger in men than in women. " It is, moreover," says he, " larger in negroes and in the Celtic tribes than in the Teutonic races ; in the French, for instance, it is larger than in the Germans. The national character of these nations not only does not confirm the opinion of Mr. Combe, but is in direct contradiction to it." From this and some other objections of Dr. Spurzheim, which I pass over without comment, I am convinced that he has not correctly apprehended the quality of mind which I designate Concentrativeness. This must, no doubt, be my fault ; but it affords a good reason for not prolonging disputation. So far as my knowledge of French literature extends, it is not marked by deficiency of Concentrativeness. The intellectual range of the French is limited, but no nation attains to greater perfection within the sphere which their faculties are calculated to reach : they write the best elementary works on science of any people in Europe ; and to this Concentrativeness is essential. They bring their powers to bear in a regulated manner on the point under consideration, and present it clearly and definitely to the understanding. The Germans have more powerful reflecting faculties than the French, and also greater perseverance ; but, if I may judge from the limited knowledge of their literature which I have been able to obtain, they appear inferior to them in Concentrativeness. They introduce more frequently extraneous ideas and feelings, and do not present so neat and complete a whole in their compositions. The organ is large in the negroes and Scotch, full in the Germans, Chinese, and Hindoos, moderate in the ancient Greeks, and small in the Peruvians.

In regard to the tendency to " Inhabitiveness," I conceive that concentration of mind is favourable to this tendency, and that those men and animals whose faculties are most concentrated, have the greatest inclination to remain in one place ; besides, animals which browse on rocks, and which place their nests in high and difficult situations, or by the banks of rapid rivers, would require for their well-being and comfort just such a faculty as this, which should enable them to maintain their position with ease, and at the same time to provide for their food and safety. The eagle, which loves to soar aloft, requires certain faculties to be exerted to maintain his equilibrium, while at the same time his eye darts over a great expanse " through the azure deep of air," to discern his prey on the surface of the earth. There are farther required a concentration and simultaneous action of numerous faculties in the stoop which he makes upon the prey itself, and in pouncing at once upon the bird or lamb which he has selected for his victim. Something of the same kind is required in the water-fowl, whose cradle is the deep, in diving for his food through the waters. The co-operation of all his powers must be required to keep him in that situation, and at the same time enable him to secure what he wishes for food, and avoid his numerous enemies. The skulls of carnivorous animals indicate a larger developement of the brain than those of herbivorous creatures ; and the former appear to me to manifest, in their habits, more of the quality of continuousness of emotion and concentrativeness of attention than the latter. In this way I conceive that the new functions attributed to this organ do not supercede the old, nor imply any incorrectness in the observations which led Dr. Spurzheim to conjecture its uses; at the same time there may be a modification of the faculty itself in different species of animals, which may determine some to high and some to low situations; while in man it may be a more general faculty, without determining to a residence of any particular kind.

The strongest expression of this faculty which I have observed is in rope-dancers and equestrian performers. Their countenances show a great internal concentration, watching and directing the slightest motions of the body; and in the head of Ducrow, of which the Phrenological Society has a cast, the organ is very large. He manifests the faculty in the highest degree.

Since the third edition of this work was printed, Dr. Spurzheim has replied very fully to my observations on Concentrativeness, in his work on Phrenology, published at Boston, United States, in 1832, vol. i., p. 160. I have perused his statements with all the attention and respect due to a master and a most esteemed friend, and with the single object of arriving at the truth, but still I am not satisfied that my previous views were erroneous. As the functions of this organ, however, can be settled by facts alone, I consider it unnecessary to reply to the arguments brought forward by Dr. Spurzheim in opposition to my opinions. The reader must judge for himself. Dr. Spurzheim alludes to the developement of the organ in his own head. "The organ," says he, "is small in my head, and when I objected against the former definition of Concentrativeness, 'the tendency to maintain two or more powers in simultaneous and combined activity, so that they may be directed toward one object,' considering such an operation of the mind rather as intellectual than affective, I was told that I could not easily conceive this primitive power, since the organ is small in my brain. I confess that this answer never satisfied my mind. I allow that several feelings and their respective organs are small in my head; but this did not prevent me to conceive their existence in others, being guided by reasoning and by facts." P. 174. In this last observation Dr. Spurzheim is in the right. If I had succeeded in determining accurately the primitive function, in defining it, and in proving its truth by sufficient facts and arguments, he would unquestionably have understood what I meant. But I have all along confessed that I have not succeeded in accomplishing so much. Nevertheless, in consequence probably of the organ being large in my own brain, I have a strong feeling of the mental quality connected with it; while, in conversing with Dr. Spurzheim on the subject, he appeared to me to have so weak a consciousness of the quality, that we never could succeed in understanding each other's experience in regard to it, and this is the circumstance to which he alludes. There is no indelicacy in now adding, that the deficiency of Concentrativeness appeared to me to be a striking feature in Dr. Spurzheim's mental manifestations, whether as a lecturer, as an author, or in conversation; and that if a large developement of this organ had been added to his splendid moral and intellectual gifts, the powers of his mind as a public teacher would have been rendered still more efficient than they were.

The leading object of these discussions is, to enable the reader to form an idea of the mental quality, if it be such, intended to be designated by Concentrativeness, so that he may be able to decide on the function of the organ by his own observations. It acts along with the feelings as well as with the intellect, and prolongs emotions. Abstract reasoning is not admitted in Phrenology as proof in favour of any organ or faculty; and I have observed that, by leading the mind insensibly to adopt a conclusion for or against particular ideas, it produces a tendency to seek support for opinions rather than truth, and thereby retards the progress of accurate investigation. This is an additional reason for abstaining from farther argument on the subject. The reader who wishes for additional informa- tion in regard to it, may consult the following able communications on Concentrativeness, in the ninth volume of the *Phrenological Journal :* " Remarks on Inhabitiveness and Concentrativeness," p. 330 ; and two letters, p. 612, one anonymous, and the other by Mr. William Hancock, jr., suggesting that *the love of pursuit*, or *constancy*, is the function of the organ. The faculty is stated as only probable, and stands open for farther elucidation.

4. ADHESIVENESS.

This organ is situated at the middle of the posterior edge of the parietal bone, on each side of Concentrativeness, higher up than Philoprogenitive- ness, and just above the lambdoidal suture. When it is very large two annular protuberances will be observed there ; or a general fulness if the neighbouring organs be large : when the organ is small, that part of the head is narrow or depressed.

Dr. Gall was requested to mould for his collection the head of a lady, who was described to him as a model of friendship. He did so, more through complaisance than in expectation of making any discovery. On examining the head, he found two large prominences, in the form of a segment of a sphere, at the sides of the organ of Philoprogenitiveness. These prominences, which he had not previously observed, were symme- trical, and manifestly formed by parts of the brain ; and he therefore con- cluded that they indicated organs. But the question was, What are their functions ? He inquired at the friends of the lady concerning her dispo- sitions and talents, and also obtained her own opinion of the feelings and capacities which she most strongly possessed. All the information concurred in regard to the fact, that she was distinguished by inviolable attachment to her friends. Although, at different periods of her life, her fortune had undergone great changes, and on several occasions she had passed from poverty to riches, her affection for her former friends was never forgotten. The idea naturally presented itself, that the disposition to attachment might be connected with a particular part of the brain. This inference acquired greater probability from the circumstance, that the prominences on the head of this lady were placed in the immediate neighbourhood of the organs of Amativeness and Philoprogenitiveness, and that the three feelings have obviously some analogy to each other. Many subsequent observations confirmed Dr. Gall's conjecture, and the organ has long been regarded as established.

The faculty gives the instinctive tendency to attachment, and causes us to experience the greatest delight in a return of affection. Those in whom it is strong feel an involuntary impulse to embrace and cling to any object which is capable of experiencing fondness. It gives ardour and a firm grasp to the shake with the hand. In boys it frequently displays itself in attachment to dogs, rabbits, birds, horses, or other animals. In girls it adds fondness to the embraces bestowed upon the doll. The feelings which it inspires abound in the poetry of Moore. He beautifully describes its effects in the following lines :

" The heart, like a tendril accustomed to cling,
  Let it grow where it will, cannot flourish alone ;
  But will lean to the nearest and loveliest thing
  It can twine with itself, and make closely its own."

It also inspires the verse—

"The heart that loves truly, love never forgets,
But as truly loves on to the close ;
As the sun-flower turns to her god as he sets,
The same look that she turned when he rose."

The old Scotch ballad, "There's nae luck about the house," breathes the very spirit of this faculty.

The organ is generally larger and the faculty stronger in women than in men ; and the extreme constancy with which, in general, they adhere to the objects of their attachment may be attributed to this faculty. "Man boasts of his capacity for friendship," says Mr. Scott, "and falsely speaks of its joys as the purest of all human enjoyments. But it is only in the heart of feeling, confiding, generous woman, that friendship is to be found in all the fulness of perfection. It was part of the doom pronounced upon her at the fall, that ' her desire should be to her husband, and that he should rule over her ;' and, conformably to the first clause in this sentence, we find Adhesiveness to be, in general, far more powerful in the woman than in the man. The most generous and friendly man is selfish in comparison with woman. There is no friend like a loving and an affectionate wife. Man may love, but it is always with a reserve, and with a view to his own gratification ; but when a woman bestows her love, she does it with all her heart and soul."*

Even in the most degraded criminals this faculty sometimes manifests itself with a fervour and constancy of affection worthy of a better fate. Mary Macinnes, executed in Edinburgh for murder, had gained the affection of a person whose name needs not here be mentioned ; and her attachment to him continued strong in death, and assumed even a romantic appearance in the last moments of her mortal career. He had sent her a pocket-handkerchief, having his name written in one corner, and also half an orange, with a request that she would eat the latter on the scaffold, in token of their mutual affection, he having eaten the other half the preceding morning at the corresponding hour. She held the corner of the napkin in her mouth almost all the night preceding her execution, and even on the scaffold. When seated on the drop, the turnkey gave her the half orange. She took it out of his hand, and, without the least symptom of fear, said, "Tell him (the object of her attachment) that I die perfectly satisfied that he has done all in his power for my life, and that I eat the orange as he desired me. May God bless him. Say to him that it is my dying request that he may avoid drink and bad company, and be sure never to be late out at night." She seemed to forget eternity in the ardour of her attachment to earth. The organ is very large in the cast of her head.†

This great proneness to, and ardour in, attachment on the part of the female sex, render these men doubly guilty who, on the false hypothesis that affection readily and warmly bestowed may be lightly withdrawn and directed to another, sport with this beautiful trait of female nature, and gain the affections of women to betray their honour, or gratify a silly vanity by being loved.

There is a great difference among individuals in regard to the strength of this feeling. Some men have many acquaintances but no friends ; while others remain attached to certain individuals during every change of circumstances, and do not readily enlarge the circle of their intimates. When the organ is large great delight is felt in friendship and attachment, the idea of distant friends often presents itself, and the glow of affection rushes into the mind with all the warmth and vivacity of a passion. Those in whom it is small care little for friendship ; out of sight, out of mind, is their maxim. We frequently see individuals of very different characters

* Phren. Journ., vol. ii., p. 280.   † Trans. of the Phren. Soc., p. 3

and genius, lastingly attached to each other. Adhesiveness, strong in both, seems to be the bond of union. They perhaps feel many points of repulsion, and are not happy if too long and too closely united; but still, on being separated, they experience a longing for each other's society, which makes them forget and forgive everything to obtain its gratification. There are husbands and wives who cannot live together, and who yet become miserable when long separated. I conceive this to arise from strong Adhesiveness in both, combined with other faculties in each, which do not harmonize.

This faculty is clearly distinguishable from Benevolence, for many persons are prone to attachment who are not generous. It, however, has a more extensive influence than the production of friendship among individuals, and appears to give rise to the instinctive tendency to congregate, whence society has originated. Man is created obviously with a view to the social state. His feelings of benevolence, love of praise, and justice require intercourse with intelligent beings for their gratification, as indispensably as the stomach requires food to enable it to perform the process of digestion; and Nature, by means of this faculty, seems to give the instinctive tendency to associate, by means of which the whole powers of the mind may find scope for exercise If this view be correct, deficiency in the organ must be essential to an anchorite or hermit.

Some of the lower animals possess this propensity as well as man : it is remarkably strong in the dog; and horses and oxen sometimes become sick and pine, when deprived of accustomed companions. "It is to be observed, however," says Dr. Spurzheim, "that the instinct of being attached for life, and that of living in society, are not mere degrees of energy of the faculty of attachment. For there are animals which live in society without being attached for life, as the bull, the dog, cock, &c.; others which live in society and in families, as starlings, ravens, crows, &c.; and others again which are attached for life without living in society, as the fox, magpie, &c." The instinct, therefore, of living in society, and that of living in family, he regards as *modifications* of the faculty in question; just as smell and taste, although the same senses in herbivorous and carnivorous animals, are modified in the former to relish vegetable substances, and, in the latter, animal fibre and effluvia. "Man belongs to the class of animals which is social and attached for life; society and marriage are consequently effects, not of human reflection, but of an original decree of nature."[*]

Dr. Gall does not coincide in the opinion that attachment for life in man and animals results from this organ. It appears to him, as far as his knowledge of natural history extends, that, in all species where both the male and female concur in rearing the young, marriage for life exists; and that, on the other hand, where the unaided female is sufficient for this end, the connexion is temporary. At the same time, he speaks with much reserve on the subject, and is not prepared to decide, whether there is a separate organ for attachment for life, or whether it is the result of a combination of several organs, or a modification of Adhesiveness.[†]

Excessive energy of this faculty produces extreme regret at the loss of friends, or at leaving our country. Nostalgia is supposed to result from disease of the organ.[‡]

Mr. Stewart[§] and Dr. Thomas Brown[‖] admit this tendency as a primitive instinct of our nature, and concur in general with the views of phrenologists in regard to it.

[*] *Phrenology*, p. 152.
[†] See a Letter on Marriage, in the *Phrenological Journal*, ii., 178.
[‡] Some interesting observations on the insanity of Adhesiveness will be found in Dr. Andrew Combe's *Observations on Mental Derangement*, pp.167, 248.
[§] *Outlines*, p. 87. [‖] *Lecture* 67.

J. J. Rousseau founds his celebrated Essay on the Origin of the Inequality of Ranks, which obtained the prize from the Academy of Dijon, on the non-existence of such a propensity in the human mind. He views man in his natural state as an isolated ·and wandering animal, satisfying his hunger by the chase or by the fruit of· the forest, and quenching his thirst at the spring or the brook, and having no more need or desire of society with his kind than the eagle or the wolf. He conceives, that the individual who first enclosed a spot of ground and called it mine, and who first cajoled his fellow-men to settle around him and assist him in his projects, was the author of all the evil with which human nature is now afflicted. Many volumes have been written in answer to this absurd lucubration; but I submit, that Phrenology, by showing that those who have this part of the brain large are inspired with an instinctive tendency to associate with their fellows, affords a brief and satisfactory refutation of the hypothesis.

The great activity of this organ disposes persons to embrace and cling to each other; two children in whom it is active will put their arms round each other's necks, and lay their heads together, causing them to approach in the direction of the organ of Adhesiveness, or assuming this attitude as nearly as possible. A dog, when anxious to show his attachment, will rub his head at the seat of this organ on his master's leg. When two persons, in whom this organ is very large, meet, they feel an involuntary attachment springing up in their minds toward each other, unless their other faculties be very incongruous.

The organ is established.

5. COMBATIVENESS.

This organ is situated at the posterior-inferior angle of the parietal bone, a little behind and up from the ear.

Dr. Gall gives the following account of its discovery: After he had abandoned all the metaphysical systems of mental philosophy, and become anxious to discover the primitive propensities of human nature by means of observation, he collected in his house a number of individuals of the lower classes of society, following different occupations, such as coachdrivers, servants, and porters. After acquiring their confidence, and disposing them to sincerity, by giving them wine and money, he drew them into conversation about each other's qualities, good and bad, and particularly about the striking characteristics in the disposition of each. In the descriptions which they gave of each other, they adverted much to those who everywhere provoked quarrels and disputes; they also distinguished individuals of a pacific disposition, and spoke of them with contempt, calling them poltroons. Dr. Gall became curious to discover whether the heads of the bravoes whom they described differed in any respect from those of the pacific individuals. He ranged them on opposite sides, and found that those who delighted in quarrels had that part of the head immediately behind and a little above the ear much broader than the others.

He observes, that there could be here no question about the influence of education, and that this prominent feature in the character of each could·never be attributed to the influence of external circumstances. Men in the rank to which they belonged abandoned themselves without reserve to the impulses of their natural dispositions.

The spectacle of fighting animals was, at that time, still existing at Vienna. An individual belonging to the establishment was so extremely intrepid, that he frequently presented himself in the arena quite alone, to sustain the combat against a wild boar or a bull. In his head the organ was found to be very large. Dr. Gall next examined the heads of several of

12

his fellow-students, who had been banished from universities for exciting contentions and continually engaging in duels. In them also the organ was large. In the course of his researches he met with a young lady who had repeatedly disguised herself in male attire, and maintained battles with the other sex ; and in her, also, the organ was large. On the other hand, he examined the heads of individuals who were equally remarkable for want of courage, and in them the organ was small. The heads of the courageous persons varied in every other point, but resembled each other in being broad in this part. Equal differences were found in the other parts of the heads of the timid, when compared with each other, but all were deficient at Combativeness.

This faculty has fallen under the lash of ridicule, and it has been objected that the Creator cannot have implanted in the mind a faculty for fighting. The objectors, however, have been as shallow in learning as in observation of human nature. The profoundest metaphysicians admit its existence, and the most esteemed authors describe its influence and operations. The character of Uncle Toby, as drawn by Sterne, is in general true to nature ; and it is a personification of the combative propensity, combined with great benevolence and integrity. " If," says Uncle Toby, ." when I was a school-boy, I could not hear a drum beat but my heart beat with it, was it my fault ? Did I plant the propensity there ? Did I sound the alarm within, or Nature ?" He proceeds to justify himself against the charge of cruelty supposed to be implied in a passion for the battle-field. " Did any one of you," he continues, " shed more tears for Hector ? And when King Priam came to the camp to beg his body, and returned weeping back to Troy without it—you know, brother, I could not eat my dinner. Did that bespeak me cruel ? Or, because, brother Shandy, my blood flew out into the camp, and my heart panted for war, was it a proof that it could not ache for the distress of war too ?"

Tacitus, in his history of the war by Vespasian against Vitellius, mentions, that " Even women chose to enter the capitol and abide the siege. Among these the most signal of all was Verulana Gracilia, a lady, who followed neither children, nor kindred, nor relations, but followed only the war."—Lib. iii. " Courage," says Dr. Johnson, " is a quality so necessary for maintaining virtue, that it is always respected, even when it is associated with vice."

Mr. Stewart and Dr. Reid admit this propensity under the name of " sudden resentment ;" and Dr. Thomas Brown, under the name of " instant anger," gives an accurate and beautiful description of it when acting in combination with Destructiveness. " *There is a principle in our mind*," says he, " *which is to us like a constant protector ;* which may slumber, indeed, but which slumbers only at seasons when its vigilance would be useless, which awakes therefore at the first appearance of unjust intention, and which becomes *more* watchful and *more* vigorous in proportion to the violence of the attack which it has to dread. What should we think of the providence of nature, if, when aggression was threatened against the weak and unarmed at a distance from the aid of others, there were instantly and uniformly, by the intervention of some wonder-working power, to rush into the hand of the defenceless, a sword or other weapon of defence ? And yet this would be but a feeble assistance, if compared with that which we receive from those simple emotions which Heaven has caused to *rush*, as it were, into our mind, for repelling every attack." Vol. iii., 324. This emotion is exactly the phrenological propensity of Combativeness aided by Destructiveness. The chief difference between Dr. Brown's views and ours is, that he regards it as a mere susceptibility of emotion, liable to be called into action when provocation presents itself, but slumbering in quiescence in ordinary circumstances ; while we look upon it as also a spontaneously active impulse, exerting an influence on the mental constitution, independently of unjust attack. It is to express this active quality that the term *Combativeness* is used to designate the faculty.

Combativeness, then, confers the instinctive tendency to oppose. In its lowest degree of activity it leads to simple resistance ; in a higher degree to active aggression, either physical or moral, for the purpose of removing obstacles. Courage is the feeling which accompanies the active state of this propensity. Hence an individual with predominating Combativeness anticipates in a battle the pleasure of gratifying his ruling passion, and is blind to all other considerations. His love of contention is an instinct. He is a fighting animal. Courage, however, when properly directed, is useful to maintain the right. On this account a considerable endowment of it is indispensable to all great and magnanimous characters. Even in schemes of charity, or in plans for the promotion of religion or learning, opposition will arise, and Combativeness inspires its possessor with that instinctive boldness which enables the mind to look undaunted on a contest in virtue's cause, and to meet it without shrinking. Were the organ very deficient in the promoters of such schemes, they would .be liable to be overwhelmed by contending foes, and baffled in all their xertions. I conceive that Mrs. Fry would require no small Combativeness to give her courage to undertake the reformation of Newgate. Without it, her mind could not have felt that boldness to encounter difficulty which must have preceded the resolution to undertake so great an enterprise. Howard the philanthropist, also, must have been supported by it in the perils he voluntarily confronted in visiting the dungeons of Europe. Indeed, I have observed that the most actively benevolent individuals of both sexes—those who, in person, minister to the relief of the poor, and face poverty and vice in their deepest haunts, to relieve and correct them —have this organ fully developed. Luther and Knox must have had a large portion of it to enable them to perform the services which they rendered to Christendom.

The organ is large in valiant warriors. In the skulls of King Robert Bruce,[*] and General Wurmser, who defended Mantua against Bonaparte, it is exceedingly conspicuous. The subjoined figures represent Wurmser's skull contrasted at this organ with the skull of a Cingalese boy, in which it is small. The figures of Hare and Melancthon, on pp. 85 and 86,

GENERAL WURMSER.   CINGALESE BOY.

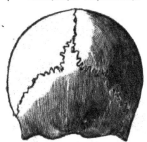 

exhibit Combativeness largely and moderately developed ; and the reader will find additional examples of its great developement in the heads of Caracalla and the Roman Gladiator, delineated in Dr. Spurzheim's *Physiognomy*, plates 14 and 32. It is very large in Linn, and moderate in the Rev. Mr. M., whose heads are represented on p. 108 of the present volume.

In feudal times great Combativeness was more essential to a leade·

* *Trans. of the Phren. Soc.*, p. 247.

than it is in modern warfare. Richard Cœur de Lion, Bruce, and Wallace could command the fierce barbarians whom they led to the field only by superior personal prowess; and, indeed, hope of victory was then founded chiefly on the dexterity with which the chief could wield his sword. In modern warfare comprehensiveness of intellect is more requisite in a general; but still Combativeness is a valuable element in his constitution. Napoleon distinguished accurately between these two qualities. He describes Ney and Murat as men in whom animal courage predominated over judgment; and notices their excellence in leading an attack or a charge of cavalry, accompanied by incapacity for conducting great affairs. The most perfect military commander, he says, is formed when courage and judgment are *in æquilibrio*—in phrenological language, when the organs of Combativeness, moral sentiment, and reflection are in just proportion to each other.

This faculty is of great service to a barrister: it furnishes him with the spirit of contention, and causes his energies to rise in proportion as he is opposed.

Combined with Destructiveness, it inspires authors with the love of battles. Homer and Sir Walter Scott are fired with more than common energy, when describing the fight, the slaughter, and the shouts of victory. From this sympathy of historians, orators, and poets, with deeds of arms, warriors are too inconsiderately elevated into heroes, and thus the trade of butchery is fostered and rendered glorious, with little reference to the merits of the quarrel. Phrenology, by revealing the true source of the passion for war, will, it is to be hoped, one day direct the public sentiment to mark with its highest disapprobation every manifestation of this faculty that is not sanctioned by justice, and then we shall have fewer battles and inflictions of misery on mankind.

When too energetic and ill-directed, it produces the worst results. It then inspires with the love of contention for its own sake. In private society it produces the controversial opponent, who will wrangle and contest every point, and, "even though vanquished, will argue still." When thus energetic and active, and not directed by the Moral Sentiments, it becomes a great disturber of the peace of the domestic circle: contradiction is then a gratification, and the hours which ought to be dedicated to pure and peaceful enjoyment, are imbittered by strife. On the great field of the world its abuses lead to quarrels, and, when combined with Destructiveness, to bloodshed and devastation. In all ages countless thousands have thronged round the standard raised for war, with an ardour and alacrity which showed that they experienced pleasure in the occupation.

Persons in whom the propensity is strong, and not directed by superior sentiments, are animated by an instinctive tendency to oppose every measure, sentiment, and doctrine advocated by others; and they frequently impose upon themselves so far as to mistake this disposition for an acute spirit of philosophizing, prompting them to greater vigour of investigation than other men. Bayle, the author of the Historical Dictionary, appears to have been a person of this description; for, in writing, his general rule was, to take the side in opposition to every one else: and hence it has been remarked, that the way to make him write usefully was, to attack him only when he was in the right, for he would then combat in favour of truth with all the energy of a powerful mind. William Cobbett mentions, that, in his youth, the rattle of the drum inviting him to war was enchanting music to his ears, and that he ardently became a soldier. In his maturer years the combative propensity seemed to glow with equal activity in his mind, although exerted in a different direction. By speech and writing he contended in favour of every opinion that was interesting for the day. To Combativeness was owing no small portion of that boldness which even his enemies could not deny him to possess.

The organ is large also in persons who have murdered from the impulse of the moment, rather than from cool deliberate design. The casts of Haggart and Mary Macinnes are examples in point. The same is the case in several casts of Caribs' skulls, a tribe remarkable for the fierceness of their courage. The ancient artists have represented it large in their statues of gladiators. The practice of gladiatorship, as also the prize-fights of England, have for their object the gratification of this propensity.

When the organ is very large and active, it gives a hard thumping sound to the voice, as if every word contained a blow. Madame de Stael informs us, that Bonaparte's voice assumed this kind of intonation when he was angry; and I have observed similar manifestations in individuals whom I knew to possess this part of the brain largely developed. When predominant, it gives a sharp expression to the lips, and the individual has the tendency to throw his head backward, and a little to the side, in the direction of the organ, or to assume the attitude of a boxer or fencer.

When the organ is small, the individual experiences great difficulty in resisting attacks; and he is not able to make his way in paths where he must invade the prejudices or encounter the hostility of others. Excessively timid children are generally deficient in this organ and possess a large Cautiousness; their heads resembling the figure of the Cingalese boy on p. 135. I conceive the extreme diffidence and embarrassment of Cowper the poet, to have arisen from such a combination; and in his verses he loathes war with a deep abhorrence. Deficiency of Combativeness, however, does not produce fear; for this is a positive emotion, often of great vivacity, which cannot originate from a mere negation of an opposite quality.

Combativeness is generally more developed in men than in women; but in the latter it is sometimes large. If it predominates, it gives a bold and forward air to the female; and when a child she would probably be distinguished as a romp.

In society it is useful to know the effects of this faculty, for then we can treat it according to its nature. When we wish to convince a person in whom the organ is large and Conscientiousness deficient, he will never endeavour to seize the meaning or spirit of our observations, but will pertinaciously put these aside, catch at any inaccuracy of expression, fly to a plausible, although obviously, false inference, or thrust in some extraneous circumstance, as if it were of essential importance, merely to embarrass the discussion. Individuals so constituted are rarely convinced of anything, and the proper course of treatment is, to drop the argument and leave them in quiet possession of the field. This, by withdrawing the opportunity for exercising their Combativeness, is really a punishment to them; and our views will have a better chance to sink into their minds, unheeded by themselves, than if urged by us, and resisted by them, which would infallibly be the case if we showed anxiety for their conviction. The test of a combative spirit is to state some clear and almost self-evident proposition as part of our discourse. The truly contentious opponent will instinctively dispute or deny it; and we need proceed no farther.

When the organ is large, and excited by strong potations, an excessive tendency to quarrel and fight is the consequence. Hence some individuals, in whom it is great, but whose moral and intellectual faculties are capable of restraining it when sober, appear, when inebriated, to be of a different nature, and extremely combative.* The organ is liable also to excessive excitation through disease. Pinel gives several examples of monomania clearly referable to it and Destructiveness. "A maniac," says he, "naturally peaceful and gentle in disposition, appeared inspired

* On the question, why intoxication excites, in a particular manner, the organs of Combativeness and Destructiveness? see The Phren. Journ., ix., 306.

12*

by the demon of malice during the fit. He was then in an unceasingly mischievous activity. He locked up his companions in their cells, provoked and struck them, and at every word raised some new quarrel and fighting." Another individual, who, during his lucid intervals, was mild, obliging, reserved, and even timid in his manners, became, during the fit, highly audacious, "and experienced the most violent propensity to provoke those who approached him, and to irritate and fight them *avec outrance*." On visiting London Bedlam in 1824, I examined the head of a male patient, and pronounced Combativeness and Destructiveness to be uncommonly large. I was desired to look at his hands. They were fastened to rings in an iron girdle round his waist. He had committed murder in an access of fury, and was liable to relapses, in which he manifested these propensities with inordinate vehemence.

This organ is found also in the lower animals; but there are great differences among them in respect to its energy. Rabbits, for instance, are more courageous than hares; and one dog looks incessantly for an opportunity of fighting, while another always flies from the combat. The bull-dog forms a contrast in this propensity to the greyhound; and the head of the former is much wider between and behind the ears than the latter. "This also," says Dr. Spurzheim, "is an unfailing sign to recognise if a horse be shy and timid, or bold and sure. The same difference is observed in game-cocks and game-hens, in comparison with domestic fowls. Horse-jockeys, and those who are fond of fighting cocks, have long made this observation."

The name given to this faculty by Dr Gall is *the instinct of self-defence and defence of property*; but Dr. Spurzheim justly regards this appellation as too narrow. "According to the arrangement of nature," says he, "it is necessary to fight in order to defend. Such a propensity must, therefore, exist for the purposes of defence; but it seems to me that it is, like all others, of general application, and not limited to self-defence: I therefore, call the cerebral part in which it inheres the organ of the *propensity to fight*, or of *Combativeness*." Mr. Robert Cox has published a minute analysis of the faculty in the ninth volume of *The Phrenological Journal*, (p. 147,) and arrives at the conclusion, that, when stripped of all accidental modifications, it is "neither more nor less than *the instinct or propensity to oppose*, or, as it may be shortly expressed, *Oppositiveness*." He regards "Combativeness," or the tendency to fight, as the result of the combined action of the organ now under discussion, and that of Destructiveness.

Sir George Mackenzie, unknown to Mr. Cox, had previously expressed a similar view in his *Illustrations of Phrenology*, published in 1820. "We are inclined," says he, "to consider a propensity to fight as a compound feeling; and also that desire which some persons appear to have, of being objects of terror to others. A propensity to fight implies a desire to injure. No man can feel a desire to attack another, and say that he has no desire to hurt him." P. 99. Cases illustrative of the organ of Combativeness will be found in *The Phrenological Journal*, v., 570; vii., 638; viii., 206, 406, 596; ix., 61.

6. DESTRUCTIVENESS.

THIS organ is situated immediately above, and extends a little backward and forward from, the external opening of the ear, and corresponds to the lower portion of the squamous plate of the temporal bone. In Dr. Gall's plates it extends a few lines farther back than in those given by Dr. Spurzheim: and Dr. Gall mentions, that, when it is excessively large, the whole portion of the skull from the inferior margin of the parietal bones to the ears is elevated; and that in cases of smaller developement the prominence is confined to the lower part of the temporal bones. I have seen examples of both kinds. The external opening of the ear is much lower in some individuals than in others. Its depression is caused by the great size of the cerebral convolutions which lie over the petrous portion of the temporal hone and in the middle fossa of the skull, and is one sign of Destructiveness being large.

Dr. Gall gives, in substance, the following account of the discovery of this organ: In comparing attentively the skulls of several of the lower animals, he observed a characteristic difference between those of the carnivorous and the graminivorous tribes. In graminivorous animals only a small portion of the brain lies behind the external opening of the ear; while in the carnivorous a considerably larger mass is situated there. He found also that the skulls of the latter were more prominent above the ear than those of the former. For a long time he merely communicated these observations to his hearers, without making the least application of them to Phrenology. He only pointed out that, by inspecting the cranium, even when the teeth are wanting, it is possible to distinguish whether the animals belong to the graminivorous or carnivorous genera. It happened, at length, that some one sent him the skull of a parricide; but he put it aside, without imagining that the skulls of murderers could be of any use to him in his researches. Shortly afterward he received also the cranium of a highwayman, who, not satisfied with robbing, had murdered several of his victims. He placed these two crania side by side, and frequently examined them. Every time that he did so he was struck with this circumstance, that, although they differed in almost every other point, each of them presented a distinct and corresponding prominence immediately above the external opening of the ear. Having observed, however, the same prominence in some other crania in his collection, he thought that it might be by mere accident that this part was so much developed in the skulls of the murderers. It was only after a considerable time, therefore, that he began to reflect upon the different conformation of the brain in carnivorous and graminivorous animals; and having then observed that the part which was large in carnivorous animals, was precisely that which was so much developed in the murderers, the question occurred to him, Is it possible that there can be any connexion between the conformation of brain thus indicated and the propensity to kill? "At first," says Dr. Gall, "I revolted from this idea; but as my only business was to observe and to state the result of my observations, I acknowledged no other law than that of truth." "Let us not, therefore," says he, "fear to unfold the mysteries of nature, for it is only when we shall have discovered the hidden springs of human actions that we shall know how to guide the conduct of men."

This faculty has been subjected to much ridicule, owing partly to its having been named by Dr. Gall the *penchant au meurtre*, or propensity to kill. It is a mistake, however, to suppose that he spoke of the organ of murder. Killing being a necessary operation, he regarded this as a legitimate aim of the faculty when rightly directed; but "I have never," says he, "in speaking of the *instinct du meurtre*, meant a propensity to homicide." The word Destructiveness employed by Dr. Spurzheim is a more comprehensive appellation, and the propensity thus designated is recognised by many authors as existing in the human mind. Lord Kames observes, that "there is a contrivance of Nature, no less simple than effectual, which engages men to bear with cheerfulness the fatigues of hunting and the uncertainty of capture; and that is an *appetite for hunting*."—"It is an illustrious instance of providential care, the adapting the internal constitution of man to his external circumstances. The appetite for hunting, though among us little necessary for food, is to this day remarkable in young men, high and low, rich and poor. Natural propensities may be rendered faint or obscure, but never are totally eradicated."* Vicesimus Knox, in his *Essays*, gives a similar theory of hunting. The delight felt in this sport has been ascribed to the excitement of the chase, to emulation, and to the pleasure of succeeding in our aim ; but if these were the only sources of the enjoyment, it ought to be as pleasant to gallop over hill and dale, and leap hedge and ditch, without as with an animal in chase, and as agreeable to shoot at any inanimate object thrown into the air as at a bird. This, however, is not the case : unless there is a creature to suffer the effects of hunting and shooting, little pleasure is derived from these laborious pastimes.

The feeling is familiar to poets and authors who delineate human nature. The description by Sir Walter Scott, of King Robert Bruce avenging on Cormac Doil the death of Allan, is written in the very spirit of Destructiveness.

> " Not so awoke the King! his hand
> Snatched from the flame a knotted brand;
> The nearest weapon of his wrath ;
> With this he crossed the murderer's path,
> And venged young Allan well !
> The spattered brain and bubbling blood
> Hissed on the half-extinguished wood ;
> The miscreant gasp'd and fell."

The same author recognises several of the phrenological faculties in the following lines—in particular, Love of Approbation and Destructiveness ; the latter, however, only in a state of abuse. The verses refer to the battle of Bannockburn :

> " But O ! amid that waste of life,
> What various motives fired with strife !
> The aspiring noble *bled for fame*,
> The patriot for his *country's claim ;*
> This knight his youthful strength to prove,
> And that to earn his lady's love :
> *Some fought from ruffian thirst of blood ;*
> From habit some, or hardihood.
> But ruffian stern, and soldier good,
> The noble, and the slave,
> From various cause the same wild road,
> On the same bloody morning trode,
> To that dark Inn, the grave."

In *Recollections of the Peninsula*, by the author of *Sketches in India*, the following passage occurs : " As the chill dews of evening were descending on our bivouac, a staff-officer, with a courier, came galloping into it, and alighted at the quarters of our general. It was soon known among us that a severe and sanguinary action had been fought by our brother-soldiers at Talavera. Disjointed rumours spoke of a dear-bought field, a heavy loss, and a subsequent retreat. I well remember how we all gathered round our fires to. listen. to conjecture, and to talk about this glorious but bloody event. We regretted that we had borne no share in the honours of such a day ; and *we talked with an undefined pleasure about the carnage.* Yes ! strange as it may appear, soldiers, and not they alone, talk of the slaughter of battle-fields with a sensation which partakes of pleasure." (P. 39.) In confirmation of this remark, I may notice that I have met with some young men who possessed good moral qualities, but whose thoughts ran habitually on killing and slaughtering. The impulse was restrained, but they confessed that it would have given them great momentary gratification to smash and slay. In them the organ was decidedly large

Sketches, B. i.

The purpose of this faculty in the human mind, and its utility, are easily discoverable. In regarding this scene of creation, we perceive man surrounded by ferocious animals, such as lions, tigers, bears, and wolves; which not only are incapable of being tamed and put to use, but would be fatal to him if he did not destroy them. To maintain himself in existence, therefore, he must put many animals to death. Moreover, he has received from nature a stomach fitted to digest animal food, and a bodily system that is nourished, excited, and preserved in health and activity by the aliment which it affords. To gratify this appetite, he must bereave animals of life by sudden destruction; for their flesh is unwholesome and unfit for use, if they die of old age or disease. In the last place, some human beings themselves are so inspired by evil passions, that only the certainty that aggression would be repelled by the infliction of pain or death, is sufficient to curb their appetites and prevent them from injuring their fellow-men. Now, let us consider in what condition man, placed in these circumstances, would have stood, if he had been without this propensity. He would have been the timid prey of every ferocious animal in want of a meal. With Destructiveness in his mind, the lion and tiger read their fate in his eye, and shrink from the encounter, unless irresistibly impelled by starvation.

Let us, moreover, imagine a community of men in whom no Destructiveness was found; who would reason with, entreat, or flee from their adversaries, but never raise a weapon in their own defence: how speedily would the profligate and unprincipled flock to the mansions of such a people, as to their appropriate prey; and what contumelies and sufferings would they compel them to endure? But let them possess the propensity in question; let them, in short, raise their standard, and, like Scotland's monarch, inscribe on it, "*Nemo me impune lacesset*"—a motto inspired by Destructiveness and Conscientiousness combined; and let them act up to the spirit of the words, by hurling vengeance on every wanton aggressor; and such a people will subsequently live in peace under their olive and their vine, protected by the terror with which this faculty inspires those who, but for it, would render the world a scene of horror and devastation. When any power is indispensable to human safety, Nature implants it in the mind; and such an instinct is Destructiveness.

Combativeness, then, gives courage to meet danger unappalled, and to resist it. Destructiveness makes the onset perilous and terrible to the aggressor. Combativeness enables us to meet and overcome obstacles, and, having surmounted them, desires no more. Destructiveness prompts us to chastise or even exterminate the causes of them, so that they may never rise up again to create fresh annoyance. Combativeness would inspire Luther and Knox with courage to oppose the doctrines of the church of Rome, and to maintain the truth as revealed in the Scriptures; Destructiveness would prompt them utterly to destroy the Roman Hierarchy, and to trample its insignia under foot.

When the energy of this faculty is great and Benevolence moderate, indifference to pain and destruction is the result. When too weak, Benevolence being strong, poignant distress is felt at the sight of death and suffering of every kind. We are surrounded by death in all its forms, and by destruction in its every shape; and Nature, by means of this faculty, steels our minds so far as to fit us for our condition, and to render scenes which our situation constrains us to witness, not insupportable. A certain degree of obduracy of feeling, regardlessness of suffering, and indifference to the calamities of our race, is absolutely necessary to render existence tolerable in this world of mingled joy and wo. I have seen individuals miserable from too great feebleness of this faculty. Every being in a state of pain harrowed up their feelings, lacerated their hearts, and produced a degree of continued uneasiness scarcely conceivable by persons of more obdurate dispositions.

Mr. Robert Cox, in an ingenious essay on "The Laws of Activity of Destructiveness," published in *The Phrenological Journal*, vol. ix., p. 402, regards the primitive feeling manifested by this organ to be "the propensity to injure." "Let me not," says he, "be misapprehended. Injury does not necessarily imply malice or mischief. There are occasions when it is beneficial to injure ; though doubtless the propensity is manifested less frequently in its uses than in its abuses. We may destroy, kill, or chastise for good purposes as well as bad ; nay, we are compelled to do so : and the faculty which prompts to such conduct needs only to be regulated by morality and reason. Destruction is *extreme injury ;* to kill is to *injure mortally ;* slander and reproach are *verbal injuries ;* chastisement is *injurious* to bodily comfort ; we *injure* a statue by breaking off its nose." Mr. Cox remarks, that "it seems to be a law of the human constitution, that, when any of our faculties is pained or disagreeably active, this propensity instantly comes into play ; that is to say, there is immediately excited in the mind of the sufferer *an inclination to injure—* having for its object the inflicter of the pain, if one exist, but not frequently vented, where the feeling is uncontrolled by the moral sentiments and intellectual powers, upon neutral individuals, or even inanimate objects." A foolish nurse beats the ground on which a heedless child has fallen, and thereby gratifies its feeling of revenge, or its desire to injure the object which occasioned the pain. I concur in Mr. Cox's view, in so far that I regard the desire to injure as one form of manifestation of Destructiveness ; but I doubt whether in every individual this desire is instinctively felt on every occasion when pain is experienced. This appears to me to be the case only when Destructiveness has been trained to act on such occasions, or when the organ is very large and active. But if in any individual it is moderate, and Benevolence and Veneration are very large, I think that the first emotions of such a person in experiencing pain are, resignation, meekness, and submission. To this, however, Mr. Cox replies, that, on the contrary, it is only as the result of moral training, and of religious and philosophical impressions, that resignation and meekness in such circumstances are found ; the *natural* and *immediate* tendency of pain and grief being to excite Destructiveness. This, he argues, is distinctly seen in the conduct of ill-educated people, and especially of children and savages—a class of persons who act almost exclusively from impulse of the animal feelings, unrestrained and unmodified by the moral and intellectual powers. A large Destructiveness is *most easily* roused.

The organ is large in the heads of cool and deliberate murderers. It is very large, and Benevolence small, in the skull of Bellingham, who murdered Mr. Perceval.[*] The temporal bones protrude very much in the situation of the organ of Destructiveness, on each side, and the frontal bone presents a receding surface at the organ of Benevolence, where the skulls of individuals remarkable for benevolence generally rise into an elevation of an inch or more. A cast of Bellingham's skull may be inspected in the Phrenological Society's collection. The organ of Destructiveness is largely developed also in the skull of Gordon, who accompanied a poor half-fatuous pedlar boy, and, in the middle of a muir, beat out his brains with the heel of his clog, and robbed him of his pack, not worth twenty shillings.[†] The skull itself is in the Society's collection, and the bones protrude considerably on each side at the region in question. The protrusion in these instances arises from its excess over the neighbouring organs. If they had been equally large, there would have been great general breadth, but no particular elevation. Inexperienced observers often fall into great errors by looking for protrusion alone. The organ is large in Charles Rotherham, who pulled a stake from a hedge and beat out the brains of a poor woman on the highway, and robbed her of some very trifling articles. It is large also in the skulls of Hussey, Nisbet, and Lockey, who were executed for murder. It is very large, with deficient moral organs, in William Hare, who murdered sixteen human beings, for the sake of the price of their dead bodies as subjects for dissection; and also in Gottfried, already mentioned on pages 86 and 87; Vitellius, page 89; and Linn, page 108. It, and the organ of Acquisitiveness, appear to have been largely developed in the head of Heaman, executed at Edinburgh for piracy and murder; also in the head of Robert Dean, executed for murdering a child without any rational motive; and in the head of Mitchell, executed for murdering a young woman whom he had seduced. In the heads of David Haggart and Mary Macinnes, executed at Edinburgh, and of Booth, a poacher, executed at York, all for murders committed on the impulse of the moment, it appears considerably developed; while in them Combativeness also is large. In the skull of Tardy, an atrocious pirate, murderer, and suicide,* the developement of Destructiveness is enormous. It is large also in the skull of Robert Burns.† The reader may contrast, at situation of this organ, the skulls represented on p. 135 of the present work.

The Phrenological Society possesses casts of the skulls of five Caribs, who are well known to be a ferocious tribe, and in all of them the organ of Destructiveness is decidedly large. On the other hand, Dr. George Murray Paterson, surgeon in the Honorable East India Company's service, mentions, as the result of three thousand actual examinations, that the organ is small in the heads of Hindoos in general, who are known to

ESQUIMAUX.   PAPUAN.

be extremely tender in regard to animal life.   In the skulls of thirty-seven
Hindoos, twelve of which were presented to the Society by this gentleman, two by Dr. J. S. Combe, of Leith, and the others by Sir George
Mackenzie, the developement of the organ is in general decidedly less
than in the crania of most Europeans.   The organ is moderately developed
in the Esquimaux and Cingalese, and they are strangers to cruelty and
ferocity.   It is very large in the Papuan Islanders, who are very prone
to murder.*   In the casts of three Swedish Laplanders presented to the
Society by Mr. G. M. Schwartz, of Stockholm, the organ is large ; and
accordingly the temper of that people is very passionate.†   The subjoined
figures represent the skulls of Tardy and a Cingalese.   A section of the
latter will be found on page 87.

TARDY.   CINGALESE.

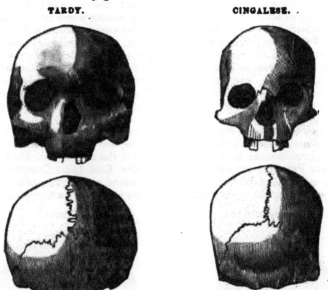

When excited by intoxication, the organs sometimes becomes ungovernable ; and hence arises the destruction of glasses, mirrors, chairs, and
every other frangible object, at the close of many a feast.   Hence also
the temptation, often almost irresistible, experienced by many a worthy
citizen, when inebriated, to smash a lamp in his progress home.   One
gentleman assured me that the lamps have appeared to him, when in this
state, as it were, twinkling on his path with a wicked and scornful gleam,
and that he has frequently lifted his stick to punish their impertinence,
when a remnant of reason restrained the meditated blow.   In him Destructiveness is decidedly large, but, when sober, there is not a more
excellent person.

This organ is larger in the male head than in the female ; and hence
the male head is in general broader.   The manifestations correspond ;
for the propensity is less vigorously manifested by woman than by man.

In active life a good endowment of the organ is an indispensable requisite to a proper discharge of the duties of several situations.   What
restrains the domination of the proud, but a knowledge that, if they press

* *Phrenological Journal*, ii., 264 ; vii., 638 ; viii., 299.

† Ib., ix., 329 ; and Malte-Brun's *Universal Geography*, (Edinburgh édition,)
vi., 466.   As to the Destructiveness of the Scotch and Peruvians, see *The
Phren. Journ.*, viii., 182, and ix., 160.

too heavily even on the meanest, the feeling of resentment will start into activity to repel the insult! and resentment is the result of Destructiveness excited by wounded Self-Esteem. In the case of officers conducting difficult and dangerous enterprises, what weight would the word of command carry, if every stubborn mind that received it knew, for certain, that the leader's dispositions were so soft that he would inflict no punishment for disobedience? and punishment flows from Destructiveness directed by justice : the sword, accordingly, is carried before the supreme magistrate, and is an emblem of Destructiveness ready to fall on the contemners of the law.

These are not mere theoretical ideas, but views founded on actual observations. The Hindoo head is smaller than the European, and in particular Combativeness and Destructiveness are less in it in proportion to the other organs ; and we see millions of the former conquered by thousands of the latter. I have met with persons who were so soft that they scarcely struck fire, however hardly they were hit ; who shrunk and retreated, yet agonized under every insult that was offered ; whose anger was so feeble that its manifestations excited only a deeper scorn, and incited to farther outrages. Such individuals possessed small Combativeness and Destructiveness, and were carried through life on the shoulders of others, being incapable of fighting their own way amid the turmoils of the world. Men who have an ample endowment of these organs, well regulated by superior sentiments, are not aware how much they owe to them. In civilized society we pass years without a contest ; but it is because all know that the sentinels are at their post, and that attack is dangerous. A man in whom society recognises a deficiency of these powers, is not equally safe from aggression.

Destructiveness has been regarded by some phrenologists as communicating a more general energy to the mind. Endeavouring to trace analytically the manner in which it produces this effect, they have supposed it to give an impatient craving appetite for excitement ; a desire to vent the mind, as it were, on something ; a feeling which would be delighted with smashing and turmoil, or with any irregular commotion, rather than with the listlessness of repose : and hence a large developement of it is held to be incompatible with that drowsiness of disposition which dreams life away in vapid inactivity, is contented to accept absence of suffering for enjoyment, and feels pain rather than pleasure in excitement. In this view it is supposed to give a general stir and impetus to the mental faculties. The Hindoos, in whom the organ is small, are remarkable, not only for great tenderness of animal life, but for deficiency in energy of character. In point of fact, however, the brain in general must be large and active, before great general power can be manifested ; and the real effect of Destructiveness appears to me to be to communicate ability to act with energy in certain situations in which, were that organ small, the individual would be completely paralyzed. In this view, it may add efficiency even to Benevolence, to which, at first sight, it appears directly opposed ; but it does so, not by increasing the positive amount of that feeling, which depends on its own organ, but by fitting the possessor to perform acts of real kindness, which require severity as their means.

As much ill-nature as wit is necessary for satire, and Destructiveness gives to it, to sarcasm, and to invective, their edge. It prompts also to the conception of images of terror, which become sublime or horrible, according as they are clothed with Ideality, or presented in naked deformity. In Lord Byron's works it is strongly manifested. His appetite for fierce excitement—the dark and dismal scenes of suffering and murder which generally abound in his stories—together with the deadly venom and the

fearful vehemence of his pen, when directed against his enemies—could
proceed from no source but the faculty in question. It leads a poet in
general to imagine scenes of devastation and destruction, and to delight
in the description of them. Byron's poem of *Darkness* exhibits the very
form and pressure of Destructiveness.

The abuses of this faculty are easily recognised in society. There
are persons who fly into a passion upon every trifling occurrence, and
vent their rage on all who are subjected to their authority. This is a rude
and vulgar manifestation of it. There are others, however, who avoid this
form of misapplication, but who indulge in making severe remarks and
cutting observations, altogether uncalled for, and introduced with no view
but to give pain; others issue their commands in harsh and angry terms,
backed by loud threatenings and terrible gesticulations; others are severe
to excess on account of failures in duty, and little mindful of the happiness of those who live under their control: all these manifest abuses of
Destructiveness.

When very active, this propensity produces a quick step, a drawing up
of the body to the head, and a stamping or striking downward; also a
wriggling of the head like the motion of that of a dog in the act of worry-
ing. It gives a dark expression to the countenance, and harsh and dis-
cordant tones to the voice. If, in a friendly converse with a person in
whom the organ is large and Secretiveness small, one happens to touch
on some irritating topic, in an instant the softness of Benevolence and
the courtesy of Love of Approbation are gone, and the hoarse growl of
Destructiveness indicates an approaching storm. I have seen it stayed,
by referring the rising wrath to its source in this propensity, and calling on
reflection to subdue it.

Cursing is an abuse of this faculty; and I have observed among the lower
orders, that some boys who attempted to practise this abominable vice
through imitation, deeming it manly, could never infuse in their imprecations
that force and expression which seemed to come quite naturally to others;[*]
and this incapacity for swearing proceeded from Destructiveness being moderately developed in proportion to the organs of the moral sentiments.

I have said that this faculty furnishes the threat which gives force
to command. In the Bible every variety of motive is held out to deter
men from sin; and I have noticed that those individuals in whom
Destructiveness predominates, have a natural tendency to dwell on the
threatenings of the Gospel, while those in whom Benevolence, Hope, and
Veneration are large, and Destructiveness deficient, hold out almost exclusively its promises—or, if they do mention its denunciations, they are
so diluted by the softness of their own minds, that more than half their
terrors are abated. Preachers of the first class frequently mistake the
fervours of Destructiveness for the inspirations of moral eloquence; and
while, by their vehemence, they gratify men of sterner natures, they harrow up amiable and susceptible minds, and cause them great uneasiness.
Preachers of the latter class, on the other hand, are acceptable to persons
naturally mild in disposition, but to the others appear insipid. Love is a
higher motive than fear, and where the mind can be led by the higher, it
ought always to be preferred; but many are open to the influence of terror,
who are not alive to Hope and Veneration, and hence the use of both is
necessary. It is only inordinate dwelling upon the one to the exclusion
of the other that is reprehensible. The higher the cultivation of the
audience, the less is fear requisite to make an impression. Fear is only
aversion to personal suffering, and is totally different from the love of good.

---

* *Stephen.* I would rather than forty shillings I could swear as well as that
gentleman. " Body of Cæsar—St. George—and the foot of Pharaoh." No,
I haven't the right grace   *Every Man in his Humour.*

The pleasure which even humane and cultivated individuals experience in witnessing an execution, is inexplicable on any principle, except that of the existence of such a faculty as this, aided no doubt by the love of excitement, arising from Wonder and some other faculties. " We have," says Mr. Scott, in an admirable essay on this propensity, " too much humanity ourselves to put a man to death. But, if a man is to be killed, we have no objection to witness the fact, or, if I may be allowed to say so, to enjoy the pleasure of seeing it performed."—" Were Destructiveness wanting, and Benevolence favourably developed, in persons present at an execution, they would be horrified, not delighted, by such a scene."* A blind man in Edinburgh attended the public executions. His Destructiveness was probably gratified by descriptions given to him by those who saw, and by their emotions when excited by the scene.

, In children, and even in adults, Destructiveness frequently vents itself in destroying inanimate objects. The people deface mile-posts, bridges, statues, and public buildings, wherever they can get access to them; and " no object of art, or even of utility," says a late writer, " is safe from their depredations." He ascribes this tendency to " the spirit of pure mischief,"—a correct designation for unguided Destructiveness. The statute 3d Geo. IV., chap. 71, which ordains, " that, if any person or persons shall wantonly and cruelly beat, abuse, or ill-treat any horse, mare, gelding," &c., he shall pay certain penalties to the king, is clearly directed against the abuses of this propensity, and, of course, supposes its existence. The adjectives *severe, harsh, angry, cruel, fierce, ferocious, savage, brutal, barbarous, atrocious,* indicate states of mind all originating from it.

Metaphysical authors in general do not treat of any power resembling this propensity, considered as a spontaneously active power. Accustomed to reflect in the closet more than to observe actions, they were not likely to discover it. At the same time, it is surprising that the contemplation of the pages of history did not suggest the existence of a tendency of this kind to their minds. Caligula is represented as cutting out the tongues of his victims—delivering them to be devoured by wild beasts—forcing individuals to assist in executing their relations—torturing and putting to the rack unhappy wretches as an amusement to his own ferocious spirit— and finally expressing a wish that the Roman people had but one head, that he might cut it off by one blow. Turning our eyes to Nero, we discover him indulging in equal atrocities—causing Britannica to be poisoned —murdering his own mother—setting fire to Rome in four quarters at once, and ascending a tower to enjoy the spectacle of the conflagration. In modern times we are presented with the horrors of the Sicilian Vespers, the carnage of St. Bartholomew's, the cruelties of the Spaniards in America, the burning of witches, and the massacres of the French revolution. These actions are inexplicable, on the supposition that no propensity like Destructiveness exists : if the metaphysicians had applied their systems to human conduct, they would have discovered that they contained no principle capable of accounting for the atrocities alluded to. In the ancient busts of Nero the organ of Destructiveness is represented as enormously large.

The organ is liable to excitement by disease, and then the propensity is manifested with irresistible vehemence. The author of *Sketches of Bedlam* describes the case of Pat Walsh, a ferocious maniac, who had been deranged altogether about twelve years, and had, it is said, uniformly evinced a character of desperation, vengeance, and sanguinary cruelty, scarcely conceivable even in madness. Notwithstanding every precaution that was taken, he had killed three persons since his confinement. " His propensity to mischief, malice, and personal abuse is as incessant as his taste for bloodshed and slaughter. He has contrived, notwithstanding his restriction of hands and feet, to break about seventy panes of glass within the last two years, in the dining-room windows, although guarded on the inside by a strong iron-wire lattice-work. This amusement he contrived to effect by standing on a form placed at some distance from the windows, and, taking the bowl of his wooden spoon in his mouth, he poked the handle through the meshes of the wire-work, and thus broke the pane." As this man is said to be confined in an iron cincture that surrounds his waist, with strong handcuffs attached to it, I infer that he is the same whose head I examined in Bedlam in 1824, and in whom the organs of Combativeness and Destructiveness were inordinately large.

When these two organs are very much developed, and the moral and intellectual organs very deficient, there is an innate disposition to mischief and violence, which renders the individual dangerous to society. In visiting the Richmond Lunatic Asylum at Dublin, in 1829, a man was presented to me by Dr. Crawford, substitute-physician, concerning whom I made the following remarks :   . '

" This is the worst head I ever saw. The combination is worse than Hare's. Combativeness and Destructiveness are fearfully large, and the moral organs altogether very deficient ? Benevolence is the best developed of them, but it is miserably small compared with the organs of Combativeness and Destructiveness. I am surprised that that man was not executed before he became insane."

, Dr. Crawford had previously written down, and then exhibited, the following observations :
" Patient E. S., aged 34. Ten years since first admission.
Total want of moral feeling and principle ; great depravity of character, lead-
· ing to the indulgence of every vice, and to the commission even of crime.
Considerable intelligence, ingenuity, and plausibility; a scourge to his family from childhood ; turned out of the army as an incorrigible villain ; attempted the life of a soldier ; repeatedly flogged ; has since attempted to poison his father."

In preparing a report of this and other cases for The Phrenological Journal, (vol. vi., p. 80,) I sent the proof-sheet to Dr. Crawford for revisal, which he returned along with a letter to the following effect : " I have a few remarks to make on the lunatic lettered E. S. You observe in your own notes, ' I am surprised he was not executed before he became insane.' This would lead to the supposition, that he had been afflicted with some form of insanity in addition to a naturally depraved character. Such, however, is by no means the case : he never was different from what he now is ; he has never evinced the slightest mental incoherence on any one point, nor any kind of hallucination. It is one of those cases where there is great difficulty in drawing the line between extreme moral depravity and insanity, and in deciding at what point an individual should cease to be considered as a responsible moral agent, and amenable to the laws. The governors and medical gentlemen of the asylum have often had doubts whether they were justified in keeping E. S. as a lunatic, thinking him a more fit subject for a bridewell. He appears, however, so totally callous with regard to every moral principle and feeling—so thoroughly unconscious of ever having done anything wrong—so completely destitute of all sense of shame or remorse when reproved for his vices or crimes— and has proved himself so utterly incorrigible throughout life—that it is almost certain that any jury before whom he might be brought would satisfy their doubts by returning him insane, which in such a case is the most humane line to pursue. He was dismissed several times from the asylum, and sent there the last time for attempting to poison his father, and it seems fit he should be kept there for life as a moral lunatic; but there has never been the least symptom of *diseased* action of the brain, which is the general concomitant of what is usually understood as *insanity*. This I consider might with propriety be made the foundation for a division of lunatics into two great classes; those who were *insane* from *original constitution*, and never were otherwise, and those who had been *insane* at some period of life from diseased action of the brain, either permanent or intermittent. There would be room for a few additional notes to the case of E. S., explanatory of what I have said, if you think fit.—*Dublin, 20th July*, 1829."

Dr. Gall cites a variety of cases of diseased manifestations of this propensity, which had fallen under his own observation, and quotes several others highly illustrative from Pinel. I select one of these, in which the organ of Destructiveness seems to have been affected singly, the other organs remaining entire. The patient, during periodical fits of insanity, was seized with an "uncontrollable fury, which inspired him with an irresistible propensity to seize an instrument or offensive weapon, and to knock on the head the first person who presented himself to his view. He experienced a sort of internal combat between this ferocious impulse to destroy, and the profound horror which rose in his mind at the very idea of such a crime. There was no mark of wandering of memory, imagination, or judgment. He avowed to me, during his strict seclusion, that his propensity to commit murder was absolutely forced and involuntary, and that his wife, whom he tenderly loved, had nearly become his victim, he having scarcely had time to bid her flee to avoid his fury. All his lucid intervals were marked by melancholy reflections and expressions of remorse; and so great did his disgust of life become, that he had several times attempted an act of suicide " (this is common in the excess of Destructiveness) " to bring it to a close. ' What reason have I,' said he, ' to cut the throat of the superintendent of the hospital, who treats us with so much kindness? and yet in my moments of fury I am tempted to rush upon him, as well as others, and plunge a dagger in his bosom. It is this unhappy and irresistible propensity which reduces me to despair, and makes me attempt my own life.' "*

Individuals who occasionally commit murder, or set fire to property, without any rational motive, sometimes ascribe their actions to the temptation of the devil; asserting that he whispered into their ears, " Kill him, kill him," and never ceased to repeat the exhortation till they had complied with it. Diseased activity of this organ, filling the mind habitually with a desire to destroy, probably gives rise to such an impression. In ages when belief in witchcraft was common among religious persons, impulses of the propensities, arising from spontaneous activity of the organs, appear to have been frequently mistaken for suggestions of evil spirits.

One form in which disease of this organ sometimes appears, requires particular notice; it is when it prompts females of the most unquestionable reputation to child-murder. I cite the following from the public newspapers of May, 1822 : " On Sunday morning, about half-past ten o'clock, a most horrid murder of unparalleled inhumanity, was perpetrated on the body of a fine female infant, about eight months old, named Sarah Mountfort, by her own mother, wife of Mr. Mountfort, weaver, No. 1 Virginia Row, Bethnal Green. The husband, who is a Methodist, had gone to chapel, leaving his wife to clean, and send to the Sunday school, her young

* *Sur l'Alienation Mentale,* deuxième édition, p. 102 et 103, sect. 117. See other cases of the same kind in Gall *sur les Fonctions du Cerveau,* i., 399, 417 –423, 447–457; ii., 470; iii., 174; iv., 99–110, 170;—Spurzheim's *Phrenology,* section on Destructiveness;—Dr. A. Combe's *Observations on Mental Derangement, p.* 258 ;—Simpson's *Necessity of Popular Education,* Appendix, No. II; —and *Phren. Journ.,* viii., 144, 189.

13*

family. Having done this, it appeared she cleaned herself and her infant, when, overcome by some extraordinary aberration of intellect, she cut off the head of the child with a razor, and, besmeared with the blood, immediately told the persons in the house of the bloody deed, desiring to be given into custody, as she wanted to be hanged. From the conduct of the wretched woman after the transaction, no doubt can be entertained of her insanity. Mrs. Mountfort underwent a short examination on Monday, and was committed for trial. A coroner's inquest has been held, which returned a verdict of wilful murder against the wretched woman. The distress of the family is extreme. The unhappy husband and two of the eldest daughters are seen running about the streets in a state of distraction. One of the latter has been deprived of utterance since the horrid transaction." This woman is said to have been "overcome by some extraordinary aberration of intellect ;" a mode of expression which may be forgiven in the writer of a newspaper paragraph, although, viewed philosophically, it is absurd. The intellectual powers enumerated by the metaphysicians, such as Perception, Conception, Memory, Imagination, and Judgment, furnish no propensities to action which, being deranged, could produce such a piece of barbarity. Derangement of intellect causes the patient to reason incorrectly and speak incoherently ; but if his *feelings* be sound, he is not mischievous. Here, however, the unhappy woman seems to have been inspired with a blind and irresistible impulse to kill, arising from disease of Destructiveness.

These details are exceedingly painful, and the reader may question the taste which permits their insertion ; but great ignorance prevails in the public mind on this subject, and the records of our criminal courts still show cases of wretches condemned to the gallows, who, if Phrenology were known to the judges and juries, would be consigned to lunatic asylums.

As already noticed, the organ is common to man and carnivorous animals.[*] Dr. Gall, however, remarks, that "the organ is not, in all carnivorous animals, situated with rigorous exactness above the external opening of the ear. Among some species of birds—for example, in the stork, the cormorant, the heron, the gull, &c.—the external opening of the ear is considerably removed back, and the organ of the propensity to kill is placed immediately behind the orbits, forming a large prominence upon each side, the size of which is found to bear an uniform proportion to the degree in which the animal manifests the propensity to kill. In comparing the crania of carnivorous birds with the skulls of those which can live indifferently upon either animals or vegetables, this prominence is found to be less conspicuous in the latter—in the duck, for example, and in the different species of thrushes ; and it becomes less and less prominent, in proportion as the birds exhibit a more distinct preference for vegetables, such as the swan, the goose," &c. The differences are illustrated by plates in Dr. Gall's work. If the brain of a sheep and that of a dog be compared, a great deficiency will be discovered in the former at Destructiveness.

In 1827 Dr. Joseph Vimont presented to the Royal Institute of France a memoir on Comparative Phrenology, in which he brings forward a vast collection of most interesting facts, in regard to the dispositions and forms of the brain in the lower animals. In regard to Destructiveness he says : "All animals which live on flesh, or which have a propensity for destroying, have a particular part of the cranium whose developement corresponds with that of this faculty. Thus all the *feræ*,[†] without exception, have the squamous portion of the temporal bone[‡] enlarged in a perceptible

* Mr. Robert Cox maintains that herbivorous animals are not wholly destitute of Destructiveness. See *Phren. Journ.*, ix., 406. It is certainly not easy to deny that the bull and ram sometimes display the faculty in a high degree.

† Beasts of prey.   ‡ Situated immediately outward of Destructiveness.

manner. We may cite, as examples, the tiger, the cat, the fox, the martin, the weasel, the ermine.

" In the carnivorous birds properly so called, the portion of the cranium situated behind the orbit corresponds with the organ of carnivorous instinct, and presents a remarkable developement. In the omnivorous birds the enlargement is a little more posterior."

The organ is established.

ALIMENTIVENESS, OR ORGAN OF THE APPETITE FOR FOOD.

It early occurred to Drs. Gall and Spurzheim that the appetite for food is an instinct not referable to any of the recognised faculties of the mind, and they therefore were disposed to view it as a primitive power, having a separate organ; but they did not discover its situation.

In the sheep the olfactory nerves, which are very large, are perceived to originate from two cerebral convolutions, laying at the base of the middle lobe of the brain, adjoining and immediately below the situation occupied by the organ of Destructiveness in carnivorous animals. The sheep is guided in the selection of its food by the sense of smell; and the inference occurred to me, that these parts might be the organs of the instinct which prompts it to take nourishment. Corresponding convolutions occur in the human brain, but the functions of them are not ascertained, owing to their situation presenting obstacles to the determination of their size during life. The conjecture, however, seemed to be plausible, that they might serve a similar purpose to that which they were supposed to perform in the sheep.

This subject has attracted the notice of that ingenious phrenologist, Dr. Hoppe, of Copenhagen, and he has treated of it in two valuable communications, published in The Phrenological Journal, vol. ii., pp. 70, 484. (See also vol. iv., p. 308.) He is of opinion that, besides the nerves of the stomach and palate, of which alone he conceives the sensations of hunger and thirst to be affections, there must be also an organ in the brains of animals for the instinct of nutrition, (taking nourishment for the preservation of life,) which incites them to the sensual enjoyments of the palate, and the activity of which is independent of hunger and thirst. " How," says he, December, 1823, " should the mere sense of hunger, more than any other disagreeable or painful sensation, make the animal desire food, the necessity of such not being known to him by experience? This could only be effected by instinct; because either an instinct, i. e., the immediate impulse of an organ, or else experience and reflection, are the causes of all actions.

" We observe that the chicken is no sooner out of the egg, than it picks the grain that lies on the ground, and the new-born babe sucks the nipple. Is this to be explained without the supposition of an organ analogous to that which makes the duckling immediately plunge into the water, or makes the kitten bite the first mouse it meets with?

" Neither am I able otherwise to conceive how the new-born animal can discriminate what is useful for its nutrition; that, for instance, the chicken never mistakes gravel for grain, and that the wild beasts always avoid poisonous plants without ever tasting them.

" When the child, even enjoying perfect health, sucks till the stomach is filled, in a literal sense of the word, it surely feels no hunger or thirst; yet, if laid to the breast, it will continue sucking, even sometimes having thrown off the last draught from overfilling.

" If nothing but hunger and thirst impelled man to take food, he would, when satiated, have no appetite for meat and drink; yet we every day observe people that cannot resist the temptation of surfeiting themselves both with meat and drink, though they know it to be noxious, and others again that never are tempted to gluttony."

Dr. Hoppe adds several other reasons in support of an organ of the instinct of nutrition, and sums up his views in the following words : " According to my opinion, *hunger* and *thirst* must be discriminated from the desire of food which we call *appetite ;* for those I consider as only affections of the stomachical and palatic nerves, caused by the defect of necessary supply; but appetite as an activity of a fundamental animal instinct, which has in the brain an organ analogous to the rest of the organs. Yet there is a very intimate connexion between these; thus, nothing can more effectually rouse appetite than hunger."

In lecturing on Phrenology, I had for some years pointed out the part of the brain above alluded to as the probable seat of this faculty ; and Dr. Hoppe, without being aware of this circumstance, or the reasons on which the conjecture was founded, arrived at a similar conclusion with respect to a neighbouring part of the base of the brain. He proceeded even so far as to point out an external indication of the size of the organ. " Regarding the organ for taking nourishment," says he, 28th December, 1824, " I have been led to think, since I wrote last, that the place where its different degrees of developement are manifested in the living body, is in the *fossa zygomatica, exactly under the organ of Acquisitiveness, and before that of Destructiveness.* Before I had thought at all of Phrenology, I was struck with the remarkable breadth of the face or head of a friend of mine, caused, not by prominent cheek-bones, as in some varieties of mankind, but more toward the ears, by the great convexity of the zygomatic arch. Knowing that this individual was exceedingly fond of good living, and that, even in spite of a very powerful intellect, and propensities moderate in almost every other respect, he was prone to indulge too frequently in the joys of the table, I afterward thought that this form of the head and tendency of the mind might bear a nearer relation to each other than had at first occurred to me; and in some other persons, notoriously fond good eating and drinking, I found a confirmation of my suppositions. This prominence of the bony arch, I think, must be an absolute consequence of the part of the cranium lying under the temporal muscle being pushed outward, and diminishing, in that direction, the space of the *fossa.* Besides this greater convexity of the arch, the part also of the skull situated immediately above it, under the organ of Acquisitiveness, will in this case be observed to be more full and protruding. The breadth of head produced in this way can by no means be mistaken for a mere prominent cheek-bone, nor for the organs of Acquisitiveness, or Destructiveness, or Constructiveness, situated higher, behind, and in front of it. Having found the said parts in some persons much compressed, in others less so, and, as I think, the disposition of mind always proportionate to it, and not yet having met with any exceptions, I cannot but hold my opinion to be true."

Dr. Hoppe considers that the organ of Alimentiveness is likewise the organ of the sense of taste. "That the sensation of taste," says he, "only passes through the nerves, and is perceived in a part of the brain, is a supposition, I think, sufficiently proved. Now, it appears to me as highly probable, and by analogy agreeing with other experiences, that it is one and the same organ which *tastes* (viz., distinguishes and enjoys) and *incites* us to taste, or, in other terms, to take food and drink. This, according to my opinion, is the organ of appetite for food, and consequently it may also be named the organ of Taste, (gustus,) and stands in the same relation to this of the external senses as the organ of Tune to the sense of Hearing."

Dr. Crook, of London, mentions that, several years before the publication of Dr. Hoppe's papers, he himself had arrived at similar conclusions with respect to this faculty and the position of its organ. "Three persons," says he, "with whom I had become acquainted in the year 1819, first led me to suspect that a portion of the brain situated near the front of the ear (next to Destructiveness) was connected with the pleasures of the festive board. From that time to the end of 1822, above a thousand observations were made; as they tended to confirm this view, several phrenological friends were informed of the result. From 1823 I no longer doubted that the anterior portion of the middle lobe was a distinct organ, and that its primary use was the discrimination and enjoyment of meats and drink. It was difficult, however, to hit the fundamental power. The situation of the organ, under the zygomatic process and the temporal muscle, frequently precluded the possibility of accurate observation. But, notwithstanding, well-marked cases, both of a positive and a negative kind, were investigated. These conclusions were imbodied, and read to the Phrenological Society of London, on the 8th of April, 1825. Two months before, though it was not known in London, a letter had been received in Edinburgh from Dr. Hoppe, of Copenhagen, giving the same portions of the brain to the sensations of hunger and thirst. The coincidence was felt to be remarkable, and by myself particularly so, as I had, in 1821, conceived a similar idea, but discarded it upon considering the dependence of these feelings upon the stomach and tongue."

Dr. Crook, misled, no doubt, by the erroneous title (" On the Conjectural Organs of Hunger and Thirst ") prefixed to Dr. Hoppe's communications in *The Phrenological Journal*, errs in supposing him to consider those sensations as connected with the organ in question. On the contrary, he and Dr. Crook concur in rejecting this idea, and in there locating the sense of taste.

The external part to which Dr. Hoppe alludes, was formerly included by Dr. Spurzheim within the limits of Destructiveness; but in Dr. Gall's busts and plates that organ was not carried so far forward, and the function of the part in question was marked by Dr. Gall as unascertained. Dr. Spurzheim latterly coincided in the soundness of the views of Dr. Hoppe, in so far as to regard the organ as that of " the propensity or instinct to feed;" but he dissented from Dr. Hoppe's opinion that this propensity discriminates what is useful for nutrition, and likewise from the notion that it produces delicacy and nicety of taste. " All," says he, " concurs to prove that the above-mentioned portion of the brain is the organ of the instinctive part of nutrition, or of the desire to feed. It exists not only in carnivorous, but also in herbivorous animals. The goose, turkey, ostrich, kangaroo, beaver, horse, &c., &c., have a middle lobe as well as the duck, eagle, pelican, tiger, lion, dog, &c. The desire to feed is common to all animals, and the carnivorous animals require the organ of Destructiveness in addition to that of the instinct to feed." He remarks, as a corroborative circumstance, that the anterior convolutions of the middle lobes are developed from the earliest age, sooner than many other parts, and both in man and in the lower animals are proportionally larger in the young than in adults. " This propensity," he adds, " is particularly assisted by the smell, and the olfactory nerve is in all animals in the most intimate communication with the middle lobes ; so much so, that, in the ox, sheep, horse, dog, fox, hare, rabbit, &c., the internal part of the middle lobes seems to be almost a mere continuation of the olfactory nerve. In man also the external and greater root of the olfactory nerve is in connexion with the anterior convolutions of the middle lobes. Farther, the middle lobes are in particular communication with the nervous bundles, which constitute the anterior lobes and the anterior external portion of the crura—in other words, the organs of the intellectual faculties; and the propensity to feed puts into action many of the perceptive powers, and the voluntary motion of many parts, before the food is transmitted to the stomach for digestion."

This faculty is termed Gustativeness by Dr. Crook; but Dr. Spurzheim confines the sense of taste to the gustatory nerve, regarding the propensity to feed as the whole amount of the function. "This view," says Dr. Crook, "approximates so closely to my own, that it is only in very extraordinary cases that the manifestations of the one can be clearly distinguished from those of the other; but one decided case I met with in 1827, in which no part of the *cerebrum* existed, yet, during the eight days' life of this imperfectly formed creature, there had been incessant craving for food, which it took in very considerable quantity, but without any apparent discrimination as to taste or flavour. To admit the instinct to eat to be the primitive power, would subvert the first principle of physiology—the inseparable connexion between organ and function."

If this case was really as here reported, it would unquestionably form a serious obstacle to the admission of the view taken by Dr. Spurzheim; but so many facts of an opposite tendency have been observed, that it is not unreasonable to suspect that, in a case so anomalous, the organ may have been confounded with some other part at the base of the skull.

An interesting case of disease of this organ, observed in the Royal Infirmary of Edinburgh, is recorded in *The Phrenological Journal*, vol. vii., p. 64. The patient had awakened at five o'clock on the morning of the day of his admission, "craving for food," as his sister related, and had been "eating continually" from that time till sent to the infirmary about noon. His stomach was greatly distended by the quantity of food he had swallowed, yet he still complained that he was dying of hunger. At this time, and till next morning, he was delirious, but subsequently he became dull. Twenty-four hours after his admission, when roused by loud or repeated questions, he answered imperfectly, but to the point, and frequently muttered, "hunger, hunger, hunger, it's hunger." He complained of pain at the exact locality of the organ of Alimentiveness, and there alone. The reporter of this case has appended to it his observations in regard to the points to be attended to in estimating the size of the organ; which, from its situation, is a matter of difficulty. "It is nearly parallel," says he, "to the zygomatic arch, which is often rendered prominent by it when large; but, the distance of the arch from the proper parietes of the skull being variable, this is not a certain guide. The temporal muscle opposes an obstacle, but may itself be used as a means of removing the difficulty in part. When the organ is larger than its neighbours, the lower part of the temporal muscle is pushed outward, making it appear as if lying on a pyramidal instead of a vertical-sided cranium, the base of the pyramid being downward; when small, the reverse occurs. If the organ be very large, it will affect the socket of the eyeball, pushing the latter up and forward, not as in Language down and forward: when both are large (at least in one instance I have seen this) the eye looks imprisoned by a fulness extending almost around it."

In the *Journal de la Société Phrénologique de Paris*, vol. ii., Number 5, the case of a woman called Denise, detailed in the *Annales de la Médicine Physiologique*, (Oct., 1832,) is taken notice of, as furnishing a curious example of insatiable appetite for food. In infancy she exhausted the milk of all her nurses, and ate four times more than other children of the same age. At school she devoured the bread of all the scholars; and in the Salpétrière it was found impossible to satisfy her habitual appetite with less than eight or ten pounds of bread daily. Nevertheless, she there experienced, two or three times a month, great attacks of hunger, (*grandes faims*,) during which she devoured twenty-four pounds of bread. If, during these fits, any obstacle was opposed to the gratification of her imperious desire, she became so furious, that she used to bite her clothes, and even hands, and did not recover her reason till hunger was completely satisfied. Being one day in the kitchen of a rich family, when a dinner-party was expected, *she devoured, in a very few minutes, the soup intended for twenty guests, along with twelve pounds of bread!* On another occasion she drank all the coffee prepared for SEVENTY-FIVE of her companions in the Salpêtrière! Her skull is small; the region of the propensities predominates; and the organ of Alimentiveness is largely developed. Many similar instances of voracity are recorded by medical writers.[*]

The same *Journal* (October, 1835) contains an interesting paper by MM. Ombros and Théodore Pentelithe, "On Alimentiveness, or the Sense of Hunger and Thirst, as a primitive cerebral Faculty." These gentlemen, besides referring the sense of Taste to the organ under discussion, maintain with much reason that it is the cerebral seat also of hunger and thirst. That these sensations are in reality cerebral phenomena, is evident from various conclusive facts and experiments ;[†] and the identity of the organ of the propensity to feed with that of the sensation of hunger, appears from the circumstance, that hunger and the desire to eat always go together—just as courage is the concomitant of the propensity to oppose, and anger is universally attended by the propensity to inflict suffering. MM. Ombros and Pentelithe mention several cases of voracity where pain or heat was felt at the temples, or disease of the organ of Alimentiveness was found after death. In other cases they observed a great and small developement of it in combination with much and little fondness for eating. They conceive that drunkenness and the love of smoking tobacco arise from this faculty, and that hydrophobia and various other diseases are affections of the organ. The latter conclusion receives countenance from a case reported by M. David Richard, in the same number of the *Journal de la Société Phrénologique*, p. 490.

Several years ago Dr. Caldwell published in *The Transylvania Journal of Medicine* (for July, August, and September, 1832) the opinion, that the passion for intoxicating liquors arises from derangement of Alimentiveness. Instead of mere remonstrance with the drunkard, therefore, he recommends "seclusion and tranquillity, bleeding, puking, purging, cold water, and low diet" as the means of cure. These, he states, have been found successful by the physician of the Kentucky Lunatic Asylum. Dr. Caldwell's view is confirmed by the fifth case published by MM. Ombros and Pentelithe—that of an old and confirmed drunkard, in whose brain they found a distinct erosion of the left organ of Alimentiveness. There are cases of morbid voracity on record, where *post mortem* examination has shown disease in the brain, and none in the stomach.[‡]

On the whole, there seem to be very strong grounds for holding that the part of the brain above described is the organ of the propensity to eat and drink, of the sensations of hunger and thirst, and perhaps also of the sense of taste. "This organ," however, says Dr. Spurzheim, "though indicated by reason and comparative anatomy, is merely probable, and can be confirmed or rejected like every other, according to direct observations alone, in comparing cerebral developement in relation to the special propensity I possess many facts in confirmation."

---

[*] See *Phil. Trans.*, vol. xliii., p. 366; Good's *Study of Medicine*, 2d edit., vol. i., p. 111, 112; Elliotson's *Blumenbach*, 4th edit., p. 304; and Dr. A. Combe's *Physiology of Digestion considered with Relation to the Principles of Dietetics*, p. 32.

[†] See Dr. A. Combe's *Physiology of Digestion*, chap. ii., and his *Observations on Mental Derangement*, p. 246.

[‡] See Monro's *Morbid Anatomy of the Gullet, &c.*, 2d edit., p. 271.

ORGAN OF THE LOVE OF LIFE.

In conversing with a variety of individuals about their mental feelings, no fact has more forcibly arrested my attention than the difference which exists in the love of life. It will be assumed by many, that this is an universal desire, glowing with equal intensity in all ; but the fact is otherwise. All possess the feeling, but its degrees vary much more than is generally imagined. Some individuals desire life so intensely, that they view death as the greatest calamity ; they declare that, rather than part with existence, they would submit to live in endless misery : the bare idea of annihilation is unsupportable to their imaginations ; and they found an argument for immortality on the position, that God cannot be guilty of the injustice of making them conscious of so great a boon as life, and subsequently depriving them of it : to have lived, according to them, gives an indefeasible title to continue to live for ever.

> " Could'st thou persuade me the next life could fail
> Our ardent wishes, how should I pour out
> My bleeding heart in anguish, new as deep !
> Oh ! with what thoughts thy hope, and my despair,
> Abhorr'd annihilation, blasts the soul,
> And wide extends the bounds of human wo !"
>
> *Young's Night Thoughts*, B. vii., v., 645.

Other individuals, again, experience no such passion for existence ; they regard pain and parting with the objects of their affections as the chief evils of death : so far as the mere pleasure of living is concerned, they are ready to surrender it with scarcely a feeling of regret ; they discover nothing appalling in death, as the mere cessation of being ; and do not feel the prospect of immortality to be essential to their enjoyment of the present life. I have found these different feelings combined with the most opposite dispositions in all other respects : the great lovers of life were not always the healthy, the gay, and the fortunate ; nor were those who were comparatively indifferent to death always the feeble, the gloomy, and the misanthropic : on the contrary, the feeling existed strongly and weakly in these opposite characters indiscriminately.

Neither does the difference depend on the moral and religious qualities of the individuals ; for equal morality and religion are found in combination with either sentiment. This is a point in human nature not generally adverted to ; nevertheless, I have obtained so many assurances of the existence of these different feelings from individuals of sound judgment and unquestionable veracity, that it appears to me highly probable that there is a special organ for the Love of Life. We seem to be bound to existence itself by a primitive and independent faculty, just as we are led by others to provide for its continuance and transmission. Byron expresses his surprise at his own instinctive efforts to preserve himself from drowning, when, in his moments of reflection, he wished to die. The late excellent Dr. John Aikin could hardly comprehend the feeling of the Love of Life." " I have conversed," says he, " with persons who have avowed a sentiment of which I confess I can scarcely form a conception— a strong attachment to existence abstractedly considered, without regarding it as a source of happiness."* Dr. Thomas Brown treats of this faculty under the name of Desire of our own continued Existence. This desire, he beautifully remarks, " is, as a general feeling of our nature, a most striking proof of the kindness of that Being, who, in giving to man duties which he has to continue for many years to discharge in a world

---

* *Letters to his Son*, vol. ii., Letter on the Value of Life, in which the origin of the feeling is discussed at some length.

which is preparatory to the nobler world that is afterward to receive him, has not left him to feel the place in which he is to perform the duties allotted to him as a place of barren and dreary exile. He has given us passions which throw a sort of enchantment on everything which can reflect them to our heart, which add to the delight that is felt by us in the exercise of our duties ; a delight that arises from the scene itself on which they are exercised—from the society of those who inhabit it with us—from the offices which we have performed, and continue to perform."*

The organ is probably situated in the base of the brain. The only fact tending to illustrate its position is one observed by Dr. A. Combe, and recorded in *The Phrenological Journal*, vol. iii., p. 471. In describing the dissection of the brain of a lady upward of sixty, who for many years had been remarkable for continual anxiety about her own death, he observes, that " the enormous developement of one convolution at the base of the middle lobe of the brain, the function of which is unknown, was too striking not to arrest our attention ; it was that lying toward the mesial line, on the basilar and inner side of the middle lobe, and consequently of Destructiveness. The corresponding part of the skull showed a very deep and distinctly-moulded cavity or bed running longitudinally, with high and prominent sides, and presenting altogether an appearance much more striking than in any skull I ever saw. From the situation of this convolution, its developement cannot be ascertained during life, and hence its function remains unknown. Whether it may have any connexion with the Love of Life, is a circumstance which may be determined by future observations ; all that we can say at present is, that the Love of Life seems to be a feeling *sui generis*, and not proportioned to any faculty or combination of faculties yet known—that in the subject of this notice it was one of the most permanently active which she possessed—and that in her the convolution alluded to was of very unusual magnitude ; but how far the coincidence was fortuitous, we leave to time and observation to determine."

Dr. Spurzheim was disposed to admit the existence of this faculty, which he calls Vitativeness. " It is highly probable," says he, " that there is a peculiar instinct to live, or Love of Life ; and I look for its organ at the basis of the brain, between the posterior and middle lobes, inwardly of Combativeness."

7. SECRETIVENESS.

THE organ is situated at the inferior edge of the parietal bones, immediately above Destructiveness, or in the middle of the lateral portion of

the brain. When the organ of Destructiveness is much developed, it may be mistaken by the inexperienced observer for the organ of Secretiveness ; so that it is necessary to remark, that the latter organ is placed higher, and rather farther forward, than the former ; and that, instead of presenting the form of a segment of a circle, it is extended longitudinally. When both organs are highly developed, the lower and middle portion of the side of the head is characterized by a general fulness. The reader may contrast the skulls represented

* *Lectures* 65, vol. iii., p. 390.

on pages 143 and 144. The foregoing figure is a sketch of the shaven head of a secretive gentleman with whom I am acquainted, and of whose character an account will be found in *The Phrenological Journal*, viii., 206.

Dr. Gall gives the following history of the discovery of this organ: In early youth he was struck with the character and form of the head of one of his companions, who, with amiable dispositions and good abilities, was distinguished by cunning and finesse. His head was very broad at the temples, and in his natural attitude it projected forward. Although a faithful friend, he experienced an extraordinary pleasure in employing every possible device to make game of his school-fellows and to deceive them. His natural language was absolutely the expression of cunning, such as Dr. Gall had often observed in cats and dogs when, playing together, they wished to give each other the slip. At a subsequent period he had another companion, who, at first, appeared candour personified; no one had ever distrusted him: but his gait and manner were those of a cat watching a mouse; he proved false and perfidious, and deceived, in an unbecoming manner, his young school-fellows, his tutors, and his parents. He carried his head in the same attitude as that before-mentioned; his face was handsome, and his head exceedingly broad at the temples. One of Dr. Gall's patients, who died of phthisic, generally passed for a very honest man: after his death Dr. Gall was struck with the breadth of his head in the temporal region; and shortly afterward learned that he had cheated his acquaintances, and even his mother, of considerable sums of money. At Vienna he was often in the company of a physician possessed of much information, but who, on account of his character of a cheat, was generally despised. Under pretence of dealing in objects of art, and lending on pledges, he robbed all who put confidence in him. He carried his tricks and cheats to such a length, that the government warned the public, through the medium of the public journals, to beware of him; for he had practised his arts with such dexterity that he could never be legally condemned. He often told Dr. Gall that he knew no pleasure equal to that of deceiving, especially persons who distrusted him most. As the head of this individual also was very broad at the temples, Dr. Gall was impressed with the idea that there might be a primitive tendency toward cunning in the mind, and that it might be connected with this particular cerebral organ. An immense number of observations have confirmed his conjecture.

The nature and object of this propensity appear to be the following: The various faculties of the human mind are liable to involuntary activity from internal causes as well as from external excitement. Thus, Amativeness, becoming active, gives feelings corresponding to its nature; Acquisitiveness inspires with strong desires for property; and Love of Approbation fills the mind with projects of ambition. Every one must be conscious that these or similar feelings at times rush into his mind involuntarily, and frequently refuse to depart at the command of the will. Thoughts of all kinds, moreover, arise in the intellectual organs, and facts which ought not to be divulged occur to the recollection. If outward expression were given to these impulses and ideas, in all their vivacity, as they arise, social intercourse would be disfigured by a rude assemblage of disgusting improprieties, and man would shun the society of his fellows as more loathsome than pestilence or famine. Shakspeare, with that accuracy of observation which distinguishes him, has portrayed this feature of the human mind. Iago says:

" Utter my thoughts! Why, say they're vile and false—
As where's that palace whereinto foul things
Sometimes intrude not? Who has a breast so pure,
But some uncleanly apprehensions

"Keep leets and law-days, and in sessions sit
With meditations lawful?"—*Othello*, Act iii., Scene 3.

Some instinctive tendency, therefore, to restrain within the mind itself
—to conceal, as it were, from the public eye—the various emotions and
ideas which involuntarily present themselves, was necessary to prevent
their outward expression ; and Nature has provided this power in the faculty of Secretiveness. It is an instinctive tendency to conceal, and the
legitimate object of it is, to restrain the outward expression of our thoughts
and emotions, till the understanding shall have pronounced judgment on
its propriety. "A fool," says Solomon, "uttereth all his mind ; but a wise
man keepeth it in till afterward."[*]

Besides, man and animals are occasionally liable to the assaults of enemies, which may be avoided by concealment, in cases where strength is
wanting to repel them by force. Nature, therefore, by means of this propensity, enables them to add prudence, slyness, or cunning, according
to the direction given to it by other faculties of the individual, to their
means of defence.

A sufficient endowment of this organ is essential to the formation of a
prudent character. It then imposes a salutary restraint on the manifestations of the other faculties, and serves as a defence against prying curiosity.
"When Napoleon," says Sir Walter Scott, "thought himself closely
observed, he had the power of discharging from his countenance all expression, save that of a vague and indefinite smile, and presenting to the
curious investigator the fixed eyes and rigid features of a marble bust."[†]
I have observed this power to be conferred by large Secretiveness. Those
in whom it is deficient are too open for the general intercourse of society ;
they are characterized by deficiency of tact—a headlong bluntness of
manner, and the instantaneous expression of every thought and emotion
as it flows into the mind, without regard to the proprieties required by
time, place, or circumstances.

Mr. Scott, in an excellent essay on this propensity, published in the
Transactions of the Phrenological Society, observes, that it communicates
the desire to discover the secrets of others as well as to conceal our own.
The author of *Waverley*, in his novel of *Quentin Durward*,[‡] draws the
character of Louis XI. with exact fidelity to this principle of our nature.
The king, says he, was "calm, crafty, and profoundly attentive to his own
interest. He was careful in disguising his real sentiments and purposes
from all who approached him, and frequently used the expressions—that
the king knew not how to reign who knew not how to dissemble ; and
that, for himself, if he thought his very cap knew his secrets, he would
throw it into the fire. Like all astutious persons, he was as desirous of
looking into the hearts of others as of concealing his own." The representation here given is historically correct. According to this view,
even a large developement of the organ, if combined with high morality
and an enlightened understanding, is a valuable endowment. Persons so
constituted, possessing themselves the natural talent requisite for intrigue,
are well fitted to divine and discover intrigues and secret machinations in
others, and to defeat them. From the same cause they read, with great
acuteness, the natural language of concealment in other people, and are able
to discover, by the very air and manner of a man, that he is hiding some
object or intention, when a person in whom the organ is small could not
perceive such a purpose. In many of the affairs of life also, secrecy is indispensable both to prudent conduct and to success. As a duty of friendship it has ever been considered of prime importance. "Though thou
drewest a sword at thy friend," says the son of Sirach, "yet despair not,

---

[*] Prov. xxix., 11.　　　　　　　　[†] *Life of Napoleon*, iv., 37.
[‡] Vol. i., p. 7, &c.　See *Phren. Journ.*, i., 177.

for there may be a returning to favour ; if thou hast opened thy mouth against thy friend, fear not, for there may be a reconciliation ; excepting for upbraiding, or pride, or *disclosing of secrets*, or a treacherous wound —for, for these things, every friend will depart."[*] Secretiveness is an essential element of politeness, much of which consists in avoiding the expression of what is likely to be disagreeable. Montaigne has well distinguished the use from the abuse of this faculty : "A man," says he, "must not always tell all, for that were folly. But what a man says should be what he thinks, otherwise 'tis knavery."[†] Fielding's Parson Adams is a character in which Secretiveness is greatly defective. He had no power of concealment himself, and never suspected hidden purposes in others, or "saw farther into people than they desired to let him." Othello, in like manner, is thus described by Iago :

> "The Moor is of a free and open nature,
> That thinks men honest that but seem to be so ;
> And will as tenderly be led by th' nose,
> As asses are."   *Othello.* Act i., sc. 11.

When too energetic, or not properly directed, Secretiveness is liable to great abuses. It then leads to a liking for concealment, intrigue, and crooked policy, for their own sakes ; and to a feeling that it is wise and proper to wrap up the purposes of the mind in the profoundest mystery : cunning is mistaken for ability, and deceit for practical wisdom. It may prompt to the use of lies, hypocrisy, intrigue, or dissimulation, as means to gain an end. Persons in whom it predominates, judging of mankind in general by themselves, are never able to see the affairs of the world or the conduct of others in a plain and simple point of view, but imagine life to be a continual stratagem, in which every one is endeavouring to overreach his neighbour. Such persons conceive that the eye of the world is always looking into their breasts, to read the purposes that are there hatched, but the discovery of which they are resolved to prevent. In an argument a secretive man will evade all admissions.

The propensity in some instances finds gratification in the most trifling mysteries : an individual under its predominating influence will conceal his going out, his coming in, his engagements, and all his transactions ; even although communication of these would greatly facilitate domestic arrangements. Dr. Johnson mentions of Pope, that he took so "great delight in artifice, that he endeavoured to attain all his purposes by indirect and unsuspected methods ; he hardly drank tea without a stratagem. He practised his arts on such small occasions, that Lady Bolingbroke used to say in a French phrase, that he played the politician about *cabbages and turnips.*"

Dr. King relates, in his *Anecdotes of his own Times*, (p. 237,) a remarkable instance of secretive conduct in a gentleman named Howe, with whom he was acquainted. One morning Mr. Howe rose very early, and told his wife that he was obliged to go to the Tower to transact some particular business ; and the same day, at noon, she received from him a note, stating that he was under the necessity of going to Holland, and should probably be absent three weeks or a month. He continued absent from her seventeen years, during which time she heard neither of nor from him. Instead, however, of going to Holland, he went no farther than to a street in the vicinity of his house, where he took a room, and remained in disguise during the whole time of his absence. In the second or third year after his disappearance his wife was obliged to apply for an act of Parliament, to procure a proper settlement of his estate, and a provision out of it for herself ; this act he suffered to be solicited and passed, and enjoyed the

---

[*] Ecclus. xxii., 21.   [†] Essays, B. ii., ch. 17. *Cotton's Transl.*

pleasure of observing the progress of it in the votes. About ten years after his disappearance he conceived to make acquaintance with the occupant of a house opposite his wife's dwelling, and frequently dined there; so that he could often see her at the window. He used also to attend the church which she frequented, and chose a seat where he had a view of her, but could not easily be observed himself. "After he returned home," says Dr. King, "he never would confess, even to his most intimate friends, what was the real cause of such a singular conduct: apparently there was none; but whatever it was, he was certainly ashamed to own it." There can be little doubt that a predominant and engrossing Secretiveness was the chief feeling by which he was impelled.

This faculty prompts, says Dr. Gall, the general of an army to the use of stratagems to deceive the enemy, and while it leads him to conceal his own forces and enterprises, and to make false attacks and counterfeit marches. Cicero remarks the difference of generals in this respect. "Among the Carthaginians," says he, "Hannibal, and among our own commanders Quintus Maximus, have the name of men extremely close and secret, silent, dissembling; notably good at stratagems, or setting spies upon an enemy and disappointing their counsels.... There are others, now, so far from this artifice, that they are simple and open, to the degree of not enduring anything but what is done above-board; they will not suffer anything that looks like treachery. These men are the servants of truth and the enemies of fraud."* The same writer observes, that "there is no greater pest in human society than a perverse craft, under the mask of simplicity."†

Mercantile men in whom this organ predominates, occasionally conceal their circumstances from their wives and children, who proceed in the unsuspecting enjoyment of imaginary prosperity, till bankruptcy, like the explosion of a mine, involves them in instantaneous ruin. These individuals generally plead regard to the feelings of their relatives as their excuse; but the distrust implied in such conduct is a greater injury to sensitive minds than the evils they attempt to veil. The real sources of their conduct are an overweening Self-Esteem, which cannot stoop to acknowledge misconduct or misfortune, and an inordinate Secretiveness, inspiring them with an instinctive aversion to candid and unreserved communication. A favourite maxim with such men is, that secrecy is the soul of trade. It is so regarded only in narrow minds, misguided by this propensity.

Persons in whom Secretiveness is large, and who believe that they really conceal their true character from the world, are much startled at the exposure which Phrenology is said to make of the dispositions of the mind; and they feel great difficulty in believing it practicable to compare genuine mental feelings with development of brain, because they imagine that real motives and dispositions are never exhibited in conduct. Such persons err, however, in their estimate even of their own powers of concealment; for Secretiveness does not alter the aim, but affects only the means of obtaining gratification of our ordinary desires: and, besides, if disguise be really the forte of their character, Phrenology has the advantage of them still; for it discovers the organ of Secretiveness large in their brains; and in their very concealment they manifest most powerfully the faculty whose organ is most fully developed.

Innumerable abuses of this propensity occur in the ordinary intercourse of society. How polite, acquiescent, and deferential are some persons in their manners to all who are present; and how severe in their vituperations when the same individuals are gone! This conduct results from Secretiveness and Love of Approbation, aided perhaps by Veneration addressing itself to Love of Approbation in others, and endeavouring to please them by professions of respect. Conscientiousness in such indi-

* De Officiis, lib. 1.   † Ibid., lib. iii.
14*

viduals is always deficient. Many persons would not, for any consideration, mention a disagreeable truth to an acquaintance. This also arises
from an abuse of Secretiveness, combined with great Love of Approbation.
To Mr. Scott is due the merit of throwing great light on the influence
of Secretiveness in producing humour. The power of representing, with
a face of perfect gravity, some ludicrous incident, is one species of
humour. The grave exterior, while the most ludicrous ideas are internally perceived, is a species of slyness, and is clearly attributable to
Secretiveness. This kind of humour also is absolutely addressed to
Secretiveness in others. We, as spectators, see the internal absurdity
through the external gravity, and this gratifies our Secretiveness, which
likes to penetrate disguises assumed by others, as well as to disguise
itself. Another species of humour consists in detecting and exposing
little concealed purposes and intentions in our friends, and holding them
up to view in all their nothingness, when they are mystifying or concealing them as matters of real importance. "The man of humour," says
Mr. Scott, "delights in detecting these little pieces of deception; and
the *ludicrous* effect of this seems to arise from the incongruity which
appears between the real and the assumed character—the contrast between
what is intended to be apparent at the surface, and that which is seen to
be at the bottom."[*] Secretiveness, however, affords only the slyness,
the *savoir faire*, together with the tact of detecting little concealed weak-
nesses implied in humour; and the faculty of Wit is necessary, in addition, to produce ludicrous effect in the representation. Thus, a person
with much Wit and little Secretiveness will not excel in humour, although
he may shine in pure wit. A person, on the other hand, with much
Secretiveness and moderate Wit may excel in humour, although, in
intellectual witty combinations, he may make but an indifferent figure.
It is a curious fact, that the Italians and English, in whom Secretiveness is large, delight in humour, while the French, in whom the organ is
moderate, can scarcely imagine what it is. In conformity with these
differences in national developement, the English and Italians practise a
prudent reserve in their intercourse with strangers, while the French are
open to excess, and communicate even their private affairs to casual
acquaintances. The French also delight to live, and even to die, in
public; while the Englishman shuts himself up in his house, which he
denominates his castle, and debars all the world from observing his conduct. Other faculties contribute to these varieties of taste, but Secretiveness is an essential element in the relish for retirement.
I have uniformly found Secretiveness large in the heads of actors and
artists, of which I have been permitted to examine a considerable number.
In the cast of Miss Clara Fisher's head[†] it will be seen amply developed.
The theory of its effects in aiding the former seems to be this: The
actor must conceal or shade his real character, and put forth the natural
language of an assumed one. Now, Secretiveness will enable him to
suppress the manifestations of all the faculties which are not essential to
the character of the personage whom he, for the time, represents; while,
by withdrawing its restraint from other faculties, it will allow them to develope themselves with full energy. Thus, suppose an actor, in whom
Benevolence and Conscientiousness are large, to be called on to play Iago,
a character in which selfishness and villany predominate, then Secretiveness will enable him to suppress the natural language of his own superior
faculties, while, by withdrawing its influence from Combativeness, Destructiveness, and Self-Esteem, it will permit the most forcible expression

* *Phren. Trans.*, p. 174. See illustrative cases in *Phren. Journ.*, ii., 596,
iv., 503, and viii., 216, 221.
† *Transactions of the Phrenological Society*, p. 281.

of these in looks, tones, and gestures; and this will be Iago to the life. It aids the artist in a similar way. A painter or sculptor, in working a figure, first studies the mental feelings which he intends to portray, then goes to a mirror and produces the expression of them in his own person, and copies it in his picture or block of marble. In this process he resembles an actor, and Secretiveness assists him in the manner before explained.

In this analysis I differ in one point from Mr. Scott. He thinks that Secretiveness confers not only the negative power of suppressing the real character, but also the positive power of calling up, at will, the natural language of such faculties as we wish to exhibit for the time. Thus, some persons are able to load others with expressions of great esteem, attachment, and good will, when internally they hate them. Mr. Scott conceives that Secretiveness enables such individuals not only to disguise their enmity, but to call up, for the occasion, the natural language of Adhesiveness, Benevolence, Veneration, and Love of Approbation, and to use these as instruments of deception. This latter effect appears to me to depend on Imitation and Secretiveness combined.

When both Secretiveness and Cautiousness are very large, there is a tendency to extreme reserve, and even, when little knowledge of the world is possessed, to suspicion and terror of dark designs and sinister plots, hatching on every hand against the unhappy possessor of this combination. In general these plots have no existence beyond the internal feeling produced by those faculties.

Secretiveness, with small Conscientiousness, predisposes to lying, and, combined with Acquisitiveness, to theft. Indeed, Secretiveness is more invariably large in thieves than Acquisitiveness; and it prompts to this crime, probably by the feeling of secrecy which it generates in the mind. It gives the idea that all is hidden, that no eye sees, and that no intellect will be able to trace the fraud. It produces also that capacity for sly cunning which is essential to a thief. An excellent elucidation, by Dr. Andrew Combe, of the effects of Secretiveness, as a constituent element in the character of a thief, will be found in The Phrenological Journal, vol. i., p. 611. The organ is large in David Haggart, and in a variety of executed thieves, whose casts have been obtained. It is very large in Linn, (see cut on p. 108,) who, though ostensibly most artless, contrived to escape from confinement, without giving rise to suspicion, and managed matters so dexterously that no trace of him could be found. In Gottfried and Tardy (pp. 87 and 144) the organ is much developed, and both were excessively cunning. Destructiveness also being very large, they murdered by means of poison, a mode of committing the crime usually preferred by secretive persons. On 3d December, 1823, I visited, in Edinburgh jail, John Reid, a lad of sixteen, under sentence of death (but subsequently respited) for housebreaking and theft. His head was uncommonly large for his years, and the organ of Secretiveness, in particular, was enormously developed. Acquisitiveness also was large, and Conscientiousness deficient. The Reverend Mr. Porteous, chaplain to the jail, mentioned that Reid's power of concealing his thoughts and feelings was most extraordinary, and that daring and secrecy were manifested in his crime in a degree that was almost inconceivable. He had mounted on the shoulders of an accomplice to the second story of a dwelling-house, entered by a window, and, although persons slept in the bed-rooms of that floor, and the lamp in the lobby was burning, proceeded down stairs, reached the dining-room, robbed the side-board of plate, and got clear off without being heard.

Another effect of great Secretiveness, especially when aided by much Firmness, is to produce the power of repressing, to an indefinite extent, all outward expressions of pain, even when amounting to torture. Ann Ross, (whose case is reported by Mr. Richard Carmichael, of Dublin,[*]) with a view to excite the compassion of some pious and charitable ladies, thrust needles into her arm to produce disease, and carried the deception so far as to allow the limb to be amputated without revealing the cause. The needles were found on dissection, and she was more mortified by the discovery of the trick than afflicted by the loss of her arm. She manifested the same faculty in a variety of other deceptions. I examined her head, and Mr. Carmichael presented a cast of it to the Phrenological Society ; and in it the organs of Secretiveness and Firmness are decidedly large. The North American Indians are celebrated for their power of enduring torture, and the same combination occurs in casts of two of their skulls in the Society's collection.[†] It is not large in the negroes, and they are an open-minded race compared with the astutious varieties of mankind. It is very large in the native Peruvians, whose power of concealment is a distinguishing feature in their national character.[‡] In the Laplanders also it is largely developed.[§]

Dr. George Murray Paterson mentions that the Hindoos manifest Secretiveness in a high degree in the form of cunning and duplicity; and the organ is very large in their heads.[||]

This propensity, when predominantly active, produces a close sly look ; the eye rolls from side to side ; the voice is low; the shoulders are drawn up toward the ears, and the footstep is soft and gliding. The movements of the body are toward the side. Sir Walter Scott accurately describes the look produced by this faculty and Cautiousness in the following lines. Speaking of Cormac Doil, he says :

> " For evil seemed that old man's eye,
> Dark and designing, fierce yet shy,
> Still he avoided forward look,
> But slow and circumspectly took
> A circling never-ceasing glance,
> By doubt and cunning mark'd at once ;
> Which shot a mischief-boding ray,
> From under eyebrows shagged and gray."
> Lord of the Isles, Canto iv., p. 24.

When this organ is very large in the head of an author, it produces a curious effect on his style. The different members of his sentences are involved, parenthetical, and often obscure, as if he were in doubt whether he selected the proper place for his expressions, and hesitated between what he ought to put down and what he might leave to be understood. He is also liable to quaintness. Pope's style occasionally indicates this quality, and the faculty was strongly manifested in his character. Dr. Thomas Brown's style also is characterized by Secretiveness, and the organ was large in his head. Croly's poetry presents the expression of it. Goldsmith's writings indicate a very moderate endowment in him. This faculty, by enabling an author skilfully to work up his incidents and events, and to conceal the denouement of his plot or story till the most appropriate time and place for the elucidation, greatly aids him in producing effect. The organ was very large in Sir Walter Scott, and also in Swift and Burns.[¶]

The organ of Secretiveness is possessed by the lower animals, and Dr.

* Phrenological Journal, ii., 42.
† Ibid., ii., 535. Blumenbach, Decas Prima, tab. ix
‡ Robertson's History of America, b. iv.; and Edinburgh Review, ix., 437.
§ Phrenological Journal, ix., 329. Blumenbach, Decas Quinta, p. 2.
|| Trans. of the Phren. Soc., p. 443.
¶ Phrenological Journal, ix., 64.

Gall remarks that it requires a particular study in each species. In the common species of ape, for example, it commences above the origin of the zygomatic arch, and extends forward to nearly the middle of this bone. Its situation is the same in the tiger, cat, and fox. In carnivorous animals also, and in birds distinguished for cunning, this region will in general be found large.

Manifestations of this propensity, clearly attributable to disease of the organ, are described by authors on insanity.* The cunning shown by many of the insane, especially in concealing their true state, has often excited astonishment. Foderé speaks of two patients who had been long confined in the asylum at Marseilles. After an apparent cure of considerable duration, their friends demanded their dismissal. He, however, suspected deception, and determined to hold a long conversation with them. For an hour and a half, during which he avoided the kind of ideas in regard to which he knew them to be insane, they spoke, reasoned, and acted like men of sound judgment. But when he introduced the subject which excited their deranged faculties, their eyes began to sparkle, the muscles of the face to contract, and an evident agitation took place, accompanied with an effort to preserve calmness. They were ordered to be detained. Pinel mentions the cunning and tricks of some lunatics as remarkable. Dr. Marshall† notices the case of a man in Bethlem Hospital in 1789, who fancied he was a great man. "He was very crafty, and used much flattery to the keepers, calling them ' fine men, gentlemen,' especially when he wanted any indulgence ; but when his complacent looks and genteel expressions did not avail him, he became revengeful, made up some plausible story against them, and slyly told it to the steward. When fresh patients came into the house, he always introduced himself to them ; he was very civil to them, and, after gaining their confidence, he tried to get their money from them, which, if he could not do by other means, he had recourse to stratagem to get possession of it."

The regular metaphysicians have not admitted any faculty corresponding to this propensity, nor am I aware that they give any theory of cunning, although it is an obvious ingredient in human nature. The quality, however, is familiarly recognised by a variety of writers. Lord Bacon, in his *Essay on Cunning*, graphically describes a number of the abuses of Secretiveness. "We take cunning," says he, "for a sinister or crooked wisdom, and certainly there is a great difference between a cunning man and a wise man, not only in point of honesty, but in point of ability. There be that can pack the cards, and yet cannot play well ; so there are some that are good in canvasses and factions, that are otherwise weak men." In *Peveril of the Peak* we have the following dialogue : "Your Grace holds his wisdom very high," said the attendant. "*His cunning at least*, I do," replied Buckingham, "which, in court affairs, often takes the weather-gage of wisdom."

The organ is established.

8. ACQUISITIVENESS.

THE organ of this faculty is situated at the anterior inferior angle of the parietal bone. By Dr. Spurzheim it was called Covetiveness ; Sir G. S. Mackenzie suggested the more appropriate name of Acquisitiveness, which Dr. Spurzheim subsequently adopted.

The metaphysicians have not admitted a propensity to acquire, which is gratified by the mere act of acquisition without any ulterior object, as a

* See Dr. A. Combe's *Observations on Mental Derangement*, pp. 182, 250.
† *Morbid Anatomy of the Brain*, p. 192.

faculty of the human mind. Dr. Hutcheson says : "Thus, as soon as we come to apprehend the use of wealth, or power to gratify any of our original desires, we must also desire them ; and hence arises the universality of these desires of wealth and power, *since they are the means of gratifying all other desires.*" In like manner, we are told by Mr. Stewart, that "whatever conduces to the gratification of any natural appetite, or of any natural desire, *is itself desired, on account of the end to which it is subservient;* and by being thus habitually *associated* in our apprehension with agreeable objects, it frequently comes, in process of time, to be regarded as valuable in itself, independently of its utility. It is thus that wealth becomes with many an ultimate object of pursuit ; though, at first, it is undoubtedly valued, merely on account of its subserviency to the attainment of other objects."[*]

The same author says, in another place, that "avarice is a particular modification of the desire of power, arising from the various functions of money in a commercial country. Its influence as an active principle is much strengthened by habit and association."[†]

Dr. Thomas Brown[‡] admits the desire of wealth to be a modification of the desire of power, but he endeavours to show that Mr. Stewart's theory is defective in accounting for avarice, and enters into a most ingenious argument, to explain how that feeling arises from association. He takes *time* into account as an ingredient ; and adduces the example of a boy purchasing an apple. "Before the boy lays out his penny in the purchase of an apple or orange," says he, "it appears to him valuable chiefly as the mode of obtaining the apple or orange. But the fruit, agreeable as it may have been while it lasted, is *soon devoured;* its value, with respect to him, has wholly ceased ; and the penny, he knows, is still in existence, and would have been still *his own*, if the fruit had *not* been purchased. He thinks of the penny, therefore, as *existing now*, and existing without anything which he can oppose to it as an equivalent ; and the feeling of *regret* arises—the wish, that he had *not* made the purchase, and that the penny, as still existing, and equally capable as before of procuring some new enjoyment, had continued in his pocket." This produces " a slight terror of expense, which the habits of many years may strengthen into parsimony."

Nothing can be more ingenious than this speculation, and it is a beautiful instance of the nature of metaphysical science ; but it is not sound. The question occurs, Why is this " slight terror of expense " experienced only by some boys and some men, since association and the love of enjoyment are universal qualities of human nature ?

It is proper to mention, however, that Lord Kames (who has been censured by the regular metaphysicians for admitting too many faculties) recognises the existence of this feeling as a primitive propensity in man, and calls it the "hoarding appetite. Man," says his lordship, " is by nature a *hoarding animal*, having an *appetite* for storing up things of use ; and the sense of property is bestowed on men for securing what they thus store up."[§] He adds, that " the appetite for property, in its nature a great blessing, degenerates into a great curse, when it transgresses the bounds of moderation." And in another work he observes : " The notion of property arises from an innate sense, which teaches even infants to distinguish between *yours* and *mine*."[‖]

The observer of the passion of avarice in real life is not satisfied with such theories as those of Mr. Stewart and Dr. Brown. Dr. King, in his *Anecdotes of his Times*, remarks, that an avaricious man " is *born* and

[*] *Elements*, p. 388.   [†] *Outlines*, p. 92.
[‡] *Lectures*, vol. iii., p. 474.   [§] *Sketches*, B., sect. 2.
[‖] *Loose Hints upon Education*, 2d edit., p. 100.

framed to a sordid love of money, which first appears when he is very young, grows up with him, and increases in middle age, and, when he is old, and all the rest of his passions have subsided, wholly engrosses him." (P. 101.) He mentions Lord Chancellor Hardwick, the Duke of Marlborough, Sir James Lowther, Sir Thomas Colby, and Sir William Smith, as remarkable instances of it.

The metaphysical notions of Mr. Stewart fail entirely to explain the phenomena of avarice, under which passion no enjoyment is sought, except that of accumulating wealth. The character of Trapbois, as drawn in *The Fortunes of Nigel,* and admirably represented on the Edinburgh stage by Mr. Mason, is a personification of the faculty of Acquisitiveness, operating as a blind animal instinct, exalted to the highest degree of energy and activity, and extinguishing every feeling of the mind, except that of fear, which it had cultivated and increased to minister to its protection. This character is recognised as natural; highly coloured, indeed, but true to life in its leading features. It appears absurd, therefore, to ascribe, as the metaphysicians do, so intense a passion to a mere law of association as its source—to an error of the understanding, in mistaking wealth for the objects which it is fitted to obtain. The very essence of the character is a desire for wealth, independent of every purpose of application. Phrenologists have observed that the intensity of the wish to acquire is in proportion to the size of a certain part of the brain, and they therefore regard it as an original propensity of the mind. The organ was discovered in the following manner:

When Dr. Gall was employed in comparing mental manifestations with cerebral developement, he was in the habit of collecting in his house individuals of the lower orders, with the view of more easily discovering the different primitive propensities, which he supposed would be found to operate in them with greater simplicity and vigour than in persons of higher rank. On many occasions the individuals assembled, encouraged by him to familiarity, accused each other of petty larcenies, or of what they styled *chiperies,* and took great pleasure in pointing out those who excelled in such practices; and the *chipeurs* themselves advanced in front of their companions, proud of their superior *savoir-faire.* What particularly attracted his attention was, that some of the men showed the utmost abhorrence of thieving, and preferred starving to accepting any part of the bread and fruit which their companions had stolen; while the *chipeurs* ridiculed such conduct and thought it silly.

To discover whether this tendency to pilfer was connected with any particular cerebral organ, Dr. Gall divided the persons whom he had assembled into three classes: the *first* included the *chipeurs;* the *second,* those who abhorred the very idea of stealing; and the *third,* those who seemed to regard it with indifference. On comparing the heads of these three classes, he found that the most inveterate *chipeurs* had a long prominence extending from the organ of Secretiveness, almost as far as the external angle of the superciliary ridge; and that this region was *flat* in all those who showed a horror of theft—while in those who were indifferent about it, the part was sometimes more and sometimes less developed, but never so much as in the professed thieves: and, on repeating the experiment again and again with a new assemblage, he found the same results uniformly present themselves.*

Having thus ascertained the constancy of the *facts,* the idea naturally

* The effect of the moral sentiments in directing Acquisitiveness is not sufficiently adverted to by Dr. Gall in this description. This organ may be large in an individual, who may nevertheless have an abhorrence of theft, if his organs of Conscientiousness, Benevolence, and Reflection are also large. He will be fond of property, but will desire to obtain it honestly.

occurred to the mind of Dr. Gall, that the propensity to *appropriate* must be somehow connected with the peculiarity of cerebral configuration which had so strongly attracted his notice. It could not be the effect of education, for most of the subjects of his observations had received none. They were the children of nature left to their own resources. Some who detested stealing happened to be precisely those whose education had been most completely neglected. The wants and circumstances of all of them were nearly the same—the examples set before them were the same—and to what causes, therefore, could the difference be ascribed, if not to an original difference of mental constitution?

At this time Dr. Gall was physician to the Deaf and Dumb Institution, where pupils were received from six to fourteen years of age, without any preliminary education. M. May, a distinguished psychologist, then director of the establishment, M. Venus, the teacher, and he, had it thus in their power to make the most accurate observations on the primitive mental condition of these children. Some of them were remarkable for a decided propensity to steal, while others did not show the least inclination to it; some of them were easily reformed, but others were quite incorrigible. The severest punishments were inflicted upon one of them, but without any effect. As he felt himself incapable of resisting temptation, he resolved to be a *tailor*, because, as he said, he could then indulge his inclination with impunity. On examining the heads of all these boys, the same region was found to be uniformly developed in proportion to the endowment of the propensity. Dr. Gall made casts of those of them who were confirmed thieves, in order to compare them with such other heads of thieves or robbers as might afterward fall in his way.

About this time, also, Dr. Gall met with another very decisive proof of the connexion between this propensity and a particular developement of brain. In the house of correction he saw a boy of fifteen years of age, who had been a notorious thief from his earliest infancy. Punishment having had no effect upon him, he was at last condemned to imprisonment for life, as absolutely incorrigible In a portrait of him, in the 26th plate of Dr. Gall's Atlas, a remarkable prominence in the lateral region of the head is conspicuous, corresponding to what is now ascertained to be the organ of Acquisitiveness. The forehead is low, narrow, and retreating, and his intellect is stated to have been exceedingly weak and defective; and hence the ascendency and activity of the propensity in question are easily explained.

The following cuts represent skulls in which the organ of Acquisitiveness is fully and moderately developed:

The instinctive appetite for accumulation, produced by this propensity, when viewed by itself, presents a mean and vulgar aspect, and we are apt to regard the individual in whom it predominates as a base and sordid being, cased in selfishness, and dead to every generous sentiment. But when we view it in its results, it rises vastly in dignity and importance. The first demand of nature is to live and to enjoy; the other feelings of the mind, independently of Acquisitiveness, would prompt man to kill and eat, or to weave and wear, for the satisfaction of his present wants. But if he bounded his industry by his necessities, and lolled in idleness while not employed in indispensable pursuits, he would never become rich. Wealth consists of the savings of industry, after supplying immediate demands. According to the metaphysicians, there is no instinctive propensity in man, prompting him, by a natural impulse, to save and to accumulate; they imagine that the calls of nature for immediate gratification, or the love of power, are the only motives to such exertions. In the faculty of Acquisitiveness, however, the phrenologist perceives an instinct prompting the human being, after his appetites of hunger and thirst are appeased, and his person protected against the elements of heaven, to labour, prompted by the mere delight of accumulating; and to the ceaseless industry which this instinct produces is to be ascribed the wealth with which civilized man is everywhere surrounded. It prompts the husbandman, the artisan, the manufacturer, the merchant to diligence in their several vocations; and, instead of being necessarily the parent only of a sordid appetite, it is, when properly directed, one of the sources of the comforts and elegancies of life. Its regular activity distinguishes civilized man from the savage. The prodigal, who consumes the last shilling which he can command, dies and leaves no useful trace of his existence behind him. The laborious artisan, on the other hand, who, under the impulse of this faculty, consumes only half the produce of his labour, leaves the other half, as a contribution to the stock of national capital, to set in motion the industry of unborn generations. These, if animated by the same spirit, will leave it with new accessions to their posterity; and thus the stream of public prosperity will be swelled, in an increasing ratio, to the remotest periods of time. When, however, the pursuit of wealth becomes the chief business of life, Acquisitiveness deadens the moral sentiments, engrosses the intellect, and debases the whole faculties of the mind.

The propensity takes its direction from the other faculties with which it is combined. Acquisitiveness and Individuality both large, are necessary to a spirited collector of objects in natural history: when it is combined with large Form, Colouring, and Ideality, it takes the direction of pictures; when with large Veneration, it may lead to collecting old coins. In short, in no instance where the wish to acquire and possess is strongly manifested, is this organ deficient; while, on the other hand, in those in whom there is no appetite for accumulation, who allow their substance to slip through their hands, from incapacity to retain it, I have always seen it small.

Mr. Owen, of New Lanark, maintains, that the desire for wealth or individual property is not a natural propensity of the human mind; and, in his own head, this organ (like that of Destructiveness, the feeling attached to which he also denies) is by no means largely developed. So differently do those feel in whom Acquisitiveness is large, that they wish to acquire for the mere sake of acquisition. If a person so endowed be owner of fifty acres, it will give him infinite delight to acquire fifty more; if of one thousand or one hundred thousand, he will still be gratified in adding to their number. His understanding may be perfectly convinced that he already possesses ample store for every enjoyment, and abundant provision against every want; yet, if this faculty be active, he will feel his joys impaired if he ceases to amass. This explains the insatiable nature of the passion for acquiring, and also one source of the disappointment generally experienced by persons whose lives have been devoted to commerce, when they retire from business with a view to enjoy the fruits of their industry. The gratification of Acquisitiveness in accumulating wealth constituted the chief pleasure of their previous lives; and when this propensity ceases to be indulged, and no other faculty has been cultivated with equal ardour, ennui and disgust are the natural and unavoidable results of their new situation.

It has been stated, as an objection to this propensity, that property is an institution of society, and that an organ cannot exist in the brain for a factitious desire. The answer to this argument is, that the idea of property springs from the natural suggestions of the faculty in question; and that the laws of society are the consequences, not the causes, of its existence. Laws are intended to regulate the desires of mankind for possessions: but this purpose clearly supposes such desires antecedently to exist.

Many persons, in whom Benevolence and Love of Approbation are large, as well as Acquisitiveness, can with difficulty believe that the latter influences their feelings. They are so ready to disburse and to bestow that they never accumulate, and hence persuade themselves that they have no tendency to acquire. But such persons are keen in their dealings; they cheapen in making purchases, know where bargains are to be obtained, and, on consulting their own minds, will find that schemes for acquiring property frequently haunt their imaginations. They are also prone to admire the rich. Persons, on the contrary, in whom the organ is small, think of everything with more interest, and pursue every object with more avidity, than wealth. They may be industrious in order to live, but there is no intense energy in their pursuit of gain; and their fancies, in building castles in the air, rarely erect palaces of gold, or place happiness in hoards of accumulated riches.

The effects of this faculty are greatly modified by the strength of Self-Esteem. Acquisitiveness desires to *acquire;* Self-Esteem produces the *love of self;* the two conjoined give rise to the love of acquisition for self-gratification; and if both organs be large, the individual will have a strong tendency to sordid selfishness, unless the moral powers be active and energetic. The passion for *uniques* also seems to arise from this combination.

Dr. Gall observes, that the negroes are little prone to steal, and that the organ is moderately developed in them. He had an opportunity of observing, among the Spanish troops, that both the Arragonese and Castilians have the anterior part of the temporal region a good deal flattened, denoting a small Acquisitiveness; and he was assured that they are faithful servants, and equally incapable of stealing and of lying. The Kalmuck's, again, are the very opposite. They are renowned for thieving and bad faith; and, in accordance with this, Blumenbach, in describing the Kalmuck skull, observes that it is almost globular, and projects in the region of Acquisitiveness—"*globose fere calvaria forma*"—"*capita ad latera extantia.*" Dr. Gall possessed two Kalmuck skulls, both corresponding with Blumenbach's description. Dr. Spurzheim also tells us, "that a young Kalmuck, brought to Vienna by Count Stahrenberg, became melancholy, because his confessor, who instructed him in religion and morality, had forbidden him to steal. He got permission to steal, on condition that he should give back what he had stolen. The young man, profiting by this permission, stole his confessor's watch during high mass, but joyfully returned it after mass was over."

It is difficult to conceive a miser without a great endowment of this propensity, although an individual may be a thief with a moderate portion of it. Avarice arises from Acquisitiveness, raised to the height of a passion. Theft implies a want of regulating and directing influence from the moral faculties, as much as an excessive and intense desire to acquire property for the sake of possessing it. Strong sensual propensities, which cannot be gratified without money, may lead individuals to resort to theft as a means of supplying their wants, without the love of property itself being strong; but Conscientiousness must be weak, before such an expedient can be resorted to.

The existence of this organ throws light on the tendency to steal, which some individuals, whose external circumstances place them far above temptation, manifest in a remarkable degree. In them it seems to be in a state of diseased activity, and not to be controlled by the moral and reflecting faculties. Dr. Gall mentions several cases of diseased affections of this organ. M. Kneisler, governor of the prison of Prague, spoke to him and Dr. Spurzheim about the wife of a rich merchant, who stole continually from her husband in the most adroit manner, and who was at last shut up in a house of correction, which she had scarcely left, when she stole again, and was again confined. She was condemned to a third and longer imprisonment, and again commenced her operations in the jail itself. With the utmost address, she made a hole in the stove which heated the apartment where the money was deposited, and committed repeated depredations, which were soon noticed. Every means were adopted to detect the offender, and bells were suspended at the doors and windows, but all in vain. At length a spring-gun was set, the wire of which was connected with the strong box. She was so dreadfully frightened by its explosion, that she had not time to escape through the stove. At Copenhagen Drs. Gall and Spurzheim saw an incorrigible thief, who sometimes distributed the produce of his larcenies to the poor; and, in another place, a robber, who was in confinement for the seventh time, assured them, with sorrow, that he felt himself unable to act otherwise. He begged to be detained in prison, and to be provided with the means of supporting himself.

At Munster a man was condemned to imprisonment for eight years, on account of some robberies: he was no sooner liberated than he committed fresh depredations, and was then imprisoned for life. Sixteen years afterward he revealed a conspiracy which had been formed among the criminals, and it was proposed to reward him by setting him free. The judge objected to this, that it would be dangerous to do so, as the man himself had previously assured him that his thievish propensity was so rooted in his constitution that he could not by any possibility resist it. About a year afterward he escaped from prison, betook himself to his old practices, and was again arrested; shortly after which he hanged himself. "During ten years that I have known this man in the prison," said Werneking, from whom Drs. Gall and Spurzheim got these details, "he was remarkable for activity, and also for devotion during divine service; but I learned, after his death, that he had constantly been committing theft, even in the prison itself."

Dr. Gall mentions, that among the young men confined in one of the prisons of Berlin (Stadtvogtey) one in particular attracted the attention of Dr. Spurzheim and himself. They strongly recommended that he should never be set at liberty, as they thought it impossible he could abstain from stealing. They explained their opinions to the gentlemen who accompanied them, and, on examining the registers, the latter were much surprised to find that the man had from infancy manifested the strongest tendency to thieving. The organs of the higher sentiments were extremely deficient, while that of Acquisitiveness was developed in the highest degree. There was, moreover, an immense endowment of Secretiveness. The man was little and deformed; his forehead "villanously low," retreating backward immediately above the eyebrows; but the lateral regions, or temples, were broad and prominent. In such a case no phrenologist would hesitate to give the same advice.

In the prison at Bern Drs. Gall and Spurzheim saw a rickety and badly-organized boy of twelve years of age, who could not refrain from stealing ; and who, with his pockets filled with his own bread, purloined that of others. At Haina the officers spoke to them about an incorrigible robber, named Fesselmayer, whom no punishment could amend. He stole in prison to such an extent, that a mark was put upon his arm, that all might be upon their guard against him. Before seeing him, Drs. Gall and Spurzheim stated what his developement ought to be, and their prediction was verified at the first glance. He had the appearance of being sixteen, although he was in reality twenty-six years of age. His head was round, and about the size of that of an infant of one year. He was, moreover, deaf and dumb.

Mr. Schiotz, a Danish magistrate, reports the case of an incorrigible thief, in whom he found the organ of Acquisitiveness very large.*

Numerous examples of the diseased activity of this propensity occur in all lunatic asylums, and afford strong proof of the independent existence of the faculty and organ. Pinel tells us, that it is a matter of common observation, that men who, in their lucid intervals, are justly considered as models of probity, cannot refrain from stealing and cheating during the paroxysm ; and Dr. Gall gives four cases of women, who, in their ordinary state, had no such tendency, but when pregnant manifested it in a high degree.

Two citizens of Vienna attracted his notice, both of whom had led irreproachable lives previously to becoming insane. After that time both were distinguished for an extraordinary inclination to steal. They wandered over the hospital from morning to night, picking up whatever they could lay their hands upon—straw, rags, clothes, wood, &c,—which they carefully concealed in the apartment which they inhabited in common ; and, although lodged in the same chamber, they stole from each other. In both the organ was very much developed. I have seen several patients in asylums for the insane, in whom the propensity to steal was a predominant trait, and the organ was largely developed in them all.

M. Esquirol, physician to the Salpétrière of Paris, gave Dr. Gall an account of a knight at Malta, who had quitted the army at the beginning of the French revolution, and who, from excessive indulgence and disappointed love, had become weak in intellect, violent in temper, and at last a thief. On his way to M. Esquirol's asylum he contrived to steal spoons, covers, &c., from the inns at which he dined. He then went about accompanied by a servant, and not unfrequently refreshed himself in coffee-houses, and, instead of paying, put the cup, saucer, and spoon into his pocket, and walked away. In other respects he was sufficiently reasonable. This inclination to theft was cured, although his intellect remained weak.

Acrel mentions a young man who was trepanned, in consequence of a severe wound on the temple, in the region of the organ of Acquisitiveness. After his dismissal from the hospital, he manifested an irresistible propensity to steal: after committing several larcenies, he was imprisoned, and would have been condemned, had not Acrel declared him insane.

"There are persons," says that accurate and philosophical observer and physician, Dr. Rush, of Philadelphia,† "who are moral to the highest degree as to certain duties, but who, nevertheless, live under the influence of some one vice. In one instance a woman was exemplary in her obedience to every command of the moral law except one—*she could not refrain from stealing*. What made this vice more remarkable was, *that she was in easy circumstances, and not addicted to extravagance in any-*

king. Such was the propensity to this vice, that, when she could lay her hands upon nothing more valuable, she would often, at the table of a friend, fill her pockets secretly with bread. She both confessed and lamented her crime." A case of the same kind is recorded in *The Phrenological Journal ;* and Montaigne refers to similar instances which had fallen under his own observation.†

The *Journal de Paris* of 29th March, 1816, states, that " an ex-commissary of police, Beau-Conseil, has just been condemned to eight years' confinement and hard labour, and to the pillory, for having, when still in office, stolen some pieces of plate from an inn. The accused persisted to the last in an *odd* enough species of defence. He did not deny the crime, but he attributed it to mental alienation, occasioned by wounds which he had received at Marseilles in 1815." Dr. Gall observes, that if the previous conduct of Beau-Conseil was irreproachable, and if he really did receive a wound in the head, either his counsel was inexcusable in not making the defence available, or the court was blameable for not listening to it.

This propensity is found also in the lower animals. Lord Kames observes, that " the beavers perceive the timber they store up to be their property ; and the bees seem to have the same perception with regard to their winter provision of honey." Dr. Gall mentions a variety of the lower animals which manifest the sense of property. The same pair of storks, swallows, nightingales, and red-breasts return, in spring or in autumn, to the same country in which they had passed the season in the preceding year, and establish themselves, the storks on the same steeples, the swallows under the same roofs, and the nightingales in the same bushes. If another pair of birds attempt to seize the place already appropriated, war is immediately waged against them, and the intruders are forced to depart. Cows, returning from the pasturage, occupy each, its own stall in the byre, and defend it.‡ The cat and dog, in hiding food, to be used when hunger returns—and the squirrel, hamster, and jackdaw, which collect provisions for the winter—undoubtedly have the notion of property in the stores they accumulate. These animals, however, do not enact laws ; and the sense of property is in them clearly an instinct of nature. In the human race, says Dr. Gall, the process is the same : Nature inspires the mind with the notion of property, and laws are made to protect it.

The organ of Acquisitiveness is established.

9. CONSTRUCTIVENESS.

THIS organ is situated at that part of the frontal bone immediately above the spheno-temporal suture. Its appearance and situation vary slightly, according to the developement of the neighbouring parts. If the zygomatic process is very projecting, or if the middle lobes of the brain, or the forehead in general, or the organs of Language and Order in particular, are greatly developed, its size is less easily distinguished. The leading object ought to be to determine the actual size of each organ, and not its mere prominence ; and, on this account, it is proper farther to notice, that, if the base of the brain is narrow, this organ holds a situation a little higher than usual, and there will then frequently be found a slight depression at the external angle of the eye, between the zygomatic process and the organ in question, especially when the muscles are thin. In such cases it has sometimes appeared as high up as Tune generally occurs. This slight variation from uniformity of situation occurs in the distribution of all the parts of the body : but the anatomist is not, on this account, embarrassed in his

* Vol. ix., p 459.　　　　　　　　† *Essays*, B. ii., ch. 8.
　　‡ This, however, may arise from the love of place.

operations; for the aberration never exceeds certain limits, and he acquires, by experience, the tact of recognising the part by its general appearance.

It has been objected, that the elevation or depression of this part of the brain depends on the force with which the temporal muscles, which lie over it, have acted in the individual: carnivorous animals, it is said, which masticate bones, possess those muscles in a very powerful degree, and in consequence have narrow heads, and little brain in the region of this organ. The answer to this is fourfold   First, carnivorous animals do not build, and the organ in question is wanting in them. The absence of the organ, the narrowness of their head, and their want of constructive power are facts in exact accordance with Phrenology. Secondly, the beaver cuts timber with its teeth, and its temporal muscles act with great energy; yet the organ is large, the head is broad, and the animal is highly constructive —all which circumstances harmonize with our doctrine, and contradict that of the objectors.   Thirdly, in the human race the size of the head, at the region in question, does not bear a proportion to the force with which mastication is performed; for some individuals, who live chiefly on slops, and chew little, have narrow heads and weak constructive talents, while others, who eat hard viands, have broad heads, and manifest great mechanical skill.   And, fourthly, the actual size of the head in this quarter, from whatever cause it arises, bears a regular proportion to the actual endowment of constructive ability.

The temporal muscles differ in thickness in different persons, and the phrenologist ought to desire the individual observed to move the lower jaw, and, while he does so, to feel the muscle, and allow for its size.   The uncertainty in regard to the dimensions of the temporal muscle, renders it unsafe to predicate the size of the organs of Constructiveness and Acquisitiveness from casts of the head, unless information as to the thickness of the fleshy fibres be communicated.   This organ, therefore, is best established by examining living heads, or skulls, or casts of skulls.

When Dr. Gall first turned his attention to the talent for construction, manifested by some individuals, he had not discovered the fact that every primitive faculty is connected with a particular part of the brain as its organ; and, on this account, he directed his observations to the whole heads of great mechanicians.   He was frequently struck with the circumstance, that the heads of such artists were as broad in the temporal region as at the cheek-bones.   This, however, although occurring frequently, was not a uniform characteristic; and hence he was led by degrees to believe, that the talent depended on a particular power.   In order to find out an indication of it in the head, he sought acquaintance with men of distinguished mechanical genius wherever he found them, studied the forms of their heads, and moulded them.   He soon met with some in whom the diameter from temple to temple was greater than that from the one zygomatic bone to the other; and at last found two celebrated mechanicians, in whom there appeared two swellings, round and distinct, at the temples.   These heads convinced him that it is not the circumstance of equality in the zygomatic and temporal diameters which indicates a genius for mechanical construction, but a round protuberance in the temporal region, situated in some individuals a little behind, in others a little behind and above, the eye.   This developement is always found in concomitance with great constructive talent, and when the zygomatic diameter is equal to it, then there is a parallelism of the face; but, as the zygomatic bone is not connected with the organ, and projects more or less in different individuals, this form of countenance is not invariably the concomitant of constructive talent, and ought not be taken as the measure of the developement of the organ.

Having thus obtained some idea of the seat and external appearance of the organ, Dr. Gall assiduously multiplied observations At Vienna some gentlemen of distinction brought to him a person, concerning whose talents they solicited his opinion. He stated that he ought to have a great tendency toward mechanics. The gentlemen imagined that he was mistaken, but the subject of the experiment was greatly struck with this observation: he was the famous painter Unterbergen. To show that Dr. Gall had judged with perfect accuracy, he declared that he had always had a passion for the mechanical arts, and that he painted only for a livelihood. He carried the party to his house, where he showed them a multitude of machines and instruments, some of which he had invented, and others improved. Besides, Dr. Gall remarks that the talent for design, so essential to a painter, is connected with the organ of Constructiveness, so that the art which he practised publicly was a manifestation of that faculty.*

Several of Dr. Gall's auditors spoke to him of a man who was gifted with an extraordinary talent for mechanics ; Gall described to them beforehand what form of head he ought to have, and they went to visit him : it was the ingenious mathematical instrument-maker, Lindner, at Vienna ; and his temples rose out in two little rounded irregular prominences. Dr. Gall had previously found the same form of head in the celebrated mechanician and astronomer, David, Augustine friar, and in the famous Voigtlænder, mathematical instrument-maker. At Paris, Prince Schwartzenberg, then Minister of Austria, wished to put Drs. Gall and Spurzheim to the test. When they rose from table, he conducted Dr. Gall into an adjoining apartment, and showed him a young man : without speaking a word, he and the Prince rejoined the company, and he request Dr. Spurzheim to go and examine the young man's head. During his absence, Dr. Gall told the company what he thought of the youth. Dr. Spurzheim immediately returned, and said that he believed him to be a great mechanician, or an eminent artist in some constructive branch. The prince, in fact, had brought him to Paris on account of his great mechanical talents, and supplied him with the means of following out his studies.

Dr. Gall adds, that, at Vienna, and in the whole course of his travels, he had found this organ developed in mechanicians, architects, designers, and sculptors in proportion to their talent.

He mentions, that, at Mulhausen, the manufacturers do not receive into their employment any children except those who, from an early age, have displayed a talent for the arts, in drawing or clipping figures ; because they know, from experience, that such children alone become expert and intelligent workmen.

* Dr. Scheel, of Copenhagen, had attended a course of Dr. Gall's lectures at Vienna, from which city he went to Rome. One day he entered abruptly, when Dr. Gall was surrounded by his pupils, and, presenting to him the cast of a skull, asked his opinion of it. Dr. Gall instantly said, that he " had never seen the organ of Constructiveness so largely developed as in the head in question." Scheel continued his interrogatories. Dr. Gall then pointed out also a large developement of the organs of Amativeness and Imitation. " How do you find the organ of Colouring ?"—" I had not previously adverted to it," said Gall, " for it is only moderately developed." Scheel replied, with much satisfaction, " that it was a cast of the skull of Raphael." The skull from which the cast was taken was preserved in the Academy of St. Luke, at Rome, and was universally mentioned as being that of Raphael ; so that Dr. Scheel acted in perfect good faith on this occasion. It has been since discovered that the skull was not that of Raphael. Dr. Gall merely stated the developement which he observed in it ; and it remains as striking an example of that developement as ever. As, however, the mental qualities of the individual are unknown, it affords no evidence for or against Phrenology, and I therefore omit farther mention of it in this edition. It is now said to have been the skull of Adjutorio, a celebrated amateur in the fine arts, who founded St. Luke's Academy. See *Phrenological Journal*, vol. ix., p. 92.

Dr. Spurzheim mentions the case of a milliner of Vienna, who was remarkable for constructive talent in her art, and in whom the organ is large. A cast of her skull is in the Phrenological Society's collection, and it presents two small round eminences at the situation of the organ.

ANCIENT GREEK.   NEW HOLLANDER.

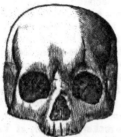 

These figures represent the skulls of an ancient Greek and a New Hollander. In the New Hollanders the skull at Constructiveness falls greatly within the line of the cheek-bones ; while in the Greek the skull swells out at that organ. "The natives of New Holland," says Sir Walter Scott, "are, even at present, in the very lowest scale of humanity, and ignorant of every art which can add comfort or decency to human life. These unfortunate savages use no clothes, construct no cabins nor huts, and are ignorant even of the manner of chasing animals or catching fish, unless such of the latter as are left by the tide, or which are found on the rocks."

When Dr. Spurzheim was in Edinburgh in 1817, he visited the workshop of Mr. James Milne, brass-founder, (a gentleman who himself displays no small ingenuity in his trade, and in whom Constructiveness is largely developed,) and examined the heads of his apprentices. The following is Mr. Milne's account of what took place upon the occasion :

"On the first boy presented to Dr. Spurzheim, on his entering the shop, he observed, that he would excel in anything he was put to. In this he was perfectly correct, as he was one of the cleverest boys I ever had. On proceeding farther, Dr. Spurzheim remarked of another boy, that he would make a good workman. In this instance also his observation was well-founded. An elder brother of his was working next him, who, he said, would also turn out a good workman, but not equal to the other. I mentioned that, in point of fact, the former was the better, although both were good. In the course of farther observations, Dr. Spurzheim remarked of others, that they ought to be ordinary tradesmen, and they were so. At last he pointed out one, who, he said, ought to be of a different cast, and of whom I would never be able to make anything as a workman, and this turned out to be too correct ; for the boy served an apprenticeship of seven years, and, when done, he was not able to do one-third of the work performed by other individuals, to whose instruction no greater attention had been paid. So much was I struck with Dr. Spurzheim's observations, and so correct have I found the indications presented by the organization to be, that, when workmen, or boys to serve as apprentices, apply to me, I at once give the preference to those possessing a large Constructiveness ; and if the deficiency is very great, I would be disposed to decline receiving them, being convinced of their inability to succeed."

The organ of this faculty is very largely developed in Mr. Brunel, the celebrated engineer of the Thames Tunnel, and the inventor of machinery for making blocks for the rigging of ships, by means of steam ; and who has, besides, shown a great talent for mechanics in numerous departments of art. It is large in Edwards, an eminent engraver; in Wilkie, Haydon, and J. F. Williams, celebrated painters; in Sir W. Herschel, whose great discoveries in astronomy arose from the excellence of his telescopes, made by his own hands; and in Mr. Samuel Joseph, an eminent sculptor. Masks of all these individuals are to be seen in the Phrenological Society's collection. In the late Sir Henry Raeburn, who was bred a goldsmith, but became a painter by the mere impulse of nature, without teaching and without opportunities of study, I observed it large. It is large also in Mr. Scoular, a very promising young sculptor, who displayed this talent at a very early age. I have noticed it large in all the eminent operative surgeons of Edinburgh, in distinguished engravers, and also in cabinet-makers and tailors who excel in their art. It and Form are large in children who are fond of clipping and drawing figures. The organ is well developed in many of the Esquimaux, who show considerable constructive talent.* It is large in most of the ancient Greeks. The busts also of eminent artists of former ages display a great developement of this organ; in particular, in that of Michael Angelo, in the church of Santa Croce, at Florence, the breadth from temple to temple is enormous. The reflective organs, situated in the forehead, and likewise Ideality, are in him very large; and these add understanding and taste to the talent and love of constructing works of art.

On the other hand, I possess a cast of the head of a very ingenious friend, distinguished for his talents as an author, who has often complained of so great a want of constructive ability, that he found it difficult even to learn to write; and, in his head, although large in other dimensions, there is a conspicuous deficiency in the region of Constructiveness. Among the negative instances are the casts and skulls of the New Hollanders, in the Phrenological Society's collection, which are remarkably narrow in the situation of this organ; and their low condition in the constructive arts has been already mentioned. Contrasted with them are the Italians and French. An accurate and intelligent phrenologist authorizes me to state, that, during his travels in Italy, he observed a full developement of Constructiveness to be a general feature in the Italian head; and the same holds, but in a less degree, in the French. Both of these nations possess this organ and constructive ingenuity in a higher degree than the English.

These are positive facts in regard to the organ of Constructiveness. I shall now advert to a few circumstances illustrative of the existence of a talent for construction, as a distinct power of the mind apart from the general faculties of the understanding; from which the reader may form an opinion of the extent to which the phrenological views agree or disagree with the common phenomena of human nature. This is the more necessary, as metaphysical philosophers in general do not admit a primitive faculty of Constructiveness, and hold the mechanical arts to be the result exclusively of reflection.

Among the lower animals, it is clear that the ability to construct is not in proportion to the endowment of understanding. The dog, horse, and elephant, which in sagacity approach very closely to the more imperfect specimens of the human race, never, in any circumstances, attempt a work of art. The bee, the beaver, and the swallow, on the contrary, with far less general intellect, rival the productions of man. Turning our attention to the human race, we observe that, while, among children of the same family or the same school, some are fond of a variety of amusements unconnected with art, others constantly devote themselves, during their leisure hours, to designing with chalk various objects on the boards of books, walls, and paper; or occupy themselves with fashioning in wax

* *Phren. Journ.*, viii., 425.

or clay, or clipping in paper, the figures of animals, trees, and men. Children of a very tender age have sometimes made models of a ship of war, which the greatest philosopher would in vain strive to imitate. The young Vaucanson had only seen a clock through the window of its case, when he constructed one in wood, with no other utensils than a bad knife. A gentleman with whom I was intimately acquainted constructed, at an early age, a mill for making pot-barley, and actually set it in operation by a small jet from the main stream of the Water of Leith. Lebrun drew designs with chalk at three years of age, and at twelve he made a portrait of his grandfather. Sir Christopher Wren, at thirteen, constructed an ingenious machine for representing the course of the planets. Michael Angelo, at sixteen, executed works which were compared with those of antiqity.[*]

The greater number of eminent artists have received no education capable of accounting for their talents; but, on the contrary, have frequently been compelled to struggle against the greatest obstacles, and to endure the most distressing privations, in following out their natural inclinations.[†] Other individuals, again, educated for the arts, and on whom every advantage has been lavished, have never surpassed mediocrity. Frequently, too, men whom circumstances have prevented from devoting themselves to arts to which they were naturally inclined, have occupied themselves with mechanics as a pastime and amusement. An eminent Scotch barrister, in whom Constructiveness is largely developed, has informed me, that occasionally, in the very act of composing a written pleading on the most abstruse questions of law, vivid conceptions of particular pieces of mechanism, or of new applications of some mechanical principle, dart into his mind, and keep their place so as to interrupt the current of his voluntary thoughts, until he has imbodied them in a diagram or description, after which he is able to dismiss them, and proceed with his professional duties. Leopold I., Peter the Great, and Louis XVI. constructed locks. The organ of Constructiveness was largely developed in the late Lord President Blair of the Court of Session, as appears from a cast of his head, his statue, and also his portraits: and it is said that he had a private workshop at Avendale, in Linlithgowshire, in which he spent many hours during the vacations of the court, constructing pieces of mechanism with his own hands. The predilection of such individuals for the practice of mechanical arts cannot reasonably be ascribed to want, or to their great intellectual faculties; for innumerable objects, more directly fitted to gratify or relieve the understanding, must have presented themselves to their notice, had they not been led by a special liking to the course they followed, and felt themselves inspired by a particular talent for such avocations. Not only so, but examples of an opposite description are met with; namely, of men of great depth and comprehensiveness of intellect, who are destitute of manual dexterity. Lucian and Socrates renounced sculpture, because they felt that they possessed no genius for it. M. Schurer, formerly Professor of Natural Philosophy at Strasburg, broke every article he touched. There are persons who can never learn to make a pen or sharpen a razor; and Dr. Gall mentions that two of his friends, the one an excellent teacher, the other "grand ministre," were passionately fond of gardening, but he could never teach them to ingraft a tree. Montaigne says of himself—"I cannot handsomely fold up a letter, nor could ever make a pen, or carve at table worth a pin, nor saddle a horse."[‡] As a contrast to these, men of conside-

[*] Gall *Sur les Fonctions du Cerveau,* tome v.
[†] A striking case of this nature is reported in *The Phrenological Journal,* i., 509.
[‡] *Essays,* B. ii., ch. 17, Cotton's Transl.

rable mechanical dexterity are frequently found to be remarkably destitute of talent for every other pursuit, and to possess very limited understandings.

Cases of disease also tend to prove that Constructiveness is a special faculty, and not the result merely of general intellect. Dr. Rush men·tions two cases in which a talent for design had unfolded itself during a fit of insanity ; and he adds, that there is no insane hospital in which examples are not found of individuals who never showed the least trace of mechanical talent previously to their loss of understanding ; but who have subsequently constructed the most curious machines, and even ships completely equipped.* Fonderé, in his *Traité du Goitre et de la Cretinisme,* p. 133, remarks, "That, by an inexplicable singularity, some of these individuals, (Cretins,) endowed with so weak minds, are born with a particular talent for copying paintings, for rhyming, or for music. I have known several who taught themselves to play passably on the organ and harpsicord ; others who understood, without ever having had a master, the repairing of watches and the construction of some piece·of mechanism." He adds, that these powers could not be attributed to the intellect, for the individuals in question not only could not read books which treated of the principles of mechanics, " mais ils etaient deroutés lorsqu'on en parlait, *et ne se perfectionnaient jamais.*"

In the lower animals Nature has implanted a propensity to construct, but in them it is always specific ; while in man a similar tendency is found, but general in its application. For example, nature inspires the beaver not only with a desire to build, but also with an instinctive and unerring impulse, independent of acquired knowledge and experience, to construct a dwelling of a particular form ; and the power of the animal to build is confined entirely within the limited sphere of its intuitive inspiration. Man, on the other hand, has received from Nature a propensity to construct, but not a limited instinct to build a house or a ship, or to weave a coat or a vest, or, in short, to.fashion any *particular* object. The beaver possesses no general reflecting powers to direct its propensity, and hence it was necessary to inspire it not only with a desire to build, but with a plan of architecture. To man, on the contrary, reflection and the power of amassing knowledge are given ; and the faculties of the understanding enable him to invent plans, and to employ his impulse to construct in a great variety of ways.

Constructiveness, then, confers only the love and power of constructing in general ; and the results which it is capable of producing are influenced by other faculties. For example, intellect alone, with extreme deficiency of Constructiveness, will never enable an individual to become an expert handicraftsman ; but, if the developement of Constructiveness be equal in two individuals, and the intellectual organs be large in the one and small in the other, the former will accomplish much higher designs than the latter. And the reason is obvious. The primitive talent for construction is the same in both ; but the one, by means of his intellect, is endowed with the perception of the relation of means to an end, and hence is able to select, from the wide circle of nature and of art, every object and appliance that may extend and elevate his conceptions and aid their execution ; while the latter is limited to a mere mechanical talent, never stretching beyond the imitation of objects previously existing.

The word *Constructiveness* has been objected to as not sufficiently comprehensive. To construct is to take detached materials and put them together, so as to form a single object out of the whole. Thus we may be correctly said to construct a house, a machine, or a ship. The faculty, however, goes farther than this ; it seems to be a tendency to *fashion* in

* Rush's *Medical Inquiries and Observations on the Diseases of the Mind.* Philadelphia, 1812. P. 153.

general—in other words, to alter the shape or appearance of objects—whether by combining detached materials, or by chipping off fragments, or by drawing lines and laying on colours. It is not the province of this faculty to *invent*, but merely to *fashion* or *configurate.*[*] Invention is an act of the understanding alone ; so that we find ingenious inventors who are destitute of mechanical skill, and excellent handicraftsmen without any power of invention. It is probable, however, that Constructiveness, when powerful, stimulates the understanding to invent what will give itself agreeable employment in the process of construction. When the organ of Weight is large, machinery is the department preferred.[†]

Dr. Gall mentions, that it is difficult to discover the position of this organ in some of the lower animals, on account of the different arrangement of the convolutions, their small size, and the total absence of several of those which are found in man. The organ of Tune in the lower creatures is situated toward the middle of the arch of the eyebrow, and that of Constructiveness lies a little behind it. In the hamster, marmot, and beaver, of whose crania he gives plates, it is easily recognised ; and at the part in question the skulls of these animals bear a close resemblance to each other. In the beaver and other *rodentia*, the organ will be found immediately above and before the base of the zygomatic arch, and the greater the talent for construction the more this region of their head projects. The rabbit burrows under ground, and the hare lies upon the surface ; yet their external members are the same. On comparing their skulls, this region will be found more developed in the rabbit than in the hare. The same difference is perceptible between the crania of birds which build nests, and those of such as do not build. Indeed the best way to become acquainted with the appearance of the organ in the lower animals is, to compare the heads of animals of the same species which build, with those of such as do not manifest this instinct ; the hare, for example, with the rabbit, or birds which make nests with those which do not. Between the brains of animals of different species it is impossible to make a very accurate comparison.

The organ is established.

GENUS II.—SENTIMENTS.

THIS genus of faculties embraces certain feelings which correspond to the " emotions " of the metaphysicians. They differ from intellectual perceptions, in being accompanied with a peculiar vividness, which every one understands, but which it is impossible to express by any verbal definition.[‡] They may be excited by the presentment of the external objects naturally related to them, as danger is to fear, and august appearance to reverence ; or by the spontaneous activity of the organs. Dr. Spurzheim has named these faculties Sentimenta, because they produce an emotion or feeling of a certain kind, joined with a propensity to act ; but, as shown in the Appendix No II , the detail of his classification is here by no means accurate. Several of them are common to man and the lower animals ; others are peculiar to man. The former, styled the Inferior or Lower Sentiments, shall be first treated of.

* Mr. Richard Edmondson, of Manchester, in an essay, " On the Functions of the Organs called Weight and Constructiveness," published in the ninth volume of *The Phrenological Journal*, p. 624, views the elementary function of the organ in a new light, but I am not yet satisfied of the accuracy of his analysis.
† See *Phrenological Journal*, ii., 415; and iii., 190.
‡ *Lectures* by Dr. Thomas Brown. Lecture 52.

1. *Sentiments common to Man and the lower Animals.*

10. SELF-ESTEEM.

THIS organ is situated at the back part of the mesial region of the vertex, where the coronal surface begins to decline toward the occiput, and a little above the posterior or sagittal angle of the parietal bones. When it is large the head rises far upward and backward from the ear, in the direction of it.

POPE ALEXANDER VI.[*]

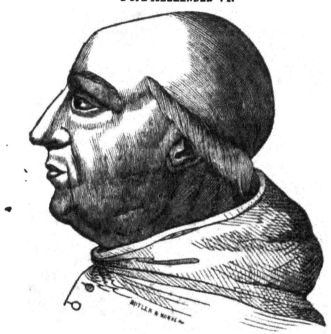

Dr. Gall gives the following account of the discovery of the organ : A beggar attracted his attention by his extraordinary manners. He reflected on the causes which, independently of an absolutely vicious conformation or of misfortunes, could reduce a man to mendicity, and believed that he had found one of the chief of them in levity and waht of foresight. The form of the head of the beggar in question confirmed him in this opinion. He was young and of an agreeable exterior, and the organ of Cautiousness was very little developed. Dr. Gall moulded his head, and, on examining it with attention, remarked, in the upper and back part of the 'middle line, a prominence extending from above downward, which could arise only from developement of the cerebral parts there situated. He had not previously observed this prominence in other heads ; and, on this account, he was very anxious to discover what it indicated. The head, moreover, was small, and announced neither strong feelings nor much intellect. After many questions, addressed to him with a view to discover the re-

[*] Phrenological observations on the head and character of this arrogant and dissolute pope will be found in Dr. Spurzheim's *Phrenology in Connexion with the Study of Physiognomy*, p. 71. It was Alexander who assumed the power of dividing the new world between the kings of Spain and Portugal, granting to the former the territory on the west of an imaginary line running from north to south through the Atlantic Ocean.

markable traits of his character, Dr. Gall requested him to relate his history. The beggar said that he was the son of a rich merchant, from whom he had inherited a considerable fortune ; that he had always been so proud as not to be able to condescend to apply to business, either for the preservation of his paternal fortune, or to acquire a new one ; and that this unhappy pride was the only cause of his misery. This, says Dr. Gall, " called to my recollection those persons who forbear to cut their nails, with the view of supporting the idea that they never need to work." He made several remarks to the beggar, and showed him that he doubted his veracity ; but the man always reverted to his pride, and seriously stated, that even now he could not resolve to follow any kind of labour. Although it was difficult to conceive how pride should cause any one to prefer begging to working,* yet Dr. Gall was led, by this person's reiterated assurances, to reflect upon the sentiment, and to observe the organ ; and he found, at length, incontrovertible proofs of their connexion.

He mentions a variety of cases in illustration, of which I select only the following :

A young man, endowed with faculties above mediocrity, had manifested, from his infancy, insupportable pride. He constantly maintained that he was of too good a family to work, or apply himself to anything. Nothing could free him from this absurdity ; he was even put, for eighteen months, into a house of correction at Hainar. A physician of Vienna, an otherwise amiable man, carried the feeling of pride to such a height, that every time when called to a consultation, even with practitioners older than himself, or with public professors, he regularly took the precedence, both in entering and coming out of the apartment. When any document was to be subscribed, he insisted on affixing his signature first. He had connected himself with the director of the great hospital, but solely, as he himself told afterward, for the purpose of supplanting him. At Heidelberg Dr. Gall saw a girl of eighteen, of a remarkable character. Every word or gesture in the least familiar revolted her. She called on God on every occasion, as if he took a special interest in her affairs. When she spoke, assurance and presumption were painted in her features ; she carried her head high, and a little backward, and all the movements of her head expressed pride. She was not capable of submission ; when in a passion, she was violent, and disposed to proceed to all extremities. Although only the daughter of a quill-merchant, she spoke her native language with extraordinary purity, and communicated with none but persons of a rank superior to her own. In all these individuals the organ of Self-Esteem was very largely developed. Dr. Gall mentions, that he had examined also the heads of a number of chiefs of brigands, remarkable for this quality of mind, and that he had found the organ large in them all.

The faculty inspires with the sentiment of Self-Esteem or Self-love, and a due endowment of it produces only excellent effects. It imparts that degree of satisfaction with self which leaves the mind open to the enjoyment of the bounties of Providence and the amenities of life ; it inspires us with that degree of confidence which enables us to apply our powers to the best advantage in every situation in which we are placed. It also aids in giving dignity in the eyes of others ; and we shall find, in society, that that individual is uniformly treated with the most lasting and sincere respect, who esteems himself so highly as to contemn every action that is mean or unworthy of an exalted mind. By communicating this feeling of self-respect, it frequently and effectually aids the moral senti-

* From the description given of this individual's head, it is plain that he must have approached to idiocy ; and his beggary seems to have been the result of a general imbecility of mind, accompanied with an inordinate endowment of Self-Esteem.

ments in resisting temptation to vice. Several individuals in whom the organ is large, have stated to me that they have been restrained from forming improper connexions, by an overwhelming sense of the degradation which would result from doing so ; and that they believed their better principles might have yielded to temptation, had it not been for the support afforded to them by the instinctive impulses of Self-Esteem.*

When the organ is too small, a predisposition to humility is the result. In such a case the individual wants confidence and a due sense of his own importance. He has no reliance upon himself ; if the public or his superiors frown, he is unable to pursue even a virtuous course, through diffidence of his own judgment. Inferior talents, combined with a strong endowment of Self-Esteem, are often crowned with far higher success than more splendid abilities joined with this sentiment in a feebler degree. Dr. Adam Smith, in his *Theory of Moral Sentiments*, remarks, that it is better, upon the whole, to have too much, than too little, of this feeling ; because, if we pretend to more than we are entitled to, the world will give us credit for at least what we possess ; whereas, if we pretend to less, we shall be taken at our word, and mankind will rarely have the justice to raise us to the true level.

It is only when possessed in an inordinate degree, and indulged without restraint from higher faculties, that it occasions abuses. In children it then shews itself in pettishness and a wilful temper. Those children in whom the organ is small are generally obedient, and easily directed according to the will of others. In later life a great developement of the organ, with deficiency of the moral powers, produces arrogance, superciliousness of deportment, and selfishness. The first thought of persons so endowed is, how the thing proposed will affect themselves ; they see the world and all its interests only through the medium of self. When it is very large, and Love of Approbation small, it prompts the individual to erect himself into a standard of manners and morals. He measures himself by himself, and contemns the opinions of all who differ from him. Men of this character sometimes marry beneath their rank, through sheer Self-Esteem. They cannot risk the mortification of a refusal from a lady of their own grade, and therefore address an inferior. They also set the opinions of society proudly at defiance.

I have seen individuals mistake the impulses of the sentiment under discussion for the inspiration of genius, and utter common-place observations with a solemnity and emphasis suitable only to concentrated wisdom. The musician, under its predominating influence, is sometimes led to embellish a tune with decorations of his own inventing, till its character is changed and the melody destroyed. In short, when the organ is inordinately large, it communicates to the individual a high sentiment of his own importance, and leads him to believe that whatever he does or says is admirable, because it proceeds from *him*. It inspires him with magnificent notions of his own respectability, and prompts him, on comparing himself with others, to depreciate them, in order to raise himself in the scale of comparative excellence. It is an essential element in the disposition to censoriousness and envy. Persons who are fond of discussing the characters of others, and feel the tendency to vituperate rather than to praise them, will be found to have this organ large. It is the comparison with self, and a secret satisfaction at fancied superiority, that gives pleasure in this practice. Envy is the result of Self-Esteem, offended by the excellencies or superior happiness of others, and calling up Destructiveness to hate them.† To make way for this effect, however, Benevolence and Conscientiousness must be deficient.

* See *The Phrenological Journal*, iii., 85.
† See *Phren. Journ.*, ix., 413. Jealousy arises from the same combination, with the addition of Secretiveness and Cautiousness.—*Ibid.*

Another effect of a predominating Self-Esteem is, to render the individual extremely well satisfied with whatever belongs to himself. An eminent phrenologist sailed as a passenger from the Clyde to a foreign port, in a vessel commanded by a person in whose head the organ was very largely developed, and saw many striking manifestations of it on the voyage. The captain said, that he estimated the vessel very lightly when he first saw her, but, after commanding her for some time, he thought her the first ship belonging to the Clyde. This was evidently because she had become his vessel. On his voyage he assumed the most dictatorial airs; told the passengers he would send them before the mast, that he was sole commander here, and that all must obey; spoke habitually of himself, and seemed to have an insatiable appetite for power. He possessed little reflection, and was deficient in Conscientiousness.*

When Self-Esteem predominates, it gives an intense feeling of egotism; there is a proneness to use the emphatic I: "I did this, I said the other thing." The faculty then gives a solemn gravity to the manners, an authoritative commanding tone to the voice, and a kind of oracular turn to the mind, which frequently shows itself in the most ludicrous manner. Cobbett's whole life and writings indicate an extensively active Self-Esteem, aided by Combativeness;† and he maintained, at different times, every variety of opinion that could enter the human imagination, and upon every point of his changeful creed he dogmatized with more than oracular assumption. Madame de Stael describes most graphically another illustrious example of the effects of an inordinate Self-Esteem, even on a powerful mind. Speaking of one of the heroes of the Revolution, she says, that he possessed considerable talents, "mais au lieu de travailler il s'etonnoit de lui même." Some individuals manifest a solemn good-natured patronising tendency toward others, indicated in discourse by epithets such as "my good sir," "my good fellow," and the like. This arises from Self-Esteem and Benevolence both large.

Self-Esteem enters largely into the composition of that intolerant zeal which is so frequently displayed by professing Christians on behalf of their sectarian views. "There is no grace," says Cowper in one of his Letters, "that the spirit of self can counterfeit with more success than a religious zeal. A man thinks he is fighting for Christ, and he is fighting for his own notions. He thinks that he is skilfully searching the hearts of others, when he is only gratifying the malignity of his own; and charitably supposes his hearers destitute of all grace, that he may shine the more in his own eyes by comparison. When he has performed this noble task, he wonders that they are not converted: 'he has given it them soundly, and if they do not tremble, and confess that God is in him of a truth, he gives them up as reprobate, incorrigible, and lost for ever.'"

Under the influence of this faculty some authors fall unconsciously into the excessive use of pronouns of the first person. The following example is taken from the works of Dugald Stewart, who was familiarly known among his friends by the appellation of "the amiable egotist:" "When I first ventured to appear before the public as an author," says he, "I resolved that nothing should ever induce me to enter into any controversy in defence of my conclusions, but to leave them to stand or fall by their own evidence. From the plan of inductive investigation which I was conscious of having steadily followed, as far as I was able, I knew that whatever mistakes might be detected in the execution of my design, no such fatal consequences were to be dreaded to my general undertaking, as might have been justly apprehended, had I presented to the world a connected system, founded on gratuitous hypothesis or on arbitrary definitions. The detections, on the contrary, of my occasional errors would, I flatter myself, from the invariable consistency and

* See details in The Phrenological Journal, i., 259.   † Ib., ii., 216.

harmony of. truth, threw new lights on those inquiries which *I* had conducted with greater success ; as the correction of a trifling mis-statement in an authentic history is often found, by completing an imperfect link or reconciling a · seeming contradiction, to dispel the doubts which hung over the more faithful and accurate details of the narrative.

" In this hope *I* was fortified by the following sentence of Lord Bacon, which *I* thought *I* might apply to *myself*, without incurring the charge of presumption : · Nos autem, si qua in re vel male credidimus, vel obdormivimus et minus attendimus vel defecimus in via et inquisitionem abrupimus, nihilo minus iis MODIS RES NUDAS ET APERTAS EXHIBEMUS, ut errores nostri notari et separari possint ; atque etiam, ut facilis et expedita sit laborem nostrorum continuatio.'

" As this indifference, however, about the fate of *my* particular doctrines arose from a deep-rooted conviction, both of the *importance* of *my* subject and of the *soundness* of my plan, it was impossible for *me* to be insensible to such criticisms as were directed against either of these two fundamental assumptions. Some criticisms of this description *I* had, from the first, anticipated ; and *I* would not have failed to obviate them in the introduction to *my* former work, if *I* had not been afraid to expose *myself* to the imputation of prolixity, by conjuring up objections for the purpose of refuting them," &c.

Another amusing instance of a similar style of writing will be found in an account of himself by Flechier, Bishop of Nismes, prefixed to an edition of his " Oraisons Funebres," printed at Paris in 1802. I infer this to arise from a great endowment of Self-Esteem. A portrait of the author last-named is prefixed to his work, and a strong expression of Self-Esteem appears depicted on the countenance. The portraits of Gibbon also indicate this expression in a remarkable degree.* By pointing out these tendencies of the faculty, persons in whom the organ is large will be put upon their guard to avoid such ludicrous modes of its manifestation.

Mr. William Scott has published, in the first volume of *The Phrenological Journal*, p. 378, an able exposition of the effects of a large Self-Esteem upon the character, when combined with each of the other faculties greatly developed ; and additional illustrations will be found in vol. ii., pp. 57, 58, 60, 213; iv., 495; viii., 306, 496, 592; ix., 64, 258, 412. Perhaps there is no faculty of which a weak endowment is so rarely found as of Self-Esteem.

The feeling of individual personality has been supposed by some phrenologists to arise from this faculty ; and they have been led to this conjecture by the undoubted fact, that the prominence which the first person assumes in the mind bears a proportion to the size of the organ of Self-Esteem.

Self-Esteem is an ingredient in the love of *uniques*. The high value attached by some persons to objects which no other person can possess, seems resolvable, to a great extent, into a gratification of this feeling. In possessing the article they enjoy a superiority over the whole world.

* A ludicrous example of egotism in an antiphrenological Essay by the Rev. R. W. Hamilton, of Leeds, is quoted in *The Phrenological Journal*, (vol. iii., p. 473,) where the following remark was made by the editor : " We have heard of an author whose MS, was detained in the press from his printer wanting a sufficient stock of capital *I*'s to set up a single sheet of his work ; but Mr. Hamilton, it appears, far surpasses that famed composer. The present article has actually been returned to us, with an intimation, that it is difficult for our printers to find so many Roman capital *I*s, *ME*'s, and *MY*'s, as we had marked, and he has solicited to be allowed to use Italics. Our extracts extend to only *four pages* of Mr. Hamilton's pamphlet ; what a store of *I*'s the sheet would have required !"

and the consciousness of this confers great importance on it in their estimation. Acquisitiveness is the other element of the taste.

The love of power and dominion owes its origin to Self-Esteem. The organ is large in the busts of Augustus Cæsar and of Bonaparte; and I have observed that the same configuration occurs in those individuals who, in private life, aspire most eagerly to office, and who are most delighted with the possession of a little brief authority. From this faculty producing the love of power, it happens that those who are fondest of exercising dominion themselves, are the most violent opponents of authority when vested in other hands. They are the great advocates for liberty ; but are no sooner placed in possession of power themselves than they abuse it and become tyrants. In short, when two individuals equally thirst for dominion, and when the one can rule only by the other obeying, it is easy to perceive that the subject will, in such a case, manifest little satisfaction under the yoke, and that his very love of authority will make him the most determined opponent of it in others. Self-Esteem gives rise to the spirit of independence.*

Nations differ with regard to the degrees in which they possess this organ. It is large in the Chinese and Hindoos, and the English have more of it than the French : hence the manner of a genuine Frenchman appears to an Englishman to be fawning and undignified ; while the manner of an Englishman appears to the French cold, haughty, and supercilious. The great Self-Esteem of the English, and their consequent innate aversion to all stretches of power, is probably one important cause of their political liberty. Dr. Adam Ferguson has recognised the operation of this sentiment in maintaining their freedom. Alluding to the *habeas corpus* act, he remarks, that " it requires a fabric no less than the whole political constitution of Great Britain, *a spirit no less than the refractory and turbulent zeal of this fortunate people*, to secure its effects."† Among savages this organ is in general extremely active,‡ ignorant persons being usually found to have the highest opinion of themselves.

Self-Esteem, when eminently powerful, and not combined with the higher sentiments equally strong, causes the individual to carry his head high and reclining backward. It gives a cold and repulsive expression to the manner, and it is particularly offensive to other individuals greatly endowed with the same faculty.

Dr. Reid and Mr. Stewart treat of this sentiment under the designation of the Desire of Power. Dr. Thomas Brown calls it " pride," and defines it as that feeling of vivid pleasure which attends the contemplation of our excellence.§ Dr. Brown views the desire of power as a distinct primitive emotion ; but Self-Esteem appears to me to be the fundamental feeling, and the love of power to be only one of the forms of its manifestation. It is quite conceivable, that a private individual, removed from all means of acquiring public authority, may manifest little appetite for dominion over the nation, though Self-Esteem is large ; but he will be found to be proud, and to exercise a sovereign sway over his own household. This is the same principle differently directed. I have never seen a man fired with ambition for situations of command, in whom Self-Esteem was defective or even moderate in size ; so that there appears no adequate ground for assuming pride to be one primitive sentiment, and the love of power another and distinct original desire.

In treating of Acquisitiveness, I mentioned that the practical effects of that faculty are much modified by the endowment of Self-Esteem, with

* See *The Phrenological Journal*, iii., 224.
† *History of Civil Society*, part iii., sect. 6.
‡ See instances, collected by Mr. Robert Cox, in the *Phrenological Journal*, viii., 305.
§ *Lectures*, vol. iii., p. 297.

which it is combined—selfishness being greatly increased by the combination of both in a full degree of developement. Acquisitiveness desires to acquire wealth, and Self-Esteem to hold and apply it to selfish gratification. This organ appears to be possessed by the lower animals. The turkey-cock, peacock, horse, &c., manifest feelings resembling pride or Self-Esteem. "The master-ox," says Lord Kames, "leads the rest into the stable, or into the fold, and becomes unruly if he be not let first out; nay, he must be first yoked in the plough or wagon."*

Dr. Gall, however, entertained views on this subject peculiar to himself. He mentions that, after having studied the sentiment of pride as a primitive mental quality, and its organ in the human race, he wished to ascertain whether his observations would be confirmed by the lower animals. He therefore examined the heads of such of them as we are accustomed to call proud—the race-horse, the cock, and the peacock. He did not find in any of these a remarkable developement of the cerebral parts corresponding to the organ of Self-Esteem in man; but he found a considerable developement of these parts in animals in which he would never have thought of looking for it—that is to say, in those which voluntarily remain in the higher regions of the air, living on mountains and other elevated situations; for example, in the roebuck, the chamois, the wild goat, and certain species of eagles and falcons: and what struck him most was, that the parts in question were the more developed in proportion to the greater height of the dwelling-places of the animals. Dr. Gall himself was astonished at this observation. That a predilection for physical heights should, in animals, depend on the same organ as that to which the sentiment of Self-Esteem is referrible in man, appeared to him, at first, altogether improbable and inadmissible; yet, says he, "I have laid down the rule to communicate the progress of my observations, as well as the manner in which they had given rise to my opinions. Opinions which have not facts for their basis, if not erroneous, are at least very likely to be so; and a natural historian ought to be less ashamed of committing an error in his interpretations of facts, than of founding his opinions on reasoning alone." He accordingly enters into some interesting observations on the various dwelling-places of animals; directing the attention of his readers both to those which inhabit elevated regions, and to others which prefer the lowest situations: and he states, that, in all animals which have their abodes in high places, there is a lengthened eminence in the middle of the head, immediately above the organ of Philoprogenitiveness, and which entirely resembles the organ of Self-Esteem in man.†

Dr. Spurzheim holds that this prominence in the brains of the lower animals corresponds to the organ No. III. in man, (named by him Inhabitiveness, and in this work Concentrativeness;) and, while he admits the accuracy of the facts stated by Dr. Gall, he differs from his conclusions, and says, that it is not the same organ which produces in man the sentiment of Self-Esteem, and, in the lower creatures, the love of physical heights; but that there are distinct organs both in man and the lower animals for these separate mental qualities. It appears to me, that Dr. Spurzheim is correct in maintaining that the organ No. III. is distinct from that of Self-Esteem, both in the lower animals and in man; and the real extent of the difference between him and Dr. Gall is this—Dr. Spurzheim admits two organs lying between Firmness and Philoprogenitiveness, but Dr. Gall only one: Dr. Gall considers the whole of the intermediate cerebral parts as the organ in man of Self-Esteem, and, in animals, of the love of physical elevation; while Dr. Spurzheim regards the upper portion of these parts as the organ of Self-Esteem, and the lower portion as the organ of Inhabitiveness, in both cases. I am satisfied

* *Sketches,* B. ii., Sk. 1.　　† *Sur les Fonctions du Cerveau,* tome iv., p. 279.

that the organs are distinct in the human species, and that the upper serves
to manifest Self-Esteem. Farther observations must determine the function of the lower organ, or No. III.

When Self-Esteem becomes excited by disease, the individual imagines
himself to be a king, an emperor, a transcendent genius, or even the Supreme Being. Dr. Gall mentions the case of a Monsieur B., in whom
the organ was very large, and who was accidentally wounded by a nail in
this part of the brain. While labouring under the influence of the wound,
he felt himself, as it were, elevated above the clouds, and carried through
the air, retaining, at the same time, and also manifesting during his convalescence, the same proud and haughty manners which had distinguished
him during health.

"The organ," says Dr. G., "was equally conspicuous in an insane
patient at Baden, near Rastadt. This man's insanity consisted in believing himself a major. He had a small head, and the only organ which was
developed in a high degree was that of Self-Esteem; the whole other
convolutions of the brain being very small. In the charity work-house
of Fribourg we saw an insane man who was extremely proud. He declared, in a vehement and pathetic tone, ' qu'il est la souche ' by the aid
of which God created and preserves the world, that he has been crowned
by Jesus Christ; that he is the young man whom the Queen of Heaven
has selected for her spouse. His attitude is that of an arrogant despot.
Deeply inspired with sentiments of his high importance, he crosses his
arms, and, to give an idea of the astonishing power which he possesses,
he strikes his breast and sides with violence. In general, he stands with
one foot placed before the other, the body erect, and a little inclined
backward. When I requested him,' continues Dr. Gall, " to allow me to
touch his head, he replied, with astonishing arrogance, ' Ich habe keinen
Kopf, sondern ein Haupt,' I have no head such as common men possess,
but a Haupt, or head peculiar to kings and gods, He turned away, holding
us to be totally unworthy of approaching him. We observed, however,
distinctly, that he had the organ of Self-Esteem very largely developed."

Pinel, Foderé, and other writers on insanity, mention cases equally
characteristic of disease of this organ. "A patient," says Pinel, " confined in a private asylum in Paris, during his fits, believed himself to be
the prophet Mahomet, assumed an attitude of command, and the tone of
the Most High ; ses traits étaient rayonnans, et sa démarche pleine de
majesté. One day when cannon were fired in Paris on account of some
events of the Revolution, he persuaded himself that it was to render him
homage; he caused silence to be observed around him, and could not
restrain his joy." ' "A woman," continues the same author, " extremely
imperious, and accustomed to make her husband obey with even more
than docility, remained in bed part of the morning, and then insisted that
he should come, and on his knees present her with drink. She ended by
believing herself, in the ecstasies of her pride, to be the Virgin Mary."
I have seen many cases similar to the foregoing, some of which are
reported in The Phrenological Journal, vol. vi., p. 80.*

This organ is generally larger in men than in women ; and more males
are insane through pride than females. The organ is regarded as established. It is large in Haggart, Bellingham, and Dempsey, and moderate
in Dr. Hette. Dr. Spurzheim's Phrenology in Connexion with the study
of Physiognomy contains many examples of its large developement. See
plate x., fig. 1 ; xv., 1 ; xvi., 1 ; xvii., 1 ; xxii., 1 ; xxv., 2 ; xxvi., 2 ;
xxvii., 1 ; xxviii., 1 and 2 ; xxix., 1, 2, 3, 4, 5, 6. The organ is represented
small in plate x., fig. 2 ; and xv., 2.

* See also Dr. A. Combe's Observations on Mental Derangement, p. 175.

11. LOVE OF APPROBATION.

This organ is situated on each side of that of Self-Esteem, and commences about half an inch from the lambdoidal suture. When large, it
produces a remarkable fulness and breadth in the upper and back part of
the head. From its situation, it cannot be brought into line, so as to be
represented successfully by figures, similar to those used in illustration
of the other organs. The reader may, however, inspect the valuable
work of Dr. Spurzheim, just referred to, plate xvi., fig. 1 ; xxii., 1 ; xxiv.,
2 ; xxvii., 1 ; and particularly xxviii., 1, representing the head of Lalande.
When Dr. Gall was occupied in making observations on the organ of
Self-Esteem, he met with a woman in a lunatic asylum who conceived
herself to be the Queen of France. He expected to find the organ of that
sentiment largely developed ; but, in place of this, there was a very distinct hollow in the situation of it, and a round and considerable prominence
presented itself on each side. This circumstance at first caused him
considerable embarrassment. He soon perceived, however, that the character of this woman's insanity differed materially from that of men alienated
through pride. The latter were grave, calm, imperious, elevated, arrogant ;
and they affected a masculine majesty. Even in the fury of their fits
all their motions and expressions bore the impress of the sentiment of
domination which they imagined themselves to exercise over others. In the
patients insane through vanity, on the other hand, the whole manner was
different. There was then a restless frivolity, an inexhaustible talkative-
ness, the most affected forwardness ; eagerness to announce high birth and
boundless riches, promises of favour and honour—in a word, a mixture of
affectation and absurdity. From that time Dr. Gall perceived the difference
between the sentiment of Self-Esteem and that of Love of Approbation.
He draws, with great accuracy, the distinction between pride, which is
an abuse of Self-Esteem, and vanity, an abuse of Love of Approbation.
The *proud* man, says he, is imbued with a sentiment of his own superior
merit, and, from the summit of his grandeur, treats with contempt or indifference all other mortals ; the *vain* man attaches the utmost importance
to the opinions entertained of him by others, and seeks with eagerness to
gain their approbation. The *proud* man expects that mankind will come
to him and acknowledge his merit ; the *vain* man knocks at every door to
draw attention toward him, and supplicates for the smallest portion of
honour. The *proud* man despises those marks of distinction, which on
the *vain* confer the most perfect delight. The *proud* man is disgusted by
indiscreet eulogiums ; the *vain* man inhales with ecstasy the incense of
flattery, although profusely offered, and by no very skilful hand. *
Dr. Gall treats of the abuses of this sentiment under the names of
vanity, ambition, and the love of glory, rather than of the primitive sentiment itself. To Dr. Spurzheim is due the merit of elucidating the ultimate principle of many of the faculties, and in particular the one under
consideration.
This faculty produces the desire of approbation, admiration, praise, and
fame. Hence it renders us anxious to please those whose approval is
valued, and makes us attentive to the opinions which others entertain of
us. The object of its desire is approbation in general, without determining the means or the manner of acquiring it. The direction in which its
gratification will be sought depends on the faculties with which it is combined in the individual. If the moral sentiments and intellect are vigorous,
it will prompt to moral emulation and the desire of honourable fame. It

* Gall *Sur les Fonctions du Cerveau*, tome iv., p. 297.

may thus animate the poet, the painter, the orator, the warrior, and the statesman. In some individuals it attains the height of a passion, and then glory is pursued at the hazard of life and of every enjoyment which it affords, and fame is sought for even in the cannon's mouth. " Themistoclem illum," says Cicero, " summum Athenis virum, dixisse aiunt,–cum ex eo quæreretur, quod acroama, aut cujus vocem libentissime audiret ! Ejus, à quo sua virtus optimè prædicaretur." Cicero himself seems to have possessed this sentiment in a very high degree : " Trahimur omnes laudis studio," says he, " et optimus quisque maxime gloriâ ducitur. Ipsi illi philosophi, etiam in illis libellis quos de contemnenda gloria scribunt, nomen suum inscribunt ; in eo ipso, in quo prædicationem nobilitatemque despiciunt, prædicari de se'ac nominari volunt."* The same ideas are thus expressed by Montaigne : " Of all the follies of the world, that which is most universally received is the solicitude of reputation and glory ; which we are fond of to that degree, as to abandon riches, peace, life, and health, which are effectual and substantial goods, to pursue this vain phantom and empty word. And of all the irrational humours of men, it should seem that even the philosophers themselves have the most ado, and do the latest disengage themselves from this, as the most resty and obstinate of all human follies."† The organ is very large in the American Indians ;‡ and the love of decorations and ornaments, whether these consist of stars, garters, and medals, or of tatooed faces, bored noses, and eagles' feathers, springs from it. The faculty is strongly displayed by the Cingalese.§ If the lower propensities predominate, the individual may be pleased by the reputation of being the best fighter or the greatest drinker of his circle.

There is a great difference in regard to the degree of endowment of this faculty in different individuals. Some watch, with the most animated anxiety, every motion and every look, and intuitively feel when we approve or disapprove. When we approve, the eye sparkles, the countenance opens, and the individual approaches us with a pleasing courtesy, expressive at once of the pleasure he has received from our approbation, and of his desire to retain it. He, on the other hand, in whom the faculty is naturally feeble, shows, by the undisturbed fixture of his countenance, that our censure and applause are alike unimportant to him. When we censure, he stares us in the face with calm indifference, or gapes in stupid wonder.

A due endowment of this faculty is indispensable to an amiable character. It gives the desire to be agreeable to others ; it is the drill-sergeant of society, and admonishes us when we deviate too widely from the line of march of our fellows ; it induces us to suppress numberless little manifestations of selfishness, and to restrain many peculiarities of temper and disposition, from the dread of incurring disapprobation by giving offence ; it is the butt upon which wit strikes when, by means of ridicule, it drives us from our follies. To be laughed at is worse than death to a person in whom this sentiment is strong.

The feeling which is most commonly experienced when this organ is large, even when favourably combined with other organs, is anxiety about what the world will think of us. A youth in whom it is powerful cannot do this thing, because everybody will look at him ; or cannot do the other, because people will wonder. In older persons it produces a fidgety anxiety about the opinion of the public, or of the circle of acquaintances who compose the public to them. If Self-Esteem also is powerful, they

* Oratio pro Archia.   † Essays, B. i., ch. 41, Cotton's Translation.
‡ See Phren. Journ., ii., 537.
§ Phren. Journ., vii., 639. Various illustrations of Love of Approbation will be found in vol. ii., p. 64 ; viii., 590, 592, 428 ; ix., 66, 414.

imagine themselves' continually before the public eye, and that the world is occupied with little else than weighing their motives, speculating on their conduct, and adjusting the precise point in the scale of importance and respectability at which they ought to be placed. A great portion of this feeling, however, is the mere inspiration of great Self-Esteem and Love of Approbation in their own heads. . The public are too much engrossed with themselves and their own affairs, to bestow so minute and permanent a degree of attention upon an individual. This anxiety about public opinion, when too great, is subversive of happiness and independence. It renders the mere *dicta* of the society in which the individual moves, his code of morality, religion, taste, and philosophy ; and incapacitates him from upholding truth and virtue, if disowned by those whom he imagines influential or genteel. The want of a philosophy of mind allows wide scope to the aberrations of this faculty ; for, in the absence of well-defined principles of taste and conduct, individuals of high pretension dictate, with success, fashions, however absurd, which the herd of mankind follow.

The characteristic difference between the disposition to oblige conferred by this sentiment, and the feeling of genuine kindness which springs from Benevolence, is, that Love of Approbation prompts us to do most for those who least require our aid, whereas Benevolence takes exactly the opposite direction. Men, in general, care little for the approbation of their inferiors, their own household, or those of whom they are altogether independent ; and he whose exertions are inspired chiefly by this faculty, will do extremely little to benefit them. To serve or please the great and the splendid, on the other hand, or strangers whose voice may raise or depress his fame, he will make the most animated exertions. Persons, accordingly, in whom Love of Approbation is very strong, and Benevolence and Conscientiousness deficient, are frequently the most agreeable acquaintances to those who are altogether independent of them ; "they smile on all who care not for their frowns," while they neglect or torment their inferiors and equals.

No faculty is more prone to run into excess than Love of Approbation ; and hence it has served as a fertile theme to the satirist in every age. The *Characters* of Theophrastus contain some happy sketches in ridicule of its inordinate manifestations. In Young's *Love of Fame* also there are many striking passages descriptive of the absurdities into which it leads mankind. The diversified forms in which its activity appears are well exposed by the following lines in Satire First :

> " The love of praise, howe'er conceal'd by art,
> Reigns, more or less, and glows in every heart :
> The proud, to gain it, toils on toils endure ;
> The modest shun it, but to make it sure.
> O'er globes and sceptres, now on thrones it swells,
> Now trims the midnight lamp in college cells ;
> 'Tis Tory, Whig ; it plots, prays, preaches, pleads,
> Harangues in senates, squeaks in masquerades :...
> It aids the dancer's heel, the writer's head,
> And heaps the plain with mountains of the dead
> Nor ends with life, but nods in sable plumes,
> Adorns our hearse, and flatters on our tombs."

This faculty is too much cultivated in education, by being almost universally appealed to as the chief stimulus to exertion and good behaviour. In infant-schools, however, conducted on Mr. Wilderspin's plan, prizes and place-taking are dispensed with, and the result is most satisfactory. It is only where the subjects of study are unsuitable to the minds of children, or improperly taught, that Love of Approbation requires to be strongly appealed to.*

Combined with Secretiveness large and Conscientiousness deficient, it prompts its possessor to pay to others those unmeaning compliments which pass current in society, and which most persons receive well when addressed to themselves, but treat with ridicule when bestowed lavishly on others. It prompts to the equivocation of "not at home," when the person is otherwise engaged. The faculty of Conscientiousness would desire that the plain fact should be stated; but Love of Approbation produces an instinctive feeling that the Self-Esteem of the person calling will be offended, if any engagement can render it inconvenient to see him. To save this pang, Love of Approbation and Secretiveness prompt to the invention of the little *equivoque*. The deceit is seen through by all, and nevertheless the use of it is more pleasing to persons in whom Self-Esteem and Love of Approbation are very large, than the announcement of the simple truth. Some individuals state candidly that they are " engaged ;" and I have asked persons in whom the organs above-mentioned are large, whether they felt more annoyed by this reply than by "not at home," even when they suspected that the latter meant really the former. They acknowledged that, on the first occasion, they did feel slightly irritated; but that a moment's reflection satisfied them that forcible reasons must exist for the refusal, and that the very announcement of the truth was an appeal to their higher feelings, and a proof of unhesitating confidence in their attachment and good sense ; and ever after they were not offended by the reply, "Engaged." It is the same concomitance of Love of Approbation with Secretiveness which prompts some individuals to pursue the practice of calling on those whom they are pleased to style their friends, when they think that they are not at home, for the purpose of leaving their card. This proceeding is an offer of flattery to the Self-Esteem and Love of Approbation of the persons called upon ; but as in the fashionable code it is not intended to imply either affection or esteem for them, but mere civility or attention, it is, in truth, a very slender compliment. The real import of these conventional ceremonies is universally understood, so that philosophy sees in them only ludicrous attempts at gratifying Love of Approbation, attended with no success.

When the developement of Love of Approbation is excessive, while the regulating organs are deficient, it is the cause of great unhappiness. It renders the little girl at school miserable, if her dress and the style of living of her parents are not equal to those of the parents of her associates. It overwhelms the artist, author, or public speaker with misery, if a rival is praised in the journals in higher terms than himself. A lady is tormented by perceiving in the possession of her acquaintance finer dresses or equipages than her own. It excites the individual to talk of himself, his affairs and connexions, so as to communicate to the auditor vast ideas of his greatness or goodness ; in short, vanity is one form of its abuse. "Sir," says Dr. Johnson, "Goldsmith is so much afraid of being unnoticed, that he often talks, merely lest you should forget that he is in the company." When not combined with Conscientiousness and Benevolence, it leads to feigned professions of respect and friendship ; and many manifest it by promises and invitations, never intended to be fulfilled or accepted. It, as well as Self-Esteem, prompts to the use of the first person ; but its tone is that of courteous solicitation, while the *I* of Self-Esteem is presumptuous and full of pretension.

When, on the other hand, the organ is deficient, and the sentiment, in consequence, is feeble, the individual cares little about the opinion enter-

* Phren. Journ., v., 613; x., 9; and Simpson's *Necessity of Popular Education*, p. 148.

tained of him by others; and, provided they have not the power to punish his person or abridge his possessions, he is capable of laughing at their censures, and contemning their applause. Persons of this sort, if endowed with the selfish propensities in a strong degree, constitute what are termed "impracticable" men; their whole feelings are concentrated in self, and they are dead to the motive which might induce them to abate one iota of their own pretensions to oblige others. If actuated by any strong passion, and endowed with intellect, it is astonishing what they are sometimes able to accomplish in attaining their objects. Strangers to ceremony and indifferent to censure, they meet with a thousand rebuffs which they never feel, and are loaded with a hundred indignities which never affect them: free from the restraints which delicacy imposes upon others, they practise upon the benevolence, the disposition to oblige, or the interest of mankind, and succeed in circumstances in which a sensitive mind would have found only obstacles unsurmountable.

Philosophers and acute observers of human nature have long distinguished between pride and vanity;[*] but, nevertheless, no error is more frequently committed by ordinary minds than to confound them; and no mistake is more common than to imagine that beaux and belles, and all who are very tasteful and particular about their personal appearance or equipages, are necessarily extremely conceited. A large Love of Approbation and much Ideality, joined with Individuality, which produces attention to details, and Order, will, in general, give rise to the passion for neatness, propriety, and ornament; but such a combination, instead of producing a proud or conceited character, inspires with the very opposite dispositions. I rarely see a dandy who is not at bottom a polite, obliging, good-natured, but probably weak, individual; and it is only when large Self-Esteem, which is not an indispensable ingredient in beauxism, is added to the combination, that the common opinion will be justified by the result.

This faculty corresponds to the Desire of Esteem of Dr. Reid and Mr. Stewart, and to the Desire of Glory of Dr. Thomas Brown. The observations of these philosophers on its functions are generally correct; but here, as in the case of Self-Esteem, they treat chiefly of its heroic manifestations, and present us with almost no views of its operations in the more interesting theatre of private life.

The faculty, when powerful, gives a tendency to carry the head backward, and a little to the side; it communicates a soft soliciting tone to the voice, puts smiles into the countenance, and produces that elegant line of beauty in the lips which resembles Apollo's bow.

As formerly mentioned, the French are remarkable for a large developement of this organ, while the English excel in Self-Esteem. The influence of the Love of Approbation shows itself in the manners, institutions, and daily literature of France in an extraordinary degree. Compliments and praises are the current coin of conversation; and a late writer most justly observes, that, "in France, glory is the condiment to the whole feast of life, and the trumpet of fame is that which makes the sweetest music to their ears."[†] In private life also, an individual who has much Love of Approbation himself, is extremely prone to pay compliments to others, from an instinctive feeling of the pleasure of being praised, and to believe that in this way he renders himself highly agreeable.

The faculty is generally more active in women than in men; and it is observed, that a greater number of women than of men become insane from this feeling. Dr. Spurzheim mentions, that he had met with only one

* "Pride makes us esteem ourselves; vanity makes us desire the esteem of others. It is just to say, as Dean Swift has done, that a man is too proud to be vain."—*Blair's Lectures*, lect. 10.
† *Edinburgh Review*, Nov., 1820, p. 294.

man who had become deranged from this cause. Its effects, when diseased, have already been described in the history of the discovery of the organ.†

The organ is possessed by the lower animals. The dog is extremely fond of approbation, and the horse displays the sentiment, not only in his sensibility to marks of affection, but in his spirit of emulation in the race. Dr. Gall mentions, that, in the south of France, the peasants attach a *bouquet* to the mules when they have acquitted themselves well, and that the animals understand it as a mark of approbation, and feel afflicted when it is taken away. He mentions also, that he had a female monkey, who, on receiving a handkerchief, put it on as a robe, and took extraordinary delight in seeing it trail behind her as a train. In all these creatures the organ is largely developed.

The organ is large in Dr. Hette, the Reverend Mr. M., King Robert Bruce, and Clara Fisher; and deficient in D. Haggart and Dempsey. It is established.

12. CAUTIOUSNESS.

This organ is situated near the middle of each parietal bone, where the ossification of the bone generally commences.

The figures represent its appearance when large and small.

Dr. Gall was acquainted at Vienna with a prelate, a man of excellent sense and considerable intellect. Some persons had an aversion toward him, because, through fear of compromising himself, he infused into his discourses interminable reflections, and delivered them with unsupportable slowness. When any one began a conversation with him, it was very difficult to bring it to a conclusion. He paused continually in the middle of his sentences, and repeated the beginning of them two or three times before proceeding farther. A thousand times he pushed the patience of Dr. Gall to extremity. He never happened by any accident to give way to the natural flow of his ideas; but recurred a hundred times to what he had already said, consulting with himself whether he could not amend it in some point. His manner of acting was in conformity with his manner of speaking. He prepared with infinite precautions for the most insignificant undertakings. He subjected every connexion to the most rigorous examination and calculation before forming it.

CINGALESE BOY.

12   12

GIRL.

12   12

This case, however, was not by itself sufficient to arrest the attention of Dr. Gall; but this prelate happened to be connected in public affairs with a counsellor of the regency, whose eternal irresolution had procured for him the nickname of *Cacadubio*. At the examination of the public schools these two individuals were placed side by side, and Dr. Gall sat in the seat immediately behind them. This arrangement afforded him an excellent opportunity of observing their heads. The circumstance which most forcibly arrested his attention was, that both their heads were very broad in the upper, lateral, and hind parts, the situation of the organ in

† See also Dr. A. Combe's *Observations on Mental Derangement*, p. 174.

question. The dispositions and intellectual qualities of these two men were, in other respects, very different; but they resembled each other in circumspection, and also in this particular development of head. The coincidence between them in this point suggested the idea to Dr. Gall, that irresolution, indecision, and circumspection might be connected with certain parts of the brain. Subsequent reflections on this disposition, and observation of additional facts, converted the presumption into certainty.

It is a principle in Phrenology, that absence of one quality never confers another. Every feeling is something positive in itself, and is not a mere negation of a different emotion. Fear, then, is a positive sentiment, and not the mere want of courage; and it appears to me that the faculty now under discussion produces that feeling. The tendency of the sentiment is to make the individual apprehend danger; and this leads him to hesitate before he acts, and to look to consequences that he may be assured of his safety. Dr. Spurzheim names it "Cautiousness," which appellation I retain as sufficiently expressive, although the primitive feeling appears, on a rigid analysis, to be simply fear. Dr. Gall says, "It was requisite that man and animals should be endowed with a faculty to enable them to foresee certain events, to give them a presentiment of certain circumstances, and to prompt them to provide against danger. Without such a disposition, their attention would have been occupied only with the present; and they would have been incapable of taking any measures with reference to the future." Accordingly, he describes the faculty which prompts to these actions, as if it comprised something intellectual; and he calls it "Circumspection, Foresight." Dr. Spurzheim "does not believe that it foresees; it is, in his opinion, blind, and without reflection, although it may excite the reflective faculties." This observation appears to me correct.

A full development of this organ is essential to a prudent character. It produces a cautious, circumspect, and considerate disposition of mind. Persons so organized, says Dr. Gall, "are habitually on their guard; they know that it is more difficult to sustain than to acquire reputation, and, consequently, every new undertaking is prosecuted as carefully as the first. They look forward to all possible dangers, and are anxious to anticipate every occurrence; they ask advice of every one, and often, after having received much counsel, remain undecided. They put great faith in the observation, that, of a hundred misfortunes which befal us, ninety-nine arise from our own fault. Such persons never break any article; they may pass their lives in pruning trees, or in working with sharp tools, without cutting themselves. If they see a vessel placed near the edge of the table, their nerves shrink. If they give credit, or indulge in gambling, they never lose large sums of money. Finally," says he, "they form a standing subject of criticism to their less considerate neighbours, who look on their forebodings as extravagant, and their precautions as trifling and absurd."*

When the organ is too large, it produces doubts, irresolution, and wavering; and may lead to absolute incapacity for vigorous and decisive conduct. A great and involuntary activity of it produces a panic—a state in which the mind is hurried away by an irresistible emotion of fear, for which no adequate external cause exists.

The organ is almost uniformly large in children, and appears, from this circumstance, to be developed at an earlier age than many of the other organs. This is a wise provision of nature; as caution is never more indispensable to the safety of the individual than during the helpless years of infancy and childhood. The cut represents a top view of the skull of

* Sur les Fonctions du Cerveau, tome iv., p. 339.

the Cingalese boy already figured on p. 194.
Children possessing a large endowment may
be safely trusted to take care of themselves;
they will rarely be found in danger. When,
on the other hand, the organs are small in a
child, he will be a hapless infant; fifty
keepers will not supply the place of the instinctive guardianship performed by adequate
Cautiousness. In a boy of six years of age
it was very small, and he took off his clothes
to leap into an old quarry full of water to recover his cap, which the wind had blown into
it; totally insensible to the danger, which was
imminent, of being drowned. In some very
young children the organs are so prominent as to alarm mothers with the
fear of disease or deformity. Water in the head indeed frequently shows
itself by an enlargement of this part of the skull, but it is not uncommon
for unskilful persons to mistake a natural and healthy developement of
the organ in question for an indication of that malady.

In mature age, when the organ is very deficient, the individual is rash
and precipitate. He is never apprehensive about the results of his conduct, and often proceeds to act without due consideration. Persons of
this description are frequently of a gay, careless disposition, and engrossed entirely with the present; they adopt rash resolutions, and enter upon
hazardous enterprises, without deliberation or advice. In domestic life misfortunes overtake them in consequence of their want of precaution. From
constitutional recklessness, they precipitate themselves against objects in
the dark; they break frangible articles, owing to want of precaution in arranging them; and lose the money which they lend, by omitting to take
proper security for repayment. Riding upon a slippery path, quite insensible to danger, their horse falls and deprives them of life. A cat, or other
animal, overturns the candle which they have left burning, and sets their
house on fire. In short, they are subject to interminable misfortunes,
through want of caution in their conduct.[*]

This faculty produces a repressing influence, and, in estimating its
effects, the faculties with which it is combined ought to be kept in view.
An individual with large Acquisitiveness and Self-Esteem, which produce
instinctive selfishness, was pointed out to me as remarkably careful of his
own interest, although the organ of Cautiousness was deficient in his
head. It was admitted, however, that his prudence consisted chiefly in
resisting solicitations to perform generous actions, and to enter into
suretyship; but that, when a tempting prospect of gain was held out to
him, although attended with great risk, he was liable to dash into the
adventure, and, in consequence, frequently sustained severe losses. His
natural dispositions rendered him little prone to excessive generosity, and
in that respect no danger awaited him; but if Cautiousness had been large,
it would have rendered him alive to the perils of speculation, and prompted
him to prefer small and certain profits, to the chances of great but uncertain gain.

Extreme and involuntary activity of this faculty produces internal sensations of dread and apprehension, highly distressing to the individual,
although often very ridiculous in the eyes of ignorant spectators. The
character of "the fearful man," depicted by Theophrastus, may be referred
to as an excellent illustration. Many persons believe that the feelings
of the mind depend upon the dictates of the understanding, and that indi-

[*] Gall, Sur les Fonctions du Cerveau, tome iv., p. 319.

viduals, if they would allow themselves to be convinced of the groundlessness of their apprehensions, might, by an act of volition, remove the terrors which oppress them. Such notions argue great ignorance of human nature. As easily can we remove a pain from the leg, by resolving to be quit of it, as can the unhappy sufferer, under diseased Cautiousness, dispel the mental gloom by which he is afflicted.

A large development of this organ, combined with much Destructiveness, predisposes to self-destruction. Cautiousness does not produce suicide as a specific act; but the sentiment, when stimulated to excess by disease of the organs, gives rise to intense melancholy, anguish, and anxiety, and, by rendering life extremely miserable, indirectly prompts to this result. Hence the fact, that the best of men, and those in whose external circumstances no adequate motive can be found, are sometimes led to that fatal deed. Let no one suppose such an act done from mere error in judgment. It proceeds from internal and involuntary feelings of a diseased nature, of the misery and torment of which no man, who has never felt anything similar, can form an accurate conception. The great ignorance of mankind in general, regarding the state of mind which predisposes to suicide, has arisen from the influence of the organs being entirely overlooked, and from the fact not being known, that disease in any of them deranges the character of the same feeling which it serves to manifest, and often renders it independent of the will. Dr. A. Combe examined a number of suicides in the Morgue at Paris, and found in them, Hope generally small, with Cautiousness and Destructiveness large; and I have seen several similar examples.*

Many instances of disease of this organ occur, not only in hospitals for the insane, but in private life. Dr. Gall mentions, that, at Vienna, he attended two fathers of families in easy circumstances, who, nevertheless, were tormented night and day by the apprehension that their wives and children were exposed to die of hunger. The most earnest assurances of their friends were insufficient to make them comprehend that this fear was altogether chimerical. After their recovery, they could not bear to hear their condition mentioned, through terror of a relapse. Before their malady, they were known to be men of gloomy dispositions.

Pinel, under the head of Melancholy, mentions a variety of cases referrible to diseased Cautiousness. "A distinguished military officer," says he, "after fifty years of active service in the country, was attacked with disease. It commenced by his experiencing vivid emotions from the slightest causes: if, for example, he heard any disease spoken of, he immediately believed himself to be attacked by it; if any one was mentioned as deranged in intellect, he imagined himself insane, and retired into his chamber full of melancholy thoughts and inquietude. Everything became for him a subject of fear and alarm. If he entered into a house, he was afraid that the floor would fall, and precipitate him amid its ruins. He could not pass a bridge without terror, unless impelled by the sentiment of honour for the purpose of fighting."

The forms in which this affection shows itself are numberless. It is in vain to address the understanding of the patient by argument; because the disease consists in a disordered state of a corporeal organ, and the only consequence of the most irresistible demonstration to the intellect would be a change of the object of terror, but no alleviation of the feelings of painful apprehension itself.†

* See *Phrenological Journal*, vi., 77; ix., 136.
† See Dr. Andrew Combe's *Observations on Mental Derangement*, pp. 151, 267; and an Essay by him on the Seat and Nature of Hypochondriasis, in *The Phrenological Journal*, iii., 51. See also vol. ii., pp. 75-8, ix., 66; and *Transactions of the Phrenological Society*, p. 313.

Dr. Gall mentions, that this organ is possessed in a high degree by those of the lower animals which venture out only during the night, as owls and bats; and also by those animals which place sentinels to warn them of approaching danger, as the wild goose, chamois, crane, starling, and buzzard. Among the lower animals it is generally larger in females than in males; and Dr. Gall mentions some curious facts, illustrative of the greater manifestation of the faculty by the former than by the latter. He happened to kill so many as twenty squirrels, without finding a single female among them; although it was not the season in which they are confined by the care of their young. He caught, during three years, forty-four cats in his garden, among which he found only five females. During one winter five hundred bears were killed in two provinces of Virginia, among which only two females were discovered. An account of the wolves destroyed in France from 1st January, 1816, to 1st January, 1817, was published officially by Count Gerardin, captain of the Royal Chase: it showed 1894 males, and only 522 females. Among the goats the leader is always a female, and their safety, it will be recollected, arises from a high degree of circumspection. Among wild cattle, horses, and other animals which are defended by courage, the leader is uniformly a male, for, in this sex, Combativeness is usually larger. This fact, of females in general being more cautious than males, is corroborated by Captain Franklin, in his *Journey to the Arctic Regions:* " It is extraordinary," says he, " that, although I made inquiries extensively among the Indians, I met with but one who said that he had killed a she bear with young in the womb."

It has been remarked, in the way of criticism on these statements, that more males are produced by nature than females; which is quite correct: but this excess of males does not extend to the twentieth part of the difference in the number of their deaths by violence.

The metaphysicians, in general, do not treat of " fear," nor of the instinctive tendency to take precautions against danger, as an original principle of the mind; but its existence and utility are recognised by Lord Kames.[*] " It is not," says he, " within the reach of fancy to conceive anything more artfully contrived to answer its purpose, than the instinctive passion of fear, which, upon the first surmise of danger, operates instantaneously. So little doth the passion, in such instances, depend on reason, that it frequently operates in contradiction to it: a man who is not upon his guard cannot avoid shrinking at a blow, though he knows it to be aimed in sport; nor avoid closing his eyes at the approach of what may hurt them, though conscious that he is in no danger."[†] Dr. Thomas Brown ranks melancholy among the primitive emotions, which is one of the effects of this faculty in a state of constant, but not violent, activity.

The organ is larger in the Germans, English, and Scotch, than in the Celtic French; and it appears to be larger in the English than in the Turkish head. Mr. Forster, a civil servant on the Madras Establishment, travelled overland from Bengal to England in the year 1782, disguised as a Turk. In all the numberless scenes through which he passed, he had the address successfully to maintain his disguise, except in one single instance, in which he was detected by an individual who was led to certainty in the discovery which he made, by examining the shape of the traveller's head. " A Georgian merchant," says Mr. Forster, " who occupied the room next to mine, (it was at Cashmere,) and was a very agreeable neighbour, did not, I observed, give a ready credit to my story, which he cross-

---

[*] As to the manifestations of Cautiousness in the lower animals, see Lord Kames' *Sketches*, B. ii., Sk. i.
[†] *Elements of Criticism*, 8th edit., 1805, vol. i., p. 68.

examined with some tokens of suspicion ; and one day, having desired to look at my head, he decidedly pronounced it to be that of a Christian. In a future conversation he explained to me, and proved by comparison, that the head of a Christian *is broad behind*, and *flatted out at the crown* ; that a Mahomedan's head grows narrow at the top, and, like a monkey's, has a conic form."* This description indicates Cautiousness to be larger in the Christian.

The organ is large in Bruce, Hette, Burns, the Swiss, Scotch, Mummies, Hindoos,† Cingalese,‡ Peruvians, and Papuans ;§ moderate in Bellingham, Mary Macinnes, and negroes. The subjoined figures represent two skulls indicating a great developement of the organ. These on the left are views of the skull of a Candian, one of the Cingalese tribes in Ceylon ; the others, of the skull of a Papuan, or inhabitant of New Guinea.

KANDIAN.   PAPUAN.

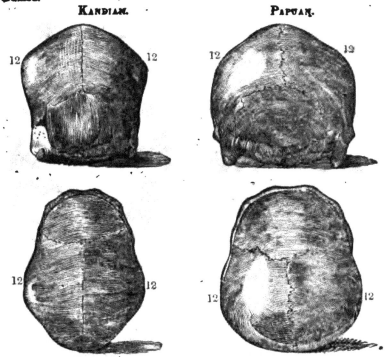

The difference of breadth at this part between heads of the same general size, but presenting a large and small developement of Cautiousness, frequently exceeds an inch and a half ; and as the organ is particularly easy of observation, it deserves the attention of beginners.

The organ is ascertained.

II.—SUPERIOR SENTIMENTS.

HITHERTO we have considered man so far as he is animal. But besides the organs and faculties already spoken of, common to him and the brutes, he is endowed with a variety of sentiments, which constitute the peculiar-

* Forster's *Journey*, vol. ii., p. 33.
† *Transactions of the Phren. Soc* , p. 440, and *Phren. Journ.*, viii., 569.
‡ *Phrenological Journal*, vii., 638.   § Ib., viii., 298

ly human character. Of these the lower animals appear to be destitute. The convolutions which form the organs of Veneration, Hope, and Conscientiousness in the human brain run transversely; and in the brains of the lower animals, so far as I have observed, no corresponding convolutions appear. The organs of Benevolence and Imitation, however, which are here classed among the superior sentiments, run longitudinally, and corresponding parts are found in the brains of the lower animals.

13. BENEVOLENCE.

This organ is situated at the upper part of the frontal bone, in the coronal aspect, and immediately before the fontanel. When it is large, the frontal bone rises with an arched appearance, above the organ of Comparison; when small, the forehead is low and retreating. The following cuts exhibit a contrast in this respect; the skull of Burns being elevated far above the eyes, while that of Griffiths (a murderer) is low and narrow in front. The figures of Gottfried and Eustache, on pp. 86 and 87, may likewise be compared at this organ:

ROBERT BURNS.   GRIFFITHS.

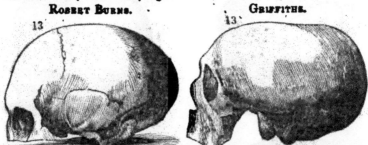

One of Dr. Gall's friends frequently said to him, that, as he sought for external indications of mental qualities, he ought to examine the head of his servant named Joseph. "It is impossible," said his friend, "to find a greater degree of goodness than that young man possesses. For more than ten years, during which he has been in my service, I have seen him manifest, on all occasions, only benevolence and sweetness of disposition. This is the more surprising, as he does not possess the advantages of education, and has grown up to manhood among servants of very inferior habits." Dr Gall adds, that, previously to that time, he had been far from supposing that what is called goodness of heart could have any organ in the brain, and, consequently, had never looked for indications of it in the head. The repeated solicitations of his friend, however, at length awakened his curiosity.

He immediately recollected the habitual conduct of a young man whom he had known from his most tender infancy, and who was distinguished from his numerous brothers and sisters by his goodness of heart. Although he was passionately fond of the games proper to his age, and delighted in scouring the forests in search of birds' nests, yet no sooner did any of his brothers and sisters become sick, than an inclination still more powerful kept him at home, and drew from him the most assiduous attentions toward the sufferer. When grapes, or apples, or cherries were distributed among the children, his share was always the least, and he rejoiced in seeing the others partake more largely than himself. He was never more pleased than when some good fortune happened to those whom he loved, on which occasions he often shed tears of joy. He was fond of taking charge of sheep, dogs, rabbits, pigeons, and birds; and if one of these birds happened to die, he wept bitterly, which did not fail to draw upon him the ridicule of his companions. Up to the present time, continues Dr. Gall, benevolence and goodness are the distinguishing characteristics of this individual. These dispositions certainly did not arise from education; on the contrary, he had been all along surrounded by those whose conduct was calculated to produce the very opposite results. Dr. Gall then began to suspect, that what is called *goodness of heart* is not an acquired, but an innate, quality of the mind.

On another occasion, amid a very large family, he spoke of the boasted *goodness of heart* of the servant Joseph. "Ah!" said the eldest daughter, "our brother Charles is exactly like him; you must positively examine his head—I cannot tell you how a good a child he is." .

"I had thus in my eye," says Dr. Gall, "three cases in which goodness of disposition was strongly marked. I took casts of the head, placed them beside each other, and continued to examine them until I should discover a developement common to the three. This I at last found, although the heads were in other respects very differently formed. In the meantime I tried to find similar cases in families, schools, &c., that I might be in a condition to multiply and correct my observations. I extended my investigations to animals also, and, in a short time, collected so great a number of facts, that there is no fundamental quality or faculty whose existence and organ are better established than those of Benevolence."

The faculty produces desire of the happiness of others and delight in the diffusion of enjoyment. It disposes to active goodness, and, in cases of distress, to compassion. It is easy to distinguish kindness flowing from this sentiment, from acts of attention arising from Love of Approbation or more interested motives. A warmth and simplicity of manner, and a directness of purpose, are communicated by this faculty, that touch the mind at once. We feel its character, and recognise it as genuine, unalloyed goodness, aiming at no end but the welfare of its object. There is, on the other hand, an air of "*empressement*" evidently assumed, or of coldness and constraint, attending deeds of kindness proceeding from interested motives, betraying the source from which they flow. The secret spring and ulterior object are apparent, notwithstanding the efforts made to conceal them. St. Paul gives a beautiful description of the genuine character of this sentiment in his account of Christian charity: "Charity," says he, "suffereth long and is kind; charity envieth not; charity vaunteth not itself; is not puffed up," &c. The good Samaritan mentioned in Scripture, is a delightful instance of the disposition formed by Benevolence when eminently powerful. It is a leading feature also in the character of Addison's Sir Roger de Coverley.

This faculty is a great source of happiness to the possessor. It communicates a lively, amiable, delightful tinge to the impressions received by the mind from without. It produces liberality of sentiment toward all mankind, a disposition to love them, and to dwell on their virtues rather than their vices. A person in whom this feeling is strong, rarely complains of the ingratitude or heartlessness of others. His goodness provides its own reward. The organ appears very large in the mask of Henri Quatre. When one some spoke to him of an officer of the League, by whom he was not loved, he replied, "*Je veux lui faire tant de bien, que je le forcerai de m'aimer malgré lui.*" A person thus endowed is so conscious of wishing well to others, that he hardly doubts of their good-will toward himself. Adhesiveness attaches us to friends and to countrymen; but Benevolence brings the whole human race within the circle of our affections. Fenelon exhibited a beautiful manifestation of it, when he said, "I am a true *Frenchman*, and love my country; but I love *mankind* better than my country." It inspired Henri-Quatre also, when he replied to those who exhorted him to rigour toward some places which had joined the League; "La satisfaction qu'on tire de la vengeance ne dure qu'un moment; mais celle qu'on tire de la clemence est eternelle." The organ is large, and very distinctly marked, in the mask of Jacob Jervis, presented by Dr. Abel to the Phrenological Society. That individual possessed the sentiment in so high a degree, that he was obliged to hide himself when he saw persons coming to make improper solicitations, being conscious of his inability to resist them. The organ is extremely developed also in the head of a negro called Eustache, who lived for a considerable time in Paris, and in whom the feeling was excessively strong. The cut represents a section of his head across Benevolence. During the insurrection of the blacks in St. Domingo, the disinterested exertions of Eustache on behalf of his master were unbounded; and when the latter, in consequence of weakness of the eyes, became unable to amuse himself by reading, he taught himself to read, in order that he might have the satisfaction of whiling away his master's long and sleepless hours. In Paris he was constantly occupied in doing good, and, on meeting a beggar, could hardly refrain from giving away all that was in his possession. His merits were publicly recognised by the institute, from whom he obtained the *prise of virtue* on the 9th of August, 1832 [*]

It is a vulgar idea that this faculty cannot be manifested, except in bestowing alms or money. It may be exerted in the domestic circle and in society in a thousand ways, productive of advantage, without being accompanied by donation. It is benevolence to those with whom we live to order our arrangements with a due regard to their comfort and happiness, and not to deny them proper gratifications; it is benevolence to suppress our own humours and tendencies, when these would give unnecessary pain to others; to restrain Self-Esteem and Destructiveness in our commands; to be mild and merciful in our censures; to exert our influence and authority to promote the welfare of others: and one of the most benevolent of all exercises is, to visit the poor and vicious, when suffering and wretched, even with the view of administering only the pecuniary bounty of others. It is an essential element also in true politeness.

Deficiency of Benevolence does not produce cruelty nor any positively bad sentiment; but it leads to regardlessness of the welfare of others. When the organ is small, a powerful restraint is withdrawn from the lower propensities. In Bellingham, Hare, Griffiths, and other cold-blooded and deliberate murderers, the organ is decidedly deficient. Those in whom this organ is less than Acquisitiveness and Self-Esteem, rarely feel themselves called on to join in works of charity, to contribute to subscriptions, or to bestow personal exertions for the benefit of others; they generally urge the apology, that they have enough to do with themselves, and that nobody manifests benevolence toward them. This latter excuse may be just; for it is in the nature of all the higher sentiments to be doubly rewarded—*first*, in the enjoyment which attends the very exercise of them; and, *secondly*, in the kindly feelings which the manifestation of them generates in others. Closely connected as men are in society, and dependent, in a greater or less degree, on each other for prosperity and

* *Journal de la Soc. Phrén. de Paris* for 1824, and April, 1836; also *Phren. Journ.*, ix., 134, and Vimont's *Treatise on Phrenology.*

happiness, no individual can enjoy, or leave to his children, a richer and more valuable treasure, than the esteem and affection of his fellows, founded on respect and gratitude for his own virtues and generosity. Such advantages, indeed, the selfish man cannot enjoy ; for his conduct excites no benevolence in others toward him, and his selfishness becomes the more necessary, as he has chosen it as his stay. When large Acquisitiveness and Self-Esteem are combined with this organ small, the individual will be an utter disbeliever in disinterested goodness, and will regard generosity, which has no selfish end, as imbecility. Such a combination, also, if joined with much Destructiveness, probably leads its possessor to doubt of the benevolence of the Supreme Being. Deficiency of the organ, in short, exposes the mind to the predominance of the lower feelings, and the temper is then apt to become cold, harsh, sour, and unhappy. There is little sympathy with enjoyment ; the face of creation does not appear to smile ; moral and physical objects are viewed on their darkest sides ; and if Destructiveness be large, the mind steels itself with malignity, as a defence against their imagined evil qualities—misanthropy, in short, is the result. The character of Lucifer, as drawn by Milton, and by Byron in his drama of Cain, is a personification of great Destructiveness and Intellect, with an utter destitution of Benevolence.

The organ is small in tribes of men remarkable for cruelty ; for example, in the Caribs. In the representations of Tiberius, Caligula, Caracalla, Nero, Catharine of Medicis, Christian the Cruel, Danton, and Robespierre, says Dr. Gall, the organ is deficient ; while it is large in Trajan, Marcus Aurelius, Henri Quatre, and other individuals distinguished for benevolent feelings.

Benevolence, admirable as it is in its own nature, requires to be directed by Conscientiousness and Intellect, otherwise it produces abuses. When too powerful, and not so guided, it leads to profusion. This kind of facility is not the effect of mere weakness of reasoning power ; it arises from an over-ready disposition to give, without an adequate motive or consideration, but merely for the pleasure of bestowing. Benevolence very powerful, with deficient Firmness, may lead also to the sacrifice of the just interests of the individual, to the necessities or cupidity of others. In short, this sentiment, indulged without consideration, may produce many evil consequences : indiscriminate donations to beggars in the street, for example, encourage profligacy ; and compulsory assessments for support of the poor have often fostered recklessness and idleness. It can never be sufficiently inculcated, that the functions of the different faculties of the mind are distinct, that those which feel give merely an impulse in general, and that Nature intended them to be placed under the direction of the faculties which reason. Hence, the individual who instinctively feels a vivid compassion for every object in distress, ought to be aware, that this impulse is not the voice of inspiration directing him to the mode in which it should be indulged. On the contrary, the stronger the emotion, the power of direction is not unfrequently the weaker ; because the feeling is in itself of so excellent a character, and so delightful, that the man who is inspired by it is the last to suspect the necessity of much consideration in regard to the mode in which it is employed. On the other hand, however, it must also be remembered, that the faculties which reason do not feel Benevolence, and that, hence, that individual is most fitted to mature wise plans of charity who enjoys a large endowment of this sentiment, combined with powerful intellectual faculties duly cultivated.

It has been objected, that Nature cannot have placed a faculty of Benevolence, and another of Destructiveness, in the same mind. But man is confessedly an assemblage of various qualities. The great modern novelist speaks of "the well-known cases of men of undoubted benevolence of character and disposition, whose *principal delight is, to see a miserable criminal*, degraded alike by his previous crimes and the sentence which he has incurred, *conclude a vicious and a wretched life by an ignominious and cruel death.*"[*] This indicates Benevolence coexisting in the same individual with Destructiveness. The greatest of poets has said :—

> "O thou goddess,
> Thou divine Nature, how thyself thou-blazon'st
> In these two princely boys! They are as *gentle*
> As zephyrs, blowing below the violet,
> Not wagging his sweet head ; and yet as rough,
> Their royal blood enchaff'd, as the rud'st wind,
> That by the top doth take the mountain-pine,
> And make him stoop to the vale."

Here Shakspeare informs us, that these boys manifested much Combativeness and Destructiveness, combined with great Benevolence.

The skull of Burns indicates large Combativeness, Destructiveness, and Self-Esteem, combined with large Benevolence and full Conscientiousness ; and Dr. Currie, his accomplished biographer, describes his character thus': "By nature kind, brave, sincere, and in a singular degree compassionate, he was, on the other hand, proud, irascible, and vindictive ;" indicating, in the clearest manner, the coexistence in him of the organs before-named.

The sword is one of the emblems of State, and what is it but the symbol of destruction ready to fall on the heads of those who offend against the laws ?—ministering thus, in its very severity, to purposes of Benevolence and Justice. What are the implements of war but instruments of destruction ? and for what end do soldiers take the field, but to destroy their enemies ? And yet surgeons and numerous assistants attend on armies, to succour those on whom the calamities of war have fallen ; the two faculties, which are deemed incompatible, being thus manifested together, with deliberate design. Without Combativeness and Destructiveness there would be no war ; and without Benevolence, if these existed, there would be neither mercy nor compassion. Instead, therefore, of the coexistence of these faculties forming an objection to the phrenological system, it proves its harmony with nature.[†]

Benevolence cannot be compensated by Adhesiveness and Conscientiousness, nor any other faculties. A daughter, wife, or sister, who possesses large Benevolence, will, at a sick-bed, show an anxiety to alleviate suffering, a softness and sympathy of manner, and, if intellect is possessed, a fertility of invention in devising means of relief, that will be truly admirable, and to the patient invaluable : but if this organ be deficient, although the attendant may, through Intellect and Conscientiousness, do everything that is suggested by others, she will neither sympathize with, nor spontaneously labour to assuage, the patient's pain. This observation applies to every department of life in which Benevolence can be manifested. When it is small, the well-spring of goodness flowing toward misery is absent.

Dr. Gall refers not only the feeling of benevolence, but the sentiment of justice, to the faculty now under consideration. "The reader will remember," says he, "that I could not discover the functions of the different organs, except when I met with them in a state of extreme developement, and when, consequently, the faculties were manifested with excessive energy. A mental power, in a state of high excitement, sometimes exhibits a character quite different in appearance from its ordinary

* *St. Ronan's Well*

† Lord Kames mentions several instances of the combined action of Destructiveness and Benevolence in his *Sketches*, B. i., Sk. b. See also *Phren. Journ.*, i., 193 ; ix., 67, 417.

form of manifestation. Libertinism is the consequence of over-activity of Amativeness, and theft of Acquisitiveness. It is the same with Benevolence. The individuals who had become remarkable on account of uncommon goodness of heart, presented an extreme developement of the organ in question. Consequently, goodness, benevolence, sensibility to distress, are not the primitive destination or ordinary function of this organ; but the manifestation of its exalted condition. Benevolence, therefore, is something more than the primitive function of the organ from which it proceeds. What is the original sentiment? It being extremely difficult to make positive observations on the fundamental destination of an organ, I am obliged," continues Dr. Gall, " to resort to reasoning ; and I think there are plausible grounds for holding, that the primitive tendency connected with this organ is that which disposes man to conduct suitable to the maintenance of social order :, I call it *the moral sense, the sentiment of justice and injustice.*" He proceeds with a variety of arguments, and arrives at the conclusion, that Benevolence " n'est qu'un degré d'action plus élevé du sens moral."*

Dr. Spurzheim dissents from this view, and holds Conscientiousness to be a distinct sentiment, of which he has discovered and established the organ ; although it was not admitted by Dr. Gall. There are only two ways of settling this dispute ; the one by metaphysical analysis of the feeling, and the other by observation of the organ. The result of both appears to me to be in favour of Dr. Spurzheim. I shall revert to the subject when treating of the organ of Conscientiousness.

In another point, also, in regard to this organ, Dr. Spurzheim differs from Dr. Gall, and apparently on good grounds. "An opinion of Dr. Gall," says he, " of which I cannot approve, is, that Benevolence may degenerate into bad temper, and into the propensity to rejoice in the evil that happens to others, in the same way as the sense of taste may degenerate into disgust at food, physical love into aversion to the other sex, and the sense of melody to aversion to music. The inactivity of Benevolence, or its exhausted state, may produce indifference to its functions, and make us avoid any opportunity of doing beneficent actions ; but active wickedness, and pleasure in the pains of others, like cruelty, depend on inferior feelings, unaccompanied by superior sentiments."†

This organ is found in the lower animals, and, when it is largely developed, they are mild and docile ; whereas, when it is deficient, they are vicious, ill-natured, and intractable. Dr. Gall gives some interesting illustrations of this fact. The head of the tiger, says he, is more flat at this part than that of the lion ; and the heads of the hyæna and wolf are more depressed than that of the dog. The organ is greatly depressed immediately above the level of the eyes in the baboon ; while, on the contrary, it is elevated in the ouran-outang ; and the dispositions of all these animals are in accordance with their developement. In the horse the organ is placed in the middle of the forehead, a little above the eyes. When this region is hollow and narrow, a horse is invariably vicious, and disposed to bite and to kick. In mild and good-natured horses, on the contrary, this part stands as far out as the eyes, or even farther. The driver of a cabriolet of Neuilly, says Dr. Gall, bought, at a low price, a horse which nobody could use on account of its extremely bad temper ; but it was an excellent runner. In the first week it bit off two of the driver's fingers and one of his ears. He attempted to correct it by redoubled blows, but these rendered it only more vicious. He then resolved to try the effect of gentle treatment, and this succeeded to a certain extent. The organ in question was very small in this animal ; and the same

* *Sur les Fonctions du Cerveau,* tome v., p. 273, *et sequen.*
† *Phrenology,* p. 190.

conformation will be found in all horses which require to be muzzled, to prevent them from biting. On one occasion, a gentleman in the country mentioned at his dinner-table, that he had two horses, one extremely mild, and the other very vicious in temper. They were brought out into the stable-yard, and, by examining their heads according to Dr. Gall's directions, I pointed out each, without having previously seen them. The difference was so great, that several persons who were present recognised it the moment they were told where to look for it. I have seen this experiment repeated with invariable success.

The same rule holds in regard to dogs. Dr. Gall saved two puppies of a litter of five, and watched their dispositions with the closest attention. Even before their eyes were opened he remarked a great difference between them; one of them, when taken into the hand, testified, by its gestures, that it was pleased; the other growled, whined, and struggled till it was put down. Scarcely were they fifteen days old, when one indicated, by the motions of its tail, contentment and gentleness, not only toward other little dogs, but to persons who approached it; the other, on the contrary, never ceased to grumble, and to bite every one within its reach. Aware how much was attributed to education, Dr. Gall charged those who habitually approached these animals to bestow equal caresses on each. He himself took the greatest pains to soften the disposition of the ill-natured one; but nothing could change its character. It bit even its mother, if she chanced to incommode it. In the sixth month the dogs were seized with distemper, and with whatever degree of gentleness they were treated, the one never ceased to growl and bite, till death put an end to its efforts; while the other, on the contrary, till its last moment, gave the most striking marks of attachment and gratitude to those who took charge of it. Even the servants were forcibly struck with the difference in the dispositions of these animals. Dr. Gall states, that the difference in their heads was equally conspicuous.

In observing this organ in the lower animals, it is necessary to be acquainted with the osteology of their skulls, to be able correctly to distinguish its place. In some of them, such as the elephant, the sow, &c., the two tables of the skull are not parallel at this part, and hence the size of the organ in them cannot be ascertained except by dissection. In the bull and cow the inner table is separated to some distance from the external table, but the two tables are parallel in the region of this organ, and on this account its size may be judged of during life. The same is the case, says Dr. Gall, with the cat.*

"There are examples," says Dr. Spurzheim, "on record, where animals have shown high degrees of benevolence to others, and even to man. A respectable family of Paris told me, that they had a horse and a cow living together in the same stable; that the horse several times got untied, went to the corner where the sack of oats stood, and drew it in his teeth near the cow; probably to make her partake of the good cheer. Many dogs also exhibit the same feeling. Dupont de Nemours saw a swallow caught by one foot in the noose of a pack-thread attached to the roof of the French Institute at Paris. The prisoner screamed, and attracted all the swallows of the neighbourhood. After a long and tumultuous consultation, a great number formed a line, one after another darted at the pack-thread with their bills, and in half an hour delivered the captive."†

Some incidents of a similar nature have happened in this country. Dr. Millar favoured me with the following statement: "The Reverend Dr. Wodrow, late of Stevenston, in Ayrshire, when clergyman of Dunlop, a parish in the same county, narrated a curious fact, concerning swallows,

* Sur les Fonctions du Cerveau, tome v., p. 327.
† Phrenology, p. 188.

in a letter to his relative, Mrs. Thomson, of Edinburgh. ' At Dunlop manse,' says he, ' in a very dry summer, one of their nests, attached to the corner of the parlour-window, fell down, and lay on the window-sill, without any damage done either to the nest or its helpless inhabitants, four or five young ones. It was a few minutes before breakfast, when I observed the accident ; and, soon after it happened, I went out, and carefully placed it on the top of a cut hedge, and I waited to see the event. It was pleasant to see the young ones fed at proper intervals, and, at the same time, a great number of other swallows jointly and busily employed, in a warm summer morning, in building a new nest in the same place with the former ; some of them bringing clay, straws, &c. ; others making use of these materials ; others dipping themselves into an open well, and plashing the walls of the nest ; and all of them cheering one another to the useful work. In two hours the new nest was completely finished, and then the young ones were carried through the air under the wings of one, sometimes two, old swallows, and safely placed in their lodging ; after which the noise and cheering of the troop ceased.' " Dr. Poole also stated to me, that a cat having seized a young sparrow, a flock of these birds perceiving it, attacked the cat, fastened on its back, pecked and flapped till they made it quit its prey, and rescued the intended victim. This happened in a garden behind St. John-street, Edinburgh, and was witnessed by a neighbour of Dr. Poole's, who communicated the circumstances to him. Dogs also are known to precipitate themselves into water, to save persons in danger of being drowned ; and they attack with fury assassins who assail their masters.

The activity of this sentiment is productive of so much benefit in society, that its cultivation ought to be specially attended to in the training of children. The experience of the teachers of infant-schools shows how much may be done in adding to its energy.*

I have mentioned before, that stimulating liquors, by exciting the organs, give energy to the feelings or propensities which depend on them for the means of manifestation. Some individuals become excessively profuse when intoxicated. They would then give the world away ; or, if they had the power, they would create a new one, in which every individual should enjoy infinite happiness. On the principle that intoxication can never create any feeling, I am inclined to think that such persons have naturally a large endowment of Benevolence, the organ of which is stimulated to this great activity by strong potations. This, however, is only a conjecture.

The organ is liable to excessive excitement by disease. Dr. Gall mentions the case of a hussar, who had always manifested great benevolence of disposition, and subsequently became insane. He gave away all his clothes, and left himself absolutely naked ; he never ceased repeating that he wished to make every one happy, and he introduced into all his projects of beneficence the Holy Trinity. In his head the organs of Benevolence and Veneration were extremely developed. Idiots in whom this organ is large are good-natured and harmless ; while those in whom it is small, if Destructiveness be large, are mischievous and wicked.

The existence of Benevolence, as an innate sentiment of the human mind, is distinctly recognised by Lord Bacon in one of his *Essays*. "I take goodness," says he, "in this sense, the affecting of the weal of men, which is that the Grecians call *philanthropia* ; and the word humanity (as it is used) is a little too light to express it. Goodness I call the habit, and goodness of nature the inclination. This, of all virtues and dignities of the mind, is the greatest, being the character of the Deity ; and, without it, man is a busy, mischievous, wretched thing, no better than a kind of vermin....The inclination to goodness is imprinted deeply in the nature of man, insomuch that if it issue not toward men, it will take unto other living creatures; as it is seen in the Turks, a cruel people, who, nevertheless, are kind to beasts, give alms to dogs and birds; insomuch that, as Busbechius reporteth, a Christian boy in Constantinople had like to have been stoned for gagging, in a waggishness, a long-billed fowl."

The Scotch metaphysicians in general admit the existence of this sentiment; but Hobbes, and many other metaphysical writers, who resolve all our actions into selfishness, deny it. Dr. Thomas Brown successfully and beautifully answers the objection, that we are selfish even in our feelings of good will. "The analysis of love," says he, "as a complex feeling, presents to us always at least two elements; a vivid delight in the contemplation of the object, and a desire of good to that object....Though we cannot, then, when there is no interfering passion, think of the virtues of others *without pleasure*, and must, therefore, in loving virtue, *love what is by its own nature* pleasing, the love of *the virtue which cannot exist without the pleasure*, is surely an affection very different from the love of the mere pleasure existing, if it had been possible for it to exist, *without the virtue*—a pleasure that accompanies the virtue, only as the soft or brilliant colouring of nature flows from the great orb above—a gentle radiance that is delightful to our eyes, indeed, and to our heart, but which leads our eye upward to the splendid source from which it flows, and our heart, still higher, to that Being by whom the sun was made."*

Mr. Robert Cox has published, in the tenth volume of *The Phrenological Journal*, p. 1, an elaborate essay on the "laws of action of Benevolence;" in which he adduces a variety of facts and arguments, to shew that the power and activity of this organ are increased by the *agreeable* or pleasurable action of the organs of the other mental powers, in the same way as Destructiveness receives excitement when their action is *disagreeable*. Hence he regards happiness as conducive to generosity and sweetness of temper, and misery as tending to render the disposition sour and irritable; and from these principles practical results of great importance are deduced.

14. VENERATION.

This organ is situated in the middle of the coronal region of the brain, at the bregma or fontanel of anatomists. The figures represent it large and small.

PAPUAN.   GRIFFITHS.
14   14

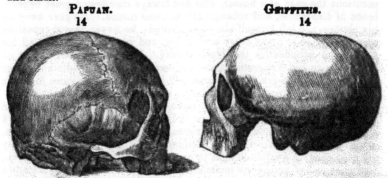

Dr. Gall gives the following account of the discovery of this organ: His father's family consisted of ten children, who all received the same

* *Lecture* 59, vol. iii., p. 241.

education, but their talents and dispositions were very dissimilar. One of his brothers manifested from infancy a strong tendency toward religion. "Ses jouets étaient des vases d'église qu'il sculptoit lui-même, des chasubles et des surplis qu'il faisait avec du papier." He was constantly engaged in prayer and in saying mass; and when obliged to be absent from church, he spent his time in ornamenting and gilding a crucifix of wood. His father had intended him for a merchant, but he himself disliked that occupation, because, said he, it exposed him to the necessity of lying. At the age of twenty-three years he abandoned merchandise; and having lost all hope of being then able to pursue the studies requisite for the church, he fled from his father's house, and became a hermit. His father at length allowed him to study—at the end of five years he took orders, and continued, till the period of his death, to live in the exercise of devotion and the practice of penance.

Dr. Gall farther remarked, that, in schools, some of the children took no interest in religious instruction, while others received it with avidity; also, that those individuals in the classes who voluntarily devoted themselves to the church, were either studious, pious, virtuous, and honourable young men, or idlers of the worst description, indolent, and totally destitute of talent. The latter, he observes, obviously had no other aim than that of living at the expense of their fellow-citizens; while the former felt a lively interest in the vocation to which they aspired. This commendable feeling sprang up in them, says he, nobody knew how; and it certainly was not attributable to example or education, nor to the circumstances in which they had been placed; for many of them had embraced the clerical profession, even contrary to the intention of their parents and guardians. These facts convinced him that the disposition to religion is innate.

At a later period, no sooner had he fixed his attention on some of the primitive qualities of the mind, than he recollected these observations made in his youth, and immediately examined the heads of persons eminent for devotion. He visited the churches of every sect, and particularly observed the heads of individuals who prayed with the greatest fervour, or who were the most completely absorbed in their religious contemplations. The result was the establishment of the part of the brain in question as the organ of Veneration.

Catholic countries afford particularly favourable opportunities for such observations. Dr. Bright, a traveller in Lower Hungary, informs us, that, in Vienna, "the churches are almost constantly open, and enter them when you will, servants, who have been sent on errands, are seen kneeling before the altars or the images, with their baskets or parcels by their sides. Thus prayer, by its frequency, becomes a habit and recreation, rather than the performance of a duty; and I have often been truly astonished to observe, in the coldest weather, little children, when far from the restraints of their parents, fall down upon their knees before the images which adorn many of the corners of the streets and passages in Vienna, and there remain fixed for several minutes, as in serious devotion."* I have observed similar facts in Catholic cities on the continent.

The function of the faculty is to produce the sentiment of Veneration in general; or an emotion of profound and reverential respect, on perceiving an object at once great and good. It is the source of natural religion, and of that tendency to worship a superior power, which manifests itself in almost every tribe of men yet discovered. The faculty, however, produces merely an emotion, and does not form ideas of the object to which adoration should be directed; and hence, if no revelation have reached the individual, and if the understanding be extremely limited, the unfor-

* Pages 43, 44.
18*

tunate being may worship the genius of the storm; the sun, as the source of light, heat, and vegetable life; or, if more debased in intellect, brutes, and stocks, and stones:

> " Lo! the poor Indian, whose untutored mind,
> Sees God in clouds, or hears him in the wind."

The organ is large in King Robert Bruce, who, it is mentioned in history, was strongly alive to religious feelings, and ordered his heart to be carried to the Holy Land, because he had not been able to fulfil a vow to visit it in person.

This faculty, when unenlightened, may lead to every kind of religious absurdity; as worshipping beasts, and stocks, and stones. The negroes, American Indians, and even the Hindoos, have a poor intellectual developement compared with Europeans, and their superstitions are more gross. Socrates did not assent to the popular religious errors of the Greeks, and in the ancient busts of him he is represented with a splendid forehead.*

It is large also in the negroes, who are extremely prone to superstition.

It has been objected, that, if an organ and faculty of Veneration exist, revelation was unnecessary. But Dr. Gall has well answered, that the proposition ought to be exactly reversed: for unless a natural capacity of feeling religious emotion had been previously bestowed, revelation would have been as unavailing to man as it would be to the lower animals; while, if a mere general sentiment of devotion, or an instinctive, but blind, tendency to worship, which Veneration truly is, was given, nothing was more reasonable than to add instruction how it ought to be directed. Dr. Gall observes, farther, that the existence of the organ is an indirect proof of the existence of God. Destructiveness is implanted in the mind, and animals exist around us, to be killed for our nourishment: Adhesiveness and Philoprogenitiveness are given, and friends and children are provided as objects on whom they may be exercised: Benevolence is conferred on us, and the poor and unhappy, on whom it may shed its soft influence, are everywhere present with us: in like manner, the instinctive tendency to worship is implanted in the mind, and, conformably to these analogies of nature, we may reasonably infer that a God exists whom we may adore. As, however, Veneration has likewise objects on earth, this argument cannot be regarded as conclusive.

The organ is possessed by all men, but in different degrees by different persons: and, on the principle that the natural power of experiencing an emotion bears a proportion *cæteris paribus* to the size of its organ, every sane individual will be naturally capable of joining in religious worship; but the glow of devotional feeling experienced by each will be greater or less in intensity, according to the developement of this part of his brain. The difference in the strength of the emotion is certain, independently of Phrenology; so that this science only reveals the relation between its intensity and the size of the organ.

Dr. Gall mentions, that, in the portraits of saints remarkable for devotional feeling, this organ is represented as large, and that the same configuration of head has been given by the ancient artists to their high priests. It is large in the portraits of Constantine, Marcus Aurelius, St. Ambrose, Charles I. of England, and Malebranche. In the portrait of St. John, in the Last Supper, by Leonardo da Vinci, on the succeeding page, it and Benevolence are represented as very large.

It is also greatly developed in philosophers and poets who are distinguished for piety, as in Newton, Milton, and Klopstock; while it is flat in the head of Spinosa, who professed atheism. The same configuration is found in the heads of Christ represented by Raphael. In these the

* A copy of his bust may be seen in the Phrenological Society's Hall.

parts behind the ear, or the organs common to man and the lower animals, are small ; whereas the organs situated in the forehead and in the coronal region, connected with intellect and the moral sentiments, are very large. This organization indicates great intellectual penetration, with exalted Benevolence and Veneration. Dr. Gall puts the question, Has this divine form of head been invented, or may we presume that it is a faithful copy of the original? It is possible, says he, that the artists may have imitated the heads of the most virtuous, just, and benevolent men whom they could find, and thence drawn the character of the head of Christ. In this case the observation of the artists coincides with that of Dr. Gall —a circumstance which supposes either a kind of presentiment of organology on their part, or an accuracy of observation scarcely admissible. He considers it more probable that the general type, at least, of the head of Christ has been transmitted to us. St. Luke was a painter, and how should he fail to preserve the features of his Master? It is certain that this form of the head of Christ is of a very high antiquity. It is found in the most ancient pictures and specimens of mosaic work. The Gnostics of the second century possessed images of Christ and of St. Paul ; hence Dr. Gall concludes, that neither Raphael nor any other artist has invented this admirable configuration.*

The metaphysicians in general do not treat of Veneration as an original emotion. They trace the belief in God to the perceptions of the understanding. We perceive order, beauty, harmony, power, wisdom, and goodness in the works of creation, and infer from these qualities that a supreme creating and directing Mind exists. In this view the phrenolo-

* *Sur les Fonctions du Cerveau,* tome v., p. 389. See also a Brief Notice of some Ancient Coins and Medals, as illustrating the Progress of Christianity, by the Rev. R. Walsh, LL.D. Chaplain to the Embassy at Constantinople.

gists concur: the understanding, however, only perceives facts and draws inferences, but does not feel emotions; and, therefore, after this deduction was completed, it would experience no tendency to adore the God whom it had discovered. Now, in point of fact, the tendency to worship is a stronger principle than the understanding itself; for the most ignorant and stupid men are prone to venerate, while their intellects are incapable of directing them to an object worthy of their homage. Under the influence of a blind Veneration, they cut branches from trees, and fall down and worship them; or they adore monsters and reptiles as deities —facts which were utterly inexplicable, till, Phrenology pointed out an instinctive tendency to venerate, altogether apart from understanding. This tendency is produced by the faculty in question, and it is a great omission on the part of the old philosophers, that no such power is to be found in their systems.

Hitherto we have considered Veneration only as directed to religion, which is undoubtedly its noblest end; but it has also objects and a wide sphere of action in the present world. It produces the feeling of deference and respect in general; and hence may be directed to every object that seems worthy of such regard. In children it is a chief ingredient in filial piety, and produces that soft and almost holy reverence with which a child looks up to his parent as the author of his days, the protector of his infancy, and the guide of his youth. A child in whom this organ is small, may, if Benevolence and Adhesiveness are large, entertain great affection for his parent as a friend; but, in his habitual intercourse, there will be little of that deferential respect which is the grand feature of the mind when the organ is large. Children who are prone to rebellion, regardless of authority, and little attentive to command, will generally be found to have Self-Esteem large and this organ proportionally deficient.

Veneration leads to deference for superiors in rank as well as in years, and prompts to the reverence of authority. The organ is generally largely developed in the Asiatic head, and the tendency to obedience is strong in the people of that quarter of the globe. Indeed, the hereditary slavery which has descended among them through so many generations, may be connected with the prevalence of this disposition.

A lady who is in the habit of examining the heads of servants before hiring them, informed me, that she has found, by experience, that those in whom Veneration is large are the most deferential and obedient; and that one with large Combativeness and Destructiveness, and small Veneration, became angry and abusive when her conduct was censured. This occurred, even although Love of Approbation and Conscientiousness were both large; but the passion speedily subsided, and was followed by self-reproach and repentance. If Veneration also had been large, it would have produced that instinctive feeling of respect which would have operated as instantaneously as Combativeness and Destructiveness, and restrained the ebullitions.

Veneration may produce also respect for titles, rank, and power; for a long line of ancestry, or mere wealth; and it frequently manifests itself in one or other of these forms, when it does not appear in religious fervour. Individuals in whom Love of Approbation and Veneration are very large, and Conscientiousness and intellect not in proportion, venerate persons of higher rank than their own, and are fond of their society. People of rank, who do not possess high virtues or talents, like the society of those in whom this combination occurs. It inspires its possessor with an habitual deference toward them, which is felt as a constant homage. On the occasion of King George the Fourth's visit to Scotland in 1822, some individuals experienced the profoundest emotion of awe and respect beholding him; while others were not conscious of any similar ex citement, and were surprised at what appeared to them to be the exaggerated enthusiasm of the first. I examined the heads of several of both classes, and, in the former, found the organ of Veneration uniformly larger, in proportion to the other organs, than in the latter.

This faculty is likewise the source of the profound awe which some persons feel in visiting ancient temples, Gothic cathedrals, and places of sepulture for the illustrious dead. It gives reverence for churchyards, and other burial-places of our ancestors. A person in whom it is small experiences a comparatively feeble emotion, even in viewing Westminster Abbey, and the monuments of departed genius there preserved. Veneration is one ingredient in the love of old coins, and in the tendency generally to antiquarianism.

Like other powers, this sentiment is liable to abuse. When not subjected to the guidance of Reflection and Conscientiousness, it may produce a bigoted respect for old customs and absurd institutions, if only sanctified by time; and a blind tendency to admire the wisdom of our ancestors beyond its real worth.* It gives reverence for great names and authorities in religion and philosophy, and thus often presents a strong obstacle to the progress of truth. It seems to maintain the unenlightened devotee in a state of bigoted subjection to his priests : an emotion of profound and sanctified respect springs up in his mind on contemplating the doctrines which they have instilled into him in his youth ; and every suggestion of the understanding, in opposition to this feeling, is expelled as profane. In short, Veneration, when vigorous and unenlightened, produces complete prostration of the mind before the object to which it is directed. A few years ago the despotic sovereigns of Europe, under the name of the Holy Allies, were bent upon cultivating this sentiment to the highest possible degree in their subjects ; prostrating reason, they encouraged monks, processions, and superstitious observances, while they banished philosophers and excluded books of science. If it had been possible to succeed, these sovereigns would have rendered their people blind worshippers of their own power, and trained them to bow in humble subserviency to their will. The French Revolution of 1830 gave a deathblow to their projects. The Spaniards are a noble people, but, while their intellects have been shackled for many centuries, Veneration has been cultivated to an extravagant height, and misdirected ; in consequence of which they have fallen into a state of benighted and ferocious superstition.

Defect of Veneration does not necessarily produce profanity, but only indifference to religious exercises, and little reverence for power and ancestry. On the other hand, a man may possess a large organ of Veneration, and, nevertheless, have no reverence for the Christian religion, if he disbelieve in its divine origin ; but he will venerate something else. Voltaire's Veneration was large, and he was an unbeliever ; but he is known to have venerated the Supreme Being, and to have paid great deference to persons of high rank.† He was even accused of fanaticism by some of the Parisian sçavans, on account of his respect for God. I have found Veneration large, in the head of the genuine Tory—in him who really delights in contemplating kings and nobles, and who regards them as invested with a degree of sanctity by being able to trace their descent through a long line of ancestry, and by the possession of hereditary authority. In the genuine Whig or republican, who sees in kings and nobles only men liable to all the frailties of human nature, and requiring checks to prevent them from abusing power, Veneration is generally smaller, in proportion to their intellectual endowment. When Veneration, Self-Esteem, Con-

* See *Phrenological Journal*, viii., 598.
† See "Observations on some recent Objections to Phrenology, founded on a part of the Cerebral Developement of Voltaire," by Mr. Simpson, *Phren. Journ.*, iii., 564.

scientiousness, and Intellect are all well developed, the individuals are moderate Whigs or moderate Tories, and readily approximate in their sentiments. They ought to exercise mutual forbearance, their different feelings being the result of different natural constitutions. These observations are limited to genuine Tories and genuine Whigs ; for a man may profess whiggery through love of place, and toryism through mere factiousness, and in such cases other organs will predominate.

As Nature has implanted the organs of Veneration and Wonder in the brain, and the corresponding sentiments in the mind, it is a groundless terror to apprehend that religion can ever be extinguished, or even endangered, by the arguments or ridicule of the profane. Forms of worship may change, and particular religious tenets may now be fashionable, and subsequently fall into decay ; but while the human heart continues to beat, awe and veneration for the Divine Being will ever animate the soul : the worshipper will cease to kneel, and the hymn of adoration to rise, only when the race of man becomes extinct.

The natural language of this faculty carries the head upward in the direction of the organ. The voice is soft, subdued, reposing, and adoring. The greatest difference is perceptible in the tones and manner of prayer of clergymen in whom the organ is large, compared with those in whom it is small ; there is a soft breathing fervour of devotion in the former, and a cold reasoning formality in the latter. I have found the organ uniformly large in clergymen who selected the clerical profession from natural liking, and not merely as a means of subsistence.

The organ is generally larger in the female head than in the male ; and women are more obedient and prone to devotion.

Dr. Gall treats of this sentiment as producing religious feeling alone ; to Dr. Spurzheim is due the merit of analyzing it, and. describing it as the source of the emotion of reverence and respect in general.

Nothing is more common in the hospitals for the insane, says Pinel, than cases of alienation produced by devotional feelings excessively exalted, by conscientious scruples carried to prejudicial excesses, or by religious terror. As this kind of insanity, says Dr. Gall, is often present without derangement of the other faculties, physicians ought to have inferred that it is connected with disease of a particular part of the brain. He and Dr. Spurzheim saw, in the hospital of Amsterdam, a patient who was tormented with the idea that he was compelled to sin, and that he could not possibly be saved. In him the organ of Veneration was very largely developed. In a priest who despaired of salvation, and in another patient who had the confirmed idea that he was condemned to eternal punishment, the organ was also very large. A woman, named Elizabeth Lindemann, was brought to Dr. Gall. At the first glance he perceived that she possessed this organ in an extraordinary degree ; she continued standing before him lifting her eyes from time to time to heaven, and indicating, by all her gestures, sadness and anguish. From her youth she had been excessively addicted to prayer. For some time previous to the interview with Dr. Gall, she "had been subject to convulsions, and maintained that she was possessed ; the devil, she said, entered into her heart by her mouth, and made efforts to carry her to hell." Dr. Gall mentions also, that he had seen, in the collection of M. Esquirol, casts of the heads of three persons subject to religious insanity. In all the three the organ of Veneration was largely developed. If, says he, M. Esquirol continues for some time to mould the heads of the insane and to preserve their skulls, he will not fail to become one of the most zealous and enlightened disciples of Organology. Esquirol very justly remarks on the subject, that although a particular sermon has often been blamed for producing this species of insanity, yet it would not have had

that effect, unless there had been a predisposition to the disease, probably
a pre-existence of it, in the individual.
I have seen patients insane from Veneration in several lunatic asylums
in this country. In Mr. Drury's establishment, near Glasgow, I saw, in
1836, a patient whose tendency to prayer, when labouring under a fit of
insanity, was irresistible. He prayed on his knees all the day. The organ
of Veneration was not large in his head. It has always been stated, that
although large organs, from their superior energy of function, are more
prone to fall into a state of diseased activity than small ones, yet that
small organs also may become diseased. This patient enjoyed a lucid
interval when I conversed with him, and in answer to the question, Whether
he enjoyed his devotional exercises when excited? he replied, No—that he
was unhappy, and that the object of his prayers was to implore the turning
away of the divine wrath. His organs of Cautiousness and Destructiveness were very large ; and my impression is, that he prayed through fear.
When religious insanity arises from the diseased excitement of Veneration,
Hope, and Wonder, the patient enjoys a supernatural beatitude. Respecting religious insanity, the reader may consult Dr. A. Combe's *Observations on Mental Derangement*, p. 184 ; and a series of articles in the
ninth volume of *The Phrenological Journal*, pp. 289, 532, 577, entitled
" Observations on Religious Fanaticism ; illustrated by a Comparison of
the Belief and Conduct of noted Religious Enthusiasts with those of
Patients in the Montrose Lunatic Asylum. By W. A. F. Browne, Esq.,
Medical Superintendent of that Institution."

The organ of Veneration is large in the following heads, represented in
Dr. Spurzheim's *Phrenology in Connexion with the Study of Physiogno-
my* : Oberlin, plate xvii., fig. 2 ; President Jeannin, xviii., 2 ; Francis
Paris, xxi., 1 ; Augustus Baker, xxi., 2 ; Paul Lejeune, xxiv., 2 ; and
Sully, xxxiv., 2. Small in Nero, xv., 1, and Pope Alexander VI., xvii.,
1, copied on p. 181 of this work.

15. FIRMNESS.

THIS organ is situated at the posterior part of the coronal region of the
head, close upon the middle line.

Dr. Gall observed, that persons of a firm and constant character have
this part of the brain much developed ; and Lavater had previously distinguished the same configuration in concomitance with that kind of disposition. It is difficult to determine, by analysis, the ultimate principle of
this faculty. Dr. Gall remarks, that, properly speaking, Firmness is
neither an inclination nor a power ; " *c'est une manière d'être qui donne à
l'homme une empreinte particulière que l'on appelle le caractère :* he who
is deficient in it," says he, " is the sport of external circumstances, and
of communicated impressions." Its effects, says Dr. Spurzheim, are
mistaken for will ; because those in whom it is large are prone to use the
phrase " I will " with great emphasis, which is the natural language of
determination ; but this feeling is different from proper volition. It gives
fortitude, constancy, perseverance, determination ; and, when too energetic, produces obstinacy, stubbornness, and infatuation. Its organ will
be found large in stubborn and untractable children.

Firmness seems to be a faculty which has no relation to external
objects ; its influence terminates on the mind itself, and adds only a quality
to the manifestations of the other powers : thus, acting along with Combativeness, it produces determined bravery ; with Veneration, sustained
devotion ; and with Conscientiousness, inflexible integrity. It gives perseverance, however, in acting only on the other faculties which are
possessed in an available degree. An individual having much Firmness

and considerable Tune, may persevere in making music : if Tune were greatly deficient, he would not be disposed to persevere in that attempt ; but if he possessed much Causality, he might persevere in abstract study. At the same time Dr. Gall justly remarks, that firmness of character ought not to be confounded with perseverance in gratifying the predominating dispositions of the mind. Thus an individual in whom Acquisitiveness is the strongest propensity, may, although Firmness be deficient, exhibit unceasing efforts to become rich, but he will be vacillating and unsteady in the means which he will employ ; he will to-day be captivated by one project, to-morrow by another, and the next day by a third ; whereas, with Firmness large, he would adopt the plan which appeared to him most promising, and steadily pursue it to the end. We may persevere in a course of action from two motives—either, first, because it is of itself agreeable, or, secondly, because we have resolved so to act. It is Firmness which gives origin to the latter motive, and enables us to persist with vigour in conduct once decided upon, whether agreeable or the reverse.

When this organ predominates, it gives a peculiar hardness to the manner, a stiffness and uprightness to the gait, with a forcible and emphatic tone to the voice.

A due degree of it is essential to the attainment of eminence in any difficult pursuit. Dr. Gall observes, that, when it is large, the motto of the individual will be, " Tu ne cede malis, sed contra audacior ito." It produces the " tenax propositi vir." The organ is larger in the British than in the French, and the latter are astonished at the determined perseverance of the former, in the prosecution of their designs, whether these relate to the arts, sciences, or war. Napoleon knew well the weakness of the French character in this point, and in his conversations recorded by Count Las Cases, frequently complained of it. In war the effects of this organ are very conspicuous in the conduct of the two nations. The French, under the influence of large Combativeness and moderate Cautiousness, make the most lively and spirited attacks, shouting and cheering as they advance to the charge : but, if steadily resisted, their ardour abates ; and, from deficiency in Firmness, they yield readily to adversity. The British, on the other hand, advance to the assault with cool determination, arising from great Firmness and considerable Cautiousness and Secretiveness ; and, although repulsed, they are not discomfited, but preserve presence of mind to execute whatever may appear most advisable in the circumstances which have occurred.

This faculty contributes greatly to success in any enterprise, by communicating the quality of perseverance. Fatigue will damp the ardour of the bravest after much exertion ; and hence he who is able to maintain his faculties in a state of vivid application for the greatest length of time, will frequently succeed at last, merely by wearying out his opponent. Fortitude and patience, also, as distinguished from active courage, result from this faculty. The organ is large in the American Indians, and their powers of endurance appear almost incredible to Europeans.* Dr. Gall found it very large in a highwayman, who was exceedingly hardened in crime. He was kept in close confinement for a considerable time, with the view of forcing him to disclose his accomplices ; but this had no effect, and he was then put to the torture of beating. Finding this infliction intolerable, he strangled himself with his chain. After his death the parietal bones were found separated precisely at the point where the organ of Firmness is situated. Dr. Gall could not determine whether the separation arose from the violent strangulation, from the excessive energy of the organ, or from accident ; but records the fact, to call attention to similar cases, should they occur in future. This organ, and that of De-

* See Phrenological Journal, ii., 535.

structiveness, are very large also in John Thurtell, executed for the murder of Weare, and he manifested both powerfully in his conduct. The organ is very large in King Robert Bruce, and he was distinguished for unshaken firmness in circumstances in which an ordinary mind would have been overwhelmed by despair. It is large in Haggart, who also manifested a remarkable degree of determination in crime and constancy in suffering. The subjoined cuts represent a cast of the head of a gentleman in whom the faculty is very strong, and whose character is described in *The Phrenological Journal*, vol. viii., p. 206.

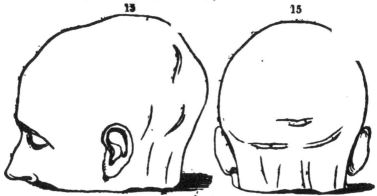

13   15

When the organ is small, the individual is prone to yield to the impulses of his predominating feelings. When Benevolence assumes the sway, he is all kindness; when Combativeness and Destructiveness are excited, he is passionate, outrageous, and violent: and thus he will afford a spectacle of habitual vacillation and inconsistency. If Love of Approbation and Benevolence are large, and Firmness small, solicitation will with great difficulty be resisted. The organ is very small in the cast of Mrs. H., and she manifested much unsteadiness of purpose.

The figures introduced on p. 224 represent this organ large and small. It is large in Rammohun Roy, p. 46, and Dr. Spurzheim, p. 51; also in Oberlin, Ramus, Stubbs, and Schlabrendorf, of whose heads representations are given in Dr. Spurzheim's *Phrenology in Connexion with the Study of Physiognomy*, pl. xvii., fig. 2; xxv., 2; and xxvi., 1 and 2. The following cuts shew the appearance of the skull when it is very large and very small:

FRENCH SOLDIER.   GIRL.
15   15

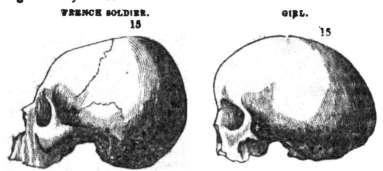

I am not aware that the metaphysicians admit any faculty corresponding to this sentiment. It exercises a great influence in forming the character, and its omission is very important in any system of mental philosophy.

The effects of disease of the organ seem to have been little observed.

We may infer, that they will be the axaltation of the function—namely, extreme stubbornness and infatuation.   One case in which the organ was very large, and apparently at the same time diseased, is reported by Professor Otto, of Copenhagen, in *The Phrenological Journal,* vol. viii., p. 66. The organ is established.

16. CONSCIENTIOUSNESS.

This organ is situated on the posterior and lateral parts of the coronal region of the brain, upward from Cautiousness, and backward from Hope. In Dr Gall's plates the function of the part is marked as unascertained, and the merit of the discovery and establishment of the organ is due to Dr. Spurzheim.

The dispute among philosophers about the existence of a moral faculty in the human mind is of very ancient standing, and it has been conducted with great eagerness since the publication of the writings of Hobbes in the middle of the seventeenth century.   This author taught, " that we approve of virtuous actions, or of actions beneficial to society, from self-love ; because we know, that whatever promotes the interest of society, has on that very account, an indirect tendency to promote our own." He farther taught, that, " as it is to the institution of government we are indebted for all the comforts and the confidence of social life, the laws which the civil magistrate enjoins are the ultimate standards of morality."[*]

Cudworth, in opposition to Hobbes, endeavoured to show that the origin of our notions of right and wrong is to be found in a particular power of the mind, which distinguishes truth from falsehood.

Mandeville, who published in the beginning of the last century, maintained, as his theory of morals, That by nature man is utterly selfish ; that, among other desires which he likes to gratify, he has received a strong appetite for praise ; that the founders of society, availing themselves of this propensity, instituted the custom of dealing out a certain measure of applause for each sacrifice made by selfishness to the public good, and called the sacrifice Virtue.   " Men are led, accordingly, to purchase this praise by a fair barter ;" and the moral virtues, to use Mandeville's strong expression, are " the *political offspring which flattery begot upon pride.*"   And hence, when we see *virtue*, we see only the indulgence of some selfish feeling, or the compromise for this indulgence in expectation of some praise.[†]

Dr. Clarke, on the other hand, supposes virtue " to consist in the regulation of our conduct, according to certain *fitnesses* which we perceive in things, or a peculiar congruity of certain relations to each other ;" and Wollaston, whose views are essentially the same, " supposes virtue to consist in *acting* according to the *truth of things*, in treating objects according to their *real character*, and not according to a character or properties which they truly have not."[‡]

Mr. Hume, it is well known, wrote an elaborate treatise, to prove " that utility is the constituent or measure of virtue ;" in short, to use the emphatic language of Dr. Smith, " that we have no *other* reason for praising a man than that for which we commend a chest of drawers."[§]

There is another system " which makes the *utility* according to which we measure virtue, in every case our own individual advantage."   Virtue, according to this system, is the mere search of pleasure, or of personal gratification.   " It gives up *one* pleasure, indeed, but it gives it up for a *greater.*   It sacrifices a present enjoyment ; but it sacrifices it only to

* Stewart's *Outlines*, p 128.
† *Fable of the Bees*, vol. i., pp. 28-30.   8vo.   London, 1728 ; and Brown's *Lectures*, vol. iv., p. 4.   ‡ Brown's *Lectures*, vol. iv., p. 17.
§ Brown's *Lectures*, vol. iv., p. 22.

obtain some enjoyment which, in intensity or duration, is fairly worth the sacrifice." Hence, in every instance in which an individual seems to pursue the good of others, *as good,* he seeks *his* own personal gratification, and nothing else.*

Dr. Hutcheson, again, strenuously maintains the existence of a moral sense, on which our perceptions of virtue are founded, independently of all other considerations.

Dr. Paley, the most popular of all authors on moral philosophy, does not admit a natural sentiment of justice as the foundation of virtue, but is also an adherent of the selfish system, under a modified form. He makes virtue consist in " the doing good to mankind, in obedience to the will of God, and *for the sake of everlasting happiness.*"† According to this doctrine, " the will of God is our rule, but private happiness our motive ;" which is just selfishness in another form.

Dr. Adam Smith, in his *Theory of Moral Sentiments,* endeavours to show that the standard of moral approbation is *sympathy,* on the part of the impartial spectator, with the action and object of the party whose conduct is judged of.

Dr. Reid, Lord Kames, and Mr. Stewart maintain the existence of a faculty in man which produces the sentiment right and wrong, independently of any other consideration.

These disputes are as far from being terminated among metaphysicians at present as they were a century ago ; a writer on the subject, the author of the article MORAL PHILOSOPHY in The *Edinburgh Encyclopædia,* disputes the existence of a moral sense, and founds virtue upon religion and utility. Sir James Mackintosh, in his Dissertation on the progress of Ethical Philosophy, prefixed to the *Encyclopædia Britannica,* gives an account of conscience which I confess myself unable to comprehend. He speaks of it as formed of " *many elements,*" and by " the combination of elements so unlike as the private desires and the social affections." " It becomes," says he," " from these circumstances, more difficult to distinguish its separate principles, and it is impossible to exhibit them in separate action." (P. 409.)

I have introduced this sketch of conflicting theories, to convey some idea of the boon which Phrenology would confer upon moral science, if it could fix on a firm basis this single point in the philosophy of mind— That a power or faculty exists, the object of which is to produce the sentiment of justice or the feeling of duty and obligation, independently of selfishness, hope of reward, fear of punishment, qr any extrinsic motive ; a faculty, in short, the natural language of which is, " Fiat justitia, ruat cœlum." Phrenology does this by a demonstration, founded on numerous observations, that those persons who have the organ now under consideration large, experience powerfully the sentiment of justice, while those who have that part small, are little alive to the emotion. This evidence is the same in kind as that adduced in support of the conclusions of physical science.

The sentiments of Benevolence and Veneration produce moral emotions ; and actions done in opposition to their dictates are felt by the mind to be improper, wrong, or unbecoming : but they do not seem to give rise to the peculiar sentiment of duty. It is the faculty of Conscientiousness which produces the feeling of obligation or incumbency, for which we have no single definite expression in the English language. Justice is the result of this sentiment, acting in combination with the intellectual powers. The latter investigate the motives and consequences of actions ; but, after having done so, they, of themselves, experience no emotions. In surveying human conduct, however, as soon as the intellect has tho-

* Brown's *Lectures,* vol. iv., p. 64. † Ib., pp. 100, 101.

roughly penetrated into the springs from which it proceeds, a feeling of decided approval or condemnation, distinct from all other sentiments, and from pure intellection, arises in the mind; and this is produced by the faculty of Conscientiousness.

This faculty is of the very highest importance as a regulator of all the others. If Combativeness and Destructiveness be too active, Conscientiousness prescribes a limit to their indulgence; it permits, defence, but no malicious aggression: if Acquisitiveness urge too keenly, it reminds us of the rights of others: if Benevolence tend toward profusion, this faculty issues the admonition, Be just before you are generous: if Ideality aspire to its high delights, when duty requires laborious exertions in an humble sphere, Conscientiousness supplies the curb, and bids the soaring spirit restrain its wing.

Nay, not only does it operate as a curb upon our too active desires, but it may lead us to do acts as duties, which other faculties, if powerful, would have prompted us to do with inclination. If Benevolence be weak, Conscientiousness proclaims, in a voice of authority, that it is our DUTY to relieve the miserable; if Acquisitiveness be too feeble to prompt to industry, this sentiment calls aloud on us to labour, that we may do justice to those around us. From this regulating quality, Conscientiousness is an important element in constituting a practical judgment and an upright and consistent character, Hence its cultivation in children is of great importance.*

When this faculty is powerful, the individual is disposed to regulate his conduct by the nicest sentiments of justice: there is an earnestness, integrity, and directness in his manner, which inspire us with confidence, and give us a conviction of his sincerity. Such an individual desires to act justly from the love of justice, unbiassed by fear, interest, or any sinister motive.

The activity of Conscientiousness takes a wider range than regard merely to the legal rights and property of others. It prompts those in whom it is strong to do justice in judging of the conduct, the opinions, and the talents of others. Such persons are scrupulous, and as ready to condemn themselves as to find fault with others. When predominant, it leads to punctuality in keeping appointments, because it is injustice to sacrifice the time and convenience of others, by causing them to wait till our selfishness finds it agreeable to meet them. It prompts to ready payment of debts, as a piece of justice to those to whom they are due. It will not permit even a tax-collector to be sent away unsatisfied, from any cause except inability to pay; because it is injustice to him, as it is to clerks, servants, and all others, to require them to consume their time in unnecessary attendance for what is justly due and ought at once to be paid. It leads also to great reserve in making promises, but to much punctuality in performing them. It gives consistency to the conduct; because, when every sentiment is regulated by justice, the result is that "daily beauty in the life" which renders the individual in the highest degree amiable, useful, and respectable. It communicates a pleasing simplicity to the manners, which commands the esteem and wins the affection of all well-constituted minds.

In practical life, when it predominates over Benevolence, it renders the individual a strict disciplinarian, and a rigid, although a just, master. It disposes him to invest all actions with a character of duty or obligation, so that if a servant misplace any article, it is not simply an error, but a fault. Some very estimable persons, by giving way to this tendency in matters of trivial importance, render themselves not a little disagreeable.

* Much attention is paid to the training of Conscientiousness in the infant-schools of Mr. Wilderspin. See *Phren. Journ.*, vi., 429.

A deficiency of Conscientiousness produces effects exactly opposite. The weakness of the faculty appears in the general sentiments of the individual, although circumstances may place him beyond the reach of temptation to infringe the law. The predominant propensities and sentiments then act without this powerful regulator. If Adhesiveness and Benevolence attach him to a friend, he is blind to all his imperfections, and extols him as the most matchless of human beings. If this model of excellence happen to offend, he becomes a monster of ingratitude and baseness; he passes in an instant from an angel to a demon. Had Conscientiousness been large, he would have been viewed all along as a man; esteem toward him would have been regulated by principle, and the offence candidly dealt with. If Love of Approbation be large and Conscientiousness deficient, the former will prompt to the adoption of every means that will please, without the least regard to justice and propriety. If an individual have a weak point in his character, Love of Approbation will then lead to flattering it; if he have extravagant expectations, it will join in all his hopes; if he be displeased with particular persons, it will affect to hate with his hatred, altogether independently of justice. In short, the individual in whom this faculty is deficient is apt to act and also to judge of the conduct of others exactly according to his predominant sentiments for the time: he is friendly when under the impulse of Benevolence, and severe when Destructiveness predominates: he admires when his pride, vanity, or affection gives him a favourable feeling toward others; and condemns when his sentiments take an opposite direction, always unregulated by principle. He is not scrupulous, and rarely condemns his own conduct or acknowledges himself in the wrong. Minds so constituted may be amiable, and may display many excellent qualities; but they are never to be relied on where justice is concerned. As judges, their decisions are unsound; as friends, they are liable to exact too much and perform too little; as sellers, they are prone to misrepresent, adulterate, and overcharge—as buyers, to depreciate quality and quantity, or to evade payment.

The laws of honour, as apprehended by some minds, are founded on the absence of Conscientiousness, with great predominance of Self-Esteem and Love of Approbation. If a gentleman is conscious that he has unjustly given offence to another, it is conceived by many that he will degrade himself by making an apology; that it is his duty to fight, but not to acknowledge himself in fault. This is the feeling produced by powerful Self-Esteem and Love of Approbation, with great deficiency of Conscientiousness. Self-Esteem is mortified by an admission of fallibility, while Love of Approbation suffers under the feeling that the esteem of the world will be lost by such an acknowledgment; and if no higher sentiment be present in a sufficient degree, the wretched victim will go to the field and die in support of conduct that is indefensible. When Conscientiousness is strong, the possessor feels it no degradation to acknowledge himself in fault, when he is aware that he is wrong: in fact, he rises in his own esteem by doing so, and knows that he acquires the respect of the world; while, if fully conscious of being in the right, there is none more inflexible than he.

This sentiment is essential to the formation of a truly philosophic mind, especially in moral investigations. It produces the desire of discovering truth, the tact of recognising it when discovered, and that perfect reliance on its invincible supremacy, which gives at once dignity and peace to the mind. A person in whom Conscientiousness is deficient, views all propositions as mere opinions; esteems them exactly as they are fashionable or the reverse, and cares nothing about the evidence on which they are based. Love of Approbation and Secretiveness, joined with deficiency of this sentiment, lead to paradox; and if Combativeness added, there will be a tendency to general scepticism, and the denial or disputation of the best-established truths on every serious subject.

No sentiment is more incomprehensible to those in whom the organ is small than Conscientiousness. They are able to understand conduct proceeding from ambition, self-interest, revenge, or any other inferior motive; but that determination of soul, which suffers obloquy and reproach, nay, death itself, from the pure and disinterested love of truth, is to them utterly unintelligible. They regard it as a species of insanity, and look on the individual as "essentially mad, without knowing it." Madame De Stael narrates of Bonaparte, that he never was so completely at fault in his estimate of character, as when he met with opposition from a person actuated by the pure principle of integrity alone. He did not comprehend the motives of such a man, and could not imagine how he might be managed. The maxim, that "every man has his price," will pass as profoundly discriminative with those in whom Acquisitiveness or Love of Approbation is very large and Conscientiousness moderate; but there are minds whose deviation from the paths of rectitude no price can purchase and no honours procure; and those in whom Conscientiousness, Firmness, and Reflection are powerful will give an instinctive assent to the truth of this proposition.

I have observed that individuals in whom Love of Approbation was large and Conscientiousness not in equal proportion, were incapable of conceiving the motive which could lead any one to avow a belief in Phrenology, while the tide of ridicule ran unstemmed against it. If public opinion should change, such persons would move foremost in the train of its admirers: they instinctively follow the doctrines that are most esteemed from day to day; and require our pity and forbearance, as their conduct proceeds from a great moral deficiency, which is their misfortune rather than their fault.

The fact, that this organ is occasionally deficient in individuals in whom the organs of intellect are amply developed and the animal propensities strong, accounts for the unprincipled baseness and moral depravity exhibited by some men of unquestionable talents. It is here, as in other cases, of the greatest importance to attend to the distinct functions of the several faculties of the mind. No mistake is more generally committed than that of conceiving that, by exercising the faculty of Veneration, we cultivate those of Benevolence and Justice: but if Veneration be large and Conscientiousness small, a man may be naturally disposed to piety and not to justice; or if the combination be reversed, he may be just and not pious, in the same manner as he may be blind and not deaf, or deaf and not blind. Deficiency of Veneration, as before observed, does not necessarily imply profanity; so that, although an individual will scarcely be found who is profane and at the same time just, yet many will be found who are just and not pious, and vice versa.

Conscientiousness, when powerful, is attended with a sense of its own paramount authority over every other faculty, and it gives its impulses with a tone which appears like the voice of Heaven. The scene in The Heart of Mid-Lothian, in which Jeanie Deans is represented giving evidence on her sister's trial at the bar of the High Court of Justiciary, affords a striking illustration of its functions and authority when supported by piety. A strong sense of the imperious dictates of Conscientiousness, and of the supreme obligation of truth, leads her to sacrifice every interest and affection which could make the mind swerve from the paths of duty; and we perceive her holding by her integrity, at the expense of every other feeling dear to human nature.

Repentance, remorse, a sense of guilt and demerit, are the consequences of this faculty, when the actions have been in opposition to its dictates

It is a mistake, however, to suppose that great criminals are punished by the accusations of conscience ; for this organ is generally very deficient in men who have devoted their lives to crime, and, in consequence, they are strangers to the sentiment of remorse. Haggart felt regret for having murdered the jailer at Dumfries, but no remorse for his thefts. His large Benevolence induced the uneasy feeling on account of the first crime, and his small Conscientiousness was the cause of his indifference to the second. If Conscientiousness had been strong, he could not have endured the sense of the accumulated iniquities with which his life was stained. In Bellingham both Benevolence and Conscientiousness are small, and he manifested equal insensibility to justice and mercy, and testified no repentance nor remorse.

Dr. Gall did not admit a faculty and organ of Conscientiousness. He formerly considered remorse as the result of the opposition of particular actions to the predominant dispositions of the individual ; and, according to him, there are as many consciences as faculties. For example, if a person in whom Benevolence was large injured another, this faculty would be grieved ; and the feeling so arising he considered to be regret or repentance. If a usurer or a libertine neglected an opportunity, he would repent, the former for not having gratified Acquisitiveness, the latter for not having seduced some innocent victim. Dr. Gall called this natural conscience, and said that we could not trust to it, and that hence laws and positive institutions became necessary. Dr. Spurzheim answered this argument in an able manner, and showed that the mere feeling of regret is totally different from that of remorse. We may regret that we lost a pair of gloves, or spent half a crown ; but this feeling bears no resemblance to the upbraidings of conscience for having robbed a neighbour of his right, committed a fraud, or uttered a malevolent falsehood. Dr. Gall latterly regarded Benevolence as the moral faculty ; but the sentiment of duty and incumbency is as clearly distinguishable from mere goodness or kindness, as hope is from fear ; and, besides, positive facts prove that the two feelings depend on different organs.

When this organ is deficient and Secretiveness large, and especially when the latter is aided by Ideality and Wonder, a natural tendency to lying is produced, which some individuals, who have possessed the advantages of education and good society, have never been able to overcome.

Some criminals, on being detected, confess, and seem to court punishment as the only means of assuaging the remorse with which their minds are devoured. The Phrenological Society has a cast of the skull of one person who displayed this desire to atone for his crime. It is that of John Rotherham, who met a servant girl on the highway and murdered her, out of the pure wanton impulse of Destructiveness ; for he did not attempt to violate her person ; and, of her property, he took only her umbrella and shoes. When apprehended, he confessed his crime, insisted on pleading guilty, and with great difficulty was induced by the judge to retract his admission. The organ is large in him. He appears to have acted under the influence of excessive Destructiveness. James Gordon, on the contrary, who murdered a pedlar boy in Eskdale Muir, stoutly denied his guilt, and, after conviction, abused the jury and judge for condemning him. Before his execution, however, he admitted that his sentence was just. In him the organ of Conscientiousness is defective.

The organ is very large in Mrs. H., the Rev. Mr. M., Dr. Hette, and Rammohun Roy, who all manifested the sentiment powerfully. Considerable attention is requisite to discriminate accurately the size of this organ. When Firmness is large and Conscientiousness small, the head slopes at an acute angle downward from Firmness, as in Haggart and King Robert Bruce. When both Firmness and Conscientiousness are large, the head rises considerably from Cautiousness to Firmness, with a full and rounded swell, as in the Rev. Mr. M., p. 108. When both of these organs are small, the head rises very little above Cautiousness, but runs flat across to Cautiousness on the other side, as in the boy.

Mrs. H.

Firmness small and Conscientiousness large.

Boy addicted to falsehood.

Firmness and Conscientiousness deficient.

DAVID HAGGART.

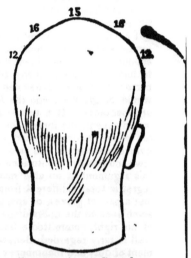

Firmness large, Conscientiousness deficient.

In Mrs. H. Firmness, 15, is small, and Conscientiousness, 16, large : in D. Haggart Firmness, 15, is large and Conscientiousness, 16, deficient ; and in the boy both of these organs are deficient, which is indicated by the head rising very little above 12, Cautiousness. If in Mrs. H. Firmness had been as large as Conscientiousness, or in Haggart Conscientiousness had been as large as Firmness, the heads would have presented a full and elevated segment of a circle passing from Cautiousness to Cautiousness, the very opposite of the flat and low line in the head of the boy. It is of great importance in practice to attend to these different forms.

The *difference of developement* of this organ in different nations and individuals, and its combinations with other organs, enable us to account for the differences in the notions of justice entertained at different times, and by different people. The sentiment of truth is found by the English judges to be so low in the Africans, the Hindoos, and the aboriginal Americans, that such individuals are not received as witnesses in the colonial courts ; and it is a curious fact, that a defect in the organ of Conscientiousness is a reigning feature in the skulls of these nations in possession of the Phrenological Society.* It is small likewise in the Esquimaux, who are notoriously addicted to dishonesty and theft.† The notions of justice of that individual are most fit to be assumed as a standard, in whom this organ is decidedly large, in combination with a large endowment of the other moral sentiments and reflection ; just as we hold the person possessed of the greatest organ of Tune, in combination with the organs of the moral sentiments and reflection, to be the best judge of musical compositions

* See *Phren. Journ.*, viii., 515, 530, 581.   † Ib., p. 301.

ESQUIMAUX.

It is obvious also, that laws or positive commands, ordering and forbidding certain actions, become necessary as rules to those who do not possess a sufficient endowment of this sentiment from nature to regulate their conduct. Those who are favourably gifted are, in the language of St. Paul, "a law unto themselves."

It has been objected, that persons possessing a large developement of this organ, not unfrequently act in opposition to the dictates of sentiment, and practise selfishness, or sacrifice justice to ambition, exactly as those do in whom the organ is small; and it is asked, What becomes of the organ in such instances? The plurality of organs and faculties explains this phenomenon. Conscientiousness is not the only faculty in the mind, and, although it is paramount in authority, it is not always so in strength. A person in whom Benevolence and Destructiveness are both large, may, under special circumstances which strongly excite Destructiveness, manifest that faculty in rage, revenge, or undue severity, in direct opposition to Benevolence. In like manner, an individual in whom Acquisitiveness and Self-Esteem are large, may, if these are very forcibly addressed, obey their impulses in opposition to that of Conscientiousness. But the benevolent man, when the temptation is past, feels the opposition between his conduct and the dictates of Benevolence; and, in like manner, the individual here supposed, on cool reflection, becomes conscious of the opposition between his unjust preference of himself and the dictates of Conscientiousness: both will repent, and will make atonement, and desire to avoid repetition of such offences. If Benevolence and Conscientiousness had been small, they would not have felt that their actions were wrong; they would have experienced no remorse; and their lower faculties would have operated with greatly increased violence. I have observed in practical life that, when Conscientiousness is large in any individual, he yields compliance to demands made on him whenever a strong case in justice is made out by the applicant; but when the organ is not large, he is moved only by favour or partiality. It is of the utmost importance to the respectability of government and the welfare of the people, that public functionaries should possess the former character. The necessity of it in persons in authority will be more and more felt as society advances in knowledge, discrimination, and morality.

Another difficulty is experienced in the doctrine, that Conscientiousness is merely a sentiment, and does not by itself lead to the perception of what is just. This will be best removed by an example. A judge hears one side of a cause, and Conscientiousness, acting on the statement presented to it through the medium of the intellect, produces the feeling that this party is in the right. The other litigant is heard, new facts appear, and Conscientiousness may now produce the feeling that justice lies on his side. If this faculty itself had formed specific ideas of what is just, it would have been an intellectual power, and reasoning would have been in proportion to it, which is not the case; but, as it is only a sentiment, its real function is to produce an emotion of justice or injustice, on the particular case or assemblage of facts being presented to it by the intellect. An illustration of this doctrine is found in Parnell's *Hermit*. The angel throws the servant over the bridge, and this is felt to be unjust while nothing more is known than the result; but when the intellect is afterward informed that he intended next night to murder his master, Conscientiousness feels that his destruction by the angel was just. This is not Conscientiousness giving opposite decisions on the same case; but the intellect presenting different cases, or different views of the same case, and Conscientiousness producing its peculiar emotion in regard to each, according as it is laid before it.

This organ is occasionally found diseased, and then the most awful sentiments of guilt, generally imaginary, harrow up the mind. I have seen two individuals labouring under this disease. One of them believed himself to be in debt to an enormous amount, which he had no means of paying; the other imagined himself to be guilty of murder, and of every variety of wickedness contained in the records of iniquity; whereas, in fact, the whole conduct of both, while in health, has been marked by the greatest humanity, honour, and scrupulosity. When this organ and that of Cautiousness are diseased at the same time, the individual imagines himself to be the most worthless of sinners, and is visited with fearful apprehensions of punishment. Such patients sometimes present a picture of despair which is truly appalling. Slight degrees of disease of these organs, not amounting to insanity, are not unfrequent in this country, and produce an inward trouble of the mind, which throws a gloom over life, and leads the patient to see only the terrors of religion. Such persons are greatly relieved by being convinced that the cause of their unhappy feeling is disease in the mental organs, and that they may in general be restored to health by proper medical treatment. If they are religiously disposed, their anxiety will probably be directed to their salvation. If they are worldly-minded, the fear of ruin, or of inability to meet their engagements, will probably be the form in which the disease will appear. In all cases, however, where there are no adequate external causes for the impressions, they may be regarded as really arising from disease of the mental organs, the feelings only being differently directed, according to the character of each individual. I have known great injury done to the health, by treating these depressions, when they occurred in amiable persons, on exclusively religious principles; and very respectfully, but earnestly, recommend to the friends of such patients to call in a physician as well as a clergyman for their relief.*

In the first edition of this work I stated that gratitude probably arises from this faculty; but Sir G. S. Mackenzie, in his *Illustrations of Phrenology*, has shown that gratitude is much heightened by Benevolence—a view in which I now fully acquiesce.

It is premature to speak of the combinations of the faculties before we have finished the detail of the simple functions; but this is the most proper occasion, in other respects, to observe, that Phrenology enables us to account for the origin of the various theories of morals before enumerated.

Hobbes, for instance, denied every natural sentiment of justice, and erected the laws of the civil magistrate into the standard of morality. This doctrine would appear natural and sound to a person in whom Conscientiousness was very feeble; who never experienced in his own mind a single emotion of justice, but who was alive to fear, to the desire of property, and to other affections which would render security and regular government desirable. It seems to me probable that Hobbes was so constituted.

Mandeville makes selfishness the basis of all our actions, but admits a strong appetite for praise; the desire for which, he says, leads men to state other enjoyments for the sake of obtaining it. If we conceive Mandeville to have possessed a deficient Conscientiousness and a large Love of Approbation, this doctrine would be the natural product of his mind.

Mr. Hume erects utility, to ourselves or others, into the standard of

* See Dr. A. Combe's *Observations on Mental Derangement*, pp. 187, 196.

virtue; and this would be the natural feeling of a mind in which Benevolence and Reflection were strong, and Conscientiousness weak.

Paley makes virtue consist in obeying the will of God, as our rule, and doing so for the sake of eternal happiness as the motive. This is the natural emanation of a mind where the selfish or lower propensities are considerable, and in which Veneration is strong and Conscientiousness not remarkable for vigour.

Cudworth, Hutcheson, Reid, Kames, Stewart, and Brown,* on the other hand, contend most eagerly and eloquently for the existence of an original sentiment or emotion of justice in the mind, altogether independent of other considerations; and this is the natural feeling of persons in whom the faculty is powerful. A much respected individual, in whom this organ is predominantly large, mentioned to me, that no circumstance in philosophy occasioned to him greater surprise, than the denial of the existence of a moral faculty; and that the attempts to prove it appeared to him like endeavours to prop up, by demonstration, a self-evident axiom in mathematical science.

The organ is regarded as established.

17. HOPE.

This organ is situated on each side of that of Veneration, and extends under part of the frontal and part of the parietal bones. It cannot be brought into outline in a drawing, and on this account no figure is given.

Dr. Gall considered hope as belonging to every faculty; but Dr. Spurzheim very properly observes, that although every faculty being active produces *desire*—as Acquisitiveness the desire for property, and Love of Approbation the desire for praise; yet this is very different from hope, which is a simple emotion *sui generis*, susceptible of being directed in a great variety of ways, but not desiring any one class of things as its peculiar objects. Nay, desire is sometimes strong, when hope is feeble or extinct: a criminal on the scaffold may ardently desire to live, when he has no hope of escaping death. Dr. Spurzheim was convinced, by

* I embrace this opportunity of paying an humble tribute to the talents of the late Dr. Thomas Brown. The acuteness, depth, and comprehensiveness of intellect displayed in his works on the mind, place him in the highest rank of philosophical authors; and these great qualities are equalled by the purity and vividness of his moral perceptions. His powers of analysis are unrivalled, and his eloquence is frequently splendid. His *Lectures* will remain a monument of what the human mind was capable of accomplishing, in investigating its own constitution, by an imperfect method. In proportion as Phrenology shall become known, the admiration of his genius will increase; for it is the highest praise to say, that, in regard to many points of great difficulty and importance in the Philosophy of Mind, he has arrived, by his own reflections, at conclusions harmonizing with those obtained by phrenological observation. Of this, his doctrine on the moral emotion, discussed in the text, is a striking instance. Sometimes, indeed, his arguments are subtle, his distinctions too refined, and his style circuitous; but the phrenologist will pass lightly over these imperfections, for they occur only occasionally, and arise from mere excess of the faculties of Secretiveness, Comparison, Causality, and Wit; on a great endowment of which, along with Concentrativeness, his penetration and comprehensiveness depended. In fact, he possessed the organs of these powers largely developed, and they afford a key to his genius. Whether he drew any of his lights from Phrenology is uncertain. He was acquainted with the philosophy of Dr. Gall, for he wrote the *critique* on his doctrines, which appeared in the 3d No. of *The Edinburgh Review* in 1803, but he then condemned them. He survived the publication of Dr. Spurzheim's works in English; but I have been told that he did not alter his lectures from the first form in which he produced them.

analysis, that hope is a distinct primitive sentiment ; and was led to expect that an organ for it would be found. Numerous observations have since determined the situation of the organ, on the sides of Veneration ; and it is now admitted by phrenologists in general as established. Dr. Gall, however, continued till his death to mark the function of this part of the brain as unascertained.

The faculty produces the sentiment of Hope in general, or the tendency to believe in the future attainment of what the other faculties desire, but without giving the conviction of it, which depends on the intellect. Thus a person with much Hope and much Acquisitiveness, will expect to become rich ; another, with much Hope and great Love of Approbation, will hope to rise to eminence ; and a third, with much Hope and Love of Life, will hope to enjoy a long and a happy existence. It inspires with gay, fascinating, and delightful emotions ; painting futurity fair and smiling as the regions of primitive bliss. It invests every distant prospect with hues of enchanting brilliancy, while Cautiousness hangs clouds and mists over remote objects seen by the mind's eye. Hence, he who has Hope more powerful than Cautiousness, lives in the enjoyment of brilliant anticipations which are never realized ; while he who has Cautiousness more powerful than Hope, habitually labours under the painful apprehension of evils which rarely exist except in his own imagination. The former enjoys the present, without being annoyed by fears about the future ; for Hope supplies his futurity with every object which his fancy desires, undisturbed by the distance or difficulty of attainment : the latter, on the other hand, cannot enjoy the pleasures within his reach, through fear that, at some future time, they may be lost. The life of such an individual is spent in painful apprehension of evils, to which he is, in fact, very little exposed ; for the dread of their happening excites him to ward them off by so many precautions that it is scarcely possible they can overtake him.

When predominant and too energetic, this faculty disposes to credulity with respect to what we desire to attain, and, in mercantile men, leads to rash and inconsiderate speculation. Persons so endowed never see their own situation in its true light, but are prompted by extravagant Hope to magnify tenfold every advantage, while they are blind to every obstacle and abatement. They promise largely, but rarely perform. Intentional deception, however, is frequently not their object ; they are misled themselves by their constitutional tendency to believe everything possible that is future, and they promise in the spirit of this credulity. Those who perceive this disposition in them, ought to exercise their own judgment on the possibility of performance, and make the necessary abatement in their anticipations. Experience accomplishes little in improving the judgment of those who possess too large an organ of Hope : the tendency to expect immoderately being constitutional, they have it not in their power to see both sides of the prospect ; and, beholding only that which is fair, they are constitutionally led to form extravagant expectations. When the organ is very deficient and that of Cautiousness large, a gloomy despondency is apt to invade the mind ; and if Destructiveness be strong, the individual may resort to suicide in order to escape from wo.

This faculty, if not combined with much Acquisitiveness or Love of Approbation, disposes to indolence, from the very promise which it holds out of the future providing for itself. If, on the other hand, it be combined with these organs in a full degree, it acts as a spur to the mind, by uniformly representing the objects desired as attainable. An individual with much Acquisitiveness, great Cautiousness, and *little Hope*, will *save* to become rich ; another, with the same Acquisitiveness, little Cautiousness, and *much Hope*, will *speculate* to procure wealth. I have found Hope and Acquisitiveness large in persons addicted to gaming.

Hope has a great effect in assuaging the fear of death. I have seen persons in whom it was very large die by inches, and linger for months on the brink of the grave, without suspicion of the fate impending over them. They *hoped* to be well, till death extinguished the last ember of the feeling. On the other hand, when Hope, and Combativeness, which gives courage, are small, and Cautiousness and Conscientiousness large, the strongest assurances of the Gospel are not always sufficient to enable the individual to look with composure or confidence on the prospect of a judgment to come. Several persons in whom this combination occurs, have told me that they lived in a state of habitual uneasiness in looking forward to the hour of death; while others, with a large Hope and small Cautiousness, have said that such a ground of alarm never once entered their imaginations. Our hopes or fears, on a point of such importance as our condition in a future state, ought to be founded on grounds more stable than mere constitutional feeling; but I mention these cases to draw attention to the fact, that this cause sometimes tinges the whole conclusions of the judgment. When the existence of such a cause of delusion is known, its effects may more easily be resisted.

In religion this faculty favours the exercise of faith; and, by producing the natural tendency to look forward to futurity with expectation, disposes to belief in a happy life to come.

The metaphysicians admit this faculty, so that Phrenology only reveals its organ and the effects of its endowment in different degrees. I have already stated an argument in favour of the being of a God, founded on the existence of a faculty of Veneration conferring the tendency to worship, of which God is the proper and ultimate object. May not the probability of a future state be supported by a similar deduction from the possession of a faculty of Hope? It appears to me that this is the faculty from which originates the notion of futurity, and which carries the mind forward in endless progression into periods of everlasting time. May it not be inferred, that this instinctive tendency to leave the present scene and all its enjoyments, to spring forward into the regions of a far distant futurity, and to expatiate, even in imagination, in the fields of an eternity to come, denotes that man is formed for a more glorious destiny than to perish for ever in the grave? Addison beautifully enforces this argument in the *Spectator*, and in the soliloquy of Cato; and Phrenology gives weight to his reasoning, by showing that this ardent hope and "longing after immortality" are not factitious sentiments, nor a mere product of an idle and wandering imagination, but that they are the results of two primitive faculties of the mind, Love of Life and Hope, which owe at once their existence and their functions to the Creator.

Pope beautifully describes the influence of the sentiment of Veneration in prompting us to worship—blindly indeed, when undirected by information superior to its own. He also falls into the idea now started in regard to Hope, and represents it as the source of that expectation of a future state of existence, which seems to be the joy and delight of human nature, in whatever stage of improvement it has been found.

"Lo! the poor Indian whose untutored mind
Sees God in clouds, or hears him in the wind;
His soul proud science never taught to stray
Far as the solar walk, or Milky Way;
Yet simple nature to his *hope* has given,
Behind the cloud-topp'd hill an humbler heaven:
Some safer world, in depth of woods embraced;
Some happier island in the watery waste;
Where slaves once more their native land behold,
No fiends torment, no Christians thirst for gold."

The organ is established.
20

18. WONDER.

THIS organ is situated immediately above Ideality, in the lateral parts of the anterior region of the vertex.

Dr. Gall observed, that some individuals imagine themselves to be visited by apparitions of persons dead or absent; and he asks, How does it happen that men of considerable intellect often believe in the reality of ghosts and visions? Are they fools, or impostors? or is there a particular organization which imposes, in this form, on the human understanding? and how are such illusions to be explained? He then enters into an historical sketch of the most remarkable instances of visions. Socrates spoke frequently and willingly to his disciples of a demon or spirit, which served him as a guide. Dr. Gall remarks, that he is quite aware of the common explanation, that Socrates referred only to the force and justness of his own understanding; but adds, that if he had not himself believed in a genius communicating with him, the opinion that he had one would have been lost in the twenty-three years during which Aristophanes made it a subject of ridicule, and his accusers would not have revived it as a charge against him. Joan of Arc also related an appearance of St. Michael to her, who told her that God had pity on France, and that she was commissioned to raise the siege of Orleans, and to install Charles VII. as king, at Rheims. Tasso asserted himself to have been cured by the aid of the Virgin Mary and St. Scholastic, who appeared to him during a violent attack of fever. In the historical notes which accompany the Life of Tasso, the following anecdote appears, extracted from the Memoirs of Manso, Marquis of Villa, published after the death of Tasso, his friend:

Tasso, in his delirium, believed that he conversed with familiar spirits. One day, when the marquis endeavoured to drive these ideas from his mind, Tasso said to him, "Since I cannot convince you by reason, I shall do so by experience; I shall cause the spirit, in which you refuse to believe, to appear before your own eyes." "I accepted the offer," says the marquis; "and next day, when we sat by the fire conversing, he turned his eyes toward the window, and, looking with steadfast attention, appeared so completely absorbed, that when I called to him he did not answer. 'See!' said he, at length, 'See! my familiar spirit comes to converse with me.' I looked with the greatest earnestness, but could see nothing enter the apartment.' In the meantime, Tasso began to converse with this mysterious being. I saw and heard himself alone. Sometimes he questioned, and sometimes answered; and from his answers I gathered the sense of what he had heard. The subject of his discourse was so elevated, and the expressions so sublime, that I felt myself in a kind of ecstasy. I did not venture to interrupt him, nor to trouble him with questions, and a considerable time elapsed before the spirit disappeared. I was informed of its departure by Tasso, who, turning toward me, said, 'In future you will cease to doubt.' 'Rather,' said I, 'I shall be more sceptical; for although I have heard astonishing words, I have seen nothing.' Smiling, he replied, 'You have perhaps heard and seen more than—' He stopped short; and, fearing to importune him by my questions, I dropped the conversation."[*]

Dr. Gall quotes this dialogue from "La Vie du Tasse, publiée à Londres en 1810;" and I have translated from his French version.[†]

Swedenborg believed himself miraculously called to reveal to the world the most hidden mysteries. "In 1743," says he, "it pleased the Lord to manifest himself to me, and appear personally before me, to give me a

---

[*] *Sur les Fonctions du Cerveau*, tome v.; p. 341.
[†] For the original, see Rev. Mr. Black's *Life of Tasso*, vol. ii., p. 240.

knowledge of the spiritual world, and to place me in communication with angels and spirits, and this power has been continued with me till the present day." Swedenborg, says his biographers, was a man of unquestionable sincerity, but one of the most extravagant enthusiasts that ever existed.*

Dr. Gall remarked, in the first fanatic who fell under his observation, a large developement of the part of the brain lying between the organs of Ideality and Imitation, and subsequently met with many similar instances. Dr. Jung Stilling, whom he often saw with the late Grand Duke of Baden, was a tailor in his youth, then a tutor, afterward doctor in medicine, moralist, divine, journalist, illuminatus, and visionary; and in him this part of the brain was largely developed. He believed firmly in apparitions, and wrote a book in exposition of this doctrine. In the *Maison de Detention*, at Berne, Dr. Gall saw a fanatic who believed that Jesus Christ, surrounded by a brilliant light, as if a million of suns had combined their splendours, had appeared to him to reveal the true religion. A gentleman who moved in the best society in Paris, asked Dr. Gall to examine his head. The doctor's first remark was, "You sometimes see visions, and believe in apparitions." The gentleman started from his chair in astonishment, and said that he *had* frequent visions; but that never, up to this moment, had he spoken on the subject to any human being, through fear of being set down as absurdly credulous. On another occasion, Dr. Gall, when he observed the developement of the head of a Dr. W., told him that he ought to have a strong liking for the marvellous and supernatural. "For once," replied he, "you are completely mistaken, for I have laid down the rule to believe in nothing which cannot be mathematically demonstrated." After talking with him on various scientific subjects, Dr. Gall turned the conversation toward animal magnetism, which appeared a fit topic to put the mathematical rigour of his proofs to the test. He instantly became greatly animated; assured Dr. Gall again very solemnly, that he admitted nothing as true that was not mathematically demonstrated; but added, he was convinced that a spiritual being acted in magnetism— that it operated at great distances—that no distance, indeed, presented an obstacle to its action—and that, on this account, it could sympathize with persons in any part of the world. "It is the same cause," continued he, "which produces apparitions. Apparitions and visions are rare, no doubt, but they undoubtedly exist, and I am acquainted with the laws which regulate their production." "On this occasion," says Dr. Gall, "I thought, within myself, that my inference from his developement was not so very erroneous as the worthy doctor wished me to believe."

A man named Halleran, at Vienna, imagined himself continually accompanied by a familiar spirit; he saw the spirit, and conversed with it. When he reached his sixtieth year his genius appeared as if he wished to leave him, and only on certain days in the month was he favoured with his presence. At Gersbach, near Durlach, in the Grand Duchy of Baden, Dr. Gall knew a curate who was confined because he conceived himself to have a familiar spirit. At Manheim there was a man who saw himself continually attended by several spirits: sometimes they marched at his side in visible forms; at other times they attended him under ground. In these persons Dr. Gall found the part of the brain in question largely developed. He states as questions for consideration, "Does this convolution form part of the organ of Imitation? and does its extreme developement exalt the talent for mimicry to such a degree, as to personify simple ideas, and to give them, thus metamorphosed, a locality out of the individual? Or does it constitute parts both of Ideality and Imitation? Or, finally, does it constitute a separate organ? These points can be determined only by farther researches."†

* Gall, tome v., p. 342.
† *Sur les Fonctions du Cerveau*, tome v., p. 346.

Sir Walter Scott observes, that "no man ever succeeded in imposing himself on the public as a supernatural personage who was not to a certain degree the dupe of his own imposture."*

Dr. Gall mentions, that the organ appears large in the busts of Socrates, Joan of Arc, Cromwell, Swedenborg, and other individuals by whom the tendency before described has been manifested. In the portrait of Tasso it and Ideality (18 and 19) both appeared largely developed.

TASSO.

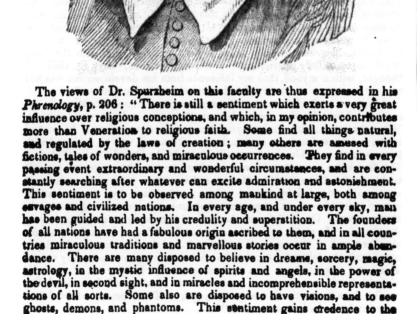

The views of Dr. Spurzheim on this faculty are thus expressed in his *Phrenology*, p. 206 : "There is still a sentiment which exerts a very great influence over religious conceptions, and which, in my opinion, contributes more than Veneration to religious faith. Some find all things natural, and regulated by the laws of creation ; many others are amused with fictions, tales of wonders, and miraculous occurrences. They find in every passing event extraordinary and wonderful circumstances, and are constantly searching after whatever can excite admiration and astonishment. This sentiment is to be observed among mankind at large, both among savages and civilized nations. In every age, and under every sky, man has been guided and led by his credulity and superstition. The founders of all nations have had a fabulous origin ascribed to them, and in all countries miraculous traditions and marvellous stories occur in ample abundance. There are many disposed to believe in dreams, sorcery, magic, astrology, in the mystic influence of spirits and angels, in the power of the devil, in second sight, and in miracles and incomprehensible representations of all sorts. Some also are disposed to have visions, and to see ghosts, demons, and phantoms. This sentiment gains credence to the

* *Life of Napoleon Bonaparte*, vol. iv., p. 88.

true and also to the false prophet, aids superstition, but is also essential to faith and refined religion. It is more or less active, not only in different individuals, but also in whole nations. Its functions are often disordered, constituting one species of insanity.

"The legislators of antiquity, aware of the great influence of this faculty, made frequent use of it to enforce and to confirm their laws. They spoke in the name of God, of angels, or of supernatural powers. In our own days the religious sects of Swedenborgians, Methodists, Quakers, and many others, particularly demonstrate its influence and presence. In dramatic representations the introduction of ghosts, angels, transformations, and supernatural events proclaims its activity both in the author and in the public, by whom such exhibitions are relished and sought after.

"The existence of this feeling is certain. Its organ is situated anterior to Hope, and a great developement of the convolutions on which it depends enlarges and elevates the superior and lateral parts of the frontal bone. It is remarkably prominent in the heads of Socrates, of Torquato Tasso, Dr. Price, Jung Stilling, Wesley, &c. My observations on it are extremely numerous, and I consider it as established."

My own observations on this organ are the following : I have met with persons excessively fond of news, which, if extravagant, were the more acceptable ; prone to the expression of surprise and astonishment in ordinary discourse ; deeply affected by tales of wonder ; delighting in the Arabian Nights' Entertainments, and the mysterious incidents abounding in the Waverley Novels ; and in them I have uniformly found the part of the brain in question largely developed. When the organ predominates, there is a peculiar look of wonder, and an unconscious turning up of the exterior portions of the eye-lashes, expressive of surprise. In other persons I have found the part of the brain in question small, and in them it was accompanied with a staid soberness of feeling, diametrically opposite to the manifestations above described. Such individuals were annoyed by everything new or strange ; they scarcely felt or expressed surprise, and had no taste for narratives leaving the beaten track of probability or reality, and soaring into the regions of supernatural fiction. On analyzing these manifestations, they all appear to be referrible to the sentiment of Wonder, an emotion which is quite distinguishable from these hitherto enumerated.

Philosophers have long been puzzled to account for the circumstance, that a particular form of furniture or dress is pleasing, and is regarded as even beautiful when first introduced, but that it appears ridiculous and antiquated after it has been superseded by a newer fashion. Probably one cause of this feeling may be found in the faculty now under consideration ; and the agreeable impressions made on it by new objects may be one source of the gratification which a change of fashion affords. Love of Approbation unquestionably prompts multitudes to *follow* the fashion, without much relish for novelty itself ; but some individuals must take the lead, and there must be some principle in the mind to be gratified by mere change, which excites them to do so ; and Wonder may contribute to this effect. Indeed, as every faculty has a useful and legitimate sphere of action, I am disposed to infer, that the legitimate tendency of this sentiment is to inspire the mind with a longing after novelty in everything, and that its proper effect is to stimulate to invention and improvement. Fashion is not a real element of beauty in external objects ; and to persons who possess a good endowment of Form and Ideality, intrinsic elegance is much more pleasing and permanently agreeable, than forms of less merit, recommended merely by being new. Hence there is a beauty which never palls, and there are objects over which fashion exercises no control. A Chinese teapot may be rendered agreeable by being fashionable, but will look ugly when the mode changes; while a vase of exquisite form will please in all countries and in all ages. The teapot I conceive to owe its attraction to the impression which its novelty makes on the faculty of Wonder : but when this has ceased, it is judged of by its proper qualities, and disliked on account of its inherent inelegant proportions ; while the vase, by gratifying the faculties which take cognizance of intrinsic beauty, continues always to please. This view is strengthened by the fact, that the greatest votaries of fashion have frequently execrably bad taste ; a circumstance perfectly accordant with the supposition, that the mere love of novelty is the chief element in this disposition of mind.[*]

The French in general possess a considerable developement of the organs of Ideality, Wonder, and Love of Approbation ; and they have long been celebrated as leaders of fashion. Their ordinary discourse also is replete with terms of admiration and approbation, which to Englishmen appear excessive. Every object is *superbe, magnifique ;* and the terms *bon, beau, excellent,* express such faint praise as almost to imply disapprobation.

Sir John Ross, R. N., mentioned to me that young men, born and bred up in inland situations, who enter the navy voluntarily, generally possess a large developement of this organ, the gratification of which, he inferred, incites them to choose the sea as a profession.

According to this view, Wonder may aid genius, by prompting to novelty in all the conceptions of the mind. Kepler, Napier, Newton, and Davy, all of whom were fond of diving into abstruse and unexplored regions of science, were inclined to superstition. Dr. Samuel Johnson is strongly suspected of having believed in ghosts, a trait which indicates an excessive endowment of this faculty ;[†] and his style is full of new words and unusual forms of expression, to which he was probably led by the same feeling. Dr. Chalmers also shows a strong tendency to coin new vocables, and occasionally to give strange turns to his discourse ; which perhaps originates from Wonder acting with Comparison, as his brilliancy and elevation spring chiefly from Ideality. Mr. Tennant, the author of *Anster Fair,* and Mr. Hazlitt show some degree of the same disposition in their writings ; and I have observed the organ full in the heads of both. The faculty prompts, as Dr. Spurzheim remarks, to the use of machinery in poetry, and to the introduction of supernatural agency. In the portraits of Shakspeare and the busts of Sir Walter Scott it is large ; moderate in the head of Rammohun Roy. The feeling was strong in Robert Burns, and the cast of his skull indicates a large developement of the organ.[‡]

The following lines of the poet Akenside finely delineate the manifestations of the sentiment of Wonder :

> " Witness the sprightly joy, when aught unknown
> Strikes the quick sense, and wakes each active power
> To brisker measures. Witness the neglect
> Of all familiar prospects, though beheld
> With transports once; the fond attentive gaze
> Of young astonishment ; the sober zeal
> Of age, commenting on prodigious things.
> For such the bounteous providence of Heaven,
> In every breast implanting this desire
> Of objects new and strange, to urge us on
> With unremitted labour to pursue

[*] Concentrativeness has been supposed to act as the antagonist of Wonder, in giving the love of sameness of object and pursuit. See *Phren. Journ.,* ix., 619.

[†] Respecting the sources of credulity, see *Phren. Journ.,* ix., 642.

[‡] See *Phren. Journ.,* ix., 69, note.

Those sacred stores, that wait the ripening soul
In Truth's exhaustless bosom. What need words
To paint its power? For this the daring youth
Breaks from his weeping mother's anxious arms,
In foreign climes to rove : the pensive sage,
Heedless of sleep or midnight's harmful damp,
Hangs o'er the sickly taper ; and, untired,
The virgin follows, with enchanted step,
The mazes of some wild and wondrous tale
From morn to eve....Hence, finally, by night,
The village matron, round the blazing hearth,
Suspends the infant audience with her tales,
Breathing astonishment ! of witching rhymes,
And evil spirits ; of the death-bed call
Of him who robbed the widow, and devoured
The orphan's portion ; of unquiet souls
Risen from the grave to ease the heavy guilt
Of deeds in life concealed ; of shapes that walk
At dead of night, and clank their chains, and wave
The torch of hell around the murderer's bed.
At every solemn pause the crowd recoil,
Gazing each other speechless, and congealed
With shivering sighs ; till, eager for the event,
Around the beldame all erect they hang,
Each trembling heart with grateful terrors quelled."[*]

Dr. Spurzheim concludes his account of this faculty with the following remarks : " The preceding facts," says he, " determined me formerly to designate this feeling by the name of Supernaturality ; and it is certain that it is *principally manifested by a belief in miraculous and supernatural circumstances*, in the foundation of religion by supernatural means, and in its dogmatical points. As, however, the feeling may be applied both to natural and supernatural events, and in every case fills the mind with amazement and surprise, I do not hesitate to change the name of Supernaturality into that of *Marvellousness*. This name I prefer to that of *Wonder*, adopted by Mr. Combe, because, according to Dr. Johnson's Dictionary, *wonder* is applicable only to surprise excited by natural objects, while *marvellousness* embraces both kinds of astonishment caused by natural and supernatural circumstances."

When Dr. Spurzheim observes, in the foregoing passage, that this faculty is " *principally* manifested by a belief in miraculous and supernatural circumstances," I do not understand him to mean that this belief is its *legitimate function*. The period when Divine Power manifested itself by extraordinary means was limited, and is long since past ; and philosophy cannot acknowledge any object or event that occurs in the present day as miraculous or supernatural : a special faculty, therefore, for belief in such objects appears inadmissible. The fact, however, mentioned by Dr. Spurzheim, that persons in whom this organ is large have a natural disposition to believe in the wonderful and miraculous is certain. Some individuals, so endowed, have informed me, that, when any marvellous circumstance is communicated to them, the tendency of their minds is to believe it *without examination* ; and that an effort of philosophy is necessary to *resist* the belief, instead of evidence being requisite to produce it. This tendency appears to me to arise from too great energy in this faculty, not directed by reflection ; but it is not inconsistent with the idea, that the primitive sentiment is that of Wonder. Every propensity and sentiment desires objects suited to afford it gratification : Acquisitiveness longs for wealth, and Love of Approbation for praise ; and, in like manner, Wonder will ardently desire the marvellous. Individuals, therefore, in

* *Pleasures of Imagination*, B. i., v., 232-270.

whom the organ is large, will delight in extraordinary narratives, and the
pleasure felt in them will render the intellect little prone to enter on a
severe scrutiny of their truth : hence the tendency to believe in such
communications is easily accounted for. Still, however, this longing for
the marvellous appears to be an abuse of the sentiment. Philosophy does
not recognise the "supernatural," while it admits wonder at new and
extraordinary circumstances as a legitimate state of mind. With the
greatest deference to Dr. Spurzheim, therefore, I continue to regard Wonder as the more correct name ; and in this analysis I am supported by the
authority of the metaphysicians.

The organ, in a state of exaltation, is the great source of fanaticism in
religion.   When largely developed, it is liable to energetic activity, from
its mere size ; and the impressions which it then excites are mistaken, by
persons ignorant of its nature, for direct communications from heaven, and
reason is contemned.   It is then also liable to be vividly called into action
by external communications of a marvellous and fanatical character ; and
hence the wildest dogmatist, pretending to superior illumination, finds no
difficulty in drawing after him a crowd of devoted admirers.   I examined
the head of the late Reverend Edward Irving, before he was established
as a preacher, and when his peculiarities were unknown ; and observed
that the organs of Wonder and Self-Esteem were very large.   They gave
a tinge to his whole public life.   The organs of Benevolence, Conscientiousness. Veneration, and Intellect were also amply developed, so that he
possessed the natural elements of the Christian character in great strength,
but their direction was rendered unprofitable by the predominance of
Wonder and Self-Esteem.

The organ of Wonder is large in the skulls of the ancient Greeks, and
small in the Esquimaux.   The sentiment is
much weaker among the latter than in savages
generally.*   When the organ is small, the skull
slopes rapidly on each side, but when large, the
vertex is broad, as seen in the annexed cut.

Dr. Adam Smith, in his *History of Astronomy,†* calls Wonder a sentiment, and attempts
to distinguish it from surprise. "We *wonder*,"
he says, "at all extreme and uncommon objects ;
at all the rarer phenomena of nature ; at me-
teors, comets, eclipses ; at singular plants and
animals ; and at everything, in short, with which
we have before been either little or not at all
acquainted ; and we still wonder, though fore-
warned of what we are to see." "We are *surprised*," he continues,
"at those things which we have seen *often*, but which we least of all
expected to meet with in the place where we find them ; we are surprised
at the sudden appearance of a friend, whom we have seen a thousand
times, but whom we did not imagine we were to see then."

Lord Kames observes, that "of all the circumstances that raise emotions, not excepting beauty nor even greatness, novelty hath the most
powerful influence. A new object produceth instantaneously an emotion
termed *wonder*, which totally occupies the mind, and for a time excludes
all other objects. Conversation among the vulgar never is more interesting
than when it turns upon strange objects and extraordinary events. Men
tear themselves from their native country in search of things rare and
new ; and novelty converts into a pleasure the fatigues and even perils
of travelling. To what cause shall we ascribe these singular appearances?
To curiosity undoubtedly, a principle implanted in human nature for a

GREEK.

21 13 21

18   18

purpose extremely beneficial, that of acquiring knowledge; and the emotion of *wonder*, raised by new and strange objects, inflames our curiosity to know more of them."*

Dr. Thomas Brown† also admits Wonder as a primitive emotion, and contends, with success, that surprise and wonder are intrinsically the same feeling, only excited by different objects or occurrences. We wonder at the comet, from its novelty; we are surprised to meet a friend in Edinburgh, whom we believed to be in London: but it is the novel and unexpected *situation* in which we meet him, that causes the surprise, and not his appearance itself.

Dr. Brown‡ somewhat strangely observes, that " it seems most probable that the feeling of *wonder*, which now attends any striking event that is unexpected by us, would *not* arise in the infant mind on the occurrence of events, all of which might be regarded as equally new to it; since *wonder* implies, not the mere feeling of *novelty*, but the knowledge of some *other circumstances* which were expected to occur, and is, therefore, I conceive, inconsistent with *absolute ignorance*." The facts which we daily observe prove the very opposite of this doctrine. The organ of Wonder existing, every *new* object excites it, and calls forth the emotion; and hence, the greater the ignorance, the more frequent and more intense is the astonishment, for then almost every occurrence is novel.

Dr. Brown§ observes more justly, that " we may be struck at the same time with the beauty or grandeur of a new object, and our mixed emotion of the novelty and beauty combined, will obtain the name of *admiration*."

Mr. Stewart and Dr. Reid do not treat of this emotion. Their writings (especially those of Dr. Reid) indicate very little of the quality existing in their own minds, and this probably was the cause of their omitting to enrol it among the primitive mental emotions.

The subject of visions is still attended with considerable difficulty. I have met with cases similar to those recorded by Drs. Gall and Spurzheim. In the London Bedlam I examined the head of a patient whose insanity consisted in seeing phantoms, and being led to act as if they were realities; although, as he himself stated, he was convinced by his understanding, at the very time, that they were mere illusions; but could not regulate his conduct by this conviction. In him the organ of Form was well developed, and that of Wonder was decidedly large. When asked whether he experienced any sensation in the head when afflicted with visions, he pointed to the spot on each side where the organ of Wonder is situated, and said that he felt an uneasy sensation there.

In the Richmond Lunatic Asylum, at Dublin, I saw several patients in whom this organ predominated, and whose insanity consisted in believing themselves to be supernatural beings, or inspired.‖ In the Lunatic Asylum, at Newcastle, I saw a Miss H., in whom this organ was exceedingly large in the left hemisphere, and her insanity consisted in believing herself under the influence of spiritual beings.¶

An interesting case of derangement of the organ of Wonder is reported in *The Phrenological Journal*, vol. v., p 585. The patient, Dr. Anderson, of Cupar-Fife, devoted much attention to the study of animal magnetism, and at length imagined himself under its influence—an opinion which gradually acquired an ascendency over him, till it became so strong as to haunt him continually. His nights became disturbed, and when he did sleep he was tormented by oppressive dreams and other strange phantasms.

* *Elements of Criticism*, vol. i., p. 241.　　　† Vol. iii., p. 59.
‡ Vol. iii., p. 55.　　　 § Vol. iii., p. 57.
‖ See *Phrenological Journal*, vol. vi., p. 84.
¶ See a paper on Demonology and Witchcraft, by Mr. Simpson, *Phren. Journ.*, vi., 504; Mr. W. A. F. Browne's Observations on Fanaticism, vol. ix., pp. 289, 522, 577; x., 45; and a case mentioned in vol. v., p. 84.

His notion of animal magnetism was, that certain individuals who had an
antipathy to him, could wield over him at will an influence of so malignant
a nature as to deprive him of every kind of enjoyment. " He invested
these *invisibles*, as be called them, with vast power.   No place was proof
against their malignity, nor could distance restrain it.   He went to Paris
in the year 1822, with the view of escaping from it, but he found its influence there as great as at home.   He frequently during the night could
hear his enemies planning schemes for his annoyance.   In his imagination
they had recourse to every kind of torment which the most wicked and
inquisitorial minds could invent, and were inexorable and persevering in
their attacks....Several times he made application to the local authorities
to control their malignity, and even took bond from some of his acquaintances that they should cease to disturb him.   On all other subjects
saving animal magnetism his judgment was sound. and indeed in reasoning
he evinced much acuteness ; a stranger, in short, when the peculiar subject was not agitated, could not detect anything unusual about him."
On opening the head after death, the skull-cap was found very thick and
hard, affording evidence of long-continued disease; and over the organ
of Wonder was " an inflammatory deposit, apparently of old standing,
under the arachnoid coat, with thickening of the membrane itself, and
adhesion to the parts beneath for about the space of an inch and a half in
length, and one in breadth."   Dr. Scott, who reports the case, does not
specify the organ of Wonder as the exact seat of the affection ; because,
from not being acquainted with Phrenology, he did not know the situation
of that organ.   But Dr. A. Combe received a letter (quoted in *The Phrenological Journal*) from a gentleman who was present at the dissection,
and who had studied the subject, stating explicitly that the deposit had
its seat precisely at the organ of Wonder ; and adding, that the pain
complained of during eight years was " confined to the forehead and coronal surface, but *principally* to the latter region," and that it was Dr.
Anderson's invariable practice to apply cold water to these parts every
night, to abate the annoying heat which he felt in them.
   In the Edinburgh Pauper Lunatic Asylum Dr. Spurzheim saw a woman who was visited by ghosts and spectres.   In her the organ of Wonder was remarkably developed.   He asked her if she ever complained of
headache.   She answered that she did ; and being requested to put her
hand on that part of the head where she felt the pain, she did so on the
very spot where the organ is situated.*
   Several years ago I saw a person in the west of Scotland, who was
liable to spectral illusions.   He was then thirty-eight years of age, in sound
health, remarkably intelligent, and by no means liable to extravagance
either in his sentiments or ideas.   He mentioned that there was almost
constantly present to his mind the appearance of a carpet in motion, and
spotted with figures.   On visiting Glasgow, he saw a large log of wood,
mounted on two axles and four wheels, passing along the street ; and, on
returning home, the apparition of the timber and its vehicle, with the
horses, driver, &c., stood before him in the dimensions and hues of actual
existence.   On another occasion, he saw a funeral pass by the end of
Queen-street, in Glasgow ; and for some time afterward, whenever he shut
his eyes or was in darkness, the procession moved before his mind as
distinctly as it had previously done before his eyes.   These are merely a
few instances, out of many, of beings and objects which he had seen,
reappearing to his fancy.   He was not conscious of the appearance of the
phantom of any object which he had not previously seen ; and he was
rarely, or almost never, troubled with these visions when actual existences
were before his eyes in broad light : but at all times they appeared to

a greater or less extent when his eyes were shut, or darkness prevailed. His head was in general well formed ; the different organs, with the exception of the organ of *Wonder*, (which was decidedly large, and which seems to have been the origin of this affection,) were fairly proportioned ; the knowing organs preponderated a little over the reflective.

He mentioned, that this peculiarity had descended to his son. On one occasion, the boy had made up to what he conceived to be a beggar-man, and endeavoured to speak to him. The figure retired ; and the boy followed, till it disappeared at a high wall, seeming to glide into it. The boy ran up the wall, and groped it with his hands, when he discovered that the beggar was a spectral illusion. I had not an opportunity of examining the head of the son ; but the father stated, that, in other respects, there was no peculiarity about his mental constitution.

This tendency of mind, occurring in remote and secluded districts of the Highlands, has probably given rise to the *second sight*. The individual above described, if placed in a situation where his chieftain, his clansmen, their dogs and their flocks, were almost the only animated objects presented to his eyes, would have been visited with frequent spectral appearances of them. If, after the occurrence of such apparitions, the chief had been killed, or the clansmen drowned, or the flock buried in the snow, the coincidence would have been remarked, and the event would have been regarded as having been predicted by an exercise of the second sight. Where nothing followed the spectres, nothing would be said of their appearance, just as happens in the case of dreams. A correspondent of *The Phrenological Journal** gives an account of a Highland gentleman, who believed that an apparition of the second sight had occurred to himself ; and he states, that, in his head, the organ of Wonder is large.

At the same time, it is difficult to comprehend how an exalted state of this organ should produce these effects, unless we suppose it to excite the organs of Form, Colouring, Size, and Individuality, so as to prompt them to conjure up illusions of forms and colours, fitted for the gratification of Wonder ; just as the involuntary activity of Cautiousness, during sleep, excites the intellectual organs to conceive objects of terror, producing thereby frightful dreams. This theory is rendered probable by the fact, that morbid excitement of the knowing organs produces spectral illusions, independently of an affection of the organ of Wonder. Mr. Simpson has communicated an admirable paper on this subject to *The Phrenological Journal*,† to which I shall have occasion afterward to refer.

The natural language of this faculty is nodding the head obliquely upward, in the direction of the organ. I have observed a person telling another, in whom this organ predominated, a wonderful story. At the end of each head of the narration the listener nodded his head upward two or three times, and ejaculated an expression of surprise. An individual in whom the organ is small will not naturally do this.

The general function of the organ is regarded as ascertained ; but its metaphysical analysis is still incomplete.

19. IDEALITY.

THIS organ is situated nearly along the temporal ridge of the frontal bone. Dr. Gall gives the following account of its discovery :

The first poet whose head arrested his attention by its form was one of his friends who frequently composed *extempore* verses when least expected to do so ; and who had thereby acquired a sort of reputation, although in other respects a very ordinary person. His forehead, immediately above the nose, rose perpendicularly, then retreated, and extended

* Vol. ii., p. 362.   † Vol. ii., p. 290.

itself a good deal laterally, as if a part had been added on each side. He
recollected having seen the same form in the bust of Ovid. In other
poets he did not find, as a constant occurrence, the forehead first perpendicular and then retreating, so that he regarded this shape as accidental;
but in all of them he observed the prominences in the anterior lateral parts
of the head, above the temples. He then began to look upon these
prominences as the distinctive marks of a natural talent for poetry; but
still he spoke to his hearers on the subject with a degree of doubt, especially as, at this period, he was not convinced that a talent for poetry
depended on a primitive mental faculty. He waited, therefore, before
deciding definitely, till he had made a greater number of observations.

A short time afterward he got the head of the poet Alxinger, in which
this part of the brain and also the organ of Adhesiveness were very much
developed, while the other portions were so only in a small degree. A
little after this the poet Jungar died, and Gall found the prominences
also in his head. He found the same parts still larger in the poet Blu-
mauer, with a large organ of Wit. At this time Wilhelmine Maisch
acquired reputation at Vienna by her poetry; and the same enlargement
was found in her head, above the temples. Dr. Gall observed the same
organization in Madame Laroch, at Offanbach, near Francfort; in Ange-
lique Kaufmann; in Sophia Clementina, of Meaklen; in Klopstock; in
Schiller, of whom he had a mask; and also in Gesner, of Zurich. In
Berlin he continued to speak of this organ still with considerable reserve,
when M. Nicolai invited him and Dr. Spurzheim. to see a collection of
about thirty busts of poets in his possession. They found, in every one
of them, the part in question projecting more or less considerably, according as the talent was manifested in a higher or lower degree in each
poet. From that moment he taught boldly, that the talent for poetry
depends on a primitive faculty, and that it is connected with this part of
the brain as its special organ.

In Paris Dr. Gall moulded the head of Legouvé after his death, and
found this organ large. He and Dr. Spurzheim opened the head of the
late Delille, and pointed out to several physicians who were present the
full developement of the convolutions placed under the external prominences at this part; these convolutions projected beyond all the others.
Dr. Gall preserved a cast of one of the hemispheres of the brain; so that
this statement may still be verified. In a pretty numerous assemblage,
Dr. Gall was asked what he thought of a little man, who sat at a considerable distance from him? As it was rather dark, he said, that, in truth,
he could not see him very distinctly, but that he nevertheless observed
the organ of poetry to be greatly developed. He was then informed that
this was the famous poet François, generally named *Cordonnier*, from his
having been bred a shoemaker.* "If we pass in review," says Dr. Gall,
"the portraits and busts of the poets of all ages, we shall find this configuration of head common to them all; as in Pindar, Euripidés, Sophocles,
Heraclides, Plautus, Terence, Virgil, Tibullus, Ovid, Horace, Juvenal,
Boccacio, Ariosto, Aretin, Tasso, Milton, Boileau, J. B. Rousseau,
Pope, Young, Gorsset, Voltaire, Gesner, Klopstock, Wieland." &c. Dr
Bailly, in a letter, dated Rome, 30th May, 1822, addressed to Dr. Brayer,
says: "You may tell Dr. Gall that I have a mask of Tasso, taken from
nature, and that, although part of the organ of poetry be cut off, neverthe-
less, the lateral breadth of the cranium in this direction is enormous."
Mr. Lawrence Macdonald, sculptor, who visited Tasso's tomb at the Mo-

---

* A cast of the head of this individual is in the Phrenological Society's
collection, Edinburgh, and in De Ville's, at London. The organ in question
is large. Some particulars respecting him will be found in *The Phrenological Journal*, vi., 495.

nastery of St. Onofrio, in Rome, has favoured me with the following particulars: "In the library of the Monastery of St. Onofrio there is preserved,
along with an original letter of the poet, a cast in wax of his head, evidently
taken after death. The brain is very large in proportion to the face, and
the head altogether is above the ordinary size. The knowing organs are
very large, the reflecting large. The organs of the sentiments are full,
those of the propensities large. The most striking characteristic, however, is the breadth at the region of Ideality, which is extremely large."

The bust of Homer presents an extraordinary developement at this part
of the head. It is doubted whether it be authentic; but be it real or
ideal, the existence of the prominence is remarkable. If it be ideal, why was
the artist led to give this particular form, which is the only one in accordance with nature? If he modelled the head of the most distinguished
poet of his day as the best representative of Homer, the existence of this
developement is still a fact in favour of the organ.

We owe to Dr. Spurzheim the correct analysis of this faculty, and the
elegant and appropriate name by which it is designated. "It is impossible,"
says he, "that poetry in general should be confined to one single organ;
and I therefore think that the name 'Organ of Poetry' (used by Dr. Gall)
does not indicate the essential faculty."—"In every kind of poetry the
sentiments are exalted, the expressions warm; and there must be rapture,
inspiration, what is commonly called imagination or fancy."

This faculty produces the desire for exquisiteness or perfection, and is
delighted with what the French call "Le beau idéal." It gives inspiration to the poet. The knowing faculties perceive qualities as they exist
in nature; but this faculty desires, for its gratification, something more
exquisitely perfect than the scenes of reality. It desires to elevate and
endow with a splendid excellence every object presented to the mind.
It stimulates the faculties which form ideas to create scenes, in which
every object is invested with the perfection which it delights to contemplate. It is particularly valuable to man as a progressive being.
It inspires him with a ceaseless love of improvement, and prompts him
to form and realize splendid conceptions. When predominant it gives
a manner of feeling and of thinking befitting the regions of fancy rather
than the abodes of men. Hence those only on whom it is largely bestowed can possibly be poets; and hence the proverb, "Poëta nascitur,
non fit."

Those who experience a difficulty in conceiving what the faculty is,
may compare the character of Blount with that of Raleigh in Kenilworth:
"But what manner of animal art thou thyself, Raleigh," said Tressilian,
"that thou holdest us all so lightly?"—"Who I?" replied Raleigh,
"An eagle am I, that never will think of dull earth, while there is a heaven to soar in and a sun to gaze upon." Or they may compare the poetry
of Swift with that of Milton; the metaphysical writings of Dr. Reid with
those of Dr. Thomas Brown; the poetry of Crabbe with that of Byron;
or Dean Swift's prose with that of Dr. Chalmers.

It was this faculty "by whose aid" Shakspeare imagined the characters
of Ariel and Prospero. Prospero's concluding speech in The Tempest is
a beautiful specimen of the style of writing which it produces:

"I have bedimmed
The noon-tide sun, call'd forth the mutinous winds,
And 'tween the green sea and the azured vault
Set roaring war; to the dread rattling thunder
Have I giv'n fire, and rifted Jove's stout oak
With his own bolt; the strong based promontory
Have I made shake, and by the spurs pluck'd up
The pine and cedar: graves at my command
21

Have waked their sleepers ; oped and let them forth
By my so potent art.   But this rough magic
I here adjure : and when I have required
Some heavenly music, which even now I do,
To work mine end upon their senses, that
This airy charm is for ; I'll break my staff ;
Bury it certain fathoms in the earth ;
And, deeper than did ever plummet sound,
I'll drown my book."   *Act* v., *Sc.* 6.

Individuals differ exceedingly with respect to the degree in which they possess this faculty. According to the energy and activity of it, poetry is prized or relished. I have met with persons who declare that they could perceive no excellence in poetical compositions, and could derive no gratification from them ; and yet they were endowed with every degree of understanding and penetration, according as they possessed the other faculties strongly or weakly, and were not uniformly deficient either in moral sentiment or in judgment, in proportion to their want of poetic fire. An amusing case of its deficiency is recorded in *The Phrenological Journal,* viii., 411.

This faculty gives a particular tinge to all the other faculties. It makes them, in everything, aspire to exquisiteness. A cast of the human head is a plain transcript of nature ; a bust is nature, elevated and adorned by the Ideality of a Chantry, a Joseph, or a Macdonald. Add a large developement of this organ to the other propensities, sentiments, and reflecting powers, and it expands the field of their interest ; carries them outward, and forward, and-upward ; and causes them to delight in schemes of improvement. In common life we easily distinguish those who have, from those who have not, a considerable endowment of it. The former speak, in general, in an elevated strain of language, and, when animated, show a splendour of eloquence and of poetical feeling, which the latter are never able to command. It gives to conversation a fascinating sprightliness and buoyancy, the very opposite of the qualities expressed by the epithets *dryness* and *dulness.*

Some sects in religion, and, among others, that most respectable body The Society of Friends, declaim against ornament in dress, furniture, and other modes of life ; they renounce these as vanity, while they hold up the solid and the useful as alone worthy of rational and immortal beings. Now, this is the natural feeling of persons in whom Benevolence, Concientiousness, and Veneration are large, and Ideality very deficient ; and perhaps the original propounders of these notions possessed such a combination : but this is not the language of universal human nature, nor of physical nature either.   Where Ideality exists to a considerable extent, there is an innate desire for the beautiful, and an instinctive love and admiration of it ; and so far from the arrangements of the Creator in the material world being in opposition to it, he has scattered, in the most profuse abundance, objects calculated, in the highest degree, to excite and gratify the feeling.   What are the flowers that deck the fields, combining perfect elegance of form with the most exquisite loveliness, delicacy, and harmony of tint, but objects addressed purely to Ideality and the subordinate faculties of Colouring and Form?   They enjoy not their beauty themselves, and afford neither food, raiment, nor protection to the corporeal frame of man ; and, on this account, some persons have been led to view them as merely nature's vanities and shows, possessed of neither dignity nor utility. But the individual in whom Ideality is large, will in rapture say, that these objects, and the lofty mountain, the deep glen, the roaring cataract, and all the varied loveliness of hill and dale, fountain and fresh shade, afford to him the banquet of the mind ; that they pour into his soul a stream of pleasure so intense, and yet so pure and elevated, that, in comparison with it, all the gratifications of sense and animal propensity sink into insipidity and insignificance. In short, to the phrenologist, the existence of this faculty in the mind, and of external objects fitted to gratify it, is one among numberless instances of the boundless beneficence of the Creator toward man; for it is a faculty purely of enjoyment—one whose sole use is to refine, and exalt, and extend the range of our other powers, to confer on us higher susceptibilities of improvement, and a keener relish for all that is great and glorious in the universe.

In conformity with this view, the organ is found to be deficient in all barbarous and rude tribes of mankind, and large in the nations which have made the highest advances in civilization. It is small in atrocious criminals; and I have observed, that persons born in the lower walks of life, whose talents and industry have raised them to wealth, are susceptible of refinement in their manners, habits, and sentiments, in proportion to the developement of this organ, and that of Love of Approbation. When it is small, their primitive condition is apt to stick to them through life; when large, they make rapid advances, and improve by every opportunity of intercourse with their superiors.

This faculty, then, joined with Love of Approbation, Form, Colouring, and the other knowing faculties, and using Constructiveness as their instrument, produces all the ornaments of dress and architecture; and is the fountain of painting and sculpture. Those persons, therefore, who declaim against ornament, ask us to shut up one of the greatest sources of enjoyment. An elegant vase, couch, or chair, fashioned in all the delicacy of form and proportion which Constructiveness, aided by Ideality and Form, can attain; or the human form attired in dress, in which grace, utility, and beauty are combined, is an object which our faculties *feel* to be agreeable; the pleasure arising from it is natural, and of so excellent a quality, that it is approved of by intellect and by all the moral powers. Ideality is one element in correct taste. Great Love of Approbation may give a passion for finery; but we observe that intended ornaments, in the hands of some persons, occasionally produce the effect of deformities, through want of taste in their selection and arrangement; a result which arises partly from a defective endowment of Ideality. If, on the other hand, we enter a house in which exquisite taste reigns in every object; in which each particular ornament is made subservient to the general effect, and the impression from the whole is that of a refined and pleasing elegance; we may be certain of finding Love of Approbation combined with large Ideality in one or both of the possessors. Indeed, where the degree of wealth is equal in different persons, we might almost guess at the extent of these two faculties by the different degrees of splendour in their domestic establishment; and in cases where homeliness is the prevailing feature, while affluence is enjoyed, we may predicate a very moderate Ideality in the one or other of the heads of the family. I have frequently observed, in persons who, from an humble origin, have become rich by commerce, an intense passion for domestic splendour; and, without a single exception, I have remarked Love of Approbation and Ideality largely developed in their heads.

The figures on subsequent page represent the organ large in Chaucer, and deficient in Locke.

The relish for poetry and the fine arts is generally in proportion to the developement of Ideality. Temperament, however, modifies the effects of this as well as of all the other organs. The nervous temperament, being most favourable to refinement and susceptibility, greatly enhances the practical effects of this faculty.

Ideality is necessary to a tragic actor. The tone of voice suitable to it is elevated and majestic, and hence it is essential to enable the performer to feel and express the greatness of the personages whom he represents.

In some individuals the front part of this organ is most developed, in others the back part; and, from a few cases which I have observed, there is reason to believe that the latter is a separate organ. The back part is left without a number on the bust, and a mark of interrogation is inscribed on it, to denote that the function is a subject of inquiry. The back part touches Cautiousness; and I suspect that excitement of this organ, in a moderate degree, is an ingredient in the emotion of the sublime. The roar of thunder, or of a cataract—the beetling cliff suspended high in air, and threatening to cause ruin by its fall—impress the mind with feelings of terror; and it is only such objects that produce the sentiment of sublimity. It would be interesting to take two individuals with equal Ideality, but the one possessed of much and the other of little Cautiousness, to the vale of Glencoe, the pass of Borrowdale, the cave of Staffa, or some other scene in which the elements of the sublime predomi-

CHAUCER.

19

LOCKE.

19

nate, and to mark their different emotions. I suspect that the large Cautiousness would give the more profound and intense emotions of sublimity.

Like all other faculties, Ideality may be abused. When permitted to take the ascendency over the other powers, and to seek its own gratification to the neglect of the serious duties of life—or when cultivated to so great an excess as to produce a finical and sickly refinement—it becomes a source of great evils. It appears to have reached this state of diseased excitement in Rousseau. "The impossibility of finding actual beings, (worthy of himself,) threw me," says he, "into the regions of fancy; and seeing that no existing object was worthy of my delirium, I nourished it in an ideal world, which my creative imagination soon peopled to my heart's desire. In my continual ecstasies I drank in torrents of the most delicious sentiments which ever entered the heart of man. Forgetting altogether the human race, I made society for myself of perfect creatures, as celestial by their virtues as their beauties, and of sure, tender, and faithful friends, such as I have never seen here below. I took such delight in gliding along the air with the charming objects with which I surrounded myself, that I passed hours and days without noticing time ; and losing the recollection of everything, scarcely had I eaten a morsel, but I burned to escape," and return to this enchanted world. The theory of this condition of mind appears to be, that Rousseau invigorated and refined every faculty in his imaginary personages, till it reached the standard of excellence fitted to please his large Ideality, and then he luxuriated in contemplating the perfection which he had created.

The passion for dress, ornament, and finery, which in some individuals goes beyond all reasonable bounds, and usurps the place of the serious and respectable virtues, results from an abuse of Ideality, Wonder, and Love of Approbation, and is generally accompanied by a deficient development of the organs of Conscientiousness and reflection. In an hospital Dr. Gall found this organ considerably developed in a man who was insane ; and remarked to the physicians who accompanied him, that he observed the external sign which indicted a talent for poetry. The patient, in point of fact, possessed this talent ; for, in his state of alienation, he continually composed verses, which sometimes were not deficient in point and vigour. He belonged to the lowest class, and had received no education. In the collection of M. Esquirol Dr. Gall saw a mask of an insane person, who also was habitually occupied in versifying ; and in it the organ in question is considerably larger than any of the others. Dr. Willis mentions a patient of his, who, during his paroxysms of insanity, which were anxiously expected, was conscious of the most delightful and elevated emotions, and wrote poetry and prose with equal facility. This state of feeling always disappeared when the fit went off.

The sentiment of Ideality corresponds in some degree to that of "Taste," admitted by Mr. Stewart ; only he regards taste as one of the powers acquired by habits of study or of business.

Mr. Stewart has written an Essay on Beauty, in which he arrives at the conclusion, that this word does not denote one single and simple emotion, but that external objects are said to be beautiful in a variety of instances in which they excite agreeable feelings, although the kinds of emotion which they call forth are very different. Thus, it is correct speech to call a mathematical theorem beautiful, a rose beautiful, and a lovely woman beautiful ; yet the qualities of these three objects, and the kinds of emotion which they excite, are so different, that they have no common property, except that of the feeling excited by all of them being agreeable.

Mr. Stewart appears to be correct in this observation, and it is valuable, in so far as it directs our attention to the vagueness of the word beauty ; but it throws no light on the theory of the beautiful itself. Phrenology, however, enables us to supply Mr. Stewart's deficiency in this respect. Every faculty is gratified with contemplating the objects to which it is naturally related. A grand and solemn hymn pleases the faculty of Veneration, and is, on account of raising this delight, pronounced to be beautiful. A symmetrical figure gratifies the faculty of Form, and, on account of the pleasure it produces, is also termed beautiful. A closely logical discourse pleases Causality and Comparison, and, on this account, is in like manner said to be beautiful. Hence, the inventors of language, little prone to nice and metaphysical distinctions, framed the word beauty, to express only the general emotion of pleasure, of a calm and refined nature, arising in the mind on contemplating outward objects of various kinds; and in this sense a person may be alive to beauty, who enjoys a very imperfect endowment of Ideality. But the function of this faculty is to produce a peculiarly exquisite and intense emotion of pleasure, on surveying certain qualities in external objects; and it surpasses so vastly in strength and sublimity the perceptions of beauty communicated by the other faculties, that it may itself be regarded as the fountain of this delightful emotion, and be styled the Faculty of the emotion of Beauty. When active from internal causes it desires beauty, splendour, grandeur, and perfection for its gratification, and prompts the other faculties to produce and seek out objects invested with these qualities.

Dr. Thomas Brown[*] treats of the sentiment of beauty as an original emotion of the mind; and his doctrine might, with the change of names, almost be adopted by a phrenologist in speaking of Ideality. According to our doctrine, the knowing faculties perceive objects as they exist—such as a landscape, a statue, or a Grecian temple; and the faculty of Ideality, excited by their features, glows with a delightful and elevated emotion; and to the qualities in the external objects which kindle this lively sentiment of pleasure, we ascribe the attribute of beauty. Beauty, therefore, though appreciated in the first instance by the perceptive faculties, is enjoyed as a strong emotion only when these act in conjunction with Ideality. If the intellect acts alone, Ideality remaining quiescent, the feeling of beauty experienced will be less vivid. Hence, if a person be extremely deficient in Ideality, the most lovely objects in external nature may appear to him invested with all their pleasing attributes of form, colour, size, and arrangement; but he will never thrill with that sublime emotion, or that ecstatic delight, which prompts the exclamation that the object contemplated is exquisitely beautiful. Dr. Thomas Brown, in perfect conformity with this doctrine, says: "You are now in no danger of confounding that view of beauty, which regards it as an *emotion*, dependent on the existence of certain previous perceptions or conceptions, which may induce *it*, but may also, by the operation of the common laws of suggestion, induce, at other times, in like manner, *other* states of mind, exclusive of the emotion—with the very different doctrine, that regards beauty as the object of a peculiar internal *sense*, which might, therefore, from the analogy conveyed in that name, be supposed to be as uniform in its feelings as our other senses, on the presence of their particular objects, are uniform, or nearly uniform, in the intimations afforded by *them*. Such a *sense* of beauty," says he, "as a fixed regular object, we assuredly have not; but it does not follow, that we are without such an original susceptibility of a mere emotion, that is not, like sensation, the direct and uniform effect of the presence of its objects, but may vary in the occasions on which it rises, like our other emotions; love, for example, or hate, or astonishment, which various circumstances may produce, or various other circumstances may prevent from arising."

If Dr. Brown had added to his theory the statement, that some individuals possess from nature a great susceptibility of experiencing the emotion of beauty, while others appear almost insensible to it, as is the case also with the emotions of love, hate, and astonishment, which he mentions—and that this constitutional difference is one great cause of the different perceptions of beauty enjoyed by different persons—he would have rendered his explanation of the phenomenon nearly complete.

The question has been much agitated, What constitutes poetry? The answer afforded by Phrenology is, that the elements of poetry are all the feelings and perceptions of the human faculties, imbued with the quality of Ideality. Ideality itself is a primitive emotion, which may be described, but cannot be defined. It harmonizes, and may therefore blend, with every emotion and conception whose striking qualities are not in opposition to its own nature. If it is the feeling of the beautiful, then it will naturally combine with the highest and best manifestations of the other faculties, and stand opposed to all imperfection.

By communicating the desire of perfection, Ideality erects a high standard in the mind, by which to compare actual attainments. Viewed in this light, it appears to be an important element in the mental constitution of man, as a progressive being. To the lower animals, which cannot pass beyond their primitive condition, a desire of arriving at a more perfect state would have been a source of pain; whereas to man, with an undefined scope of improvement before him, no feeling could be more useful and delightful. When regulated by reason, the perfection which it aims at is not that which belongs to God or to superior beings; but that which results from the best action of all the faculties of man as a being of limited power.

Lord Jeffrey's article on Beauty, in the *Supplement to the Encyclopædia Britannica*,* appears to me to proceed on a misconception of the theory of Dr. Brown, and to be unsound and inconsistent with human nature. His lordship conceives that all "emotions of beauty and sublimity must have for their objects the sufferings or enjoyments of sentient being;" and he rejects, "*as intrinsically absurd and incredible*, the supposition, that material objects, which obviously do neither hurt nor delight the body, should yet excite, by their mere physical qualities, the very powerful emotions which are sometimes excited by the spectacle of beauty." Accordingly he lays it down, that the pleasure we enjoy in contemplating a Highland landscape arises from associating, with the wilds which we gaze upon, ideas of the rude sons of the mist and the mountain who inhabit them; from our conjuring up, while we look upon their scenes, recollections of their loves, their hates, their strifes, their shouts of victory, and their lamentations over the dead; and from our ascribing the delight occasioned by these emotions to the external objects themselves, as their cause, and conceiving them to possess the quality of beauty, when, in truth, they are only the occasions which excite these other emotions in our minds. In the bust of Lord Jeffrey Ideality is not the most prominent feature; but the organs of Eventuality, Comparison, and Causality are large; and this combination would produce precisely such a state of mind, on surveying a mountain-pass, as what he here describes. Ideality not being very energetic, the emotions of sublimity and grandeur would be only secondary in power; whereas Eventuality, Comparison, and Causality, being more vigorous, and in ceaseless activity, would suggest a thousand incidents, and their *relations*, connected with the scene. This state of mind, however, would be peculiar to persons possessing this combination.

To put this theory to the test of experiment, I accompanied a French gentleman to the Trosachs, and marked his emotions as he stood in the gorge of the pass leading toward Lock Katrine. He was comparatively a stranger to the manners, customs, and history of Scotland; although, at the same time, from acquaintance with English literature, he had some few ideas concerning the inhabitants of the mountains, which he might have associated with the rocks which he beheld. He possessed, however, considerable Ideality and a cultivated understanding. When the scene burst upon him in the full effulgence of its glory, he stood in mute astonishment and delight, until I asked him what *ideas* were passing in his mind. His answer was, "Mon Dieu, je sens, et je ne pense pas." I explained to him the motive of the question, and he declared that he experienced only feelings of the most intense and elevating description; that every nerve thrilled with pleasure, and that he thought of nothing, but resigned

* Page 181.

himself entirely to these delightful emotions. On analyzing them, he said that he felt his mind excited to rapture by the richness and exquisite elegance of the trees and shrubs with which the mountains were clothed; that his soul was awed into sublimity by the stupendous and broken cliffs which towered in magnificence to the clouds; and that even the chill of fear crept silently along his nerves, as the projecting precipices were perceived threatening to fall, and to cut off communication with the world around: and again he declared, that he thought not, and cared not, who inhabited the wilds, until the force of the first and most exquisite emotion was spent; after which his mind began to be occupied with ideas of collateral objects, or coolly to think; and that then the emotion diminished rapidly in intensity, till at last it ceased entirely to exist.

On another occasion I accompanied a gentleman, also of education and a cultivated understanding, but with little Ideality, to the same spot. He looked calmly around, and exclaimed, " Pretty trees these! High hills! Terrible uproar of elements been here! Difficult pass for the Highlanders!" &c.; but he exhibited no emotion and no deep-toned sentiment of the sublime, like the other.

The former of these instances showed that the supposition " that material objects, which obviously do neither hurt nor delight the body, should yet excite, by their mere physical qualities, the very powerful emotions which are sometimes excited by the spectacle of beauty," is not quite so " intrinsically absurd and incredible " as Lord Jeffrey imagines; while the second instance indicated that Ideality is truly the faculty which feels the beautiful and the sublime, and that, where it is not powerful, the most magnificent scenes may be regarded with pleasure, but with no intense emotions of beauty.

In composition this faculty imparts splendour and elevation to the style, and it manifests itself in prose as well as in poetry. The style of Lord Bacon is remarkably imbued with the splendour of Ideality, sometimes to excess, while that of Locke is as decidedly plain; and the portraits of both show that their heads corresponded with these different manifestations. Hazlitt's head indicated a large developement of Ideality, and the faculty glows in his compositions. It was the sustaining power which gave effect to his productions; for he was eminent for neither sound principles, correct observations, nor extensive knowledge. He seems to have relied chiefly on his imagination and language for success; and his works are already sinking into the shades of oblivion. In Lord Jeffrey's head, as it appears in the bust, Ideality does not predominate. The report was current at the time, that the review of Lord Byron's Tragedies, which appeared in No. lxxii. of the *Edinburgh Review*, (February, 1822,) was the joint production of these two celebrated authors; and keeping in view the fact that Mr. Hazlitt's Ideality is larger than Lord Jeffrey's, it would not be difficult, by a careful analysis of the article, to assign to each the sentences which he wrote. Lord Jeffrey's predominating intellectual organs are Eventuality, which treasures up simple incidents or events; Comparison, which glances at their analogies and relations; and Causality, which gives depth and logical consistency to the whole. Hazlitt, on the other hand, possessed a large Comparison, respectable Causality, with a decidedly large Ideality, elevating and adorning his intellectual conceptions. Proceeding on these views, I would attribute the following sentence to Lord Jeffrey's pen, as characteristic of his manner. Speaking of the qualities of Shakspeare's writings, the reviewer says: " Though time may have hallowed things that were at first but common, and accidental associations imparted a charm to much that was in itself indifferent, we cannot but believe that there was an original sanctity which time only matured and extended, and an inherent charms from which the association derived all its power. And when we look candidly and calmly to the works of our early dramatists, it is impossible, we think, to dispute, that, after criticism has done its worst on them; after all deductions for impossible plots and fantastical characters, unaccountable forms of speech, and occasional extravagance, indelicacy, and horrors ; there is a facility and richness about them, both of thought and of diction ; a force of invention, and a depth of sagacity ; an originality of conception, and a play of fancy ; a nakedness and energy of passion, and, above all, a copiousness of imagery, and a sweetness and flexibility of verse, which is altogether unrivalled in earlier or in later times ; and places them, in our estimation, in the very highest and foremost place among ancient or modern poets."* In this passage we have the minuteness of enumeration of Eventuality, the discrimination of Comparison and Causality, and the good taste of a fair, but none of the elevation, ornament, and intensity of a large, Ideality. In another part of the same review† we find the following sentences : In Byron, "there are some sweet lines, and many of great weight and energy ; but the general march of the verse is cumbrous and unmusical. His lines do not vibrate like polished lances, at once strong and light, in the hands of his persons, but are wielded like clumsy batons in a bloodless affray... He has too little sympathy with the ordinary feelings and frailties of humanity to succeed well in their representation. ' His soul is like a star, and dwells apart.'... It does not ' hold the mirror up to nature,' nor catch the hues of surrounding objects ; but, like a kindled furnace, throws out its intense glare and gloomy grandeur on the narrow scene which it irradiates." Here we perceive the glow of Ideality : the simplicity of the former style is gone,-and the diction has become elevated, figurative, and ornamental. I am not informed regarding the particular sentences which each of the above-named gentlemen wrote in this review : but these extracts will serve as brief examples of the differences produced on the style when Ideality sheds few or many beams on the pen of the author ; and I regard the probabilities as very strong, that the passages are assigned to their actual sources.

The organ is ascertained.

20. WIT, OR MIRTHFULNESS.

EVERY one knows what is meant by wit, and yet no word presents more difficulties in its definition. Dr. Gall observes, that, to convey a just idea of the faculty which produces it, he could discover no better method than to describe it as the predominant feature in the minds of Rabelais, Cervantes, Boileau, Racine, Swift, Sterne, Voltaire. In all these authors, and in many other persons who manifest a similar talent, the anterior-superior-lateral parts of the forehead are prominent and rounded. When this developement is excessively large, it is attended with a disposition, apparently irresistible, to view objects in a-ludicrous light.

Wit, however, is not the only cause of laughter Laughing, like crying, may arise from a variety of faculties. I am acquainted with a boy in whom Acquisitiveness is large, and who laughs when one gives him a penny. Another youth, who possesses a large Love of Approbation, laughs when unexpected praise is bestowed upon him. These facts, to which many more might be added, show that we may smile from any pleasing affection of the sentiments, or even of some of the propensities ; and that the cause of a smile is not always the ludicrous. This view is confirmed by the circumstances which occur in hysterical affections. It is not uncommon to see a lady or child laugh and cry alternately and involuntarily, apparently on account of some varying affection of the whole mental system, rather than from any particular ludicrous or distressing idea presenting itself by turns to the fancy. I have noticed farther, that a large developement of Hope, Benevolence, and Wonder, producing happy emotions, predisposes the possessor to laugh; while Cautiousness, Veneration, Conscientiousness, and Reflection, when predominant, give rise to a natural seriousness and gravity, adverse to laughter, the tone of these faculties being grave and solemn.

There may be much excellent wit, without exciting us to laugh. Indeed Lord Chesterfield lays it down as a characteristic feature of an accomplished gentleman, that he should never laugh; and although this rule is absurd, yet there may be a high enjoyment of wit without laughter. The following are instances in point: There is a story of a Nottinghamshire publican, *Littlejohn* by name, who put up the figure of *Robin Hood* for a sign, with the following lines below it:

> "All ye that relish ale that's good,
>   Come in and drink with *Robin Hood*;
> If *Robin Hood* is not at home,
>   Come in and drink with *Littlejohn*."

This is genuine wit, what even Chesterfield would allow to be so; and yet it does not force us to laugh. Another instance is the following: Louis XV. once heard than an English nobleman (Lord Stair) at his court was remarkably like himself. Upon his lordship's going to court, the king, who was very guilty of saying rude things, observed, upon seeing him, "A remarkable likeness, upon my word! My lord, was your *mother* ever in France?" To which his lordship replied, with great politeness, " No, please your majesty, but my *father* was." This also is admirably witty; but it does not excite laughter. In Prior's song upon a young lady entreating her mother to allow her to *come out*, (as it is called,) there is an allusion which, likewise, is very fine wit, although it is not laughable. The lady is alluding to the liberty enjoyed, and the conquests made, by her elder sister. The last two stanzas are these:

> "Dear, dear mamma, for once let me
>   Like *her* my fortune try,
> I'll have an earl as well as she,
>   Or know the reason why.
> The fair prevailed—mamma gave way,
>   And Kitty, at her desire,
> OBTAINED THE CHARIOT FOR A DAY,
>   AND SET THE WORLD ON FIRE."

In all these instances every one must perceive wit, although no inclination to laughter is excited. In the following cases, again, the risible muscles are affected, though, in fact, the real point of wit contained in them is infinitely less:

The story of the Nottingham publican, named Littlejohn, who erected the sign of *Robin Hood*, goes on to say, that Mr. Littlejohn having died, his successor thought it a pity to lose so capital a sign and so much excellent poetry, and accordingly retained both; only, erasing his predecessor's name, he substituted his own in its place. The lines then ran thus:

> "All ye who relish ale that's good,
>   Come in and drink with *Robin Hood*;
> If *Robin Hood* is not at home,
>   Come in and drink with *Samuel Johnson*."

The whole wit is now gone, and yet the lines are much more laughable than before. In like manner, when a servant let a tongue fall from a plate, and a gentleman at the table said, "Oh, never mind; it's a mere *lapsus linguæ*," there was genuine wit in the remark; but when another servant, who had heard that this was witty, let fall a shoulder of mutton, and thought to get off by styling this accident, too, a *lapsus linguæ*, the whole wit was extinguished, but laughter would be more irresistibly provoked. Now, in what does the wit of the first instances consist? and what is the cause of the more laughable effect of the second class of cases, in which the wit is actually extinguished?

This leads me to a definition of wit. Locke describes it as " lying most in the assemblage of ideas, and putting those together with quickness and variety, wherein can be found any *resemblance* or *congruity*, *thereby* to make up pleasant pictures and agreeable visions in the fancy."[*] Now, it may be demonstrated, that this definition is erroneous. For example, when Goldsmith, in his beautiful verses on hope, compares that great blessing of humanity to the light of a taper, he adds a circumstance of resemblance, which, according to Locke's definition, is the perfection of wit:

> " Hope, like the glimmering taper's light,
> Adorns and cheers the way,
> *And still, as darker grows the night,*
> *Emits a brighter ray.*"

But this, in point of fact, is only exquisitely beautiful, and not in the least witty. In like manner, Moore, in the following verses, introduces comparisons, which also have great beauty, but are entirely destitute of wit. In his song on music's powers to awaken the memory, he says:

> " *Like* the gale which sighs along
> Beds of oriental flowers,
> Is the grateful breath of song
> That once was heard in happier hours.
> Filled with balm, the gale sighs on,
> When the flowers have sunk in death,
> So when pleasure's dream is gone,
> Its memory lives in music's breath."

Again, in speaking of the pains of memory, he says:

> " When I remember all
> The friends so link'd together,
> I've seen around me fall
> *Like* leaves in wintry weather
> I feel *like* one who treads alone
> Some banquet hall deserted;
> Whose lights are fled, whose garland's dead,
> And all but he departed."

In these instances we have the most unexpected resemblances presented to the mind, beautiful, as I have said, but not witty; and when we analyze the images, we are able to refer them all to Comparison and Ideality as their origin; the suggestion of simple resemblance, adorned with beauty, being their constituent elements.

Wherein, then, do the comparisons which are witty, such as those already cited, or *Hudibras's* famous simile,

> " When, like a lobster boiled, the morn
> From black to red began to turn,"

differ from those which are not witty? This brings us at last to the consideration of the real nature of wit, and to the main object of all these remarks, the function of the organ now under consideration.

The authority of the metaphysicians tends to support the idea that the talent for perceiving resemblances is distinct from that which discriminates differences. Malebranche observes, that " There are geniuses of two sorts. The one remarks easily the *differences* existing between objects

* *Essay on the Human Understanding*, b. ii., c. xi., § 2.

and these are the excellent geniuses. The others imagine and suppose resemblances between things, and these are the *superficial* minds."[*] Locke makes the same distinction. After speaking of wit as "lying most in the assemblage of ideas wherein any resemblance or congruity can be found," he proceeds thus: "Judgment, on the contrary, lies quite on the other side, in *separating carefully, one from another*, ideas wherein can be found *the least difference*, thereby to avoid being misled by *similitude and by affinity to take one thing for another*."[†] Lord Bacon says, that "the chief and (as it were) radical distinction between minds, in regard to philosophy and science, is this—that some minds have greater power and are more fitted for the observation of the *differences*, others for the observation of the *resemblances*, of things."

These ideas will be better understood by an illustration. The objection is sometimes stated, that Phrenology is no science, because a large organ of Destructiveness and a large organ of Benevolence may be found in the same head, and then they will *neutralize each other, like an acid and an alkali*. This objection would spring from a mind in which the power of perceiving resemblances was greater than that which perceives differences, and would appear conclusive at first sight to minds similarly constituted. But a person having a large endowment of the faculty for perceiving distinctions, would discriminate in a moment the *difference* between two chemical substances, placed in a state of mechanical mixture, and two organs subsisting separately, having distinct functions, and calculated for acting on different occasions ; and he would see that the analogy had no force whatever.

Supposing, then, that the faculty of Comparison, to be afterward treated of, perceives resemblances, the question occurs, Which is the faculty that perceives *differences* ? Mr. Scott has been led to believe, that this depends upon the faculty of Wit, and that the primitive function of the power is to distinguish differences. He conceives that, in all the foregoing instances in which wit is recognised, there is "a mixture of congruity and incongruity, or that incongruity appears where congruity was expected," which in principle is the same thing. This is nearly the definition of wit given by Beattie, and it approaches closely to that given by Campbell and Dr. Thomas Brown. Now, he says that the proper function of the faculty under discussion is to perceive *difference*—to observe, in short, *incongruity* —and that it is only when this is done that wit is at all recognised. The wit in Lord Stair's reply lies in the incongruity between the answer which Louis received and that which he expected. He evidently anticipated that Stair would say that his mother had been in France ; and the king meant it to be inferred, that she had been false, and that Stair was his brother. His lordship's reply, on the contrary, completely turned the tables on the king. "No, but *my father* was," implied that Louis, by parity of reason, was descended of Stair's father. In like manner, when Kitty

> "Obtained the chariot for a day,
> And set the world on fire,"

we perceive the comparison between the young beauty's exploit and that of *Phæton* with the chariot of the Sun ; and the difference or incongruity is so striking, that we feel it as an essential ingredient in the description, and relish it as wit. In the comparison of hope to the taper, on the other hand,

> "Which still, as darker grows the night,
> Emits a brighter ray,"

* *Rech. de la Verité*, liv. ii., 2d part, c. ix.
† *Essay*, &c., b. ii., c. xi., sect. 2.

we attend only to the *resemblance*, which is very striking and beautiful, and *not to the points of difference*; and then the image strikes us as a *pure comparison*, and not as implying any incongruity—and, in consequence, it is not felt as witty.

Wit, therefore, appears to consist chiefly in an *intellectual perception of difference*, of incongruity amid congruity; and hence wit, like an argument, may be retailed a thousand times, from mind to mind, without losing its intrinsic qualities; while humour, which is ascribed chiefly to Secretiveness, is entirely personal, and must be witnessed at the first hand to be at all enjoyed.* These are the ideas of Mr. Scott, who has treated the subject at great length in *The Phrenological Journal.* It is impossible to give here a comprehensive abstract of his views, and I shall, therefore, quote only one paragraph. " I strongly incline," says he, " to think that this is an intellectual faculty, and that, while its function, as well as that of Comparison and Causality, is to compare ideas or feelings together, its special function consists in the peculiar manner of comparing. It does not compare, as Comparison does, to discover resemblances or analogies, nor, as Causality does, to draw refined distinctions, or to observe close philosophical relations; but it compares for the purpose of discovering broad, violent, extravagant contrasts, and of bringing together ideas the most incongruous, disproportionate, and opposite in existence." (Vol. iv., p. 195.)

Dr. Spurzheim, on the other hand, is of opinion that " the same power which perceives resemblances perceives differences also. I see no reason," says he, " for adopting two faculties for the act of discrimination. The same power perceives the harmony and disharmony of tones; there is only one power of Colouring; and the proportion and disproportion in dimensions are felt by the same faculty of Size; in the same way, I think that Comparison alone distinguishes similitudes and dissimilitudes, differences, analogies, or identities." It must, however, be remarked on this passage, that the ultimate or simple function of Comparison is still under discussion, and that there seems to be a difference between the comparisons made by it and those made by Size, Form, Tune, and Colouring.†

Dr. Spurzheim considers the faculty now under consideration to be " a *sentiment* which disposes men to view everything in a gay, joyful, and mirthful manner." He regards it as " given to man to render him merry and gay—feelings not to be confounded with satisfaction or contentment: these are affections of every faculty, while gayety and mirthfulness belong to that which now occupies our attention." According to this view, wit consists in conceptions formed by the intellectual powers, imbued with the sentiment of the ludicrous; in the same way as poetry consists in the productions of the other faculties, acting in combination with, and elevated by, Ideality. Dr. Spurzheim observes, that, even granting Mr. Scott's supposition that one faculty perceives resemblances and another differences, it still appears necessary to admit a special feeling of Mirthfulness. " We may excite Mirthfulness, it is true, by making comparisons of things which differ; but," says he, " we may do so also by comparing things which resemble each other. If, amid incongruity and difference, we seek for analogies, the faculty of Comparison is active, and, combined with Mirthfulness, it will undoubtedly make us laugh. But we may laugh heartily at a single object, without allusion to any difference. Those who are the most disposed to laugh and to be merry, are not always the most intelligent and the most skilful in distinguishing either analogies or differences. The feeling of Mirthfulness, therefore, seems to be special. It

---

* The theory of humour is explained on p. 162.

† On this point, which it is unnecessary to discuss here in detail, see *The Phrenological Journal,* vi., 384, and ix., 435, 495; also the section on Comparison in this work.

may be excited by pointing out differences or resemblances, by the agency of various feelings, by playing tricks, or by inspiring fear. The fundamental power, then, cannot be wit. This is only one of its applications, and results from its combination with intellect." An ingenious writer in *The Phrenological Journal*, vol. iv., p 364, supports, with much ability, Mr. Scott's opinion, that the power of discrimination arises from the organ No. 20 ; but also states weighty reasons for considering the sense of the ludicrous as a distinct mental power, not intellectual, but affective, the organ of which is not yet ascertained, but which he is disposed to look for between the organs of Wit, Wonder, and Imitation. The locality of the organ No. 20 in the forehead, among those of the intellectual faculties, certainly is a ground for presuming that its function is not affective. Mr. Hewett Watson, however, thinks that Mr. Scott's ideas are untenable, " inasmuch as the poet Moore, in whose mask Wit is but moderately developed, evinces a very considerable perception of difference."*

In *The Phrenological Journal*, vol. vi., p. 451, Mr. Watson has given a different analysis of this faculty from that of Mr. Scott, and ably illustrated it. He regards it as an intellectual power, whose function is to take cognizance of the nature or intrinsic properties of things, the office of Causality being to perceive the " relations of causation and dependence in general." According to him, the ludicrous is a *mode* of manifestation of all the intellectual faculties, and he gives examples in which Sheridan and Moore display great wit, chiefly from Individuality and Comparison. The faculty now under discussion also produces wit as a *mode* of manifestation ; but he conceives that it does so always by comparing or contrasting the *intrinsic qualities* of objects. The study of character " is included in the functions of Wit, not merely the actions performed, but the real dispositions." " Let us now take up," says he, " the Sentimental Tour of Sterne, in whose mask Causality and Wit are predominating organs. Almost the whole tenor of this work, unlike that of most tourists, consists of disquisitions concerning the dispositions and inherent qualities of persons and things ; for, instead of narrating whom and what he saw, his attention seems to have been absorbed in speculations as to their conditions, dependences, nature, and qualities. We wish to condense the evidence in support of the views now advanced concerning the organ of Wit, and shall, therefore, be sparing in our quotations from each author, and, indeed, select them rather as examples than evidence, leaving to those who may feel inclined the office of trying their soundness, by reference to the general writings of the authors enumerated. In the Preface written for the Sentimental Journey we have the following disquisition :

" ' Your idle people leave their native country, and go abroad for some reason or reasons, which may be derived from one of these general causes —Inferiority of body ; Imbecility of mind ; or inevitable necessity.

" ' The first two include all those who travel by land or by water, labouring with pride, curiosity, vanity, or spleen, subdivided and combined *ad infinitum.*

" ' The third class includes the whole army of peregrine martyrs ; more especially those travellers who set out upon their travels with the benefit of clergy, either as delinquents travelling under the direction of governors recommended by the magistrates—or young gentlemen transported by the cruelty of parents and guardians, and travelling under the direction of governors recommended by Oxford, Aberdeen, and Glasgow.

" ' There is a fourth class, but their number is so small that they would not deserve a distinction, were it not necessary in a work of this nature to observe the greatest precision and nicety, to *avoid a confusion of character.* And these men I speak of are such as cross the seas, and sojourn in a land of strangers, with a view of saving money for various reasons and upon various pretences ; but as they might also save themselves and others a great deal of unnecessary trouble by saving their money at home, and as their reasons for travelling are the least complex of any other species of emigrants, I shall distinguish these gentlemen by the name of ' Simple Travellers.' '

" ' Thus the whole circle of travellers may be reduced to the following heads :

Idle Travellers,	Proud Travellers,
Inquisitive Travellers,	Vain Travellers,
Lying Travellers,	Splenetic Travellers.

" ' Then follow

The Travellers of Necessity,
The Delinquent and Felonious Traveller,
The Unfortunate and Innocent Traveller,
The Simple Traveller; and, lastly,
The Sentimental Traveller, (meaning thereby myself.')

" There is in these distinctions an admixture both of philosophy and wit, but certainly more of the former ; and if our readers have gone along with our previous conclusions, they will scarcely hesitate to attribute both the one and the other to the organ bearing the cognomen of the latter. Again he says :

" ' The sons and daughters of service part with liberty, but not with nature, in their contracts ; they are flesh and blood, and have their little vanities and wishes in the midst of the house of bondage, as well as their task-masters.'

" Sheridan enjoyed no slight imputation as a wit ; but any one taking the trouble to analyze his manifestations in that way, will soon perceive that the wit of this remarkable individual almost always consists of comparisons, or contrasts of proportion, position, objects, and events, with little or no reference to their attributes or inherent properties. For instance, he compares a tall thin man with a short fat wife, to a church and steeple ; beaux flirting with a lady seated in a very high carriage, to supporters hanging half-way up the door ; a tall thin man, to a tree run up against a wall ; and such a one with his arms spread, to a cross on a Good-Friday bun."

" As, therefore, in the works of individuals noted for the large development of Wit, we find a peculiar tendency to dwell on the essential properties of things, and, at the same time, in some of them an equal tendency to ridicule all fancy, philosophy, and reasoning, wherein there appears neglect or ignorance of these attributes ; as we are not aware of any other organ which can include perceptions of this nature in its function ; and as the inherent properties of the constituent parts of creation seem to be intellectual perceptions, equally distinct from those of condition or dependence as those of objects are from those of their position and physical properties ; there seems no slight probability for supposing the existence of some distinct organ for such perceptions ; and, farther, if we find them manifested strongly when the organ of Wit is large; if the peculiar wit and satire believed to be connected with the function of this organ is found to depend essentially on such perceptions; and if other kinds of wit—that of Curran and Sheridan, for instance—may exist with a moderate or deficient endowment of this organ ; we shall be almost necessarily forced to the conclusion that perception of inherent properties does depend on the organ of Wit, unless it can be shown to exist powerful when the organ is feebly developed, which we have in vain looked for.

" It hence appears that the range of this faculty is far more extensive, and that it forms a much more essential ingredient in our philosophic capacities, than could be predicated from only observing its manifestations

when acting along with Secretiveness, Self-Esteem, Combativeness, and
Destructiveness, to produce irony, sarcasm, ridicule, and satire ; or, with
other intellectual powers, to sparkle in the sallies of wit. Directed toward
man, it probably gives a tendency to investigate the real character, instead
of resting content with observing appearances or actions, which seems to
have been greatly the bent of Sterne's mind, and considerably, so of that
of Franklin. Taking the direction of religion, it will inquire into the
nature and attributes of God, as manifested in creation. Cowper affords
an example of this, and Socrates may be also named. In physiology
primary or essential function, as distinct from modes of manifestation, and
particular actions and directions, will be its aim. To the metaphysician
it will impart a strong desire for ascertaining the nature and inherent
powers of mind, and of creation in general. Phrenology, being a union
of the latter two—the metaphysician and the physiologist—its founders
will afford us a suitable illustration. In the bust of Dr. Gall the organ is
represented much less developed than in that of Dr. Spurzheim ; and the
superiority of the latter in discriminating modes of manifestation, and particular directions of the mental powers, from the powers themselves, is
familiar to all phrenologists. Perhaps, too, we shall not err in adducing
Locke as a negative instance of the faculty. In the portraits of this
philosopher Comparison and Causality appear greatly larger than Wit ;
and his system derives not only ideas, but the mental feelings, from external impressions ; but as he was obliged to give the mind a capability
of being affected by impressions on the external senses, he endowed it
with the faculties of perception, contemplation, memory, comparison, and
abstraction, which are in reality but modes of activity, not inherent powers.
His grounds for denying the innateness of ideas were their non-manifes-
tation, or various modifications in different individuals, from which it
would seem that modes of being were to him in lieu of innate powers.

" It has been supposed that the organ of Wit gives a tendency to view
everything in a ludicrous light ; but if the ideas here proposed concerning
its functions prove correct, such a supposition must be untenable ; and
that it is so, in point of fact, may be shown by reference to nature. The
masks of Drs. Cullen, Franklin, and Spurzheim exhibit a greater developement of the organ than do those of Curran, Swift, and Sheridan. And
farther, let any one appeal to his own private friends in whom the organ
is largely developed, and ask whether they are not oftener pained than
pleased by things of opposite and unharmonizing nature brought into
unnecessary contact ; and, on the other hand, delighted by harmonies
between the properties or attributes, whether real or imaginary, of different objects."

" It seems that almost all amusing wit consists in a slight resemblance
addressed to the function of one organ, and at the same time a difference
to that of another—thus coming still nearer to Mr. Scott's theory of
laughter than his own view of wit could do. For, if there were distinct
organs to perceive resemblance and difference, each would be similarly
excited by the specimens of wit ; but if these be modes of activity common
to all the intellectual powers, then one of them is agreeably excited by
the similarity, and the other jarred by the contrast, producing different
states of excitement. We say ' jarred,' because the more any organ is
developed, the more are similarities and harmonies between its perceptions
sought after ; Tune, Colour, and Number, for example."

My own views coincide with those of Dr. Spurzheim, that the organ in
question manifests the sentiment of the ludicrous, and that wit consists
in any form of intellectual conception combined with this sentiment. If
this opinion is adopted, however, another question arises, namely, What
are the objects of the sentiment of the ludicrous ? We are able to point

out certain forms, colours, and proportions, which are intrinsically beautiful, and to specify them as the external objects to which Ideality is related. An ingenious friend stated the idea that there are also external objects which, in their own nature, are ludicrous, and which stand in an established relation to the sentiment of gayety. He specified night-caps, the nose, the elbow, a sailor with a wooden leg, and a windmill, as examples. It appears to me that the ludicrous is merely *a mode of existence*, of which almost all natural objects are susceptible, but which is not the sole or necessary characteristic of any of them. The nose, for example, when perfect in form and harmonious in colouring, in relation to the other features, naturally excites the sentiment of the beautiful, and calls up emotions of pleasure and admiration, and not at all any ludicrous feeling : let its proportions, however, or its colour, be changed, so that it shall be too long or too short, too high or too low, too red or too white, and it will instantly excite the sentiment of the ludicrous. There are several other sentiments which possess the characteristic of having no special objects in nature related to them, but of being liable to be excited by certain modes of existence. There is no object, for instance, that, in all its modes of existence, is especially and directly terrible, or instituted apparently for the direct purpose of rousing Cautiousness. A lion in a cage, or the sea in a calm, is not terrible ; but both become highly so when lashed into fury, and threatening to devour us. The conclusion which I draw from this view is, that although a sentiment of the ludicrous has been bestowed on us by a benignant Creator, to render us merry and gay, yet there is no object in nature which in itself is essentially and necessarily ludicrous or absurd. If any part of the human form, for example, or any imperfection or disproportion in its parts, were necessarily ludicrous, he in whom such aberrations occurred would be doubly afflicted—first by the physical inconvenience ; and, secondly, by being a natural and inevitable object of merriment to the whole human race, the latter being by far the greater evil of the two. Byron seems to have entertained the notion that some such impression was excited in the minds of spectators by his lame foot, and it rendered him extremely miserable. It would be in vain to attempt to educate a child by precept and example to feel compassion instead of mirth, on seeing an old sailor with a wooden leg, if a maimed man, supplying his defect by art, were necessarily a ludicrous object. But it would be quite possible to do so, if the ludicrous be only a mode of existence, and not an inherent quality in objects. By directing the child's attention to the cause of the sailor's imperfection, probably fighting in defence of his country, and to the inconvenience which he suffers from it, he might be rendered an object of interest to Benevolence and Veneration, and thus excite feelings of kindliness and respect, instead of those of the ludicrous.

This view explains also why the most acute writers have failed in giving a satisfactory definition of wit. If no object whatever be in its own nature-ludicrous, and if every mundane object may assume the ludicrous as one of its modes of existence, it is clear that any definition, or even description of the ludicrous, as a specific entity, must be impossible.

The different degrees of developement of the organ, in different individuals, explains why some men see the ludicrous in objects in which it is not perceived by others—the larger the organ, the greater being the tendency to discover ludicrous appearances.

I agree with Mr. Watson, that some individuals, in whom both Wit and Causality are largely developed, have a great talent for investigating the intrinsic qualities of things, including the primitive functions of the mental faculties and bodily organs, yet are not distinguished for wit ; while this analytic capacity is less conspicuously displayed by other persons in whom Causality is large and Wit deficient. The organs of Causality were much larger than those of Wit in the heads of Dr. Reid and Mr. Dugald Stewart, and neither of them was distinguished for the power of discriminating between primitive faculties, the laws of their operation, and the results of their acting in combination. Mr. Stewart indeed was remarkably deficient in this quality.[*] Dr. Thomas Brown possessed much more of this discriminating talent, and the organ of Wit was larger in his head. These and several other examples which I have observed, appear to support Mr. Watson's views ; but as the essential function of a faculty is most strikingly manifested when its organ is in excess, I have observed the manifestations of several individuals in whom Wit predominated over Causality, and in them. I perceived a striking love of the purely ludicrous, with a regardlessness equally of the intrinsic and of all the other philosophical qualities of things. Their great delight was to heap absurd and incongruous ideas together, to extract laughter out of every object, and to enjoy the mirth which their sallies had created. In consequence of

[*] The following sentence, which occurs in the very threshold of his philosophical writings, affords a striking illustration of the remark in the text : " Upon a slight attention to the operations of our own mind," says he, " they appear to be so complicated and so infinitely diversified, that it seems to be impossible to reduce them to any general laws: In consequence, however, of a more accurate examination, the prospect clears up ; and the phenomena which appeared at first to be too various for our comprehension, are found to be the result of a comparatively small number of simple and uncompounded faculties, or of simple and uncompounded principles of action." It is extremely difficult to comprehend the *distinction* between " *faculties* " and " *pr inciples of action*," which is obviously implied in the terms of this sentence. Mr. Stewart proceeds : " These *faculties and principles are the* GENERAL LAWS *of our constitution*, and hold the same place in the philosophy of mind that the general laws we investigate in physics hold in that branch of science."[*] This is evidently erroneous. The propensity of Destructiveness, for example, is a primitive faculty, and it acts according to certain laws. One of these laws is, that it is excited by injury or provocation ; and that it lies dormant when its possessor is gratified. Under certain influences it may become diseased; and then it is a law of its constitution that it becomes extremely vigorous and ungovernable by the other faculties, and that it adds greatly to the energy of muscular action. The propensity itself is a primitive faculty of our nature, and the phenomena which it exhibits take place regularly, and this regularity is metaphorically expressed by saying that it acts according to certain laws, which are called laws of our constitution; but there is a want of discrimination in mistaking the laws which the propensity observes, or its mode of action, for the propensity itself, which Mr. Stewart here obviously does. The same want of penetration is apparent in his remark in regard to the objects of our investigation in physical science. It is true, that, in astronomy, the objects of our investigation are the *laws* which the principle of gravitation obeys ; but in chemistry, which is equally a physical science, the elements and the inherent properties or qualities of substances, whatever these may be, are the ultimate objects of investigation, just as the primitive faculties are in mind. The modes of action of chemical substances, and the laws which they obey, are obviously distinct objects of study from the substances themselves. The mineralogist, for instance, studies the diamond simply as it exists ; while the chemist investigates its elements, and its modes of action when exposed to heat and other external influences. Again, it has long been disputed; what *caloric* is in itself; whether it is a *substance*, or a *state* merely arising from certain modes of action in matter. But the laws which it obeys in being radiated, in being reflected, and in being concentrated, are clearly distinct objects of consideration from its substance, and yet Mr. Stewart confounds them. This incapacity to discriminate between primitive faculties and their modes of action runs through almost all his writings. Sometimes he recognises original principles distinctly, as in pp. 367, 371, 372. On other occasions, he loses sight of the distinction between them and modes of action, I shall revert to this subject when treating of association.

* *Elements of the Philosophy of the Human Mind*, 2d edit., p. 10.

these observations, I embrace Dr. Spurzheim's view that the sentiment of the ludicrous is the primitive function of the organ. The facts brought forward by Mr. Watson remain to be accounted for, and seem to give plausibility to the idea that there may be a special organ for taking cognizance of intrinsic qualities.

I do not regard the cases of Curran and Sheridan as attended with much difficulty. In Curran's mask the organs of Eventuality and Comparison are large, while those of Causality and Wit are only full. He had a reputation for wit; but I suspect that he manifested chiefly burlesque humour; for I have searched in vain in his speeches, reported in the Life written by his Son, for proofs of the former quality. I find in his speeches very few of the witty contrasts which distinguish the writings of Sterne, Voltaire, and the Reverend Sidney Smith. He does not display either philosophical profundity or comprehensiveness of mind. I am led by Curran's biography to infer that he possessed a very active temperament, and large Destructiveness, Secretiveness, and Imitation; and that these organs, combined with large Eventuality and Comparison, gave him fertility of invention, copiousness of illustration, savoir-faire, and a command, to a certain extent, of a coarse satirical humour. By dint of these talents he appears to have addressed himself dexterously to the prevailing sympathies of his audience for the time, and to have produced an effect on their minds much greater than the intellectual qualities displayed in his speeches would lead a modern reader to expect.

Sheridan's literary works contain more examples of genuine wit than the remains of Curran. He had a large developement of Individuality, Eventuality, and Comparison, but Causality and Wit were scarcely full. The wit in Sheridan's works is more abundant, and of a higher character, than the organ of the faculty in his head would lead us to expect; but in his biography by Mr. Moore, an instructive light is cast on this apparent anomaly. Much of the wit which sparkles in Sheridan's pages was not his own, but collected in the intellectual circles in London in which he moved, noted down by him when uttered by his friends, and subsequently wrought up into his own productions. His speeches partake much of the general character which distinguishes those of Curran. They are brilliant and clever, adapted to the day and place which gave them birth, but meager in philosophic principles, and also in genuine and underived wit. I cannot, therefore, regard either Sheridan or Curran as witty men, in the same sense of the word in which we pronounce Voltaire and Sterne, and the author of Hudibras, to have been witty. The Reverend Sidney Smith is a living example of a really witty mind. His wit is always pertinent to the object about which he reasons. It is the seasoning to solid argument, and, in fact, is often in itself argument. Sheridan, when he drew on his own resources, manifested Individuality, Eventuality, and Comparison in enumerations and descriptions of physical objects and events, 'and by means of a moderate organ of Wit he tinged them with the ludicrous. Sidney Smith, on the other hand, impregnates the abstract deductions of reason with wit, presenting the strongest arguments in the most ludicrous attire, yet keeping the wit always subordinate to the logic. Causality, combined with a large organ of Wit, appears to me to be indispensable to the manifestation of these qualities.

Some individuals who possess a large developement of Individuality, Eventuality, and Comparison, particularly when Secretiveness and Imitation (which are great elements in the talent for acting) are also large, often enjoy a great reputation for wit and drollery among their companions, although in them the organ of the ludicrous is by no means large. Two explanations may be given of this fact. First, the conceptions formed by the faculties here named are palpable and striking; and, if even a mo-

derate portion of the ludicrous be infused into them, they produce a great
effect on ordinary minds. Secondly, many persons mistake everything for
wit which makes them laugh ; and, in consequence, dignify with that name
mere imitations, and sometimes even absurdities, when uttered with a confident air, as if they had legitimate pretensions to be considered ludicrous.

Dr. Spurzheim, in the dissection of the brain, shows that, anatomically,
Ideality and Wit belong to the same department of convolutions ; whence
a presumption in his opinion arises that their functions belong to the same
class of mental faculties : and as Ideality has been uniformly regarded as
a sentiment, Wit may with propriety be placed under the same head. It
will be observed, that all these differences relate to the metaphysical
analysis of the faculty, and that phrenologists are agreed on the fact, that
witty and mirthful manifestations are connected with the organ now under
consideration. The organ and its function, therefore, may, to this extent,
be regarded as ascertained.

21. IMITATION.

Dr. Gall gives the following account of the discovery of this faculty
and organ : One day, a friend with whom he was conversing about the
form of the head, assured him that his had something peculiar about it,
and directed his hand to the superior-anterior region of the skull. This
part was elevated in the form of a segment of a sphere ; and behind the
protuberance there was a transverse depression in the middle of his head.
Before that time Dr. Gall had not observed such a conformation. This
man had a peculiar talent for imitation. Dr. Gall immediately repaired
to the institution for the deaf and dumb, in order to examine the head of a
pupil named Casteigner, who only six weeks before had been received into
the establishment, and, from his entrance, had attracted notice by his
amazing talent for mimicry. On the mardi-gras of the carnival, when a
little play was performed at the institution, he had imitated so perfectly
the gestures, gait, and looks of the director, inspector, physician, and
surgeon of the establishment, and above all of some women, that it was
impossible to mistake them. This exhibition was the more amusing, as
nothing of the kind was expected from the boy, his education having been
totally neglected. Dr. Gall states, that he found the part of the head in
question as fully developed in this individual as in his friend Hannibal,
just mentioned.

Is the talent for mimicry, then, said Dr. Gall, founded on a particular
faculty and organ ? He sought every opportunity of multiplying observations. He visited private families, schools, and public places, and everywhere examined the heads of individuals who possessed a distinguished
talent for mimicry. At this time Monsieur Marx, secretary to the
minister of war, had acquired a great reputation by playing several characters in a private theatre. Dr. Gall found in him the same part of the
head swelling out as in Casteigner and Hannibal. In all the other persons
whom he examined he found the part in question more or less elevated,
in proportion to the talent for imitation which they possessed. It is told
of Garrick, says Dr. Gall, that he possessed such an extraordinary talent
for mimicry, that, at the court of Louis XV., having seen for a moment
the king, the Duke D'Aumont, the Duke D'Orleans, Messrs. D'Aumont,
Brissac, and Richelieu, Prince Soubise, &c., he carried off the manner
of each of them in his recollection. He invited to supper some friends
who had accompanied him to court, and said, " I have seen the court only
for an instant, but I shall show you the correctness of my powers of observation and the extent of my memory ;" and placing his friends in two
files, he retired from the room, and, on his immediately returning, his

friends exclaimed, "Ah! here is the king, Louis XV., to the life!" He imitated in succession all the other personages of the court, who were instantly recognised. He imitated not only their walk, gait, and figure, but also the expression of their countenances. Dr. Gall, therefore, easily understood how greatly the faculty of Imitation would assist in the formation of a talent for acting; and he examined the heads of the best performers at that time on the stage of Vienna. In all of them he found the organ large. He got the skull of Jünger, a poet and comedian, and afterward used it to demonstrate this organ. Subsequently, he and Dr. Spurzheim, in their travels, met with many confirmations of it. In particular, in the house of correction, at Munich, they saw a thief who had it large. Dr. Gall said he must be an actor: surprised at the observation, he acknowledged that he had for some time belonged to a strolling company of players. This circumstance was not known to Dr. Gall made the observation. On these grounds, Dr. Gall conceived himself justified in admitting the existence of a special talent for imitation; that is to say, a faculty which enables the possessor in some degree to personify the ideas and sentiments of others, and to exhibit them exactly by gestures; and he considered this talent to be connected with the particular organ now pointed out.

This organ contributes to render a poet or author dramatic; such as Shakspeare, Corneille, Moliere, Voltaire, &c. It is large in the portraits of Shakspeare, and also in the bust of Sir Walter Scott, whose productions abound in admirable dramatic scenes.

This faculty produces the talent for imitation alone; and Mr. Scott observes, that, in perfect acting, there is more than imitation. There is expression of the propensities and sentiments of the mind in all the truth and warmth of natural excitement; and this power of throwing real expression on the outward representation he conceives to depend upon Secretiveness.* Thus, says Mr. Scott, a person with much Imitation and little Secretiveness could represent what he had seen, but he would give the externals only in his representation; add Secretiveness, and he could then enter into any given character as it would appear if existing in actual nature: he could, by means of this latter faculty, call up all the internal feelings which would animate the original, and give not a copy merely, but another of the same—a second edition, as it were, of the person represented. In this analysis of acting perhaps too much influence is ascribed to Secretiveness and too little to Imitation: my own opinion, as expressed on p. 163, is, that Secretiveness produces chiefly a restraining effect, and that Imitation enables its possessor to enter into the spirit of those whom it represents.

As imitation consists in reproducing existing appearances, it will easily be understood that its effects should be greatly augmented by vigorous powers of observation; and, accordingly, this faculty is greatly aided by a large endowment of Individuality and Eventuality. In the heads of Garrick, of the late Mr. Matthews, the comedian, these organs were very largely developed in addition to Imitation.

While, however, Secretiveness and Imitation together may thus be regarded as general powers, without which no talent for acting can be manifested, it is proper to observe, that the effect with which they can be applied in representing particular characters will depend on the degree in which other faculties are possessed in combination with them. They confer on the individual only the capacity of applying, in this particular way, the other powers of the mind, so far as he possesses them; but they do not supply the want of these powers. For example; an actor very deficient in Tune, however highly he may be endowed with Secretiveness

* Trans. of the Phren. Soc., p. 169.

and Imitation, could not imitate Malibran; nor, what is the same thing, perform her parts on the stage : neither could an individual possessing little Self-Esteem and Destructiveness, represent, with just effect, the fiery *Coriolanus*; because the natural language of haughty indignation can no more be called up by Imitation and Secretiveness, without Destructiveness and Self-Esteem, than can melody without the aid of Tune. Hence, to constitute an accomplished actor, capable of sustaining a variety of parts, a generally full endowment of the mental organs is required. Nature rarely bestows all these in an eminent degree on one individual; and, in consequence, each performer has a range of character in which he excels, and out of which his talents appear to be greatly diminished. I have found, in repeated observations, that the lines of success and failure bear a decided reference to the organs fully or imperfectly developed in the brain. Actors incapable of sustaining the dignity of a great character, but who excel in low comedy, will be found deficient in Ideality ; while, on the other hand, those who tread the stage with a native dignity of aspect, and seem as if born to command, will be found to possess it largely developed ; and also Firmness, Self-Esteem, and Love of Approbation. It does not follow, however, from these principles, that an actor, in his personal conduct, must necessarily resemble most closely those characters which he represents to the best advantage on the stage. To enable an individual to succeed eminently in acting *Skylock*, for example, Firmness, Acquisitiveness, and Destructiveness are indispensable ; but it is not necessary, merely because *Skylock* is represented as deficient in Benevolence, Conscientiousness, Veneration, and Love of Approbation, that the actor should also be so. The general powers of Imitation and Sensitiveness, although they do not supply the place of faculties that are deficient, are quite competent to suppress the manifestations of incongruous sentiments. Hence, in his private character the actor may manifest, in the highest degree, the moral sentiments ; and yet, by shading these for the time, by the aid of Secretiveness, and bringing into play only the natural language of the lower propensities, which also we suppose him to possess, he may represent the scoundrel to the life.

This faculty is indispensable to the portrait painter, the engraver, and the sculptor ; and, on examining the heads of Mr. W. Douglas, Mr. Joseph, Mr. Uwins, Mr. W. Allan, Mr. James Stewart, Mr. Shelby the ornithologist, and Mr. Lawrence Macdonald, I found it large in them all. Indeed, in these arts Imitation is as indispensable as Constructiveness. It also aids the musician and linguist, and, in short, all who practise arts in which expression is an object. On this faculty, in particular, the power of the ventriloquist depends.*

Dr. Spurzheim, alluding to Imitation, Wonder, Ideality, Wit, and Tune, observes, that " it is remarkable that the anterior, lateral, and upper region of the brain contains the organs of such powers as seem to be given particularly for amusements and theatrical performances."

Imitation gives the power of assuming those gestures which are expressive of the thoughts and feelings of the mind, and hence is requisite to the accomplished orator. In private life some individuals accompany their speech with the most forcible and animated expressions of countenance ; the nascent thought beams from the eye, and plays upon the features, before it is uttered in words ; this is produced by much Imitation and Ideality.

In children Imitation is more active than in adults. Young persons are very apt to copy the behaviour of those with whom they associate ;

* See " Phrenological explanation of the vocal illusions commonly called Ventriloquism," by Mr. Simpson, *Phren. Journ.*, vol. i., p. 466 ; and additional illustrations, vol. ii., p. 583.

and hence the necessity of setting a good example before them, even from the earliest years. "Children," says Locke, "(nay, men too,) do most from example; we are all a sort of chameleons, that still take a tincture from things near us."[*]

Cabanis relates a case in which the organ of Imitation seems to have been diseased. The patient felt himself impelled to repeat all the movements and attitudes which he witnessed. "If at any time they prevented him from obeying that impulse, either by constraining his limbs or obliging him to assume contrary attitudes, he experienced insupportable anguish; here it is plain, the faculty of imitation was in a state of morbid excitement."[†] "A young idiot girl," says Pinel, "whom I have long had under my care, has a most decided and irresistible propensity to imitate all that is done in her presence; she repeats automatically everything she hears said, and imitates the gestures and actions of others with the greatest accuracy."[‡]

This organ is possessed by some of the lower animals, such as parrots and monkeys, which imitate the actions of man. The faculty is very powerful in the *Turdus Polyglottus*, or mocking-bird. "Its own natural note," says Dr. Good, "is delightfully musical and solemn; but, beyond this, it possesses an instinctive talent of imitating the note of every other kind of singing bird, and even the voice of every bird of prey, so exactly as to deceive the very kinds it attempts to mock. It is, moreover, playful enough to find amusement in the deception, and takes a pleasure in decoying smaller birds near it by mimicking their notes, when it frightens them almost to death, or drives them away with all speed, by pouring upon them the screams of such other birds of prey as they most dread."[§]

When this organ and that of Benevolence are both large, the anterior portion of the coronal region of the head rises high above the eyes, is broad, and presents a level surface, as in Miss Clara Fisher, who, at eight years of age, exhibited great talents as an actress. When Benevolence is large and Imitation small, there is an elevation in the middle, with a rapid slope on each side, as in Jacob Jervis. The organ is regarded as ascertained.

JACOB JERVIS.

CLARA FISHER.

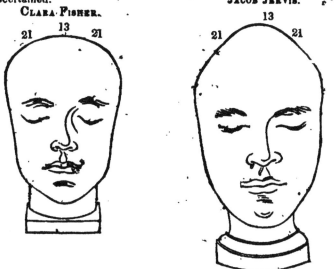

* Locke's *Thoughts concerning Education*, § 67.
† Cabanis, *Rapports du Physique et du Moral de l'Homme*, tome i., p. 195.
‡ *De l'Aliénation Mentale*, 2d edit., p. 99, § 115.
§ Good's *Study of Medicine*, 2d edit., vol. i., p. 463.

In both of these figures the head rises to a great height above the eyes ; but in Jervis it slopes rapidly on the two sides of 13, Benevolence, indicating Imitation deficient ; whereas in Miss Clara Fisher it is as high as 21, Imitation, as at Benevolence, indicating both organs to be large.

ORDER II.—INTELLECTUAL FACULTIES.

THESE faculties communicate to man and animals knowledge of their own internal sensations, and also of the external world ; their object is to know existence and to perceive qualities and relations.   Dr. Spurzheim's latest division of them is into three genera :

" I.   The External Senses.

" II.   The Internal Senses, or perceptive faculties which procure knowledge of external objects their physical qualities, and various relations.

" III.   The Reflective Faculties."*

For the sake of uniformity, I here adopt the same classification ; although, as noticed in the Appendix, No. II., it is far from being unexceptionable.   But until the analysis of the faculties themselves shall be more complete than at present, an accurate arrangement of them cannot be attained.

GENUS I.—EXTERNAL SENSES.

BY means of the Senses man and animals are brought into communication with the external world.   Dr. Spurzheim. in his *Physiognomical System*, and, in his more recent work, *Phrenology*, gives admirable treatises on the senses ; of which I shall avail myself largely in the following pages.

The opinions entertained by philosophers in regard to the functions of the senses have, in many instances, been whimsical, extravagant, and contradictory.

Since the time of Bacon and Locke, the greater number of philosophical systems rest on the axiom of Aristotle, that all ideas come into the mind by means of the external senses.   According to this notion, he who possesses them in the highest state of perfection, is able to manifest most powerfully the intellectual faculties of the mind ; or, in other words, the faculties, both of man and animals, ought to be proportionate to the perfection of the senses, and to the education bestowed upon them.   Daily experience, however, contradicts this hypothesis.   Dr. Thomas Brown's doctrine is, that in the sensations " we find the rude elements of all our knowledge, the materials on which the mind is ever operating, and without which it seems to us almost impossible that it could have operated at all, or could, even in its absolute inactivity, have been conscious of its own inert existence."†

Philosophers of another class maintain, that the mind acts independently of all organization, and that the senses, instead of being instruments of action, are rather impediments to it.   They complain much of the illusions of the senses ; and despise all testimony, and all conclusions grounded upon sensation.   Such notions are unworthy of being refuted.

Other philosophers, again, have attributed to the external senses many acts which are performed by the internal faculties alone.   For instance, Helvetius has said, that man owes his arts to the structure of his hands ; and that, if the hoof of the horse had been joined to the human arm, he would have been still wandering wild in the woods.   But many animals

* *Philosophical Principles of Phrenology.* Boston, United States, 1832.
52.   † *Lectures*, vol. i., p. 398.

have instruments equally curious and perfect in structure with those to which peculiar capacities of mind have been attributed in man ; and yet these instruments do not produce in them the corresponding functions. Monkeys have hands almost as nicely formed as those which are attached to the human arm ; but do monkeys put wood upon the fire to support combustion ? or do they construct works of art ? According to this theory, also, insects, craw-fish, lobsters, and still more the cuttle-fish, ought to have exact ideas of extension, of size, and of the theorems of geometry, in consequence of their numerous and perfect organs of touch.

In point of fact, however, the external instruments are often similar, while the functions performed by them are quite different. The hare and rabbit have similar feet ; yet the hare lies on the surface of the fields, while the rabbit burrows under ground. We have also examples of similar functions observed in animals which have instruments quite different. The proboscis is to the elephant what the hand is to man and to the monkey. The hands of monkeys and the feet of parrots and squirrels are certainly different ; yet, by means of these instruments, they all move their food to their mouths in eating. In order to dig up truffles, the hog ploughs the earth with his snout, and the dog scratches it with his feet.

Some have taught that the functions of the senses are not ordained by nature, but acquired by experience. Much, for example, has been written about the *rectification* of the sense of sight by means of touch ; and about what they call the *acquired perceptions* of sight.

Each sense, however, performs its functions in consequence of its own innate constitution alone ; and the relations of every sense to external impressions are determinate, and subjected to positive laws. If an odour make an impression upon the olfactory nerve, the impression is immediately found to be agreeable or disagreeable ; and this feeling arises from the constitution of the sense, and the relation established between it and the odorous particles which excite it to activity. The functions of every sense depend only on its peculiar organization ; and hence no preceding exercise or habit is necessary, in order to acquire the special power of any sense. If the organization be perfect, the functions are perfect also ; and if the organization be diseased, the functions are deranged, notwithstanding all preceding exercise. If the optic apparatus be perfect in newly-hatched birds, their sight is perfect ; as is the case with chickens, ducks, partridges, and quails : if, on the contrary, at the first entrance into life, the organization of the eyes or the ears be imperfect, the power of the animal to see or hear is proportionally deficient. In adult persons vision is deranged if the eyes be diseased. In old persons the function of the five senses lose their energy, because the vital power of the organs is diminished.

It is indeed ridiculous to suppose that Nature should have produced any sense which could not perform its functions without being supported by another and a different sense ; that, for example, we should not be able to see without feeling, or to hear without seeing. Hence the propositions appear self-evident,—that no sense acquires its functions by means of any other sense, and that any one sense cannot be the instrument of producing the sensations experienced by means of all the senses collectively. But we must observe, that different senses may enable us to perceive the same object ; and that one sense is more fitted than another to make us acquainted with different objects and their qualities. For example, we may obtain a conception of the figure of a book by means of the sense of touch, and also by means of the sense of sight.

Each sense, as already observed, is subject to its own positive laws. For example, we see according to the laws of the refraction of light ; and hence, a straight rod half plunged in water appears crooked, although touch proves that, in this situation, the rod continues straight.

This is a kind of rectification; but it must not be confounded with the doctrine which maintains that one sense acquires its functions by means of the rectification of another sense. Touch may show that a red which is plunged in water, and looks crooked, is straight; but the eyes will see it crooked as before. The rectifications thus effected by the senses are mutual, and not the prerogative of one sense. In this view the eyes may rectify the sense of touch. If, without our knowledge, a piece of thin paper be placed between one of our fingers and the thumb, we may not *feel* but we may *see* it. Even smell and taste may rectify the senses of seeing and of touch. Thus, many fluids *look* like water, and it would be impossible to discover them to be different substances by the sense of touch; but it is easy to do so by smell and taste. Thus each sense has its peculiar and independent functions, and each is subject to positive laws. But every sense also perceives impressions of which another is not susceptible; and it is in consequence of this circumstance that the external senses rectify one another; or rather produce, by their co-operation, an extent of accurate conception, which, in an unconnected state, they would have been incapable of producing.

It is a task of considerable difficulty to point out accurately the precise limits of the functions of the senses; because, in every act of perception their instrumentality is combined with that of the internal faculties of the mind; and it is not easy to discriminate to what extent the act depends upon the one, and to what extent upon the other. For the elucidation of this point, I submit the following considerations to the reader:

The external organs of the senses do not *form ideas*. For example, when an impression is made upon the hand, it is not the nerves of touch which form the conception of the objects making the impression; they merely receive that impression, and communicate it to the brain, and *an internal faculty of the mind* perceives, or forms an idea of the object by which the impression is caused. Without the nerves of feeling, the internal faculty could not experience the perception; because the medium of communication between it and the object would be wanting.

Hence, previously to every perception, there must be an impression on the external organs of sense; and the function of these organs appears to consist in receiving and transmitting this impression to the brain and internal faculties. The nature of the impression depends on the constitution of the organs of sense, and on the relations established between them and external objects; and, as it is absolutely impossible for the human will to change either the constitution of the senses or the relations between them and the external world, it is clearly absurd to speak of acquired impressions.

But, as the senses are constituted with a determinate relation to external objects, so the brain and internal faculties are constituted with a determinate relation to the organs of sense. In virtue of the first relation, a certain object makes a certain impression; and in virtue of the second, a certain impression gives rise to a certain perception: and both depend on nature, and not on the will, nor on exercise or habit.

But we must distinguish between the perceptions we experience of external objects, and the inferences concerning their qualities which we draw by reasoning from these perceptions. All those ideas which are pure perceptions are formed intuitively, on the presentation of objects fitted to excite them. Inferences from these, on the other hand, are the result of our reasoning powers. What are sometimes called "acquired perceptions" are merely *habits of reasoning* from the impressions naturally made on the senses; and these habits are just as much a part of our *nature* as the original perceptions. It appears to me, that the visible and tangible appearances of bodies are simple perceptions, because, after the amplest experience of some of these being deceitful, we cannot, in the slightest degree, alter our perceptions of them. For example, a rod half immersed in water appears crooked, in defiance of every endeavour to see it straight. When we stand three or four yards distant from a mirror, and perceive our image in it, we cannot, by any efforts, succeed in perceiving the image as if formed on the surface of the mirror, although we know perfectly that it is so. It appears always at the same distance behind the surface as we are before it. If a picture be painted according to the rules of perspective, so as to represent a vista in the country, or a long street in a city, we are altogether incapable, when in the proper position for viewing it, of perceiving the surface to be plain. The picture appears to us to represent objects at different distances, and the most determined resolution to see them all equally near is of no avail, although we know that, in point of fact, they are so.[*]

If, previously to experience, all objects seen by the eye appear only as of different colours and shades, and all equally near, although really at different distances ; and if we learn by experience only, that this natural appearance is deceitful, and that, in point of fact, one object is near and another distant ; I cannot perceive a reason why we might not learn, by experience, also to perceive pictures as plain surfaces, and images as if formed on the surfaces of mirrors—in short, to get quit altogether of the illusions of optics. If it be easy to acquire, by habit, the power of perceiving objects as at different distances, which naturally appear to the eye as all equally near, it ought to be no difficult matter to learn by experience to perceive a surface to be plain which really is so, after we are certain of the fact ; and yet I have never been able to do so. Colour, form, magnitude, and distance appear to be objects of intuitive perception, when the organs which take cognizance of them are adequately possessed ; and, accordingly, no experience, and no repetition of acts of volition, can alter such appearances, if the refraction of light, the state of the eye, and the internal faculties continue the same.

The following appears to me to be a correct mode of ascertaining the limits of the functions of the senses : Whatever perceptions or impressions received from external objects can be fully renewed by an act of recollection, cannot depend exclusively upon the senses ; because the organs of sense are not subject to the will, and in the healthy state never produce the impressions which depend upon their constitution, unless excited by an external cause. On the other hand, whatever impressions we are unable to recall must, for the same reason, depend on the senses alone.

These principles will be best elucidated by examples. In hearing, I call that part of the impression which is occasioned by the vibrations of the air, and of the tympanum, simply noise ; and that part which is dependent on the activity of the brain, a note. When a noise has been made by striking a table with a hammer in our presence, and the sound has ceased, the noise cannot be reproduced by an effort of the will ; because its existence depended on the apparatus of the ear being in a certain state of excitation, which cannot be reproduced by an act of volition. But if an individual is endowed with the internal faculty of Tune, and if a piece of music be played over in his presence, then, after the noise of the instrument has ceased, although he cannot recall that noise, he can with facility reproduce the internal impressions which the notes made upon his mind ; in short, he can enjoy the tune internally anew, by an act of recollection.

* I am informed that there are individuals, enjoying perfect vision, who see their own image always on the surface of a mirror, at whatever distance they stand from it ; who naturally see paintings (a diorama of a valley, for instance) as plain surfaces, and who find it necessary to make a mental effort to perceive perspective ; but this is not the general case. The organ of size was deficient in the only two individuals thus constituted whom I have seen.

And as most sounds have something musical in them, he may also recall the *note* made by the hammer in striking the table, but not the *noise*. The power of experiencing the perception of melody, and of enjoying the impressions which it makes, appears, therefore, to depend on the internal faculty of Tune, while the noise alone depends upon the ear. Hence the perfection of the power of perceiving melody in any individual is not in proportion to the perfection of the external ear alone, but in proportion to the joint perfection of that organ and the internal faculty of Tune. Without the auditory apparatus the internal faculty could not receive the impressions; but that apparatus could never of itself produce the perception of melody. Accordingly, we see every day that many individuals enjoy the sense of hearing, unimpaired, who have no perception of melody. The same principles, applied to the other senses, will point out distinctly the precise limit of their functions. We may take an example from the sense of touch. If we embrace a square body with the hands, certain impressions are made on the nerves of touch, called sensations, in consequence of which the mind forms an idea of the figure of the body. Now, we can recall the conception of the figure, but not the sensation which excited it. The conception, therefore, depends on an internal faculty; the sensation on the nerves of touch. The perception, however, depends as entirely on nature as the sensation; and the power of perceiving the form of the body is not acquired by experience.

Dr. Spurzheim observes on this head, that, where the *same ideas* are acquired by the instrumentality of *two* or more senses, the ideas cannot possibly be formed by the *senses*; because Nature, so far as man has discovered, never endows *different instruments* with the *same functions,* in the same individual. For example, we can acquire ideas of form by the instrumentality of the sense of Sight, and likewise by means of Touch. Now, from this circumstance alone, it is evident that the conception of figure is formed, not by the eyes, nor by the nerves of Touch, because this would be an instance of two separate senses performing the same function; but by an internal faculty, which perceives figure, in consequence of impressions made on either of these two different senses. The impressions made upon the eye are totally different from those made upon the nerves of Touch, but the internal faculty is adapted by nature to both; and hence the same perceptions are experienced by means of the same faculty, although through the instrumentality of different media. The same function, however, is not performed by distinct senses.

These views of the functions of the senses are illustrated and confirmed by the phenomena which take place when the organs of sense are diseased. For example, when the ear becomes inflamed, it often happens that noises having no external causes are heard; when too much blood flows into the eye, impressions like those of light are perceived; when the nerves of Taste become diseased, there is a consciousness of disagreeable savours; when the nerves of Touch are excited by internal causes, a tickling or disagreeable sensation is felt; when the muscular system is relaxed by nervous diseases, and flying spasms occur over the body, impressions occasionally arise from these spasmodic affections, so precisely resembling those of touch, that the individual is at a loss to distinguish them.

There is reason to conjecture, that particular parts of the brain receive the impressions transmitted by the different external senses, and that it is by their instrumentality that the gourmand, for instance, recalls the flavour of a particular dish, He cannot reproduce the sensation, which depends on the activity of the nerves of taste; but he can recall all that —mental in the perception, or that depends on the activity of any part e brain.

Every one is acquainted with the ridiculous theories which have been framed by philosophers, to account for the phenomena of perception. Aristotle taught, says Dr. Reid, "that, as our senses cannot receive external material objects themselves, they receive their species, that is, their images or forms without the matter, as wax receives the form of the seal, without any of the matter of it."* The Platonists differed from Aristotle in maintaining, "that there exist *eternal and immutable ideas*, which were prior to the objects of sense, and about which all science was employed." They agreed with him, however, as to the manner in which these ideas are perceived. Two thousand years after Plato, Mr. Locke represents our manner of perceiving external objects by comparing the understanding to a "closet, wholly shut from light, with only some little opening left, to let in external visible resemblances or ideas of things without." The notion of all these philosophers was, that, from the existence of these images or ideas, the mind inferred, by a process of reasoning, the existence of the external objects themselves.

Dr. Ried refuted, by a very simple process, these doctrines. He pointed out merely the fact, that the mind is so formed, that certain impressions, produced by external objects on our organs of sense, are followed by certain sensations; that these sensations are followed by perceptions of the existence and qualities of the bodies by which the impressions are made; and that all the steps of this process are equally involuntary and incomprehensible to us.

It will be perceived, that the doctrine above laid down regarding the functions of the senses, corresponds precisely with the philosophy of Dr. Reid.

The organs of each sense are double; and yet the consciousness of all impressions experienced by the mind is single. Various theories have been propounded to account for this fact; but none of them is satisfactory. Dr. Gall ventured to give an explanation different from them all. "He distinguishes two states of activity in the organs of the senses, calling one active, the other passive. The functions are passive, if performed independently of the will; the eye, for instance, necessarily perceives the light which falls upon it, and the ear the vibrations propagated to it. Now, we perceive *passively* with both organs, says he; we see with both eyes, hear with both ears, but the active state is confined to one organ, and commonly to the strongest. We see with both eyes at the same time, but we look with one only; we hear with both ears, we listen only with one; we feel with both hands, we touch with but one, &c.

"There is no doubt that we look with one eye only. In placing a pencil or any other thin body between us and a light, keeping both eyes open, and throwing the axis of vision, the stick, and the light into a right line, did we look with both eyes, the pencil should occupy the diagonal, and its shadow fall on the nose. But this always falls on one eye, on that which the person, who makes the experiment, ordinarily uses in looking with attention. If the pencil be kept in the same position, and the eye not employed in looking be shut, the relative direction of the objects will seem to remain the same; but if he shut the eye with which he looked, it will be altered, and the pencil will appear removed far from its former place. Again, let any one look at a point but a little way distant, both eyes will seem directed toward it; let him then shut his eyes alternately. If he close the one with which he did not look, the other remains motionless; but if he shut that with which he looked, the other turns immediately a little inward, in order to fix the point. Moreover, the eyes of many animals are placed laterally, and cannot both be directed at once to the same object. Finally, the gestures of man and animals prove

* *Essay on the Intellectual Powers*, p. 25.
23*

that they look with one eye and listen with one ear; for they direct one eye or one ear toward the object to be seen or heard."*

"Notwithstanding what has been said, Dr. Gall's explanation seems to me," says Dr. Spurzheim, "little satisfactory. Indeed it is very remarkable, that, passively, we perceive, at the same time, the impressions of both organs of any sense, not only if one, but also if different objects impress the two. Even different impressions of different objects may be perceived by both organs of two-senses at once. We may, for instance, with both eyes see different objects at the moment that with both ears we hear different sounds. As soon as we are attentive, however, as soon as we look or listen, we perceive but one impression. It is impossible, therefore, to attend to two different discourses at once. The leader of an orchestra hears passively all the instruments, but he cannot be attentive except to one. The rapidity of mental action deceives several, and makes them think it possible to attend to different objects at the same moment. It follows, that there is a difference between the active and passive state of the senses; but whether this difference suffices to explain the single consciousness of every sense is another question; I think it does not.

"First, this explanation would apply only to functions in their active, not at all in their passive, state; and the cause of single consciousness must be the same in both. Farther, the active state is not produced by the external senses themselves, any more than voluntary motion by the mere muscles. Some internal power renders the senses active; they themselves are always passive, and merely propagate external impressions; they appear active only when something internal employs them to receive and to transmit impressions to the brain. It is, therefore, probable that the internal cause, which excites only a single organ of the external causes to activity, is also the cause of the single consciousness of different impressions. Dr. Gall's explanation of single consciousness is, consequently, not only grounded upon an inaccurate notion, but would be far from satisfactory, were the supposition even true."†

The mind has no consciousness either of the existence of the organs of sense, or of the functions performed by them. When the table is struck, and we attend to the subject of our own consciousness, we perceive the impression of a sound; but by this attention we do not discover that the impression has been experienced by the instrumentality of any organ whatever. Hence the perceptions of the mind are always directed to the objects which make the impression, and not to the instruments by means of which the impressions are experienced. The instruments perform their functions under Nature's care, and, as already observed, are not subject to the will. We should have been distracted, not benefited, by a consciousness of their action. When they become diseased we obtain this consciousness, and it is painful. Every one must be sensible of this fact, whose eyes or ears have been inflamed.

Dr. Spurzheim observes, that "the brain seems to be necessary to every kind of perception, even to that of the immediate functions of the external senses; but it is not yet ascertained, though it is probable, that one fundamental power, inherent in a particular part of the brain, knows and conceives, as sensations, all the varied impressions made on the external senses. Some phrenologists think that each external sense has a peculiar portion of brain for this end, and that the combined action of its nerve and of this cerebral part is necessary to the accomplishment of its functions—that the nerve of taste and a portion of brain, for instance, are necessary to perceive savours; the olfactory nerve and a cerebral part, distinguish colours, &c. I do not believe that consciousness happens without brain, but I see no reason to surmise that the immediate functions of each external sense require a particular portion of the brain, in order to be recognised as determinate sensations."* Dr. Caldwell, on the other hand, I think with justice, regards the opinion here expressed by Dr. Spurzheim as at variance with sound physiology,† and the facts which I shall adduce on p. 276 will show that, in the case of the sense of sight, there is an internal organ in the brain which is connected with vision.

After these general considerations, which apply to all the external senses, a few words may be added on the specific functions of each sense in particular.

FEELING OR TOUCH.

Dr. Spurzheim inferred, from pathological facts, that the nerves of motion must be distinct from the nerves of feeling ;‡ and subsequent experiments have proved his inferonce to be well founded. This subject has been treated of on page 65. The sense of feeling is continued, not only over the whole external surface of the body, but even over the intestinal canal. It gives rise to the sensations of pain and pleasure ; of the variations of temperature ; and of dryness and moisture. These cannot be recalled by the will ; and I therefore consider them as depending on the sense alone.

This sense is usually supposed to convey to us impressions, not merely of heat and cold, pain and pleasure, but also of the resistance met with by the body when in contact with external objects. This, however, seems to be a mistake ; and, in reality, there is a sense altogether distinct from that of feeling properly so called, and of which the nerves are those already mentioned on page 68, as conveying to the brain a knowledge of the state of the muscles—in other words, of the degree of contraction or force which they are exerting at the time. The existence of such a sense is distinctly maintained by Dr. Thomas Brown. "The feeling of resistance," says he, "is, I conceive, to be ascribed, not to the organ of touch, but to our muscular frame, to which I have already more than once directed your attention, as forming a distinct organ of sense ; the affections of which, particularly as existing in combination with other feelings, and modifying our judgments concerning these, (as in the case of distant vision, for example,) are not less important than those of our other sensitive organs."§ This passage, it is worthy of remark, was written about fifteen years before the nerve of the sense was discovered by Sir Charles Bell. Mr. Simpson, in a very ingenious and elaborate essay on this subject, published in The Phrenological Journal,‖ has adduced many facts and arguments confirmatory of Dr. Brown's opinion. One case communicated to the Journal¶, by a medical gentleman of Edinburgh, seems quite decisive. "I was consulted," says he, "by the son of a gentleman in the country who has had a singular paralytic affection. He lost the power of motion in his arms, but retained sensation acutely, and felt another person's hand cold or warm, as the case might be. (This indicated the *nerves of feeling*, distributed to the skin, to be uninjured, while the *motor*

* Spurzheim's *Phrenology*, p. 257.
† Caldwell's *Elements of Phrenology*, 2d edit., p. 21.
‡ See Spurzheim's *Physiognomical System*, 1815, p. 23, and *Phrénolbgie*, 1818, p. 236. Also his *Anatomy of the Brain*, sect. iii., p. 37, et seq.
§ *Lectures*, vol. i., p. 496.
‖ Vol. ix., p 193; see also his other papers there referred to, particularly that on the sense of equilibrium, vol. iv., p. 266. Sir George Mackenzie has commented on Mr. Simpson's essay mentioned in the text, in vol. ix., p. 349.
¶ Vol. iv., p. 315.

nerves, which convey the mandates of the will to the muscles and cause them to contract, were impaired.) Now, at the distance of three weeks, he has regained the power of motion, but has lost the sense of the state of the muscles so completely that he cannot adapt his muscular contractions to the purpose he has in view. (The motor nerve had recovered its health, but the *nerve of the sense of resistance* continued powerless.) In seizing a small object, he bears down upon it with his extended hand, gathers it in, and grasps it like a vice, not aware of the disproportion of his effort. He has at the same time the complete command of his muscles as to contraction and relaxation, but wants only the sense of their state."

Hunger and thirst seem to constitute a peculiar sense, of which the stomach and throat, and nerves connecting them with the brain, are the external organs, and the organ of Alimentiveness the cerebral part in which the sensations are experienced.*

Thus the number of the senses appears to be seven, instead of five.

TASTE.

THE function of this sense is to produce sensations of taste alone ; and these cannot be recalled by the will. We may judge of the qualities of external bodies by means of the impressions made on this sense ; but to form ideas of such qualities is the province of the internal faculties.

SMELL.

By means of smell the external world acts upon man and animals from a distance. Odorous particles are conveyed from bodies, and inform sentient beings of the existence of the substances from which they emanate. The functions of smell are confined to the producing of agreeable or disagreeable sensations, when the organ is so affected. These cannot be reproduced by an effort of the will. Various ideas are formed of the qualities of external bodies, by the impressions which they make upon this sense ; but these ideas are formed by the internal faculties of the mind.

HEARING.

In new-born children this sense is not yet active ; but it improves by degrees, and in proportion as the vigour of the organ increases. It is a very common opinion, that music and the faculty of speech are the result of the sense of hearing ; but this notion is erroneous

As already mentioned, the auditory apparatus, being excited to activity by an external cause, produces only the impression of noise ; and here its functions terminate. If, besides, the faculty of Tune be possessed by any individual, melody in sounds is perceived by that faculty. If the faculty be not possessed, such perceptions cannot exist. Hence, among birds, although the female hears as well as the male, yet the song of the male is very much superior to that of the female, and in him the organ of Tune is larger. Among mankind, also, many individuals hear, and yet are insensible to melody. Thus, both in man and other animals, there is no proportion between the perfection of hearing and the perfection of the power of perceiving melody. If it were part of the function of the auditory apparatus to give the perception of melody, how could it happen that, in one individual, the apparatus can perform only one-half of its function, while in others it performs the whole ? This is not like Nature's work.

* See p. 155 of this work ; and a paper on Alimentiveness, by Mr. Robert Cox, in *The Phrenological Journal*, vol. x.

Farther, hearing cannot produce music ; because the auditory apparatus is excited only by sounds which are already produced ; while the first musician must have begun to produce music before he had heard it, and therefore he must have done so from an internal impulse of the mind. Singing-birds also, which have been hatched by strange females, sing naturally, and without any instruction, the song of their species as soon as their internal organization is active. ·Hence the males of every species preserve their natural song, though they have been brought up in the society of individuals of a different kind. Hence also, musicians who have lost their hearing continue to compose. They possess the internal faculty; and it, being independent of the auditory apparatus, conceives the impressions which different sounds naturally produce, long after the ear has ceased to be capable of allowing these sounds to be heard anew. Hence, likewise, deaf and dumb persons have an innate feeling of measure and cadence. Though, however, hearing does not produce music, yet, without an auditory apparatus fitted to receive the impressions made by tones, melody could not be perceived : and, unless that apparatus had been once possessed, neither could melody be produced, because the individual could not judge of the impressions which the sounds he made were fitted to make upon those who hear.

Another common opinion is, that hearing alone, or hearing and voice jointly, produce the faculty of speech. This error will be refuted, by considering in what any language consists, and how every language is produced. Language has been divided into two kinds, natural and artificial. In both kinds a certain sign is used to indicate to others certain feelings or ideas of the mind. Various motions of the body and expressions of the countenance, the moment they are beheld, indicate certain emotions and sentiments. In this case the expression of the countenance or the motion of the body is a sign fitted by nature to excite in us the perception of the feeling. The meaning of the sign is understood by all men, without instruction or experience. It is obvious that its power, in this case, to excite the perception, does not depend either upon hearing or voice ; for neither is employed in producing it : but that the effect is an ultimate fact of our constitution, which must be referred to the will of the Creator. Besides these signs, however, we make use of many others to communicate our thoughts, which have no original connexion with the things signified. For example, the word *table* has no necessary connexion with the thing upon which I now write. How, then, does the word happen to indicate the thing? The internal faculties first conceive the object : having done so, they wish to fix upon a sign by which that conception may be recalled or communicated. They therefore *employ the organs of voice* to make the sound which we express when we utter the word *table*. The thing itself being pointed out, and the sound being uttered at the same time, the meaning of the sound becomes understood ; and hence every time it is pronounced, the idea of the thing is suggested. But we are not to suppose that the auditory apparatus, or the organs of voice, conceive the idea of the table. This is done by the internal faculties alone ; and these merely make use of the organs of voice as instruments for producing a sign. Hence, the reason why monkeys do not speak is, not that they want the sense of hearing and organs of voice, but that they have not the internal faculty which fixes upon artificial signs to indicate the conceptions formed by the mind.

The proper function, then, of the sense of hearing is confined to the production of the impressions which we call sounds ; yet it assists a great number of internal faculties.

The auditory nerve has a more intimate connexion with the organs of the moral sentiments, than with those of the intellectual faculties.

SIGHT.

THIS last of the senses is the third of those which inform man and other animals of the existence of remote objects by means of an intermedium ; and the intermedium, in this instance, is light.

This sense has been said to acquire its functions by touch or by habit. Bishop Berkeley is supposed by the metaphysicians to have discovered the true theory of vision, and the result of his investigation is, " that a man born blind, being made to see, would not at first have any idea of distance by sight. The sun and stars, the remotest objects as well as the nearest, would all seem to be in his eye, or rather in his mind "[*] Dr. Reid and many other philosophers have written ingenious disquisitions, to show that our perceptions of distance, figure, and motion are acquired. " Philosophy," says Mr. James Mill, " has ascertained that we derive nothing from the eye whatever but sensations of colour ; that the idea of extension, in which size, and form, and distance are included, is derived from sensations, not in the eye, but in the muscular part of our frame. How, then, is it that we receive accurate information by the eye of size, and shape, and distance ? By association merely."[†] These speculations proceed on the principle, that Nature has done little for man, and that he does a great deal for himself, in endowing himself with perceptive powers. But vision depends on the organization of the eye ; and is energetic or weak, as the organization is perfect or imperfect. Some animals come into the world with perfect eyes ; and these see perfectly from the first. The butterfly and honeybee fly at the first attempt, through fields and flowery meadows ; and the young partridge and chicken run through stubble and corn-fields. The sparrow, on taking its first flight from the nest, does not strike its head against a wall, nor mistake the root of a tree for its branches ; and yet, previously to its first attempt at flight, it can have no *experience* of distance.

- On the other hand, animals which come into the world with eyes in an imperfect state, distinguish size, shape, and distance only by degrees. This last is the case with new-born children. During the first six weeks after birth their eyes are almost insensible to light; and it is only by degrees that they become fit to perform their natural functions. When the organs are sufficiently matured, however, children see, without habit or education, as well and as accurately as the greatest philosopher.

Indeed, as has been formerly mentioned, the kind of perception which we enjoy by means of the eyes is dependent solely on the constitution of the eyes, and the relation established between them and the refraction of light. So little power has experience to alter the nature of our perceptions, that even in some cases where we discover, by other senses, that the visible appearance of objects is illusive, we still continue to see that appearance the same as before. The greatest philosopher, standing at one end of a long alley of trees, cannot see the opposite rows equally distant from one another at the farther end, as they appear to be at the end nearest to him, even after experience has satisfied him that the fact really is so   He must see according to the laws of perspective; which make the receding rows appear to approach ; and there is no difference in this respect between his perceptions and those of the most untutored infant. In like manner, a philosopher, on looking into a concave spoon, cannot see his right hand upon the right side, and his left upon the left, even after he has learned, by the study of the laws of optics, that the image of himself, which he sees in the spoon, is reversed.

[*] Stewart's *Dissertation*, ii., p. 109.
[†] *Analysis of the Phenomena of the Human Mind*, vol. i., ch. iii., p. 73.

So confident, however, is Mr. Stewart in the opinion that we learn to see, and do not see by nature, that, after remarking that "Condillac first thought that the eye judges *naturally* of figures, of magnitudes, of situations, and of distances : he afterward was convinced that this was an error, and retracted it,"—he adds, "Nothing short of his own explicit avowal could have convinced me that a writer of such high pretensions, and of such unquestionable ingenuity as Condillac, had really commenced his metaphysical career under so gross and unaccountable a delusion." Mr. Stewart also expresses his surprise, that Aristotle should maintain "that it is not from seeing often nor from hearing often that we get these senses; but, on the contrary, instead of getting them by using them, we use them because we have got them."

It is worth while to inquire into the grounds on which the metaphysicians maintain such extraordinary opinions. They are two : *first*, The fact that new-born children miss the object they mean to seize, and show clearly that they do not accurately appreciate size, distance, and relative position ; and, *secondly*, The fact that a blind-man couched by Chesselden, on the first influx of light to the retina, saw all external objects as situated in his eye, and after a few weeks perceived distance and magnitude like ordinary persons. From these facts the metaphysicians infer that the human being does not naturally perceive distance, size, and form, but learns to do so by experience. The answers are obvious The eye in the child is not perfect till six weeks after birth. The eye newly-couched is not a sound eye instantly, nor do the muscles and various parts which had lain dormant for thirty years, act with perfect effect at the first attempt, after the irritation and torment of a painful operation ; and, even admitting that the eye was perfectly sound, the internal organs which perceive distance are not so. By disuse, every organ of the body becomes unfitted for the due performance of its functions. In civilized nations the muscles of the external ear, being prevented, by the head-dress, from acting during childhood, not only lose all contractile power, but almost dwindle into nothing. In the savage state the power of moving the ear is often as perfect in man as in the lower animals. After long confinement of a limb for the cure of fracture, the muscles diminish in size, and unfitness for action is observed. In the same way, during blindness, the organs which judge of colour and distance are never called into action, and therefore become, to a certain extent, unable to execute their functions, and it is only by degrees that they acquire sufficient energy to do so. In visiting several asylums for the blind, I observed that the organ of Colouring was imperfectly developed in those patients who had lost their sight in infancy. If in middle life their vision had been restored by an operation, the organ of Colouring would not have become at once as perfect in size and activity as if no previous impediment to the exercise of its function had existed.

Dr. Thomas Brown, whose acuteness I have repeatedly had occasion to praise, admits that the lower animals perceive distance intuitively ; and, although, on the whole, he agrees in the opinions of Berkeley, Reid, and Stewart, yet he considers the opposite opinion, which the phrenologists maintain, as far from ridiculous. "It is," says he, "not more wonderful, *à priori*, that a sensation of colour should be *immediately followed* by the notion of a mile of distance, than that the irritation of the nostril, by any very stimulant odour, should be immediately and involuntarily followed by the sudden contraction of a distant muscular organ, like the diaphragm, which produces, in sneezing, the violent expiration necessary for expelling the acrid· matter."*

It is very true that Nature does not give us intuitive perceptions of the number of feet or inches which any object is distant from us ; because

* *Lectures*, vol. ii., p. 69.

those are artificial measures, with which nature has nothing to do. · But when two objects, equal in size, are presented to the eye, the one being · twice as far distant as the other, the mind has an intuitive perception that they are not equally near, unless the external or internal organs, or both, be deficient or deranged.

What, then, are the true functions of the eye? No external organ of sense *forms ideas:* The eye, therefore, only receives, modifies, and transmits the impressions of light; and here its functions cease. Internal faculties form conceptions of the figure, colour, distance, and other attributes and relations of the objects making the impression : and the power of forming these conceptions is in proportion to the perfection of the eyes and the internal faculties jointly, and not in proportion to the perfection of the eyes alone. *

The anterior pair of the *corpora quadrigemina* seem to have an intimate connexion with the sense of sight, and indeed to form part of its organic apparatus. Sœmmering states that he found them atrophied in blind horses, and Dr. Gall made similar observations. Dr. Vimont found in fourteen old horses which were one-eyed, a diminution of the anterior corpus quadrigeminum opposite to the lost eye; in two of them the atrophy was complete. To obtain farther light on this subject, he put out the left eyes of four rabbits, and the right eyes of other four; and deprived another of both eyes. Ten months afterward they were all put to death. In the four deprived of the left eye he found the anterior corpus quadrigeminum on the right side much smaller than that on the left, while the opposite appearance presented itself in those which had lost the right eye. In the blind rabbit both of the anterior corpora were much smaller than the sound one in any of the other rabbits. Compared with the corresponding parts in a rabbit of the same litter, whose eyes were sound, they presented a very perceptible difference of volume. Dr. Vimont adds : " M. Magendie has told me, that he had observed a diminution of a bigemina body in birds, a short time after having put out one of their eyes. I have repeated the experiment; it is exact; the diminution even takes place a great deal sooner than in quadrupeds."† He mentions farther, that, according to the observations of Wenzel,‡ there is atrophy of the optic thalami in blindness, and when that state is of long continuance the thalami become narrower and flatter. These facts account satisfactorily for Chesselden's patient not being able to see perfectly, immediately after being couched.

The senses may be exercised, and their powers greatly improved by exercise. The taste of the gourmand is more acute than that of the peasant, and the touch of the artisan than that of the ploughman.

GENUS II.—INTELLECTUAL FACULTIES WHICH PROCURE KNOWLEDGE OF EXTERNAL OBJECTS, THEIR PHYSICAL QUALITIES, AND VARIOUS RELATIONS.

THE faculties now to be treated of take cognizance of the existence and qualities of external objects They correspond, in some degree, to the Perceptive Powers of the metaphysicians ; and form ideas. Their action is attended with a sensation of pleasure, but (except in the case of Tune) it is weak compared with the emotions produced by the faculties

* See two papers by Dr. A. Combe, " On the Functions of the Sense of Sight, considered chiefly in its relations to ideas of Form, Colour, Magnitude, and Distance ;" *Phren. Journ*, vol. iv., p. 608, and vol. v., p. 286.
† *Treatise on Human and Comparative Phrenology*, i., p. 310 ; French edit., p. 298.
‡ *De Penit. Struct. Cerebri*, p. 125.

already treated of. In judging of the size of these organs, the rules laid down on page 85 require to be particularly attended to. The organs of the intellectual faculties are small, but active. If they had been as large as those of the propensities, we should have been liable to intellectual passions. The comparative calmness of our reasoning processes is probably the result of the small size of these organs.

22. INDIVIDUALITY.

This organ is situated in the middle of the lower part of the forehead, immediately above the top of the nose. When large, it produces breadth, projection, and descent between the eye-brows, at that part; when small, the eye-brows approach closely to each other, and lie in a horizontal line. It is very large in the portrait of Michael Angelo.

MICHAEL ANGELO.

In surveying the external world, we may consider, first, objects simply as substances or existences, such as a rock, a horse, a tree, a man; these perceptions are designated by substantives;—in the next place, the properties and relations of things which exist, such as their form, size, weight, and colour. After these perceptions, we may notice their active phenomena; the rock falls, the horse runs, the tree grows, the man walks— these actions are designated by active verbs. As size, form, weight, and colour are adjuncts of physical existence, time is an adjunct of action. Now, the faculty of Individuality renders us observant of objects which exist; it gives the notion of substance, and forms the class of ideas represented by substantive nouns when used without an adjective, as *rock*, *man*, *horse*.

The faculty gives the desire, accompanied with the ability, to know objects as mere existences, without regard to their modes of action or the purposes to which they may be subservient. Individuals in whom it is large will observe and examine an object with intense delight, without the least consideration to what it may be applied—a quality of mind which is almost incomprehensible to persons in whom this organ is small and Causality large. It prompts to observation, and is a great element in a genius for those sciences which consist in a knowledge of specific existences, such as natural history. It leads to giving a specific form to all the ideas entertained by the mind. A student in whom this organ is small and the reflecting organs large, may have his mind stored with general principles of science and with abstract ideas, but will experience much difficulty in reducing them into precise and specific forms. Another, in whom this organ is large, will have all his knowledge individualized : if he hear lectures or conversation in which general views chiefly are presented, he will render them specific for himself; but unless his reflecting organs also be large, he will be prone to miss the essential principle, to seize upon the most palpable circumstance attending it, and to embrace this as his conception of it. Such persons are learned; and, owing to the store of facts with which their memories are replenished, the great definiteness and precision of their ideas, and the readiness with which they command them, they often take a lead in public business : but if their reflecting organs be deficient, they show no depth or comprehensiveness of understanding ; they do not advance the principles of science, and rarely acquire a permanent reputation.

In common life a great development of this organ confers a talent for observation, curiosity to know, and aptitude for acquiring knowledge of details. The character of *Miss Pratt*, as drawn by the author of *The Inheritance*, a novel, is a personification of Individuality when predominantly powerful, and not directed by higher faculties.[*] "But people who make use of their eyes," says this author, " have often much to see, even between two doors ; and, in her progress from the hall-door to the drawing-room, *Miss Pratt* met with much to attract her attention. True, all the objects were perfectly familiar to her ; but a real *looker*, like a great genius, is never at a loss for a subject—things are either better or worse since they saw them last—or if the things themselves should happen to be the same, they-have seen other things, either better or worse, and can, therefore, either approve or disapprove of them. . *Miss Pratt's* head then turned from side to side a thousand times as she went along, and a thousand observations and criticisms about stair-carpets, patent-lamps, hall-chairs, slab-tables, &c., &c., &c., passed through her crowded brain."—" At length *Miss Pratt* and *Mr. Lindsay* were announced, and thereupon entered *Miss Pratt* in a quick paddling manner, as if in all haste to greet her friends."—" *Miss Pratt* then appeared to her (*Gertrude*) a person from whom nothing could be hid. Her eyes were not by any means fine eyes—they were not reflecting eyes—they were not soft eyes—they were not sparkling eyes—they were not penetrating eyes ; neither were they restless eyes, nor rolling eyes, nor squinting eyes, nor prominent eyes—but they were active, brisk, busy, vigilant, immoveable eyes, that looked as if they could not be surprised by anything—not even by sleep. They never looked angry, nor joyous, or perturbed, or melancholy, or heavy.; but morning, noon, and night they shone the same, and conveyed the same impression to the beholder, viz., that they were eyes that had a look—not like the look of Sterne's monk, beyond this world—;

* See *The Phrenological Journal*, ii., 65.

but a look into all things on the face of this world. Her other features had nothing remarkable in them ; but the ears might evidently be classed under the same head with the eyes—they were something resembling rabbits'—long, prominent, restless, vibrating ears, for ever listening. and never shut by the powers of thought."

From communicating this talent of observation, Individuality greatly assists Imitation in promoting mimicry. The organ was large in Garrick and Matthews ; and it is obvious that accurate observation of the manners and appearances of men was a fundamental element in a talent such as theirs, of pourtraying on the stage living individuals in their minutest peculiarities.

When the organ is deficient, the individual fails to observe things that exist around him ; he may visit a house, and come away without knowing what objects were in the room. A person thus deficient walks in the streets, or through the country, and observes nothing. In short, although the external senses are in perfect health—owing to the feebleness of this observing power, they are not called into activity for the purpose of acquiring knowledge.

This organ, when large, prompts to discovery by observation of things which exist. Persons so constituted do not seek to arrive at new truths by reasoning, but inquire of nature, of men, of books for information ; and hence, many brilliant physical discoveries have been made by persons largely endowed with these and the other perceptive organs, whose reflecting faculties have not passed mediocrity. Since BACON's rules of philosophizing have been duly appreciated and become fashionable, science has been extensively and successfully cultivated by a class of minds, which, while the method of speculative reasoning prevailed, was excluded from such pursuits. This class is composed of persons in whom the organ under consideration greatly predominates over those of the reflecting powers. Such individuals are constituted by nature to become observers ; and natural history, particularly botany,* anatomy, mineralogy, and even chemistry, are great departments of knowledge fitted for the exercise of their peculiar talent. The substance of these sciences consists in a knowledge of the existence, appearances, and properties of natural objects as *facts ;* and we need not be surprised to meet with eminent professors of them, in whose heads the reflecting organs are greatly inferior to the knowing.

To the artist this organ is of great importance. It enables him to give body and substance to the conceptions of his other faculties, and confers on him a capacity for attending to detail. In the pictures of an artist in whose head Individuality is deficient, there is an abstractness of conception and a vagueness of expression that greatly detract from their effect. In the works of an individual in whom these organs are large, every object appears full of substance and reality ; and if he paint portraits, the spectator will be so impressed with their individuality, that he will be apt to fancy himself acquainted with the originals.

Persons who excel at whist generally possess Individuality and Eventuality large. If both of the organs be deficient, eminence will not easily be attained in this game.

This faculty gives the tendency to personify nations and phenomena, or to ascribe existence to mere abstractions of the mind, such as Ignorance, Folly, or Wisdom.

The organ was large in Sheridan and Sir Walter Scott. It is small in the Scots in general ; it is larger in the English, and still larger in the French.

In adults the frontal sinus is generally present at the situation of this

* See Letter by Mr. Hewett Watson, on the heads of botanists, *Phrenological Journal,* vol. viii., p. 101.

organ, and this throws a difficulty in the way of judging of its size. The function, however, is ascertained by observing young persons in whom the sinus is not formed, and by the negative evidence; that is, when the external part of the skull at the top of the nose-is narrow, contracted, and depressed, the portion of brain below is necessarily small, and then the mental power is found invariably weak. This concomitance of large size and great power in young persons, and of deficiency of size and feebleness of power in all ages, proves the function. In certain cases the sinus may throw a difficulty in the way of determining the exact size of the organ, but this does not prevent the possibility of ascertaining the function by observations made in other cases in which this obstacle does not exist.

The organ and the mental qualities conferred by it are established; but the metaphysical analysis of the faculty seems to require farther elucidation.*

23. FORM.

Dr. GALL was struck with the circumstance, that certain persons and animals recognise, with the greatest facility, individuals whom they have not seen for years, and even then seen only in passing. In himself this faculty was weak, and frequently, on rising from table, he had no recollection of the person who had set next to him, so as to be able to recognise him again in society; and he was, in consequence, exposed to many painful embarrassments and awkward mistakes. Being desired to examine the head of a young girl who had an extreme facility of distinguishing and recollecting persons, he found her eyes pushed laterally outward, and a certain squinting look: after innumerable additional observations, he spoke of an organ of the knowledge of persons.

The organs lie on the two sides of, and contiguous to, the *crista galli*. When small, the orbitar plate approaches close to the sides of the crest, and then the external width across the nose from eye to eye is small: when large, there is a considerable space between the orbitar plate and the crest, and a great external breadth across the nose; in general there is also a depression of the internal part of the eyes.

In some instances the frontal sinus is found at the situation of this organ, but it very rarely leads to difficulty in observing its size. The organ was large in King George III., and, combined with his large organ of Individuality, gave him that extraordinary talent for recollecting persons for which he was celebrated. It is very moderately developed in Curran.

Dr. Gall observes, that those individuals who never bestow more than a superficial attention on phenomena, and who have always reasonings, or at least sophisms, ready in explanation of every fact, pretend that a deficiency, such as he experienced in recognising persons, is owing to the eyes; that, in such cases, the vision is indistinct, or there is a squint. His personal experience, he adds, affords a refutation of this hypothesis; for he never had a squint, and his vision was particularly acute and clear.†

* Mr. Scott has published an elaborate essay on In ividuality in *The Phrenological Journal*, vol. v., p. 226. See also remarks on it by Mr. Schwartz, of Stockholm, vol. vi., p. 328; and by Mr. Hewett Watson, vol. vii., p. 213.

† Dr. Gall mentions, that, although he could neither paint nor design, he was able to seize, with great facility, the numerous forms of the head; which statement is at variance with great deficiency in the organ of Form: but, from the general tenor of his observations, it appears that his power of distinguishing forms was not so great as he imagined it to be. Dr. Spurzheim gives the following note in his reprint of the article " Phrenology " in the 3d number of *The Foreign Quarterly Review*:

"The phrenological faculties of Dr. Gall's infantile genius were, Individuality, Eventuality, and Causality, in an eminent degree.

Often children from three to five years of age have a great memory of persons. Some dogs, at the distance of years, recognise an individual whom they have only once seen; while others, after a few days' absence, do not know again persons whom they have seen frequently. Monkeys, dogs, horses, elephants, and even birds, distinguish, with greater or less facility, their master, and those who have been kind or cruel to them among a thousand. All the animals which belong to a herd, and also all the bees in a hive, from 20,000 to 80,000 in number, know each other. When a stranger attempts to introduce himself, they drive him away, or kill him.[*]

Dr. Spurzheim has analyzed the mental power connected with the organ in question, and considers it in the following manner: "To me," says he, "there seems to exist an essential and fundamental power, which takes cognizance of configuration generally, and one of whose peculiar applications or offices is recollection of persons; for persons are only known by their forms. I separate the faculty which appreciates configuration from that of Individuality, since we may admit the existence of a being without taking its figure into consideration. Individuality may be excited by every one of the external senses, by smell and hearing, as well as by feeling and sight;'while the latter two senses alone assist the faculty of configuration. It is this power which disposes us to give a figure to every being and conception of our minds; that of an old man to God; to Death, that of a skeleton, and so on. The organ of Configuration is situated in the internal angle of the orbit; if large, it pushes the eyeball toward the external angle a little outward and downward. It varies in size in whole nations. Many of the Chinese I have seen in London had it much developed. It is commonly large in the French, and bestows their skill in producing certain articles of industry. Combined with Constructiveness, it invents the patterns of dress-makers and milliners. It leads poets to describe portraits and configurations, and induces those who make collections of pictures and engravings to prefer portraits, if they have it in a high degree. It is essential to portrait-painters. Crystallography also depends on it; and to me it appears that conceptions of smoothness and roughness are acquired by its means."[†] I have met with numerous facts in proof of this faculty and organ.

In *The Phrenological Journal*, vol. viii., p. 216, a case is recorded of a literary gentleman who always associated a particular form with certain words. "Words," says he, "are associated in my mind with shapes, and shapes with words; a horse's mouth, for instance, I always associate

"It has been remarked as singular, that Dr. Gall should have been the first founder of this new science while he could not recollect persons after dinner, though they had been near him at table, and since he could not find his way again to places where he had been before; or, in phrenological terms, since he had Form and Locality very small. Those who make that remark, can neither know the proceeding of Dr. Gall nor understand the true meaning of the two phrenological denominations. Dr. Gall compared the size of individual cerebral portions with certain talents or characters eminent in any way; and he was not deficient in the power of perceiving size and its differences. The want of Locality did not prevent him from making discoveries, any more than the want of seeing certain colours hinders any one to cultivate geometry or mathematics in general. Dr. Gall's deficiency in Form explains why he constantly attached himself to isolated elevations and depressions on the surface of the head, rather than to their general configuration, and left this rectification of Phrenology to my exertions; he, nevertheless, has the great merit of having discovered first, certain relations between cerebral development and mental manifestations."

[*] *Sur les Fonctions du Cerveau*, tome v., p, 1, 2, &c..
[†] *Phrenology*, p. 274.

with the word *smeer*. As instances of the association of words with forms,
take the following examples :

    " *Combe* resembles

    " *Cox* resembles

    " *Simpson* resembles

The late Mr. Thomas Allan, of Edinburgh, who had a passion for mineralogy from early youth, had a very large developement of this organ, as also of Comparison. I have seen many children who were expert at cutting figures in paper, possess it, with the organs of Imitation and Constructiveness large. A gentleman called on me in whom Constructiveness, Locality, and other organs which go to form a talent for drawing landscape and botanical figures, are large, but in whom Form is deficient ; and he said, that he could not, except with great difficulty and imperfection, draw or copy portraits.

The celebrated Cuvier owed much of his success as a comparative anatomist to this organ. De Candolle mentions that " his memory was particularly remarkable in what related to forms, considered in the widest sense of that word ; the figure of an animal, seen in reality or in drawing, never left his mind, and served him as a point of comparison for all similar objects." This organ, and also the organs lying along the superciliary ridge, were largely developed in his head.

Mr. Audubon says of the late Mr. Bewick, the most eminent woodengraver whom England has produced—" His eyes were placed farther apart than those of any man I have ever seen."*

Children in whom the organ of Form is very large learn to read with great facility, even in languages of which they are totally ignorant, and although the book be presented to them upside down.†

In the casts of two Chinese skulls in the Phrenological Society's collection, the organ is greatly developed ; and it is said to be large in the Chinese in general. Their use of characters for words may have sprung from the great size of this organ, which would enable them easily to invent and remember a variety of forms. In a collection of portraits of eminent painters, presented by Sir G. S. Mackenzie to the society, the organ appears uncommonly large in those who excelled in portrait painting. The metaphysicians do not admit a faculty of this kind.

Dr. Gall remarks, that some authors present the reader with descriptions of the persons whom they introduce, drawn with great minuteness and effect. Montaigne and Sterne, for example, are distinguished for this practice, and in the portraits of both the organ of Form is conspicuously large.

I subjoin a copy of the portrait of William Dobson, an English painter in the reign of Charles II., in whom the width between the eyes at this organ (28) is very great.

---

* Audubon's *Ornithological Biography*, vol. iii., p. 300.
† See two illustrative cases in *The Phrenological Journal*, vol. viii., p. 65, and vol. ix., p. 344.

WILLIAM DOBSON.

Lord Jeffrey, in the article "Beauty" in the *Supplement to the Ency-clopædia Britannica*, agrees with another author, whom he quotes, Mr. Knight, in maintaining, that "there are no *forms* that have any *intrinsic beauty*, or any power of pleasing or affecting us, *except through their asso-ciations or affinities to mental affections*, either as expressive of fitness and utility, or as types and symbols of certain moral or intellectual qualities, in which the sources of our interest are obvious." From these obser-vations one would suspect Lord Jeffrey and Mr. Knight to be endowed with small organs of Form themselves, and that they have taken their own experience as that of mankind in general. The notion which Lord Jeffrey has erected into a fundamental principle, and on which his whole essay on Beauty is built—that external objects possess no qualities of their own fitted to please the mind, but that all their beauty and interest arise from human feelings which we have associated with them—is con-tradicted by daily experience. The mineralogist, when he speaks of the beauty of his crystals, has a distinct and intelligible feeling to which the name of Beauty is legitimately applied; and yet he connects no human emotions with the pyramids, and rhombs, and octagons, which he contem-plates in the spars. Persons in whom this organ is large declare that they enjoy a perceptible pleasure from the contemplation of mere form, altogether unconnected with ideas of utility and fitness, or of moral or intellectual associations; and that they can speak as intelligibly of elegant and inelegant, beautiful and ugly shapes, regarded merely as shapes, as of sweet and bitter, hard and soft. The organ is regarded as established.

24. SIZE.

THE faculty of distinguishing form differs from that of distinguishing size; because there is an essential difference between the idea of size and that of form. The form may be the same, and the size different. One of these kinds of knowledge may exist without the other; and there is no proportion between them. Besides, as formerly mentioned, the nerves of touch and the organs of sight do not form ideas of any kind; so that the power of conceiving size cannot be in proportion to the endowment of them. Dr. Spurzheim, therefore, inferred, by reasoning, that there must be a faculty, the function of which is to perceive size; and observation has proved the soundness of this conclusion, for the situation assigned by him to the organ has been found correct, and it is regarded as ascertained. In dissecting the brain, the convolutions which constitute Size and Form are found intimately connected. The organ is placed at the internal extremity of the arch of the eyebrow, on the two sides of Individuality.

A member of the Phrenological Society called on Dr. Spurzheim in Paris, and the latter remarked that he had the organ of Size largely developed. This proved to be a correct indication of the talent in his case; for he possessed the power of discriminating size with great nicety. He was able to draw a circle without the aid of any instrument, and to point out the centre of it with mathematical accuracy. Being in the army, he found himself able to make his company fall from column into line with great exactness; estimating correctly by the eye the space to be occupied by the men, which many other officers could never learn to do. Locality, which also he largely possessed, would aid him in this practice.

Sir G. S. Mackenzie is "inclined to think, that magnitude, size, length, breadth, thickness, height, depth, distance, being all, strictly speaking, referrible to extension, the faculty which we are in quest of is probably that of *space* in general."* Dr. Vimont thinks he has discovered a special faculty for perceiving distance, but his arguments do not appear to me conclusive.†

There is reason to believe that the organ of size is connected with the power of perceiving distance, and that it is a chief element in the talent for perspective. Mr. Ferguson, tutor in the family of Sir G. S. Mackenzie, stated, that he had a difficulty in " understanding a landscape " in a picture; and explained, that " it appeared to him to present a group of objects on a plain surface, without any perceptible fore or back ground." He attributed this defect in his perceptions to his not having been taught the rules of perspective at school. In the course of farther interrogation, he stated, that he sees the forms of objects distinctly, as also their colours; that he likes brilliant tints best, and that in nature he perceives distances also. He has visited Roslin, (in the neighbourhood of Edinburgh,) and not only perceived the beauty which characterizes that delicious spot, but enjoyed it with a keen relish. He has also seen many pieces of Highland scenery, and been delighted with them. Rivers, meadows, trees, and cultivated ground are, however, the objects which interest him most. On turning his back upon any natural landscape, or shutting his eyes, his recollections instantly become very confused. He is not able to recall to his mind the " relative positions " of the objects, while he distinctly recollects the *pleasing impressions* which they made upon him; this remembrance does not soon fade. His *recollection* of Roslin, for example, is like that of a confused picture of rocks and trees, and a river winding

* *Illustrations of Phrenology*, p. 159.
† Vimont, *Traité de Phrénologie*, tome ii., p. 294.

through them; but his remembrance of the impressions of grandeur and beauty produced by the objects, is vivid and distinct.

For a long time it was difficult to account for this curious deficiency of mental power. Mr. Ferguson permitted a cast of his face and forehead to be taken, (which is sold in the shops;) and in it the organ of *Size* appeared to be decidedly small, and Form and Locality not very fully developed ; while, by examining his head, it was found that Ideality, Wonder, and Benevolence, with the organs of the other sentiments and also of the intellectual powers, were nowise deficient ; but to which of the three organs of Size, Form, or Locality, the imperfection ought to be ascribed, it was not easy to determine.

Subsequently, however, Mr. Douglas, miniature-painter, a member of the Phrenological Society, stated, in conversation, that one of the earliest indications which he had exhibited of a liking for painting was an extraordinary interest in matters connected with perspective. When a mere child, the appearance of approach in the remote end of ploughed ridges puzzled him exceedingly, and he crawled across the fields, before he could well walk, to measure the actual distance between the ridges, with a stick, and was lost in astonishment when he found that the space between each was actually the same at both ends, notwithstanding the great difference which appeared between them to the eye. He continued from this time to take a great interest in perspective, as a quality in painting, and he subsequently gave up landscape for miniature painting, not from inclination, but from other motives. On comparing his head with Mr. Ferguson's, the organ of Size was found to differ more than any of the others ; it was very large.

On subsequently examining the head of Mr. P. Gibson, who was known greatly to excel in perspective, I again found the organ of Size very large. And, finally, in the head of a gentleman with whom I am intimately acquainted, this organ is developed rather below than above on average ; and he stated to me that, with the power of easily perceiving that one object is more distant than another, he has, nevertheless, felt great difficulty in representing distance correctly on paper ; and, while he understands the general theory of perspective, he could never learn to practise it by tact of hand, and, on this account, gave up all attempts at drawing.

In a former edition I mentioned the case of a lady who, having Form large and Size deficient, copied figures accurately in regard to form, but inaccurately in regard to size. To this statement Lord Jeffrey objected that size is necessary to proportion, and proportion to form ; and that there was inconsistency in the account of the lady's talents. His lordship is in the right : she informs me that it is only the simplest forms which have few parts that she is able to copy correctly, and in drawing even them she will err in size ; but that when a figure has detached parts, although she may give the outline of each part by itself with considerable accuracy, it will be larger or smaller than the original ; whence the whole figure will be deficient in proportion. In drawing from nature, she fails in perspective ; nevertheless, she feels great pleasure in observing forms, recollects them easily, and has a complete consciousness of the powers of Form and Size being different, and of the one being strong and the other weak in her mind.

The frontal sinus throws a difficulty in the way of observing this organ ; and the negative evidence is, therefore, chiefly to be relied on.

25. WEIGHT.

THERE seems to be no analogy between the weight or resistance of bodies, and their other qualities. They may be of all forms, sizes, and colours, and yet none of these features would necessarily imply that one was heavier than the other. This quality, therefore, being distinct from all others, we cannot logically refer the cognizance of it to any of the faculties of the mind which judge of the other attributes of matter; and, as the mental power undoubtedly exists, there appears reason to conjecture that it may be connected with a special organ. Persons who excel at archery and quoits, and also those who find great facility in judging of momentum and resistance in mechanics, are observed to possess the parts of the brain lying nearest to the organ of Size largely developed; and the organ is now regarded as probable. Statica, or that branch of mathematics which considers the motion of bodies arising from gravity, probably belongs to it. Persons in whom Individuality, Size, Weight, and Locality are large, have generally a talent for engineering and those branches of mechanics which consist in the application of forces; they delight in steam-engines, water-wheels, and turning-lathes. The same combination occurs in persons distinguished for successful execution of difficult feats in skating; in which the regulation of equilibrium is an important element. Constructiveness, when Weight is small, leads to rearing still fabrics, rather than to fabricating working machinery.

Mr. Simpson has published, in *The Phrenological Journal*, (vol. ii., p. 412,) an interesting and ingenious essay on this organ, in which he enumerates a great number of examples in proof of its functions. It is large, says he, in Dr. Chalmers, Dr. Brewster, Sir James Hall, Sir George Mackenzie, Professor Leslie, and in Mr. Jardine and Mr. Stevenson, two eminent engineers. " We have lately seen," he continues, " Professor Farish, of Cambridge, who manifests a high endowment of mechanical skill, and has the organ large; as has Mr. Whewell, of the same university, who has written a work of merit on the same subject. In a visit we lately made to Cambridge, we saw much that was interesting in regard to this organ. Professor Farish's son inherits the mechanical turn and the organ. We saw both the statue and bust of Sir Isaac Newton, by Roubilliac. The bust was a likeness taken in the prime of his years, and in it the knowing organs are still more prominent than in the statue. *Weight* is very pre-eminent. The same organ is very large in the bust of the lamented Dr. Clarke, the traveller; and, as might have been expected, *Locality* quite extraordinarily developed.* We met with several persons with small Weight, who at once acknowledged deficiency in mechanical talent and awkwardness in their actions and movements. A child of two years old was mentioned to us, although we did not see it, quite remarkable to every one for the large developement of brain at this part of the frontal bone, and for the uncommon steadiness of its walk, at an age when other children totter, and it is the theme of wonder to all who know it." The organ is large in the mask of Maclachlan, a weaver of saltcoats, who spent much time and money in devising means to regulate the stroke of the common pump, so as to make the working-rod move with the same momentum up and down: it is large also in the mask of

* " In the numerous living heads we saw at Cambridge we met often with the organ of Number large, and found, invariably, that it was accompanied in the individual with algebraic celebrity. The organisation generally corresponded to the cause of the person's rank in the university; and, although there were exceptions, most of the persons who have achieved honours evidently owe them to the great power of their knowing organs; clearly showing that those who were also gifted with deeply-reflecting and combining powers, are not called to use them either in classical or mathematical studies. Many men, on the contrary, have figured in public life, in virtue of their great endowment of Causality and Comparison, who, from a smaller gift of the knowing organs, have held a very humble grade at Oxford and Cambridge."

Brunel, the celebrated engineer and mechanician. In examining masks, a depression of muscle which sometimes takes place at this part, in consequence of the weight of the plaster, must not be mistaken for a fulness of the organ. In blowing crown-glass, the workman dips the end of a hollow iron tube into a pot of melted glass, and takes up as much of it as will suffice to make a circle. To form a full-sized circle, the quantity raised should be nine pounds and a half; and, when visiting a manufactory at Newcastle, I was told that an expert workman will generally hit the exact quantity, and very rarely deviate to the extent of two or three ounces, either under or over it. Some men excel others in this tact, and some are wholly incapable of acquiring it. I observed the organ of Weight very largely-developed in the successful workmen.

Mr. Simpson proceeds: "The faculty now under consideration, in high endowment, manifests itself in engineering, in dynamical skill, in the knowledge and application of mechanical forces. What may be its *lesser* endowments? Where do we find the organ? Situated in the midst of that group which gives us the perception of the qualities of material objects; namely, Form, Size, Locality, Colouring, Order, and Number. It is evident there is a quality of bodies most essential to their nature, not included in these qualities, singly or combined; namely, their density and corresponding weight. As bodies gravitate in a well-known ratio to their density, and their density and weight are the same thing, weight is only one name for gravitation. Does it then serve any important purpose in our being, or is it essential to our animal existence, that we should have an instinctive perception of gravitation, operating constantly and independently of reason? That state of rest which the law of gravitation constitutes the natural state of all bodies, solid, fluid, and aëriform, is called their *equilibrium*. The simplest animal motions, what are they but alternate disturbance and restoration of *equilibrium?*"—" The land-animal walks and runs, and avails itself of the resistance of the earth—the bird flies by its instinctive perception of the resistance of the air—the fish uses its fins and tail, instintively perceiving the resistance of the water."

" Some degree, therefore, of the power of adapting motions to the law of gravitation, some power over equilibrium must be possessed by the whole animated creation—for without it, it is plain, they must perish. May the organ of Weight be the organ of this faculty? To man alone is given the capacity to aid this power, and render his motion more effectual, and force more availing by the use of instruments—and Franklin well named him a tool-making, or rather a tool-using, animal. What are his tools? They are all modifications of the elementary mechanical powers. His club and bow are levers—his axe, knife, sword, and arrow are wedges. He instinctively aids his own muscular force by the lever, when he applies a bar of wood to raise a stone from the ground; if he wishes to raise that stone to a certain height, perpendicularly, he will instinctively counteract its gravitation by forcing it up an inclined plane, instead of applying his own bodily force to lift it perpendicularly. The principle of the pulley will suggest itself whenever he has obtained a block with a cord or thong, to draw water out of a pit. The screw is only the inclined plane wrapped spirally round a cylinder; to avail himself of which he would be led, whenever he attempted, as he early did, to build a tower."

These views, says Mr. Simpson, are strongly supported by diseased affections of this part of the brain. Miss S. L. was attacked with headache and pain in the region of the organ of Weight; " her perception of equilibrium was deranged, and she experienced giddiness, inclined position of horizontal floors and ceilings, and the sensation of being lifted up, and of again falling down and forward. Her account of it is worthy of remark, for she said she felt as if she had been *tipsy*." Mr. Simpson refers to a diseased condition of this and of some of the other knowing organs, a curious mental affection, which Mr. John Hunter, the celebrated anatomist, experienced in 1776, and which is recorded in his Life, written by Sir Everard Home. " From great anxiety of mind," says he. " Mr. H. had a severe illness. It attacked him on a journey, and his first sensation, it is well worthy of remark, was that *of having drunk too much*, although he had taken nothing but a little weak punch. On going to bed, he felt as if *suspended in the air*, and soon after *the room seemed to go round* with very great rapidity. This ceased, but the strange sensation, like Miss S. L.'s, of being lifted up, continued ; and, on being brought home in his carriage, his sensation was that of *sinking or going down*. The symptoms of whirling and suspension increased ; and his own head, when he raised it from his pillow, seemed to move from him to some distance with great velocity. When he became able to stand without being giddy, he was unable to walk without support ; ' for,' says Sir E Home, ' *his own feelings did not give him information respecting his centre of gravity*, so that he was unable to balance his body and prevent himself from falling.' We need not add," continues Mr. Simpson, " the obvious comment, that the organ of *Weight* was diseased, and the very function we have imputed to it, the instinct of equilibrium, (expressed almost in our own words by Sir E. Home,) unequivocally impeded."[*]

The phenomena of intoxication are explained by Mr. Simpson in a similar way. " Both Miss S. L. and Mr. John Hunter," says he, " bore testimony to the illusive *feeling* of being intoxicated, while Miss S. L. had acute pain in the organ of the instinct or power of preserving the balance, and maintaining an upright posture. But for an innate, steady, and never-failing perception of equilibrium, animal movements would be only staggering and tumbling. The intoxicated soon lose a steady gait, fall down, see perpendiculars at other angles, believe the floor itself perpendicular, and grasp the ground to save themselves from falling off its surface ; they feel lifted up, sinking down, and whirling round. Sickness would follow these sensations, independent of the stimulus of the liquor to the stomach ; and it is extremely probable that sea-sickness results from the inverted feelings occasioned by motion which violates our habitual perception of equilibrium."[†]

A correspondent of *The Phrenological Journal* [‡] mentions, that he was struck with this remark about sea-sickness arising from the disturbance of equilibrium, and found by experience, when at sea, that, by standing at the vessel's side, directing his eyes to an object on shore perfectly still, the top of a mountain, for example, and shutting out with the palms of his hands all sight of the ship and the sea, sickness was invariably dispelled ; but always returned whenever he withdrew his hands, and allowed any part of the vessel to catch his eye.

Sir. G. S. Mackenzie has suggested the name " Resistance " as more appropriate for this faculty than " Weight." " We cannot judge," says he, " of weight as we do of form, without repeated experience. We may see before us two balls of the same size and colour. We take up one of them, and perceive that it requires a certain exertion or resistance on the part of the muscles of the arm and hand to support it. From this, however, we cannot determine that the other ball will produce the same effect, for it may be hollow. Now, although we have obtained the experience that two similar balls may not produce the same effect ; this experience is of no use to us, for we must always make the experiment of lifting both, in order to determine which is the heavier. The impression

* *Phrenological Journal*, vol. ii., pp. 302, 426.
† *Phrenological Journal*, vol. ii., p. 427.   ‡ Vol. ii., p. 645.

of resistance is, however, left with us; and probably it is the function of the faculty which Dr. Spurzheim calls that of Weight, to give us conceptions of resistance in general."[*] Mr. Simpson conceives resistance to be perceived by an external sense formerly spoken of,[†] and now calls this the faculty of Force.[‡]

Mr. Richard Edmondson, of Manchester, mentions that a great number of observations have led him to the conviction that this organ gives the perception of perpendicularity. Workmen who easily detect deviations from the perpendicular possess it large; while those who constantly find it necessary to resort to the plumb-line have it small, and vice versa.[§] The same gentleman has more recently published [||] an essay on the functions of the organs of Weight and Constructiveness, in which he maintains the same view, with this addition, that the faculty perceives not only perpendicularity, but also the *direction* of force, and in particular the direction of the gravitating force of our bodies. The perception of the *degrees* of force he refers to Constructiveness.

26 COLOURING.

Although the eyes are affected agreeably or disagreeably by different modifications of the beams of light, or by colours, yet they do not conceive the relations of different colours—their harmony or discord—and they have no memory of them. Certain individuals are almost destitute of the power of perceiving colours, who yet have the sense of vision acute, and readily perceive other qualities in external bodies, as their size and form. This fact has been remarked by Mr. Stewart. He says, " In the power of conceiving colours too, there are striking differences among individuals; and, indeed, I am inclined to suspect that, in the greater number of instances, the supposed defects of sight in this respect ought to be ascribed rather to a defect in the power of conception. One thing is certain, that we often see men who are perfectly sensible of the difference between two colours when they are presented to them, who cannot give names to these colours with confidence when they see them apart; and are, perhaps, apt to confound the one with the other. Such men, it should seem, feel the sensation of colour like other men, when the object is present; but are incapable (*probably in consequence of some early habit of inattention*) to conceive the sensation distinctly when the object is removed."[¶]

In this quotation we have a specimen of the usual mode of conducting metaphysical speculations. When the most curious and striking phenomena of the mind are mentioned, and when we look anxiously for an explanation of them, *habit* or *association* is dragged in to solve the difficulty; and this perhaps merely in a parenthesis, as if no difficulty existed.

Observation enables us to prove that individuals who have the part of the brain marked No. 26 largely developed, possess, in a high degree, the power of discriminating colours; and, on this account, the phrenologist admits that power as a fundamental faculty of the mind.

Lord Jeffrey objected to this doctrine, that light is always coloured, indeed nothing else but colour; and that it is impossible for any one to see acutely who cannot distinguish colours with equal success, because all visible objects must necessarily be distinguished by colour alone. The answer is, that the eye receives the external impression of light, and transmits it to the organ of Colouring, just as the ears transmit sound to the

* *Illustrations of Phrenology.* p. 168   † See p. 450.
‡ The matured views of Mr. Simpson respecting this faculty are fully expounded in *The Phrenological Journal*, vol. ix., p. 193.
§ *Phrenological Journal*, vol. vii., p. 166. || Ib., vol. ix., p. 624.
¶ *Elements*, ch. iii.

organ of Tune; and both are requisite to the perception of colour. If the eye be perfect and the organ of Colouring deficient, the individual may be capable of distinguishing degrees of intensity of light, although he cannot discriminate differences of tint; and the former is sufficient to acute vision, as is proved by engraving and black chalk drawing; in which form, distance, and expression are successfully represented by mere differences of light and shade, or by different degrees of light independently of colour.

The faculty, when powerful, gives a delight in contemplating colours, and a vivid feeling of their harmony and discord. Those in whom the organ is deficient experience little interest in colouring, and are almost insensible to difference of hues. In the *Transactions of the Phrenological Society*, p. 210, Dr. Butter reports the case of Mr. Robert Tucker, whose eyesight was not deficient, and who was able neither to distinguish nor to recollect many of the primitive colours, even when shown to him. "Orange he calls green, and green colours orange; red he considers as brown, and brown as red; blue silk appears to him like pink, and pink of a light blue colour; indigo is described as purple." The organ is reported to be decidedly deficient in this gentleman's head. The case of Mr. James Milne, brass-founder, in Edinburgh, is also peculiarly illustrative of this faculty; and, as I obtained the facts from himself, they may be implicitly relied on.

Mr. Milne's grandfather, on the mother's side, had a deficiency in the power of perceiving colours, but could distinguish forms and distance easily. On one occasion this gentleman was desirous that his wife should purchase a beautiful green gown. She brought several patterns to him, but could never find one which came up to his views of the colour in question. One day he observed a lady passing on the street, and pointed out her gown to his wife as the colour that he wished her to get; when she expressed her astonishment, and assured him that the colour was a mixed brown, which he had all along mistaken for a green. It was not known till then that he was deficient in the power of perceiving colours.

Neither Mr. Milne's father, mother, nor uncle on the mother's side, was deficient in this respect; so that the imperfection passed over one generation. In himself and his two brothers, however, it appeared in a decided manner; while in his sisters, four in number, no trace of it is to be found; as they distinguish colours easily. Mr. Spankie, a cousin once removed, has a similar defect. *

Mr. Milne is rather near-sighted, but never could find glasses to aid his defect. He rather excels in distinguishing forms and proportions; and, although he cannot discover game upon the ground, from the faintness of his perception of colours, yet he is fond of shooting: when a boy, he was rather an expert marksman, when the birds were fairly visible to him in the air. He sees them, however, only in the skylight; and, on one occasion, when a large covey of partridges rose within ten or twelve yards of him, the back ground being a field of Swedish turnips, he could not perceive a single bird. His eye is convex to a considerable degree.

Mr. Milne's defect was discovered in rather a curious manner. He was bound apprentice to a draper, and continued in his service for three years and a half. During two years he fell into considerable mistakes about colours, but this was attributed to inexperience, and ignorance of the names of the tints. At length, however, when he was selling a piece

* I have examined the heads of Mr. Milne's brothers, who are deficient in the power, and in them the organ is evidently little developed. I have also examined its developement in one of his sisters, and found no deficiency, but rather a fulness, in the organ. Mr. Lyon, a member of the Phrenological Society, states, that he has examined the head of Mr. Spankie, and found the organ rather deficient.

of olive corduroy for breeches, the purchaser requested strings to tie them with; and Mr. Milne was proceeding to cut off what he considered the best match, when the person stopped him, and requested strings of the same colour as the cloth. Mr. Milne begged him to point out a colour to please himself; and he selected, of course, a green string. When he was gone, Mr. Milne was so confident that he himself was right, and the purchaser wrong, that he cut off a piece of the string which he intended to give, and a piece of that which had been selected, and carried both home with a piece of the cloth also, and showed them to his mother. She then told him that his riband was a bright scarlet, and the other a grass-green. His masters would not believe in any natural defect in his power of perceiving colours; and it was only after many mistakes, and some vituperation, that he was permitted to renounce the business, and to betake himself to another, that of a brass-founder, to which he had a natural disposition; for he had used the turning-lathe in fashioning play-things, when a mere boy.

As to the different colours, he knows blues and yellows certainly; but he cannot distinguish browns, greens, and reds. A brown and green he cannot discriminate or name when apart; but when together, he sees a difference between them. Blue and pink, when about the same shade, and seen in daylight, appear to him to be of the colour of the sky, which he calls blue; but seen in candlelight, the pink appears like a dirty buff, and the blue retains the appearance which it had in daylight. The grass appears to him more like an orange than any other coloured object with which he is acquainted. Indigo, violet, and purple appear only different shades of one colour, darker or lighter, but not differing in their bases. He never mistakes black and white objects: he distinguishes easily between a black and a blue, and is able even to tell whether a black is a good or a bad one. In the rainbow he perceives only the yellow and the blue distinctly. He sees that there are other tints in it, but what they are he cannot distinguish, and he is quite unable to name them. In daylight crimson appears like blue or purple, but in candlelight it seems a bright red.

When in Glasgow, his greatcoat was carried off from the travellers' room by mistake, and, on inquiring at the waiter what had become of it, the question was naturally put, what was the colour of the coat? Mr. Milne was quite puzzled by the interrogatory; and, although he had worn it for a year, he could only reply that it was either snuff brown or olive-green, but which he could not tell. The waiter looked as if he suspected that Mr. Milne wanted to get a coat instead of wishing to recover one; but the coat was found, although even yet Mr. Milne is not able to tell the colour. He is apt to mistake copper for brass, unless he distinguish them by the file.

A mask of Mr. Milne is sold in the shops, and in it the organs of Form, Size, and Constructiveness* are well developed, while that of Colouring is decidedly deficient; there being a depression in the part corresponding to this organ, into which the point of the finger falls on passing it along. As a contrast, the reader may compare with it the masks of Sir David Wilkie, Mr. Haydon, Mr. Douglas, or Mr. Williams, all eminent painters; and as the organ is large in these masks, a very marked difference will be perceptible.

Cases of this description are not rare. In the mask of Mr. Sloane, of Leith, the developement is small, and in a letter, dated 20th February, 1822, addressed to me, this gentleman says: " When I see a piece of tartan, or any other complication of colours, I can easily distinguish the

* This is an example of the organ of Constructiveness being situated higher than usual, as noticed on p. 173.

difference of hues; but were the different colours presented to me singly,
I could not say which was which. I feel particularly at a less to distinguish between green and brown, and likewise between some shades of red
and blue. I am not sensible of being deficient in. seeing anything at a
distance, or of being-unable to perceive as small a particle as the generality of men can do." In this mask the deficiency is not so great as in
that of Mr. Milne, but the organ of Colouring is much less developed in
it than in the masks of the painters before alluded to.*

Sir John. F. W. Herschel's explanation of the cause of deficiency in
the power of discriminating between colours, seems to coincide with that
now given. " We have examined," says he, " with some attention, a
very eminent optician, whose eyes (or rather eye, having lost the sight
of one. by an accident) have this curious peculiarity, and have satisfied
ourselves, contrary to the received opinions, that all the prismatic rays
have the power of exciting and affecting them with the sensation of light,
and producing distinct vision; so that the defect arises from no insensibility of the retina to rays of any particular refrangibility, nor to any colouring matter in the humours of the eye preventing certain rays from
reaching the retina, (as has been ingeniously supposed,) but from a defect
in the sensorium, by which it is rendered incapable of appreciating exactly
those differences between rays on which their colour depends."†

There are instances of individuals who involuntarily associate particular colours with particular names, even although they have never seen
the persons named; thus all Johnsons will be blue, and all Thomsons
black, and so on with other names and colours. There appears to be an
association in activity between the organs of Colouring and Language in
such individuals, so that the one cannot act without exciting the other;
as some men cannot bend one finger without bending also the one next
to it. This, however, is only a conjecture ‡

The proper way to observe the developement of the organ of Colouring
is, to distinguish to what extent the centre of each eyebrow projects forward.
In Mr. Milne it is slightly depressed below the neighbouring parts; in Mr.
Sloane it is scarcely depressed, but it does not project, so as to over-
hang the eyeball; in the painters it is large and prominent, forming a
heavy shade above the eye. Dr. Spurzheim mentions that a large developement of it is indicated by an arched appearance in the middle of the
eyebrow, and that this sign is found in the portraits of Rubens, Titian,
Rembrandt, Salvator Rosa, Claude Lorraine, &c.; but its large size is
indicated also by the projection forward of this part of the eyebrow without arching. It presents this appearance in the masks of the late Sir
Henry Raeburn, Sir David Wilkie, Haydon, and other eminent painters.

Dr. Gall states it as an indubitable fact, that determinate laws of proportion in colours exist. The three primitive colours of blue, yellow,
and red, says he, do not harmonize. If we mix two of these, an intermediate colour is produced; blue and yellow give green; blue and red,

* A collection of similar cases has been made by Mr. Robert Cox in *The
Phrenological Journal*, vol. vii., p. 144. In addition to the works there referred
to the following, enumerated by Dr. Mackenzie, in his *Practical Treatise on
the Diseases of the Eye*, 2d edit., p. 861, may be consulted by the reader who
is curious respecting such cases. Nicholl, in *Medico-Chirurgical Transactions*, vol vii., p. 477, and vol ix., p. 359: also in *Annals of Philosophy*, New
Series, vol. iii., p. 128. Harvey, in *Transactions of the Royal Society of Edinburgh*, vol. x., p. 253; also in *Edinburgh Journal of Science*, vol. v., p. 114.
Brewster, in *Edinburgh Journal of Science*, vol. iv., p. 85. Colquhoun, in
Glasgow Medical Journal, 1829; vol. ii., p. 12.

† *Encyclopædia Metropolitana*, article " Light," p. 434, § 567.

‡ See cases of colours associated with things, persons, and musical notes,
in *The Phrenological Journal*, vol. iii., p. 420; also vol. viii., pp. 70, 216.

violet; red and yellow, orange. To obtain a harmonious combination, we must place beside a primitive colour a mixed one, into which the primitive enters as an element ; the mixed colours will always be in harmony with the two primitive colours from which it is produced. If we place, says he, a silk riband, of a blue colour and about an inch broad, on a sheet of white paper, and look at it steadfastly, at the end of a short time we shall see besides, yellow and red, and (at the side) orange, resulting from their mixture.*

Lord Jeffrey, in the article " Beauty," already alluded to, informs us that "colour is, in all cases, absolutely indifferent to the eye ;" and adds, that " it is no doubt quite true that, among painters and connoisseurs, we hear a great deal about the harmony and composition of tints, and the charms and difficulties of a judicious colouring. In all this, however, we cannot help thinking that *there is no little pedantry and no little jargon.*" Speaking of the natural gamut of colours, he continues : " We confess we have no faith in any of these fancies ; and believe that, if all these colours were fairly arranged, on a plain board, according to the most rigid rules of this supposed harmony, nobody but the author of the theory would perceive the smallest beauty in the exhibition, or he the least offended by reversing their collocation." It is a curious fact, that the organ of Colouring in Lord Jeffrey's head is actually depressed ; and it appears that, in the usual manner of metaphysical writers, he has conceived his own feelings to be an infallible standard of those of human nature in general. It is quite true that the *eye* is affected only by the degrees of light ; but by this expression the mind is here obviously meant. The author, when speaking in the next sentence of the gamut, draws no distinction between the powers of the mind and those of the eye. Those individuals, then, whose cases I have cited, and who cannot distinguish dark brown from scarlet, buff from orange, or violet from pink, would probably subscribe to Lord Jeffrey's positions. But other individuals, such as Wilkie and Haydon, have an intense sensibility to shades of every hue and of every degree ; and some painters have assured me, that they experience a very decided emotion in contemplating colours, independently of every association; and declare, that they perceive harmony, congruity, and incongruity in their arrangements, even on a plain board, as certainly and as distinctly as they distinguish harmony and discord in sound.

Lord Jeffrey, in criticising this work in *The Edinburgh Review*, No. 88, controverts these inferences. " Without meaning," says he, " to call in question the fact of the depression of his skull, we happen to *know* that the individual here mentioned has a remarkably fine and exact perception of colours, so as to be able to *match them* from memory with a precision which has been the admiration of many ladies and dress-makers. He has also an uncommon sensibility to their beauty ; and spends more time than most people in gazing on bright flowers and peacocks' necks, and *wondering,* he hopes innocently, *what can be the cause of his enjoyment.* Even the phrenologists, we think, must admit that, *in his case,* it cannot be the predominance of the appropriate faculty, since they have ascertained that he is totally destitute of the organ."

In a letter which I addressed to Lord Jeffrey, in answer to this criticism,† I asked, " How could you assert in the *Encyclopædia,* that 'colour is in all cases absolutely *indifferent* to the eye,' if you were conscious when you wrote of possessing 'an *uncommon sensibility to their beauty ?*' How could you stigmatize as, '*pedantry and jargon*' the doctrine of 'the

---

* *Sur les Fonctions du Cerveau,* tome v., p. 81.
† *Phrenological Journal,* vol. iv., p. 1, and also p. 242. I beg leave to refer the reader to these Letters for an answer to the whole of Lord Jeffrey's criticisms on this work. The first is published also separately.

harmony and composition of tints, and the charms and difficulties of a judicious colouring,' and assert, 'that if all those colours were fairly arranged, on a plain board, according to the most rigid rules of this supposed harmony, nobody but the author of the theory would perceive *the smallest beauty* in the exhibition, or be the least offended by reversing their collocation,' when all the time you enjoyed in yourself 'a remarkably fine and exact perception of colours, so as to be able to *match them* from memory with a precision which has been the admiration of many ladies and dress-makers?'"

In a note to the 89th number of the *Review* Lord Jeffrey replied to this argument as follows: "There are two questions here; *first*, whether there are any grounds, from inconsistency or otherwise, to impeach the credit of the reviewer, when he says that he can *distinguish* colours and shades of colours with more than common accuracy? and, *secondly*, whether there are any such grounds for disbelieving him, when he says that he has a strong sense of their *beauty?* The first is the main allegation, and formed the whole original subject of controversy. Mr. Combe alleged that the organ of colour was actually depressed in the head of that individual, and inferred that he probably did not know scarlet from brown: it was answered that this was a mistake, for he was known to have a remarkably fine perception of colours and their diversities: and the replication to this in the pamphlet is, that that cannot well be, since he himself had stated, in the Encyclopædia, that all colours are indifferent to the eye, and one just as beautiful as another. Well, suppose he had said so, where would have been the inconsistency? for where is the connexion between the allegations that are held to be contradictory? A man who happens to think brown as beautiful as scarlet, may surely perceive *the difference* between them—or rather, he *must* perceive it, when he compares them, in this way, as two distinct and distinguishable objects. There is not, therefore, the shadow of a pretext for discrediting the reviewer's leading allegation, that the individual alluded to, though destitute of the phrenological organ, can discriminate colours with unusual readiness and precision."

In answer to these remarks, I beg leave to observe, that Lord Jeffrey overstates my objection. The paragraph on which he comments is printed in this work *verbatim* as it stood in the edition reviewed, and the reader will perceive that I did not allege that the organ was absolutely wanting in his head, and did not infer that he was incapable of perceiving colours, or that "he probably did not know scarlet from brown," On the contrary, the statement was merely that the organ is "depressed;" that is to say, that in him it is deficient in size relatively to the other organs—whereas in the painters it is large. The work itself afforded information of the effect of a depressed organ: it is said that "PERCEPTION is the *lowest* degree of activity" of every intellectual faculty.; "when a coloured object is presented, and the individual cannot perceive, so as to distinguish the hues, he is *destitute* of the power of manifesting the faculty of colour;" "each organ will enable the mind to recall the impressions which it served at first to receive;" and memory is merely "a degree of activity to each faculty.". A friend in India, after reading Lord Jeffrey's note, wrote to me as follows: "Melody is the pleasure arising from successions of simple sounds suited to each other. Harmony is that arising from combined sounds, or from several striking the ear simultaneously, as in a band playing different parts. The former requires much less of the organ than the latter, and hence the Scotch, with no great Tune, are melodists, but nothing as musicians. In like manner, the allocation of the simple colours is their melody, and the combination of several is harmony. Lord Jeffrey might thus place one riband beside another very well, but not perceive the harmony of combined colours."* ` There is no inconsistency, therefore, between the depression of Lord Jeffrey's organ of Colouring and the manifestations which he describes. Even Mr. Milne is able to perceive some colours and to distinguish differences between them, and he has memory of some of them ; although in him the organ is considerably more depressed than in Lord Jeffrey. -

The real objection stated in the work was, that painters not only distinguish differences, but enjoy *direct* pleasure from "contemplating colours independently of every association ; and that they perceive harmony, congruity, and incongruity in their arrangements, even on a plain board, as certainly and distinctly as they distinguish harmony and discord in sounds;" which assertions Lord Jeffrey designated as pedantry and jargon.

In answer to my statement, therefore, he ought to have proved that, notwithstanding his depressed organ, he possesses the faculty in this higher degree, that he actually receives *direct* pleasure from colours, and perceives their harmonies and discord. In No. 88 of the *Review* he endeavoured to do this, by referring to his " remarkably fine and exact *perception* of colours, so as to be able to match them from memory ;" and to his delight "in gazing on bright flowers and peacocks' necks;" and in No. 89 of the *Review* he favours us with the following additional arguments in support of this position :

" But, in the next place," says he, "and this is still more material, it is certain that the individual in question *does not maintain*, in the Encyclopædia, that there is no beauty in colours or combination of colours— but the very reverse. His whole object in that treatise, as every one must know who has looked into a line of it, is, not to deny the existence of beauty, but to *explain* its nature and causes, in colours as in everything else : and, accordingly, not only is there no doubt thrown on the fact of their beauty, but its reality, and that of the peculiar pleasure afforded by it, is both expressly asserted in a variety of passages, and constantly assumed and taken for granted, as the very basis of the theory, and the test of the illustrations which are urged in its support. The theory is, that colours are beautiful, not in consequence of the mere organic operation of their physical qualities on the eye, but in consequence of their habitual *association* with certain simple emotions or mental qualities, of which they remind us in a great variety of ways. Thus blue, for example, is said to be beautiful, because it is the colour of the unclouded sky—green, because it is that of vernal woods and summer meadows—and red, because it reminds us of the season of roses, or of the blushes of youth and innocence ; and, accordingly, when these associations are disturbed, the beauty which they created disappears Green would not be beautiful in the sky, nor blue on the cheek, nor vermilion on the grass. The doctrine is precisely the same as to the beauty of combination of colours, and it is attempted to be proved by similar illustrations. Throughout it is distinctly stated, and invariably assumed as indisputable, *that they are beautiful*, and afford pleasure to those who admire them—though it is alleged that there is a good deal of pedantry in those who dogmatize on the laws of their harmony, and affect to limit their pleasing combinations exclusively to certain arrangements. It is maintained, as before, that their beauty depends *entirely* on the associations with which they are connected ; and while it is admitted that certain combinations will generally excite the same associations in those who are devoted to the same pursuits, it is denied that these are either universal or unvarying, or that the feeling they undoubtedly excite can ever be referred to the organic action of the

* I understand that this defect is apparent in some painters ; they are capable of matching a few simple colours, but when a numerous assemblage of them requires to be introduced into a picture, they fail in giving them harmony.

coloured light on the sense. These opinions may be right or wrong
the only question now at issue is,—whether they are inconsistent wi
admission of the fact, that colours are beautiful? and whether th
who holds them must be disbelieved, when he says that he has a
sense of *this kind of beauty?*"

In this note Lord Jeffrey no longer wonders what can be the .cau
his enjoyment from the bright flowers and peacocks' necks. He in
us distinctly, that he has no *direct* perception of beauty in their coloe
mere colours, but that the beauty perceived by him depends " *entirt
the associations with which they are connected.*" "Colours," say
" are *beautiful, not in consequence of the mere organic operation of •
physical qualities on the eye,* but in consequence of their habitual *associa
with certain simple emotions or mental qualities of which they remin
in a great variety of ways.*" It now turns out, accordingly, that his pl
sure in contemplating the bright flowers and peacocks' necks arose,
from any quality in these objects themselves, nor from any direct eff
produced by them on his own mind, but from something else, which t
served merely to introduce to his fancy. He was pleased, for exam
with the red of the flowers, not because it was a colour grateful in its
but because it reminded him of the lovely season in which roses are p
duced, or of the blushes of youth and innocence ; and he delighted in t
blue of the peacocks' necks, not because that colour was intrinsical
pleasing, but because it excited the recollection of the unclouded sk
The painters, on the other hand, in whom the organ is large, state, th
the source of their pleasure in colours is very different. They infor
me that Lord Jeffrey's love of bright flowers and peacocks' necks indicate
that his perception of colours is feeble ; because a strong stimulus i
necessary to excite it to action, and even when thus stimulated, he is no
capable of feeling direct pleasure from colours, nor of perceiving their har
mony and discord, but they serve merely to introduce extrinsic ideas an
emotions. His experience, therefore, corresponds in the most complet
manner with the " depressed " state of the organ in his head.

This is so plain as scarcely to admit of illustration ; but we may suppos
a young military officer to assert that there is no harmony nor discord ii
sounds, and no direct pleasure in melody ; but that, nevertheless, he enjoy
great delight in hearing a military band. If we should ask him what i
the source of his delight in the band, and he should answer, " Oh, th
notes themselves give me no pleasure, but they remind me of the ga
uniforms, the waving plumes, and the martial pomp of our regiment ; the
recall the summer evening's parade, with the fairy forms and angel smile
of female loveliness which then hover around us ; in short, with me, th
beauty of the music depends entirely on the associations which it serve
to introduce." Who that enjoys sensibility to music would not say, tha
Phrenology would be in fault if the man who made such a statement wer
not deficient in the organ of Tune? In fact, the individual suppose
would never dwell for a moment on the music itself ; to him it would b
mere sound, exciting in his mind ideas of the lancers, the parade, and
female beauty, which would be the real objects of his admiration and th
sources of his enjoyment. This case is an exact parallel to that of Lor
Jeffrey, in regard to colours. The colours themselves exhibit no beauty
to his mind : they never engage his attention by their own loveliness ; bu
merely usher in extraneous ideas and emotions, in which he finds hi
gratification. Would not Phrenology be in fault, if in him the organ of
Colouring were otherwise than " depressed ?"

A legal practitioner, in a Scotch provincial town, whom I have seen
and in whom this organ was very large, was engrossed by a passion fo
flowers, even to the neglect of his professional duties. It is probable tha

the intense sensibility to colours, which accompanies a large developement
of the organ, was the source of this interest.

Phrenologists are accustomed to infer the particular powers which are
most vigorous in an author's mind from the manifestations of them in his
works; and none affords better scope for observation than the faculty of
Colouring. Unless the impressions made on the mind of an author by
colours be very strong, he has no inducement to introduce them in his
works, for he can easily treat of a great variety of subjects without adverting to their hues. When, therefore, we find him minutely describing
shades and tints, and dwelling on colours and their effects with evident
delight, we may safely infer that the organ is large. Mr. Tennant, the
author of *Anster Fair*, frequently does so, and in his head the organ is large.
. The organ is generally larger in women than in men; and, accordingly,
some women, as *colourists*, have equalled the masters among men; while,
as *painters*, women, in general, have always been inferior to the other sex.
The faculty aids the flower-painter, enameller, dyer, and, in general, all
who occupy themselves with colours. Its great energy gives a passion
for colours, but not necessarily a delicate taste in them. Taste depends
upon a perfect rather than a very powerful activity of the faculties. In
several oriental nations, for example, the faculty appears, from their love
of colours, to be strong, and, nevertheless, they display bad taste in the
application of them.

If any conclusion may be drawn from the very limited observations
which have been made on the developement of the organ of Colouring in
different parts of the world, it appears to be large in those countries where
vegetation displays the greatest brilliance of tint, and deficient where the aspect of nature is dreary and unvariegated. The organ, for instance, seems
to be large in the Chinese; while it is small in the Esquimaux, to whom
the sky, and snow, and ice are almost the only objects of vision. Captain
Parry mentions that dying is an art wholly unknown to the Esquimaux.*

Dr. Spurzheim observed, that, in persons born blind, the organ of Colouring is in general less developed than in persons who see, or who have
become blind in mature age. I have repeatedly verified this observation
in asylums for the blind. Indeed it is possible, by observing the developement of the organ of Colouring, to distinguish individuals who have
become blind in infancy from others who have lost their sight in mature
age; in the former the organ is much less developed than in the latter.
James Wilson, of Belfast, author of *Biography of the Blind*, lost his sight
from small-pox at four years of age. His right eye was subsequently
couched, and he saw till he was seven; his vision was then again extinguished by a furious cow, and he has continued blind ever since. After
he became blind he learned to work as a carpenter; he also acquired
such an accurate and extensive knowledge of places, as to be able to act
as a kind of courier for the merchants, to the extent of thirty or forty
miles round Belfast; he boasts of considerable literary attainments, and
possesses a very extensive memory for persons, places, names, and dates.
I saw him in 1836, when he was in the 57th year of his age: at that
time his organs of Colouring were very small; while those of Individuality, Size, and Number were large, and those of Form and Locality very
large. His temperament was nervous, bilious, and a little sanguine.
The organs which had been most exercised appeared to have attained
the largest size, while the organs of Colouring, which had been dormant,
had apparently scarcely grown from infancy. A mask of him was taken,
and is in the collection of the Phrenological Society.

Dr. Gall mentions, that he had seen a bookseller of Augsburg, blind
from birth, who maintained that it is not the eye, but the intellect, which

recognises, judges, and produces proportion among colours. This individual asserted, that, by means of an internal sense, he had precise notions
of colours, and it is a fact that he determined their harmony exactly. He
had a number of glass-beads, of various colours, which he formed into
different figures, and always produced harmony in the arrangement of the
colours. After making a great effort of this kind, he experienced pain
immediately above the eye, particularly over the right eye.* I have seen
a blind man, in Stirling, who distinguished colours with great accuracy
by means of touch. Derham, in his *Physico-Theology*,† mentions a similar case, and observes, that "although the eye be the usual judge of
colours, yet some have been able to distinguish them by feeling." I have
conversed with persons born blind, who assured me that they could form
no conception whatever of colour, nor of the phenomena of sight. I cannot conceive, therefore, that the blind bookseller of Augsburg, spoken of
by Dr. Gall, had precise notions of colours, similar to those enjoyed by
persons who see. The blind man at Stirling, who distinguished colours
by the sense of touch, was guided by differences in the texture of the
objects. He practised chiefly on the dresses of the passengers in the
beautiful walk round Stirling Castle; and I have seen him, by rubbing his
hand along the pile of the sleeve, distinguish, with much readiness and
accuracy, a black coat, a brown coat, a blue coat, and a green coat. The
skin on the points of the fingers had acquired a most extraordinary softness and delicacy, from long practice of this operation. In his mind there
appears to have been a distinct tactile perception, to which he gave the
name of green, another which he designated brown, and so on; but I
cannot conceive that such impressions at all resembled the common apprehensions of colours enjoyed by persons who enjoy perfect vision. Dr.
Spurzheim says: "Many blind persons have assured me of their incapacity
to distinguish colours. A few, however, discern white from black, because
white surfaces are in general smoother than black. When the blind pretend to distinguish colours, they do no more than determine surfaces of
greater or less degrees of smoothness, without acquiring any idea of colour in itself."‡

The organ is considered as established.

27. LOCALITY.

DR. GALL mentions, that the taste which he had for natural history
induced him to go frequently into the woods in order to catch birds, or to
discover their nests; and although he was expert in accomplishing these
objects, yet, when he wished to return to the nests, he generally found it
impossible to retrace his way, or to light upon the tree which he had
marked, or the snares which he had set. This difficulty did not arise
from inattention; for, before quitting the spot, he stuck branches into the
ground, and cut marks on trees, to guide him in his return, but all in vain.
He was obliged to take constantly along with him one of his school-fellows,
named Scheidler, who, with the least possible effort of attention, went
always directly to the place where a snare was set, even although
they had sometimes placed ten or fifteen in a quarter that was not familiarly known to them. As this youth possessed only very ordinary talents
in other respects, Dr. Gall was much struck with his facility in recollecting places, and frequently asked him how he contrived to guide himself
so surely; to which he replied by asking Gall, in his turn, how he contrived to lose himself everywhere. In the hope of one day obtaining
some explanation of this peculiarity, Dr. Gall moulded his head, and after-

* *Sur les Fonctions du Cerveau*, tome v., p. 85.
† Book iv., ch. 6.   ‡ *Phrenology*, p. 296.

ward endeavoured to discover persons who were distinguished by the same faculty. The celebrated landscape-painter, Schænberger, told him that, in his travels, he was in the custom of making only a very general sketch of countries which interested him, and that afterward, when he wished to produce a more complete picture, every tree, every group of bushes, and every stone of considerable magnitude, presented itself spontaneously to his mind. About the same period Dr. Gall became acquainted with M. Meyer, author of the Romance of Dia-na-Sore, a person who found no pleasure except in a wandering life. Sometimes he went from house to house in the country, and at other times attached himself to some man of fortune, to accompany him in extended travels. He had an astonishing faculty of recollecting the different places which he had seen. Dr. Gall moulded his head also; he then placed it and the other two together, and compared them attentively: they presented great differences in many points, but he was struck with the singular form which appeared in all the three a little above the eyes, and on the two sides of the organ of Individuality; namely, two large prominences commencing near each side of the nose, and going obliquely upward and outward, almost as high as the middle of the forehead. From that time he was led to suppose that the talent for recollecting places depended on a primitive faculty, of which the organ was situated under this part of the skull; and innumerable subsequent observations confirmed this inference.[*]

Dr. Spurzheim states, that "the special faculty of this organ and the sphere of its activity remain to be determined. It makes the traveller, geographer, and landscape-painter; recollects localities; and give notions of perspective. It seems to me," says he, "that it is the faculty of Locality in general. As soon as we have conceived the existence of an object and its qualities, it must necessarily occupy a place, and this is the faculty that conceives the places occupied by the objects that surround us."[†] Sir George Mackenzie considers the primitive faculty to be that of perceiving relative position. Dr Spurzheim says, that "notions of perspective" are given by Locality, but certain facts, already noticed, appear to show that these depend rather on Size: in other respects his observations coincide with my own experience.

Persons in whom this organ is large, form vivid and distinct conceptions of situations and scenery which they have seen or heard described, and they have great power in recalling such conceptions. When the faculty is active from internal excitement of the organ, such ideas are presented to the mind involuntarily. In the mask of Sir Walter Scott the organ is large. Readers, similarly endowed, are almost as much delighted with his descriptions of scenery, as by a tour made by themselves amid the mountain glens; while those in whom the organ is small are quite uninterested by his most splendid poetical landscapes. This author wrote so pictorially, that he almost saves an artist, who means to illustrate his pages, the trouble of invention.

Authors in whom this organ is moderately developed treat of places in a very different manner. Mr. Tennant, the author of Anster Fair and The Thane of Fife, merely designates, by appropriate epithets, the leading features of a landscape, in a way which excites a pleasing and distinct recollection of it in those who have seen it, but which calls up no picture in the mind of a reader who was not familiar with it before; and in his head the organ of Locality is below an average size. The following lines are characteristic of his manner:

" Next them the troopers each on fervent steed
  That dwell *within the warm and flowery dales*
  Where Annan and where Esk, and Liddle, lead
  Their streams down tripping through the sunny vales,
  And where the *stronger and more swelling Tweed,*
  Emergent from his midland mountain, trails
  Voluminous and 'broad his waters down
  To meet the briny sea by bulwark'd Berwick town."

The organ is large in the busts and portraits of all eminent navigators
and travellers, such as Columbus, Cook, and Mungo Park; also in great
astronomers and geographers, as Kepler, Galileo, Tycho Brahé, and Newton. In Tasso the poet, also, it appears to have been very large, and he
manifested the faculty in a high degree. Several cases are mentioned
by Dr. Gall of individuals passionately fond of travelling, in whom the
organ was greatly developed ; and a similar instance is reported by Mr.
Schiotz, a Danish magistrate, in *The Phrenological Journal.*[*] This
faculty gives what is called "*coup d'œil,*" and judgment of the capabilities of ground. It is necessary to the military draughtsman, and is of
great importance to a general in war. Dr. Gall mentions, that he had
observed the organ large in distinguished players at chess ; and he conceived their talent to consist in the faculty of conceiving clearly a great
number of the possible positions of the men.

Some persons have a natural tact in discriminating and recollecting the
situation of the organs on the phrenological bust, and perceiving differences in the forms of the head, while others experience the greatest difficulty in doing so. The former have Locality, Size, and Form large ; the
latter have them small, indicated by a general narrowness at the top of
the nose. These state their own inability to observe as an objection
against the system ; but this is as if Mr. Milne were to deny the diversity
of certain colours, because his own organ of Colouring is so defective that
he cannot perceive it.

Locality appears to be an element in a genius for geometry. In the
heads or busts of six or seven eminent mathematicians which I have carefully examined, this organ, and also those of Size, Individuality, and
Comparison, are large. Indeed pure geometry treats only of the relations
of space, and does not imply agency, or any relation except that of proportion ; and hence it might be legitimately inferred to belong to the
sphere of the organs now mentioned. Negative cases also coincide with
these positive observations. Zhero Colburn, the American youth who
was celebrated for his arithmetical powers, turned his attention to mathematics, but with very little success. He stated to me that he had been
taught the first six books of Euclid, and understood the propositions, but
felt no interest in the study. He liked algebra much better ; and he has
the organ of Number large, but that of Locality deficient. The gentleman who had taken charge of his education, it is said, at first intended
him for a mathematician, but afterward, finding that his genius did not lie
that way, directed his attention to law. Mr. George Bidder, when a mere
child, displayed such astonishing talent as a mental calculator, that several gentlemen in Edinburgh were induced to take charge of his education ;
and, on the supposition that his abilities extended to mathematical science
generally, selected for him the profession of an engineer. Having heard
of this intention, and having observed that in his head the organs of the
geometrical faculties were not developed in any extraordinary degree, I
inferred that his eminence as a geometrician would not equal that which
he had attained as a calculator, and communicated this conviction in writing to Principal Baird, one of his patrons. Mr. Bidder subsequently

* Vol. viii., p. 64.

pursued the study of geometry; but, at the end of two years, both he himself and Professor Wallace informed me, that he was not distinguished for more than common ability in the class.

An opinion prevails, that mathematics afford exercise to the reflecting faculties, and that their tendency, as a branch of education, is to cultivate the talent for general reasoning: some persons regard them as the best substitute for the useless logic of the schools.. This idea appears to me to be erroneous. Geometry treats of the proportions of space, and algebra and arithmetic of the relations of numbers, and the three constitute the grand elements of the science of pure mathematics. For judging of the proportions of space, the faculties of Size, Locality, and Individuality, aided by Comparison, are those essentially required; while the faculties of Number and Order, also aided by Comparison, are the chief powers necessary for dealing with the proportions of numbers. Causation always implies power, force, or agency; and the idea of causation or efficiency does not at all enter into the propositions of pure mathematics. The popular error is not sanctioned by the authority of the masters in philosophy. Lord Bacon observes, that "the mathematical part in some men's minds is good, and the logical is bad. Some can reason well of numbers and quantities, that cannot reason well in words." Dugald Stewart remarks, that ", when it is stated in the form of a self-evident truth, that *magnitudes* which coincide, or which exactly fill the same space, are equal to one another, the beginner readily yields his assent to the proposition; and this assent, without going any farther, is all that is required in any of the demonstrations of the first six books of Euclid."[*] Mr. Stewart was a mathematician, and also a metaphysician; and this is strong testimony to the fact, that the whole of the first six books of Euclid, which constitute a large portion of a common mathematical education, relate exclusively to the proportions of space or magnitude, and do not imply causation.

Professor Leslie states, that the *whole structure of geometry is grounded on the simple comparison of triangles;* and Mr. Stewart corrects this remark by observing, that "it is expressed in terms too unqualified. D'Alembert has mentioned another principle, as not less fundamental, the measurement of angles by circular arches." It is obvious that both triangles and circular arches are mere forms of space. "Fluxions," says Professor Playfair, "were, with Newton, nothing else than *measures of the velocities* with which variable or flowing *quantities* were supposed to be generated, and they might be of any magnitude, providing they were in the ratio of those velocities, or, which is the same, in the ratio of the nascent or evanescent increments."[†] Sir John Herschel remarks, that "it must be recollected that there are minds which, though not devoid of reasoning powers, yet manifest a decided inaptitude for mathematical studies—which are *estimative*—not *calculating*, and which are more impressed by analogies, and by apparent preponderance of general evidence in argument, than by mathematical demonstration, where all the argument is on one side, and no show of reason can be exhibited on the other. The mathematician listens only to one side of a question, for this plain reason, that no strictly mathematical question *has* more than one side capable of being maintained otherwise than by simple assertion; while all the great questions which arise in busy life, and agitate the world, are stoutly disputed, and often with a show of reason on both sides, which leaves the shrewdest at a loss for a decision."[‡]

[*] *Philosophy of the Human Mind,* vol. ii., p. 174, edit. 1816.
[†] *Dissertation II.,* Encyc. Brit., p. 16.
[‡] *Views on Scientific and General Education, applied to the proposed System of Instruction in the South African College;* reprinted in *The London and Edinburgh Philosophical Magazine and Journal of Science,* vol. viii., p. 432. No. 48, May, 1836. See the note by Mr. Simpson, above, p. 286.

In these remarks I allude merely to pure mathematics, or to geometry and its branches, with algebra and arithmetic and their branches. Although these sciences do not treat of causation, yet they may be applied to measure forces, in every instance in which these operate with such undeviating regularity that their action may be measured by precise divisions of space and number. Gravitation is such a force. But wherever the agencies do not operate in this manner, mathematics are inapplicable. Human actions, for instance, proceed from intellectual perceptions, the impulses of affection, or the force of passion; all of which are causes, but none of them possesses that simplicity of character and uniformity of operation which are indispensable to the application of mathematical measurement. In judging of human conduct, the understanding must estimate, by innate sagacity improved by experience, the influence of motives and of external circumstances; and a high mathematical training, by exercising chiefly the powers conversant with space and quantity, is by no means favourable to the developement of this talent, which depends chiefly on Comparison and Causality, operating along with the affective faculties. Hence an individual may be distinguished for talent as a mathematician, and extremely deficient in this estimative sagacity.

It is worthy of remark, that the French mathematicians use the word *donc*, "then," where the English use "therefore" in their demonstrations. The French *donc* corresponds with the Latin *tunc*, and with the English *then*, or *at that time*, and it is the more correct expression. In a purely mathematical demonstration the conclusion becomes apparent at a particular point of time, when the proposition and its relations have been unfolded, without the least idea of active efficiency in the proposition to produce the conclusion as an effect; whereas the word *therefore* expresses a necessary result of efficiency. In the proposition "The sun shines brilliantly, *therefore* we are hot;" the word *therefore* implies a relation of causation; whereas in the proposition, "A is equal to B, and C is equal to B, *therefore* A and C are equal to one another;" the relation which it expresses is one of proportion merely, and the French *then* is more philosophical.

When the group of organs situated at the top of the nose, namely, Individuality, Form, Size, Weight, and Locality, are all large, there is generally a strong talent for dynamics. Persons thus endowed excel in turning and in archery; and if Constructiveness also be full, and they have been bred to professions in which they find no scope for these faculties, they frequently set up private workshops, and become inventors and improvers of machinery.

The organ of Locality is generally much larger in men than in women; and the manifestations correspond.

Dr. Gall cites several cases of diseased affection of this organ; and in *The Phrenological Journal** Mr. Simpson gives a highly interesting detail of symptoms attending disorder of this and the other knowing organs already treated of. He adverts particularly to the case of Mr. John Hunter, who, when in the house of a friend, forgot in what part of the town he was, and looked out of the window to refresh his memory in vain; for, as Sir Everard Home expresses it, "he had not a conception of any place existing beyond the room he was in, yet was perfectly conscious of the loss of memory."†

This organ is possessed by the lower animals, and many interesting facts are recorded of their manifestations of the faculty. Dr. Gall mentions several instances of dogs returning to their homes from a great

* Vol. ii., p. 303. See also vol. vii, p. 317.
† Life of John Hunter. annexed to his *Treatise on the Blood, Inflammation, and Gunshot Wounds,* published by Sir E. Home in 1794.

distance, without the possibility of their having been guided by smell or sight. "A dog," says he, "was carried in a coach from Vienna to St. Petersburgh, and at the end of six months reappeared in Vienna. Another was transported from Vienna to London : he attached himself to a traveller, and embarked along with him ; but, at the moment of landing, he made his escape and returned to his native city. Another dog was sent from Lyons to Marseilles, where he was embarked for Naples, and he found his way back by land to Lyons." An ass, shipped at Gibraltar, on board the Ister frigate, in 1816, was thrown overboard, when the vessel struck at Point de Gat, in Spain, a distance of 200 miles. There were holes in his ears, indicating that he had been used for carrying criminals when flogged ; and as such asses are abhorred by the peasantry, no one stopped him, and he immediately returned, through a mountainous and intricate country intersected by streams, to Gibraltar.* The common hypothesis, Dr. Gall observes, that dogs retrace their way by the aid of smell, appears abundantly absurd, when applied to cases in which they were transported by water, or in a coach ; and the idea that these animals can discover the effluvia of their master's person across a space of several hundred leagues, appears equally preposterous. Besides, a dog does not return home by the straightest road, nor even by the precise line in which he was carried away ; and some naturalists have, therefore, been induced to admit an occult cause of this surprising talent, and named it a *sixth sense*. Dr. Gall considers it to belong to the organ of Locality. The falcon of Iceland returns to its native place from a distance of thousands of miles ; and carrier-pigeons have long been celebrated for a similar tendency, and have occasionally been employed in consequence to convey despatches. Swallows, nightingales, and a variety of sea-fowls migrate from one climate to another at certain seasons of the year, which is attributed by Dr. Gall to periodical and involuntary excitement of the organ of Locality. This excitement occurs even in birds kept in cages, and abundantly supplied with food.†

The frontal sinus has been stated as an objection to the possibility of ascertaining the size of the organ of Locality, but it rarely ascends higher than the lower part of it ; and while prominences formed by the sinus are irregular in form, and generally horizontal in direction, the elevations occasioned by a large developement of Locality are uniform in shape, and extend obliquely upward toward the middle of the forehead. Farther, the negative evidence in favour of the organ is irresistible, and it is, therefore, held as established.

28. NUMBER.

A scholar of St. Poelten, near Vienna, was greatly spoken of in that city on account of his extraordinary talent for calculation. He was the son of a blacksmith, and had not received any particular instruction beyond that bestowed on other boys at the same school ; and in all other respects he was nearly on a footing of equality with them. Dr. Gall induced him to come to Vienna, and, when he was nine years of age, presented him to his audience. "Lorsqu'on lui donnait," says Dr. Gall, " je suppose, trois nombres exprimés chacun par dix à douze chiffres, en lui demandant de les additionner, puis de les soustraire deux à deux, de les multiplier et de ler diviser chacun par un nombre de trois chiffres ; il regardait une seule fois les nombres, puis il levait le nez et les yeux en l'air, et il indiquait le résultat de son calcul mental avant que mes auditeurs n'eussent eu le temps de faire le calcul la plume à la main. Il

* Kirby and Spence's *Entomology*, p. 496
† See Remarks on Carrier-pigeons, *Phren. Trans.*, vol. viii., p. 71.

avait creé lui-même sa méthode." An advocate of Vienna stated his
regret that his son, of five years of age, occupied himself exclusively with
numbers and calculation in such a manner that it was impossible to fix
his attention on any other object, even the games of youth. Dr. Gall
compared his head with that of the boy just mentioned, and found no particular resemblance, except in a remarkable prominence at the external
angle of the eye, and a little to the side. In both the eye was in some
degree covered by the outer extremity of the eyebrow. These cases
suggested the idea that the talent for calculation might be connected with
a particular organ ; and Dr. Gall sought for men distinguished for this
power, in order to verify the discovery. He repaired to the Counsellor
Mantelli, whose favourite occupation was to invent and solve problems in
mathematics, and particularly in arithmetic, and found the same configuration in him. He next went to Baron Vega, author of Tables of Logarithms, at that time professor of mathematics, and who, in every other
talent, " était un homme fort médiocre," and found in his head the same
peculiarity. He then visited private families and schools, and desired
the children distinguished for ability in calculation to be pointed out to
him ; and still the same developement recurred. He therefore felt himself constrained to admit a special organ and faculty for this talent.

Sir Whitelaw Ainslie reports, in *The Phrenological Journal*, the case
of a boy whom he met in a stage-coach, and who attracted his attention
by a remarkable developement of the organ of Number, which projected
so much as to be " nearly of the size of half a common marble, and not
unlike it in shape." On asking the boy's father whether he was not an
excellent arithmetician, Sir Whitelaw was informed that, in arithmetic,
he excelled all the other boys at school, and could multiply six figures by
other six without the aid of a pencil.*

The organ, when large, fills up the head above and outside of the external angle of the eye, a very little below the point called the external
angular process of the frontal bone.

The special function of the faculty seems to be calculation in general.
Dr. Gall calls it " *Le sens des nombres* ;" and, while he states distinctly
that arithmetic is its chief sphere, he regards it as also the organ of mathematics in general. Dr. Spurzheim, on the other hand, limits its functions to arithmetic, algebra, and logarithms ; and is of opinion that the
other branches of mathematics, such as geometry, are not the simple
results of this faculty. In this analysis he appears to me to be correct.
Mr. George Bidder, when only seven years of age, and without any
previous instruction, showed an extraordinary talent for mental calculation; and I have seen him, when only eleven, answer the most complicated questions in algebra in a minute or a minute and a half, without the
aid of notation. When he first came to Edinburgh, and before I had
seen him, a gentleman waited on me, accompanied by three boys of
nearly equal ages, and said: " One of these is George Bidder, the celebrated mental calculator ; can you tell which is he by his head !" On
examining the organ of Number in all of them, I replied that one of them
ought to be decidedly deficient in arithmetical talent ; that another should
possess it in a considerable degree ; but that the third must be Bidder,
because in him the organ was developed to an extraordinary extent.
The gentleman then stated that the indications were perfectly correct ;
that the first was a boy who had been remarked as dull in his arithmetical
studies ; the second was the most expert calculator selected from a school
in Edinburgh ; and the third was Bidder. Dr. Gall mentions a similar
experiment which was tried with him, and with the same result. He
gives a detailed account of Zhero Colburn, the American youth who exhi-

* *Phren. Journ.*, vi., 107. See another case, vol. iii., p. 266 ; also iii., 561

bited great talents for calculation, and in whom also the organ was found large. This young man visited Edinburgh, and afforded the phrenologists of this city an opportunity of verifying Dr. Gall's observations, which were found to be correct. Masks of him and of Bidder were taken, and now form part of the Phrenological Society's collection. These two examples, however, prove that Dr. Spurzheim is right in limiting the function of this faculty to calculation of numbers ; as neither of these young men has proved so eminent in geometry as in arithmetic and algebra.

The organ is large in the mask of Humboldt, brother of the traveller, and celebrated for his powers of calculation.

I am acquainted with other individuals in whom this organ is deficient, and who experience great difficulty in solving the most ordinary arithmetical questions—who, indeed, have never been able to learn the multiplication table, nor to perform readily common addition and subtraction, even after persevering efforts to attain expertness. The organ is small in the mask marked " French M. D. ;" which serves as a contrast, in this respect, to those just mentioned, in which it is large.

Dr. Gall observes, that, when this organ predominates in an individual, all his faculties receive an impression from it. He knew a physician in whom it was very large, who laboured to reduce the study of medicine, and even the virtue of particular medicaments, to mathematical principles ; and one of his friends, thus endowed, endeavoured to found a universal language on similar grounds.

This organ and Individuality, both large, give the talent of recollecting dates. Form, however, seems to aid them in this, by retaining the idea of the printed numerals.

Dr. Spurzheim mentions, that " certain races of negroes make five the extent of their enumeration, that is, they count only as far as five by simple terms ; all their numbers after five are compound, whereas ours are not so till they have passed the number ten ;. while our terms, six, seven, &c., are simple, they say five-one; five-two, five-three, &c. Negroes in general," he continues, " do not excel in arithmetic and numbers ; and, accordingly, their heads are very narrow in the seat of the organ of Number." Humboldt also mentions that the Chaymas (a people in the Spanish parts of South America) " have great difficulty in comprehending anything that belongs to *numerical* relations ;" and that " the more intelligent count in Spanish, with an air that denotes a great effort of mind, so far as 30, or perhaps 50 :" he adds, that the corner of the eye is sensibly raised *up* toward the temples."[*] The organ of Number is remarkably small in the skulls of the Esquimaux, and both Parry and Lyon notice that their eyes are turned up at the exterior angle : they have the peculiarity of " not being horizontal as with us, but coming much lower at the end next the nose than at the other."[†] Captain Back adverts to the same peculiarity in an Esquimaux woman whom he describes.[‡] This " remarkable formation of the eye," says Captain Lyon, " is in all alike."[§] Accordingly, Captain Parry speaks of their " imperfect arithmetic, which resolves every number above ten into one comprehensive word."[||] The Arctic Highlanders of Captain Ross are unable to reckon farther than five ; and, in answer to his inquiries concerning the numbers of the tribe, they could only say that there were " plenty people." Others, however, could reckon ten ¶ Nor is the skill of the other Greenland tribes much superior. Their numerals, says Crantz, " fall very short, so that they

* *Personal Narrative*, vol. iii., pp. 223, 241, 242.
† Parry's *Voyages*, 12mo., vol. v., p. 184.
‡ *Narrative of the Arctic Land Expedition* in 1833-4-5; London, 1836, p. 384.   § *Private Journal*, p. 309. || Vol. v., p. 319.
¶ Ross's *Voyage*, London, 1819, pp. 95, 127.

verify the German proverb, that they can scarce count five : however, they can make a shift with difficulty to mount as high as twenty, by counting the fingers of both hands and the toes of both feet. When the number is above twenty, they say, ' it is innumerable.' "*

It is mentioned by Dr. Gall, that two of his acquaintances felt pain in the region of this organ, after being occupied for several days in succession with difficult calculations. In the hospital of Vienna he saw a patient whose insanity degenerated into idiocy, but who, nevertheless, occupied himself solely with counting. He stopped, however, regularly at ninety-nine, and could never be induced to say one hundred, but recommenced counting at one. M. L. A. Gœlis, in his Treatise on Chronic and Acute Hydrocephalus, mentions the case of a boy who, though stupid in every other respect, still manifested, in his twelfth year, an astonishing memory for numbers and a strong feeling of Benevolence ; which qualities, however, he adds, disappeared in proportion as his malady, hydrocephalus, increased. In the *Journal Generale de Médecine†* a young Englishman is mentioned, who had a nervous attack each alternate day, during which he saw and heard nothing, as was verified by experiment, and who yet occupied himself particularly with mathematics, arithmetic, and logarithms, and solved with ease new and difficult problems. In October, 1835, I saw, in the lunatic asylum, at Newcastle, a patient named Marshall, in whom the organ of Number was very largely developed, and it was mentioned by Mr. Macintosh, the resident surgeon, that he was distinguished by a " love of arithmetic and accounts, and was perpetually employed in figures." His hands were confined to prevent him from scratching numerals on the walls, and he then used the tip of his tongue and traced them with saliva on the stones. I saw his tongue excoriated at the point with this exercise.

It seems difficult to determine whether or not this faculty exists in the lower animals. George Le Roy states, from observation, that magpies count three ; while Dupont de Nemours asserts that they count nine. Dr. Gall does not attempt to decide the question. Dr. Vimont mentions an experiment which convinced him that dogs have an idea of numbers. At a certain hour of twelve successive evenings, he gave a dog three balls of meat, which he threw into different parts of the room. Afterward he kept one of them on the table, and threw down the other two. The animal came for them as usual, but, not finding the third ball, began to search for it in every part of the room, and barked in order to obtain it : when Dr. Vimont threw down the third ball its cries immediately ceased. Its behaviour was the same when four or five pieces of meat were used.‡

The organ is established.

29. ORDER.

ORDER supposes a plurality of objects ; but one may have ideas about a number of things and their qualities, without considering them in any order whatever. Every arrangement of physical objects is not equally agreeable to the mind ; and the disposition to be delighted with order, and distressed by disorder, is not in proportion to the endowment of any other faculty. There are individuals who are martyrs to the love of order —who are distressed beyond measure by the sight of confusion, and highly satisfied when everything is well arranged. These persons have the

* Crantz's *History of Greenland,* vol. i., p. 225. See Remarks on the Character and Cerebral Developement of the Esquimaux, by Mr. Robert Cox, *Phren. Journ.,* vol. viii., p. 436.
† Tome xl., p. 155.   ‡ *Traité de Phrénologie,* tome ii., p. 321.

organ in question large. The sort of arrangement, however, prompted by this faculty is different from, although perhaps one element in. that philosophical method which is the result of the perception of the relations of things. The faculty of which we here speak gives method and order in arranging objects, as they are physically related ; but philosophical or logical inferences, the conception of systematizing or generalizing, and the idea of classification, are formed by the reflecting faculties. Dr. Spurzheim mentions, that the Sauvage de l'Aveyron, at Paris, though an idiot in a very high degree, could not bear to see a chair or any other object out of its place ; and that, as soon as anything was deranged, he, without being excited to it, directly replaced it. He likewise saw in Edinburgh a girl who, in many respects, was idiotic, but in whom the love of order was very active. She avoided her brother's apartment, in consequence of the confusion which prevailed in it.

Dr. Gall states, that he has met with facts which strongly indicate that " order " depends on a primitive faculty ; but that, on account of the difficulty of observing the organs placed in the superciliary ridge, and the small size of this organ in particular, as pointed out by Dr. Spurzheim, he had not been able to collect a sufficiency of determinate facts to authorise him to decide on its situation.*

I have seen several instances in confirmation of this organ. The late Mr. L., Fellow of the Royal College of Surgeons, of Edinburgh, whose mask is sold as an illustration of it, had a large developement ; and his love of regularity and order was conspicuous in all his professional and domestic occupations. He observed his appointments in the most exemplary manner ; wrote his letters and papers with the greatest neatness and care ; kept his accounts with invariable regularity ; and was remarkable for his neat style of dress, as well as for the high state of order in which his articles of apparel were always arranged in his wardrobe. On each superciliary ridge of his cast there is an elevation resembling a small pea, which is frequently mistaken for this organ ; that, however, appears to be merely a projecting point of the frontal bone, to which some fibres of the temporal muscle are attached. The developement of the organ is indicated by a great fulness, producing a square appearance at the external angles of the lower part of the forehead. This trait of character is hereditary in Mr. L.'s family : it was transmitted to him by his father, (whose portrait indicates a large developement,) and has descended in greater and less degrees to the members of a large family of sons. Every article which Mr. L.'s father carried about his person had its appropriate pocket, into which it was put with unfailing regularity. It is related of him, that, on one occasion, not finding his penknife in its accustomed place, he summoned his servants and some young relatives before him, and demanded whether they had seen it. Being answered in the negative, he at once unhesitatingly declared that the knife " *must have been* stolen," and upon being requested to search his other pockets, he actually lost his temper, and exclaimed, with great warmth, that the knife had not been in any other pocket for twenty years. At length, however, he was prevailed on to search another pocket, and blushed deeply on finding the strayed article. Mr. L. had a very equal general developement of brain, which aided Order in producing his general regularity of conduct. In the mask of Mr. Douglas, who also was very fond of order, the organ is largely developed. I have seen other cases, in which this part of the brain was very small, and the love of order was extremely deficient.

The mode in which a person is trained in youth has a marked influence on the activity of this organ. If brought up by regular and orderly,

* *Sur les Fonctions du Cerveau,* tome iv., p. 467.

parents, the individual will be much more ·distinguished by the same
qualities than if his early years had been spent in the midst of disorder
and dirt.

In the skulls of the Esquimaux the organ is small; and all the navigators who have visited them agree in describing their habits as most
filthy, slovenly, and disgusting.*

On the whole, therefore, I am disposed to admit the organ as ascertained. It is large in the mask marked "French M. D.," and in Franklin,
and Humboldt, brother of the traveller ; it is small in Anne Ormerod.

30. EVENTUALITY.

This organ, when large, gives prominence or a rounded fulness to the
middle of the forehead.   SHERIDAN.

    PITT.   MOORE.

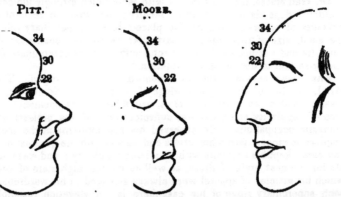

22. Individuality moderate.   22. Individuality large.   22. Individuality large.
30. Eventuality large.   30. Eventuality small.   30. Eventuality large.
34. Comparison rather large. 34. Comparison very large. 34. Comparison full.

After Dr. Gall had discovered an external sign of the talent for learning by heart, he was not long in perceiving that it by no means indicated
every species of memory. He observed, that among his school-fellows
some excelled in verbal memory, and remembered even words which they
did not understand; while others were deficient in this qualification, but
recollected, with uncommon facility, facts and events: some were distinguished by a great memory of places ; some were able to repeat, without mistake, a piece of music which they had heard only once or twice,
while others excelled in recollecting numbers and dates ; but no individual possessed *all* of these talents combined in himself. Subsequently
to these observations, he learned that philosophers before him had arrived
at similar conclusions ; and had distinguished three varieties of memory
—memory of things, " *memoria realis* ;" verbal memory, " *memoria ver-
balis* ;" and memory of places, " *memoria localis*." In society he observed
persons who, though not always profound, were learned, had a superficial
knowledge of all the arts and sciences, and knew enough to be capable
of speaking on them with facility ; and he found in them the middle of
the lower part of the forehead very much developed.   At first he regarded
this as the organ of the " memory of things ; " but, on farther reflection,
he perceived that the name " memory of things " does not include the
whole sphere of activity of the faculty now under consideration.   He
observed that persons who had this part of the brain large, not only possessed a great memory of facts, but were distinguished by prompt con-

* See ample details in *The Phrenological Journal*, vol. viii., p. 435.

ception in general, and an extreme facility of apprehension ; a strong desire
for information and instruction ; a disposition to study all branches of
knowledge, and to teach these to others : and also, that, if not restrained
by the higher faculties, such persons were naturally prone to adopt the
opinions of others, to embrace new doctrines, and to modify their own
minds according to the manners, customs, and circumstances by which
they were surrounded. He therefore rejected the name " memory of
things," and adopted the appellations " *Sens des choses, sens d'educabilité,
de perfectibilité,*" to distinguish this faculty.

These observations of Dr. Gall apply to the part of the brain comprising
the organs now designated Eventuality and Individuality ; he did not treat
of these as separate organs. We owe to Dr. Spurzheim the correct indication of the functions of each.

The function of this faculty is to take cognizance of changes, events,
or active phenomena, indicated by active verbs. In such expressions as
the ROCK *falls,* the HORSE *gallops,* the BATTLE is *fought,* the substantive
springs from Individuality, and the verb from Eventuality. It prompts to
investigation by experiment, while Individuality leads to observation of
existing things. Individuality gives the tendency to personify abstract
ideas, such as Ignorance or Wisdom ; and Eventuality to represent them
as acting. In a work written by an author with whom I was acquainted,
and in whom both of these organs were large, Ignorance and Common-
sense were represented as personages who addressed the people, excited
them to action, and themselves performed a variety of parts ; Ignorance
" stole a march on Common-sense," who, by dexterous expedients, extri-
cated himself from the difficulty. An author in whom Individuality is
large and Eventuality small, will treat his subjects by description chiefly ;
and one in whom Eventuality is large and Individuality small, will narrate
actions, but deal little in physical description.

Sheridan possessed both organs large, with those of Size and Locality
amply developed ; and the following passage affords an example of the
prominence which the physical appearances of objects obtain in his composition. Speaking of a woman and her husband, he says : " Her fat
arms are strangled with bracelets, which belt them like corded brawn.—
You wish to draw her out as you would an opera glass.—A long lean man,
with all his arms rambling ; no way to reduce him to compass, unless you
could double him up like a pocket-rule.—With his arms spread he'd lie
on the bed of Ware, like a cross on a Good-Friday bunn.—If he stands
cross-legged, he looks like a caduceus ; and put him in a fencing attitude,
you would take him for a chevaux-de-frise : to make any use of him, it
must be as a spontoon or a fishing-rod.—When his wife's by, he follows
like a note of admiration.—See them together, one's a mast, and the other
all hulk—she's a dome, and he's built like a glass-house ; when they part,
you wonder to see the steeple separate from the chancel, and were they
to embrace, he must hang round her neck like a skein of thread on a lace-
maker's bolster ; to sing her praise, you should choose a rondeau, and to
celebrate him you must write all alexandrines."

In the busts and portraits of Pope Individuality is greatly inferior in
dimensions to Eventuality ; and this author rarely excels in describing
physical appearances, while he surpasses in representing action. The
following lines from *The Rape of the Lock* are intended to describe a
beautiful lady ; but it will be observed that they represent action, condition, and quality, almost to the exclusion of substantive existence, with
its attributes of form, colour, size, and proportion :*

* Some acute and interesting observations by Mr. Hewett Watson, on the
relation between the writings of these and other authors, and their cerebral
organs, will be found in *The Phrenological Journal,* vol. vi., pp. 383, 451.

" Not with more glories in the ethereal plain,
    The sun first rises o'er the purpled main,
    Than, issuing forth, the rival of his beams
    Launched on the bosom of the silver Thames.
    Fair nymps and well-dressed youths around her shone ;
    But every eye was fixed on her alone.
    On her white breast a sparkling cross she wore,
    Which Jews might kiss, and infidels adore.
    Her lively looks a sprightly mind disclose,
    Quick as her eyes and as unfixed as those :
    Favours to none, to all she smiles extends :
    Oft she rejects, but never once offends.
    Bright as the sun her eyes the gazers strike ;
    And, like that sun, they shine on all alike.
    Yet graceful ease, and sweetness void of pride,
    Might hide her faults, if belles had faults to hide :
    If to her share some female errors fall,
    Look on her face, and you'll forget them all."

This organ is largely developed in children, and gives them an appetite
for knowledge, in the form of stories and narratives. In practical life
it gives chiefly the talent of observing, recollecting, and describing action ;
in other words, of observing the occurrences of which history is composed,
and of telling the story of what we know. When deficient, great difficulty
is experienced in observing, recollecting, and describing active phenomena.
Captain Marryat's novels exhibit the faculty strongly; and the organ appears
to be large in his portrait. The writings of Godwin show little of it, and
in his mask the organ is small.

If Eventuality be large and Concentrativeness deficient, the qualities
of observation and narration may be possessed, but the narrative will resemble a description of figures in a carnival ; it will be full of life, action,
and incident, but deficient in onward continuity : with Concentrativeness
large, the story would more nearly resemble a regular drama.

If Individuality be large, physical substances may be remembered vividly
by it, their relations in space by Locality and Order, and their causes and
effects by Causality ; but if Eventuality be deficient, extreme difficulty
will be experienced in bringing together these items of information, and
presenting them in the form of a natural narrative.

A person in whom the combination now described exists, and in whom
Concentrativeness is large, will feel strongly the desire of communicating
the quality of continuity to his narrative, and on important occasions he
will produce it by laboriously writing down all the elementary ideas of his
subject, by transposing them, by filling up, and by striking out parts, until
the whole shall cohere with neatness and consistency. Such a combination will fit its possessor for more successfully studying physical than moral
science ; because action is the primary element of the latter.

If Concentrativeness and Eventuality be both deficient, the literary or
philosophical productions of the individual will be marked by omissions
of important intermediate ideas ; in oral discourses he will combine description with inference, without taking sufficient notice of modes of action;
he will often wander from his subject ; in short, he may display great
knowledge of objects which exist, with profound reflection on their relations, and yet be unsuccessful in conveying to the minds of his readers
or auditors philosophical convictions, similar to those which exist in his
own mind. This will be owing chiefly to deficiency in the power of
representing, by Eventuality, modes of actions, and of giving, by Concentrativeness, continuity to the thread of his discourses.

Individuality, Eventuality, and Concentrativeness are indispensable
qualities to a successful teacher. I have never seen a person capable of

interesting children and exciting their intellects, who was deficient in both the first and the second. The manner of a teacher thus deficient in communicating knowledge is vague, abstract, and dry, and altogether unsuited to their mental condition. These three organs large, combined with large Philoprogenitiveness, Benevolence, and Conscientiousness, and an active temperament, constitute the leading elements of a good teacher.* Sir George Mackenzie suggests that he ought also to be gifted with a mirthful disposition.†

When both Individuality and Eventuality are large, the individual possesses two important qualities for general business. They confer that readiness of observation and talent for detail, which are essential in the management of affairs. The lawyer so endowed is able readily to apprehend the details of his cases ; to recollect the principles of law, the dicta of legal authors, and the dicisions of courts, as matters of fact ; and to reproduce the whole in a connected narrative before a judge or jury. His power of applying principles to new cases depends on the reflecting faculties ; but although these be powerful, yet, if Individuality and Eventuality be deficient, he may feel great difficulty in preparation for a trial, and in the reproduction of his ideas. In point of fact, the most eminent practical lawyers, particularly in England, are distinguished by a great developement of these organs. They are equally necessary to the public speaker, to give him a command over the *materiel* or details of his subject, and to enable him to set it forth clearly and naturally to his audience. I have observed them large also in eminent physicians ; for in the profession of medicines prompt and accurate observation is one important element in success.

Both of these organs are large in authors who acutely observe objects that exist, and also life, manners, and occurrences ; as Le Sage, Defoe, and Sir Walter Scott.‡ They are essential to the composition of such works as *Robinson Crusoe* and *Gulliver's Travels*, in which a strong impression of reality is produced by a minute description of particular objects and actions. In the skull of Swift the organs appear very large.§

When both organs are small, the individual will retain only general ideas, and will experience great difficulty in becoming learned ; he may see, hear, or read many facts, but they will make only a faint impression, and soon escape from his mind ; he will feel great difficulty in commanding, without previous preparation, even the knowledge which he possesses. These faculties desire only to know existence and phenomena, and do not reason nor trace relations. A person in whom they are strong, and in whom the reasoning powers are deficient, gains his knowledge by questioning and observation. If we tell him two facts, which clearly imply a third, he will not naturally endeavour to find it out by his own suggestion, but will instantly put another question. The tendency of these faculties also, is to recollect facts according as they occur, and not ac-

* See *The Phrenological Journal,* vol. v., p 620.
. † *General Observations on the Principles of Education : for the use of Mechanics' Institutions.* By Sir G. S Mackenzie. Bart. 1836, p. 65.
‡ Sir Walter Scott was deficient in Concentrativeness, and the absence of the mental quality is very conspicuous in his writings. The first volume of each of his novels is in general consumed before he enters fairly into his subject. With Concentrativeness large, he would have dashed into it at once, and proceeded to pour forth a condensed stream of narrative and description to the close.
§ This skull, which I examined in Dublin, presents unequivocal marks of disease, and cannot therefore be cited as evidence, except in so far as supported by authentic portraits painted before his insanity commenced. In all of these the organs of Individuality and Eventuality are represented large. See *Phren. Journ.,* vol. ix., pp. 466, 603.

cording to any philosophical relations between them. *Mrs. Quickly's* speech to *Falstaff* is a beautiful illustration of this kind of understanding. She is reminding him of his promise of marriage, and says : " Thou didst swear to me *on a parcel-gilt goblet, sitting in my Dolphin-chamber, at the round table, by a sea-coal fire, on Wednesday in Whitsunweek, when the prince broke thy head* for likening his father to a singing man of Windsor ; thou didst swear to me *then, as I was washing thy wound,* to marry me, and make me my lady thy wife. Canst thou deny it ! Did not *goodwife Keech, the butcher's wife, come in then, and call me gossip Quickly? coming in to borrow a mess of vinegar* ; telling us, *she had a good dish of prawns* ; whereby thou didst *desire to eat some* ; whereby I told thee they were ill *for a green wound* ; and didst not thou, *when she was gone down stairs, desire me to be no more so familiarity with such poor people,* saying, that ere long they should call me madam ! And didst thou *not kiss me, and bid me fetch thee thirty shillings?* I put thee now to thy book-oath ; deny it if thou canst "* Here is a surprising variety of trivial circumstances, connected by no link but that of the order of their occurrence. Yet every one must perceive that they have an effect in producing the impression of reality on the mind. We feel it impossible to doubt the promise, which is substantiated by so particular a detail of facts, every one of which becomes, as it were, a witness to its truth.

Dr. Spurzheim, in treating of Eventuality, says : " It seems to me that this faculty recognises the activity of every other, whether external or internal, and acts in its turn upon all of them. It desires to know everything by experience, and consequently excites all the other organs to activity ; it would hear, see, smell, taste, and touch ; is for of general instruction, and inclines to the pursuit of practical knowledge, and is often styled *good sense* in our proceedings. It is essential to editors, secretaries, historians, and teachers. By knowing the functions of the other powers, this faculty and Individuality contribute essentially to the unity of consciousness, and to the recognition of the entity *myself* in philosophy. Eventuality seems to perceive the impressions which are the immediate functions of the external senses, to change these into notions, conceptions, or ideas, and to be essential to attention in general. Its sphere of activity is very great, and expressed by the *verbs* in their infinitive mood. Every philosophic system has taken account of some operations of this faculty."†

Dr. Gall regarded the part of the brain comprising Individuality and Eventuality as the organ of " the sense of things " in man, and of educability or perfectibility in the lower animals. While he admits that every faculty is susceptible of improvement by education, he forms a scale of the heads of animals, from the crocodile and frog up to man, with the view of proving, that the more this part of the brain is developed in each species, the higher are its natural susceptibilities of being tamed and taught. Camper and Lavater, he adds, had made similar observations ; but they did not distinguish special faculties and organs. Dr. Spurzheim acknowledges the correctness of the facts stated by Dr. Gall, that tame animals have fuller foreheads than wild ones, and that animals are generally tameable in proportion to the development of their foreheads ; but he conceives that Dr. Gall attributes to a single faculty manifestations which depend on the intellect generally. Eventuality does not fill the whole forehead ; and the other organs situated there contribute to the effects observed by Dr. Gall. The observation of the latter, therefore, is deficient in precision, rather than in truth. Dr. Gall regarded the

* Second Part of *King Henry IV.*, Act ii., Scene 2.
† *Phrenology,* last (American) edition, p. 340.

organ of Benevolence, in the lower animals, as the source of gentleness of disposition, and described it as situated in them in the middle of the upper part of the forehead. The organ of Educability, which is distinct, he says, is situated in the middle of the *lower* part of the forehead.

The older metaphysicians do not treat of any faculty distinctly analogous to Eventuality. But Dr. Thomas Brown* admits a power of the mind, under the name of "Simple Suggestion," which corresponds very closely with it ; and he reduces Conception and Memory of the metaphysicians to this principle of Simple Suggestion.

The organ is established.

31. TIME.

THE power of conceiving time, and of remembering the relation in which circumstances stand to each other in chronology, and also the power of observing time in performing music, are very different in different individuals. Many observations have been made on this organ ; and it is now regarded as ascertained. The special faculty seems to be the power of judging of time, and of intervals of duration in general. By giving the perception of measured cadence, it appears to me one source of pleasure in dancing It is essential to music and versification.

Mr. Simpson, in an excellent essay on this faculty, published in *The Phrenological Journal*,† says : " We have found the organ largely developed in those who show an intuitive knowledge of the lapse of minutes and hours, so as to name the time of the day, without having recourse to the clock ; and also in those who perceive those minuter divisions, and their harmonious relations, which constitute rhythm, and who, when they apply the tact to music, are called good timists—a distinct power from that of the mere melodist, and often wanting in him ; while it is matter of the commonest observation, on the other hand, that this sensibility to rhythm, called time, is marked in those who have a very moderate perception of melody. Such persons are invariably accurate dancers, observing delicately the time, though indifferent to the melody of the violin. We have made many observations, both in persons who have Time and Tune large, and in those who have only one of them in large endowment, and we have never found the manifestations fail. Very lately we were struck with the uncommon prominence of the organ of Time in a whole family of young people, and inquired whether or not they danced with accuracy, and loved dancing ? We were answered, that they did both in a remarkable degree ; and, as we lived near them for some weeks, we observed that dancing was a constant and favourite pastime of theirs, even out of doors. Their dancing-master informed us, that the accuracy of their time exceeded that of any pupils he had ever taught. There was thus evident in these young persons an intense pleasure in accurate rhythmical movements."

The fact, that many deaf and dumb persons dance with precision and much pleasure, is thus accounted for by Dr. Simpson : " That time," says he, " may be marked with the utmost precision to the eye, is a fact familiar to every one who has seen a regiment of soldiers go through the manual and platoon exercise, without a single word of command, by obeying the movements of the fugle-man, who gives the time to the eye ; and who that has seen this done by a practised corps, is ignorant that there is great pleasure in witnessing the exquisitely timed movements of the exercise ? Now, suppose a dancer, unaided by music, were to keep his eye on any person or object which was marking dancing-time to his sight, it cannot be doubted that he could dance to it. A deaf person could

* *Lectures*, vol. ii., p. 192.　　　　　† Vol. ii., p. 134.

perform the manual exercise from the time given by the fugle-man ; and just as easily could a deaf person dance with his eye upon the violin-bow, or the player's arm, or on the movement of the drumsticks.

" It is unnecessary to go farther, and show that the sense of touch may be the channel through which the organ of Time is excited, as well as the sense of hearing and sight. . No one will dispute that a soldier could perform the manual exercise to a succession of taps on the shoulder ; and to time, in the same way given, might a person dance.

".What we have said is confirmed by fact. It is well known that the deaf and dumb do dance, taking the time by the eye, either from the violin-player's arm, or at second hand, but instantaneously, from the other dancers. We are acquainted with a young lady and gentleman in England, both of rank, who are deaf and dumb, and who, in addition to many accomplishments, dance with the greatest grace and precision."

Individuals are occasionally met with who estimate the lapse of time so accurately that they are able to tell the hour without having recourse to a time-piece. A case of this sort was sent by M Chavannes to the Society of Natural Sciences of Switzerland. The individual, whose name is Jean Daniel Chevalley, was visited by M. Chavanues, whose account of the case is recorded in the *Bibliothèque Universelle*, vol. xxvii. An abridgment of it, in the English *Journal of the Arts and Sciences*, is copied into a valuable paper on the faculty of Time in *The Phrenological Journal*, vol. iv., p. 517. The following is a portion of this curious case : " Being on board the steamboat on the lake of Geneva, (July 14, 1823,) he soon attracted attention by his remarks, that so many minutes and seconds had passed since they had left Geneva, or passed other places ; and, after a while, he engaged to indicate to the crowd about him the passing of a quarter of an hour, or as many minutes and seconds as any one chose, and that during a conversation the most diversified with those standing by ; and farther, to indicate by the voice the moment when the hand passed over the.quarter minutes, or half minutes, or any other subdivision previously stipulated, during the whole course of the experiment. This he did without mistake, notwithstanding the exertions of those around him to distract his attention, and clapped his hands at the conclusion of the time fixed.

" M. Chavannes then reverts to his own observations. The man said, 'I have acquired by imitation, labour, and patience, an internal movement, which neither thought, nor labour, nor anything can stop ; it is similar to that of a pendulum, which, at each motion of going and returning, gives me the space of three seconds, so that twenty of them make a minute, and these I add to others continually.' The calculations by which he obtained subdivisions of the second were not clearly understood by M. Chavannes, but the man offered freely to give a proof of his power. On trying him for a number of minutes, he shook his head at the time appointed, altered his voice at the quarter, half, and three-quarter minutes, and arrived accurately at the end of the period named. He seemed to assist himself in a slight degree by an application of mnemonics, and sometimes in idea applied religious names to his minutes up to the fifth, when he recommenced : this he carried through the hour, and then commenced again. On being told that the country people said he made use of his pulse as an indicator, he laughed at the notion, and said it was far too irregular for any such purpose.

" He admitted that his internal movement was not so sure and constant during the night ; nevertheless ' it is easy to comprehend,' he said, ' that when I have not been too much fatigued in the evening, and my sleep is soft, if, after having gently awakened me, I shall reflect a second or two, my answer will not be ten minutes in error. The approach of day renews the movement, if it has been stopped, or rectifies it, if it has been deranged, for the rest of the day.' When asked how he could renew the movement when it had ceased, he said, ' Sir, I am only a poor man ; it is not a gift of Heaven ; I obtained this faculty as the result of labours and calculations too long to be described ; the experiment has been made at night many times, and I will make it for you when you please.' M. Chavannes had not, however, the opportunity of making this experiment, but he felt quite convinced of the man's powers. He states that the man is deaf, and cannot hear at present the sound of his clock or watch ; and farther, that neither of them vibrates twenty times in a minute, which is always the number indicated by the motions of Chevalley when he wishes to illustrate his internal movement : and he is convinced, according to what he has seen, that this man *possesses a kind of internal movement, which indicates minutes and seconds with the utmost exactness.*"

An illiterate Highlander, who was long in the service of Sir G. S. Mackenzie as a ploughman, could tell the hour of the day with great exactness, and also the time of high water, although he resided seven miles from the sea. Sir George had not become acquainted with Phrenology at the period of this man's death.

Dr. Hoppe, of Copenhagen, mentions an interesting case of a morbid affection of the organ of Time, which fell under his observation in 1827. "Last October," says he, " I was called to visit Mrs. G., a nervous, but very intelligent, woman of my acquaintance, labouring under a moderate degree of *delirium puerperale.* When spoken to she was quite sensible, and gave reasonable answers. She stated, *without being particularly questioned,* that, though she was perfectly conscious of herself and of everything around her, she had no conception of time ; so that sometimes an exceedingly long period, and at other times but a few moments, seemed to her to have elapsed since she fell into her present state. She experienced a like perturbation of thought when telling me what had happened since the preceding day. She expressed great astonishment at this state of her mind, of which she was perfectly aware. She knew persons and things, and reasoned and spoke as well as ever. It was only on a few occasions, when left to herself, that she fell into slight delirium. I did not at first think phrenologically about this case ; but when she, *unquestioned,* complained of pain and a ' strong sense of burning in a *line* (these were her words) across the forehead,' I was immediately struck, and asked her to point out the place with her finger. ' There,' said she, and laid the point of her finger *most exactly* upon one of the organs of Time, drawing it across the forehead to the other organ of Time. I asked if she felt pain in any other part of the head. ' No,' replied she, ' only in this line.' "*

The origin of the notion of time has greatly puzzled the metaphysicians. Lord Kames says, that we measure it by the number of ideas which pass in the mind ; but experience contradicts this supposition, for time never appears so short as when ideas are most numerous, and pass most rapidly through the mind. The opinion, that it depends on a separate faculty and organ, on the other hand, is in harmony with this fact ; for, as the organ of Time may remain inactive while the others are vividly excited, it follows, that our perceptions of duration will, on such occasions, be indistinct, and time will, in consequence, appear brief.

The talent of using tenses properly in composition appears to be dependent on this organ

The lower animals seem to be endowed with the power of perceiving and appreciating intervals of time. "Mr. Southey, in his *Omniana,* relates two instances of dogs, who had acquired such a knowledge of time, as would enable them to count the days of the week. He says : 'My grandfather had one which trudged two miles *every Saturday* to cater for himself in the shambles. I know another more extraordinary and well-authenticated example. A dog which had belonged to an Irishman, and was sold by him in England, would never touch a morsel of food *upon Friday.*' The same faculty of recollecting intervals of time exists, though in a more limited extent, in the horse. We know a horse," says the writer from whom I quote, "(and have witnessed the circumstance,) which, being accustomed to be employed once a week on a journey with the newsman of a provincial paper, always stopped at the houses of the several customers, although they were sixty or seventy in number. But, farther, there were two persons on the route who took one paper between them, and each claimed the privilege of having it first on the alternate Sunday. The horse soon became accustomed to this regulation, and, although the parties lived two miles distant, he stopped once a fortnight at the door of the half customer at Thorpe, and once a fortnight at the door of the other half customer at Chertsey ; and never did he forget this arrangement, which lasted several years, or stop unnecessarily, when he once thoroughly understood the rule."* Dr. Vimont thinks it impossible to doubt that the lower animals possess the faculty of appreciating time ; and he relates several facts in support of this opinion.†

32. TUNE.

Dr. Gall mentions, that a girl named Bianchi, of about five years of age, was presented to him, and he was asked for what talent she was most distinguished. He discovered in her no indication of an extraordinary memory ; and the idea had not then occurred to him, that the talent for music could be recognised by the conformation of the head. Indeed, he had not at that time ascertained the different kinds of memory ; but his friends, nevertheless, maintained, that the girl had an extraordinary memory for music, and, as he had not discovered that talent in her, they inferred that the doctrine which he taught of external signs for different kinds of memory was unfounded. This child repeated whatever she heard sung or played on the piano, and recollected whole concerts if she had heard them only twice. Dr. Gall asked if she learned by heart with equal facility, but he was told that she possessed this astonishing memory in music alone. He concluded that a well-marked difference exists between memory for music and the other kinds of memory with which he was then acquainted, and that every kind has its distinct organ. He prosecuted his observations with fresh ardour, and at last discovered that the talent for music is connected with the organ now under consideration. He calls it " *Le sens des rapports des tons;*" an expression, says he, " qui rattache la manière dont l'intellect du musicien met en œuvre les rapports des tons à la manière d'agir des sens en général."

The organ of Tune bears the same relation to the ears which the organ of Colouring does to the eyes. The auditory apparatus receives the impressions of sounds, and is agreeably or disagreeably affected by them ; but the ear has no recollection of tones, nor does it judge of their relations : it does not perceive the harmonies of sound ; and sounds as well as colours may be separately pleasing, though disagreeable in combination. A friend, in a letter written from India, formerly quoted, says : " Melody is the pleasure arising from successions of simple sounds suited to each

* *Library of Entertaining Knowledge,* vol. i., p. 55. Another case of a dog which obviously distinguished the days of the week, will be found in *The Phrenological Journal,* vol. viii., p. 76.

† *Traité de Phrénologie,* tome ii., p. 330.

other. Harmony is that arising from *combined* sounds, or from several
striking the ear simultaneously, as in a band playing different parts. The
former requires much less of the organ than the latter ; and hence the
Scotch with no great Tune are melodists, but nothing as musicians."

A correspondent of *The Phrenological Journal* mentions, that " he has
a most singular tendency to compare one thing with another : for instance,
if he hears the piano played, every sound seems to resemble a particular
colour ; and so uniform is this, that he thinks he could almost make a
gamut of colours. Some notes are yellow, others green, others blue,
and so forth." In him Comparison is large, but neither Colouring nor
Tune is much developed.*

A great developement of the organ enlarges the lateral parts of the
forehead ; but its appearance varies according to the direction and form
of the convolutions. Dr. Spurzheim observes, that, in Glück and others,
this organ had a pyramidal form ; in Mozart, Viotti, Zumsteg, Dussek,
Crescentini, and others, the external and lateral portions of the forehead
are enlarged, but rounded. Great practice is necessary to be able to observe this organ successfully ; and beginners should place together one
person possessing a genius for music, and another who can scarcely distinguish between any two notes, and mark the difference of their heads.
The superior developement of the former will be perceptible at a glance.

The faculty gives the perception of melody ; but this is only one
ingredient in a genius for music. Time is requisite to give a just perception of intervals, Ideality to communicate elevation and refinement, and
Secretiveness and Imitation to produce expression ; while Constructiveness, Form, Weight, and Individuality are necessary to supply mechanical expertness : qualities all indispensable to a successful performer.
Even the largest organ of Tune will not enable its possessor to play
successfully on the harp, if Weight be deficient ; the capacity of communicating to the string the precise vibratory impulse necessary to produce
each particular note will then be wanting.

Dr. Gall mentions that he had examined the heads of the most celebrated
musical performers and singers, such as Rossini, Catalani, &c., and found
the organ uniformly large ; and that the portraits and busts of Haydn,
Glück, Mozart, &c., also show it largely developed. I have examined
the heads of Madame Catalani and many eminent private musicians, and
found the organ confirmed in every instance. Dr. Gall remarks farther,
that a great developement is not to be expected in every ordinary player
on a musical instrument. With a moderate endowment, the fingers may
be trained to expertness ; but when the soul feels the inspiration of harmonious sounds, and the countenance expresses that voluptuous rapture
which thrills through the frame of the real musician, a large organ will
never be wanting.

" Il me paraît," continues Dr. Gall, " que les hommes qui sont capables
de déduire les lois le la composition des lois des vibrations sonores et des
rapports des tons, et d'établir ainsi les principes les plus généraux de la
musique, doivent être doués en même temps *d'un organe des nombres*
très developpé ; car l'exercice de ce degré du talent musical exige, sans
contredit, beaucoup de calcul ; aussi la circonvolution inférieure de l'organe musical, la plus large de toutes se continue immédiatement dans
l'organe des nombres. Ceci explique pourquoi on peut être excellent
musicien, et n'avoir pas le talent de la composition ; être grand composi-
teur sans être en même temps grand musicien."*

The heads of Italians and Germans in general are broader and fuller
at the situation of this organ than those of negroes, Spaniards, French.

* Vol. viii., p. 216.
†. *Sur les Fonctions du Cerveau*, tome v., p. 119.

men, and Englishmen in general ; and musical talent is more common in the former than the latter. The Esquimaux are very deficient both in the talent and in the organ.[*]

Mr. Scott has published, in *The Phrenological Journal*,[†] two admirable essays " on Music, and the different faculties which concur in producing it," which will be found highly deserving of attention. He conceives Tune to be the primitive faculty which distinguishes, " 1st, that agreement of component vibrations in simple sounds, which constitutes them *musical*; 2d; that, relation in separate sounds emitted together, which constitutes *harmony*; and, 3d, that relation in successive notes, which constitutes melody." He then considers the *auxiliary faculties* requisite to the practical musician, (namely those above enumerated,) and points out the effect of each in conducing to musical genius. " Imitation," says he, " is necessary, particularly to the vocal performer, to enable him to imitate the sounds he hears, and to give, by his own vocal organs, a correct copy of the music which he wishes to execute. Accordingly, it is matter of observation that all singers who sing naturally and easily, possess a considerable organ of Imitation." He next enters, at considerable length, into the subject of musical expression. " It seems to me," says he, " although I do not pretend to have made observations sufficiently accurate and numerous to prove the fact, that there is a correspondence in all cases between the voices of men and women, and their cerebral developement. The subject is a very curious one, and I mention it more for the purpose of inducing others to make observations, than from any value I attach to any observations of my own. Some facts there are, however, which are matters of common notoriety, and which go far to prove that there is at least a general correspondence ; and farther light might, doubtless, be thrown upon it by more accurate and minute observers.

· " In the first place, it is a general rule, that the heads of women are comparatively smaller than those of men, and that their voices are, in a corresponding degree, smaller and shriller than the male voice.

" Boys under puberty, who have smaller heads than full-grown men, have voices small, shrill, and soft, like a woman's.

" The voices of children of both sexes, but particularly girls, are shriller than even the adult female voice.

" As boys advance from puberty to manhood, and just at the time when the head is receiving the largest accessions, the voice is changed from the small shrill pipe of the boy to the grave tones of the man.

" In men who have small or moderately-sized heads, particularly if the lower propensities are moderately developed, the voice approaches to the shrill pitch and softness of a woman's.

" In women who have large heads, particularly if the lower propensities are fully developed, the voice is generally grave, and approaches in its tones to a man's. I have been informed, that it has been observed of women who are subject to *nymphomania*, that, when under the influence of a paroxysm, their voices are harsh, low, and rough, like those of men. This fact, if sufficiently established, would go far to prove that low and rough notes are the natural language of the lower propensities.

" So far I have observed in general ; but I would wish that those who, have an opportunity would make observations which may confirm the above, or show whether there are any exceptions to the rule. I do not recollect to have seen any. It would be desirable to ascertain whether all the bass-singers in our bands and choirs have large heads, and the counter-tenors among men small ones ; or whether the depth of voice is in proportion to the developement of the cerebellum ;—whether the women singers, whose voices are pitched low, have larger heads, or a fuller endowment of the lower propensities, than those who have treble voice.

"It is undoubted, that the quality of tone, as well as the pitch, depend considerably on the nature of the developement. In women who possess Combativeness and Destructiveness well developed, the voice, though shrill, is sharp, and the tones pierce the ear like a sword. In women who are given to scolding, this sharp piercing quality of voice will invariably be noticed; and it forms one of the most unpleasant circumstances attending it. If the lady would utter the same words in a moderate tone, the nuisance would not be nearly so great. In like manner, in men who have large Destructiveness, if the head is otherwise large and well-balanced, the voice, though grave, will be clear, and have a peculiar edge and sharpness, which Destructiveness alone seems to give.

"When the head is in general large, but Destructiveness deficient, the voice will probably be grave and full, but soft, and will want the sharp ringing quality which Destructiveness confers. This is a voice, from its rarity, much in request among singers, and is called a veiled voice (voce velata.) Madame Marconi, who sung at the first Edinburgh Festival, had a voice of this description. She was said to have been remarkable for good nature.

"In those in whom intellect predominates, the voice has a calm and composed, but not a touching expression. When Benevolence and the kindly and social affections are large, and when Tune, Imitation, and Ideality are at the same time large, the voice has a degree of bewitching softness, as may be observed in the case of Miss Stephens or Miss Tree. But there occur in private life many instances to the same effect. When Benevolence and the higher sentiments are both united in full proportion, the voice is felt to be peculiarly delightful and harmonious. In men there is generally too much of the lower propensities to admit of this in its highest degree; indeed, these seem so essential to a manly character, that in them it would not be desirable. But we have met with women whose every tone is music, and whose voices, even in ordinary discourse, have about them a delightfulness which is quite irresistible, and which makes its way directly to the heart. This softness and sweetness of voice is remarked as a great point of female excellence by *King Lear*, where the old distressed monarch is enumerating the excellencies of his favourite *Cordelia*—

'——Her voice was ever soft,
Gentle and low—an excellent thing in woman.' "*

These observations of Mr. Scott are very interesting, and numerous cases have been observed in accordance with them; but they are not absolutely correct, because I have met with decided exceptions. One gentleman, in particular, has a moderate-sized head, small cerebellum, and the other organs of the propensities below an average, whose voice is, nevertheless, a deep rich bass. It is certain that the developement of brain has some, and even an important, influence on the quality of the voice: but so have the lungs and larynx; and it is still unascertained how much of the actual effect is attributable to each.†

When an average developement of Tune is combined with large reflective organs, the superior objects with which these are conversant generally attract the mind, and music is little cultivated. When, on the other hand, these are small, and Ideality, Hope, Benevolence, Veneration, and Won-

* *Phrenological Journal*, vol. ii., p. 575.
† I have observed that large lungs, which imply a correspondingly large heart and bloodvessels, are highly favourable to intensity of action in the brain. The blood is then well oxygenated, and it is sent to the brain copiously, and with great energy.

der, which Tune is particularly calculated to gratify, are large, the tendency to practise music is much stronger. Hence, with the same absolute developement of this organ, very different practical results may ensue; but this is in exact accordance with the principles of the science : for it is the *predominance* of particular organs in an individual that decides the bias of his mind ; the largest organs always tending most powerfully to seek gratification.

Tune is occasionally found strong in idiots, and; in some insane patients, its activity remains unimpaired amid an extensive derangement of the other faculties. I have seen two idiots who manifested it in a considerable degree.

The following case is reported by Dr. Andrew Combe, and occurred in his own practice :

" A young lady of high musical and intellectual powers, and of a very active mind, and who has for some months past been subject to frequent attacks of hysteria in all its ever-changing forms and who suffers almost constantly in a greater or less degree from headache, complained, on Saturday, 22d April, 1826, of feeling acute pain at the external angle of the forehead, precisely in the situation of the organs of Tune, which are largely developed, and upon which, in describing the seat of the pain, she placed most accurately the points of the fingers. Next day the same complaint of pain in that region was made ; and about two hours after I saw her, she was suddenly seized with a spasmodic, or rather convulsive, affection of the larynx, glottis, and adjoining parts, in consequence of which a quick, short, and somewhat musical sound was regularly emitted, and continued with great rapidity, as if the breathing had been very hurried. On examination externally, the os hyoides at the root of the tongue and the thyroid cartilages were seen in constant motion, and in the act of alternately approximating and receding from each other. The will was so far powerful in controlling this motion, that the young lady was able to utter a few short sentences at a time without much difficulty ; interrupted, however, by two or three movements. After this singular state had continued for about two hours, she herself remarked, that it was become rather too musical, and wished that it would cease, which it did at the end of another half hour, from accidental pressure with the finger in pointing out the motion to another person ; she was then as well as usual, only somewhat fatigued.

" On Monday, 24th April, she still complained of pain in the situation of the organ of Tune ; and stated, that she had been dreaming a great deal of *hearing the finest music ;* that she felt quite excited by it, and could not even now get the impression out of her head. The day passed on, however, and nothing remarkable occurred.

" On Tuesday I found that I had been rather anxiously expected. During the night the young lady had been tormented with the recurrence of the musical dreams, during which she heard and performed the most beautiful airs, with a distinctness which surpassed those of the preceding night. These dreams continued for some hours, and left such an impression, that, on awaking, she thought she could almost note down one piece of composition which had particularly pleased her. But what is very remarkable, the excessive excitement of the faculty of Tune had now reached a height that could not be controlled ; the patient felt, not a desire only, but a *strong and irresistible passion or craving* for music, which it was painful beyond endurance to repress. She insisted on getting up, and being allowed to play and sing ; but that being for many reasons unadvisable, she then begged to have a friend sent for to play to her, as the only means of relief from a very painful state ; but shortly after the craving of the faculty became so intolerable, that she got hold of a guitar, lay down upon a sofa, and fairly gave way to the torrent, and, with a volume, clearness, and strength of voice, and a facility of execution, which would have astonished any one who had seen her two days before, she sung in accompaniment till her musical faculty became spent and exhausted. During this time the pain at the angles of the forehead was still felt, and was attended with a sense of fulness and uneasiness all over the coronal and anterior parts of the forehead. Regarding all these phenomena as arising from over-excitement chiefly of the organs of Tune, I directed the continued local application of cold, and such other measures as tended to allay the increased action, and soon after the young lady regained her ordinary state, and has not since had any return of these extraordinary symptoms.

" In this case the order in which the phenomena occurred put *leading queries* on my part, or exaggeration or deception on the part of the patient, alike out of the question. The pain in the organ was distinctly and repeatedly complained of for many hours (at least 36) before the first night of dreaming, and for no less than *three days* before the irresistible waking inspiration was felt. When my attention was first drawn to the existence of the pain, I imagined it to arise from an affection of the membranes covering that part of the brain, and had no conception that it was to terminate in any such musical exhibition as afterward took place ; and, in fact, although the young lady had mentioned her previous melodious dreams, my surprise was quite equal to, although, thanks to Phrenology, my alarm was not so great as, that of her relations; when, on entering the house on the morning of Tuesday the 25th, I heard the sound of the guitar mingling with the full and harmonious swell of her own voice, such as it might show itself when in the enjoyment of the highest health and vigour."

It is a prevalent error in education, to persevere in attempts to cultivate musical talent where none is naturally possessed. Dr. Neil Arnott speaks feelingly of the lamentable consequences of the ignorant prejudice " that in the present day condemns many young women, possessed of every species of loveliness and talent except that of *note-distinguishing*, to waste years of precious time in an attempt to acquire this talent in spite of nature ; and yet, when they have succeeded as far as they can, they have only the merit of being machines, with performance as little pleasing to true judges as would be the attempt of a foreigner, who knew only the alphabet of language, to recite pieces of expressive poetry in that language. Such persons, when liberty comes to them with age or marriage, generally abandon the offensive occupation ; but tyrant fashion will force their daughters to run the same course."*

The organ is large in Haydn and Macvicar ; small in Sloane, and remarkably deficient in Ann Ormerod. This girl was admitted, at twelve years of age, into the asylum for the blind at Liverpool, and, during two years, means were unsparingly employed to cultivate and improve any musical talent which she might possess : but " with such decided want of success, that her teachers, Mr. Handford and Mr. Platt, men of unceasing perseverance, and constantly accustomed to the most stubborn perverseness, were at last under the necessity of abandoning the attempt altogether."† The figures represent her head, the organ of Tune being thrown into the outline on her left side—and the head of Handel, the organ being brought into line on his right side.

Dr. Spurzheim mentions, that the heads and skulls of birds which sing, and of those which do not sing, and the heads of the different individuals of the same kind which have a greater or less disposition to sing, present a conspicuous difference at the place of this organ. · The heads of males, for instance, and those of females, of the same kind of singing birds, are

HANDEL.   ANN ORMEROD.

easily distinguished by their different developement.   Dr. Vimont protests
against Gall's practice of comparing the skulls of animals of different
species at the situation of this organ; "such a practice," says he, "is
extrêmement vicieuse; for there are many varieties of developement of organs which Gall had not studied, and which are calculated to lead into error.
The result of my anatomical researches," he adds, " to which I have given
the closest attention, is, that the difference of organization of the brain
and skull between musical birds and those which do not sing, is appre-
ciable only in comparing individuals of the same species or genus."*

33. LANGUAGE.

THE history of the discovery of this organ has already been given in
the introduction, p. 60.

A large developement of it is indicated by the prominence and depression of the eyes; this appearance being produced by convolutions of the
brain, situated in the posterior and transverse part of the upper orbitary
plate, pressing the latter, and with it the eyes, more or less forward, downward, or outward, according to the size of the convolutions.   When the
knowing organs are very large, and the eyebrows project, the eyes may
appear less prominent than they really are.   The projection of the eyes
over the cheek-bone, and their depression downward, are the proper signs
of the organs being large.

The functions of this organ will be understood by a short elucidation.
The different faculties being active, produce desires, emotions, and intellectual conceptions.   The mind, wishing to communicate a knowledge
of these to other individuals, accomplishes this end by making *signs* expressive of their existence.   These signs may consist of the peculiar
gestures, looks, and cries that naturally accompany the action of the several faculties, and which, being part of our constitution, are universally
understood, and constitute what is termed natural language.   For example,
when the mind is deeply impressed by fear, a certain terror-stricken expression is spread over the countenance, indicative of the emotion.   When
it is wrapped in pride, the head is carried high, and a cold, repulsive, arrogant aspect is presented to the spectator.   These signs need only to be
presented, and they are understood in all countries, and by all nations.

But mankind possess also the power of inventing and establishing
arbitrary signs to express their feelings and conceptions.   For example,
the words *love, compassion,* and *anger* are mere conventional signs, by
which we in Britain agree to express three internal feelings; and there

* *Traité de Phrénologie,* tome. ii, p. 371.

is no natural connexion between the signs and the things signified. The metaphysicians attribute this talent to association; but it is a peculiar power of association given by the faculty of Language only. Persons possessing much of this faculty, have a great natural power of inventing arbitrary signs, and of learning the use of them when invented by others. This faculty, however, gives the capacity of learning the *signs alone*; and the *meaning* of them is acquired by other faculties. If a horse, for instance, be presented to the mind, the faculty of Language will give the desire to find a name or sign by which to indicate it, and also the power of associating the appearance of the object with any particular sound or name when invented But the meaning or signification which the word will embrace will depend on the perfection of other faculties, and the extent to which they have been used. For example, the faculty of Form will judge of the form of the horse ; Size, of its dimensions ; Colouring, of its colour. A blind man, by the aid of the faculty of Language, may learn to connect his own notions of a horse with the sound of the name , but his conceptions will be very different from those attached to it by a person who sees ; for the blind man could not judge of its colour at all, and not very correctly of its form and size. In the same way, any individual possessing the organ of Language, may learn the manner in which the word *justice* is generally used ; but the meaning attached to it in the mind of a person like David Haggart, who was extremely deficient in the organ of Conscientiousness, will be very imperfect when compared with the notion which would be formed of it by one in whom that organ was extremely large.

Every metaphysical author complains of the ambiguity of words, and shows how the vagueness of their signification retards the progress of moral and intellectual science : the exposition now given shows whence this vagueness arises. Before individuals can attach precisely the same conceptions to words expressive of feelings and judgments of the understanding, they must possess a similar combination of faculties ; and as no two individuals do possess an exactly similar combination of faculties, so as to be capable of feeling and judging alike, there will be shades of difference in the meaning attached by different persons to such terms, in spite of every effort to define them In consequence of this difference in the faculties, the very definition itself is differently apprehended. In mathematics and algebra the things indicated by the signs are not feelings, which vary in every individual, but relations and proportions of space and numbers, which have a definite and fixed existence, and which, if apprehended at all, can be conceived only in one way. Hence arises the precision of the language of these sciences compared with that of metaphysics and moral philosophy.

If these principles be correct, they demonstrate the impossibility of framing a philosophical language, applicable, with perfect precision, to moral disquisitions To apprehend the very definitions of the words, we must be able to experience the sentiments which they are intended to indicate ; and many persons are capable of doing so only in a very imperfect degree. In attending to the style of an author, we may observe that he uses those words with most precision and felicity which express mental feelings or operations naturally vigorous in himself. Mr. Stewart, for example, writes correctly and with great beauty in narrative, and on topics connected with moral sentiment ; but his style becomes loose and inaccurate when he enters on original abstract discussion, requiring the activity of the higher intellectual powers. I infer from this, that, in him, the knowing and sentimental organs were more amply developed than those of reflection. Moore uses epithets and illustrations expressive of attachment with great frequency and inimitable beauty ; and we may conclude that, in him, Adhesiveness, which gives that feeling, is very strong. John Bellingham, on the other hand, in his voluminous memorials, petitions, and letters, was continually writing about justice and injustice, and about cruelty and oppression exercised toward him ; but the acts which he specified are discovered, by every well-constituted mind, not at all to possess the character which he ascribes to them, and his writings on these points are replete with the grossest abuses of words. This, I apprehend, arose from the great deficiency of Conscientiousness which is discernible in his head. In professional practice also every lawyer meets with individuals who pretend ardently to desire justice, and who speak incessantly about it, but who evidently do not perceive at all what it is; the selfish faculties in their case so far predominating over Conscientiousness, that they never attain correct notions of justice. The same thing happens in regard to religion. Many talk about it, and against it, without in the least comprehending the object of their vituperation. In like manner, every one will acknowledge in words that charity is a duty ; but, on inquiring of different persons what constitutes charity, we shall find their notions of the meaning of the word, and of the duty also, to vary exceedingly, according to their developement of Benevolence, in proportion to Acquisitiveness and Self-Esteem. *

The power of associating, by means of the faculty of Language, conceptions with signs is limited, however, in one respect. Any *indifferent* object may be selected and used as the arbitrary sign of a propensity, sentiment, or conception ; but if the object already stands in a *natural* relation to any faculty, it cannot, except with great difficulty, be made the arbitrary sign of an opposite emotion. For example, we might, by a mutual understanding, constitute a square figure the artificial sign of the emotion termed *rage*. After the agreement was understood, that figure would suggest the notion of rage just as well as the letters now composing that word, which are mere forms, placed in a certain order. But, if we were whimsical enough to make the outline of a sweet and smiling countenance, which likewise is merely a species of form, the sign of this emotion, we could not, without great difficulty, learn to associate the idea of rage with that figure, for it is already the natural sign of emotions entirely opposite : it would excite Benevolence *directly*, more forcibly than Destructiveness indirectly, through the medium of Language ; it would call up ideas of joyfulness and innocence, rather than of anger and cruelty. In the same way, we might associate feelings of veneration, pity, affection, or grief with soft and *slow* notes of music, because these notes, which are calculated to produce emotions of a specific kind themselves, may become arbitrary signs of any other emotions of a *homogeneous kind*. But it would be difficult to form an association, by which soft, slow, and delicate

---

* These principles enable us to explain, in a simple manner, the source and nature of eloquence. It is a trite observation, that every passion is eloquent ; that is to say, any propensity or sentiment being vividly active, excites the faculty of Language to give it utterance ; and when the mental emotion is strongly felt, the words partake of the force, and are distinguished by the precision, which characterize the feeling. Popular eloquence draws largely from the propensities and sentiments, and hence, in many distinguished orators, we do not observe so large a developement of the intellectual organs as those persons would expect who imagine that oratory is altogether an intellectual product ; but in them an ample endowment of the organs of the propensities and sentiments will be discovered. The Phrenological Society possesses masks of Burke and Curran. The former is by much the more distinguished for intellect in his printed remains, and his forehead is the better developed ; but the impression made by Curran on a popular assembly was perhaps the greater of the two. On analyzing Curran's orations, however, as formerly remarked, (section on Wit,) no higher degree of reflecting power will be discovered in them than what is indicated by his mask.

tones should become the artificial signs of violent rage, jealousy, and fury; because the *natural* character of such sounds is directly opposite to the character of such feelings.

Philosophers have written voluminous disquisitions on the influence of words on thought; but if the view now presented be correct, feelings and conceptions must, in every instance, *precede* words; and the invention of a term for which no idea exists, instead of being a step toward the advancement of knowledge, would be a simple absurdity. It is true, that the language of any nation is a correct index of its attainments; but this happens, because, in proportion as a people acquire notions, they invent words to express them, and hence their language is commensurate with their mental states.

The art of *writing* greatly facilitates the progress of knowledge; but it does so only by giving precision to words and permanence to thought. Written words are to thinking what ciphers are to calculation; they record our past attainments, and enable us to advance, unencumbered, in the path of discovery: in no instance, however, can they possibly precede the march of ideas. The new nomenclature of chemistry smooths the study of that science; but the nomenclature itself was the *result* of correct and enlarged ideas of the nature and relation of chemical substances, and could not possibly have been formed before these were obtained.

If these principles are sound, it is a grievous error in education to devote the years of youth chiefly to the study of languages. In all cases knowledge of objects and their qualities and relations should precede the study of words; for it is only in consequence of that previous knowledge that words become significant and useful; and languages are merely words. A good education should embrace the culture of *all* the faculties; which can be attained only by exercising each on its own objects, and regulating its action.

Persons who have a great endowment of the organ of Language, abound in words. In ordinary conversation their words flow like a copious stream—in making a speech they pour out torrents. When this organ is extremely large and those of reflection small, the individual is prone to repeat, to the inconceivable annoyance of the hearer, the plainest sentences again and again, as if the matter were of such difficult apprehension, that one enunciation was not sufficient to convey the meaning. This practice appears to originate in an immoderate power and activity of the faculty of Language—so great, that delight is felt in mere articulation, independently of reflection. The same combination produces a verbose, cumbersome, and inelegant style of literary composition. Thomson's *Seasons* are chargeable with a redundancy of words, and in the portraits and busts of the author the organ appears very large. In *Dramas of the Ancient World*, by David Lindsay, we meet with examples of this kind of writing:

> " My gracious kinsman,
> What good occasion now hath brought thee hither?
> Noah. Nothing of good, for good is flown for ever
> Away from this *stained* world; and *spotless* truth
> And *weeping* mercy, veiling their *bright* looks
> With their *spread* pinions, have forsaken earth,
> And sought a refuge at the sacred foot
> Of the Almighty's throne."
> *The Deluge*, p. 15.

Another example occurs in the following passage, extracted from a periodical publication:

" We hope it will prove interesting to our readers occasionally to take a *popular sketch* of the *brilliant success* attending the *meritorious actions* of the *respectable circle* of *scientific chemists*, whose pursuits, if judiciously exhibited, are fitted to interest every mind endowed with intellectual curiosity."

When the organ is very small, there is a want of command of expression, a painful repetition of the same words, and a consequent poverty of style, both in writing and in speaking. The style of that author is generally most agreeable in whom the organs of Language and of Reflection bear a just proportion to each other. If the intellectual powers are very acute and rapid, and Language not in equal proportion, a stammer in speech is frequently the consequence. Individuality, Eventuality, Time, Comparison, and Imitation greatly assist this faculty, when applied to the acquisition of foreign languages and grammar. I have observed that boys who are *duces* in classes for languages, generally possess such a combination; and that this endowment, with moderate Language, accomplishes more, in the way of scholarship, than a large developement of the latter organ, with a small endowment of the others. Such individuals have a great facility in recollecting rules, as matters of fact and detail, in tracing etymologies, and in discriminating tenses and shades of meaning: the combination alluded to gives them great readiness also in using their knowledge, whatever the extent of it may be.

The doctrine before laid down, that the signification of words is learned by other faculties, removes an apparent difficulty, in regard to learning to repeat, which occasionally presents itself. A person with a moderate organ of Language, will sometimes learn songs, poetry, or particular speeches, by heart, with considerable facility and pleasure; but in such cases the passages committed to memory will be found highly interesting to his other powers, such as Ideality, Causality, Tune, Veneration, Combativeness, or Adhesiveness; and the study and recollection of vocables only, will be difficult and disagreeable to him. To a person, on the other hand, in whom the organ is decidedly large, mere words are interesting, and he can learn them without caring much about their meaning. Hence also, a person with a moderate organ of Language and good reflecting organs, may, by perseverance, learn languages, and attain proficiency as a scholar; but he will not display copiousness, fluency, and richness of expression in his style, either in his own or in a foreign tongue.

There appears to be a quality of brain, no external indication of which is known, which communicates the character of retentiveness to all the intellectual organs, and which greatly augments their power of remembering the impressions which they have received. Sir Walter Scott appears to have possessed this quality; for it is said that he never forgot anything which he had ever heard, seen, or read.

It is difficult to determine precisely on what powers the talent for learning the *spirit* of languages depends. The fact is certain, that some individuals easily learn the spirit of different languages without having a great memory for words; while others readily acquire words, without catching the spirit of any language. Dr. Gall admits two organs of Language; one he names "*Sens des mots, sens des noms, mémoire des mots, mémoire verbale;*" and the other, "*Sens du langage de parole; talent de la philologie:*" to the latter he attributes the talent for philology, and for acquiring the spirit of languages. The former organ he describes as lying on the posterior half of the super-orbitar plate, and, when large, pushing the eyes outward; it gives a talent for learning and recollecting words, and persons possessing it large recite long passages by heart, after reading them once or twice. The latter organ, says he, is placed on the middle of the anterior part of the super-orbitar plate, and, when it is large, the eyeball not only projects, but is depressed; the depression producing the appearance of a bag or folding in the lower eyelid. Persons possessing this form of eyes, he adds, have not only an excellent memory of words, but a particular disposition for the study of languages, for criticism, and, in general, for all that has reference to literature.[*] Dr. Gall states, at the same time, that the determination of the size of the organ of words is attended with much difficulty ; as, from its situation, it may extend itself to the sides as well as forward—increasing, in the former case, the general breadth of the head across the temples, or even between the eyes ; so that much remains to be ascertained in regard to it.

Dr. Spurzheim, on the other hand, admits only one organ of Language, lying transversely on the posterior portion of the super-orbitar plates ; and holds that it takes cognizance both of words and of the spirit of languages—that it "makes us acquainted with arbitrary signs, remembers them, judges of their relations, and gives a disposition to indulge in all exercises connected with words." "It seems to me," says he, "that the organ of words must have its laws as well as those of Colour, Melody, or any other faculty. Now, the law of words constitutes the spirit of language. I am satisfied," he continues, "that this opinion is correct ; because the spirit of every language is the same, just as the essence of all kinds of music is alike ; that is, the laws or principles of music and of language rule universally, and are constant ; they are only modified in different nations, by modifications in their organs, and dissimilar combinations of these in each."[†]

I am disposed to coincide with Dr. Spurzheim in this view ; and, perhaps, by analyzing the source whence the structure of language proceeds, we may obtain some light on the origin of a taste for the spirit of languages, as distinguished from the power of learning and recollecting words. Language, then, expresses merely the feelings and conceptions produced by the various primitive faculties acting separately or in combination. Now, let us imagine the cerebral developement of a nation to be distinguished by large organs of the propensities, sentiments, and knowing faculties, small reflecting organs, and little Secretiveness. Their language, being the spontaneous growth of such a combination, would naturally abound in words expressive of simple feelings, and conceptions of individual objects and their qualities ; while it would be poor in terms of abstract relation, conceived by the faculties of reflection. For the same reason, the transitions of such a language would be like those in Mrs. Quickly's speech, rapid, and in the order of the casual occurrence of the circumstances which excited the ideas : Secretiveness being small, there would naturally be little involution in the arrangement of the words. Suppose, on the other hand, that in another nation Secretiveness and the reflecting organs predominated ; the genius of their language would differ widely from that of the people first described. Their expressions for discriminating individual conceptions would be fewer, while their stock of words and phrases, designative of abstract relations, would be more extensive, and the general structure of their sentences would be more involved. Now, suppose two individuals, with equal organs of Language, and, consequently, equal power of learning words, as mere signs, to possess, the one a head like the former, and the other a head like the latter people—and that they attempted to learn these different languages—it appears probable that the one with the first-mentioned developement would find the genius of the first language the more easy and natural to him ; he would acquire its forms of collocation and its niceties of designation with facility and delight, because they would coincide with the modes of feeling and thinking of his own mind. If, on the other hand, his at-

*. Sur les Fonctions du Cerveau, tome v., pp. 18 and 30.
†. Phrenology, p. 262.

tention were directed to the language of the second people, he would meet with greater difficulties. Although he might master the words, he would not find the idioms natural ; the forms of expression depending on the reflecting powers, and likewise the involution introduced by Secretiveness, would appear to him extremely intricate and unintelligible ; he would be obliged to learn them by *rule*, through defect of innate tact in apprehending them ; and rules alone never produce a really excellent linguist. The second language, on the other hand, would come quite naturally to the other individual possessing a head like that of the people who invented it.

If these views be correct, the talent for learning the genius or spirit of different languages will depend upon the developement of the organ of words, taken in conjunction with the power of the individual to enter into the feelings, and form the precise kinds of intellectual combinations, of different nations ; or, in short, upon the capacity to go out of himself, and to enter into the mental state of others—a capacity conferred chiefly by Secretiveness, Imitation, Individuality, and Eventuality, aided, of course, by the other primitive faculties. This will be best understood by an example. If two individuals have an equal developement of all the organs except the four now mentioned, which the one possesses in a high degree, and the other only to a very limited extent, the former will have a power of entering into the feelings and reasoning of others, which the latter will want ; and this power, according to the view now presented, will render him more apt in acquiring the spirit of different languages. This, however, is merely a theory, thrown out for the consideration of the reader ; yet it has been suggested by facts. I know an individual who has an excellent developement of many of the organs, but is a very decided character, and possesses little of the talent of entering into, or accommodating himself to, the feelings of others ; and he experienced an inconceivable difficulty in acquiring the simplest French idioms. I know another young gentleman who was in the same situation in regard to Latin, and who has little versatility. In them the organ of Language is rather deficient. On the other hand, I have met with several persons in whom the organ was equally deficient, and who possessed the power of learning foreign idioms ; in their case, however, the power of amalgamation with the mental states of others was decidedly greater, and their organs of Secretiveness, Imitation, Individuality, and Eventuality were larger.

Although the theory of the talent for philology is involved in considerable obscurity, it is quite certain that the ready command of words in speech or writing is in proportion to the developement of the organ situated above the super-orbitar plate, and that a fluent orator or author is never found deficient in it.

Numerous cases are on record of the power of using words being impaired by disease, when the ability to articulate and the powers of perception and judgment remained entire. In the *Transactions of the Phrenological Society*, p. 235, Mr. Hood, of Kilmarnock, has communicated a very interesting instance of this kind, which fell under his own notice as medical attendant. The patient, a sober and regular man of 65 years of age, possessed of the ordinary knowledge of written and spoken language, on the evening of 2d September, 1822, suddenly began to speak incoherently, and became quite unintelligible to all those who were about him. "It was *discovered that he had forgotten the name of every object in nature.* His recollection of *things* seemed to be unimpaired, but the *names* by which *men* and *things* are known were entirely obliterated from his mind, or rather he had lost the faculty by which they are called up at the control of the will. He was by no means inattentive, however, to what was going on ; and he recognised friends and acquaintances perhaps as quickly as on any former occasion; but their names, or even his own or his wife's name, or the names of any of his domestics, appeared to have no place in his recollection.

"On the morning of the 4th September," says Mr. Hood, "much against the wishes of his family, he put on his clothes, and went out to the workshop; and, when I made my visit, he gave me to understand, by a variety of signs, that he was perfectly well in every respect, with the exception of some slight uneasiness referrible to the eyes and eyebrows. I prevailed on him, with some difficulty, to submit to the reapplication of leeches, and to allow a blister to be placed over the left temple. He was now so well in bodily health, that he would not be confined to the house; and his judgment, in so far as I could form an estimate of it, was unimpaired; but his memory for words was so much a blank, that the monosyllables of affirmation and negation seemed to be the only two words in the language, the use and signification of which he never entirely forgot. He comprehended distinctly every word which was spoken or addressed to him; and, though he had ideas adequate to form a full reply, the words by which these ideas are expressed seemed to have been entirely obliterated from his mind. By way of experiment, I would sometimes mention to him the name of a person or thing—his own name, for example, or the name of some one of his domestics—when he would have repeated it after me distinctly, once or twice; but, generally, before he could do so a *third* time, the word was gone from him as completely as if he had never heard it pronounced. When any person read to him from a book, ho had no difficulty in perceiving the meaning of the passage, but he could not himself then read; and the reason seemed to be, that he had forgotten the elements of written language, viz., the names of the letters of the alphabet. In the course of a short time he became very expert in the use of signs; and his convalescence was marked by his imperceptibly acquiring some general terms, which were with him at first of very extensive and *varied* application. In the progress of his recovery time and space came both under the general appellation of *time*. All future events and objects before him were, as he expressed it, '*next time*;' but past events and objects behind him were designated '*last time*,' One day being asked his age, he made me to understand that he could not tell; but, pointing to his wife, uttered the words '*many times*' repeatedly, as much as to say that he had often told her his age. When she said he was sixty, he answered in the affirmative, and inquired what "*time*" it was; but as I did not comprehend his meaning distinctly, I mentioned to him the hour of the day, when he soon convinced me that I had not given him the proper answer. I then named the day of the week, which was also unsatisfactory; but, upon mentioning the month, and day of the month, he immediately signified that this was what he wanted to know, in order to answer my question respecting his age. Having succeeded in getting the day of the month, he then pointed out the '*time*' or day of the month on which he was born, and thereby gave me to understand that he was sixty years of age, and five days, or '*times*,' as he expressed it."

In the month of December, 1822, his convalescence was so complete, that he could support conversation without much difficulty. The headaches, with which he had been so long affected, recurred occasionally; but in other respects he enjoyed, generally, tolerably good health. On the 10th January, 1825, he suddenly became paralytic on the left side. On 17th August he had an attack of apoplexy, and on the 21st he expired. In *The Phrenological Journal*, vol. iii., p. 28, Mr. Hood has reported the dissection of his brain. In the left hemisphere lesion of the parts was found, which terminated "at half an inch from the surface of the brain, where it rests over the middle of the super-orbitar plate." Two small depressions or cysts were found in the substance of the brain, "and the cavity, considered as a whole, expanded from the anterior part of the brain till it opened into the ventricle in the form of a trumpet. The right hemisphere did not present any remarkable appearance." Another case is reported by Mr. Hood, in vol. ii., p. 82.

In July, 1836, I was present at the dissection of the brain of a gentleman who died in his 94th year, and who for several years before his death had laboured under a deficiency in the command of words, similar to that experienced by Mr. Hood's patient. His understanding was sound, and he comprehended spoken language when addressed to him ; he could articulate perfectly, but he could not command the proper words to express his ideas. A small cavity was found in the left *corpus striatum*, about an inch back from the organ of Language. There had obviously been effusion of blood into it, which had been absorbed, leaving a cavity of a quarter of an inch in diameter lined with a yellowish membrane. The right hemisphere was entire. The brain presented appearances of general chronic inflammatory action.

Dr. Spurzheim mentions having seen, at Inverness, a case closely resembling the foregoing ; and also one of the same nature at Paris. Dr. Gall cites from Pinel the case of a notary, who, after an attack of apoplexy, had forgot his own name, and those of his wife, children, and friends, although his tongue preserved all its mobility. He could no longer read or write, but, nevertheless, remembered objects which had formerly made an impression on his senses, and which related to his profession. He frequently pointed out with his finger the files which contained documents that could not be found, and indicated, by other signs, that he preserved the former train of ideas entire.* Dr. Gall mentions also the case of a soldier sent to him by Baron Larrey, whom he found to be very nearly in the same condition as the notary mentioned by Pinel. "It was not his tongue," says he, "which was the source of his embarrassment, for he was able to move it with great agility, and to pronounce well a great number of isolated words. It was not his memory either which was in fault, for he showed evident dissatisfaction with himself upon many subjects which he wished to mention. The only faculty in him which was impaired was that of speech: This soldier, like the patient of M. Pinel, was rendered incapable of reading or writing."†

M. Bouillaud, an eminent Parisian phrenologist, has made extensive investigations into the pathology of the organ of Language. In an essay which he has published on this subject,‡ a number of interesting cases of loss of the power of speech are reported, partly from his own observation, and partly from the works of MM. Rostan and Lallemand, two of the most accurate and highly-esteemed continental writers on nervous diseases. In two of the cases the anterior lobe, at the part which corresponds to the orbital arch, was reduced to soft purulent-looking matter. A third was restored to health. Not fewer than sixteen instances follow, in which the recollection of words and their relations, and the ability to use them, were altogether destroyed, although it was evident, from the looks and gestures of the patients, that their silence resulted from no want of ideas, but solely from incapacity to express them. In these cases the same organic lesion was discovered. M. Bouillaud's essay led him into a successful controversy with M. Scipio Pinel, of which some account will be found in The Phrenological Journal.§

In another volume of the same Journal‖ Mr. John Inglis Nicol, one of

* Pinel *sur l'Aliénation mentale*, 2de édition, § 105.
† *Sur les Fonctions du Cerveau*, tome v., p. 38.
‡ *Archives Generales de Médécine*, tome viii., pp. 25–45. 1825.
§ Vol. viii., p. 256.   ‖ Vol. iii., p. 616

the medical attendants of the Northern Infirmary, at Inverness, has reported two cases of a similar kind. One of the patients died ; and it was found, on dissection, that, "about the centre of the under surface of the anterior lobe, the convolutions, to the extent of half a crown, were changed in colour to a reddish brown."

In a case reported by Professor Syme* the faculty of Language was impaired, and, on dissection, both anterior lobes were found healthy, with the exception of the parts constituting the organs of Form and Language. In this, as in most of the other instances referred to, the patient seemed to understand perfectly whatever was *said* to him, but had scarcely any recollection of *written* or *printed* words. It is difficult to explain why the latter exclusively should have been unintelligible. Perhaps the disease of the organ of Form may have had some share in producing this phenomenon.

Pain over the eyes frequently accompanies derangement or deprivation of the power of speech. This is seen in certain diseases, such as plague, yellow fever, and typhus ;† and has been observed also in cases of cerebral injury.‡

In the ninth volume of *The Phrenological Journal*§ a most valuable series of papers, "On Morbid Manifestations of the Organ of Language, as connected with Insanity," has been published by Mr. W. A. F. Browne, medical superintendent of the Montrose Lunatic Asylum. He describes successively, and illustrates by numerous cases, the various kinds of symptoms by which the derangement shows itself : 1. Rapidity of voluntary utterance ; 2. Involuntary utterance ; 3. Rapidity of involuntary utterance ; 4. Total loss of verbal memory ; 5. Partial loss of memory of all words indiscriminately ; 6. Partial loss of memory of certain classes of words, such as names or substantives generally ; 7. Impaired perception of the relation of words to the things signified ; 8. Impaired perception of the relation of words to each other ; and, 9. Total loss of perception of these relations. It appears, from several cases reported by Mr. Browne, that the activity of the organ sometimes rises to so high a pitch of exaltation in lunatics, that the utmost difficulty is experienced in preserving silence, and occasionally words flow with astonishing volubility, in direct opposition to the will of the speaker.‖ Many lunatics indulge in the vociferation of most violent and disgusting language ; Mr. Browne considers it pretty certain, both from his own observation and that of others, that, in a great majority of such cases, the ejaculations are involuntary, and result from a special excitement of the organ of Language, by which certain words are called up without the assent of the patient, and sometimes even contrary to his inclination. It is important that the possibility of derangement confined to this single faculty should be generally known ; for, as Mr. Browne remarks, "little doubt can be entertained, that, in many such cases, great and irreparable injury and injustice may be committed by restraining or confining individuals as lunatics, who are merely monomaniacs in the power of Language. The effects of joy, fear, affection, and love of approbation, in suspending or limiting the exercise of language, are known and have been felt by all ; and it may readily be conceived that, in a disposition highly susceptible of such impressions, the slightest deviation from health in the organ of Language will become doubly perceptible, and may lead to misconstruction and consequences of the most melancholy kind."¶ Mr. Browne has more recently published

---

* *Edin. Med. and Surg. Journ.*, No. 117 ; and *Phren. Journ.*, ix., 17

† *Phren. Journ.*, vol. viii., p. 422.

‡ *Ibid.*, vol. viii., p. 189 ; ix., 119, 516 ; x., 118.

§ Pages 250, 306, 414.   ‖ Pages 311–13.   ¶ Page 422.

in the Journal* an instructive account of that species of insanity of which
the symptom is speech in unknown tongues, and which is not uncommon
among the fanatics of Britain.

Dr. William Gregory mentions, that he has repeatedly observed the
faculty of Language to be affected by the use of morphia. "If I take,"
says he, "from twenty to thirty drops of the solution of muriate of morphia, it produces, in the course of an hour, a very agreeable state of calm;
and, for some hours after, the organ of Language is so strongly stimulated,
that I find it difficult to stop when I begin to speak; and I have repeated
this experiment, which is attended with no inconvenience, so often, that
I am quite confident of the result."† Having, on other occasions, taken
a considerably larger quantity of the solution, he found it to produce a
marked derangement of the faculty of Language, amounting to a disso-
ciation of words from the things signified, and, in the most severe instance,
accompanied by violent headache in the situation of the organ. Dr. Gregory
considers it probable that morphia acts exclusively upon the anterior lobe,
more particularly the organ of Language; and that an over-dose causes
entire derangement of that faculty. These conclusions, he adds, will
have to be confirmed, or otherwise, by the observations of intelligent
practitioners. He justly remarks, that if medical men, acquainted with
Phrenology, were to direct their attention to the specific action of different
remedies on the minds of their patients, a new and interesting field of
inquiry would be laid open, and much light would probably be thrown on
many obscure points in mental philosophy.

Some individuals in whom Language is large, state, as an objection, that
they had a bad memory of names; but they will be found in general to
have a deficient memory of the objects which the names indicate : for example, if they cannot recollect names of persons, they will have deficient
Form and Individuality; and if they cannot recollect names of tunes, they
will be deficient in Tune. The defect lies in the faculty which apprehends and recollects the primitive idea, for which Language recollects
the name; and it is quite conceivable that, although Language may be
powerful, yet it may not furnish names, as mere words, when the thing
signified is not present in the mind.‡

The lower animals appear to have this organ in some degree; for they
learn the meaning of arbitrary signs in so far as they possess the feelings
and conceptions which these express.

The organ is large in the companion of Gall, Sir J. E. Smith, Humboldt, Pope, Voltaire, and Rammohun Roy; and small in the mask of
Fraser.—Established.

GENERAL OBSERVATIONS OF INDIVIDUALITY AND THE OTHER KNOWING OR PERCEPTIVE FACULTIES.

No objection to Phrenology is more frequently repeated than that such
and such persons have retreating foreheads, and yet are very clever. A

* Vol. ix., p. 593.   † *Phrenological Journal*, vol. viii., p. 163.
‡ See remarks by Dr. A. Combe on the talent for recollecting names, *Phrenological Journal*, vol. iii., p. 120.—In vol. v., p. 431, is recorded a case where
memory of names was impaired by a severe blow on the left eyebrow, while
the memory of other classes of words does not seem to have been injured;
another case of loss of memory of names only, is noticed in vol. viii., p. 415.
—Mr. Hewett Watson has published, in vol. vii., p. 214, some observations on
memory of names.— Mr. W. A. F. Browne states it as the result of his experience, that, in cases of partial loss of language, the words remembered
appear to be substantives when Individuality is vigorous, abstract terms when
Causality is powerful, and adjectives when the lateral knowing organs are
large and unimpaired; vol. viii., p. 423.

short explanation will serve to remove this difficulty. In the first place, a forehead may *appear* retreating, not because the reflecting organs are *greatly* deficient, but because the knowing organs are very prominently developed, so that, if the latter were diminished in size, the former would *appear* relatively larger: but every one must perceive that, in such an event, the perceptive powers would be proportionally diminished, and the talents of the individual lessened, while the unskilful observer might imagine the developement of his forehead to be improved. In the mask of Henri Quatre, for example, the forehead appears to slope ; whereas, if the knowing organs were reduced to the same state of projection beyond the cheek-bones as in the mask of Voltaire, it would appear much more perpendicular. This, however, would clearly detract from the mental power. It would cause the reflecting faculties to predominate, only by diminishing talent in the department of observation.

But, in the next place, suppose that a head does retreat considerably, still Individuality and the other knowing organs may be large ; and if we attend for a moment to the *range* of these powers, we shall perceive that the individual may be deficient in Causality and Comparison, and yet be *very clear*. A wide range of sciences, falling under the scope of Individuality and Eventuality chiefly, has already been pointed out, and in these a person so endowed may be very learned. Farther, the details of history, statistics, geography, and trade, all belong to the department of simple knowledge ; and in them also he may be eminently skilled. And, finally, in the daily occurrences of life, acuteness of observation, and the power of treasuring up the lessons of experience, which he may possess, constitute important elements in a practical judgment. If, then, to a large endowment of the knowing organs a nervous temperament be added, the individual may be observing, active, and enterprising; if Cautiousness be large, he may be prudent, and rarely venture beyond the scope of his abilities ; if Conscientiousness be large, he may enjoy that delicacy of sentiment which discriminates intuitively where the right lies, and where the path of honour terminates ; and with these endowments there will be no wonder if he act creditably and cleverly in the ordinary walks of life. These are not imaginary suppositions, but descriptions drawn from observations made on numerous individuals engaged in active business. Such persons, however, are never distinguished for profound and comprehensive views of obstract principles ; which belong to the reflecting faculties, not yet treated of.*

In the preceding pages it is stated that the faculty of Form perceives the forms of objects—Colouring, their colour—and Size, their dimensions ; that Individuality takes cognizance of things existing, and Eventuality of events in general. The question naturally occurs—If the minor knowing powers apprehend *all* the separate qualities of external objects, what purposes do Individuality and Eventuality serve in the mental economy ? One important function of Individuality is to form a single intellectual conception out of the different items of information communicated by the other knowing faculties, which take cognizance of the properties of external objects. In perceiving a tree, the object apprehended by the mind is not colour, form, and size, as separate qualities ; but a *single thing* or *being* named a tree. The mind having, by means of Individuality, obtained the idea of a tree, as an individual existing object, may analyze it, and resolve it into its constituent parts of form, colour, and magnitude ; but the contemplation of it in this manner is at once felt to be widely different from the conception attached to the word *tree* as a whole. The function of Individuality, therefore, is, to imbody the separate elements furnished

* This subject is more fully illustrated in *The Phrenological Journal*, vol. iii. pp. 48, 67.

by these other knowing faculties into one, and to produce out of them conceptions of aggregate objects as a whole; which objects are afterward viewed by the mind as individual existing things, and are remembered and spoken of as such, without our thinking of their constituent parts. Children early use and understand general terms, such as *tree, man, ship*; and the organ of Individuality is for the most part prominently developed in them.

Farther, Form, Colouring, and Size furnish certain elementary conceptions, which Individuality unites and conceives as one, such as Man. The faculty of Number, called into action, gives the idea of plurality; and that of Order furnishes the idea of gradations of rank and arrangement. Now, Individuality, receiving the intimations of all these separate faculties, *combines* them again, and contemplates the *combination* as an *individual object*, and this is an *army*. After the idea of an army is thus formed, the mind drops the recollection of the constituent parts, and thinks of the *aggregate only*, or of the combined conception formed by Individuality; and regards it as a single object.

Eventuality is surrounded by Individuality, Locality, Comparison, and Causality, and forms individual conceptions from their combined intimations. A storm is not a specific existing object, nor is it a quality of anything; yet the mind clearly apprehends it. It is the result of certain physical elements in violent commotion, and all the faculties last enumerated, together with Eventuality itself, which observes motion, combine in furnishing individual conceptions, which Eventuality unites into one idea, designated by the word *storm*. Revolution is another example: a revolution does not exist in nature as a substantive thing, but arises from the combined action of numerous moral and physical causes, the result of which Eventuality conceives as one event.

It is interesting to observe the phrenological system, which at first sight appears rude and unphilosophical, harmonizing thus simply and beautifully with nature. Had it been constructed by imagination or reflection alone, it is more than probable that the objection of the minor knowing faculties, rendering Individuality and Eventuality superfluous, would have appeared so strong and insurmountable, as to have insured the exclusion of one or other as unnecessary; and yet, until both were discovered and admitted, the formation of such terms as those we have considered was altogether inexplicable.

Genus III.—REFLECTIVE FACULTIES.

The intellectual faculties which we have considered furnish us with knowledge of objects, their qualities and relations, and also of events; those which we proceed to treat of "act," as Dr. Spurzheim expresses it, "on all the other sensations and notions;" in other words, they judge, not of the qualities and relations of external objects, but of the relations of different classes of ideas produced by the perceptive faculties. They minister to the direction and gratification of all the other powers, and constitute what we call reason or reflection.

34. COMPARISON.

Dr. Gall often conversed on philosophical subjects with a *savant*, possessing much vivacity of mind. Whenever the latter was put to difficulty in rigorously proving his positions, he always had recourse to a comparison. By this means he in a manner painted his ideas, and his opponents were defeated and carried along with him; effects which he could never produce by simple argument. As soon as Dr. Gall perceived that, in him, this was a characteristic trait of mind, he examined his head, and found an eminence of the form of a reversed pyramid on the upper and middle portion of the frontal bone. He confirmed the observation by many subsequent instances. He names the quality "perspicacity, sagacity, *esprit de comparaison.*" Examples of the appearance of the organ, when large and small, are given on page 308.

The faculty gives the power of perceiving resemblances and analogies. Tune may compare different notes; Colouring contrast different shades; but Comparison may compare a tint and a note, a form and a colour, which the other faculties by themselves could not accomplish.* "The great aim of this faculty," says Dr Spurzheim, "seems to be to form abstract ideas, generalizations, and to establish harmony among the operations of the other faculties. Colouring compares colours with each other, and feels their harmony, but Comparison adapts the colours to the object which is represented; it will reject lively colours to present a gloomy scene. The laws of music are particular, and Tune compares tones; but Comparison chooses the music according to the situations where it is executed. It blames dancing music in a church; it is opposed to walking with fine clothes in the dirt, to superb furniture beside common things; it feels the relation between the inferior and superior feelings, and gives the preference to the latter. Its influence, however, presupposes the activity of the other faculties, and it cannot act upon them if they are inactive. This explains why some persons have taste and good judgment in one respect and not in another. He who is deprived of Reverence, may not be careful enough about its application. He may deride what others respect. But if another possess it in a high degree, and at the same time Comparison, he will wish to bring his Reverence into harmony with his other powers."

Comparison thus takes the widest range of nature within its sphere. "It compares," says Mr Scott, "things of the most opposite kind, draws analogies, and discovers resemblances between them, often the most unexpected and surprising. It compares a light, seen afar off in a dark night, to a good deed shining in a naughty world; it compares the kingdom of heaven to a grain of mustard seed. If we would describe more minutely and accurately," he continues, "what are the kinds of resemblances which this faculty discovers, it will perhaps be found that they are in no case *direct* resemblances, such as are perceived by the observing powers, but *relative* resemblances, or, to speak more accurately, resemblances, not between the objects themselves, but *between their relations* to other objects. What resemblance is there, for instance, between a good action and the light of a candle! None whatever directly; but relatively there is felt to be a resemblance, when the light appears brighter because of the surrounding darkness, and when the good action is set off by the contrast afforded by the wickedness of the world."† It finds analogies between the qualities of matter and mind; and from these comparisons and analogies a great part of language, expressive of the qualities of mind, is drawn; "a great part of it being almost metaphorical, and applied originally in its literal sense to designate qualities of matter." For this reason the language of every nation proves whether this organ is much or little developed in the greatest number of its individuals. If they have this faculty in a high degree, their language is replete with figure. Dr. Murray Paterson mentions that the Hindostanee language abounds in figures, and that Comparison is larger than Causality in the heads of the Hindoos in general.‡

* See Gall *Sur les Fonctions du Cerveau,* vi., 406; *Phren. Journ.,* iv., 322; vi., 384; and ix., 435, 495. Also above, p. 253.
† Essay on the Faculty of Comparison; *Phren. Journ.,* vol. iv., p. 322.
‡ *Trans. of the Phren. Soc.,* p. 437.

This faculty gives rise to proverbs, which convey instruction under figurative expressions.

It attaches us to comparison, without determining its kinds; for every one must choose his analogies according to his knowledge, or from the sphere of activity of his other faculties. He who has Locality in a high degree, derives thence his examples; while another, in whom Form predominates, will illustrate his subject from it. Dr. Chalmers draws his illustrations from mechanics and astronomy; and the organs which take cognizance of these are large in his head.

According to Dr. Spurzheim, Comparison takes cognizance, not only of resemblances, but also of differences. This view is opposed by Mr. Scott who attributes the perception of differences to the organ of Wit; an opinion in which he is supported by several metaphysicians before quoted.[*]

This faculty gives a tendency to what is frequently called reasoning, but which is very different from the correct and severe inductions of a sound logic; namely, it endeavours to prove that one thing is of such and such a nature, because it resembles another which is so and so—in short, it reasons by analogy, and is prone to convert an illustration into an argument. The published sermons of the late Mr. Logan, minister of Leith, afford an example of the productions of this kind of intellect. He is always establishing a proposition, and, to those who do not analyze profoundly, he appears to be an argumentative preacher; but his argument is not induction—it is a mere statement of analogies, closed by an inference that the case in point must be as he views it, otherwise it would be an exception to the ordinary arrangements of nature. The tendency of Comparison is to perceive only resemblances, or rather to lose sight of the differences of things; and, as a difference in one point out of a hundred frequently destroys the whole force of the analogy, no reasoning is so often false and superficial as that of persons in whom Comparison is the leading intellectual organ, but in whom, nevertheless, it is not large. The late Professor Playfair may be cited as an example in opposition to these. In him Causality and Comparison were both large and of equal dimensions, and his comparisons are merely illustrations. His conclusions, in general, stand in the relation of necessary consequences to his premises.

This faculty is more rarely deficient than any of the other intellectual powers, and the Scripture is addressed to it in an eminent degree, being replete with analogies and comparisons. From giving readiness in perceiving analogies and resemblances, it is one element in instantaneous acuteness. The organ is largely developed in a neighbouring nation; and it is correctly observed by an anonymous writer, that "ingenuity in discovering unexpected glimpses and superficial coincidences in the ordinary relations of life, the French possess in an eminent degree."[†] In schools the best scholars generally have much Language and Comparison. In children the organ of Comparison is usually well developed; and it is remarked by a practical writer, that "children come both to understand and to relish a figurative expression much sooner than we might naturally be led to imagine."[‡] "Children," says Miss Edgeworth, "are all, more or less, pleased with the perception of resemblances and of analogy."[§] The faculty is of essential service to orators and popular preachers. It and Eventuality are the largest organs in the forehead of William Pitt. It is large also in the busts of Curran, Chalmers, Burke, and Jeffrey. In Mr. T. Moore it is very large; and, in the eighth number of The Westminster Review, it was remarked, that there are two thousand five hundred similes in his Life of Sheridan, besides metaphors and allegorical expres-

* Page 252.   † Edinburgh Review, Nov., 1820, p. 389.
‡ Wood's Account of the Edinburgh Sessional School, 1828, p. 179
§ Practical Education, vol. iii., p. 96.

sions. Dr. Gall correctly observes, that close reasoning and rigid induction are always disagreeable to a popular audience, because their faculties are not cultivated nor exercised to follow abstract conceptions. The great charm of popular speakers, therefore, consists in perspicuity of statement and copiousness of illustration.

From giving power of illustration and command of figures, this faculty is of great importance to the poet; and it aids Wit also, by suggesting analogies. By common observers, indeed, the metaphors, amplifications, allegories, and analogies, which Comparison supplies, are frequently mistaken for the products of Ideality, although they are very different. Ideality, being a sentiment, when greatly excited, infuses passion and enthusiasm into the mind, and prompts it to soar after the magnificent, the beautiful, and the sublime, as objects congenial to its constitution.* Comparison, on the other hand, being an intellectual power, produces no vivid passion, no intense feeling or enthusiasm; it coolly and calmly plays off its sparkling fire-works, and takes its direction from the other powers with which it is combined. If united with great Individuality and Causality in any individual, the comparisons employed will be copious, ingenious, and appropriate; but if Ideality be not large, they will not be impassioned, elevated, and glowing. Add to Comparison, again, a large Ideality, as in Dr. Chalmers, and its similes will now twinkle in delicate loveliness like a star, now blaze in meridian splendour like the sun, while intense feeling and lofty enthusiasm will give strength and majesty to all its conceptions.

The organ of Comparison is large in Franklin, Roscoe, Edwards, Henri Quatre, Mr. Hume, and the Hindoos; and deficient in the Caribs.

Till recently the function of this organ has been considered as limited to a perception of general resemblance between ideas compared; but a new view has been suggested by my ingenious friend, Mr. Hewett Watson. He conceives that its simple function probably is "a *perception of conditions*;" and he proposes the term *Conditionality* as its name. It is admitted, says he, that the faculty of Form compares forms, Tune compares notes, and Colouring compares colours. In these faculties comparison is a *mode of activity* only; and it is contrary to all analogy to assign comparison to another organ as its primitive function. The organ XXXIV, therefore, will probably originate some specific perceptions distinct in kind from those of any other organ; and its comparisons will be made between *its own* perceptions only, as is the case with every other intellectual faculty. A few illustrations will render these ideas more clear.

When we utter the word *man*, we address Individuality alone; we speak of a being which exists, without specifying his form, size, colour, or weight; without mentioning his actions; and without intimating his condition. When we say "the man walks," we add a new idea, that of walking: in this proposition we call in the aid of Eventuality, which conceives action or events. If we say "the *tall man* walks," we address Size, Individuality, and Eventuality; or if we say "the *black* man rides," then Colouring, Individuality, and Eventuality combine in uttering and in understanding the proposition. But, suppose that we are told that the "*miserable man* runs along the road;" here we have, first, the man—second, his condition, *miserable*—and, third, his action, *running*: now,

* It is under the influence of Ideality that

"The poet's eye, in a fine phrensy rolling,
Doth glance from heaven to earth, from earth to heaven;
And as imagination bodies forth
The forms of things unknown, the poet's pen
Turns them to shapes, and gives to airy nothing
A local habitation and a name."

what organ takes cognizance of his condition?" It is obvious that it must be an organ distinct from the other two, because the mind can conceive the man without his action; it can conceive the man and his action without thinking of his condition, and his condition without adverting to his action: his condition is, therefore, a third and separate consideration, introduced as an article of additional information. Again, suppose that we are told that Mr. A. and Miss B. were married last week at the altar of their parish church: the information would be communicated by, and addressed to, the organ of Individuality, which takes cognizance of Mr. A and Miss B. as individuals, and the altar and church as things which exist; Locality would give us the notion of the place of the marriage, and Time of the date of it; but in all this no information would be acquired of the *condition* of the parties. Now, suppose that we should meet them coming from the church, and should wish them " much happiness " in their " *new condition*," it is evident that some conceptions different from the former are added. We now contemplate them in the " married condition," and we express our wish, that they may live happily in that state.

Mr. Watson's idea is, that the primitive function of Comparison is to take cognizance of the condition (as alive, dead, warm, cold, healthy, or sick) in which beings and inanimate objects exist; and that it compares the conditions, just as Colouring compares colours, and Tune compares notes. Of all the means of creating interest or affording illustration, the specification of the condition of objects or beings is the most effectual. Thus, *the man exists*, is announced by Individuality, and produces little interest; *the man dies*, is announced by Individuality and Eventuality, and is more affecting; but the " *good* and *just young* man dies," stirs up a far deeper emotion; and it is the addition of his qualities and condition, "good, just, and young," that makes the difference. Poets and orators, therefore, in whom this faculty is strong, will possess vivid perceptions of the condition or state of objects and beings; and if every faculty compares its own objects, this will compare conditions. If Mr. Watson's view be correct, we ought to find authors in whom Individuality predominates, illustrating their subject chiefly by comparing simple individual objects; those in whom Eventuality predominates, illustrating by comparing actions; and those in whom the organ now under discussion predominates, illustrating by comparing conditions or states; and such accordingly appears to be actually the case. The following illustrations are furnished chiefly by Eventuality:

> " When Ajax strives some rock's huge weight to throw,
> The line, too, labours, and the words move slow;
> Not so when swift Camilla scours the plain,
> Flies o'er the unbending corn, and skims along the main."
>
> *Pope.*

Mr. Watson observes, that in Sheridan Individuality and Eventuality are large, and Comparison only full; and the example already given on page 309, from his works, corresponds with this developement.

In Moore Individuality is large, Eventuality deficient, and Comparison very large; and his descriptions are confined so much to conditions, that any artist who should attempt to transfer one of his beauties to canvass, would find it necessary to invent every item of form, proportion, colour, and indeed everything except condition. " The harp that once through Tara's halls " is a good example of this; the whole piece being but a description and comparison of conditions. In another short poem, " Though Fate, my girl, may bid us part," the same occurs; and the following is another example

> " When I remember all
> The friends so linked together,
> I've seen around me fall
> Like leaves in wintry weather;
> I feel like one who treads alone
> Some banquet hall deserted;
> Whose lights are fled, whose garland's dead;
> And all but he departed."

It is quite obvious, that condition is the prominent feature—indeed, almost the whole physiognomy—of these lines.

In the busts of Pope Individuality is moderately developed, Eventuality very large, and Comparison considerable. " The styles of Pope and Moore," says Mr. Watson, " seem to be quite contrasted in this respect— that Pope narrates all the circumstances of his stories in succession, as they may be supposed to occur. Moore, on the other hand, gives us a series of highly-finished pictures, describing clearly and beautifully the *state* of the earth, atmosphere, sky, clouds, and *dramatis personæ*, for the time being, but by no means with that regular sequence of occurrences which is to be found in Pope. His stories are the whole routine of real life; those of Moore stage-representations, where a good deal is done behind the scenes, and only the most effective parts brought into view. Pope writes historical documents with the minute accuracy and detail of a Welsh pedigree; Moore's pen is like the pencil of an artist, and creates a gallery of paintings, where we see the same persons in different situations at different periods, but with no more information of what becomes of them in the interim, that we can obtain concerning the noon-day dwelling of *Oberon*, or the *Ghost* of *Royal Hamlet*. Their styles being thus different, we should expect their similes to exhibit a corresponding diversity, if there be really no special organ of Comparison: those of Pope should be less strongly characterized by resemblance of condition, and show a greater and more proportional variety in the points of similitude; the comparisons should be more diversified, and the resemblances more comprehensive."[*]

I communicated Mr. Watson's ideas to Dr. Spurzheim, before they were published in *The Phrenological Journal*; and he favoured me with the following remarks, in a letter, dated Dublin, 16th May, 1830: " My description of Comparison involves the essence of Mr. Watson's ideas. Among your examples, *young* horse belongs to it, but not *lively* horse. The horse being *lively*, is known by Eventuality, in the same way as motion in general. The *generality* of attributes and all abstract ideas and general notions are conceived by Comparison. *Condition* indicates not only state, but also cause; and if *Comparison* shall be replaced by another term, it cannot be *Conditionality*. Abstraction or generalization should be preferable. *Vergleichender Scharfsinn* is very significant: it compares, discriminates, separates, abstracts, adapts, and generalizes. The philosophers styled *Nominalists* had it in an eminent degree, while Individuality was predominant in the *Realists*. Comparison compares conditions or states, and conditions or causes. Its essential result is generalization and discrimination.

In the last edition of his *Phrenology* Dr. S. adverts to Mr. Watson's view in the following terms: " I am delighted to know that this gentleman is engaged in the pursuit of Phrenology; he is destined to render great service to its cause, but my Comparison makes me differ from him as to the essential function of this faculty....In my opinion, the cognizance of different conditions is tested by Eventuality. This faculty not only shows the active, but also the passive and neutral verbs. It perceives a man walking, but also a man being carried, a man asleep, two persons being

married. To be young or old, good, just, or the contrary, are physical or
moral events, which are made known to Eventuality. Hence, there is
no necessity of a new organ of Conditionality."

Mr. Watson's latest remarks on Comparison are contained in the tenth
volume of *The Phrenological Journal.* " By comparing," says he, " the
developements of several authors and private acquaintances with their
styles of writing and thinking, I came to the conclusion that *comparison*
was only a mental process, and ought to be classed with perception, conception, memory, imagination, and other terms which appear to express a
state of functional activity, not the kind of ideas formed in the cerebral
organs. This conclusion was forced upon me by finding that the tendency
to compare was not always in proportion to the developement of the organ named Comparison, and that the sense of resemblance and difference,
like that of memory, was always manifested most strongly in the ideas
presumed to be formed by the largest organs. The next step was to
ascertain the *kind of ideas* existing or formed in the organ hitherto called
Comparison. On carefully examining the works of authors in whom this
organ was predominant, I believed to have detected a peculiar tendency
to describe and to compare certain trains of ideas, touching the condition
or states of external nature and internal feelings; while the works of
others, in whom this organ was moderately developed, were comparatively
devoid of such tendency, but were prone to describe and compare other
trains of ideas. Hence came the suggestion of this organ taking cognizance of such ideas, and remembering and comparing those ideas, just as
Form is said to remember and compare shapes. Although the works of
Spurzheim do not give this view, his own ideas about the function of the
organ seem to have approximated to it, because, in reply to Mr. Combe's
epistolary intimation of my conclusions, he wrote, ' Comparison compares
conditions or states, and conditions or causes. Its essential result is
generalization and discrimination.' " Mr. Hancock says that my term ' conditions ' does not convey to his mind any very distinct ideas. The fault
may be personal, not verbal, as it appears that Spurzheim distinctly comprehended the ideas that it should excite. I differ from Spurzheim and
Mr. Scott in still thinking that each organ (or pair of organs) generalises
and discriminates its own ideas only. The heads of several persons
eminent in the physical sciences evince only a moderate developement of
Comparison, yet these sciences require generalization and discrimination
to a great extent. Half the science of botany, and almost the whole of
entomology, turn on discriminations of objects nearly alike, or in uniting
them into general groups in accordance with certain resemblances in their
physical properties. Why, therefore, is the organ of Comparison not
always large in eminent botanists and entomologists, if this organ be
necessary to generalization and discrimination of all kinds of ideas alike ?
Again, if Comparison ' compares conditions or states,' what organ perceives and remembers them ?"*

The views of Dr. Vimont on this subject are identical with those of
Mr. Watson; he names the faculty " *Comparaison ou appréciation de
l'état des choses,*" and illustrates its nature thus: When a piece of ice
is placed in a vessel over the fire, Form, Size, and Colouring take cognizance of its appearance; and, when it melts, the change is perceived by
Eventuality. All these perceptions may take place without any idea
arising, of a relation between the state of the now liquid substance, and
the same state in other substances, such as lead, mercury, or milk. What
then, says he, is the faculty which recognises that state of one body relatively to another, so as to make known its qualities expressed by the

adjective in language ? Doubtless, he answers, Comparison ; or, as he prefers to name it, " l'appréciation de l'état des corps, mais avec l'idée de rapprochement ou de relation."* He alludes to Mr. Watson's essay in *The Phrenological Journal*, and adds the remark—ill-founded, as it appears to me—that, " although the arguments of that phrenologist are very ingenious, his theory seems to be at bottom nothing but the idea of comparison, in the sense in which the word is used by Gall."

It is not yet determined whether this organ is possessed by the lower animals. Dr. Gall says that man alone is endowed with it, but Dr. Vimont has been led, by studying the actions of certain animals, such as the dog, elephant, orang-outang, and bear, to consider these creatures as not destitute of the faculty.

35. CAUSALITY.

IT has long been a matter of general observation, that men possessing a profound and comprehensive intellect, such as Socrates, Bacon, and Galileo, have the upper part of the forehead greatly developed. At Vienna Dr. Gall remarked, that in the most zealous disciples of Kant, men distinguished for profound, penetrating, metaphysical talent, the parts of the brain lying immediately at the sides of the organ of Comparison were distinctly enlarged. He and Dr. Spurzheim subsequently saw a mask of Kant himself, moulded after death, and perceived an extraordinary projection of these parts. At a later period they became personally acquainted with Fichte, and found a developement of that region still larger than in Kant. Innumerable additional observations satisfied them concerning the function of this organ : Dr. Gall named it " *Esprit métaphysique, Profondeur d'esprit*," and Dr. Spurzheim " Causality." This organ and Comparison are large in Melancthon, p. 86, Tasso, p. 232, Chaucer and Locke, p. 244, and Michael Angelo, p. 277 ; small in Idiot, p. 46, New Hollander, p. 52, and Griffiths, p. 200.

Dr. Thomas Brown says : " A cause, in the fullest definition which it philosophically admits, may be said to be *that which immediately precedes any change, and which, existing at any time in similar circumstances, has been always, and will be always, immediately followed by a similar change.* Priority is the sequence observed, and invariableness of antecedence in the past and future sequences supposed, are the elements, and the only elements, combined in the notion of a cause." This is a definition, by means of Individuality and Eventuality, of the function of Causality, but it is not complete. When we treat of a primitive power of the mind, all that we can do is, to describe it, to state the objects which excite it, and to give it a name. We cannot, by means of a definition, enable a person who never experienced it, to understand what it is. The definition of Dr. Brown describes, with sufficient accuracy, the circumstances in which the perception of causation is excited ; but it does not convey any notion of the primitive mental faculty by which the perception is accomplished. In addition to the invariable sequence which Eventuality perceives, a notion of power or efficiency in the antecedent to produce the consequent appears to me to arise in the mind when contemplating instances of causation in nature ; and this notion seems to be the mental affection connected with the organ of Causality.

It is said, that it is only by experience, or by observing the invariableness of the sequence, that we discover the connexion of cause and effect ; and this is true : but in this respect Causality does not differ from the other faculties. Caloric, as something existing in nature, is one thing, and the sensation of heat produced by it in the human body is another. Before

* *Traité de Phrénologie,* tome ii., p. 382.
29*

the mind can experience the sensation, heat must be applied to the nerves; but even after the sensation has been felt, the mind knows nothing about what caloric is in itself, or *how* it comes to have the quality of causing the sensation. All that the mind discovers is, that caloric, be it what it may, exists; and that it is capable of producing certain effects in matter, and of exciting in the living body that peculiar feeling which is named heat or warmth. The same holds in regard to Causality. A cause must manifest itself by producing an effect, before the mind can know its presence. The application of caloric to the nerves produces the feeling of heat; and the presentment of an instance of causation excites in Causality the notion that a cause exists. Suppose a bent bow, with an arrow drawn to the head, but retained in this position, to be presented, it is said that Causality, prior to experience, could never discover that, on the restraining power being withdrawn, the bow would expand and propel the arrow; and this is quite correct; because a bow in this condition is an object which excites only the faculties of Form, Size, Colouring, and Individuality. It is an object of still life, of simple existence; when it expands, and the arrow starts from the string, it becomes an object of Eventuality, which perceives the motion; but, in addition to the perception of the bow and the motion, an impression is generated, that the expansion was the cause of the arrow's motion; and this impression is produced by Causality. The most illiterate savage would repeat the operation in the confidence that the effect would follow. A monkey, however, although it might find the arrow very useful in knocking down fruit which it could not reach with its paws, would not repeat the operation, although presented with the bow and arrow. It possesses hands and arms quite adapted to draw the string; but having no organ of Causality, it would not conceive the notion of causation: it might see the phenomena succeed each other, without any idea of efficiency being excited.*

* Beavers and others of the lower animals appear, at first sight, to have some degree of Causality. Beavers adapt the structure of their dam with surprising sagacity to the pressure of the water; and, in preparing it, they not only cut trees in such a way as to ensure their falling into the water, and not on dry land, but select trees so situated that, when they do fall, the stream shall carry them to the spot where they wish them to be placed. There appears to be a knowledge of cause and effect in these operations; and yet the beaver cannot apply this knowledge out of its own department. I am inclined, therefore, to give a different explanation. It is probable that each knowing faculty is adapted to the natural laws of its objects; the organ of Tune is fitted, not only to feel in accordance with the laws of harmony, but instinctively to seek to obey them in producing music; it desires melody, and melody cannot be produced except in conformity with those laws: it therefore tries, and tries again, until at last it succeeds in producing sounds agreeable to itself, and, just because its constitution and the laws of harmony are in accordance, it at least fulfils these laws by instinctive impulse, without knowing them. It is probable that the organs of Constructiveness and Weight, in the beaver, are in like manner adapted to the laws of motion and gravitation, and that it instinctively obeys them witnout knowing anything of the laws themselves. This would account for its powers being perfect, yet limited in their sphere. Constructiveness and Weight in man also may be adapted to these laws, but, by the addition of Causality, he may become acquainted with natural powers as general agents, and capable of tracing their general application. Thus, a beaver, an elephant, and a savage, may, by the mere instinct of Weight and Momentum, roll or pull up an inclined plain a heavy body, which they cannot lift, without knowing anything of the causes why they succeed in raising it in this way; but a philosopher, with great Causality, may recognise the existence of the cause, ascertain the laws of its operation, and then adapt it to a variety of purposes. This would account for philosophers often excelling in particular branches of science, who are moderately endowed with Causality—Newton, for example, in mathe

Individuality and Eventuality take cognizance of things obvious to the senses. Causality looks a little farther than these, perceives the dependencies of phenomena, and furnishes the idea of causation, as implying efficiency, or something more than mere juxta-position or sequence. It impresses us with an irresistible conviction, that every phenomenon or change in nature is caused by something, and hence by successive steps, leads us to the great Cause of all. In looking at the actions of men, it inclines us to consider the motives, or moving causes, from which they proceed. Individuality and Eventuality apprehend facts and events, or take cognizance of direct evidence; Causality judges of circumstantial evidence, or that by inference. In a trial, a juryman, with large Individuality and Eventuality, and small Causality, will have great difficulty in convicting on circumstantial evidence. He in whom Causality is large will often feel that kind of proof to be irresistible. This faculty induces us on all occasions to ask, Why is this so? It gives deep penetration, and the perception of logical consequence in argument. It is large in persons who possess a natural genius for metaphysics, political economy, or similar sciences. When greatly larger than Individuality, Eventuality, and Comparison, it tends to vague generalities of speculation, altogether inapplicable to the affairs of life; and hence those in whom it predominates are not calculated to shine in general society. Their sphere of thought is too abstract to be reached by ordinary minds: they feel this, and remain silent; and hence are reputed dull, heavy, and even stupid.

A great defect of the organ renders the intellect superficial; and unfits the individual for forming comprehensive and consecutive views, either in abstract science or in business. Coincidence only, and not causation, is then perceived in events. Persons in whom it is deficient are often admirably fitted for common situations, or for executing plans devised by profounder intellects; but, if they are entrusted with the duties of legis-

matics and dynamics; while no man is ever observed to be eminent for his talent of applying causation generally, who has a deficiency of that kind. Some philosophers, however, believe that the lower animals possess some degree of causality. Beavers modify their structures to adapt them to new circumstances, and I have seen a monkey run in terror when a gun was presented toward it—indicating that, from having seen it fired, it knew it to be a destructive engine. Those effects might result from a very low degree of Causality, sufficient to give perception of causation, but not enough to lead to the active employment of causes to accomplish ends; and in this case the remark in the text would be too broad. Dr. Vimont says: "I am much inclined to believe that the faculty of Causality exists in certain animals, such as the elephant, the orang-outang, and the dog; though in a degree so inferior, that they cannot in this respect be compared with man. I believe that it is to the considerable endowment of this faculty in the latter that we ought chiefly to ascribe the immense distance which exists between him and the brutes." Dr. Elliotson observes: "I see daily instances of something deserving some such name as judgment or reason in brutes. To the incredulous I offer the following anecdote in the words of Dr. Darwin: 'A wasp on a gravel walk had caught a fly nearly as large as itself. Kneeling on the ground, I observed him separate the tail and the head from the body part to which the wings were attached. He then took the body part in his paws, and rose about two feet from the ground with it; but a gentle breeze wafting the wings of the fly, turned him round in the air, and he settled again with his prey upon the gravel. I then distinctly observed him cut off with his mouth first one of the wings and then the other, after which he flew away with it unmolested with the wind.' *Zoonomia:* Instinct. The works of the two Hubers *Sur les mœurs de fourmis indigènes*, furnish an abundance of most interesting instances of reason in those insects. See also Mr. Smellie's paper in the *Transact. of Royal Society of Edinburgh*, vol. i., p. 89, sqq." Elliotson's *Blumenbach*, 4th edit., p. 543. An additional instance will be found in *The Phrenological Journal*, vol. viii., p. 73.

latose, or become directors in any public affair embracing causation, it is difficult to make them comprehend the natural dependencies of things, and to act according to them. Blind to causes and to remote consequences, they stigmatize as visionary all intellectual perceptions which their own minds cannot reach; they reject principle as vain theory, are captivated by expedients, and represent these as the *beau ideal* of practical wisdom.

Dr. Spurzheim observes, that "the faculty of Individuality makes us acquainted with objects, that of Eventuality with events; Comparison points out their identity, analogy, or difference, and finds out their harmony; finally, Causality desires to know the causes of all occurrences. Consequently, these faculties together, pointing out general principles and laws, and drawing conclusions, inductions, or corollaries, constitute the truly philosophic understanding."

It is interesting to trace the effects of this faculty, strong or weak, in the mental character, as it exhibits itself in the occurrences of life. I accompanied two gentlemen to see a great public work, in one of whom Individuality was large and Causality small, and in the other of whom the proportions of these organs were reversed. The former, in surveying the different objects and operations, put question after question to the workmen, in rapid and long-continued succession; and nearly all the information which he carried away with him was acquired in answer to specific interrogatories. His mind scarcely supplied a step by its own reflection; and did not appear to survey the operations as a systematic whole. The latter individual looked a long time in silence before he put a question at all; and when he did ask one, it was, What is the use of that? The answer enabled his own mind to supply a multitude of additional ideas; he proceeded in his examination, and it was only on arriving at another incomprehensible part of the apparatus, that he again inquired. At last he got through; then turned back, and, with the most apparent satisfaction, contemplated in silence the operations from beginning to end as an entire system. I heard him afterward describe what he had seen, and discovered that he had carried off a distinct comprehension of the principles and objects of the work. It is probable that a superficial observer would have regarded the first as the acute, intelligent, and observing man of genius—the person who noticed everything, and asked about everything; and the latter as a dull, uninteresting man, who put only two or three questions, looked heavily, and said nothing.

A gentleman in a boat was unexpectedly desired to steer. He took hold of the helm, hesitated a moment what to do, and then steered with just effect. Being asked why he hesitated, he replied, "I was unacquainted with steering, and required to think how the helm acts." He was requested to explain how thinking led him to the point, and replied, That he knew, from study, the *theory* of the helm's action; that he just ran over in his mind the water's action upon it, and its action on the boat, and then he saw the whole plainly before him. He had a full Causality, and not much Individuality. A person with great Individuality and Eventuality, and little Causality, placed in a similar situation, would have *tried the experiment* of the helm's action, to come to a knowledge of the mode of steering: he would have turned it to the right hand and to the left, *observed* the effect, and then acted accordingly; and he might have steered during his whole subsequent life, without knowing anything more about the matter.

A question arose in an evening party concerning the cause of the harvest moon. In one gentleman present Individuality and Eventuality predominated; in another, Causality was the larger intellectual organ. In an instant the former said that the long continuance of moonlight at that season was owing to the moon's advancing north to the tropic of Cancer at the time of her being full. The latter paused for a little, and added, "Yes, sir, you are quite right." Observing the difference in their heads, and perceiving by their manner that they had arrived at the result by different mental processes, I asked them to explain how they knew this to be the cause. The first said, "Oh! I recollect Professor Playfair stated it in his lectures to be so." The other replied, "I had forgot the precise fact, but I recollected the principle on which the professor mentioned it to depend, and by a moment's reflection I followed it out, and arrived at the conclusion which this gentleman has just announced." "I am not sure," said the former, "that I could now master the principle, but of the result I am quite certain, because I distinctly recollect of its being stated by Mr. Playfair." This is a striking example of the mode of action of these different faculties. -Individuality knows only facts, and Eventuality events; while Causality alone takes cognizance of principles.

Causality is the fountain of resources. Place an individual in whom it is small, in new circumstances, and he will be helpless and bewildered; place another, in whom it is large, in a similar situation, and he will show his superiority by the extent of his inventions. A mechanic, with little Causality, will be at a stand if his ordinary tools are wanting, or if employed out of his ordinary line; another, having this faculty powerful, will find a thousand substitutes. If a person deficient in Causality be placed in charge of any establishment, comprehending a variety of duties which arise the one out of the other, and all of which cannot be anticipated and specified a priori, he will be prone to neglect part of what he ought to attend to. He will probably plead forgetfulness as his excuse; but want of comprehensiveness and consecutiveness of thinking will be the real cause of his imperfections.

If a person possessing little Causality write a book, he may shine in narrative, provided Individuality, Eventuality, and Language be amply developed; but when he endeavours to reason, he will become feeble and confused. One endowed with much Causality, in reading a work written by an author in whom this organ is deficient, will feel it characterized by lightness and want of depth; it will furnish him with no stimulus to thinking. When, on the other hand, a person possessing only a small Causality, peruses a book composed by an author in whom this organ predominates, such as Locke's *Essays* or Brown's *Lectures*, he will regard it as heavy, abstract, and dry, and be oppressed by it as if a night-mare were weighing on his mind.

Among metaphysicians, Hume, Dr. Adam Smith, and Dr. Thomas Brown display great Causality, Dr. Reid not so much, and Mr. Stewart still less. In the portraits of the first three the organ is represented as decidedly large. It is large also in Bacon, Franklin, and Playfair; and likewise in the masks of Haydon, Burke, Bruhel, Wordsworth, and Wilkie. It is moderate in Pitt and Sir J. E. Smith; and very deficient in the skulls of the Caribs and New Hollanders. An anonymous writer observes, that, "of whatever has been said and written upon the moral and political sciences in France, the general characteristic is a deficiency in extensive views of human nature, in profound investigation of the heart, portrayed in all its strongest feelings and multitudinous bearings."[*] Without subscribing to the accuracy of this observation in its full extent, the fact may be mentioned as certain, that, in the French head in general, the organ of Causality is by no means largely developed.

"It is remarkable," says Dr. Spurzheim, "that the ancient artists should always have given to their busts of philosophers a large forehead,

* *Edinburgh Review*, Nov., 1820, p. 389.

and represented Jupiter Capitolinus with a forehead in the middle part more prominent than is ever seen in nature; they seem to have observed that developement of the forehead has a relation to great understanding. It is farther remarkable, that this larger developement does not extend to the lateral upper portion of the forehead. The organ of Mirthfulness, which the Edinburgh phrenologists are inclined to consider as that of perceiving differences, is small in the busts of Demosthenes, Cicero, and other great men; it is particularly defective in Jupiter. In this respect therefore, the observations of the ancient artists coincide with mine, to prove that the organ of Mirthfulness is not necessary to a philosophical mind."* The bust of Socrates (of which the Phrenological Society possesses a copy) shows a very large developement of the reflecting organs. Either it is a correct representation of his real appearance, and thus presents an interesting coincidence between his character and developement; or it is imaginary, and, in that case, shows the impression of the ancient artist, that the mind of Socrates required such a tenement for its abode.

As already mentioned, when the organ now under consideration is very deficient, the individual has great difficulty in perceiving causation; and when two events are presented to him, the one following the other, he sees only *coincidence*. Illustrations of this remark frequently occur in discussions relative to Phrenology. When Causality is well developed in an observer, and several decided instances of concomitance between particular forms of head and particular powers of mind are presented to him, the feeling of connexion between them is irresistible; he is struck with it, and declares that there is something here which ought to be followed out. When the same facts are exhibited to a person in whom Causality is deficient, he smiles surprisedly, and ejaculates, "A curious coincidence!" but his mind receives no strong impression of connexion between the phenomena; he feels no desire to follow out the ideas to their consequences, and has no wish to prosecute the investigation. It was from this class of minds, ever ready to catch superficial glimpses, that the public received the first accounts of Phrenology; and on them are chargeable the misrepresentations which so long impeded its course.

This faculty is an ingredient in the judgment of the metaphysicians. As there are individuals so deficient in the organ of Tune as to be incapable of perceiving melody, so there are some in whom Causality is so defective that they are incapable of perceiving causation, except of the most obvious kind. If such persons are not aware of their own deficiency, they are often intolerable dogmatists, as they hold fast by all notions that have been infused into them by authority, and show an utter incapacity for reasoning. There are others in whom the organ is large enough to render them capable of apprehending an exposition of causation, when clearly unfolded to them; but in whom it is still so moderate that they cannot reproduce the steps of the argument by which they were convinced. Such men often possess sound opinions on abstract subjects, without being able to assign sufficient reasons for them.

Causality is also, to a certain extent, the fountain of abstract ideas, namely, those of the relation of cause and effect, and bears, in this respect, an analogy to their abstraction. It and Comparison correspond to the Relative Suggestion of Dr. Thomas Brown; "a tendency of the mind," as he explains it, "by which, on perceiving or conceiving objects together, we are instantly impressed with certain feelings of their mutual relation."† By dispensing with Perception, Conception, &c., as separate faculties of the mind, and dividing the intellect into the two faculties of Simple Suggestion and Relative Suggestion, Dr. Brown has made an interesting

* *Phrenology*, last edition, Boston, U. S., 1832, p. 356
† *Lectures*, vol. iii., p. 14.

approach to the results of phrenological discovery, and to a correct analysis of the actual constitution of the human intellect. It was impossible, by means of the old faculties of Conception, &c., to point out the characteristics of a mind which collected only facts in the order in which they were presented to it; and of another, which struck out a multitude of new ideas from every object which it contemplated, and instinctively inquired from what causes all phenomena proceeded, and to what results they tended. Dr. Brown's Simple Suggestion denotes the one, and his Relative Suggestion the other; and, in Phrenology, the perspective faculties correspond pretty closely to the former, and the Reflective powers to the latter.

We are now prepared to consider some points which have occasioned great and animated discussions among the philosophers of the old schools. It has been stated, that Individuality takes cognizance of objects that exist. A tree, a ship, a mountain, are presented to the mind, and ideas or conceptions of them are formed; and the conception is followed by an intuitive belief in their existence. Bishop Berkeley objects to the belief in their existence as unphilosophical; because, says he, the conception or idea is a mere mental affection, and no principle or reason can be assigned, why an external object must be believed to exist, merely because we experience a mental affection. A smell, for example, is nothing more than a certain impression on the mind, communicated through the olfactory nerves. But no necessary connexion can be perceived between this affection and belief in the existence of a rose: the mind may undergo the affection called a smell, just as it experiences the emotion called joy, and a material object may have as little to do in causing the one as the other. Hence Dr. Berkeley concluded, that we have philosophical evidence for the existence only of mind and mental affections, and none for the existence of the material world. Hume carried this farther, and argued, that as we are conscious only of ideas, and as the existence of ideas does not necessarily imply the existence of mind, we have philosophical evidence for the existence of ideas only, and none for that of either matter or mind. Dr. Reid answered Berkeley's objection by observing, that the belief in external objects, consequent on perceiving them, is intuitive, and hence requires no reason for its support.

Phrenology enables us to refer these different speculations to their sources in the different faculties. Individuality, (aided by the other perceptive faculties,) in virtue of its constitution, perceives external objects, and its action is accompanied by intuitive belief in their existence. But Berkeley employed the faculty of Causality to discover why it is that this perception is followed by belief; and because Causality could give no account of the matter, and could see no necessary connexion between the mental affection called perception, and the existence of external nature, he denied that nature exists. Dr. Reid's answer, translated into phrenological language, was simply this: The cognizance of the existence of the outward world belongs to Individuality: Individuality has received its own constitution and its own functions, and cannot legitimately be called on to explain or account for these to Causality. In virtue of its constitution, it perceives the existence of external objects, and belief in that existence follows; and if Causality cannot see how this happens, it is a proof that Causality's powers are limited, but not that Individuality is deceitful in its indications.

Another class of philosophers, by an error of a similar kind, have denied causation. When Eventuality contemplates circumstances connected by the relation of cause and effect, it discovers only one event following another in immediate and invariable sequence. For example, if a cannon be fired, and the shot knock down a wall, Individuality and some other perceptive faculties observe only the existence of the powder. Eventuality perceives the fire applied to it, the explosion, and the fall of the building, as events following in succession; but it forms no idea of power in the gunpowder, when ignited to produce the effect. When Causality, on the other hand, is joined with Eventuality in contemplating these phenomena, the impression of *power* or *efficiency* in the exploding gunpowder to produce the effect, arises spontaneously in the mind, and Causality produces an intuitive belief in the existence of this efficiency, just because it is its constitution to do so; and it is as absurd for Eventuality to deny the existence of some quality in the power which gives rise to this feeling, because only Causality perceives it, as for Causality to deny the existence of the external world because only the knowing faculties perceive it.

A practical application of much importance follows from these doctrines.

Some men deny the existence of God; and others strenuously maintain that his existence is demonstrable by a legitimate exercise of reason. The former, who deny God, say, that all we perceive in nature is existence and the *succession* of phenomena; that we can form no idea of efficiency or power; and that, therefore, all we know philosophically is, that matter exists, and undergoes certain changes. This is the natural conclusion of men in whose heads Individuality and Eventuality are large, and Causality small; and, accordingly, atheists are generally very deficient in the organ of Causality, and show its weakness in their general arguments on other topics. If, on the other hand, a mind in which Causality is very powerful, surveys the phenomena of nature, the conviction of a Cause of them arises irresistibly and intuitively from the mere exercise of the faculty. Benevolence and design, in the arrangements of the moral and physical world, are clearly perceived by it; and it therefore instinctively infers, that benignity and intelligence are attributes of the Cause which produced them. Hence the fact is phrenologically explained, why all master spirits are believers in God. Socrates, Plato, and the ancient philosophers are represented as endowed with large organs of Causality; and they all admit a Deity. Voltaire had too large a Causality to doubt of the existence of God; and Franklin continued to reverence the Supreme Being, although he had renounced Christianity.

To some who, perhaps for the sake of argument, have seemed inclined to deny the existence of a Deity, I have made the following appeal, without receiving any satisfactory answer: A tree with roots exists; the earth exists; and there is exquisite adaptation of the one to the other. The adaptation is not a quality of the tree nor of the earth; but a relation between them. It has no physical existence, but is clearly apprehended by the mind. Adaptation and its design being obvious, an intelligent mind must have contrived it; and this mind we call the Deity. Causality perceives the adaptation.

Another argument resorted to by atheists finds an answer in the principles now explained. They object that we have no evidence, from reason, of the *self-existence* of God; and affirm, that, for anything we know to the contrary, the Maker of the world may himself own a superior, and have been created. Their objection is stated in this form: "You who believe in God infer his existence from seeing his works, on the principle that every effect must have a cause. But," say they, "this Being himself *is an effect.* You have no evidence from reason of his *self-existence* or *self-creation;* and, as he does exist, you must assign *a cause of him,* on the same principle that you regard him as the cause of the material creation." The atheists carry this argument the length of a denial of God altogether, in respect that it is only the *first cause* that, according to them, can be entitled to be regarded as Deity; and the first cause, say they, is to us unknown.

This speculation may be answered as follows : The knowing faculties *perceive existence directly*, and Causality *infers* qualities from the manifestations of qualities. To be able to judge thoroughly of any object, the *whole* of these faculties must be employed on it. When a watch, for example, is presented to us, the knowing faculties perceive its spring, lever, and wheels, and Causality discerns their object or design. If the question is put, Whence did the watch proceed ? from the nature of its materials, as perceived by the knowing faculties, Causality infers that it could not make itself ; and, from discovering intelligence and design in the adaptation of its parts, this faculty concludes, that its cause must have possessed these qualities, and therefore assigns its production to an intelligent artificer. Suppose the statement to be next made—" This artificer himself is an existence, and every existence must have a cause ; who, then, made the watch-maker ?" In this case, if no farther information were presented to Causality than what it could obtain by contemplating the structure of the watch, the answer would necessarily be, that it could not tell. But let the artificer, or man, be submitted to the joint observation of the knowing faculties and Causality, and let the question be then put, Who made him ? the knowing powers, by examining the structure of his body, would present Causality with data from which it could unerringly infer, that although it perceived in him intelligence and power sufficient to make the watch, yet, from the nature of his constitution, he could not possibly make himself. Proceeding in the investigation, Causality, still aided by the knowing faculties, would perceive the most striking indications of power, benevolence, and design in the human frame ; and, from contemplating these, it would arrive at a complete conviction, that the watch-maker is the work of a great, powerful, and intelligent Being. If, however, the question were repeated, " Whence did this Being proceed ?" Causality could not answer. It would then be in a situation similar to that in which it would be placed, if required to tell, from seeing the watch alone, who made the watch-maker. The perceptive faculties cannot observe the substance of the Maker of the human body : his existence is the object of Causality alone ; and all that it can accomplish is, to infer his existence, and his qualities or attributes, from perceiving their manifestations. I have stated the argument in the plainest language, but with perfect reverence ; and we are arrived at the conclusion, that this faculty is silent as to the cause of the Creator of man, and cannot tell whether he is self-existent, or called into being by some higher power. But thus far it can go, and it draws its conclusions unhesitatingly, that he *must exist*, and *must possess the attributes* which it perceives manifested in his works : and, these points being certain, it declares that he is God *to us ;* that he is *our* Creator and Preserver ; that all his qualities, so far as it can discover, merit our profoundest respect and admiration ; and that, therefore, he is to man the highest and most legitimate object of veneration and worship.

It has been objected, that, although Causality may discover that God *has* existed, it sees no evidence that he *now* exists. The answer to this remark appears to me to be, that the manifestations of his power, wisdom, and goodness *continue* to be presented to Causality every moment, and that it has no data for concluding that the *cause* of them has ceased, while their effects remain monuments of his being. The organ is established.

ADAPTATION OF THE EXTERNAL WORLD TO THE INTELLECTUAL FACULTIES OF MAN.

THE human mind and the external world, having emanated from the same Creator, ought, when understood, to be found wisely adapted to each other ; and this accordingly appears, in an eminent degree, to be the case.

If the reader will direct his attention to any natural or artificial object, and consider, 1st, its existence; 2d, its form; 3d, its size; 4th, its weight; 5th, its locality, or relation in space to other objects; 6th, the number of its parts; 7th, the order or physical arrangement of its parts; 8th, the changes which it undergoes; 9th, the periods of time which these require; 10th, the analogies and differences between the individual object under consideration and other individuals; 11th, the effects which it produces; and, lastly, if he will designate this assemblage of ideas by a name—he will find that he has obtained a tolerably complete notion of the object.

This order ought to be followed in teaching the sciences. Botany and mineralogy are rendered intolerably tedious and uninteresting to many persons, who really possess sufficient natural talents for studying them, by names and classifications being erroneously represented as the chief ends to be attained. A better method would be, to make the pupil acquainted with his own mental powers, and to furnish him with experimental knowledge that these stand in definite relations to external objects, and feel a positive pleasure in contemplating them. His attention ought then to be directed to the existence of the object, as in itself interesting to Individuality; to its form, as interesting to the faculty of Form; to its colour, as pleasing to the faculty of Colouring; and so on with its other qualities: while the name, order, genus, and species ought to be taught in the last place as merely designative of the relationship of the objects with which he has become conversant. Practice in this mode of tuition will establish its advantages. The mind which, unexercised, regarded all forms, not extravagantly ugly or beautiful, with indifference, will soon experience delight in discriminating minute degrees of elegance and expression; and the same effect will be produced by following a similar process of cultivation in regard to the other powers. The larger the organs, the greater will be the delight experienced in study; but even with a moderate developement much may be attained. Nor is it necessary to resort to schools and colleges for this exercise of the intellect. Objects in nature and art everywhere surround us, calculated to stimulate our faculties; and if the reader, as he walks in the country or in the town, will actively apply his various powers in the manner now pointed out, he will find innumerable sources of pleasure within his reach, although he should not know scientific names and classifications.

MODES OF ACTION OF THE FACULTIES.

ALL the faculties tend to action, and, when active in a due degree, produce actions good, proper, or necessary: it is excess of activity and ill direction that occasion abuses. It is probable that Phrenology has been discovered only in consequence of some individuals, in whom particular organs were very largely developed, having yielded to the strongest propensities of their nature. The smallness of a particular organ is not the cause of a faculty producing abuses. Although the organ of Benevolence be small, it will not occasion cruelty; but, as it will be accompanied with indifference to the miseries of others, its deficiency may lead to the omission of duties. When, also, one organ is small, abuses may result from another being left without proper restraint. Thus, large organs of Acquisitiveness and Secretiveness, combined with small organs of Reflection and Conscientiousness, may, in certain circumstances, lead to theft. Powerful Destructiveness, with weak Benevolence, may produce cruel actions.

Every faculty, when in action, from whatever cause, produces the kind of feeling, or forms the kind of ideas, already explained as resulting from its natural constitution. Large organs have the greatest tendency to act; small organs the least. Since every organ tends to action, it is clear that there must be a legitimate sphere of action for them all. None of them is necessarily and inherently bad, otherwise God must have deliberately created organs for no other purpose but to lead us into sin.

The PROPENSITIES and SENTIMENTS cannot be excited to action directly by a mere command of the will. For example, we cannot conjure up the emotions of fear, compassion, and veneration by merely willing to experience them; and hence we are not to blame for the absence of any emotion at a particular time. These faculties, however, may enter into action from an internal excitement of the organs; and then the desire or emotion which each produces will be felt, whether we will to experience it or not. Thus, the cerebellum being active from internal causes, produces the corresponding feeling; and this cannot be avoided if the organ be excited. We may have it in our power to permit or restrain the manifestation of it in action; but we have no option, if the organ be excited, to experience, or not to experience, the feeling itself. The case is the same with the organs of Cautiousness, Hope, Veneration, and the others. There are times when we feel involuntary emotions of fear, or hope, or awe, arising within us, for which we cannot account by reference to external causes; such feelings depend on the spontaneous action of the organs of these sentiments, depending on an increased force of the circulation in their bloodvessels.

"We cannot Nature by our wishes rule,
Nor, at our will, her warm emotions cool."
Crabbe.

In the second place, these faculties may be called into action independently of the will, by the presentation of the external objects fitted by nature to excite them. When an object in distress is presented, the faculty of Benevolence starts into activity, and produces the feelings which depend upon it. When an object threatening danger is perceived, Cautiousness gives an instantaneous emotion of fear. And when stupendous objects are contemplated, Ideality inspires us with a feeling of sublimity. In all these cases the power of acting, or of not acting, is dependent on the will; but the power of feeling, or of not feeling, is not so. When the temperament is active, emotions are much more easily excited, both by external and internal causes, than where it is sluggish.

"It seems an unaccountable pleasure," says Hume,* "which the spectators of a well-written tragedy receive from sorrow, terror, anxiety, and other passions, that are in themselves disagreeable and uneasy. The more they are touched and affected, the more are they delighted with the spectacle. The whole art of the poet is employed in rousing and supporting the compassion and indignation, the anxiety and resentment, of his audience. They are pleased in proportion as they are afflicted, and never are so happy as when they employ tears, sobs, and cries, to give vent to their sorrow, and relieve their hearts, swollen with the tenderest sympathy and compassion."

Many volumes have been written to solve this problem. Those authors who deny the existence of benevolent and disinterested feelings in man, maintain, that we sympathize with Cato, Othello, or King Lear because we conceive the possibility of ourselves being placed in similar situations, and that then all the feelings arise in us which we would experience, if we were ourselves suffering under similar calamities. Mr. Stewart, who, on the other hand, admits the existence of generous emotions in the human mind, states it as his theory, that we, for an instant, believe the distress to

* Essay 22.

be real; and under this belief feel the compassion which would naturall start up in our bosoms, if the sufferings represented were actually en dured. A subsequent act of judgment, he says, dispels, in an almost imperceptible portion of time, the illusion, and restrains the mind from *acting* under the emotion; which, if the belief of reality continued, it would certainly do, by running to the relief of the oppressed hero or heroine: but still he considers that a momentary belief is necessary to call up the emotions which we experience.

The phrenological doctrine just delivered appears to me to furnish the true explanation. Each propensity and sentiment may be called into action by presentation of its object, and, when active, the corresponding feeling or emotion attends it, in virtue of its constitution. Happiness consists in the harmonious gratification of all the faculties; and the very essence of gratification is activity. "Thus, the muscular system," says Dr. A. Combe, "is gratified by motion, and pleasure arises; the eye is gratified by looking at external objects; Combativeness, by overcoming opposition; Destructiveness, by the sight of destruction and the infliction of pain; Benevolence, by the relief of suffering; Hope, by looking forward to a happy futurity; Cautiousness, by a certain degree of uncertainty and anxiety, &c. As the degree of enjoyment corresponds to the number of faculties simultaneously active and gratified, it follows, that a tragic scene, which affords a direct stimulus to several of the faculties at the same moment, *must be agreeable*, whatever these may be; 1st, if it do not, at the same time, outrage any of the other feelings; and, 2dly, if it do not excite any faculty so intensely as to give rise to pain; just as too much light hurts the eye, and too much exertion fatigues the muscles." In the play of *Pizarro*, for example, when the child is introduced, its aspect and situation instantly excite Philoprogenitiveness, and individuals possessing this organ largely feel a deep interest in it; the representation of danger to which it is exposed rouses Cautiousness, producing *fear for its safety*; when *Rolla* saves it, this fear is allayed, Philoprogenitiveness is highly delighted, and Benevolence also is gratified; and the excitement of these faculties is pleasure. All this internal emotion takes place simply in consequence of the constitution of the faculties, and the relation established by nature between them and their objects, without the understanding needing to be imposed on, or to form any theory about the scenes, whether they are real or fictitious. A picture raises emotions of sublimity or beauty on the same principles. "The cloud-capt towers and gorgeous palaces" are fitted by nature to excite Ideality, Wonder, and Veneration; and, these faculties being active, certain emotions of delight are experienced. When a very accurate representation of the towers and palaces is executed on canvass, their appearance in the picture excites into action the same faculties which their natural lineaments would rouse, and the same pleasures kindle in the soul. But what should we think if Mr. Stewart assured us that we needed to believe the paint and the canvass to be real stone and mortar, and the figures to be real men and women, before we could enjoy the scene? And yet this would be as reasonable as the same doctrine applied to tragedy. We may weep at a tragedy represented on canvass, and know all the while that there are only colours and forms before us. On the same principle we may shed tears at seeing a tragedy acted—which is merely a representation by means of words and gestures, of objects calculated to rouse the faculties—and yet suffer no delusion respecting the reality of the piece.

If the propensities and sentiments become excessively active from these representations, they may overpower the intellect; a temporary belief may follow, and the feeling will be the stronger: but, in this case, it appears to me, that the strong emotion does not *arise* from a *previous* *illusion of the understanding;* but that misconception in the intellect is the *consequence* of the feeling having become overwhelming. This remark is illustrated and confirmed by the following extract from the Life of Mrs. Siddons: "It was my custom," says she, "to study my characters at night, when all the domestic cares and business of the day were over. On the night preceding that in which I was to appear in this part for the first time, I shut myself up, as usual, when all the family were retired, and commenced my study of *Lady Macbeth.* As the character is very short, I thought I should soon accomplish it. Being then only twenty years of age, I believed, as many others do believe, that little more was necessary than to get the words into my head; for the necessity of discrimination and the developement of character, at that time of my life, had scarcely entered into my imagination. But, to proceed, I went on with tolerable composure in the silence of the night, (a night I never can forget,) till I came to the assassination scene, when the horrors of the scene rose to a degree that made it impossible for me to get farther. I snatched my candle, and hurried out of the room, in a paroxysm of terror. My dress was of silk, and the rustling of it, as I ascended the stairs to go to bed, seemed to my panic-struck fancy like the movement of a spectre pursuing me. At last I reached my chamber, where I found my husband fast asleep. I clapped my candlestick down upon the table, without the power of putting the candle out; and I threw myself on my bed, without daring to stay even to take off my clothes."*

Excessive action of the affective faculties, or the removal of their objects, causes uneasiness or pain.

The law of our constitution above explained, accounts also for several of the phenomena of insanity. All the organs are liable to become strongly and involuntarily active through disease; this produces mental excitement, or violent desires to act in the direction of the diseased organs. If Destructiveness be affected in this manner, fury, which is just an irresistible propensity to violence and outrage, will ensue. If the organ of Cautiousness become involuntarily active through disease, fear will constantly be felt; and this constitutes melancholy. If Veneration and Hope be excited in a similar way, the result will be involuntary emotions of devotion, the liveliest joy and anticipations of bliss; which feelings, fixed and immoveable, amount to religious insanity. It occasionally happens that a patient is insane on a single feeling alone, such as Cautiousness, Hope, or Veneration, and that, if the sphere of activity of this faculty be avoided, his understanding on other subjects is sound, and his general conduct rational and consistent. Thus, a person insane in Self-Esteem, sometimes imagines himself to be a king; but on other topics evinces sound sense and consecutiveness of judgment. This results from the organs of intellect being sane, and only the organ of Self-Esteem diseased. Sometimes well-meaning individuals, struck with the clearness of the understanding in such patients, set themselves to point out, by means of argument, the erroneous nature of the notions under which they suffer, supposing that, if they could convince their intellect of the mistake, the disease would be cured; but the malady consists in an unhealthy action of the organ of a sentiment or propensity; and, as long as the disease lasts, the insane feeling, which is the basis of the whole mental alienation, will remain, and argument will do as little to remove it, as a speech would accomplish in curing gout.

The converse of the doctrine now explained also holds good; that is to say, if the organ be not active, the propensity or emotion connected with it cannot be felt; just as we cannot hear a sound when the auditory apparatus is not excited by vibrations of the air.

* Campbell's *Life of Mrs. Siddons,* vol. ii., p. 55.

The most important practical consequences may be deduced from the exposition of our mental constitution. The larger any organ is, the more it is prepared to come into activity; and the smaller, the less so. Hence, an individual prone to violence, to excessive pride, vanity, or avarice, is the victim of an unfavourable developement of brain; and in our treatment of him we ought to bear this fact constantly in mind. If we had wished, for example, to render Bellingham mild, the proper proceeding would have been, not to abuse him for being ill-tempered, for this would have directly excited his Destructiveness, the largeness of which was the cause of his wrath; but to address ourselves to his Benevolence, Veneration, and Intellect, that, by rousing them, we might assuage the vehemence of Destructiveness. In a case like that of David Haggart, in whom Conscientiousness was very deficient, we ought always to bear in mind that, in regard to feeling the obligation of justice, such an individual is in the same state of unhappy deficiency, as Mr. Milne is in perceiving colours, and Ann Ormerod in perceiving melody; and our treatment ought to correspond. We would never think of attempting to improve Ann Ormerod's organ of Tune by beating her; and, Haggart's Conscientiousness being naturally as deficient, we could as little have succeeded in enabling him to feel and act justly by inflicting severe punishment. The reasonable plan in such cases is, first, to avoid placing the individual in circumstances demanding the exercise of the deficient faculty—not to place Ann Ormerod, for instance, in a band of singers, or David Haggart in a confidential situation, where property is intrusted to his care; and, in the next place, to present to all the organs of the higher sentiments which are largely possessed, motives calculated to excite them and to control the propensities, so as to supply, as far as possible, by other means, the directing power of the feeble Conscientiousness.

If the principle be correct, that large organs give strong desires and small organs weak impulses, Phrenology must be calculated, in an eminent degree, to be practically useful in society. If, in choosing a servant, we are afraid or ashamed to examine the head, and engage one with a brain extremely deficient in the moral organs, and large in those of the animal propensities, like that of Mary Macinnes, and if certain strong animal feelings accompany this developement, we shall unquestionably suffer annoyance as the consequence. If we select an individual very deficient in Conscientiousness as a child's maid, she will labour under a natural blindness to truth, and not only lie herself, but teach the children intrusted to her care this abominable vice. If a merchant select a clerk with a head like David Haggart's, and place money at his disposal, the strong animal feelings, unrestrained by Conscientiousness, may prompt him to embezzle it. It is incredible to what an extent evils might be mitigated or prevented in society, by the practical application of this principle. I have applied it in the selection of servants with great advantage.

In the next place, if the presentation of the object of a faculty rouses it into instant action—as suffering, Benevolence—or danger, Cautiousness—this becomes a highly important principle in the education of the children. If we put on the natural language of Destructiveness and Self-Esteem in our intercourse with them, we shall cultivate these faculties in their minds, by exciting the organs; if we manifest Benevolence and Veneration in their presence, we shall excite the same faculties in them; if we discourse constantly about money, the desire of increasing it, and the fear of losing it, we shall stimulate the organs of Acquisitiveness and Self-Esteem in them, and increase the power of these propensities.

In the third place, the faculties of which we are now speaking may be excited to action, or repressed, indirectly, by an effort of the will

Thus, if the knowing faculties (which have the function of forming ideas) be employed to conceive internally objects fitted by nature to excite the propensities and sentiments, the latter will start into action in the same manner, though not with so much intensity, as if their appropriate objects were externally present. For example, if we conceive inwardly an object in distress, and Benevolence be powerful, compassion will be felt, and tears will sometimes flow from the emotion produced. In like manner, if we wish to repress the activity of Ideality, we cannot do so by merely willing that the sentiment be quiet ; but if we conceive objects fitted to excite Veneration, Cautiousness, Self-Esteem, or Benevolence, the organs of these feelings will then be excited, and Ideality will sink into inactivity. The vivacity of the feeling, in such cases, will be in proportion to the strength of the conception, and the energy of the propensities and sentiments together.

If the organ of any propensity or sentiment enter into vigorous action from internal causes, it will prompt the intellectual faculties to form conceptions fitted to gratify it ; or, in other words, the habitual subjects of thought will be determined by the organs which are predominantly active from internal excitement. If the cerebellum be permanently active, the individual will be prone to collect pictures, books, and anecdotes fitted to gratify the feeling ; his mind will be much occupied with such ideas, and they will afford him delight. If, in another individual, Constructiveness, Ideality, Imitation, and the knowing organs be internally active, he will desire to see pictures, busts, and works of art, in which skill, beauty, and expression are combined ; or he will take pleasure in inventing and constructing them. He will know much about such objects, and be fond of possessing them, and of talking of them. If, in another individual, Acquisitiveness be internally active, he will feel a great and natural interest in all matters connected with wealth, and be inspired with an eager curiosity to know the profits of different branches of trade, and the property possessed by different individuals. If Benevolence be internally active, the mind will run habitually on schemes of philanthropy, such as those of Howard, Mr. Owen, or Mrs. Fry. In these cases the *liking* for the object or pursuit will depend upon the particular propensities or sentiments which are active ; the intellectual faculties serving merely as the ministering instruments of their gratification. If the pursuit be purely intellectual, such as the study of mathematics or algebra, the *liking* will arise from the activity of the intellectual faculties themselves.

These principles explain readily the great variety of tastes and dispositions among mankind ; for in no two individuals are all the organs to be found combined in the same relative proportions, and hence every one is inspired with likings in some degree peculiar to himself.

As the propensities and sentiments do not form ideas, and as it is impossible to excite or recall directly, by an act of the will, the feelings or emotions produced by them, it follows that these faculties have not the attributes of Perception, Conception, Memory, and Imagination. They have the attribute of Sensation alone ; that is to say, when they are active, a sensation or emotion is experienced. Hence, Sensation is an accompaniment of the action of all the faculties which feel, and of the nervous system in general ; but Sensation is not a faculty itself.

The laws of the KNOWING and REFLECTING faculties are in several respects different. These faculties form ideas and perceive relations ; they are subject to the will, or rather constitute will themselves, and minister to the gratification of the other faculties which only feel.

1st, These faculties also may become active from excitement of the organs by internal causes, and then the kinds of ideas which they are fitted to form are presented involuntarily to the mind. The musician feels the

notes flowing on him uncalled for. A man in whom Number is powerful
and active, calculates by a natural impulse. He in whom Form is vigorous, conceives figures by internal inspiration. He in whom Causality is
powerful and active, reasons while he thinks, without an effort. He in
whom Wit is energetic, feels witty conceptions flowing into his mind
spontaneously, and even at times when he would wish them not to be
present.

2dly, These faculties may be excited by the presentation of external
objects fitted to call them into action ; and,

3dly, They may be excited to action by an act of the will.

When excited by the presentation of external objects, the objects are
PERCEIVED, and this act is called PERCEPTION. Perception is the
lowest degree of activity of these faculties ; and if no idea is formed
when the object is presented, the individual is destitute of the power of
manifesting the faculty. Thus, when tones are produced, he who cannot
perceive the melody of them, is incapable of manifesting the faculty of
Tune. When a coloured object is presented, and the individual cannot
perceive, so as to distinguish the tints, he is destitute of the faculty of
Colouring. When the steps of a simple argument are logically and distinctly stated, he who cannot perceive the relation between the steps
and the necessity of the conclusion, is destitute of the faculty of Causality ; and so on. Thus, Perception is a mode of action of the faculties
which form ideas, and implies the lowest degree of power ; but Perception is not a separate faculty.

This doctrine is not theoretical, but is clearly indicated by facts. In
the case reported by Mr. Hood,* a patient who lost the *memory* of words,
yet enjoyed *perception* of their meaning. He understood language spoken
by others ;—or, the organ of Language retained so much of its power as
to enable him to *perceive* the meaning of words when presented to his
mind, but so little of its energy as not to be adequate to the act of recalling words by an act of his will, so as to express his thoughts. The
case of Mr. Ferguson† is another in point. He enjoyed so great a degree
of the organ of Size as to be able to perceive distance when natural
scenery was presented, but so little as to be quite unable to recollect it
when the objects were withdrawn. Mr. Sloane‡ is in a similar situation
in regard to colours. He *perceives* the *differences* of hues when they are
before his eyes, but has so little of the organ of Colouring that he does
not recollect, so as to be able to name them separately. Many persons
are in a similar condition in regard to music ; they perceive melody and
enjoy it when presented to the ear, but have so little of the faculty of
Tune as to be unable afterward to recall the notes. The same phenomena are seen in the case of the reflecting powers. Many persons enjoy
reflective faculties acute and vigorous enough to perceive an argument
if placed before them, who are quite incapable of inventing, or even reproducing, it themselves. They ascribe their defect to a bad memory ;
but they often show no lack of memory for music, or mechanics, or botany, or other subjects not involving Causality.

Here, again, a highly valuable practical result presents itself. If we
place a person with a forehead like Fraser's, in whom the reflecting
organs are deficient, in a situation, or apply to him for advice in circumstances, in which great natural sagacity and depth of intellect are necessary to acting or advising successfully, we shall assuredly be disappointed ;
whereas, if we apply to one having such a combination as that of Dr.
Franklin, in whom the organs of reflection were very large, there will be
much more of the instinctive capacity of tracing out beforehand the probable chain of causation, and anticipating the effects of measures which

* Page 328.   † Page 284.   ‡ Page 292.

we propose to follow. Fraser might show good sense and sound judgment *after* the consequences were pointed out to him, because he possesses a developement of the reflecting organs sufficient to give him *perception* of causation when presented ; but he could not, like Franklin, anticipate effects, as this demands a higher degree of power.

According to this view, which regards Perception as a mode of action of *every* intellectual faculty, an individual may possess acute perception as to one class of objects, and be very deficient as to others. Thus, Milne has an acute perception of form, although he cannot perceive some colours ; other individuals perceive symmetry distinctly, who cannot perceive melody. This exposition has the merit of coinciding with nature ; for we frequently meet with such examples as those I have now cited.

The metaphysicians, on the other hand, treat of Perception as a *general faculty ;* and, when their doctrine is applied to nature, the extraordinary spectacle is presented, of their *general power* performing in the same individual half its functions with great effect, while it is wholly inefficient as to the other half ; just as if a leg could walk east and be quite incapable of walking west. Dr. Thomas Brown has abandoned this absurdity ; and differs from Reid, Stewart, and all his predecessors, in denying perception to be anything more than an act of the general power of the mind. We call it an act of several special faculties of the mind ; but with these Dr. Brown was not acquainted.

CONCEPTION. When the knowing or reflecting organs are powerfully active from internal excitement, whether by the will or from natural activity, ideas are vividly and rapidly conceived ; and the act of forming them is styled CONCEPTION : if the act amounts to a very high degree of vivacity, it is called IMAGINATION. Thus perception is the lowest degree of activity of any of these faculties excited by an external object ; and conception and imagination are higher degrees of activity depending on internal causes, and without the interference of an external object. Each faculty performs the act of conception in its own sphere. Thus, if one person have a powerful organ of Tune, he is able to conceive, or call up in his own mind, the notes of a tune, when no instrument is sounding in his ears. If his organ of Form be very small, he may not be able to bring shapes before his mind with equal facility. Some persons read music like a book, the written sign of a note being sufficient to enable them to call up the impression of the note itself in their minds. This is the result of a very high degree of activity of the faculties of Form and Tune. Temperament has a great effect on activity ; the lymphatic temperament needs external objects to rouse it to vivid action, while the sanguine and nervous glow with spontaneous and constitutional vivacity. Hence imagination, which results from a high degree of activity, is rarely found with a temperament purely lymphatic, but becomes exalted in proportion to the approach of the temperament to the nervous.

In treating of Colouring, I cited a passage, in which Mr. Stewart, after stating the fact, that some men are able to distinguish different tints when presented together, who cannot name them when separate, attributes this want of discrimination to defect in the power of *conception*, probably arising, he supposes, from early habits of inattention. To a certain extent he is correct : an individual like Mr. Sloane may be found, whose organ of Colouring enables him to distinguish hues when seen in juxta-position, and is yet so weak as not to give him *conception* or memory of them when seen apart, and this would certainly indicate a deficient power of *conception;* but then the power of conception may be deficient in this faculty alone, and very vigorous in all the others. On Mr. Stewart's principle, that conception is a general power, we here meet with the anomaly of its performing one portion of its functions well, while it is very deficient in another; which defect is accounted for by him, by ascribing it to early habits of inattention: whereas, if a faculty be naturally strong, it as eagerly attends to its objects, as a vigorous and empty stomach craves for food.

When any of the knowing or reflecting faculties is internally active, it conceives, or is presented with ideas of the objects of which it takes cognizance. Thus, Locality, Colouring, and Size being active, we are able, with our eyes closed, to conceive a landscape in all its details of hill and dale, sunshine and shade. If this internal action become morbid through disease of the organs, then ideas become fixed, and remain involuntarily in the mind; and if this be long continued, it constitutes insanity. Many persons have experienced, when in the dark, vivid impressions of figures of every variety of colour and form passing before the mind, sometimes invested with alarming brilliancy and vivacity. I conclude that this arises from internal excitement of the organs situated at the superciliary ridge, namely, Form, Locality, Colouring, and others. This affection is, in most instances, only momentary; but suppose that it were to become fixed and continuous, then the mind would be haunted by permanent and vivid conceptions of fantastic beings, invested with more than the form and hues of reality. This would be insanity; not a morbid feeling, such as melancholy, or fury, or religious joy, but an intellectual delusion. Every sentiment might be sound, yet this aberration of intellect might remain fixed, and immoveable by the will. If we suppose this disease to take place in several knowing organs, leaving the organs of reflection entire, it is quite possible to imagine that the individual may have false perceptions on some points, and not only be sane on all others, but be able, by means of the faculties that remain unaffected, to distinguish the erroneous impressions. Such cases actually occur.

The phenomena of apparitions or spectral illusions may be accounted for by the principles now explained. If several organs become active through internal excitement, they produce involuntary conceptions of outward objects, invested with all the attributes of form, colour, and size, which usually distinguish reality. Many interesting examples of this affection are given in *The Phrenological Journal.*[*]

The organs of the knowing faculties seem, from the descriptions of the apparitions, to be the seats of these diseased perceptions. Nicolai, the Berlin bookseller, saw the *form* as of a deceased person, within eight steps of him—*vast numbers* of human and other forms equally in the day and night—crowds of both sexes—people on horseback—birds and dogs—of natural size, and distinct as if alive—of natural colour, but paler than reality. He then *began to hear them talk.* On his being blooded with leeches, the room was crowded with spectres—in a few hours their *colour* began to fade, but in a few more they were white. They dissolved in air, and *fragments* of them were visible for some time. Dr. Alderson, of Hull, furnishes other two cases. Mr. R. left his wife and family in America, but saw them and conversed with them in this country—saw *trains* of living and dead persons—in a *bright brass lock* again saw his transatlantic friends, and always in that lock—had violent headache. A pot-house-keeper in Hull saw a soldier in his cellar whom he endeavoured to seize, but found to be an illusion—he attempted to take up oysters from the ground, which were equally unreal—he saw *crowds* of the living and dead—he scarcely knew real from spectral customers—and suffered repeated flogging from a wagoner with a whip, who was an illusion.[†] I have given above, page 288, the case of a man in the west of Scotland with a large organ of *Wonder,* who saw inanimate things and persons in

* Vol. i., p. 541; ii., 111, 293, 362; v., 210, 319, 430; vi., 260, 515; vii., 162; x., 47, 217.

† Alderson's *Essay on Apparitions,* London, 1823.

visions—he had a *spotted carpet* for a long time before his eyes, a funeral, and a log of wood on wheels. His son had the same tendency—he followed a beggar, who glided and vanished into a wall. All these perceptions are clearly referrible to the knowing organs.

In July, 1836, I was present at the examination of the brain of an old gentleman, who for several years before his death saw spectral illusions, knowing them to be such. They presented themselves in the costumes of the various countries which he had visited, and even Greek and Roman statues appeared. Their dresses were often rich in colouring, and the figures were of all sizes, from gigantic to miniature beings. An old woman wrapped in a cloak, such as is generally worn by Scotch female peasants, was his most frequent visiter. There was great vascularity in the bloodvessels of the brain generally, and the falx, and the *dura mater* lying over the organs of Veneration, Benevolence, Wonder, and Imitation, were thickened and opaque, of the colour and appearance of moistened vellum ; exhibiting strong marks of chronic inflammation.

Mr. Simpson communicated to *The Phrenological Journal*, vol. ii., p. 294, the following case, which is particularly interesting and instructive. Concomitance of pain in the precise seat of the organs, with disorder of their functions, forms a striking feature in it ; and the author states, that he is ready to afford the means of verification of the facts to any philosophical inquirer :

" Miss S. L.," says Mr. Simpson, " a young lady, under twenty years of age, of good family, well educated, free from any superstitious fears, and in perfect general health of body and soundness of mind, has, nevertheless, been for some years occasionally troubled, both in the night and in the day, with visions of persons and inanimate objects, in almost all the modes and forms which we have already related. She was early subject to such illusions occasionally, and the first she remembers was that of a *carpet* spread out in the air, which descended near her, and vanished away.

" After an interval of some years, she began to see human figures in her room as she lay wide awake in bed, even in the daylight of the morning. These figures were *whitish*, or rather *gray* and *transparent* like *cobweb*, and generally above the *size* of life. At this time she had acute headaches, very singularly confined to one small spot of the head ; on being asked to point out the spot, the utmost care being taken not to lead her to the answer, our readers may judge of our feelings as phrenologists, when she touched, with her fore-finger and thumb, *each side of the root of the nose, the commencement of the eyebrows, and the spot immediately over the top of the nose, the ascertained seats of the organs of Form, Size, and Individuality !* Here, particularly on each side of the root of the nose, she said the sensation could only be compared to that of running sharp knives into the part. The pain increased when she held her head down, and was much relieved by holding her face upward.* Miss S. L., on being asked if the pain was confined to that spot, answered, that some time afterward *the pain extended to right and left along the eyebrows, and a little above them, and completely round the eyes, which felt often as if they would burst from their sockets.* When this happened, her visions were varied precisely as the phrenologist would have anticipated, and she detailed the progress without a single leading question. *Weight, Colouring, Order, Number, Locality,* all became affected ; and let us observe what happened. The whitish or cobweb spectres assumed the natural *colour* of the objects, but they continued often to present themselves, though not always, above the *size* of life. She saw a beggar one day out of doors, natural in size and colour, who vanished as she came up to the

---

* " *Quere*—Does not this look like a pressure of blood on that region of the brain ?"

spot. *Colouring*, being over-excited, began to occasion its specific ar fantastical illusions. Bright spots, like stars on a black ground, filled th room in the dark, and even in daylight ; and sudden and sometimes gra dual illumination of the room during the night often took place, so tha the furniture in it became visible. Innumerable balls of fire seemed on day to pour like a torrent out of one of the rooms of the house down th staircase. On one occasion, the pain between the eyes and along th lower ridge of the brow struck her suddenly with great violence—wher *instantly* the room filled with stars and bright spots. On attempting, on that occasion, to go to bed, she said she was conscious of *an inability to balance herself, as if she had been tipsy,* and she fell, having made repeated efforts to seize the bed-post ; which, in the most unaccountable manner, eluded her grasp. *by shifting its place,* and also by presenting her with a *number of bed-posts instead of one.* If the organ of *Weight,* situated be- tween *Size* and *Colouring,* be the organ of the instinct to preserve, and power of preserving equilibrium, it must be the necessary consequence of the derangement of that organ to overset the balance of the person. Over-excited *Number* we should expect to produce multiplication of objects, and the first experience she had of this illusion was the multi- plication of the bed-posts, and subsequently of any inanimate object she looked at—that object being in itself real and single ; a book, a footstool. a work-box, would increase to twenty, or fifty, sometimes without order or arrangement, and at other times piled regularly one above another. Such objects deluded her another way, by increasing in *size,* as she looked at them, to the most amazing excess—again resuming their natural size —less than which they never seemed to become—and again swelling out. *Locality,* over-excited, gave her the illusion of objects, which she had been accustomed to regard as fixed, being out of their places ; and she thinks, *but is not sure, that,* on one occasion, a door and window in one apart- ment seemed to have changed places—but, as she added, she might have been deceived by a mirror. This qualification gave us the more confi- dence in her accuracy, when, as she did with regard to all her other illu- sions, she spoke more positively. She had not hitherto observed a great and painful confusion in the visions which visited her, so as to entitle us to infer the derangement of *Order.* *Individuality, Form, Size, Weight, Colouring, Locality,* and *Number* only, seemed hitherto affected.

　" For nearly two years Miss S. L. was free from her frontal headaches, and—mark the coincidence—untroubled by visions, or any other illusive perceptions. Some months ago, however, all her distressing symptoms returned in great aggravation, when she was conscious of a want of health.* The pain was more acute than before along the frontal bone, and round and in the eyeballs ; and all the organs there situated recom- menced their game of illusion. Single figures of absent and deceased friends were terribly real to' her, both in the day and the night, sometimes *cobweb,* but generally coloured. She sometimes saw friends on the street, who proved phantoms when she approached to speak to them ; and in- stances occurred where, from not having thus satisfied herself of the illu- sion, she affirmed to such friends that she had seen them in certain places, at certain times, when they proved to her the clearest *alibi.* The *confusion* of her spectral forms now distressed her. (*Order* affected.) The oppression and perplexity was intolerable when figures presented themselves before her in inextricable disorder, and still more when they changed—as with Nicolai—from whole figures to parts of figures—faces, and half faces, and limbs—sometimes of inordinate size and dreadful deformity. One instance of illusive *disorder,* which she mentioned, is

* " Constitutional irregularity would, it is very probable, explain the whole disorder."

curious; and has the farther effect of exhibiting (what cannot be put in terms except those of) the derangement of the just perception of gravitation or equilibrium (*Weight*.) One night, as she sat in her bed-room, and was about to go to bed, a *stream* of spectres, persons' faces, and limbs, in the most shocking confusion, seemed to her to pour into her room from the window, in the manner of a cascade! Although the cascade continued apparently in rapid descending motion, there was no accumulation of figures in the room, the supply unaccountably vanishing after having formed the cascade. *Colossal* figures are her frequent visiters. (*Size*.)

" Real, but inanimate, objects have assumed to her the form of animals; and she has often attempted to lift articles from the ground which, like the oysters in the pot-house cellar, eluded her grasp.

" More recently she has experienced a great aggravation of her alarms; for, like Nicolai, she *began* to hear her spectral visiters speak! With Mr. R., of Hull, the spectres always spoke. At first her crowds kept up a buzzing and indescribable *gibbering*, and occasionally joined in a loud and terribly disagreeable *laugh*, which she could only impute to fiends. These unwelcome sounds were generally followed by a rapid and always alarming advance of the figures, which often on these occasions presented very large and fearful faces, with insufferable glaring eyes close to her own. All self-possession then failed her, and the cold sweat of terror stood on her brow. Her single figures of the deceased and absent then began to gibber, and soon more distinctly to address her; but her terror has hitherto prevented her from understanding what was said.*

" Of the other illusive perceptions of Miss S. L. we may mention *the sensation of being lifted up*, and of *sinking down*, and *falling forward*, with the puzzling perception of objects off their perpendicular; for example, *the room, floor and all, sloping to one side*. (*Weight*.")

Mr. Simpson concludes, by remarking " how curiously the old-established phenomena of ghosts are *seriatim* explained by this case. White or gray ghosts—the *gray bodach* of *M'Ivor* in Waverley—result from excited *Form*, with quiescent *Colouring*, the transparent cobweb effect being colourless. Pale spectres and shadowy, yet coloured, forms are the effect of partially excited *Colouring*. Tall ghosts and dwarf goblins are the illusions of over-excited *Size*. *Creusa* appeared to *Æneas* colossal in her size:

'Infelix simulacrum atque ipsius umbra Creusæ,
Visa mihi ante oculos et nota *major imago*.'

" The ghosts of *Ossian* are often colossal. Gibbering and speaking ghosts, with an unearthly confusion of tongues and fiend-like peals of laughter, as if the demons revelled, are illusions which many have experienced."

The illusions of the English opium-eater are no longer a horrible mystery; they are explained in Mr. Simpson's paper here quoted.

Mr. Macnish, in the later editions of his deservedly popular work on sleep,† has given a chapter on spectral illusions, in which the foregoing theory is adopted, as the only one capable of explaining them. " If the brain," says he, " be brought, by internal causes, to a degree of excitement, which, in general, is the result only of external impressions, ideas not less vivid than sensations ensue; and the individual has the same

* " We may here mention, that the phrenological explanations of the distressing affection which have been given Miss S. L., have had the happy effect of affording her much more composure when visited by her phantoms than she thought possible. She is still terrified with their speaking; but her mind, on the whole, is greatly eased on the subject."

† *The Philosophy of Sleep*, by Robert Macnish; 2d and 3d editions, chap. xv. See also his *Introduction to Phrenology*, p. 136.

consciousness as if an impression were transmitted from an actual object through the senses. In other words, the brain, in a certain state, perceives external bodies; and any cause which induces that state, gives rise to a like perception, independently of the usual cause—the presence of external bodies themselves. The chief of these internal causes is inflammation of the brain; and, when the organs of the perceptive faculties are so excited—put into a state similar to that which follows actual impressions from without—the result is a series of false images or sounds, which are often so vivid as to be mistaken for realities. During sleep the perceptive organs seem to be peculiarly susceptible of such excitement. In dreaming, for instance, the external world is inwardly represented to our minds with all the force of reality: we speak and hear as if we were in communication with actual existences. Spectral illusions are phenomena strictly analogous; indeed they are literally nothing else than involuntary waking dreams." Mr. Macnish gives the following interesting account of a vision seen by himself: "In March, 1829, during an attack of fever, accompanied with violent action in the brain, I experienced illusions of a very peculiar kind. They did not appear except when the eyes were shut or the room perfectly dark; and this was one of the most distressing things connected with my illness; for it obliged me either to keep my eyes open, or to admit more light into the chamber than they could well tolerate. I had the consciousness of shining and hideous faces grinning at me in the midst of profound darkness, from which they glared forth in horrid and diabolical relief. They were never stationary, but kept moving in the gloomy back-ground: sometimes they approached within an inch or two of my face; at other times they receded several feet or yards from it. They would frequently break into fragments, which, after floating about, would unite—portions of one face coalescing with those of another, and thus forming still more uncouth and abominable images. The only way I could get rid of these phantoms was, by admitting more light into the chamber and opening the eyes, when they instantly vanished; but only to reappear when the room was darkened or the eyes closed. One night, when the fever was at its height, I had a splendid vision of a theatre, in the arena of which Ducrow, the celebrated equestrian, was performing. On this occasion I had no consciousness of a dark back-ground like to that on which the monstrous images floated; but everything was gay, bright, and beautiful. I was broad awake, my eyes were closed, and yet I saw with perfect distinctness the whole scene going on in the theatre—Ducrow performing his wonders of horsemanship—and the assembled multitude, among whom I recognised several intimate friends; in short, the whole process of the entertainment as clearly as if I were present at it. When I opened my eyes the whole scene vanished like the enchanted palace of the necromancer; when I closed them, it as instantly returned. But, though I could thus dissipate the spectacle, I found it impossible to get rid of the accompanying music. This was the grand march in the opera of Aladdin, and was performed by the orchestra with more superb and imposing effect, and with greater loudness, than I ever heard it before; it was executed, indeed, with tremendous energy. This air I tried every effort to dissipate, by forcibly endeavouring to call other tunes to mind, but it was in vain. However completely the vision might be dispelled, the music remained in spite of every effort to banish it. During the whole of this singular state, I was perfectly aware of the illusiveness of my feelings, and, though labouring under a violent headache, could not help speculating upon them, and endeavouring to trace them to their proper cause. This theatrical vision continued for about five hours; the previous delusions for a couple of days. The whole evidently proceeded from such an excited state of some parts of the brain as I have already alluded to. *Ideality, Wonder, Form, Colour,* and *Size* were all in intensely active operation; while the state of the reflecting organs was unchanged. Had the latter participated in the general excitement to such an extent as to be unable to rectify the false impressions of the other organs, the case would have been one of pure delirium." To show how little spectral illusions are dependent on sight, Mr. Macnish adverts to the fact, that the blind are frequently subject to them : " A respected elderly gentleman, says he, " a patient of my own, who was afflicted with loss of sight, accompanied by violent headaches and severe dyspeptic symptoms, used to have the image of a black cat presented before him, as distinctly as he could have seen it before he became blind. He was troubled with various other spectral appearances, besides being subject to illusions of sound equally remarkable ; for he had often the consciousness of hearing music so strongly impressed upon him, that it was with difficulty his friends could convince him it was purely ideal."*

There are persons who imagine themselves to be made of glass, and who refuse to sit down, or assume any position in which glass would not be safe, lest they should break their bodies in pieces ; others have conceived that some object was attached to their nose, or that some figure was impressed upon their forehead ; who in every other respect were sound in mind. Such aberrations appear to be fixed and permanent conceptions of a diseased nature, resulting from morbid and involuntary activity of the organs of the knowing faculties. The cure will be accomplished by removing the organic cause, and not by a logical demonstration that the object does not exist ; fitted perhaps to convince a sound understanding, but altogether inefficient for the removal of illusions springing from a diseased brain.

Another form of mental derangement, arising from internal excitement of the organs, is the tendency to involuntary and sometimes unconscious manifestations of the faculties. Some insane patients talk night and day to themselves ;† and in hysterical affections the individual often alternately laughs and cries involuntarily. The last phenomena are explicable by the supposition of different organs becoming active and quiescent in turns, in consequence of some irregular action in the brain. Dr. A. Combe saw in Paris a lady who, when just emerging from insensibility, occasioned by a fit of apoplexy, manifested the faculties of Wit and Imitation quite unconsciously, but with so admirable an effect, that her relations were forced into fits of laughter, mingled with floods of tears for her unhappy condition : on her recovery, she did not know of the exhibitions she had made. The organs of Wit and Imitation were large. Phrenology accounts for such facts in a simple and natural manner, by the effects of diseased activity of the organs.

DREAMING may now be analyzed. If the greater number of the organs remain inactive, buried in sleep, and if two or three, from some internal excitement confined to themselves, become active, these will present the mind with corresponding conceptions, and their action being separated from that of the other organs, which, in the waking state, generally co-operate with them, the result will be the creation of disjointed and fantastic impressions of objects, circumstances, and events ; in short,

---

* The true theory of apparitions was acutely conjectured by Hobbes, Voltaire, Shenstone, and Hume ; but the late Dr. Alderson, of Hull, was the first to *establish* that such illusions are the result of cerebral disorder, although this honour has been claimed by Dr. Ferriar, of Manchester. See " Notes, chiefly historical, on the Philosophy of Apparitions," by Mr. Robert Cox; *Phren. Journ.,* vol. viii., p. 538.

† See before, p. 331.

all the various phenomena of dreams. Thus every circumstance whic disturbs the organization of the body may become the cause of dreams: a heavy supper, by encumbering the digestive powers, affects the brain pain fully by sympathy; and hence the spectres and "chimeras dire" created by the dreaming fancy. Fever, by keeping up a morbid excitement in the whole system, sustains the brain in a state of uninterrupted action; and hence the sleeplessness which attends the higher, and the disturbed dreams which accompany the lower, degrees of that disease. Thus also is explained another familiar fact relative to the mind. If, during day, we have been excessively engaged in any particular train of studies, it haunts us in our dreams. During day the organs of the faculties chiefly employed were maintained in a state of action, intense and sustained in proportion to the mental application. By a general law of the constitution, excessive action does not subside suddenly, but abates by insensible degrees; on going to sleep, so much activity continues in the organ, that the train of ideas goes on; till, after long action, it at last entirely ceases.

In dreams we are sometimes overwhelmed with terror, and cannot discover the object which occasions it. This may be accounted for by supposing the organ of Cautiousness to be violently excited by some internal cause, while the organs of the intellectual faculties continue asleep. In other instances we dream of seeing the most alarming or wonderful appearances without feeling any emotion. This seems to arise from several of the intellectual organs being awake, while those of the sentiments remain dormant. A remarkable dream of this description is narrated in *The Phrenological Journal*, vol. ix., p. 278.

On inquiry I find, what indeed might have been anticipated *a priori*, that dreams in different individuals have most frequently relation to the faculties whose organs are largest in their brains. A friend, in whom Tune is large and Language deficient, tells me that he has frequently dreamed of hearing and producing music, but very rarely of composing discourses, written or oral. Another gentleman, in whom Language is full and Tune deficient, states that he never but once in his life dreamed of hearing a musical note, while many a laborious page he has imagined himself writing, reading, and speaking in his dreams; nay, he has repeatedly dreamed of conversing with foreigners in their own tongue, with a degree of fluency which he could never command while awake. In the same way, a person, in whom Locality is large, assured me, that he had very frequently dreamed of travelling in foreign countries, and enjoyed most vivid impressions of the scenery; while another, in whom that organ is small, never dreamed of such a subject. One friend, in whom Combativeness is large, told me that he had fought many a tough and long-contested battle in his dreams; while another, in whom that organ is moderate, stated that he had never dreamed of fighting but once, and that was when his imagination placed him in the hands of murderers whose heads he attempted to break with a poker, and wakened in terror at his own combative effort.

If, in persons of an active temperament, the reflective organs chiefly be exercised during day, it is not unusual for the organs of Form, Locality, and Colouring to disport themselves in dreams. I have known examples of literary men and lawyers, who, in their dreams,
"Flew to the pleasant fields traversed so oft,
In life's morning march when the bosom was young,"
and enjoyed scenery which they loved, but which their avocations prevented them from visiting in their waking hours.

A curious illustration of the effect of the predominating organs in determining the character of dreams, occurs in the case of Scott, who was executed in 1823, at Jedburgh, for murder. It is stated in his Life, that some years before the fatal event, he dreamed that he had committed a murder, and was greatly impressed with the idea. He frequently spoke of it, and recurred to it as something ominous, till at last it was realized. The organ of Destructiveness was large in his head, and so active, that he was an enthusiast in poaching, and prone to outrage and violence in his habitual conduct. This activity of the organ might exist during sleep, and then it would inspire his mind with destructive feelings, and the dream of murder would be the consequence. From the great natural strength of the propensity, he probably may have felt, when awake, an inward tendency to this crime ; and, by joining this and the dream together, the strong impression left by the latter on his mind is easily accounted for.

I presume, although I do not know it as a fact, that persons in whom Cautiousness is small, and Hope and Benevolence large, will, when in health, generally enjoy brilliant and happy dreams ; while others, in whom Cautiousness is very large and Hope small, will be wading in difficulties and wo.

Mr Andrew Carmichael, of Dublin, in " An Essay on Dreaming, including Conjectures on the Proximate Cause of Sleep,"* suggests the idea that sleep may be the chief occasion when the waste of substance in the brain is repaired by the deposition of new particles of matter. There is no direct evidence of the truth of this conjecture ; but the brain, like every other part of the animal structure, is furnished with bloodvessels and absorbents, and is known to waste like them : that the waste should be repaired, therefore, is a fact of necessary inference ;"and Mr. Carmichael conceives, that the period of sleep, when the mental functions are suspended, is particularly suitable for this operation. Mr. Carmichael's views have been controverted by Mr. Macnish, chiefly on the following grounds : First, It is inconceivable that a natural and healthy deposition of new particles should cause a cessation of the functions of the brain ; before such a deposition can take place, there must be an augmented circulation of blood through its vessels, and increased circulation implies increased activity of function ; besides, the circulation in the brain, in place of being augmented during sleep, is greatly diminished. Secondly, On Mr. Carmichael's supposition, that the process of assimilation in the brain is the proximate cause of sleep, how are we to account for people being so easily awakened ? It is difficult to conceive the assimilative process to be so suddenly arrested or completed. Thirdly, Dreaming is inconsistent with the theory ; for assimilation must be supposed to take place in the whole brain at the same time, in which case the activity of one organ, while others are asleep, is impossible. Lastly, and above all, an inclination to sleep is felt immediately after taking food, and long before the chyle has reached the bloodvessels, by which it is deposited previously to assimilation.† To these arguments Mr. Carmichael has published, in the same volume,‡ a very ingenious reply.

The preceding view of the phenomena of dreaming gives a death-blow to the superstitious notion of warnings and supernatural communications being now made to the mind in sleep ; while it explains naturally the occasional fulfilment of dreams, as in the case of Scott.

Thus, the internal excitement of the intellectual organs produces conception ; the ideas conceived always bearing relation to the particular organ or organs called into action. This excitement, when morbid and involuntary, produces fixed conceptions or ideas, which is a species of insanity ; and the same excitement taking place in some organs during sleep, while others remain in a state of inaction, produces dreams. When,

* _Tilloch's Phil. Mag._, vol. liv., pp. 252, 324 ; or _Transactions of the King and Queen's College of Physicians_, vol. ii., p. 48 : Also Mr. Carmichael's _Memoir of the Life and Philosophy of Spurzheim_, p 91.
† _Phrenological Journal_, vol. ix., pp. 175-181.   ‡ _Ibid._, p. 318.

during periods of wakefulness, the excitement is inordinately great, the conception of apparitions ensues. Hence these phenomena are all connected in their cause, however dissimilar in their external appearance.

IMAGINATION. The metaphysicians frequently employ the words Imagination and Fancy, but neither of them is synonymous with the phrenological term Ideality. *Imagination* is defined to be, " The power of forming ideal pictures ; the power of representing things absent, to one's self." In this sense, which I hold to be the primitive and most correct, there is scarcely a shade of difference between Conception and Imagination. Locality, Size, Colouring, and Individuality, being active by command of the will, call up the features of a landscape, and we may then be said to *conceive* it. If to this act the word *imagine* were applied, and we were said to *imagine* a landscape, the expression would not be felt as improper. Mr. Stewart, therefore, if he had confined Imagination to the limits here pointed out, namely, to " the power of representing things absent, to one's self," would not have been censurable for doubting if it were a faculty distinct from Conception, which he has ranked as such. At the same time, his notion, that " Imagination is not the gift of nature," but formed " by particular habits of study or of business," is even on this supposition erroneous ; for there is no mode of action of the mind which is not the gift of nature, however much it may be improved by judicious exercise. There is, however, a difference between Conception and Imagination. The former is the cool and methodical representation of things absent, as they exist in nature, to one's self. Imagination is the impassioned *representation* of the same things—not merely in the forms and arrangements of nature, but in new combinations formed by the mind itself. In Phrenology, therefore, Conception is viewed as the *second* degree of activity of the knowing and reflecting faculties, and Imagination as the third. Imagination is nothing but intense, glowing, forcible conceptions, proceeding from great activity of the intellectual faculties, not confined to real circumstances, but embracing as many new combinations as they are capable of calling forth. In this way, Imagination may be manifested without ornament or illustration ; and this is the case when such faculties as Form, Locality, Colouring, and Causality act by themselves, unaided by Ideality and Comparison. Hence, the assertion of D'Alembert,[*] that " metaphysics and geometry are of all the sciences belonging to reason those in which Imagination has the greatest share," is quite intelligible, and may have been seriously made. If, in that philosopher, Form, Size, Locality, Number, and Causality—in short, the faculties which go to constitute a genius for mathematics and metaphysics—were very active, he would be conscious of imagining, with great interest and vivacity, many new relations of space, magnitude, and causation ; and, looking to the usual definitions of Imagination, he was entitled to designate these acts as operations of that faculty.

The metaphysicians attach a different and more extensive meaning to the word Fancy, and, according to my understanding of the functions described by them to this supposed power, it embraces a wider range than Imagination, and necessarily implies ornament and illustration. Hence Comparison, and probably Ideality, must be combined with the knowing and reflecting faculties to constitute Fancy. The latter faculties will call up ideas of objects as they exist in nature, Ideality will invest them with beauty, Comparison will cull similes and trace analogies throughout the boundless fields of space, and the intellectual compound may be designated as the creation of Fancy. The significations commonly attached to the words Imagination and Fancy are, however, by no means precise. The conceptions of the knowing and reflecting faculties, illustrated and diversi-

* Stewart. *Prelim. Dissert. to Sup. Encyclop. Brit.*, Part i., p. 6.

fied by Comparison alone, are frequently designated as Fancy ; and in this sense an author or orator may be said to possess a brilliant fancy, although Ideality be by no means a predominant organ in his head. On the other hand, many passages of Milton are the result merely of the knowing faculties and Causality, imbued with intense Ideality, and in them Comparison supplies but few illustrations ; nevertheless, these are said to be highly imaginative, and certainly are so. Thus, in judging of genius, Phrenology teaches us to be discriminative in our analysis, and to avoid the error of inferring the presence of *all* the powers of the mind in an eminent degree, because one great talent is possessed.

Improvisatori are able, without study or premeditation, to pour out thousands of verses *impromptu*, often of no despicable quality, upon any subject which the spectators choose to suggest. I have not seen any of these individuals ; but Phrenology enables us to conjecture the constituent elements of their genius. In the first place, we may infer that they possess a high nervous or sanguine temperament, communicating great activity to the brain ; and, in the next place, Language, Individuality, Eventuality, Comparison, Tune, Time, and Ideality all large. The great and uncommon activity supposed, would produce the readiness of conception and warmth of feeling which are the first requisites ; large endowment of Individuality and Eventuality would supply facts and incidents necessary to give substance and action to the composition ; Comparison would afford similes, metaphors, and illustrations ; Ideality would contribute elevation, Tune and Time give rhythm, and Language afford expression to the whole ideas so formed and combined. Observation only can determine whether these conjectures be correct ; but the causes here assigned appear to be adequate to the effects—and this, in a hypothesis, is all that can be expected.

MEMORY also is a mode of action of the faculties. In most individuals the mind has no power of calling up, into fresh existence, the emotions experienced by means of the propensities and sentiments, by merely willing them to be felt, and hence we hold these faculties not to possess Memory. The ideas, however, formed by the knowing and reflecting faculties can be reproduced by an act of recollection, and these powers are, therefore, said to have Memory. Memory is thus merely a mode of action of the knowing and reflecting faculties. I have said that Conception and Imagination also result from the internal action of these organs ; and the question naturally arises, In what respect does Memory differ from them? The difference appears to be this : In Conception and Imagination new combinations of ideas are formed, not only without regard to the time or order in which the elementary notions had previously existed, but even without any direct reference to their having formerly existed at all. Memory, on the other hand, implies a new conception of impressions previously received, attended with the idea of past time, and consciousness of their former existence ; and it generally follows the order of the events as they happened.

Each organ enables the mind to recall the impressions which it served at first to receive. Thus, the organ of Tune will recall notes formerly heard, and give the memory of music. Form will recall figures previously observed, will give the memory of persons, pictures, and crystals, and will produce a talent for becoming learned in matters connected with such objects. Individuality and Eventuality will confer memory for facts, and render a person skilled in history, both natural and civil. A person in whom Causality is powerful, will possess a natural memory for metaphysics. Hence there may be as many kinds of memory as there are knowing and reflecting faculties ; and an individual may have great memory for one class of ideas, and very little for another : George Bidder had an almost inconceivable power of recollecting arithmetical calculations, while in memory of history or languages he did not surpass ordinary men. As the recollection of facts and occurrences is what is commonly meant, in popular language, by a great memory, individuals so gifted will generally be found to possess a good developement of Individuality, Eventuality, and probably of Language.

There appears to be a quality of brain which gives retentiveness to memory, so that one individual retains impressions much longer than another, although their combination of organs be the same. It is said that Sir Walter Scott possessed this characteristic in a high degree ; but the cause of it is unknown. This fact does not invalidate the theory of Memory now given ; because in every individual the power of retaining one kind of impressions is greater than that of retaining another, and this power bears a uniform relation to the size of the organs.

The celebrated Cuvier affords another striking illustration of this remark. He possessed the quality of retentiveness, the cause of which is unknown, in an extraordinary degree ; but the power was strongest in his largest intellectual organs. De Candolle describes his mental qualities as follows : " His range of knowledge was surpassingly great He had all his life read much—seen much—and never forgotten anything. A powerful memory, sustained and directed by sound judgment and singular sagacity, was the principal foundation of his immense works and his success. This memory was particularly remarkable in what related to forms, considered in the widest sense of that word ; the figure of an animal, seen in reality or in drawing, never left his mind, and served him as a point of comparison for all similar objects. The sight of a map of the plan of a city seemed sufficient to give him an almost intuitive knowledge of the place ; and, among all his talents, that memory which may be called *graphic* seemed most apparent : he was consequently an able draughtsman, seizing likenesses with rapidity and correctness, and had the art of imitating with his pencil the appearance of the tissue of organs, in a manner peculiarly his own, and his anatomical drawings were admirable."[*]

The knowing and reflecting organs were both large in his head, and, judging from his portraits, his temperament seems to have been nervous, or nervous and sanguine.

Dr. Watts seems to have anticipated, by a very acute conjecture, the real philosophy of Memory. He says : " It is most probable that those very fibres, pores, or traces of the brain which assist at the first idea or perception of any object, are the same which assist also at the recollection of it ; and then it will follow, that the memory has no special part of the brain devoted to its own service, but uses all those parts in general which subserve our sensation as well as our thinking and reasoning powers."[†] This conjecture coincides exactly with Mr. Hood's case, of the person in Kilmarnock, who, although able to articulate, lost all power of recollecting arbitrary signs, and, with a sound judgment and clear understanding, forgot, through disease, his own name and the names of every person and thing with which previously he was most familiar. This could be accounted for only on the principle that the organ of Language had lost the power of internal activity at command of the will, while the organs of the other intellectual powers remained entire. The fact, also, of the memory failing in old age, before the judgment is impaired, is accounted for on the same principle. "Age diminishes the *susceptibility* and *activity* of the organs ; and hence they are unable to receive and to reproduce impressions with the vivacity of youth. Judgment is an exercise of the faculties on present objects, and does not require the same portion of internal and spontaneous excitement for its execution. It is known, that, after the mind has become dead to the recollection of recent occurrences, it recalls, with great vivacity, the impressions of youth and boyish years. These were imprinted at a time when the whole system was extremely susceptible, and subsequently have been often recalled; and hence perhaps it is that the organs are capable of resuming the state corresponding to them, after they have ceased to be capable of retaining impressions from events happening when their vigour has decayed.

The doctrine, that memory is only a degree of activity of the faculties, is illustrated by the phenomena of diseases which particularly excite the brain. Sometimes, under the influence of disease, the most lively recollection of things will take place, which had entirely escaped from the memory in a state of health. "A most remarkable example of this kind occurred some years ago at St. Thomas's Hospital. A man was brought in, who had received a considerable injury of the head, but from which he ultimately recovered. When he became convalescent, he spoke a language which no one about him could comprehend. However, a Welsh milk-woman came one day into the ward, and immediately understood what he said. It appeared that this poor fellow was a Welshman, and had been from his native country about thirty years. In the course of that period he had entirely forgotten his native tongue, and acquired the English language. But when he recovered from his accident, he forgot the language he had been so recently in the habit of speaking, and acquired the knowledge of that which he had originally acquired and lost!"[*] Such a fact as this is totally inexplicable, on any principle except that of the existence of organs by which the faculties are manifested: for it could not be the mind itself which was affected, and its faculties impaired by the fever, or which recovered long lost knowledge by the influence of disease. At the same time, the manner in which such an effect is produced is entirely unknown. Old people, when feeble, often relapse into the use of the dialect of their youth.

The case of which the following is an abstract, was communicated by Dr. Dewar to the Royal Society; and, although highly interesting, is at present inexplicable:

In a "Report on a communication from Dr. Dyce, of Aberdeen, on Uterine Irritation, and its effects on the female constitution,"[†] Dr. Dewar states, that "It is a case of mental disease, attended with some advantageous manifestations of the intellectual powers; and these manifestations disappeared in the same individual in the healthy state. It is an instance of a phenomenon which is sometimes called *double consciousness*, but is more properly a *divided consciousness*, or *double personality*, exhibiting, in some measure, two separate and independent trains of thought, and two independent mental capabilities, in the same individual; each train of thought and each capability being wholly dissevered from the other, and the two states in which they respectively predominate subject to frequent interchanges and alternations."

The patient was a girl of sixteen; the affection appeared immediately before puberty, and disappeared when that state was fully established. It lasted from the 2d of March to the 11th of June, 1815, under the eye of Dr. Dyce. "The first symptom was an uncommon propensity to fall asleep in the evenings. This was followed by the habit of *talking* in her

<hr/>

[*] Tupper's *Inquiry into Gall's System*, p. 33; Good's *Study of Medicine*, 2d edit., vol. iv., p. 190; and Article DELIRIUM, by Dr. Prichard, in *Cyclop. of Prac. Med.*, vol. i., p. 506. Dr. Prichard adds to his account of the case, that "this statement, which was first given to Mr. Tupper, has been confirmed to the writer of this article by a personal witness."

[†] Read to the Royal Society in February, 1822.

sleep on these occasions. One evening she fell asleep in this manner, imagined herself an Episcopal clergyman, went through the ceremony of baptizing three children, and gave an appropriate *extempore* prayer. Her mistress took her by the shoulders, on which she awoke, and appeared unconscious of everything, except that she had fallen asleep, of which she showed herself ashamed. She sometimes dressed herself and the children while in this state, or, as Mrs. L. called it, 'dead sleep;' answered questions put to her, in such a manner as to show that she understood the question; but the answers were often, though not always, incongruous." One day, in this state, she "set the breakfast with perfect correctness, with her eyes shut. She afterward awoke with the child on her knee, and wondered how she got on her clothes." Sometimes the cold air awakened her, at other times she was seized with the affection while walking out with the children. "She sang a hymn delightfully in this state, and, from a comparison which Dr. Dyce had an opportunity of making, it appeared incomparably better done than she could accomplish when well."

" In the meantime a still more singular and interesting symptom began to make its appearance. *The circumstances which occurred during the paroxysm were completely forgotten by her when the paroxysm was over, but were perfectly remembered during subsequent paroxysms ;*" and it is on this account that I have introduced the case under the head of Memory. "Her mistress said, that, when in this stupor on subsequent occasions, she told her what was said to her on the evening on which she baptized the children." Other instances of this kind are given. "A depraved fellow-servant, understanding that she wholly forgot every transaction that occurred during the fit, clandestinely introduced a young man into the house, who treated her with the utmost rudeness, while her fellow-servant stopped her mouth with the bed-clothes, and otherwise overpowered a vigorous resistance which was made by her, even during the influence of her complaint.. Next day she had not the slightest recollection even of that transaction, nor did any person interested in her welfare know of it for several days, till she was in one of her paroxysms, when she related the whole facts to her mother. Next Sunday she was taken to the church by her mistress, while the paroxysm was on her. She shed tears during the sermon, particularly during the account given of the execution of three young men at Edinburgh, who had described in their dying declarations the dangerous steps with which their career of vice and infamy took its commencement. When she returned home, she recovered in a quarter of an hour, was quite amazed at the questions put to her about the church sermon, and denied that she had been in any such place ; but next night, on being taken ill, she mentioned that she had been at church, repeated the words of the text, and, in Dr. Dyce's hearing, gave an accurate account of the tragical narrative of the three young men, by which her feelings had been so powerfully affected. On this occasion, though in Mrs. L.'s house, she asserted that she was in her mother's."

Drs. Dyce and Dewar do not give any theory to account for these very extraordinary phenomena. They mention that the girl complained of confusion and oppression in her head at the coming on of the fits, and that, after the periodical discharge had been fairly established, the whole symptoms disappeared. We are unable phrenologically to throw more light on the case than these gentlemen have done ; and the only conclusion which seems to arise from it is, that, before memory can exist, the organ must be affected in the same manner, or be in a state analogous to that in which they were when the impression was first received. This inference is supported by several other facts. Dr. Abel informed me of an Irish porter to a warehouse, who forgot, when sober, what he had done when drunk; but, being drunk, again recollected the transactions of his former state of intoxication. One one occasion, being drunk, he had lost a parcel of some value, and in his sober moments could give no account of it. Next time he was intoxicated he recollected that he had left the parcel at a certain house, and there being no address on it, it had remained there safe, and was obtained on his calling for it. The same phenomena present themselves in the state of somnambulism, produced by animal magnetism. In the works on this subject it is mentioned, and the fact has been confirmed to me by a very intelligent friend who has observed it in Paris, that a person who is magnetized so as to produce the magnetic sleep termed somnambulism, acquires, like the girl in Aberdeen, a new consciousness and memory; he does not recollect the transactions of his ordinary state of existence, but acquires the power of speaking and of thinking in his induced state of abstraction from the external world. When this state has subsided, all that passed in it is obliterated from the memory, while the recollection of ordinary events is restored. If the magnetic state be recalled, memory of the circumstances which formerly happened in that state is restored; and thus the individuals may be said to live in a state of divided consciousness. In this country the doctrine of animal magnetism is treated with the same contempt which was formerly poured on Phrenology. I am wholly unacquainted with its merits; but several eminent French physicians entertain a favourable opinion of them,[*] and the circumstance now stated, of alternating memory and forgetfulness, not only is mentioned in the books on this subject which I have consulted, but has been certified to me as true by a gentleman whose understanding is too acute to allow me to believe that he was deceived, and whose honour is too high to admit of his deceiving others. These facts cannot at present be accounted for in a satisfactory way; but, by communicating a knowledge of their existence, attention will be drawn to them, and future observations and reflection may ultimately throw light upon the subject.

Mr. Hewett Watson has published a valuable essay on the peculiarities of memory, in the 29th number of *The Phrenological Journal.*[†] It is unphilosophical, he remarks, to use such phrases as *a good memory* or *a great memory*, these expressions being susceptible of very different interpretations. With the view of drawing the attention of phrenologists to the necessity of exactness in their descriptions, he specifies some of the principal varieties of memory, throwing out at the same time suggestions as to the conditions on which they depend. "For the more easy illustration," says he, "it will be convenient to distinguish the varieties of memory in two leading subdivisions, which may be termed 'Simple Memory,' and 'Memory by Association.'" Simple memory is that wherein the idea of a sound, colour, object, or event appears to recur directly and spontaneously; as for instance, having once seen a house or a tree, and the idea or mental impression returning afterward, we are then said to remember it. Memory depending on association is indirect, and may be exemplified by the fact, that we can scarce think of the summer sky, or the roses that bloom beneath it, without immediately remembering the concave form and blue tint of the former, or the peculiar shape and blushing dyes of the latter. The inseparable connexion that comes to be established between the arbitrary sounds and shapes used in speech and writing, and various mental ideas, so that the mere sound or sight of a word

* See Mr. Colquhoun's translation of the Report of the Committee of the Royal Academy of Sciences on Animal Magnetism; Georget, *De la Physiologie du Systeme Nerveux*, tome i., p. 267; and *The Cyclopædia of Practical Medicine*, article SOMNAMBULISM.　　　　　† Vol. vii., p. 212.

inevitably recalls its appropriate idea, is another familiar illustration of memory by association. Such associations vary from the closest possible approximation with simple memory to the most remote, incongruous, and artificial associations that exist.

"To commence with Simple Memory. One of the most striking varieties entitled to be ranked in this division, is that wherein an individual is capable of remembering a *great number* of ideas, whether they be chiefly of shapes, sounds, objects, colours, or whatever else. The remembrance of them may be lasting or transitory; it may be orderly or without arrangement; the individual may be rapid or slow in reproducing impressions previously formed. Such a memory, in short, may be indefinitely varied in every other respect, excepting that named as its distinguishing mark, viz., the multiplicity of ideas remembered. I have seen several individuals exhibiting a memory of this kind, but varying greatly among themselves in the duration, clearness, readiness, and other peculiarities of the ideas remembered. It is this variety which is commonly meant by the frequent expressions 'a good' or 'a great memory,' although by no means invariably so. It appears essential to attaining a first rank in most departments of science and literature, and is the variety which led Gall to the discovery of the intellectual organs, the condition on which it depends seeming to be large organic developement. They who take in and remember the greatest number of ideas at once, whether the same ideas be remembered for a long period, or be shortly supplanted by others, have, *cæteris paribus*; the largest organic developement. I have observed in botanists, having Language and Individuality but moderately developed, the power of remembering for a long period, and with accuracy, a limited number of plants, their names and peculiar distinctive characteristics, as, for instance, those of a particular garden, district, or country; but, on expanding their range of observation, they forget the former, apparently from a difficulty of retaining a multiplicity of ideas in a small organ. Others, on the contrary, will write systems embracing the whole of the vegetable kingdom, which implies an amount of individual knowledge almost incomprehensible to a small developement. The mask of Sir James Smith, whose principal botanical skill lay in a knowledge of the various names which botanists and others had, at different periods, applied to the same plant, shows Language to have been large, and, in consequence, he remembered many names. Individuality and Form are both well developed, but these two organs I have seen relatively superior in some of the best *specific* botanists of Britain, who remember the plants themselves better than their names. This variety of memory would be appropriately distinguished by the epithet *extensive*. As, however, it depends essentially on large organic developement, which scarcely any person possesses in every faculty, this memory is more or less partial, that is, limited in respect to the kind of ideas remembered; so that, in order to characterize it with precision, it would be necessary to say, an extensive memory of words, of colour, of sounds, or whatever else it might happen to be. Many persons mistake the limit in kind for one of degree only, and lament in general terms their deficiency of memory, when in reality they possess an extensive memory for one range of ideas combined with a limited memory for another; the deficiency, being most felt by the inconvenience it occasions, is taken as the general criterion. Exercise seems to have less influence on this variety than it has over others presently to be mentioned, probably more influencing the direction than the quantity of ideas remembered. Linnæus, Sheridan, Newton, Johnson, Cuvier, and Sir Edward Coke may furnish examples of the extensive memory, and that chiefly in one particular range or direction.

"A second variety of memory is that of men who are capable of remembering what they see, hear, or do *during a very long period;* their mental impressions appear to bid defiance to time, and to bear its daily attritions almost without change. Whether the subjects remembered be few or many, and of whatever kind or nature, still mental images of them once formed remain deep and distinct. Individuals endowed with this variety of memory in its highest degree, will often converse nearly as easily and correctly of occurrences years gone by, as others do of those which happened but a week before. There are boys who will learn their school tasks with ease and rapidity, but just as easily and rapidly forget them ; the lesson which was perfect last week, is to-day a dim and scarce perceptible outline of something that has once been, but is now almost effaced from the soft-moulded tablets of memory.

" On the other hand, we may find some of their school-fellows, whose tasks are the same, whose instructions are scarce in the slightest degree different, yet in this respect attended with the most dissimilar results. The task of last week or month is nearly as fresh in memory as though it had been learned but yesterday, and they wonder how others *can* forget so quickly, while these in turn are astonished that such retentiveness of memory can exist in any one. It seems yet an unsolved problem on what organic peculiarity this depends. That it is not attributable to size, or at least to size alone, every day's experience must assure us ; and all that can at present be suggested in regard to it is, that *quality* rather than *quantity* of brain is the condition whereon it is dependent. It seems to be almost invariably accompanied by a degree of slowness in action, a want of that rapidity in the flow of ideas characteristic of the next variety to be mentioned. The slowness and tenacity may perhaps depend on the same peculiarity in the composition or quality of brain, the retentiveness of former ideas being connected with the slowness in acquiring new ones. On reading this to the Phrenological Society, a case was mentioned of a gentleman who, after learning to repeat long passages in a short space of time, found that he very soon forgot them, and that, when acquired with more slowness, they were long remembered.* It would appear from this, that the slowness in acquiring ideas is an antecedent to retentiveness; we are scarcely authorized to say a *cause,* for both the one and the other may, and most likely do, depend on some (general or temporary) constitutional condition checking rapidity. The epithet *retentive* would pretty correctly designate this variety of memory, and distinguish it from the former, with which it may or may not be combined. I have noticed it in men with a limited, as well as in those who possess an extensive, memory ; but, *cæteris paribus,* it seems most marked in such individuals as engage in the smallest variety of pursuits ; whether it is an effect or a cause of uniformity in taste and pursuit may admit of doubt. The inhabitants of the country seem to remember with more tenacity than such as live in large towns; and certainly they are more apt to imbibe ideas with slowness and deliberation. Joined with an extensive memory, it constitutes the man of knowledge, and is therefore an essential element in forming a scientific character, but will scarcely make a witty or showy one. Joseph Hume, Julius Cæsar, and perhaps Napoleon, may be cited as examples of it.

" A third variety of Simple Memory is characterized by the rapidity with which previous ideas are reproduced in the mind. One after another, or one dozen after another dozen, previous thoughts and impressions are renewed, and come floating athwart the mental eye in perpetual change-

* Dr. Abercrombie, in his work on the Intellectual Powers, p. 100, mentions the case of an actor who, on an emergency, committed his part to memory with surprising quickness, but in a very short time completely forgot it. Those parts, on the other hand, which he learned with slowness and deliberation, were accurately retained for many years.

ability and succession. They may arise in a regular, connected, and systematic series, or be poured forth in the most mixed and heterogeneous assemblages, like the multitudinous *olla podrida* of a masquerade, or the endlessly varied hues and objects of an extensive landscape. Rapidity of ideas is the essential character of this modification. Whether such ideas be correct or erroneous, limited or general, connected or disordered, seems to be determined by other conditions different from those on which depends the mere quickness of their reproduction......Large Language and Individuality, with great rapidity, tend to promote punning and that style of wit designated as 'good things,' 'apropos remarks,' ' clever hits,' &c., which I have seen greatly manifested when the organ called Wit has been of very moderate developement. It is perhaps this rapidity of memory occurring in cases of deficient developement of Concentrativeness that causes what is commonly termed 'far-fetched wit,' or that conjunction of widely dissimilar and unrelated ideas called up by rapidity unrestrained by concentrated action.......Rapidity of memory is probably influential in determining to the production of poetry, being evinced in the variety of its imagery, and what one of the fraternity has well exemplified in the expression ' thronging fancies.'......Rapidity in excess, implying a perpetual transition of ideas, incapacitates for science ; hence we rarely, if ever, find first rank in science and poetry, or science and wit, in the same person. Intermediate gradations may unite both in nearly equal degree. In noticing the former variety, I had suggested the rarity, if not incompatibility, of the rapid and the retentive memories coexisting in a great degree ; but was informed, on reading the remark, that Professor Mezzofante, of Bologna, combines both rapidity and retentiveness of verbal memory. The nervous temperament seems instrumental in giving this quality of brain, or perhaps might, with more correctness, be regarded as the effect ; but it is certainly not peculiar to the dark varieties of that temperament : some of the most striking examples of rapid memory I have met with occur in persons of light complexion. An appropriate mode of distinguishing this modification of memory from those previously mentioned, would be by attaching to it the epithet *rapid*. Miss Pratt, quoted in the phrenological works as an example of large Individuality, may be cited as an instance of rapid combined with extensive memory of objects and occurrences.

" Nearly allied to, but by no-means always coexistent with, the rapid memory is *readiness* of memory, or the power of immediately directing it to any given subject. There are men of considerable rapidity and diversity of ideas, who, if suddenly asked the simplest question concerning any matter not just then occupying their thoughts, find great difficulty in turning the current of their ideas into a new channel, or opening a new spring. They thus seem, both to themselves and others, to be remarkably deficient in memory. Inequality of developement probably tends to increase this peculiar defect, but it appears to me that Concentrativeness and Secretiveness, one or both, are also concerned......I have but few observations on the developement of individuals whose memory presents this modification, but it seems in perfection when large Secretiveness, Concentrativeness, and the anterior lobe, especially Individuality, are combined with rapidity, and to be proportionally injured by the abduction of any one of these requisites. I have seen an instance of this promptness of memory in a case where the knowing organs, particularly Individuality and Eventuality, with Secretiveness, were large, Concentrativeness and the reflecting organs rather above moderate, with a medium degree of rapidity and retentiveness of memory. The epithet *ready* or *prompt* may designate this variety of memory, which probably occurred in Burke, Pitt, Curran, and Sheridan.

"To the preceding peculiarities of memory there yet remains to be added another, which, from its influence over memory, by association, may be viewed as the transition and connecting link between the two artificial divisions here made. I mean partial memory, or that limited to particular ranges of ideas. The connexion between partial memory and proportionate developement of the cerebral organs is so completely one of the foundation-stones of Phrenology, that it must be quite unnecessary to say anything about it here; but we must never lose sight of the fact, that partial memory, dependent on this cause, is exhibited only in the *nature* of the ideas, as those of colour in contradistinction to shape, or shape in opposition to dimensions, and not merely in the peculiar direction."

JUDGMENT, in the metaphysical sense, belongs to the REFLECTING faculties alone. The knowing faculties, however, may also be said to judge; the faculty of Tune, for example, may be agreeably or disagreeably affected, and in this way may judge of sounds; but Judgment, in the proper acceptation of the word, is a perception of adaptation, of relation, of fitness, or of the connexion between means and an end, and belongs entirely to the reflecting powers. These, as well as the knowing faculties, have Perception, Memory, and Imagination. Causality, for example, *perceives* the relation of cause and effect, and also *remembers* and *imagines* that relation, just as Locality perceives, remembers, and imagines the relative position of objects. Hence, Judgment is the decision of the reflecting faculties upon the feelings furnished by the propensities and sentiments, and upon the ideas furnished by the whole intellectual faculties. This I conceive to be the strictly phrenological analysis of Judgment; but this term, in the popular sense, has a more extensive signification. It is a common observation to say of an individual, that he possesses an acute or even profound intellect, but that he is destitute of judgment. This apparent paradox may be explained in two ways. First: by "an acute or profound intellect" is frequently meant a great, but limited, talent, which would refer to some of the knowing faculties. Thus, a person may be distinguished for ability in mathematics or painting, and not be eminent for reflection or judgment, in the stricter sense. There is, however, a second explanation, which is preferable. To judge of the line of conduct proper to be followed in the affairs of life, it is necessary to *feel* correctly as well as to reason deeply; or rather, it is *more* necessary to feel rightly than to reflect. Hence, if an individual possess very powerful reflecting faculties, such as Lord Bacon enjoyed, and be deficient in Conscientiousness, as his lordship seems to have been, he is like a fine ship wanting a helm, liable to be carried from her course by every wind and current. The reflecting faculties give the power of thinking profoundly, but Conscientiousness and the other sentiments are necessary to furnish correct feeling, by which practical conduct may be regulated. Indeed, Lord Bacon affords a striking example, how poor an endowment intellect—even the most transcendent—is, when not accompanied by upright sentiments. That mind which embraced, in one comprehensive grasp, the whole circle of the sciences, and pointed out, with a surprising sagacity, the modes in which they might best be cultivated—that mind, in short, which anticipated the progress of the human understanding by a century and a half—possessed so little *judgment*, so little of sound and practical sense, as to become the accuser, and even defamer, of Essex, his early patron and friend; to pollute the seat of justice by corruption and bribery; and to stoop to the basest flattery of a weak king, all for the gratification of a contemptible ambition. Never was delusion more complete. He fell into an abyss of degradation from which he never ascended; and to this day the darkness of his moral reputation forms a lamentable contrast to the brilliancy of his intellectual fame. There was here the most evident defect of *judgment*; and with such reflecting powers as he possessed, the source of his errors could lie only in the sentiments, deficiency in some of which prevented him from *feeling* rightly, and of course withheld from his understanding the data from which sound conclusions respecting conduct could be drawn.

In common life the effect of the feelings in originating opinion is by far too little attended to. We frequently hear persons carrying on angry disputations, with a view to convince each other's understandings ; when, in fact, the cause of their difference lies in a feeling, so that, if it could be made the same in both, no disagreement would exist. It is common in such cases to say, " My sentiments are entirely different from yours ;" a form of expression which is strictly philosophical, and harmonizes with the explanation now given : but the parties do not perceive that a " sentiment," in the strict sense, or in popular language a " feeling," cannot be communicated by *argument*; and hence they maintain the controversy by an address to the understanding alone, and generally with no satisfactory result. If, on the other hand, two persons meet, whose propensities and sentiments harmonize, their " sentiments," in the popular sense, generally coincide, although, in the depth of their intellectual powers, there may be considerable disparity. In estimating, therefore, the degree of sound and practical judgment for the affairs of life, the good sense or mother-wit, of any individual, we ought not to confine our attention to the forehead alone, under the notion that it is exclusively the seat of judgment ; but to look first to the temperament, that we may judge of the activity of the brain, and next at the combination of organs ; for we shall invariably find sound sense to be the accompaniment of an equable developement of all the organs, those of the moral sentiments and intellect rather predominating. There are then no exaggerated and no defective powers ; so that no desires assume an undue ascendency, and no emotions are so feeble as not to be adequately experienced. This combination is rare, and hence high practical sense is more uncommon than great partial talent. A person was pointed out to me as possessing the forehead of an idiot, who yet had conducted himself with remarkable prudence and success in trade, and, by his estimable qualities, had gained the esteem of the little circle in which he moved. On examination, I found a fine nervous and sanguine temperament, and a forehead greatly retreating indeed, but with a full developement of the knowing organs ; and, on turning to the region of the propensities and sentiments, the former were found in fair proportion, with an excellent developement of the latter. Conscientiousness, Veneration, Benevolence, Love of Approbation, Adhesiveness, and Cautiousness were all large ; and the sources of his prudence, good sense, and amiable qualities were at once apparent. To show that Phrenology and the head were not at variance, I inquired into his powers of logical or profound argumentation ; when his friend said, that, although he was fond of reading, his acquaintances were surprised that he never learned the meaning of a great many plain words ; and, on asking what these were, I found them to be abstract terms and expressions, significant of ideas formed by Causality and Comparison. The individual in question not only could not reason consecutively, but in ordinary discourse misapplied, and seemed not to understand, the terms now adverted to. This was exactly what a phrenologist would have predicted.

In describing, therefore, the effect of the reflecting faculties in ordinary life, I would say that the propensities and sentiments furnish the chief desires which prompt to action, and the feelings which regulate conduct ; while reflection, without being able to alter their nature, judges of the motives presented by them to its consideration—taking in an extent of view, greater or less, in proportion to the size of the intellectual organs.

The intellect becomes acquainted with the mental faculties and their desires, with the external world, and with the relations subsisting between it and the mind, and judges of the means by which the desires may obtain gratification, and also of the consequences of indulgence ; and, by presenting a prospect of good or evil as the ultimate result, it thus constitutes the regulating and directing power.   The influence of the propensities and sentiments in biassing the judgment may be thus explained : If Cautiousness be excessively large and Hope small, this combination will present dismal forebodings to the mind ; and the understanding will not be able to alter the feelings so as to render cheery and brilliant scenes which they tinge with melancholy and gloom.   If Hope be very large and Cautiousness very small, then the most delusive anticipations of felicity will be suggested, and the understanding will see objects under this impression. If, again, both Cautiousness and Hope be large, each will furnish its own emotions on the objects of contemplation ; and the understanding now having two views, will possess elements for judging, and be able, by comparing, to come to a sound determination between them.   Hence, as already observed, a sound practical judgment is the result of a favourable combination of all the organs, sustained by an active temperament and experience.

If these principles be correct, they enable us to explain why, among lawyers, a bad pleader sometimes makes a good judge, and *vice versa.* To a pleader intellect and propensity are more essential than Conscientiousness.   To a judge, on the other hand, great moral organs are indispensable ; for, without an ample developement of them, his intellect is liable to be led astray by subtleties and false views, and in his decisions the grand element of justice will be wanting.   I have noticed, that, where Conscientiousness is large in a lawyer, and he is pleading a bad cause, he cannot avoid betraying, by his natural manner, his impression that he is in the wrong.   He in whom this organ is deficient, views all cases as questions of opinion, and contends for victory with that ardour which the other can display only when advocating the cause of truth.

The same principles enable us to judge of the propriety of a very important regulation in one of the institutions of our country—I mean the requisite of *unanimity* in juries in civil causes.   If two individuals were constituted umpires on a claim of damages for defamation, and if one of them possessed from nature an immense Love of Approbation—judging from his own feelings, he would rather suffer death than live defamed ; while the other, if he was, by natural constitution, extremely deficient in this sentiment, could pass his days unmoved by the censures or applauses of the world : and the two could not, by any efforts of their understandings, come to view the injury sustained by the plaintiff in the same light, or agree about the amount of damages which would constitute an equitable compensation for the slander.   The one must either surrender his conscience to the other, or allow a third party to decide between them ; for real unanimity is excluded by the very constitution of their minds.   No exercise of the *understanding* will produce it.   Even the intellectual perceptions of jurymen differ.   If one be very deficient in the reflecting organs, he will forget the inferential evidence and conclusions as fast as they are stated to him, and hence he may regard a point as not proved, which appears demonstrated to another in whom the reflecting organs are large.   It is difficult to admire the wisdom of that legislature which is so ignorant of the human mind as to imagine that men can by argument, if they will, arrive at one conclusion in such cases ; or which, if it knows that they cannot agree, nevertheless conceives it profound and beneficial to require a verdict in direct opposition to the constitution of the mind— to produce an *appearance* of unanimity, where the *substance* is unattain-

able.   Many arguments have been brought forward on the opposite sides
of this question : but it appears to me that the mode of judging of a
afforded by Phrenology carries us to the ultimate principles at once. If
it be naturally in the power of men, by honest efforts, to see questions
of conduct, such as occur before jury-courts, in the same light, then
unanimity should be required ; but if this perfect harmony of sentiment
be excluded by nature, it is mere imbecility to pretend to bring it
about by an act of parliament.   Accordingly, nature prevails here as
in every other case; for all sensible jurors, before commencing their
deliberations, arrange that the minority shall yield to the majority ; and
the only effects of the law are to put it in the power of some very obstinate or very wicked individual to force his fellows into the adoption
of his opinion—which, from his standing alone, will, on the ordinary
chances, be placed at an extreme point in the scale of absurdity ;—or else
to defeat the object of the parties, by depriving them altogether of a verdict.

It has been said, that the requisite of unanimity produces attention in
the jury to the case, and discussion of the subject among themselves.
This I have no doubt may be true, but even with every degree of attention and discussion, unanimity in general is morally impossible.   They
are not obvious questions of evidence or right, in which all men may
agree, that comes most frequently before courts of justice ; but difficult
cases, in which the most conscientious and enlightened may differ in
opinion.   Out of twelve or fifteen persons there is always a risk that two
or more may be the antipodes of moral and intellectual constitution to
each other.   Under the present system such individuals must yield un-
convinced.   It appears to me that, by leaving out the extremes, and requiring a majority of three-fourths, or some such proportion, the advantages
of discussion would be gained, and the evil of the great body of the jury
being forced into a verdict by one obstinate individual, might be avoided.
A proposition *voluntarily* assented to by nine men out of twelve, would
be nearer the truth than one modified by mutual concessions to conciliate,
but not to satisfy, the whole.

Having now discussed the metaphysical faculties of Perception, Conception, Imagination, Memory, and Judgment, and shown them to be
merely modes of action of the faculties disclosed by Phrenology, with
which the metaphysicians were unacquainted, I proceed to notice several
other mental operations and affections, which make a figure in the common systems of mental philosophy, and to refer them also to their principles in this science.

CONSCIOUSNESS means the knowledge which the mind has of its
own existence and operations.   Dr. Thomas Brown denies that it is a
power, or anything different from sensation, emotion, or thought, existing at any moment in the mind.   It gives us no intimation of the existence of the organs, and reveals to us only the operations of our own minds,
leaving us entirely in the dark regarding the mental affections of others,
where they differ from our own.   Hence, by reflecting on consciousness,
which the metaphysicians chiefly did, as their means of studying the
mind, we can discover nothing concerning the organs by which the faculties act, and run great risk of forming erroneous views of human nature,
by supposing mankind in general constituted exactly like ourselves.

Each organ communicates consciousness of the feelings and ideas
which it serves to manifest: thus, if the organ of Tune be extremely deficient, the individual will not be able to attain consciousness of melody ;
a person in whom Conscientiousness is extremely small, will not be conscious of the sentiment of justice, or of its obligations ; one in whom
Veneration is very feeble, will not be conscious of the emotion of piety.
If we place individuals so constituted in situations requiring vivid con-

sciousness of these emotions for the direction of their conduct, we shall be disappointed. The metaphysicians who studied the philosophy of mind by reflecting on their own consciousness, could not succeed in discovering the primitive faculties, because they were not conscious of those whose organs were very deficient in their own brains, nor of those which did not give their impulses in the retirement of a philosophical study ; such as Combativeness, Secretiveness, and Acquisitiveness. Farther, consciousness being single, they could not discover a plurality of powers attached to a variety of organs. On the other hand, when the organs are large and the temperament active, intense consciousness of the corresponding feelings and ideas is experienced ; and some persons, mistaking the emotions arising in this manner from Wonder, Veneration, and other faculties, for supernatural communications, fall into fanaticism and superstition.

No satisfactory explanation has yet been given why consciousness is single when the organs of all the mental faculties, external and internal, are double. There are cases on record of double consciousness, apparently from the two hemispheres of the brain being in opposite conditions. " Tiedemann," says Dr. Spurzheim, "relates the case of one Moser, who was insane on one side, and observed his insanity with the other. Dr. Gall attended a minister similarly afflicted: for three years he heard himself reproached and abused on his left side ; with his right he commonly appreciated the madness of his left side—sometimes, however, when feverish and unwell, he did not judge properly. Long after getting rid of this singular disorder, anger, or a greater indulgence in wine than usual, induced a tendency to relapse."* Dr. Caldwell states, in allusion to these instances, that " another case perfectly analogous, produced by a fall from a horse, exists in Kentucky, not far from Lexington."† I have received a communication of a case of a similar nature from a gentleman who was the subject of it. In a letter, dated 25th June, 1836, the Reverend R—— B —— writes to me thus : " You have heard, no doubt, of persons being deranged with one hemisphere of the brain, and setting themselves right with the other. Gall and Tissot, I think, both mention such cases. A circumstance, however, of this kind occurred to myself a few months ago, which may perhaps strike you as singular. I was reading in my bed-room one night, after a day of unusually hard labour and excitement. All at once I seemed to read my author with *two minds*. To speak more intelligibly, I read at the same time a sentence in my ordinary way, i. e., I understood the sense of what I was reading in a plain, matter-of-fact way, and I read it likewise in a more than usually imaginative way. There appeared to be two distinct minds, in fact, at work at the same page, at the same time, which continued after I closed my book and went to bed. The next morning the sensation was gone, and I have not distinctly experienced anything of the kind since. Do you not think that a different state of activity in the two hemispheres of the brain—perhaps in the region of Ideality and Marvellousness—may account for this ? It is certainly different from what is called double vision, for I felt conscious of reading only one page." Additional facts, illustrative of divided consciousness, are given at pages 102 and 369.

It has been argued by some skeptics that the human mind possesses no certain knowledge ; because, not only the senses and understanding occasionally deceive us, but even Consciousness itself gives false intimations : thus, a man whose leg has been amputated, is sometimes conscious, years after the operation, of a pain in the toe of the lost foot ; or a patient suffering under chronic disease of the liver, feels no uneasiness in it, but is conscious of a pain at the top of the right shoulder. The answer to this argument is, that each nerve and faculty has received a

* *Phrenology*, p. 37. † *Elements of Phrenology*, 2d edition, p. 82.

definite constitution, in virtue of which it gives certain intimations when affected in a particular manner; when the nerve of the toe, for example, is affected, the nerve itself gives consciousness of pain, accompanied by an instinctive reference to its seat. After the leg has been amputated, part of the nerve remains, and, when affected in the same manner as while the toe existed, it communicates the impression which belonged to it in its entire state. In this there is no deception; because the nerve which originally intimated pain in the toe, is affected in the same manner as it was when the toe existed. In like manner, the liver itself possesses little sensibility, but the phrenic nerve which is ramified on it communicates with the shoulder; and the nerve, being highly sensitive, is affected by the state of the liver, and produces pain in the shoulder. The nerve in this case is really affected, and the pain is the correct indication of its state. It is the office of Causality to discover the causes of these affections, that of Consciousness being limited to the intimation of the sensations themselves. Every derangement of an organ of sensation or perception is accompanied by disorder of consciousness to a corresponding extent: thus, in jaundice the mind has consciousness of all objects being yellow; in cases like that of Miss S. L., detailed on p. 359, there is consciousness of disturbed equilibrium; in such cases as that of Mr. Macnish, p. 361, consciousness of hearing music exists; but Causality refers these perceptions to diseases as their causes. When the derangement embraces the organs of Causality themselves, the power of discriminating the impression to be a morbid one is lost, and insanity is established.

It would be of much practical utility to teach individuals the dependence of consciousness on the states of the mental organs, as a means of inducing them, when under morbid excitement, to distrust their own impressions, and seek relief from sensible advisers. In the present system of education, the connexion of the feelings and intellect with material organs is so totally overlooked, and every emotion and perception is represented as so purely mental, that, when these become exalted or disordered, it is extremely difficult to enable the individual to comprehend how they can be delusive, or in any way affected by corporeal conditions: and hence he suffers much uneasiness in secret, avoids recourse to a physician, and persists in acting on his morbid impressions as if they were sound; till at last disease is permanently established, which, under more enlightened guidance, might easily have been averted, or cut short at its commencement.

It is extremely difficult to determine whether the feeling of personal identity indicated by the pronoun *I* is connected with a particular organ, or the result of the general action of the whole organs. The reader is referred to what is said on this subject on pages 102, 185, 312.

ATTENTION is not a faculty of the mind, but consists merely in the application of the knowing or reflecting faculties to their objects. Thus, the faculty of Tune, excited by melody, *attends* to notes; Causality, addressed by a demonstration, *attends* to the steps of the argument; and the other faculties of the intellect, in like manner, attend to their various objects. Concentrativeness gives continuity to the impressions of the faculties; Individuality and Eventuality direct them to their objects, and Firmness maintains them in a state of application—and these greatly aid attention; but still attention, in itself, is a mere act of the different intellectual faculties, and not the attribute of any particular power, established exclusively for its production.

ASSOCIATION. The metaphysicians have endeavoured, by reflecting on their own consciousness, to discover universal laws, by which the succession of ideas in mankind in general is regulated. They imagine our thoughts to follow each other in an established order, and have attempted to find out the causes and circumstances which determine the train. Success in such an attempt appears to me to be impossible. If we wished to ascertain the laws by which the succession of notes emitted by an Æolian harp is regulated, we should endeavour to discover the causes which produced them. Similar causes, acting in similar circumstances, produce similar effects; but if we vary one circumstance out of a thousand, we cannot calculate on the result. Now, the causes which determine the succession of notes from an Æolian harp are, the structure of the harp, the impetus of the air, and the order in which it excites the various strings. Render all these circumstances the same in the case of every harp, and the same succession of notes may be assuredly predicted. But if the air, that emblem of inconstancy, does not blow twice with the same force on the same spot in a month, or will not excite the same strings twice in the same order of succession in a year; and if no two Æolian harps can be made, in every particular of string, form, and substance, alike—who, by observing the notes arising from one harp, will succeed in unfolding the laws by which the succession of notes from Æolian harps in general may be determined, whatever may be their size, structure, and number of strings, and the circumstances in which they are placed? This illustration is completely applicable to the case of the intellectual faculties. Ideas are affections of these, just as notes are affections of the strings of the harp. These affections may arise from the internal activity of the faculties, or from impressions made on them by external objects; and there is as little regularity in the order in which the excitement occurs, as in the breathing of the air on the strings. And, lastly, if harps may vary in structure, human beings do positively differ in the relative strength of their powers. Hence the same impressions must produce very different effects, or introduce very different ideas into minds dissimilarly constituted; and how, amid such a countless variety of causes, can similarity of effects be expected?

If we place a number of persons on a hill-top, say Arthur's Seat, overlooking a champaign country and the sea, and bid each declare his thoughts, we shall find that one, with Ideality predominant, will think of the magnificence of nature, the boundless extent of the ocean, the vastness of the mountains; and, on recalling the scene, these ideas and emotions will be associated with it in his mind: another, with great Causality and Constructiveness, and little Ideality, will admire the skill which he sees displayed in the cultivation of the fields, and in the construction of the houses and the ships: one, with Benevolence large, will think of the happiness enjoyed by the people who inhabit the plain: another, with Acquisitiveness active, will think how the various branches of industry will pay: one, with a strong Veneration, will probably take occasion to admire the greatness and goodness of God; and some youthful lover may seize the opportunity afforded by the remoteness of the spot from human observation, to declare a passion for the lovely companion of his excursion. Now, the metaphysician expects to find out laws, by which, on Arthur's Seat being afterward mentioned in the presence of these individuals, the train of the thoughts of each in relation to it will be regulated; and he hopes to arrive at this result, by studying the train which arises in his own mind on the hill being referred to as an object of thought. Such an expectation must necessarily be futile. Each of the individuals supposed would, on the mention of the hill, experience a train of ideas corresponding to the first impressions which he received from it, and nothing can be more dissimilar than these. As well, therefore, (to use the words of an ingenious phrenologist,) may we expect, by studying the forms and hues of the clouds which flit along the sky to-day, to be able to discover laws by which their succession will be regulated to-morrow ; as, by reflecting on the ideas which pass in one mind, to discover links of association, by which ideas in the minds of mankind in general will be uniformly connected, and introduced in a determinate succession.

Mr. Stewart, in his *Elements of the Philosophy of the Human Mind,* (chap. v., part ii., sect. iii.,) speaks of " the association of ideas operating in producing *new* principles of action," and names *avarice* as one of them. He says, that " it cannot be doubted that this principle of action is artificial ;" (p. 392.)   In the same page he adds, that " there must be some limit, beyond which the theory of association cannot possibly be carried ; for the explanation which it gives, of the *formation of new principles of action,* proceeds on the supposition that there are *other* principles previously existing in the mind.   The great question, then, is, when are we arrived at this limit ? or, in other words, when are we arrived " (*not at the primitive faculties, but*) " at the simple and original *laws* of our constitution ?"   " It is on account of the enjoyments," says he, " which it enables us to purchase, that *money* is originally desired ; and yet, in process of time, by means of the agreeable impressions which are associated with it, it comes to be desired for its own sake ; and even continues to be an object of our pursuit long after we have lost all relish for those enjoyments which it enables us to command."   The erroneous nature of this mode of philosophizing may be illustrated by directing our attention to the mental organs.   Is it conceivable that any habits of association should create a new organ ? and yet this is what Mr. Stewart's hypothesis necessarily leads to, if by *principles of action* he means faculties of the mind. The love of distinction, for example, is a primitive desire arising from Love of Approbation, and it has a specific organ.   Money serves to gratify this desire.   According to Mr. Stewart, however, there is no organ giving rise to the love of money : but, in consequence of " the agreeable impressions which are associated with it," as a means of gratifying the love of distinction, the love of money becomes itself a new principle of action ; and, as all principles of action have organs, it must be presumed to create an organ for itself.   This new organ, we must suppose, causes money " to be an object of our pursuit long after we have lost all relish for those enjoyments which it enables us to command," and which first called the organ into existence.

It is evident that Mr. Stewart never saw clearly the difference between primitive faculties and their modes of action, and that he did not comprehend the real philosophy of association.   The new principles of action supposed by Mr. Stewart and other metaphysical authors to be produced by association, are either primitive propensities or sentiments, which they have erroneously imagined to be factitious, or the results merely of combinations in action among the primitive powers.   Mr. Stewart, as we have seen, describes the love of money ; and Sir James Mackintosh states conscience, as new principles of action produced by association, both of which, however, are referrible directly to primitive faculties having distinct organs. Mr. Stewart regards the power of Taste as a faculty formed by particular habits of study ; whereas Taste is not a primitive faculty at all, but the result of harmonious action in the primitive powers.   Mr. Stewart also, as remarked on p. 258, confounds, throughout his writings, primitive faculties, modes of action, laws of action, and results of combinations of faculties ; mistaking the one for the other, and applying the same language to all, in such a manner as to set consistency at defiance.

Although it is in vain to expect to find any law or principle regulating the association of one idea with another, the mutual influence of organs by association is determinate.   There are also natural associations between certain external objects and the internal faculties : and, lastly, artiicial associations may be formed between objects and the feelings of the mind ; and the laws which regulate the constitution of these associations are ascertainable and interesting. Let us, therefore, inquire briefly into hese laws of association.

First, in regard to single organs. Each, by frequently repeating any given mode of action, comes to perform it with greater facility and rapidity. For every idea formed and every emotion felt, there must be an affection of an organ. If, therefore, any organ has been trained to act in a certain manner—as the organ of Language to repeat certain verses, or he organ of Tune to reproduce a certain air—it will acquire additional acility in repeating the act ; or, in other words, the verses or notes will be presented in the order of succession, or be associated, so that, when one is produced, the others will have the tendency to follow in the accustomed order of succession.

Secondly, We are able to perform anew, when we wish to do so, any voluntary motion which we have performed before. This shows that the nerves of motion are so associated or connected with the organs of the mind, as to be at the command of the will.

In the *third* place, by conceiving an object in distress, we can raise the emotion of pity in the mind ; by conceiving a splendid scene in nature, we can excite the emotions of sublimity and beauty produced by Ideality ; by reading a terrific story, we are able to experience the chilling emotions of fear creeping along the nerves. These facts point out a close connexion between the organs of intellect and those of the different propensities and sentiments. Indeed, in the dissection of the brain, the closest relation between its different parts is perceived, combined with arrangements for separate functions ; but this is connexion rather than association.

Farther, in surveying the cerebral organs, we perceive them to be beautifully associated, in point of arrangement, for the purposes of mutual assistance in their action. "When I began," says Mr. Scott,* " to consider the schedule or map presented to us by Drs. Gall and Spurzheim, I could at first see none of this beauty in it. In looking over their list of powers, I could observe no order or connexion between them. The whole presented to me a rude appearance, quite different, as I then thought, from what is commonly found in nature. After a more attentive consideration, however, light began to dawn upon me, and, beginning to consider the faculties in a certain way, and to group them after a certain order, the whole gradually formed themselves before me into a system of surprising symmetry ; and, like the disjointed parts of an anamorphosis, when seen from the proper point of view, collecting themselves into one elegant design, delighted me with the appearance of that very order and beauty which I should beforehand have expected to find in them. In a scheme such as this, where we find powers which are analogous, which resemble one another in their nature and uses, or which act upon, and co-operate with, one another, or mutually aid and assist, or control and balance, each other, we should naturally expect the organs of these powers to be situated near one another, and in such a way as either to adjoin, or at least to admit of an easy communication. Accordingly, we find this to be the case." Immediately above Amativeness, for example, we see, in the bust, Philoprogenitiveness, giving the love of offspring, and Adhesiveness, producing the propensity to attachment, the three together constituting the group of the domestic feelings. Next to them we find Combativeness as if there were no dearer objects than those for which our courage could be exerted. Adjoining to Combativeness is Destructiveness ; the former giving bold-

* *Observations on Phrenology, as affording a Systematic View of Human Nature.* Edinburgh, 1822. Dr. Gall has a section on this subject, *Sur les Fonctions du Cerveau*, tome iii., p. 206.

ness to meet the enemy, the latter putting peril in the onset, and threatening him with destruction.

Amid the difficulties of life it is necessary to use, not only caution, but also so much of secrecy regarding our own purposes, as not to carry "our hearts on our sleeves for daws to peck at," and we find Secretiveness surmounted by, and in, juxtaposition with Cautiousness.

Turning to the region of the sentiments, we find Veneration, which produces the tendency to religion, surrounded by Benevolence, Hope, Perseverance, and Justice ; or the fountains of the whole charities and duties of life associated in a group, and beautifully arranged for reciprocal aid and combined action.

We find Ideality approaching these, but a little below them, yet so near to, and above, Constructiveness as to elevate its designs. Ideality also adjoins to Wit and Tune, as if to give soul and fancy to poetry.

In like manner, we find the organs which simply perceive, or the knowing organs, arranged together, along the superciliary ridge, and those of reflection occupying the summit of the forehead, like the powers which govern and direct the whole.

Mr. Scott, after exhibiting these views, observes, that such an arrangement is more beautiful, systematic, and appropriate, than human ingenuity could have devised ; and taken in connexion with the fact, that the organs were discovered at different times, and in separate situations, and that order and beauty appeared only after the ultimate filling up of the greater part of the brain had taken place, it affords a strong argument *a priori*, that the organs were *discovered*, not *invented*, and that the system is the work of *Nature*, and not of Drs. Gall and Spurzheim.

In treating of the organ of Language, I have explained the association of Ideas with signs. I may here add, that the science of Mnemonics is founded on this power of the mind to associate ideas with other ideas, or with arbitrary signs. In devising means for aiding the memory, it ought constantly to be kept in view, that every individual will, with the greatest ease, associate ideas with such external objects as he has the greatest natural facility in perceiving. For example, sometimes notions of place are used as the medium of recalling the ideas which we wish to remember. The room is divided, in imagination, into compartments, and the first topic of the discourse is placed in the first compartment, the second in the second, and so on ; so that, by going over the spaces, the different heads of the discourse with which they were associated will be recalled. It is obvious, however, that it is only when Locality is large that such a device can be serviceable ; because, if this faculty be weak, it will be as difficult to imagine and recollect the position of the compartments as the discourse itself. If, in like manner, numbers be resorted to as the connecting medium, with the view that, on hearing one idea which we wish to recollect, we shall associate it with the number one, and, on hearing another which we wish to recollect, we shall associate it the number two—it is obvious, that, unless the faculty of Number be powerful, this will be a more difficult task than that of simple recollection. Hence, different modes of recollection should be used for different individuals. He who has Number most powerful, will associate words most easily with numbers ; he who has Form most energetic, will associate words most easily with figures ; he who has Locality most vigorous, will associate words most easily with positions ; and he who has Tune most powerful, will associate words most easily with musical notes. Hence, also, the influence of associations on our judgment is accounted for. He in whom Veneration is powerful, and to whom the image of a saint has been from infancy presented as an object to be venerated, experiences an instantaneous and involuntary emotion of Veneration every time the image is presented to him, or a conception of it formed; because it is now the sign which excites in him that emotion, altogether independently of reflection. Until we can break this association, and prevent the conception of the image from operating as a sign to excite the faculty of Veneration, we shall never succeed in bringing his understanding to examine the real attributes of the object itself, and to perceive its-want of every quality that ought justly to be venerated. In the same way, when a person is in love, the perception or conception of the object beloved stirs up the faculties which feel into vivid action; the consequent emotion is so delightful, and the reflecting faculties have so little consciousness that the real source of the fascination is in the faculties which feel, that it is impossible to make the lover see the object with the eyes of a disinterested spectator. If we could once break the association between the object and the faculties which feel, the reflecting faculties would then perform their functions faithfully, and the object would be seen in its true colours. But, while we are unable to break this link and to prevent this fascination, we may reason *ad sempiternum*, and our conclusions will never appear to be sound; because the premises, that is, the appearance of the object, will never be the same to the party most interested in the argument, and to us.

Thus, the associations which mislead the judgment, and perpetuate prejudices, as those of words or things with *feelings* or *sentiments*, and not associations of conceptions with conceptions, or merely of ideas with ideas. The whole classes of ideas formed by the knowing and reflecting faculties may be associated *ad infinitum*, and no moral prejudices will arise, if these ideas do not become linked with the propensities and sentiments

In studying the laws of association, therefore, we must go beyond the ideas themselves, and consider the faculties which form them. If the faculties be kept in view, the whole phenomena of association will appear lucid and intelligible; and we shall find nature confirming our principles, because they will be founded on her laws. We shall see the individual who has the *reflecting* faculties most powerful, associating ideas according to the relation of necessary consequence; we shall perceive him who has the *knowing* faculties most powerful, associating ideas according to the relations of time, place, and circumstances;* and very often, though not always, we shall find each individual associating with most facility, and recollecting most perfectly, those ideas which minister to the gratification of his most powerful propensities or sentiments. If we seek only for relations among individual ideas themselves, or for general laws, according to which ideas are associated in all individuals, our researches will never be crowned with success. No stronger proof of this fact could be found than the circumstance, that, although different individuals will use the same process of reasoning to produce the same conviction, yet no two will state their arguments in the same words, nor make use of the same illustrations. The general similarity of the reasoning process depends on the similarity of the constitution of the faculties which reason; but differences in words and illustration arise from particular combination of organs belonging to different individuals, and from the circumstances in which they have been placed, which afford materials of thought in some degree peculiar to each.

In all ages unprincipled individuals have availed themselves of the law of association before explained, to enslave the minds of their fellow-men. By means of early impressions they have connected certain practices and notions favourable to their own power, with the sentiments of Cautiousness, Conscientiousness, and Veneration in the people, and thereby caused them to fear objects existing only in imagination, and to perform actions inconsistent with the welfare of society. Phrenology will tend to bring

* See examples of association of colours on page 292 of this work.

33

this species of tyranny to an end. Each faculty has a sphere of legitimate action, established by the Creator, which is in harmony with every interest, that He acknowledges as pure and beneficial ; but there is also a boundless field of abuse of each, favourable to base and selfish purposes. While the faculties themselves, and their relations to each other and to external objects, are unknown, and the human intellect is uncultivated and ignorant, it is extremely difficult for ordinary minds to distinguish accurately the boundaries of right ; and hence a wide door is opened to abuse of every power. From this cause error is largely mixed up with truth, and deliberately so, by the unprincipled, who hope to profit by delusion. Hence the opinions and institutions of society, in most countries present a feeble and inconsistent appearance. In the moral world, in consequence of our own ignorance, we perceive little of that magnificient power and comprehensive design, applied by the Deity for benevolent ends, which are so conspicuous in physical creation. In this state of things it is not difficult to impress false and prejudicial notions on the minds of youth, and to support them through life by observances fitted to give them permanence. and on this basis individual interest erects its baneful structures. But when the faculties and their relations shall be generally studied, and knowledge of their legitimate spheres of action shall be obtained, the discovery will be made, that creation is constituted in harmony only with their proper manifestations ; and then acute perception of right, with high determination to pursue it, will take the place of groping blindness and irresolute imbecility, which now characterize the moral aspects of society in many countries of the world.

In treating of the circumstances which modify the effects of size upon the power of the celebral organs,* I enumerated " *constitution*, health, exercise, excitement from without, and, in some cases, the mutual influence of the organs." The effects of the first three circumstances were considered in the introductory chapter ; and in the present section I have introduced various observations on the other two. The laws of the mutual influence of the organs form a department of Phrenology to which close and particular attention has been too little directed. Mr. Robert Cox, however, has recently been engaged with the investigation of these laws, and some of his conclusions are published in *The Phrenological Journal* " There are different modes," he observes, " in which one cerebral organ may be said to influence another. First, it may restrain us from *acting* under the other's impulse, without in any degree lessening the force of that impulse itself ; as when a person who ardently desires to strike his neighbour is prevented by Cautiousness from gratifying this inclination Or, in the second place, it may direct the other to seek gratification *in a particular line of conduct* ; as when an avaricious man is led by Conscientiousness to amass wealth by honest industry rather than by theft. In such cases, however, it is only the *result* of the activity that is modified, not the activity itself ; so that, strictly speaking, the mutual influence of the organs is *the production, increase, diminution, or extinction of the activity of one organ, consequent upon certain states of other organs.* As already hinted, this department of Phrenology, though a most interesting field of inquiry, has hitherto been greatly overlooked. Dr. Spurzheim adverts to it in a brief and somewhat unsatisfactory manner in his work on Education, a chapter of which is devoted to ' the mutual influence of the faculties as a means of excitement ;' and the subject is touched upon in a cursory way also by Mr. Combe, in his analysis of Association in the ' *System of Phrenology*.' It is intricate and bewildering in no ordinary degree, but, being also of very great importance, obviously deserves to be minutely and carefully investigated. I have of late bestowed considerable

* See Introduction, p. 48.

attention upon this department of the physiology of the brain, and am convinced that phrenologists may labour in it with every encouragement to hope for useful and valuable discoveries. Such data as I have been able to collect appear to show that the mutual influence of the organs is regulated by general laws—which, however, are, for special purposes, subject to modification by *particular laws*, regulating only *certain organs.* My speculations concerning the former class of laws here alluded to, although they have made some progress, are not yet sufficiently mature for publication ; but, in regard to at least one department of the *particular laws*, precise and definite conclusions are believed to have been arrived at."* · The laws whose existence Mr. Cox conceives himself to have established are, 1st, That, when any of our faculties is *pained* or *disagreeably* active, Destructiveness is excited sympathetically, in a degree varying with the intensity of the existing pain ; and, 2dly, That, by a law perfectly analogous, the organ of Benevolence receives excitement from the *agreeable* or *pleasurable* action of the organs of the other mental powers. In support of these propositions Mr. Cox has adduced many facts and arguments, for which I am obliged to refer to the pages of the Journal.†

PASSION is the highest degree of activity of every faculty ; and the passions are as different as the faculties : Thus, a passion for glory is the result of a high activity of the Love of Approbation ; a passion for money, of Acquisitiveness ; a passion for music, of the faculty of Tune ; a passion for metaphysics, of Causality. Lord Byron says, " I can never get people to understand that poetry is the expression of *excited passion*; and that there is no such thing as a life of passion, any more than a continuous earthquake, or an eternal fever."‡ This is correct ; but, among the faculties excited to passion, Ideality must be one before beautiful or exquisite poetry can be produced. Hence there can be no such thing as *factitious* passions, although such are spoken of in various books. Man cannot alter his nature ; and every object that he can desire must be desired in consequence of its tending to gratify some natural faculty.

" Locke, and many modern writers," says Dr. Spurzheim, " maintain that children are destitute of passion ; and it is true, that there is, in adults, one passion which is not observed in children, the passion of love. There have been, however, some individuals who, at three or four years of age, have felt passionately this propensity ; and, in general, the greater number of inclinations manifest themselves with energetic activity in children. The opponents of Phrenology, for the most part, confound the objects upon which the particular faculties act at different ages, with the inclinations themselves. Children, it is true, have no inclination to defraud the orphan of his inheritance, or to conquer kingdoms ; but they sometimes deceive one another for a bird's nest ; they fight for playthings, and they are proud to occupy the first place at school." The same faculties which give desires for these objects, when differently directed in after-life, produce the various passions which characterize our maturer years. The boy who is extremely mortified at losing a place, and burns with desire to stand at the top of his class, will not be destitute of ambition when a man.

PLEASURE and PAIN are affections of every faculty. Each, when indulged in its natural action, says Dr. Spurzheim, feels pleasure ; when disagreeably affected, feels pain : consequently the kinds of pain and pleasure are as numerous as the faculties. Hence one individual delights in generously pardoning offences, and another in taking revenge ; one is happy in the possession of riches, and another glories in disdaining the vanities of mankind." Thus, " pain and pleasure are the result, and not the cause, of the particular faculties."

* *Phrenological Journal*, vol. ix., p. 403. † See vol. ix., p. 406 ; and vol. x., p. ‡ Letter 436, Moore's *Life*, vol. v., p. 197.

PATIENCE and IMPATIENCE. Patience, as a positive feeling, arises from a large developement of Benevolence, Veneration, Hope, Conscientiousness, and Firmness, combined with small Self-Esteem. This combination is accompanied with meekness, humility, constancy, and resignation ; the constituent elements of a patient and enduring spirit. Apathy may arise from a highly lymphatic temperament, or great deficiency of brain. By persons ignorant of human nature, this state is sometimes mistaken for patience ; just as the extinction of thought and feeling in a nation is called by a despot repose.

An individual possessing an active temperament, and Self-Esteem, Combativeness, and Destructiveness larger than Benevolence, Veneration, and Conscientiousness, will be impatient of opposition and contradiction ; one in whom Tune, Time, and Ideality are large, will be impatient of bad music ; one in whom Benevolence, Conscientiousness, and Causality are large, will be impatient of hypocritical and selfish conduct. If the nervous and sanguine temperaments predominate, the organs will be very active, and the individual will be impatient of all slow prosing movements, whether in speech or in actions.

JOY and GRIEF. Mr. Hume enters into a very accurate and refined analysis, to show that grief and joy are merely *mixtures* of *hope* and *fear*. After treating of several passions, he continues thus : " None of these passions seem to contain anything curious or remarkable, except *hope* and *fear*, which, being derived from the probability of any good or evil, are mixed passions, that merit our attention."

" Probability," says he, " arises from an opposition of contrary chances or causes, by which the mind is not allowed to fix on either side, but is incessantly tossed from one to another, and is determined one moment to consider an object as existent, and another moment as the contrary."

" Suppose, then, that the object concerning which we are doubtful produces either desire or aversion, it is evident that, according as the mind turns itself to one side or the other, it must feel a momentary impression of joy or sorrow."

" The passions of fear and hope may arise when the chances are equal on both sides, and no superiority can be discovered in one above the other. Nay, in this situation the passions are rather the strongest, as the mind has then the least foundation to rest upon, and is tossed with the greatest uncertainty. Throw in a superior degree of probability to the side of grief, you immediately see that passion diffuse itself over the composition, and tincture it with fear. Increase the probability, and by that means the grief ; the fear prevails still more, till at last it runs insensibly, as the joy continually diminishes, into pure grief. After you have brought it to this situation, diminish the grief by a contrary operation to that which increased it, to wit, by diminishing the probability on the melancholy side, and you will see the passion clear every moment, till it changes insensibly into hope ; which again runs, by slow degrees, into joy, as you increase that part of the composition by the increase of the probability." Mr. Hume concludes by this question : " Are not these as plain proofs that the passions of fear and hope are mixtures of grief and joy, as in optics it is a proof that a coloured ray of the sun, passing through a prism, is a composition of two others, when, as you diminish or increase the quantity of either, you find it prevail proportionally, more or less, in the composition ?"*

These views are exceedingly ingenious, and, to a certain extent, sound ; but Phrenology presents us with a still more distinct and accurate elucidation of the nature of grief and joy. Each propensity desires to attain its object, and the attainment affords to the mind a feeling of gratification. Acquisitiveness desires wealth ; Love of Approbation longs for praise and

* Hume's *Dissertation on the Passions*, sect. i.

distinction, and Self-Esteem pants for authority or independence. The *obtaining of wealth* gratifies Acquisitiveness ; this is attended with a pleasing emotion, and this emotion constitutes joy. The *losing of wealth* robs Acquisitiveness of its object ; this,-again, is accompanied with a painful emotion, which is grief. The same remarks may be applied to Love of Approbation, Self-Esteem, or Philoprogenitiveness. When a lovely child is born, the delight experienced by the parents will be in proportion to the ardour of their desire for offspring ; or, in other words, their *joy* will be great in proportion to the gratification of their Philoprogenitiveness. If they lose the child, their *grief* will be severe in proportion to the intensity of this feeling, lacerated by the removal of its object. In all these instances we find *joy* and *grief* existing without involving either *hope* or *fear.*

Let us now advert to Mr. Hume's analysis. Cautiousness and Hope are both primitive sentiments, the former producing fear, and the latter an emotion *sui generis*, attended with delight. Both have relation to *future* objects, and in this respect differ from the other faculties, the gratification of which relates to *present* time ; but this circumstance does not change the laws of their operation. If the prospect of future evil be presented to the mind, it excites Cautiousness, and fear is produced ; this emotion is painful, but fear is not grief. It is to be observed, however, that there must be the *fear of something*; and as *evil* is that which causes a disagreeable affection of some primitive faculty, of Acquisitiveness or Philoprogenitiveness, for example, Cautiousness is rarely affected *alone*, but generally in conjunction with some other power. Thus, if a son be sick, Cautiousness fears that he will die, and Philoprogenitiveness is painfully affected by the prospect of that event—which painful emotion is grief. Here fear and grief are conjoined ; but they arise from different sources, and, although the *fear* cannot exist without *grief* in some degree or other, yet the *grief* might exist without the *fear;* and would do so, if the child were carried in a corpse without a moment's warning. In the same way, if a person hope, he must *hope for something.* If for gaining a thousand pounds, the prospect gratifies Acquisitiveness, and this is joy. Here the active Hope and gratified Acquisitiveness mingle in producing joy, but still the sources of the joy and hope are separate ; and if the money were realized, joy would exist without the hope, although hope can scarcely be active without joy. The principles here unfolded will be found to elucidate every instance of the operation of hope and fear, joy and grief, which can be supposed ; and this is a strong proof that we have found the truth. They explain beautifully, for instance, how, with many individuals, the *anticipation* of good is more delightful than the enjoyment of it. If Acquisitiveness and Hope be both strong, the *prospect* of gain excites and gratifies *both faculties at once;* whereas, the *actual attainment* pleases *only Acquisitiveness,* and excludes hope. But Hope being not less than Acquisitiveness a source of pleasure, it is easy to conceive that the *exercise of both* must be *more delightful* than that of either separately ; and that, when Hope is dropped from the combination, a great part of the pleasure will be gone.

The converse of this holds equally good. The prospect of distant evil is more painful than the experience of it when actually present. While the loss of a child is contemplated at a distance, Cautiousness, if large, adds its melancholy and heart-sinking fears to the pain of a wounded Philoprogenitiveness ; but when the event happens, the influence of Cautiousness is withdrawn, Philoprogenitiveness alone suffers, and the actual distress is frequently less grievous than the anticipation of it.

Great wisdom and benevolence on the part of the Creator are displayed in this constitution of our minds ; for we are thereby prompted, with double ardour, to avoid evil, while it is yet at a distance, and subject to control from our efforts.

SYMPATHY* may be defined to be a fellow-feeling in one person, with emotions experienced by another.   By attending to the laws which regulate the activity of the mental faculties, we shall discover the true nature of this affection, and the circumstances most favourable to its occurrence.

Every internal faculty, like each of the external senses, is most powerfully and most agreeably roused to activity by the direct presentment of its own objects ; Cautiousness, for instance, by the aspect of danger, Benevolence, by that of suffering ; and so on.   Hence, if two individuals of nearly similar constitutions of mind be exposed to the operation of the same external causes, the same faculties being called into activity in both, will give rise to similar emotions ; and they may then be said to sympathize with each other.   This is one kind of sympathy, but it is not the state of mind to which that term is most correctly applied.

The next source of stimulus to the faculties is that afforded by Natural Language.   When any faculty is predominantly active, it gives a peculiar expression to the features and certain determinate attitudes to the body, the import of which is intuitively understood by all who possess the same faculty even in a moderate degree.   Thus, Self-Esteem, being predominantly active, communicates to the body a cold, formal, erect, and haughty air.   This air is recognised intuitively by the spectator as indicating excessive pride in the individual who exhibits it ; and it is called the natural language of Self-Esteem.†   Now, by a law of our constitution, the natural language of any active faculty invariably excites the same faculty to action, and, consequently, gives rise to the same emotions, in the minds of those who witness it.   The forbidding strut of great Self-Esteem, for instance, in a person whom we never saw before, addresses itself directly to our Self-Esteem ; we instinctively draw up, and feel moved to support our own consequence by a coldness proportioned to his.   In like manner, when we meet, for the first time, with a person whose countenance and gestures express kindness, candour, and open-hearted friendship, which are the natural language of active Benevolence, Conscientiousness, and Adhesiveness, the same emotions are excited in ourselves, and we instinctively return his advances with a kindness corresponding to his own.‡   Or, let

* I am indebted to the kindness of Dr. A. Combe for the following observations on Sympathy.

† See Remarks on the Natural Language of the Faculties, p. 106.

‡ These phenomena are differently explained by Mr. Robert Cox, who regards the influence of the law of sympathy as less extensive ; but his remarks do not appear to me to be entirely sound. Commenting on the above passage in the text, he says : " It appears to me that these effects take place, not under the operation of any such law as that imagined by Dr. Combe, but simply because the natural language conveys a meaning calculated to rouse the corresponding faculty in the spectator. The forbidding strut of Self-Esteem calls that sentiment into action in ourselves only in so far as it is significant to us of an insult or assumption of superiority on the part of the strutter—these being directly calculated to stimulate the faculty in us, just as by a fine landscape the sentiment of Ideality is called into play. That the mere natural language of Self-Esteem does not excite the same faculty in the spectators, is obvious from the fact, that where circumstance put all reference to self out of the question, no such consequence ensues : thus, though we see an actor on the stage exhibiting in perfection the natural language of arrogance, yet, being ourselves not in the least offended by the exhibition, we experience no inclination to " draw up," but are satisfied with laughing heartily. In like manner, we may see one man strutting up to another on the street, without feeling at all disposed to imitate his carriage ; though, if ourselves strutted up to, Self-Esteem is touched by the insult, and its natural language of course is exhibited.   That this is the consequence of the unceremonious treatment alone, and not of mere perception of the natural language, appears from this

us imagine that we hurry to meet a friend, whom we expect to find all happiness and gayety, and that, instead of this, seriousness, anxiety, and grief are depicted on the countenance, and indicated by his gestures, these being the natural language of Cautiousness and other faculties painfully affected, will call up a corresponding affection of the same faculties in our minds, and, without knowing what has distressed him, our features and attitudes will instantly assume an expression consonant with his own. It is to this involuntary and almost unconscious communication of feelings and emotions from the mind of one individual to that of another, through the medium of natural language, that the term Sympathy is most properly applied.

An excellent illustration of this kind of sympathy is to be found in the effects of a panic, or excessively excited Cautiousness, in one individual, exciting the same feeling in all who behold it. The very sight of a panic-stricken person, when we do not know the cause which has given rise to the alarm, excites a general uneasiness about our own safety ; and if a great number of persons together, and at the same instant, perceive the terrified expression, it instantly rouses the faculty of Cautiousness to its highest pitch of activity in all of them, and produces the most intense feelings of dread and alarm. Such are the causes and origin of panics in battles and in mobs ; and hence the electric rapidity with which passions of every kind pervade and agitate the minds of assembled multitudes.

Another and very familiar example of this kind of sympathy may be seen in a crowded city. Let any one in passing along London bridge, for instance, stop short, and turn up his face, with his mouth half open, as if stupified with wonder and amazement ; and immediately the same expression, being the natural language of Individuality and Wonder, will be transferred to the countenances of nine-tenths of the passengers, not one of whom, of course, will be able to assign any *direct* cause for the emotion with which his mind will be filled. As the propensities and sentiments employ the intellect to minister to their gratification, if the wag happen to say that it is something vastly surprising in the heavens which attracts his gaze, the majority of the *curious* in wonders will soon, by a stretch of intellectual conception, come to perceive *something* where nothing actually exists.

True sympathy, then, arises from the natural language of any active feeling in one individual exciting the same feeling in another, " *antecedently to any knowledge of what excited it in the person principally concerned ;*" and, therefore, as the stimulus of natural language is secondary or inferior in power to that derived from the direct presentment of the objects of any faculty, it is easy to explain why the person who feels sym-

that an insult given quite unintentionally, and with the kindest and most respectful air, has exactly the same effect. I shall never forget the air of offended dignity with which a gentleman in a public office " drew up," when, in a moment of abstraction, half a crown was offered him as a compensation for his civility in showing the building. So it is likewise with Destructiveness and Benevolence. We may see a man furiously enraged, without having our own Destructiveness excited in the least ; while the tenth part of the concomitant verbal abuse, if lavished on ourselves, would immediately kindle our wrath into a flame. Thus also, the natural language of Benevolence fails to excite that faculty in us, if we are aware that the appearance is merely assumed. An open, sincere, and friendly countenance produces good will only in so far as it is significant of estimable qualities, and these, being agreeable to our own feelings, excite Benevolence through their medium. All the phenomena which really take place are explained by the laws whose existence I have laboured to establish—namely, that Destructiveness is roused by the disagreeable action, and Benevolence by the agreeable, of every power of the human mind." *Phrenological Journal*, vol. x., p. 13.

pathetically, feels less deeply than the person with whom he sympathizes.
The same principle explains, also, why all men do not sympathize in the
same degree, and why, in some cases, the spectator does not sympathize
at all.   If the objects presented be such as to afford a *direct* stimulus to a
different faculty in us from that exhibited in activity by another, it follows
that, in virtue of the stronger influence of the direct excitement, the particular faculty which it addresses will be roused into higher activity than
the one which has only the less powerful stimulus of natural language,
and thus a totally dissimilar emotion will be experienced.   For example,
let us suppose that a man with a good endowment of Combativeness and
Destructiveness is attacked on the highway ; the menacing looks and
gestures (the natural language of these faculties) displayed by the aggressor instantly rouse them into energetic action in the defender, and force
is repelled by force.   But, suppose that the attack is made upon a woman,
or an individual in whom Combativeness is only moderate, and in whom
Cautiousness predominates, the attack then becomes a *direct* stimulus to
Cautiousness, which, being excited, produces *fear ;* and the direct stimulus
of Cautiousness overpowering the indirect stimulus of Combativeness,
submission or flight is resorted to, rather than defence

Dr. Adam Smith* supposes that there are emotions with which we
have no sympathy.   " The furious behaviour of an angry man," says he,
" is more likely to exasperate us against himself than against his enemies."
According to the theory, however, of sympathy, that it excites in us the
same emotion which others feel, this opinion seems to be untenable.   If
Combativeness and Destructiveness in one excite by sympathy Combativeness and Destructiveness in another, which I hold them to do, it follows that, as the function of these faculties is to attack or to repel attack,
when they are roused, they must, from their very constitution, exert themselves against something or somebody.   If we know the cause of the
anger, and approve of it, and direct our Combativeness and Destructiveness against the angry man's enemies, this is clearly sympathy in every
sense of the term.   But if we disapprove of the cause, then he himself
becomes the object of our resentment ; and in popular language it may
be said, that, in this case, we do not sympathize with him ; but it must
be observed, 1*st*, that the activity of Combativeness and Destructiveness
in him is the cause of rousing the same faculties in us ; and, 2*dly*, that the
reason of anger being directed against himself is to be found in his having
outraged, by his conduct, our moral sentiments, and presented us with an
object (an unreasonably furious man) which stimulates these *directly ;*
and they being excited, determine the direction which Combativeness
and Destructiveness shall take.   The same reasoning applies to the sympathy of Self-Esteem and of other faculties, hitherto supposed not to
sympathize.

The proof, that we do sympathize with anger, when properly directed,
as well as with grief or pity, is to be found in the cordiality with which
we approve of, and indeed encourage, a just degree of it.   ·Fortunately, in
the case of Combativeness and Destructiveness, as well as of all the other
propensities, our sympathy, beyond certain limits, is soon arrested by the
direct stimulus which the moral sentiments receive from the conduct of
the angry person, and by the deep sense of their inherent supremacy which is
then felt.   In consequence we sympathize with, or approve of, the actions
produced by the lower faculties of others only when these are guided by
the faculties peculiar to man.   For example, we never sympathize with
Combativeness when indulged for the mere pleasure of fighting ; or of
Destructiveness, when gratified for the mere delight of being ferocious ;

---

* *Theory of Moral Sentiments,* p. 32.

or of Acquisitiveness, when directed to the sole purpose of accumulating wealth. But we sympathize with the action of all of these faculties when directed by justice and understanding. Such, however, is the beautiful constitution of our nature, that we sympathize with the action of the sentiments proper to man, even when unmingled with any other motive : for example, we sympathize with benevolence, from the mere glow of charity ; with veneration, from the mere inward feeling of devotion; with justice, from the pure dictates of Conscientiousness ; and actions done apparently from the impulses of these faculties lose their character of purity and excellence in our estimation, in exact proportion to the alloy of the inferior faculties which we perceive to be mingled with them. Kindness, in which we perceive interest, is always less valued than when pure and unadulterated. Activity in the service of the public loses its merit in our eyes, in exact proportion as we perceive the motive to be the Love of Approbation, unmingled with Conscientiousness and true Benevolence. These facts prove the accuracy of the phrenological doctrine, that the higher faculties are made to govern the lower; and also the curious circumstance, that man is conscious of possessing feelings, necessary, no doubt, in themselves, but of the gratification of which, when undirected by the superior powers, he himself disapproves. Even the higher sentiments, however, to be approved of, must act conformably to the understanding ; and excess of veneration, of benevolence, or of scrupolosity is regarded as weakness, as excess of any lower propensity is regarded as vice.

The doctrine of sympathy leads to valuable practical consequences. The natural language of any faculty is intelligible to, and excites the same faculty in, another, and this simple principle explains why harshness is much less powerful than mildness in commanding the services of others. Harshness is the natural language of active Self-Esteem, Combativeness, Destructiveness, and Firmness : in virtue of the above rule, it naturally excites the same faculties in those against whom it is directed, and an instinctive tendency to resistance or disobedience is the result. Among the uneducated classes this process is exhibited every day. A parent, in a harsh and angry tone, commands a child to do or to abstain from doing something ; the child instinctively resists ; and loud threatenings, and at last violence ensue. These last are *direct* stimulants to Cautiousness ; they overpower the faculties excited only by the indirect stimulus of harshness, and obedience at last takes place. This is the uniform effect of imperious commands : obedience never ensues till consequences alarming to Cautiousness are perceived, and then it is attended with a grudge. Veneration, Conscientiousness, Love of Approbation, and Benevolence, on the other hand, are the faculties which lead to willing submission and obedience, and to which, therefore, we ought to address ourselves. . If we stimulate them, compliance will be agreeable to the individual, and doubly beneficial to the person who commands.

This principle explains also the force of example in training to good conduct, and affords instructive rules for the proper education of the propensities and sentiments. Where parents and seniors act habitually under the influence of the higher sentiments, the same sentiments in children not only receive a *direct* cultivation, but are sustained in enduring vivacity by the natural expression of their activity thus exhibited. Children having the organs of the sentiments early developed, can judge of what is right and wrong long before they can reason ; and hence the importance of always manifesting before them the supremacy of sentiments. Much of the effect of example upon the future character has been ascribed to Imitation ; but, although this has an influence, I am persuaded that it is small compared with that of Sympathy as now unfolded.

There is a state of mind which has been confounded with Sympathy but which arises from the direct excitement of the faculties by their own objects. When we see a stroke aimed and ready to fall upon the arm or leg of another person, we are apt to shrink and draw back our own leg or arm, and, when it does fall, we in some measure feel it, and are hurt by it as well as the sufferer. Dr. Adam Smith proceeds to explain this by saying, that our fellow-feeling here arises from our changing places in fancy with the sufferer. Thus, if our brother is upon the rack, says he, "by the imagination we place ourselves in his situation, we conceive ourselves enduring all the same torments; we enter, as it were, into his body and become in some measure the same person with him, and thence form some idea of his sensations, and even feel something which, though weaker in degree, is not altogether unlike them. His agonies thus brought home to ourselves, when we have thus adopted and made them our own, begin at last to affect us, and we then tremble and shudder at the thought of what he feels."*

This theory, however, appears to be incorrect, for we often feel intensely for another's misery without, even in idea, changing places with him. In beholding suffering, we feel deep commiseration with its object, simply because the faculty of Benevolence, the function of which is to manifest this emotion, is a primitive mental power, having the same relation to external misery or pain that light has to the eye; and as such it is as instantly and irresistibly roused by presentment of a suffering object, as the eye is by the admission of light, or the ear by the percussion of sounds. In witnessing another's misery, we, in virtue of this constitution of mind, first feel the emotion of pity, and, in proportion to its strength, fancy to ourselves the pain which he endures: but the pity always precedes, and the effort to conceive the pain is the *effect*, and not the cause, of the pity. Hence those who are remarkable for a moderate endowment of Benevolence, although possessing superior intellectual or *conceiving* powers, never even try to fancy themselves placed in the situation of the sufferer, because they feel no motive impelling them to the attempt. The benevolent idiot, on the other hand, with scarcely any power of conception, feels the most poignant distress.

The same principle explains our shrinking from a blow impending over another. The feeling then experienced is a compound of fear and pity, Cautiousness and Benevolence. Fear is roused by the danger, and Pity is roused by the consequent pain. Danger is the direct stimulant of Cautiousness, and suffering that of Benevolence; and, therefore, when these objects are presented to the mind, we can no more help feeling the corresponding emotions, than we can help seeing or hearing. The direct chief end or function of Cautiousness is the care and preservation of *self*; therefore, when it is excited by the aspect of danger, we look eagerly to *self*, and draw in our own leg or arm as parts of *ourselves*; but this results directly from the constitution of the faculty, and not from putting ourselves in the place of another. The direct end or function of Benevolence, again, is the good and happiness of *others*, and therefore, when it is excited by the misery of another, it necessarily, from its very constitution, feels for *them*, and not for ourselves.

An active temperament greatly conduces us to sympathy, by producing vivacity in all the cerebral functions; but this does not supersede the laws of sympathy before explained.

HABIT. Next to Association, Habit makes the most conspicuous figure in the philosophy of Mr. Stewart. He refers the incapacity of some individuals to discriminate colours to habits of inattention. The powers also of wit, fancy, and invention in the arts and sciences, he informs us, are not the original gifts of nature, "but the result of acquired

* *Theory of Moral Sentiments*, p. 30.

habits."* "The power of taste, and a genius for poetry, painting, music, and mathematics," he states, " are gradually formed by particular *habits* of study or of business." And not only does Habit execute these magnificent functions in the system of Mr. Stewart, but, in the estimation of individuals in private life, it appears to be viewed as almost omnipotent. On reading to a friend the account of the boy J. G's early dishonest conduct,† he attributed them all to *bad habits* formed in the charity workhouse of Glasgow ; on exhibiting an individual whose mental character was directly opposite, he attributed the difference to *good habits*, formed under the tuition of his parents. Thus, there are no talents so transcendent, and no dispositions so excellent or so depraved, but habit is supposed by many, at once, to account for them in such a manner as to supersede the necessity of all farther investigation. What, then, *is* HABIT, and what place does it hold in the phrenological system ?

Every voluntary action is a manifestation of some one or more faculties of the mind. Habit is defined to be "a power in a man of doing anything, acquired by frequently doing it." Now, before it can be done at all, the faculty on which it depends must be possessed ; and the stronger the faculty, the greater will be the facility with which the individual will do the thing at first, and learn to repeat it afterward. George Bidder, for example, the celebrated mental calculator, acquired the habit of solving, in an incredibly short time, extensive and intricate arithmetical problems, without the aid of notation. Before he could begin to do such a thing, the organ of Number was indispensable ; possessing it largely, he made great and rapid acquisitions of skill, and at seven years of age established the *habit* which struck us with so much surprise. Other individuals are to be found endowed with a small organ of Number, who, although forced by circumstances to practise the use of figures, never succeed in acquiring a habit of performing even the simplest arithmetical questions with facility and success. This illustration may be applied to painting, poetry, music, and mathematics. Before the habit of practising these branches of art and science can be acquired, the organs on which the talents depend must be largely possessed ; and being so, the habits result spontaneously from exercising the powers. If a boy at school acquire a habit of quarrelling and fighting, it is obvious that, as these acts are manifestations of Combativeness and Destructiveness, he will the more readily acquire the habit the larger these organs are, and the less controlled by others. If these organs be small, or if the higher organs decidedly predominate, the boy will be naturally indisposed to quarrelling, and will acquire the habit of it with great difficulty, wherever he may be placed. He may repel unjust aggressions made upon him, but he will not be the promoter of mischief, or a leader in the broils of his companions. Many boys can never acquire the habit of quarrelling, even though urged to it by circumstances.‡ ·

Exercise strengthens the *organs* and causes them to act with greater facility,§ and in this way the *real* effects of habit on the mind, which are important, may be accounted for ; but the organ must possess considerable natural power and activity, to render it susceptible of the exercise by which habit is formed. The practice of debate by advocates at the bar gives them great facility in delivering extemporaneous harangues, compared with that enjoyed by persons whose avocations never lead them to make speeches ; and this facility may be said to be acquired by the habit of speaking ; but it will always bear a proportion to the original endowment of the faculties ; and we shall find that, while habit gives to one

* *Elements*, vol. i., chap. v., p. 1, sect. 4.
† See *Trans. of the Phren. Soc.*, p. 289.
‡ See these views illustrated in the case of John Linn, *Phren. Journ.*, vol. x., p. 207.   § See p. 50.

individual great fluency and copiousness of diction, it often leaves another in much poverty of speech and embarrassment of utterance. The powers of both will be greatly superior to what they would have been without the practice of speaking; but disparity in eloquence will continue to characterize them, owing to differences in their original constitution.

The metaphysicians, as we have seen, attribute many important mental phenomena to the effects of habit, and yet they altogether neglect the influence of organization on the mind. According to our views, it is the organ which acquires strength, activity, and superior facility in performing its functions, by being properly exercised, just as the fingers of the musician acquire facility of motion by the practice of playing : " The effects of habit in giving readiness and ease are thus accounted for in a manner that is at least intelligible and supported by analogy. The metaphysicians, on the other hand, must imagine that it is the immaterial principle itself which is improved by exercise and gains strength by habit—a notion that is altogether inconceivable, and in opposition to the attributes of a purely spiritual being. Farther, Phrenology teaches that the organ of Tune is distinct from that of Language; that the organs of Size, Locality, Number, Individuality, and Comparison, on which mathematical talent depends, are different from the organ of Causality, by which general reasoning is performed ; and that it is quite possible to exercise one organ, and leave another unemployed. This doctrine explains why, by practising music, we do not acquire the habit of speaking or writing with facility ; and why, by studying mathematics, we do not acquire the habit of reasoning deeply in moral or political science. Those physiologists, however, who hold the brain to be a single organ, and every part of it to be engaged in every act of the mind, ought to show how it happens, that exercising it in one way does not improve it in all ; or, to use an illustration applied by Dr. Johnson, to genius, they should inform us why the man who can walk east is unable to walk west. If the organs by means of which he walks east be *different* from those by which he walks west, no difficulty will occur ; but if they be *the same*, some portion of ingenuity on the part of the disciples of the old school will be necessary for the satisfactory solution of the question.

TASTE. Mr. Stewart speaks of Taste as a power or faculty, and, as already mentioned, supposes it to be acquired by habit. I am not aware that any other metaphysician coincides with him in these views ; but a great deal has been written on the subject, and no satisfactory theory of it, except that of Sir G. S. Mackenzie,* exists. I shall point out the manner in which it might be treated phrenologically ; but the subject is too extensive to allow me to enter into it in detail.

In the *first* place, every act of the mind must be a manifestation of some faculty or other ; and every act must be characterized either by bad taste or good taste, or be wholly indifferent in this respect. Let us inquire into the origin of bad taste, and this will lead us to distinguish its opposite or correct taste. Bad taste, then, appears to arise from an excessive or improper manifestation of any of the faculties. Lord Byron is guilty of very bad taste in some passages of *Don Juan,* in which he exhibits the passion of love in all the grossness of an animal feeling ; this arises from an excessive manifestation of Amativeness, not purified and dignified by the moral sentiments and reflection. In the same work there is a scene in a boat, in which *Don Juan* and his companions are made to devour his tutor. To a being under the sole dominion of Destructiveness, such a representation may perhaps be gratifying ; but unless this propensity be very powerful, it will be impossible for any mind deliberately to invent and enjoy such a picture of human misery. No thoughtlessness, levity,

* *An Essay on some subjects connected with Taste.* By Sir George Stewart Mackenzie, Bart. Edin., 1817.

reak of fancy, or other folly, could produce it without a predominant Destructiveness. This great defect of taste, therefore, may be ascribed to an excessive manifestation of this faculty, unrelieved by Benevolence or other higher feelings. Moore also, in his earlier verses, was guilty of sins against taste, from excessive manifestations of the amative propensity; but this error he has corrected in his later productions.

Faults in taste, however, arise, not only from unbecoming manifestations of the lower propensities, but also from an inordinate expression of the sentiments and intellectual faculties. In *Peter Bell* and *Christabell*, and in the productions of the Lake school of poetry in general, much bad taste springs from mawkish and infantine manifestations of Benevolence, Philoprogenitiveness, and Adhesiveness. Even Ideality itself may be abused. It is undoubtedly the fountain of beauty, but, in excess, it degenerates into bombast, rant, and exaggeration; or that species of composition which a contemporary critic has appropriately designated by the epithet of "drunken sublimity." Wordsworth affords examples of errors in taste arising from an abuse of Causality; he introduces abstruse and unintelligible metaphysical disquisitions into his poetry, and mystifies it, instead of rendering it profound. Homer also sometimes offends a correct taste by overloading his descriptions with similes, under the influence of Comparison.

In like manner, the expression of any sentiment or propensity in an undue degree in conversation or conduct, is essentially characteristic of bad taste. An excess of vanity, and the tendency to engross conversation, is one form of it which occurs in society, and arises from over-active Love of Approbation and Self-Esteem. The tendency to wrangle, dispute, and contradict is another fault, springing from excessive activity of Combativeness. The disposition to flatter, and utter a profusion of agreeable things to persons whom we do not esteem, but wish to please, is also characterized by bad taste, and arises from an improper manifestation of Secretiveness and Love of Approbation.

The question naturally occurs, What is the distinction between bad taste and bad morality? - I would answer, that bad morality always implies bad taste, for it springs from an improper manifestation of some lower feeling, to the outrage of the sentiments of Justice, Benevolence, and Veneration. Bad taste, however, may occur without turpitude, and this arises from an undue activity of any of the faculties, without offence against any moral sentiment. The effeminacies of *Peter Bell*, for example, stand low enough in the scale of taste; but as the greatest tenderness for asses does not necessarily imply any breach of justice, kindness, or respect to other beings, the taste only is bad, and not the morality. In like manner, when an individual, under the influence of an excessive Self-Esteem and Love of Approbation, constitutes himself the *bore* of a party —as his offence does not amount to a serious attack upon such rights as we recognise by the sentiments of Conscientiousness, Veneration, and Benevolence, we set him down as ill-bred, but not as immoral.

Chesterfield, and some dictators in manners, deliberately recommend slight offences against candour, not only as not liable to the imputation of bad taste, but as essential to good taste. Thus, Chesterfield admits a great deal of deceitful compliance into his characteristics of a gentleman; but, with great deference to his lordship's authority, I cannot subscribe to the doctrine, that bad morality and good taste are in any degree compatible in the same action. An individual may act very improperly in many parts of his conduct, and shew considerable refinement in other instances; and this is easily understood: for the higher sentiments may coexist with strong animal propensities, and one occasion may call forth the former, and another excite only the latter, so that the conduct may

34

thus assumes different aspects at different times. But the question is, Whether the *same* action can be characterized both as immoral and as distinguished by good taste? In my opinion it cannot. It is good taste to restrain the expression of our opinions or views in society, when an opposite conduct would cause only dissensions and broils; but this is good morality also. Chesterfield, however, goes further, and allows, as perfectly compatible with good manners, an expression of sentiments which we do not entertain, if they be pleasing to those to whom we address them: and this is a breach of candour. Such a practice is an insult to the person who is the object of it; and, if he saw the real motives, he would feel it to be so. Nothing which, when examined in all its lights, and seen in its true colours, is essentially rude and unprincipled, can possibly be correct in point of taste; it has only the appearance, and not the true elements, of politeness. Purity in the motive is requisite equally to good taste and to sound morality; for the motive determines the essential quality of the action.

The sources of good taste may now be adverted to. The nervous and sanguine temperaments, by giving fineness to the substance and vivacity to the action of the brain, are highly conductive to refinement. All authors and artists, whose works are characterised by great delicacy and beauty, have fine temperaments, along with Ideality. The most exquisite mental manifestations are those which proceed from a favourable combination of the whole faculties, in which each contributes a share of its own good qualities, and is restrained by the others from running into excess or abuses. If a favourable developement of this kind be possessed the higher Ideality rises—without running into excess—and the finer the temperament, the more perfect will be the taste. At the same time, and for the same reason, there may be much good taste, of a simple kind, with moderate Ideality, if the other faculties be favourably balanced.

As Taste arises from fine quality of brain and a favourable combination of organs, the explanation is simple, how it may be possessed without genius. Genius springs from great vigour and activity, depending on large size, and a high temperament: these are greater endowments than equability, and an individual may be deficient in them, and yet be so favourably constituted, with respect *to the balance of his powers*, as to feel acutely the excellencies or the faults of genius manifested by others. Hence many persons are really excellent critics, who could not themselves produce original works of value; hence also, many original authors, of great reputation, display very questionable taste.

In applying these principles to actual cases, I find them borne out by numerous facts. Dr. Chalmers occasionally sins against taste, and in his head Ideality and Comparison are out of due proportion to Causality and some other organs. In Lord Jeffrey's bust, on the contrary, there is a very beautiful and regular developement of Eventuality, Comparison, and Causality, with a fair balance between the propensities and sentiments; his temperament is nervous-bilious; and his taste is generally admirable.

As good taste is the result of the harmonious action of the faculties, we are able to perceive why taste is susceptible of great improvement by cultivation. An author will frequently reason as profoundly, or soar as loftily, in his first essay, as after practice in writing for twenty years; but he rarely manifests the same tact at the outset of his career as he attains by subsequent study and the admonitions of a discriminative criticism. Reasoning depends on Causality and Comparison, and lofty flights of imagination on Ideality; and if the organs of these faculties be large, they will execute their functions intuitively, and carry the author forward, from the first, on a bold and powerful wing: but as taste depends on the balancing and adjusting, the suppressing and elevating, the ordering and arranging of our thoughts and emotions, so as to produce a general harnony of the whole—it is only practice, reflection, and comparison with higher standards that will enable us successfully to approximate to excellence; and even these aids will suffice only when the organs are by nature equally combined; for if the balance preponderate greatly in any particular direction, no effort will produce exquisite adjustment.

Much has been written about a *standard* of taste, and, in considering his question, a distinction should be made. If, by fixing a standard, we mean determining particular objects, or qualities of objects, which all men shall regard as beautiful, the attempt must necessarily be vain. A person well endowed with Form, Size, and Ideality, may experience the most delightful emotions of beauty from contemplating a Grecian temple, in which another individual, in whom these organs are very deficient, may perceive nothing but stone and mortar. One individual may discover, in an arrangement of colours, beauty which is quite imperceptible to a person deficient in the organ of Colouring. Or one may be delighted with music, in which another, through imperfection in the organ of Tune, may perceive no melody. Thus no object, and no qualities of objects, can be fixed upon, which *all mankind*, whatever be their original constitution, will unanimously acknowledge to be beautiful; and in this view no standard of taste exists.

But *degrees of beauty* may be estimated, in which sense a scale at least, if not a standard, of taste may be framed. The more favourable the original constitution of an individual is, and the greater the cultivation bestowed on his powers, the higher authority he becomes in questions of taste. The existence of a sentiment of Justice has been denied, because individuals are found in whom it is so weak that they seem scarcely to experience the influence of it in their conduct; but Phrenology, by pointing out their defect, shows that these persons form exceptions to a general rule, and no one thinks of appealing to them as authorities to determine whether any particular action be just or unjust. In like manner, men deficient in the faculties which give the perception of beauty, are not authorities in taste; but that individual is the highest judge in whom the most favourable developement of the organs of propensity, sentiment, and intellect is combined with a fine temperament and large Ideality; and who, besides, has cultivated his faculties with the greatest assiduity. His determinations in regard to degrees of beauty in objects will form the best standards of taste which our imperfect nature is capable of attaining.

EFFECTS OF SIZE IN THE ORGANS ON THE MANIFESTATIONS OF THE FACULTIES.

Having now unfolded the primitive faculties of the mind, (so far as discovered,) with their organs and modes of action, I proceed to treat of their effects when acting in combination. In order to understand this subject, it is necessary, in the first place, to attend particularly to the effects of size in the organs on the manifestations of the faculties.

The reader is referred to the distinction between *power* and *activity* in the mind, as stated on page 98 of the present work. *Cæteris paribus*, size in the organs is the measure of power in the faculties.

As great size in the organs is an indispensable requisite to the manifestation of mental vigour, no instance ought to occur of an individual who, with a small brain, has manifested, clearly and unequivocally, great force of character, animal, moral, and intellectual, such as belonged to Bruce, Bonaparte, Cromwell, or Fox; and such, accordingly, phrenologists affirm to be the fact. The Phrenological Society possesses casts of the skulls of Bruce, La Fontaine, Rammohun Roy, and other men distintinguished by great power of mind, and they are all large. The busts and portraits of Lord Bacon, Shakspeare, and Bonaparte indicate large heads; and among living characters no individual has occurred to my observation who leaves a vivid impression of his own greatness upon the public mind, and who yet presents to their eyes only a small brain.

The European head is distinguished from the Asiatic and native American, not more by difference of form than of size; the European is much the larger, and the superior energy of this variety of mankind is known. The heads of men are larger than those of women, and the latter obey; or, to bring the point to the clearest demonstration, we need only to compare the head of a child with that of a full-grown man, or of an idiot with that of Rammohun Roy, as represented on page 46. If, then, size is so clearly a concomitant of power in extreme cases, we are not to presume that it ceases to exert an influence where the differences are so minute that the eye is scarcely able to detect them. The rule, *Extremis probatis, media præsumuntur*, is completely applicable here.

The doctrine, that power is a characteristic of mind, distinguishable at once from mere intellectual acumen and also from activity, is one of great practical importance; and it explains a variety of phenomena of which we previously possessed no theory. In society we meet with persons whose whole manner is little, whom we intuitively feel to be unfit for any great enterprise or arduous duty, and who are, nevertheless, distinguished for amiable feelings and good sense. This springs from a small brain favourably proportioned in its parts. Other individuals, again, with far less polish, inferior information, and fewer amiable qualities, impress us with a sentiment of their power, force, energy, or greatness; we feel that they have weight, and that, if acting against us, they would prove formidable opponents. This arises from great size. Bonaparte, who had an admirable tact in judging of human nature, distinguished between mere cleverness and force of character, and almost always prefers the latter. In his Memoirs he speaks of some of his generals as possessing talents, intellect, and book-learning, but as still being nobody—as wanting that weight and comprehensiveness which fit a man for great enterprises: while he adverts to others as possessing limited intellect and little judgment, but prodigious force of character; and considers them as admirably adapted by this qualification to lead soldiers through peril and difficulty, provided they be directed by minds superior to their own. Murat was such a man; and Bonaparte appears, on the whole, to have liked such officers; for they did not trouble him with thinking for themselves, while they possessed energy adequate to the execution of his most gigantic designs. The leader of a popular party, who has risen to that rank by election, or assumed it with acquiescence, will be found to have a large brain. The leaders of an army or a fleet also require a similar endowment, for otherwise they would possess artificial authority without natural weight, and would never inspire confidence in their followers. Bonaparte had a large head; and officers and soldiers, citizens and statesmen, bowed before his mental greatness, however much they might detest the use he made of his power. In him all the organs, animal, moral, and intellectual, (Conscientiousness, and perhaps Firmness, excepted,) seem to have been large; great activity was added; and hence arose commanding energy, combined with profound and comprehensive intellectual capacity.

The society possesses casts of the heads of Captains Franklin and Parry; and both are decidedly large, with an excellent proportion in the different orders of organs. These commanders displayed great force of character in their respective expeditions in quest of a north-west passage. No tendency to mutiny or insubordination occurred even in the most trying circumstances; and this would be the case, because the men under their command would instinctively feel natural superiority coinciding with artificial rank.

The men who are able to attend to their private duties, and at the same time carry a load of public business on their minds, without feeling encumbered, owe this quality to great size in the brain, with an active temperament and large knowing organs. Those who, having small brains, find their whole powers absorbed and exhausted by their particular occupations, wonder at such men, and cannot comprehend either their motives or the means by which they accomplish so much. It is power which distinguishes them; so that duties which to others would prove oppressive, press lightly on them, or afford them only amusement. Mr. Joseph Hume, M. P., is a striking illustration of this doctrine. He possesses moderate organs of Causality, little Wit, less Ideality, and no great endowment of Language; yet even his opponents allow him to

DR. SPURZHEIM.

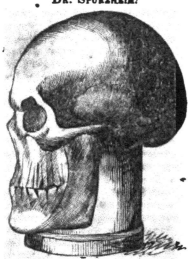

manifest great force of character, with a power of application and perseverance which, to ordinary minds, is incomprehensible. If we look at the large brain indicated in his cast, and attend to the combination of organs which it displays, we shall perceive the source of his weight. Dr. Spurzheim also showed great force of character, and his brain was large. This quality in him was the source of the intense and long enduring interest which he created and supported in the minds of those who came in contact with him. He was calm, mild, and unobtrusive, yet there was a degree of depth and power about him, which made lasting impressions on those who listened to his public discourses, or conversed with him in private.

In examining the heads of criminals in jail, I have found the most daring, desperate, and energetic to possess large brains. When great size and an unfavourable combination occur together, the officers of justice are reduced to despair in attempting to correct the offender. They feel a strength of character which they cannot subdue, and an evil bent which they cannot direct;—the result generally is a report from the police that the individual is incorrigible; his first capital offence is prosecuted to extremity, and he is hanged for the sake of protecting society from farther mischief. In professional pursuits also, the men who are indisputably paramount to their fellows, not merely in cleverness, but in depth and force of character, have large heads; and this holds, not only in the learned professions, but in mercantile avocations. I have observed that individuals who, born in indigence, have arisen to wealth by conducting great and extensive establishments, have uniformly brains above an average size; and that mercantile travellers who succeed in procuring orders, and pushing a trade amid a keen and arduous competition, are distinguished by the same quality. Such men make an impression, and act with a confidence of power which gives effect to all they say or do. In a school, if the children care nothing for the master, and treat him with disrespect, and if he fail, after using every severity, to maintain discipline and subordination, he will be found to have a small brain. In the domestic circle, if the mistress of a family (while in good health) is easily overcome, annoyed and oppressed with the cares and duties of her household, the origin of the evil will be found in too small a head.

In the church the effects of size are equally conspicuous. A preacher with a large brain is felt by his flock to possess weight, and they submit willingly to be led and taught by him, while they treat with indifference the feebleness that accompanies a little head. If, as occasionally happens, a preacher possess an excellent combination, that is, the organs of the sentiments and intellect large in proportion to those of the animal propensities, he may be acute, amiable, sensible, and interesting ; but if the general size of the brain be under an average, he will not be impressive and commanding.

The principle, that size gives power of manifestation, forms the key to the following criticism on Dr. Chalmers : " His manner, so far from being graceful," says a contemporary writer, " is very nearly uncouth ; his tones are neither musical nor under strict subordination ; in the selection of words and management of figures his taste, so far from being pure, is sometimes very much the reverse ; his pronunciation, though vigorous and distinct, is beset with provincialisms, which time and a city audience have done very little to correct ; and as to gesture, wherever we have heard him, he appeared to be totally unconscious that he had got such a thing as hands and arms to manage. In what, then, it may be asked, consists the secret of the doctor's eloquence ? Simply, as we take it, in this—that, *while his arguments* and *illustrations* are, *for the most part, striking and original*, he possesses *prodigious enthusiasm* and *energy* in enforcing them ; that the defects of his rhetoric are completely lost in the force of his ratiocination ; that, while he has *mathematics* or *logic enough to make his reasoning acute, grasping, and irresistible*, he has *poetry* enough to prevent it *from being dull* ; thus evincing the very highest species of intellect—the union of a *sound and comprehensive judgment*, with a *fertile and brilliant imagination*. We have said he possesses *energy*, and this we take to be the great and redeeming quality of his manner, compared to which the tiny graces sink into insignificance. Whether we are facile or fastidious, whether we like or dislike the preacher's doctrine, one thing is certain, *he forces us to attend to him. A man might easily get his pocket picked while listening to Dr. Chalmers, but we defy him to fall asleep."* The head of Dr. Chalmers indicates a large brain.

In authorship the same law holds good. Critics have been puzzled to account for the high rank which Dr. Samuel Johnson holds in English literature, and to discover the mental qualities on which his eminence is founded. He has made no discoveries in morals or in science to captivate the mind. His style is stately and sonorous, and his arrangement in general good ; but equal or superior graces may be found in Goldsmith, Thomson, and other authors, whom nobody would compare with him in genius. His great characteristic is force and weight ; and these are the concomitants of great size of brain. Milton's writings are highly distinguished by vigour, as are also those of Locke. Addison, on the other hand, is a specimen of genius produced by a felicitous combination of sentiment and intellect, without preponderating energy from great size. Power is the leading charm of Swift's writings : he is not graceful, and is far from elegant ; his reasoning is frequently superficial, and his conclusions questionable. But he is rarely feeble. Strength, energy, and determination mark every page. His skull indicates a large brain, particularly in the region of the propensities.

To produce its full effects, large size must be accompanied with sound health and an active temperament, as explained in p. 45 ; but these, while necessary to give it effect, will never compensate for its absence.

ACTIVITY in the organs, on the other hand, gives liveliness, quickness, or rapidity ; Dr. Spurzheim thinks that long fibres contribute to activity. The sanguine and nervous temperaments, described on pages 48 and 97, afford external indications of constitutional activity. Moderate size of brain, with a favourable combination and much activity, constitute what is commonly understood by a *clever* man in ordinary life ; such an individual will form ideas rapidly, do a great deal of work, show tact and discrimination, and prove himself really a valuable and useful member of society ; but he must not be loaded with too many duties, or opposed by obstacles, nor must the field in which he is called on to labour be too extensive.

Great errors are often committed in society through ignorance of this fact. An individual possessing a small brain, but a fine temperament, and favourable combination, perhaps distinguishes himself in a limited and subordinate sphere, or he makes one great and successful effort, in which his powers are tasked to the utmost extent of their limits ;—the notion is then adopted that he is very clever, fit for higher duties, and capable of exhibiting habitually the force of mind thus displayed on a single occasion. He is, in consequence, promoted to a more arduous station. He continues to execute small matters so well, that it is difficult to point out individual instances of failure in his more extensive duties ; yet a general impression of his incapacity arises, want of success and discontent increase, and at last, after producing great suffering to himself and annoyance to his employers, he is dismissed. The small brain is the origin of the incapacity ; and ignorance of its effects the cause of his being misplaced.

Mankind, in extreme cases, recognise energy of feebleness of mental character, and modify their conduct accordingly. Those in whom moral and religious principles do not constitute the habitual rule of conduct, treat individuals in the most different manner, according to the impression which they receive from their manner, and the estimate which they form from it of their strength or weakness of mind. There are men who carry in their very look the intimation of greatness—whose manner at once proclaims, " *Nemo me impune lacesset.*" The world reads this notice, and holds it safest to allow them to follow their own course without obstruction, while they avoid giving offence. Contrasted with them are the feeble and vacillating ; men unstable as water, unsteady as the wind. The wicked seize upon them, and make them their prey. The treatment received by different persons from society is thus widely different ; and it may be truly said, that a large portion of mankind cannot easily conceive the miseries inflicted on the weak by the powerful and unprincipled taking advantage of their deficiencies.

When a favourable combination, a fine temperament, and large size are conjoined in an individual, they constitute the perfection of genius. This I conceive to have been the case in Homer and in Shakspeare. Vivacious buoyancy, ease, and fertility, arising from the first and second causes, joined with depth, strength, comprehensiveness, and masculine energy, the result of the third, place these authors above all others whom the world has ever seen. And when we consider that these rare and splendid gifts must again be united in one individual, before their equal can appear, we shall have no difficulty in perceiving why so few Homers and Shakspeares are given by nature to the world.

In these observations I have treated of the effects of size in the brain in general on the general manifestations of the mind, to bring the doctrine clearly and forcibly before the reader ; but I beg of him not to fall into the error of taking *general* size as an indication of *particular* power, for then difficulties without end will be encountered.   For example, it has often been objected, that a particular individual wears a large hat, indicating a large brain, and that yet he has no great scope of *intellect*, and no ability, in the general sense of the term.   The answer is, that we must look for the *power* in the *direction of size*, as explained on p. 95. If the large hat is requisite on account of a great developement of the animal organs, we must expect the individual to be only a powerful *animal*; and he may be this, and at the same time a weak *man*.   If the size predominate in the region of the sentiments, we may. then look for. greatness in moral worth; but it is only when great size, combined with an active temperament, pervades the organs of the whole three classes of faculties, propensities, sentiments, and intellect, that Phrenology authorizes us to expect a general character vigorous, comprehensive, and profound.   The hat does not indicate the size either of the moral organs or of those of the intellect.

The circumstances which *modify the effects of size* have already been stated, (pp. 48 and 97,) when treating of the principles of the science.

COMBINATIONS IN SIZE, OR EFFECTS OF THE ORGANS WHEN COMBINED IN DIFFERENT RELATIVE PROPORTIONS.

THE primitive functions of each organ were *discovered* by observing cases in which it decidedly predominated over, or fell short of, other organs in point of size; and by similar observations each must still be verified. After the discovery is established, its practical application deserves attention.   Every individual above idiocy possesses all the organs; but they are combined differently in degrees of relative size in different persons, and the manifestations of each are modified in some degree by the influence of those with which it is combined.   The effect of combination, however, is not to change the proper functions of the different organs, but only to modify the *manner* in which they are manifested; or the acts in which they seek gratification.   If, for example, the organ of Tune be equally large in two individuals—but if, in one of them, the organs of the animal propensities predominate, he may manifest it in producing bacchanalian songs; while, if the organs of the moral sentiments predominate in the other, he may employ it in singing sacred melodies. In both instances Tune leads to the production of music, the only effect of the combination being to alter the direction.   This illustration is applicable to all the faculties; and shows that, although the functions of some parts of the brain are still unascertained, the discovery of them cannot alter the functions of those already known.

Dr. Gall,* in considering the combinations of the organs, divides men into six classes.

In men composing his *first* class the organs of the highest qualities and faculties are completely developed, while those of the faculties common to man with the lower animals possess only a feeble degree of developement and activity.   The dispositions and conduct of persons of this class are in accordance with reason, justice, and morality.

In the *second* class the combination is precisely reversed, and the individuals belonging to it are the slaves of sensuality and error.

In the *third* class the animal organs, and also those peculiar to man, have acquired a considerable degree of developement and activity.   Men belonging to this class may be great in virtue or vice, and often manifest the most opposite qualities.   They experience the internal struggle of the

* *Sur les Fonctions du Cerveau*, tome i., p. 319.   8vo.

higher and lower elements of our nature. Socrates, St. Paul, and St. Augustin belonged to it.

In the *fourth* class one, or a few, of the organs are highly developed, while the others are only moderately so, or even below mediocrity. This class includes men of great, but partial, genius, or men distinguished for great strength of character or for powerful dispositions of a determinate description; such as great musicians, great mechanicians, or brave warriors, who out of these lines show no superiority.

In the *fifth* class one, or several, of the organs are very little developed, and remain inactive, while the others are more favourably developed and energetic. This class includes men of general ability, who have some particular and limited deficiency. Lessing and Tischbein detested music, and Newton and Kant had no passion for women.

In the *sixth* class the animal organs and those proper to man are nearly equally moderate. In this class is comprehended the great mass of ordinary men. These six divisions, says Dr. Gall, are subject to thousands of modifications.

Dr. Vimont* observes that these divisions are insufficient to give a just and complete idea of the combinations of all the faculties, but he reproves me for having omitted to notice them in the former editions of this work. My apology is, that Dr. Gall's remarks are contained in his first volume, amid the discussion of preliminary moral, and metaphysical objections, and were overlooked by me until referred to by Dr. Vimont. Dr. Vimont makes several judicious observations on these classes, and adds to them two more, viz., Men in whom the perceptive organs predominate over those of reflection; and men who are placed a little above idiots, who have feeble perceptive powers and a nullity of reflection. This class may manifest some talent, such as that of construction, or of music; or they may be distinguished by cunning, stubbornness, or vanity; and never improve. Dr. Vimont makes also some valuable observations on the combinations of the organs in the different species of the lower animals, to which I can here only refer.

The limits of the present work prevent me from doing more than stating three rules for estimating the effects of differences in relative size occurring in the organs of the same brain.

RULE FIRST.—Every faculty desires gratification with a degree of energy proportionate to the size of the organ;† and those faculties will be habitually indulged, the organs of which are largest in the individual.‡

Examples.—If the animal organs in general be large, and the organs of the moral sentiments and intellect in general be small, the individual will be naturally prone to animal indulgence in the highest degree, and disposed to see gratification in the directest way, and in the lowest pursuits.

If, on the other hand, the organs of the moral sentiments and intellect greatly predominate, the individual will be naturally prone to moral and intellectual pursuits; such persons are "a law unto themselves."

* *Traité de Phrénologie,* tome. ii., p. 456.

† The condition, *cæteris paribus,* is always understood, and therefore needs not to be repeated in treating of the effects of size.

‡ Having been solicited to state, in methodical order, the effects of the combinations as far as observed, I tried to do so in the MS. of the present work; but found the result to be a tedious enumeration of propositions, adapted to Individuality alone, difficult to be remembered, and withal extremely incomplete. I have, therefore, preferred stating principles chiefly, accompanied by illustrations, to render them intelligible and show their application. This method was adopted in the *Elements* for the sake of brevity, and, on mature examination, it appears to be preferable in itself. The reader in whom the reflecting organs are amply developed, will not only easily comprehend the rules here laid down, but be able greatly to enlarge the sphere of their application.

In illustration of this rule, the head of Pope Alexander VI., p. 18! who was a monster of wickedness in human form, may be contrasted with that of Melancthon the reformer, p. 86; or the skull of a New Hollander may be compared with that of Dr. Spurzheim, represented on pages 51 and 52.

In farther illustration, the heads of Vitellius, and Hare the murderer, represented on pages 89 and 85, may be contrasted with those of Tasso, p. 232, Chaucer and Locke, p. 244, and Michael Angelo, p. 277. In the one class of heads the basilar and posterior regions of the brain, dedicated to the animal propensities, greatly preponderate over the anterior and coronal regions, which manifest the intellect and moral sentiments;* in the other the basilar region is large, but the intellectual and moral decidedly preponderate.

Now, under the rule before stated, the first class will be naturally prone to low and degrading pursuits, having for their object the gratification of Amativeness, Destructiveness, Acquisitiveness, and other inferior feelings; they will possess very few aspirations after the noble and beneficent virtues which dignify human nature; they will be blind to the obligations of justice, piety, and mercy, and totally incapable of appreciating the advantages of science. The second class will form a direct contrast to them. They will naturally feel the superiority of moral and intellectual pursuits, ardently desire to advance in the career of improvement, and instinctively love every virtue and attainment that is calculated to increase the true dignity and happiness of man. It is common for individuals to assume themselves as standards for judging of mankind in general'; yet no criterion can be more fallacious: the consciousness of men belonging to the inferior class would represent the race as base, grovelling, and selfish—that of the higher as elevated, benignant, and intellectual.

RULE SECOND.—As there are three kinds of faculties, propensitive, moral, and intellectual, which are not homogeneous, it may happen that several large organs of propensities are combined in the same individual with several moral and intellectual organs highly developed. The rule, then, will be, that the lower propensities will take their *direction* from the higher powers; and such a course of action will be habitually followed as will be calculated to gratify the whole faculties whose organs are large.

In this combination the strong propensities may escape, at intervals, from the control of the sentiments, and produce abuses; but as nature has rendered the moral and intellectual faculties the directing powers, the *habitual* conduct will be such as will be consistent with their dictates, and at the same time gratifying to the propensities.

Examples.—If the organs of 'Acquisitiveness and Conscientiousness were both large, stealing might gratify Acquisitiveness, but it would offend Conscientiousness. According to the rule, the individual would endeavour to gratify both, by acquiring property by lawful industry. If Combativeness and Destructiveness were large, and Benevolence and Conscientiousness also amply developed, wanton outrage and indiscriminate attack might gratify the first two faculties, but they would outrage the last two: hence the individual would seek for situations calculated to gratify all four: and these may be found in the ranks of an army imbodied for the defence of his country, or in moral and intellectual warfare against the patrons of corruption and abuse in church and state. Luther,

---

* The size of the coronal region is best judged of by the height and breadth of the brain above Cautiousness and Causality, the situation of which organs is indicated in some of the figures by asterisks. Wherever that region is shallow or narrow, the moral feelings will be comparatively feeble. See p. 86

Knox, and many other benefactors of mankind, were probably actuated by such a combination of faculties; Washington nobly displayed it.

If the cerebellum be very large, and Philoprogenitiveness, Adhesiveness, and Conscientiousness deficient, the individual will be prone to seek the directest gratifications of the animal appetite; if the latter organs be also large, he will perceive that wedlock affords the best means of satisfying the whole group.

If Benevolence, Self-Esteem, and Acquisitiveness be all large, giving charity may gratify the first; but, unless the individual be very rich, the act of parting with property may be disagreeable to the last two faculties, he will therefore prefer to gratify Benevolence by personal kindness; he will sacrifice time, trouble, influence, and advice, to the welfare of others, but not property. If Benevolence were *small*, with the same combination, he would not give either money or personal advice.

If Love of Approbation large, be combined with large Ideality and moderate reflecting organs, the individual will be ambitious to excel in the splendour of his equipage, style of living, dress, and rank. If to the same combination be added a powerful intellect and large Conscientiousness, moral and intellectual excellence will be preferred as the means of obtaining the respect of the world.

An individual in whom Benevolence and Love of Approbation are very large, and Conscientiousness deficient, will be exceedingly kind and attentive to those persons who praise him loudly and extol his benevolence; but he will overlook humble, retiring, and unostentatious merit; he will speak much of his own good deeds. If Conscientiousness and Benevolence predominate, the amiable and unpretending will be the first objects of his regard, and the good done will never be proclaimed by himself.

If Self-Esteem large, be combined with deficient Love of Approbation and Conscientiousness, the individual will be prone to gratify his selfish feelings, with little regard to the good opinion or the just claims of other men. If Self-Esteem large, be combined with large Love of Approbation and Conscientiousness, the former will produce only that degree of self-respect which is essential to dignity of character, and that degree of independence of sentiment without which even virtue cannot be maintained.

If Cautiousness large, be combined with deficient Combativeness, the individual will be extremely timid. If Combativeness be large and Cautiousness small, reckless intrepidity will be the result. If Combativeness be equally large with Cautiousness, the individual will display courage regulated by prudence. If Cautiousness, Conscientiousness, Self-Esteem, Secretiveness, and Love of Approbation be all large, and Combativeness moderate, bashfulness or *mauvaise honte* will be the consequence. This feeling is the result of the fear of not acquitting one's-self to advantage, and of thereby compromising one's personal dignity.

If Veneration and Hope be large, and Conscientiousness and Benevolence small, the individual will be naturally fond of religious worship, but averse to the practice of charity and justice. If the proportions be reversed, the result will be a constitutional disposition to charity and justice, with no great tendency to the exercise of devotion. If all the four organs be large, the individual will be naturally inclined to engage in the worship of God, and to discharge his duties to men. If Veneration large, be combined with large Acquisitiveness and Love of Approbation, the former sentiment may be directed to superiors in rank and power, as the means of gratifying the desires for wealth and influence depending on the latter faculties. If Veneration be small, combined with Self-Esteem and and Firmness large, the individual will not naturally look up with deference to superiors in rank.

The intellectual faculties will naturally tend to such employments as are calculated to gratify the predominant propensities and sentiments. If the organs which constitute a genius for painting be combined with large Acquisitiveness, the individual may paint to become rich ; if combined with Acquisitiveness small and Love of Approbation large, he will probably labour for fame, and starve while attaining it.

Talents for different intellectual pursuits depend upon the combinations of the knowing and reflecting organs in certain proportions.   Constructiveness, Form, Size, Colouring, Individuality, Ideality, Imitation, and Secretiveness large, with Locality small, will constitute a portrait, but not a landscape, painter.   Diminish Form and Imitation, and increase Locality, and the result will be a talent for landscape, but not for portrait painting.   Constructiveness and Weight, combined with Tune large, may produce a talent for *musical* instrument making : without a large Tune the other faculties could not successfully take this direction.   Constructiveness, combined with Size and Number large, may lead to *mathematical* instrument making.   Causality, combined with large Ideality and Imitation, will seek to discover the philosophy of the fine arts ; the same organs combined with large Benevolence, Conscientiousness, and Concentrativeness, will delight in moral and political investigations.   If to Individuality, Eventuality, Comparison, and Causality, all large, an equally well-developed organ of Language be added, the result will be a talent for authorship or public debate ; if Language be small, the other faculties will be more prone to seek gratification in the business of life, or in abstract philosophy.

One great difficulty frequently experienced is, to comprehend the effect of the reflecting powers, added, in a high degree of endowment, to the knowing faculties, when the latter are exercised in particular branches of art, for which they appear to be of themselves altogether sufficient.   It is stated, for example, that Constructiveness, Secretiveness, Form, Size, Ideality, Individuality, Colouring, and Imitation constitute a genius for painting ; and it may reasonably be inquired, What effect will the reflecting organs, large or small, produce on this combination ?   This question is easily answered.   When the reflecting organs are small, *form, colour beauty*, constitute the *leading* objects of the painter's productions.   There is no story, no event, no comprehensiveness of intellect displayed in his works.   These must be examined in detail, and, as single objects, unconnected with others by any of the relations perceived by the higher powers. Add the reflecting organs, however, and then outline, form, colouring, perspective, will all sink into the rank of *means*, which the intellect employs to accomplish a higher object ; such as the expression of some great action or event—some story which speaks to the judgment and interests the feelings—historical painting.

In the portraits of Raphael the organs here enumerated as essential to a painter appear to be large, and those of Causality, Comparison, and Wit are likewise far above an ordinary size.   Now, a critic on the productions of Raphael[*] says, " In *composition* Raffaello stands pre-eminent. His invention is the refined emanation of a dramatic mind, and whatever can most interest the feelings or satisfy the judgment, he selected from nature, and made his own.   The point of time, in his historical subjects, is invariably well chosen ; and subordinate incidents, while they create a secondary interest, *essentially contribute to the principal event*.   Contrast or combination of lines makes no part of his works as an artificial principle of composition ; the *nature and character of the event create the forms best calculated to express them*.   The individual expression of particular figures corresponds with their character and employment ; and, whether calm or agitated, they are at all times equally remote from affectation or insipidity.

[*] *Life of Raphael*, London, 1816, anonymous.

The *general interest* of his subject is *kept up throughout the whole composition ; the present action implies the past and anticipates the future.* If, in sublimity of thought, Raffaello has been surpassed by his great contemporary, Michael Angelo—if, in purity of outline and form, by the antique—and in colouring and chiaro-oscura by the Lombard and Venetian schools ; yet in *historical compositions* he has no rival ; and for *invention, expression,* and *the power of telling a story,* he has never been approached "

M. Fuseli, speaking of the qualities of Raphael's style as a painter, says, that " perfect human beauty he has not represented. No face of Raphael's is perfectly beautiful ; no figure of his, in the abstract, possesses the proportions that could raise it to a standard of imitation. *Form to him was only a vehicle of character or pathos ;* and to these he adapted it in a mode, and with a truth, which leaves all attempts at emendation hopeless. His composition always hastens *to the most necessary point as its centre ;* and *from* that disseminates, *to* that leads back, its rays, all secondary ones. Group, form, and contrast are subordinate to the event ; and common-place is ever excluded. His expression is unmixed and pure, in strict unison with, and decided by, character, whether calm, animated, agitated, convulsed, or absorbed by the inspiring passion : it *never contradicts its cause,* and is equally remote from tameness and grimace. The moment of his choice never suffers the action to stagnate or to expire. It is *the moment of transition,* the *crisis big with the past and pregnant with the future.* His invention connects the utmost stretch of possibility with the most plausible degree of probability, in a manner that equally surprises our fancy, persuades our judgment, and affects our hearts."

In all this criticism we have the most exact description of the manifestations of Comparison and Causality, which give scope, depth, and force of intellectual conception, the power of combining means to attain an end, and the natural tendency to keep the means in their appropriate place, as subordinate to the main design.

Raphael's genius, accordingly, can be fully appreciated only after having exercised the higher intellectual faculties on his works. Sir Joshua Reynolds acknowledges that it was only after repeated visits and *deep reflection* that he discovered their merits, his first impression having been that of mortification and disappointment, from not seeing *at once* all their greatness. The excellence of Raphael's style, says he, is not on the surface, " *but lies deep,* and at the first view is seen but mistily. It is the florid style which strikes at once, and captivates the eye for a time, without ever satisfying the judgment." If, on the other hand, the knowing and constructive organs alone had predominated in Raphael, all these accessaries would have become principles ; and the critic who possessed reflective intellect, would have felt in his paintings a decided deficiency of design, story, interest, and object. Hence high reflecting organs are indispensable to historical painting : Haydon, who has manifested great power of conception in this line, possesses them in an eminent degree. The late Sir H. Raeburn, whose style of portrait-painting, in point of dignity and force, approaches the historical, possessed also a full developement of the upper part of the forehead, as well as large pictorial organs. In sculpture the same rule holds. The artist who has Form, Size, Constructiveness, and Ideality large, without high reflecting organs, may chisel a vase or a wreath of flowers ; but he will never reach grandeur of conception, nor confer dignity and power upon his productions.

It follows from these principles, that a sculptor or painter will represent one class of objects with greater truth and fidelity than another, according to the particular organs which predominate in his head. Thus, to model the exquisite grace, elegance, and symmetry of the female form, the constructive organs, Ideality, and the moral sentiments, with a fine tempera-

ment, may suffice, without much depth and power of reflection. To
represent, on the other hand, whether on canvass or in marble, men of
superior nature, profound in thought, and elevated and intense in emotion.
the artist himself must possess great organs of sentiment and reflection,
in addition to the organs of art before described, otherwise he will never
be able adequately to conceive or to express these modes of mind, when
they occur in his subjects.   This fortunate combination occurs in conjunction with a fine temperament in Lawrence Macdonald, and hence the admirable qualities for which his sculpture is already so highly distinguished.

The same rules hold in architecture and music. An architect possessing
only the knowing organs large, may produce the plan of a common house,
or of any other simple object, with success ; but he ought never to attempt
a work in which profound thought and extensive combinations are indispensable to success. From not attending to this fact, many abortions in
architectural designs occur in this country. An artist, with a constructive
and knowing head, may produce a plan which will look beautiful on paper,
and which, as a mere drawing, is beautiful ; but if the reflecting organs
be deficient, he will be incapable of considering the fabric designed in its
relations to surrounding objects, and of divining how it will affect the
mind, when presented in contrast with them :—hence, when executed, it
may turn out a deformity. Add, however, the reflecting organs, and the
effects of collateral objects will be anticipated and provided for. An
architect, in whom the reflecting organs are large and the knowing organs
deficient, will fail in the practical arrangement of details.

The musician, in like manner, who is able to express thought, feeling,
and emotion with exquisite effect, with whom sound is subordinate to
sense, design, and expression, will be found to possess the higher powers
in addition to the merely musical faculties.

In oratory, too, a person with Individuality, Eventuality, Comparison,
Ideality, and Language, may be erudite, fluent, brilliant, and, if propensity
and sentiment be added, vehement, pathetic, or sublime ; but, to give
great comprehensiveness, deep sagacity, and a talent for profound elucidation of principle, Causality must be joined to the combination.

Taste in every branch of the fine arts is distinguishable from power and
comprehensiveness, and depends, as already explained,* on a *harmonious
combination* and due cultivation of the organs in general.   In Raphael
these requisites seem to have occurred ; and it is because nature rarely
unites the particular organs which constitute a painter—high reflecting
organs, large general size, harmonious proportion, and natural activity—
all in one individual, that so few Raphaels appear.

In no instance is it a matter of indifference to the talents and dispositions of the individual, whether any particular organ be large or small. If
it be large, although its *abuses* may be prevented by restraint imposed by
the other faculties, still its presence. will operate on the mind. If, for
instance, large Combativeness and Destructiveness be combined with a
large developement of the moral and intellectual organs, the whole life
may be passed without the occurrence of any outrage ; and it may be asked,
What effect, in this case, do the former organs produce ?   We shall find
the answer by supposing all the other organs to remain large, while those
are diminished in size, and tracing the effect of the change. The result
would be an undue preponderance of moral and intellectual qualities,
degenerating into effeminacy. Large Combativeness and Destructiveness
add the elements of repulsion and aggression to such an extent as to permit
the manifestation of manly enterprise and courage. Hence, in the case
supposed, these organs would be duly performing their functions and adding

* Page 396.

force to the character in the-struggles of active life, when the superficial observer would imagine them to be entirely useless.

In like manner, if an organ.be greatly deficient, its small size cannot be compensated by that of the other organs, however large. Suppose, for example, that, in an individual, Benevolence, Veneration, Love of Approbation, and Intellect are all large, and Conscientiousness very deficient, it may be thought that the absence of Conscientiousness will be of small importance, as its influence will be compensated by that of the other faculties here named. This, however, will not be the case. The sentiment of *duty* originates from Conscientiousness, and the individual supposed would be benevolent, when Benevolence predominated; religious, when Veneration was paramountly active; obliging, when Love of Approbation glowed with fervour; but if all or any of these were, on any occasion, counteracted by the solicitations of the inferior propensit es, he would not, if the organ of Conscientiousness were small, feel the *obligation of duty* enforcing the dictates of these other sentiments, and increasing their restraining power: he would be deficient in the sentiments of justice, duty, and incumbency: he would obey the impulses of the higher faculties *when inclined*; but if not inclined, he would not experience so strong a sense of demerit in neglecting their solicitation, as if the organ of Conscientiousness were large. Farther, the sentiments which we have supposed him to possess would themselves, if not directed by Conscientiousness, be continually prone to run into abuse. Benevolence to one would tend to trench on justice due to another; devotion might occasionally be substituted for charity, or charity for devotion.

If we take the opposite case, and suppose that an individual possesses great Intellect and Conscientiousness, with deficient Benevolence, Veneration, and Love of Approbation; then, if the propensities were strong, his conduct might be the reverse of amiable, notwithstanding his large Conscientiousness. With this combination he would be actuated by vigorous selfish feelings, which probably might overpower the single sentiment of duty, unaided by Benevolence, Veneration, and Love of Approbation; and he might act wrong in opposition to the clear dictates of his own Conscientiousness. *Video meliora proboque, deteriora sequor* would be his motto. If his propensities, on the other hand, were moderate, he would be strictly just; he would give every one his due, but he would probably not be actively benevolent and pious. The faculty of Benevolence inspires with the feeling of charity; and Conscientiousness enforces its dictates; but if (to suppose an extreme case) the feeling of charity were not inspired at all, Conscientiousness could not produce it, nor act upon it: it might impress ,the command, Do not injure another, because this is simply justice-; but it would-not-inspire with the desire to do him good, this being beyond.its limits.

Occasionally very unusual.combinations of particular organs present themselves, the effects of which cannot, by ordinary sagacity, be divined; and in such cases the phrenologist ought not to predicate anything, but to ask for information. As, however, nature is constant, he may speak with confidence the next time he meets with a similar case. Before it was ascertained that Secretiveness and Imitation confer the talent for acting, I met with an instance of this combination, and predicated something from it, which was entirely erroneous. This occurrence was loudly and extensively proclaimed as subversive of Phrenology; but to me it was a valuable lesson, and a discovery of some importance : ever afterward I found that particular talent accompany that combination.

RULE THIRD.—Where all the organs appear in nearly equal proportions to each other, the individual, if left to himself, will exhibit opposite phases of character, according as the animal-propensities or moral sentiments predominate for the time. He will pass his life in alternate sinning and repenting. If external influence be brought to operate upon him, his conduct will be greatly modified by it ; if placed, for instance, under severe discipline and moral restraint, these will cast the balance, for the time, in favour of the higher sentiments ; if exposed to the solicitation of profligate associates, the animal propensities will obtain triumphant sway. Maxwell, who was executed for housebreaking and theft, is an example of this combination. In his head the three orders of organs are well developed, but the region of the moral sentiments, lying above the asterisks, is deficient in size, in proportion to the basilar and occipital regions, manifesting the propensities. While subjected to the discipline of the army he preserved a fair reputation ; but when he fell into want, his propensities assumed the ascendency, he joined a company of thieves, adopted their practices, and was executed. The

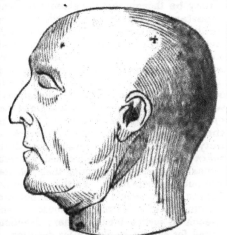

characteristic quality of men possessing this combination is their liability to be swayed by external influences.

COMBINATIONS IN ACTIVITY.

WHERE several organs are pre-eminently large in the same individual, they have a natural tendency to combine in activity, and to prompt him to a line of conduct calculated to gratify them all. Where, however, all or the greater part of the organs are possessed in nearly equal proportions, important practical effects may be produced by establishing combinations in activity among particular organs, or groups of organs. For example, if Individuality, Eventuality, Causality, Comparison, Language, and Concentrativeness be all large, they will naturally tend to act together, and the result of their combined activity will be a talent for public speaking or literary composition. If Language be small, it will be extremely difficult to establish such a combination in activity, and this talent will be deficient : but if we take two individuals, in both of whom this group of organs *is of an average size*, and if we train one of them to a mechanical employment and the other to the bar, we may accustom the Reflecting Organs and that of Language to act together in the latter, the result of which will be an acquired facility in writing and debate ; whereas, in the former individual, in consequence of the organ of Language never having been accustomed to act in combination with those of Intellect, this facility will be wanting.

On the same principle, if a person, having a favourable endowment of the organs of Propensity, Sentiment, and Intellect, were introduced for the first time into higher society than that to which he had been accustomed, it might happen that he would lose for a moment the command of his faculties, and exhibit awkwardness and embarrassment. This would arise from irregular and inharmonious action in the different organs : Veneration, powerfully excited, would prompt him to manifest profound respect ; Love of Approbation would inspire him with a desire to acquit himself to advantage; Cautiousness would produce alarm, lest he should fail in accomplishing this end; Self-Esteem would feel compromised by the consciousness of embarrassment stealing on the mind; and the intellect, distracted by these conflicting emotions, would be unable to regulate the conduct with propriety. When familiarized with the situation, the sentiments would subside into a state of less energetic and more harmonious action; the intellect, assuming the supremacy, would regulate and direct the feelings; and then the individual might become a pattern of refined manners and the ornament of the circle in which he at first made an awkward *debut*.

It is in virtue of this principle that education produces its most important effects. If, for instance, we take two individuals, in each of whom all the organs are developed in an average degree, and educate one of them among persons of sordid and mercenary dispositions—Acquisitiveness and Self-Esteem would in him be .cultivated into a high degree of activity, and self-interest and personal aggrandizement would be viewed as the great objects of his life. If the Love of Approbation were trained into combined activity with these faculties, he would desire distinction in wealth or power: if Veneration were trained to act in concert with them, it would take the direction of admiring the rich and great; and, Conscientiousness not being predominantly vigorous, would only intimate that such pursuits were unworthy, without possessing the power by itself of overcoming or controlling the whole combination against it. If the other individual, possessing the same developement, were trained in the society of moral and religious persons, in whose habitual conduct the practice of benevolence and justice toward. men, and veneration toward God, was regarded as the leading objects of human existence—the Love of Approbation, acting with this combination, would desire esteem for honourable and virtuous actions; and wealth would be viewed as the means of procuring gratification to these higher powers, but not as itself an object of paramount importance. The practical conduct of the two individuals might be very different, in consequence of this difference of training.

The change of character exhibited by some individuals appears to be referrible to new combinations in activity. It occurs generally in men in whom the organs of both the propensities and sentiments are large. In youth the propensities take the lead, and intellect acts in combination with them, producing sensual and immoral conduct. At a more advanced age, when the propensities have become less energetic, the individual may be placed in circumstances which powerfully excite his sentiments: the intellect will then act in combination with them, new interests will be felt, and higher views of duty and enjoyment arise. Life may thenceforward be regulated by reason and moral sentiment, sensual gratifications may be shunned and resisted, and the individual may appear like a different being. Religious impressions are frequently the causes which give commencement to this reformation; and this is natural, because religion addresses the most powerful motives to the higher faculties. I have observed, however, that individuals in whom the organs of the moral and intellectual faculties decidedly predominate, do not exhibit this change, because at no period are they strikingly vicious; neither do men in whom these organs are very deficient and the organs of the propensities very large, permanently undergo it; because their minds are like the stony ground mentioned in Scripture, on which good seed fell, but in which it could not take root, owing to the want of soil.

The principle now under discussion is not inconsistent with the influence of size; because it is only in individuals in whom the organs are nearly on an equality in point of size, that great effects can be produced by combinations in activity. In such cases the phrenologist, in estimating the effects of size, always inquires into the education bestowed.

The doctrine of combinations in activity explains several other mental phenomena of an interesting nature. In viewing the heads of the higher and lower classes of society, we do not perceive the animal organs preponderating in point of size in the latter, and those of the moral sentiments in the former, in any very palpable degree. The high polish, therefore which characterizes the upper ranks, is the result of sustained harmony in the action of the different faculties, and especially in those of the moral sentiments, induced by long cultivation. The rudeness observable in some of the lower orders results from a predominating combination in activity among the lower propensities; while the awkwardness that frequently characterizes them arises from the propensities, sentiments, and intellect not being habituated to act together. If, however, an individual be very deficient in the higher organs, he will remain vulgar, in consequence of this defect, although born and educated in the best society, and in spite of every effort to communicate refinement by training. On the other hand, if a very favourable developement of the organs of the higher sentiments and intellect, with a fine temperament, be possessed, the individual, in whatever rank he moves, will have the stamp of nature's nobility.

Several other phenomena, which were complete enigmas to the older metaphysicians, are explained by this principle. Dr. Adam Smith, in his Theory of Moral Sentiments, Chapter II., "On the influence of fortune upon the sentiments of mankind, with regard to the merit and demerit of actions," states the following case: A person throws a large stone over a wall into the public street, without giving warning to those who may be passing, and without regarding where it may fall; if it light upon a person's head, and knock out his brains, we would punish the offender pretty severely; but if it fall upon the ground, and hurt nobody, we would be offended with the same measure of punishment which, in the former event, we would reckon just, and yet the demerit in both cases is the same. Dr. Smith gives no theory to account for these differences of moral determination. Phrenology explains them. If the stone fall upon an unhappy passenger, Benevolence in the spectator is outraged; if the sufferer had a wife and family, Philoprogenitiveness and Adhesiveness are offended. Self-Esteem and Cautiousness also are excited, by the idea that we might have shared the same fate; all these rouse Destructiveness, and the whole together loudly demand a smart infliction on the transgressor. In the other event, when the stone falls to the ground, and hurts nobody, the only faculties excited are Intellect and Conscientiousness, and probably Cautiousness, and these calmly look at the motive of the offender, which probably was the love of mere muscular action, and award a slight punishment against him. The proper sentence, in such a case, would be one that would be approved of by Intellect and the moral sentiments acting in combination, uninfluenced by the lower propensities.

Dr. Smith states another case. One friend solicits a place for another, and, after using the greatest efforts, is unsuccessful. Gratitude in this case is less warm than if the place had been obtained; and yet the merit is the same. In the event of success Self-Esteem, Acquisitiveness, and the other animal organs are gratified, and excite Conscientiousness and Benevolence to gratitude. In the opposite result the repressing influence of these faculties, disappointed and grieved, chills the glow of Benevolence and Conscientiousness, and feeble gratitude is felt.

When a person becomes judge in his own cause, his intellect may present to him the facts exactly as they happened, but these excite in his mind, not simply the sentiment of Conscientiousness, but also Self-Love, Acquisitiveness, and, if he has been grievously injured, Destructiveness. Hence he decision of his own mind, on his own case, proceeds from Intellect, nfluenced and directed by all these lower feelings acting along with Conscientiousness. Present the same case to an impartial spectator, favourably constituted, and his decision will be the result of Conscientiousness and intellect, unalloyed by the intermixture of the selfish emotions.

Pure or abstract justice, then, in the proper sense of the term, is the result of the combined activity of intellect and Conscientiousness, uninfluenced by the animal propensities. For example, if we are called on to judge of the conduct of a person accused, in order to arrive at an absolutely just decision, the intellect must present to us a clear perception of his real motives and the tendency of this action; if either of these is wanting, the sentiment of Conscientiousness acts not on a real, but on an imperfect or imaginary case. In the next place, all the animal propensities must be quiescent; because, if offended Selfishness, or anger, or Acquisitiveness, or ambition, or Adhesiveness, mingle with Conscientiousness, the fountain is polluted, and the stream cannot be pure. It is an interesting fact, that the dictates of Conscientiousness, when perfectly enlightened, and not misled by the lower feelings, will be found always to harmonize with the enlightened dictates of Benevolence and Veneration. The moral sentiments have been so constituted as to coincide in their results; and hence, wherever any action or opinion is felt to stand in opposition to any of these sentiments, we may, without hesitation, suspect either that it is wrong, or, that the intellect is not completely informed concerning its nature and legitimate consequences.

In party-politics Adhesiveness, Love of Approbation, and Benevolence, not to mention Combativeness and Destructiveness, are extremely apt to enter into vivid activity in surveying the conduct of an individual who has distinguished himself by zealous efforts upon our own side; and our judgment of his conduct will, in consequence, be the determination of Intellect and Conscientiousness, disturbed and led astray by these inferior feelings.

The doctrine of the primitive functions of the faculties, explained in the first part of this work, and of the combinations now laid down, shows *why* Phrenology does not enable us to predict *actions*. Destructiveness, for example, is not a tendency to kill a man or a beast as a specific act, but a mere general propensity, capable of leading to destruction as its ultimate result, but which may be manifested in a great variety of ways, (many of them justifiable, others unjustifiable,) according as it is directed by the faculties which, in each particular instance, act along with it; thus, acting along with large Acquisitiveness, and in the absence of Conscientiousness, it may prompt to murder; while acting along with large Conscientiousness and Benevolence, it may prove the orphan's help and the widow's stay, by arresting the arm of the oppressor.

PRACTICAL APPLICATION OF THE DOCTRINE OF THE COMBINATIONS.

I CANNOT too earnestly repeat, that the principles now illustrated are practical and important. If any one require the assistance of a human being in affairs of moment, let him be assured that attention to the three elements—of temperament, combination of mental organs, and education or training, will afford him more certain information regarding the inherent qualities of the object and his practical capabilities, than certificates of character and attainments, such as are commonly relied on. The extent to which this work has already attained prevents me, however, from doing more than making a few observations.

In one instance I refused to hire a boy as a servant, because I found his head to belong to the inferior class, although he was introduced by a woman whose good conduct and discrimination I had long known, and who gave him an excellent character. That individual was at first greatly incensed at my refusing to engage the boy, but within a month she returned, and said that she had been grossly imposed upon herself by a neighbour, whose son the boy was; that she had since learned that he was a thief, and had been dismissed from his previous service for stealing. On another occasion I hired a female servant, because her head belonged to the superior class, although a former mistress gave her a very indifferent character—the result was equally in favour of Phrenology. She turned out an excellent servant, and remained with me for several years, until she was respectably married.*

When a servant is to be hired, the points to be attended to are the following:

First, The temperament.—If this be lymphatic, there will be little spontaneous activity; work will be a burden; and exhaustion will soon follow from forced application. If it be purely nervous, there will be great vivacity and strong natural tendency to activity; but physical strength will not be present in a corresponding degree. Combinations of the sanguine and bilious, or bilious and nervous temperaments, are the best; the bilious bestowing the quality of endurance, and the sanguine or nervous that of activity.

Second, The proportions of the different regions of the brain to each other.—If the base of the brain, the seat of the animal organs, be large, and the coronal region be shallow and narrow, the animal feelings will be strong, and the moral weak; if both of these regions be large, and the anterior lobe of the brain small, the dispositions may be good, but the intellect will be weak. If all three be large, the moral and intellectual predominating, the best combination of qualities will be present.

Third, The proportions of particular organs to each other.—If the lower region of the forehead be largely developed and the upper deficient, the intellect will execute well whatever work is placed before it; but it will be limited in its capacity of foreseeing what ought to be done, if not pointed out, and of arranging details in reference to the whole. If the upper part of the forehead be large and the lower deficient, the power of abstract thinking (which a servant rarely requires, and is almost never called on to exercise) will be considerable, but quite uncultivated, and destitute of materials to act on; while the talent for observing details, the love of order and arrangement, and, in short, the elements of practical usefulness, will be deficient. The best combination of the intellectual organs for a servant, is that which occurs when the lower region of the forehead is large, the middle region immediately above the nose, up to the line of the hair, is also large, and the upper lateral region full. The dispositions depend on the combinations of the moral and animal organs. If Acquisitiveness, Secretiveness, Love of Approbation, and Veneration be large, and Conscientiousness deficient, the servant will be selfish and cunning; but extremely plausible, deferential, and polite; eye-service will be rendered abundantly, but conscientious discharge of duty will be wanting. If Benevolence, Conscientiousness, Firmness, Self-Esteem, and Combativeness be large, in combination with Cautiousness, Secretiveness, Love of Approbation, and Veneration moderate, there may be great fidelity and honesty, with heat of temper, unbending stiffness of deportment, and, in short, an exterior

* A report of eleven cases observed in the Dublin Penitentiary is published in *The Phrenological Journal*, No. xxi., p. 88, in which the dispositions were inferred from developement of brain; and similar cases are recorded in "Testimonials" presented by me in 1836, on becoming a candidate for the chair of Logic in the University of Edinburgh.

manner the reverse of the former, but internal dispositions and practical conduct in situations of trust far superior. The combinations also determine the fitness of the individual for particular employments; a female with small Philoprogenitiveness ought never to be employed as a nursery maid; nor one deficient in Order and Ideality as a lady's maid. A man deficient in Conscientiousness is unfit to be a butler or steward. The varieties of combination are extremely numerous, and the effects of them can be learned only by experience.

Fourth, The education or training of the individual falls to be inquired into.—Phrenology shows only the natural qualities, but the direction which they have received must be ascertained by inquiry. No combination of organs will render an individual an expert cook, without having practised cookery, or an accomplished coachman, without having practically taken charge of horses, and learned to drive.

Fifth, The relation of the natural qualities of the master or mistress to those of the servant must be attended to.—If a mistress with a small brain, having Conscientiousness and Benevolence moderate, and Self-Esteem and Combativeness large, should hire a servant possessed of a large, active, and well-proportioned brain, the latter will instinctively feel that nature has made her the superior, although fortune has reversed their relative positions. The mistress will feel this too, but will maintain her authority by imperiousness, captiousness, or violence. In this condition the best dispositions of the servant may be outraged, and conduct produced of a discreditable nature, when contemplated by itself, apart from the provocation. A servant with a small brain, but favourable combination, would prove a treasure to a mistress possessed of similar qualities; whereas she would be felt to be too feeble and inefficient in her whole manner and mode of acting, by a lady whose brain was very large, very favourably combined, and very active. This principle explains why the same individual may be found to be an excellent servant in one family, and an unsuitable one in another.

Sixth, The qualities of servants, in reference to each other, ought to be considered.—Two individuals, possessing large and active brains, great Self-Esteem, Love of Approbation, and Combativeness, may, if they have large Benevolence, Veneration, and Conscientiousness, prove excellent servants to their employers, whom they regard as legitimate objects of veneration and conscientiousness; but may make very indifferent companions to each other. Each will desire deference and respect from the other, which neither will yield; and, in all probability, they will quarrel and manifest only their propensities in their mutual intercourse. Instruction in their own nature, and in the proper direction of their feelings, would, in many instances, remedy this evil. But while ignorance continues, it is advisable to rely chiefly on natural qualities: for example, if one servant has Self-Esteem large, a companion should be selected in whom this organ is moderate; and the same with Combativeness. When this is neglected, the natural language of Self-Esteem or Combativeness in the one involuntarily excites the same feeling in the other, and harmony is nearly impossible: whereas, if one has Self-Esteem large, and the other has it small, the natural expression of the former is not painful to the latter; on the contrary, the absence of pretension, which attends a small Self-Esteem, renders the latter agreeable to the former, and a sincere mutual regard may arise between them.

It will be obvious to every reflecting person, that the circumstance of a servant being rejected by a phrenologist is no proof of the individual being essentially bad; it shows only that, in one or other of the six points before mentioned, the individual did not suit the particular phrenologist, and no more. The servant may be admirably qualified for a different employer.

Similar remarks apply to the selection of clerks, partners in business and all persons required to fill confidential situations. I have been told that it is extremely difficult to prevent peculation in the post-office and other departments of public and private business, in which extensive trust is necessarily confided to the individuals employed. If only persons in whom the moral and intellectual organs decidedly predominated were chosen to fill such situations, the evil would disappear.

These observations are offered as hints of several particulars which appear to me proper to be attended to, and not as complete practical directions. The elements which compose human character are so numerous, their combinations so intricate, and so little has been done in the practical application of the science in the manner now recommended, that it is impossible to be too modest either in giving directions or in promising results. Experience is the great teacher, and my sole object is to induce phrenologists to seek experience by practice. I am aware that many of my readers will feel that much greater attainments than they at present possess would be requisite, to enable them to act on the principles unfolded even in this brief statement; and hence many of them may consider the remarks as altogether useless; but several answers may be made to this objection. *First*, There are several phrenologists who actually practise what is here recommended, and have experienced great advantages from it; and what has been done successfully and with benefit by some, may be accomplished by others. *Secondly*, Science is useless unless it be practical; all practical sciences must advance by experience; and it is only by beginning and persevering, that experience can be gained. And, *thirdly*, Even those persons who are conscious of incapacity to practise these rules must perceive the advantage of acting on them if they could; and must feel that until some mode of guiding the judgment in the selection of individuals who are to be placed in confidential situations shall be resorted to, when shall bring into view the points before treated of, uncertainty, disappointment, and annoyance must afflict both the employers and the employed. And, *finally*, Every person of common reflection will acknowledge that while it would be a great advantage to obtain the foregoing knowledge of human character, there is no system of mental philosophy in existence which affords even the least aid in attempting it, if it be not Phrenology.

This application of Phrenology has suggested the question, Are individuals with "ill-shaped heads" to become "outcasts from society?" This is precisely the evil which, under the actual system of criminal legislation, exists, and which the phrenologists are labouring to remove. An unfavourably developed brain and good natural dispositions are two conditions which do not coexist in nature. Phrenologists, therefore, by establishing the fact, that an imperfectly formed brain renders an individual naturally prone to vice, will afford an inducement to society to treat men so constituted as *moral patients*, and to use more effectual means for restraining their propensities than any that are at present adopted. This, in my opinion, would be preferable to the existing practice, which leaves individuals with the worst natural dispositions at liberty, in the most unfavourable circumstances, to follow their instinctive tendencies, and only punishes them after having committed crimes. At present these beings are surrounded by want, misery, and the means of intoxication. They transgress the criminal law, are confined in jails and bridewells, calculated to excite their propensities, and to afford little cultivation to their moral powers, and they are afterward ejected into the immoral atmosphere from which they were taken; a mode of treatment which could not exist, if Phrenology were believed and understood.

It has been farther asked, by way of objection, "Does Mr. Combe deny, that, in the case he mentions, the boy whom he rejected might have had a good character, notwithstanding the indications of his original propensities? If he denies this, he denies a proposition which he himself has always stated, and from which he derives the practical value of Phrenology ; namely, that the original propensities can be corrected, and even eradicated, by education and other means."

Answer :. I have not stated that the "original propensities can be *eradicated* by education and other means." If so, Phrenology would necessarily be a dream. What I have said is this—that all the faculties may be *directed* to proper objects,.and, when so directed, their action will become good. But to guide strong animal propensities to virtue, there must be a directing power. If there be vigorous moral and intellectual faculties in the individual, he will, in that case, be a law and a guide unto himself. If, however, the moral and intellectual faculties be deficient, which was the case with the individual under discussion, then I certainly maintain, that strong animal feelings will *not guide themselves* to virtue. In this case the directing power must be supplied *from without*. The case of E. S., mentioned in the Phrenological Journal, No. xxi., pp. 82 and 147, is exactly in point, and illustrates the positions here maintained. Now, if the boy had been placed from infancy in an asylum, from which temptation to vice was excluded, and in which the highest moral and intellectual treatment was administered, he might have had a good character, notwithstanding the form of his brain ; because, *so situated*, he *could not* have offended. But I was informed that he had been brought up in the ordinary circumstances of the labouring classes in this country ; and extensive observation had convinced me that that condition does not withdraw temptation from the propensities, and does not supply moral and intellectual stimulus to the higher faculties sufficient to direct a mind constituted like his to morality. I therefore inferred, that his good character was false ; which it actually proved to be. At present society is greatly deficient in institutions in which the moral influence of higher minds can be brought habitually to bear on inferior minds, in the absence of external temptation.

In consequence also of the lamentable ignorance of the nature of *individuals*, which too generally abounds, the mental deficiencies in which the tendency to crime originates are not understood, and still less is the immense power of moral influence which the best order of minds could wield over the inferior duly appreciated. This influence, however, cannot exert itself efficiently, unless external temptation to evil be withdrawn, which cannot be the case without institutions formed for the purpose. Phrenology will hasten the day when these shall exist. Society is in possession, from history and observation, of a pretty accurate knowledge of *human nature in general ;* but this knowledge is. *too general* to be practically useful. When an individual is presented to them, they cannot tell, previous to experience, whether he is naturally a Caligula or a Washington. Phrenology not only gives a scientific basis and form to the *general knowledge* of mankind already existing, but renders it available in *particular* instances ; it unfolds the natural qualities of *individual* men, and enables us to judge how far they will be *inclined* to one course of action or to another. I consider it, therefore, neither unjust nor unhumane to decline taking into my service individuals whom I know to be unfitted by their mental qualities for the duties which they would be called on to perform. In short, if the members of society, instead of giving false characters of profligate individuals, (through Benevolence acting without Conscientiousness,) and, in consequence, exposing each other to loss of property and life by criminal outrages, would treat as moral patients those persons whose mental deficiencies render them incapable of guiding themselves to virtue, they would benefit both themselves and the vicious.*

ON THE COINCIDENCE BETWEEN THE NATURAL TALENTS AND DISPOSITIONS OF NATIONS, AND THE DEVELOPEMENT OF THEIR BRAINS.

THE mental character of an individual, at any given time, is the result of his natural endowment of faculties, modified by the circumstances in which he has been placed. The first element, or natural constitution, is admitted, by most thinking men, to form the basis of, and prescribe the limits to, the operation of the second. If a child be by nature extremely combative, and very little cautious, highly prone to covetousness, and very insensible to justice, a reflecting guardian will adopt a different method of education and expect different consequences, than if his natural dispositions were exactly the reverse; and he will not expect education to change his nature.

A nation is composed of individuals, and what is true of all the parts (which in a nation preserve their individuality,) must hold good of the whole; nevertheless, the fashionable doctrine is, that national character depends altogether on external circumstances; and that the *native* stock of animal, moral, and intellectual powers on which these operate, is the same in New Holland and in England, in Hindostan and in France. Mr. Stewart informs us, "that the capacities of the human mind have been in all ages the same; and that the diversity of phenomena exhibited by our species is the result merely of the different circumstances in which men are placed." "This," says he, "has long been received as an uncontrovertible logical maxim; or rather, such is the influence of early instruction, that we are apt to regard it as one of the most obvious suggestions of common sense. And yet, till about the time of Montesquieu, it was by no means so generally recognised by the learned as to have a sensible influence on the fashionable tone of thinking over Europe."†

There is some ambiguity in this passage. The proposition, that "the capacities of the human mind have been *in all* AGES the same," does not necessarily imply that they have been alike *in all* NATIONS. The Hindoo mind may have been the same in the year 100 as in the year 1800, and so may the English and all other national minds; but it does not follow that either in the year 100 or 1800 the English and Hindoo minds were constituted by nature alike; and yet this is what I understand Mr. Stewart to mean: for he adds, "that the diversity of phenomena exhibited by

* The chief object of this work is to unfold the fundamental facts and doctrines of Phrenology as the science of the human mind. Its applications are treated of in other works. Besides those quoted in the work itself, the following may be consulted with advantage:

A Sketch of the Natural Laws of Man. 12mo., pp. 220. By Dr. Spurzheim.
Elementary Principles of Education. By Dr. Spurzheim.
The Constitution of Man considered in relation to External Objects. By the author of the present work. The People's Edition; price 1s 6d. The Sixth Edition, 12mo., price 4s.
Phrenology in connexion with Physiognomy. By Dr. Spurzheim.
Observations on Mental Derangement; being an application of the principles of Phrenology to the Elucidation of the Causes, Symptoms, Nature, and Treatment of Insanity. By Andrew Combe, M.D. Small 8vo., pp. 392.
The Philosophy of Education, with its practical application to a system and plan of Popular Education as a National Object. By James Simpson, Esq., Advocate.
Selections from the Phrenological Journal, consisting of the most interesting articles in the first twenty Numbers. 12mo.
† Dissertation, p. 53.

our *species* is the result *merely* of the different circumstances in which men are placed;" embracing in this proposition men of every nation as equally gifted in mental power. Now, there is reason to question this doctrine, and to regard it as not merely speculatively erroneous, but as laying the foundation of a great deal of most hurtful practice.

When we regard the different quarters of the globe, we are struck with the extreme dissimilarity in the attainments of the varieties of men who inhabit them. If we glance over the history of Europe, Asia, Africa, and America, we shall find distinct and permanent features of character which strongly indicate natural differences in their mental constitutions. The inhabitants of Europe have manifested, in all ages, a strong tendency toward moral and intellectual improvement. As far back as history reaches, we find society instituted, arts practised, and literature taking root, not only in intervals of tranquillity, but amid the alarms of war. Before the foundation of Rome the Etruscans had established civilization and the arts in Italy. Under the Greek and Roman empires philosophy, literature, and the fine arts were sedulously and successfully cultivated; and that portion of the people whose wealth enabled them to pay for education, attained a high degree of intelligence and refinement. By the irruption of the northern hordes these countries were subsequently involved in a chaos of ignorance; but again the sun of science rose, the clouds of Gothic darkness were dispelled, and Europe took the lead of the world in science, morals, and philosophy. In the inhabitants of this portion of the globe there appears an elasticity of mind incapable of being permanently repressed. Borne down for a time by external violence, their mental energies seem to have gathered strength under the restraint, and at length to have burst their fetters, and overcome every obstacle opposed to their expansion.

When, on the other hand, we turn our attention to Asia, we perceive manners and institutions, which belong to a period too remote to be ascertained, and yet far inferior to the European standard. The people of Asia early arrived at a point comparatively low in the scale of improvement, which they have never passed.

The history of Africa, so far as Africa can be said to have a history, presents similar phenomena. The annals of the races who have inhabited that continent, with few exceptions, exhibit one unbroken scene of moral and intellectual desolation; and in a quarter of the globe embracing the greatest varieties of soil and climate, no nation is at this day to be found whose institutions indicate even moderate civilization.*

The aspect of America is still more deplorable. Surrounded for centuries by European knowledge, enterprise, and energy, and incited to improvement by the example of European institutions, the natives of that continent remain, at the present time, the same miserable, wandering, houseless, and lawless savages as their ancestors were, when Columbus first set foot upon their soil. Partial exceptions to this description may be found in some of the southern districts of North America; but the numbers who have adopted the modes of civilized life are so small, and the progress made by them so limited, that, speaking of the race, we do not exaggerate in saying, that they remain to the present hour enveloped in all their primitive barbarity, and that they have profited nothing by the introduction among them of arts, sciences, and philosophy. The same

* Since the observation in the text was written, accounts have appeared of a people discovered by Major Clapperton in the interior of Africa in a state of comparative civilization. It is said, that, although they are jet black, they are not negroes, and it is conjectured that they are the descendants of the Numidians of ancient history. If the representations of their attainments be correct, I anticipate in them a brain developed like the European.

observations have occurred to a writer in the Edinburgh Review. The following remarks, on the native American character, appeared in that work in an article on "Howison's Upper Canada," June, 1822 : "From all that we learn," says the reviewer, "of the state of the aborigines of this great continent from this volume, and from every other source of information, it is evident that they are making no advances toward civilization. It is certainly a striking and mysterious fact, that a race of men should thus have continued for ages stationary in a state of the rudest barbarism. That tendency to improvement, a principle that has been thought more than perhaps any other to distinguish man from the lower animals, would seem to be totally wanting in them. Generation after generation passes away, and no traces of advancement distinguish the last from the first. The mighty wilderness they inhabit may be traversed from end to end, and hardly a vestige be discovered that marks the hand of man. It might naturally have been expected that, in the course of ages, some superior genius would have arisen among them to inspire his countrymen with a desire to cultivate the arts of peace, and establish some durable civil institution; or that, at least, during the long period since the Europeans have been settled among them, and taught them, by such striking examples, the benefits of industry and social order, they would have been tempted to endeavour to participate in blessings thus providentially brought within their reach. But all has been unavailing, and it now seems certain that the North American Indians, like the bears and wolves, are destined to flee at the approach of civilized man, and to fall before his renovating hand; and disappear from the face of the earth along with those ancient forests, which alone afford them sustenance and shelter."

The theory usually advanced to account for these differences of national character is, that they are produced by diversities of soil and climate. But, although these may reasonably be supposed to exert a certain influence, they are altogether inadequate to explain the whole phenomena. We ought ever to bear in mind, that Nature is constant in her operations, and that the same causes invariably produce the same effects. Hence, when we find exceptions in result, without being able to assign differences in causes, we may rest assured that we have not found the true or the only cause, and our diligence ought to be quickened to obtain new light, and not employed in maintaining the sufficiency of that which we possess.

If we survey a map of the world, we shall find nations, whose soil is fertile and climate temperate, in a lower degree of improvement than others who are less favoured. In Van Diemen's Land and New South Wales a few natives have existed in the most wretched poverty, ignorance, and degradation, in a country which enriches Europeans as fast as they possess it. In America, too, Europeans and native Indians have lived for centuries under the influence of the same physical causes; the former have kept pace in their advances with their brethren in the Old Continent, while the latter, as we have seen, remain stationary in savage ignorance and indolence.

Such differences are not confined to the great continents alone; but different tribes in the same hemisphere seem to possess different native minds, and these remain unchanged through numerous ages. Tacitus describes the Gauls as gay, volatile, and precipitate, prone to rush to action, but without the power of sustaining adversity and the tug of strife, and this is the character of the Celtic portion of the French nation down to the present day. He represents the Britons as cool, considerate, and sedate, possessed of intellectual talent, and says that he prefers their native aptitude to the livelier manners of the Gauls. The same mental qualities characterize the English of the nineteenth century, and they and the French may still be contrasted in similar terms. Tacitus describes the Germans, allowing for their state of civilization, as a bold, prudent, self-denying, and virtuous people, possessed of great force of character; and the same features distinguish them still. The native Irishman, in manners, dispositions, and capacities, is a being widely different from the lowland Scotchman; and if we trace the two nations to the remotest antiquity, the same characteristic differences are found.

These differences between nations living under similar climates are commonly attributed entirely to the religious and political institutions of the several countries. Presbytery and parish schools, for example, are supposed to have rendered the Scotchman habitually attentive to his own interest, but cautious, thoughtful, and honest; while Popery and Catholic priests have made the Irishman free and generous withal, but precipitate and unreflecting—ready in the gust of passion to sacrifice his friend, and in the glow of friendship to immolate himself. It is forgotten, that there were ages in which Popery and priests had equal ascendency in all the British isles, and that the Englishman, Irishman, and Scotchman were beings as specifically distinct then as at present: besides, the more correct, as well as the more profound, view, is, to regard religious and political institutions, when not forced upon a people by external conquest, as the spontaneous growth of their natural propensities, sentiments, and intellectual faculties. Hierarchies and constitutions do not spring from the ground, but from the minds of men: if we suppose one nation to be gifted with much Wonder and Veneration, and little Conscientiousness, Reflection, and Self-Esteem, and another to possess an endowment exactly the reverse; it is obvious that the first would be naturally prone to superstition in religion and servility in the state, while the second would, by native instinct, resist all attempts to make them reverence things unholy, and tend constantly toward political institutions, fitted to afford to each individual the gratification of his Self-Esteem in independence, and his Conscientiousness in equality before the law. Those who contend that institutions come first, and that character follows as their effect, are bound to assign a cause for the institutions themselves. If they do not spring from the native mind, and are not forced on the people by conquest, it is difficult to see whence they can originate.

The phrenologist is not satisfied with these common theories of national character; he has observed that a particular form of brain is the invariable concomitant of particular dispositions and talents, and that this fact holds good in the case of nations as well as of individuals. Dr. Gall[*] has treated briefly of this subject, and after noticing the effects of climate on the human faculties, he adds the following most proper caution: "It is generally believed that it is sufficient to have a few national crania before one's eyes to be in a condition to draw inductions from them. This would be the case, certainly, if the moral and intellectual character of all the individuals composing a nation were the same; but, according to the observations of Dr. Spurzheim and myself, great differences exist between individuals belonging even to nations having a very determinate character. Dr. Spurzheim saw in London twelve Chinese, and he found them to differ as much from each other as Europeans. Resemblance between the individuals held good only in the countenance, and particularly in the position of the eyes. M. Diard gave me two crania found at Coulpi, on the banks of the Ganges. If I except the organs of Philoprogenitiveness and Acquisitiveness, which are very large, all the others presented striking differences. We see the same differences among negroes, although they always resemble each other in the mouth and nose, especially when they are natives of the same country. Dr. Spurzheim

saw in London, in the establishment for mutual instruction, three negroes,
one of whom was a young man of eighteen years of age, endowed with
extraordinary talents and an agreeable countenance.   I have seen several
negroes, of both sexes, whose features were altogether agreeable.   I observe the same forms among individuals of different nations ;   so much so,
that it would be impossible to distinguish, by these alone, whether an individual was a Frenchman, German, Italian, Spaniard, or an Englsh-
man.   It is for this reason that we find individuals in all nations who
have the same moral and intellectual character.   Those, therefore, judge
precipitately, who believe that they are able to decipher the general character of a nation from a small number of skulls.   In order to discover
this general character, it is necessary to study a great number of indiv-
duals—entire regiments—the whole nation so far as possible.   With such
facilities, it will be easy for the organologist to discover in the structure
of the head the material cause of the peculiar character of the people."

    The Phrenological Society of Edinburgh possesses the largest collec-
tion of national crania in Europe, and while I am ready to admit its
importance of Dr. Gall's caution, it is proper to remark that, if one may
judge from this collection, he overstates the extent of the differences between individual skulls belonging to the same people.   The variety of
tribes of mankind is very great, and the political do not always coincide
with the natural divisions of the races.   A collection of Russian crania,
for instance, might contain almost every variety of the human species,
except negroes ; they would all be Russians politically ;   but in their
natural characteristics they would belong to the Celtic, German, Mongolian, and Circassian races, and their varieties.   Distinct and well-marked
tribes alone should be considered as nations when we are considering the
peculiarities of national skulls ; but if this be done, it appears to me that
the study is possible, because a general type pervades the great majority
of each tribe.   It is true that several individual skulls, closely resembling
each other, may be selected from a great number belonging to different
nations ;—but this is an exception to the general rule.   A common form
in the entire skull, and a common proportion in the different organs,
pervades the forty or fifty Hindoo skulls in the society's museum, acquired at different times and from different parts of Hindostan ;   to which
the head of Rammohun Roy is the sole marked exception.   The head of
this celebrated man, both in size and combination, resembles the skulls
of the mixed race of Celts and Germans in Europe ; but he was a phenomenon in his own country.   There are varieties of developement among
the other Hindoo skulls, corresponding to the differences in individual
character ; but these sink into insignificance when the Hindoo skull,
in its general form, is compared with the negro or Charib in their general
types.   The same remarks apply to the Esquimaux, the Swiss, the Peruvian, and other national skulls in the society's possession ; a peculiar
character pervades the skulls of each nation, which strikingly distinguishes
them from others.   It is not extraordinary that this should be the case,
considering that the nation consists of · ordinary beings, whose general
characteristics are closely analogous.

    I proceed, therefore, to offer a few remarks on several of the national
crania in the Phrenological Society's collection, requesting the reader to
give due weight to Dr. Gall's caution.

    In the Phrenological Transactions an account is given of the Phreno-
logy of Hindostan, by Dr. G. M. Patterson.   The HINDOOS are remarkable for want of force of character; so much so, that a handful of
Europeans overcomes in, combat, and holds in permanent subjection,
thousands, nay, millions, of that people.   Power of, mental manifestation
bears a proportion to the size of the cerebral organs, and the Hindoo head

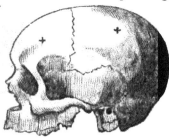

is small and the European large, in precise conformity with the different mental characters.* Farther, the Hindoo is distinguished by a great respect for animal life and absence of cruelty in his dispositions ; while, at the same time, he is destitute of fire, and of that energy of mind which overcomes obstacles and gives force to command. The European is precisely the opposite ; he lives to a' great extent upon animal food, is fierce in his anger, and is characterized by great combative and destructive vigour. The Hindoo skull indicates a manifest deficiency in the organs of Combativeness and Destructiveness ; while in the European these parts are amply developed. The Hindoo is cunning, timid, and proud ; and in him Secretiveness, Cautiousness, and Self-Esteem are large in proportion to the organs last mentioned. In intellect the Hindoo is more prone to analogical than direct reasoning, is fond of metaphors and comparisons, and little given to discriminating differences ; and the organ of Comparison is much larger in his head than those of Causality and Wit. Dr. Patterson states that these facts are drawn from upward of three thousand observations ; and they are illustrated by a collection of Hindoo skulls presented by him to the Phrenological Society. These skulls,† twelve in number, and a large addition of skulls of the same nation, acquired by the society from other quarters, have long been exhibited to public inspection. Mr. Montgomery has called in question the justness of the character assigned to the Hindoos, but his objections have been ably answered by Dr. Corden Thomson in the Phren. Journ., vol. vi., p. 244. I still regard the statements made by Dr. Patterson to be correct.

The society's collection contains other specimens of national developement of brain equally interesting. The CHARIB skulls present a striking appearance. They are

CHARIB.

much *larger* than the Hindoo heads, and, in conformity with the principle, that size indicates power, this tribe is the most remarkable among all the native Americans for force of character. The Europeans have in vain attemped to subdue them ; they have hunted them down like wild beasts, and nearly extirpated them, but failed in every attempt to enslave them in a mass, as the Portuguese and Spaniards did the natives of Mexico and Brazil. Farther, the Charib brain is prodigiously developed in the regions of Combativeness and Destructiveness, in which the Hindoo head is deficient ; and the former race is as ferocious as the' latter is mild and inoffensive. In the reflecting organs the Charib is extremely deficient ; and he is described as rushing with unbridled eagerness on present gratification, blind to every consequence, and incapable of tracing the shortest links in the chain of causation. If the ear be taken as a centre, and a line drawn from it to

* At the end of this section a table of measurements is given of all the skulls mentioned in it.

† I strongly recommend to the reader to inspect the casts of national skulls here referred to. The study of them will make an impression infinitely deeper than any description.

the most prominent part of the forehead of the Charib skulls, and another line be drawn from the same point to the most prominent part of the occiput, it will be found that by far the largest quantity of the brain is situated behind the ear. The organs of the animal propensities greatly preponderate over those of the intellectual faculties. If the region above the organs of Cautiousness and Causality be measured, the height will be found to be small, compared with that in Europeans—an indication that the organs of the moral sentiments also are deficient in size. The society possesses casts of five skulls of Charibs, all of which, with individual differences, present a general type characteristic of the whole. In St. Thomas's Hospital, London, I have seen the original of one of these casts : the whole were procured by Dr. Spurzheim from authentic skulls, and their genuineness may be relied on. In the Anatomical Museum of the Andersonian University, in Glasgow, I have seen another Charib skull, corresponding exactly with those now mentioned.

Mr. Sedgwick, Secretary to the Phrenological Society of London, communicated an interesting Essay to the Phrenological Journal, (vol vi., p. 377,) on "the artificial compression of the infant head, by barbarous nations," in which he clearly establishes that the Charib and other Indian tribes flatten the forehead of their children by compression, some of them by means of a small bag of sand, others by confinement of the infant head between two small pieces of wood, one placed before and the other behind, both being firmly bound together ; and others, on the north-west coast, by a board in the cradle brought over the forehead, and tied firmly down upon the head of the infant. The child is seldom taken from the cradle, and the compression is continued till it is able to walk. With the *cause* of the flatness, however, I am not at present dealing, the only point I wish to establish being the *fact* of concomitance between the deficiency of organization and deficiency of mental ability, which is so certain as to be altogether indisputable.

The NEW HOLLAND skull indicates a lamentable deficiency in the regions of the moral and intellectual organs. The organs of Number, Constructiveness, Reflection, and Ideality are particularly deficient, while those of the animal propensities are fully developed. The society possesses casts of two skulls of natives of New Holland, and Sir George S. Mackenzie has  presented to it the actual skulls of a chief and a female of that country ; and the whole correspond, in a striking manner, in their general features.

If these skulls were put into the hands of a phrenologist to state the dispositions which they indicate, he would say that there should be considerable energy and courage, but extreme intellectual incapacity, selfishness, stubbornness, and harshness. Every talent necessary for architecture, and the constructive arts in general, is defective, while Ideality is so small, that sentiments of refinement or elegance will scarcely be at all experienced. The most unaccustomed eye will perceive how far this skull and that of the Charib fall short of the European in the organs of Reflection, Ideality, and Constructiveness.

The following account of the actual condition of the natives of New Holland is given in Smellie's Philosophy of Natural History : "It would appear that they pull out the two fore-teeth of the upper jaw ; for in neither sex, nor at any particular period of life, are these teeth to be seen.* They are beardless: their visage is long, without exhibiting a single agreeable feature; their hair is black, short, and crisped; and their skin is equally black as that of the Guinea negroes. Their only clothing consists of a piece of the bark of a tree tied round their waist, with a handful of long herbs placed in the middle. *They erect no houses;* and, without any covering, they sleep on the ground. Men, women, and children associate promiscuously to the number of twenty or thirty. A small fish which they catch in reservoirs made with stones in arms of the sea, constitutes their chief nourishment; and with bread and every species of grain they are totally unacquainted."† I select this description on account of its brevity. Smellie refers to Dampier as his authority.

Captain Cook was the first who explored the eastern coast of New Holland, of the natives of which he gives the following account: "They appeared to have no fixed habitations; for we saw nothing like a town or a village in the whole country. Their houses, if houses they may be called, seem to be formed with less art and industry than any we had seen, except the wretched hovels at Terra del Fuego, and in some respects they are inferior even to them. At Botany Bay, where they were best, they were just high enough for a man to sit upright in, but not large enough for him to extend himself in his whole length in any direction: they are built with pliable rods, about as thick as a man's finger, in the form of an oven, by sticking the two ends into the ground, and then covering them with palm leaves and broad pieces of bark: the door is nothing but a large hole at one end, opposite to which the fire is made. Under these houses or sheds they sleep, coiled up with their heels to to their head; and in this position one of them will hold three or four persons."—"The only furniture belonging to these houses that fell under our observation, is a kind of oblong vessel made of bark," which was supposed to be used as a bucket for carrying water. Captain Cook adds, that "both sexes go stark naked;" and that he saw neither nets nor vessels in which water might be boiled. "The canoes of New Holland," he continues, "are as mean and rude as the houses," being, on the southern parts of the coast, "nothing more than a piece of bark, about twelve feet long, tied together at the ends, and kept open in the middle by small bows of wood;" and in the northern parts merely the hollow trunk of a tree. These were the inhabitants of a different part of New Holland from that visited by Dampier. Their want of curiosity also was very remarkable, and forms a good contrast with the wonder with which some American tribes regarded the Spaniards and their ships on their first appearance in the new world. Captain Cook relates that, of about twenty natives who were seen on the shore, not far from Botany Bay, "not one was observed to stop and look toward us, but they trudged along, to all appearance without the least emotion of curiosity or surprise, though it is impossible they should not have seen the ship by a casual glance, as they walked along the shore; and though she must, with respect to every other object they had yet seen, have been little less stupendous and unaccountable than a floating mountain, with all its woods, would have been to us."‡

These observations are confirmed by the Rev. Dr. Lang in the following terms:§ "Throughout the whole period of his government," says Dr.

* These teeth are wanting in the chief's skull presented by Sir George S. Mackenzie to the society.

† Vol. ii., p. 84. ‡ See Cook's First Voyage, b. ii., ch. ii. and vi.

§ An Historical and Statistical Account of New South Wales, both as a penal settlement and as a British Colony. By John Dunmore Lang, D.D., Senior Minister of the Scots Church, and Principal of the Australian College, Sydney, New South Wales. London: Cochrane and MacCrone. 1834. Vol. i., pp. 36–39.

Lang, "Captain Philip endeavoured, with a zeal and perseverance which evinced the correctness of his judgment and the benevolence of his disposition, to conciliate the aborigines of the territory. But all the efforts of the governor, as well as of other humane individuals in the colony, to effect the permanent civilization of that miserable people, proved utterly abortive. There was no difficulty in inducing individuals of their number, particularly the young, to reside for a time in European families, and to acquire the habits and learn the arts of civilization; but sooner or later they uniformly rejoined the other children of the forest, and resumed the habits of savage life. Bennelong, an intelligent native of some consequence in his tribe, had been domesticated in the governor's family, and could acquit himself at table with the utmost propriety. On returning to England, Captain Philip carried him along with him, and introduced him, as an interesting specimen of the aborigines of the colony, in many of the highest circles in the mother country. On returning, however, to his native land, Bennelong speedily divested himself of his European attire, and rejoined his tribe as a naked savage, apparently unimproved in the least degree by his converse with civilized man.

"In the year 1788 the number of the aborigines inhabiting the shores of Port Jackson was very considerable. A disease, however, somewhat resembling the small-pox, which appears to have prevailed among them to a great extent shortly after the establishment of the colony, thinned their ranks very sensibly, and left only a comparatively small number to inherit the invaded patrimony of their forefathers. Numerous dead bodies were, from time to time, found by the colonists in all directions in the vicinity of the harbour, in the very attitude in which the wretched individuals had died, when abandoned by their tribe from fear of the pestilence. Besides, the natives could not be supposed so utterly devoid of understanding as not to perceive that the occupation of their country by white men was likely to diminish their means of subsistence. 'White fellow come,' said an intelligent black native of a tribe residing beyond the Blue Mountains a few years ago—'White fellow come, kangaroo all gone!' This impression, heightened to madness, as it must often have been, by the positive aggressions of the convicts, led not unfrequently, in the earlier years of the colony, to the desultory and abortive, but murderous, efforts of savage warfare....But the vicious example of the convict population of the colony has already done much more to extinguish the miserable remnant of this degraded race, in all the more populous districts of the territory, than could have been effected, in a much longer series of years, by the united agency of war and famine and pestilential disease!

"It seems, indeed, to be a general appointment of Divine Providence, that the Indian wigwam of North America and the miserable bark-hut of the aborigines of New Holland should be utterly swept away by the flood-tide of European colonization; or, in other words, that races of uncivilized men should gradually disappear before the progress of civilization in those countries that have been taken possession of by Europeans. Humanity may interpose for a season, for the preservation of savage man, and the Christian missionary may endeavour, successfully perhaps in some instances, to raise him from the darkness and the slavery of heathenism to the light and liberty of the gospel; but European vice and demoralization will, even in free colonies, ere long infallibly produce a rich harvest of misery and death among the choicest flowers of the forest; and the miserable remnant of a once hopeful race will at length gradually disappear from the land of their forefathers, like the snow from the summits of the mountains on the approach of spring!"

In Malthus's Essay on Population* will be found a character of the

* Book i., chap. iii.

New Hollanders, founded on Cook's narrative and on Collin's "Account of New South Wales," coinciding in all important particulars with the foregoing.

The NEW ZEALANDER rises above the New Hollander. The size

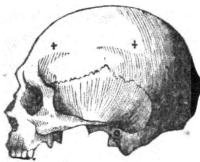

of the brain is pretty nearly the same as that of the European, but the great predominance of size is in the region of the propensities. The anterior lobe is larger than in the New Hollander, but less than in the European, while the coronal region above Cautiousness is broad, but extremely shallow. The character which this head indicates is one moderately intellectual, of considerable energy, cruel, cunning; cautious, vain, and decidedly deficient in Benevolence, Veneration, and Conscientiousness. Mr. Earle describes them as active, shrewd, and intelligent. They toil by hundreds in their forests, hewing wood for the European dock-yards established on their coast. They cultivate potatoes and Indian corn, imitate the houses built by the English, decorate the interior of them with paintings and carvings, not inferior to what is found among some of the elder labours of the Egyptians. The chiefs do not consider labour disgraceful. They are exceedingly handsome. They murdered their female infants in great numbers, until they discovered that Europeans prized their young women. They roast and eat, not only their enemies, but occasionally one of themselves. Mr. Earle saw a female slave killed for running away, roasted, and eaten. "Nine months' residence in New Zealand in 1827," pp. 10. 243.

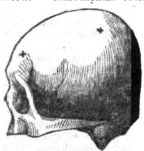

The skull of a NORTH AMERICAN INDIAN is high from the ear upward, and short from the front to the back. The forehead is not largely developed, while Firmness, Secretiveness, and Cautiousness are very prominently enlarged; as is also Destructiveness. Adhesiveness and Concentrativeness, especially the latter, are small. The society possesses only two casts of skulls of this tribe, and their general form and appearance are alike. It is impossible to draw any safe inference from so limited a collection, yet it may be worth while to notice their character, for the purpose of inducing travellers to attend to their cerebral developement in their future descriptions. As the North American Indians extend over an immense territory, it is probable that they consist of a variety of tribes; in which case we must expect to find considerable differences in their skulls. A general character, nevertheless, appears to pervade them.

"To flee from an adversary that is on his guard, and to avoid a contest where he cannot contend without risk to his own person, and consequently to his community, is the point of honour with the American. The odds of ten to one are necessary to warrant an attack on a person who is armed and prepared to resist, and even then each is afraid of being the first to advance. The great object of the most renowned warrior is, by every art of cunning and deceit, by every mode of stratagem and surprise that his invention can suggest, to weaken and destroy the tribes of his enemies with the least possible loss to his own. To meet an enemy on equal terms is regarded as extreme folly. To fall in battle, instead of being reckoned an honourable death, is a misfortune which subjects the memory of the warrior to the imputation of rashness and imprudence.   But to lie in war day after day, till he can rush upon his prey when most secure and least able to resist him ; to steal in the dead of night upon his enemies, set fire to their huts, and massacre the inhabitants as they flee naked and defenceless from the flames, are deeds of glory which will be of deathless memory in the breasts of his grateful countrymen."*

To this description it may be added, that these savages possess insuperable determination : when the fate of war has placed one of them in the power of his enemies, he knows that the most dreadful tortures await him ; but the point of honour then is to set the malignity of his tormentors at defiance, and to surpass in his powers of endurance the utmost limits of their barbarous inflictions of pain. The American savage, besides, as already noticed, has rarely been found a member of settled society, but has continued a wanderer since the sun first rose upon him in his deserts till the present day. Even contact with Europeans, surrounded by arts and enlightened by intelligence, has scarcely communicated one iota of improvement to this miserable race. When Europe has been conquered, the victorious and the vanquished have in a few ages amalgamated together, been blended into one, and have at last formed a single and united people. The native Americans have, on the contrary, uniformly receded before the Europeans ; and even in those states of the Union in which their privileges are equal with those of the whites, they rarely rise above the dignity of a barber or a shoe-black.

The exact coincidence between the developement of these skulls and the character of this people would lead us to suppose that they represent the national shape. The general size is greatly inferior to that of the average European head ; indicating inferiority in natural mental power.   The combination of Destructiveness, Secretiveness, Cautiousness, and Firmness corresponds remarkably with their timid, cunning, persevering ferocity ; while their deficiency in the moral organs, and in Concentrativeness and Adhesiveness, would account for the looseness of their social and patriotic relations.

A similar description of the American Indians is given by Timothy Flint, in his " Recollections of Ten years' Residences and Journeyings in the Valley of the Mississippi." " I have conversed," says he, " with many travellers that have been over the Stony Mountains, into the great missionary settlements of St. Peter and St. Paul. These travellers, and some of them were professed Catholics, unite in affirming, that the converts will escape from the mission whenever it is in their power, fly into their native deserts, and resume at once their old modes of life. The vast empire of the Jesuits in Paraguay has all passed away, and we are told the descendants of their convert Indians are nowise distinguished from the other savages. It strikes me that Christianity is the religion of civilized man ; that the savages must first be civilized, and that as there is little hope that the present generation of Indians can be civilized, there is but little more that they will be Christianized," p. 145. These testimonies are all confirmed, and the developement of brain is described from actual observations, by Dr. Caldwell, in the following terms :† " The aborigines of North America are to be regarded, I think, as a variety of the Mongolian race. Certainly they are not of the Caucasian. In the course of my tour I had an opportunity of examining and measuring the heads of six nations or tribes of that unfortunate family of men.

" In the city of Washington were deputations of chiefs from the Cherokee, the Creek, and the Seminole nations ; and in the state of New

* Malthus on Pop., B. i., ch. iv.
† *Phrenological Journal*, vol. iv., p. 191.

York I visited the dwellings of the Oneidas, the Tuscaroras, and the Senekas.

"Without going into *details*, I can state only the *result* of my observations and admeasurements, which were often repeated in presence of intelligent and competent witnesses.

"The average size of the head of the Indian is less than that of the head of the *white man*, by the proportion of from an eighth to a tenth, *certainly from a* tenth *to a* twelfth part of its entire bulk. The chief deficiency in the Indian head lies in the superior and lateral parts of the forehead, where are situated the organs of Comparison, Causality, Wit, Ideality, and Benevolence. The defect in Causality, Wit, and Ideality is most striking. In the organs of Combativeness, Destructiveness, Secretiveness, Caution, and Firmness, the functions of which constitute the dominant elements of the Indian character, the developement is bold. The proportion of brain behind the ear is considerably larger in the Indian than in the white man. The organ of Adhesiveness in the former is small.

"This analysis, brief and imperfect as it is, unfolds to us much of the philosophy of the Indian character, and enables us, in a particular manner, to understand the cause of the peculiar inaptitude of that race of men for civil life. For, when the wolf, the buffalo, and the panther shall have been completely domesticated, like the dog, the cow, and the household cat, then, and not before, may we expect to see the *full-blooded* Indian civilized like the white man.

"Of the mixed breed, which is very numerous, the cerebral developement and the general character approach those of the white man in proportion to the degree of white blood which individuals possess. On account of the marked superiority of his intellect, a *half-bred* seldom fails to become a *chief.*

"A chief of the Creek nation, who, on account of his pre-eminence in eloquence, held the appointment of orator of the delegation, surpassed, in a high degree, all the others in the developement of the organs of Ideality and Comparison. His addresses were replete with *metaphor*, and, for an uneducated speaker, marked with *taste.*

"Of the *full-blooded* Indians generally, permit me to remark, that such is their *entire unfitness for civilization*, that every successive effort to mould them to that condition of life more and more deteriorates their character. Of the *mixed*-bloods this is not true. Hence, the only efficient scheme to civilize the Indians is, to *cross the breed.* Attempt any other, and *you will extinguish the race.* To the truth of this the experience of every day bears ample testimony. The real aboriginal Indian is retreating before civilization, and disappearing with the buffalo and the elk, the panther and the grizly bear. Let the benevolent and enthusiastic missionary say what he may, the *forest* is the *natural home* of the Indian. Remove him from it, and, like the imprisoned elephant, he loses the strength and loftiness of his character. He becomes a hot-house plant, and dwindles in all his native efficiencies. This *problem* (for so by many it is considered) is solved *only*, but can be solved *easily*, by the lights of Phrenology. On this position it is my purpose to dwell more fully hereafter.

"The wisdom of Providence is manifested in the innumerable aptitudes of things that everywhere present themselves, and in none more clearly than in those which concern the human family. The vast American wilderness, the haunt of the deer and the elk, the bear and the buffalo, required a race of savages to people it. But converted, as it already is, in part, and rapidly as that conversion is daily extending into cultivated fields and populous towns and cities, the abode of civilization, commerce, and the arts, the mere *man of the forest* is no longer wanted, and he is, therefore, passing away. He has flourished—he was needed; but he is needed no longer, and he therefore decays."

The head of the BRAZIL INDIAN bears some resemblance to the former. The deficiency in Size is the same, indicating natural inferiority of mind, and the combination of organs is similar, only Firmness is not so great, and Concentrativeness and Philoprogenitiveness are moderate. The dimensions are annexed in the table.

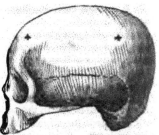

It is known that the Jesuits attempted to civilize a number of these tribes, and that, by humane and intelligent treatment, they acquired a great moral ascendency over them, induced them to settle, and established something like order and the arts of social life among them. If their brains had possessed the European developement; the seeds of improvement, sown and fostered for years by a protecting hand, would have sprung up, flourished vigorously, and produced an abundant harvest of permanent civilization; but the picture is precisely the reverse. "It must be admitted," (says the reviewer of Koster's Travels in Brazil,) "that Mr. Koster's representation of the Indians is by no means favourable; and the opinions which he expresses are of the more weight, because, as his feelings and principles are of the best kind, they load him always to judge charitably, and to look forward with hope. Infinitely meliorated as the condition of the Indians has been, theirs is still no very desirable state of existence; they are always regarded as children, and not always treated as they were by the Jesuits, with paternal kindness. But when they escape they show little capability of acting for themselves, and an evident tendency (as if instinctive) to return to a wandering and savage life: it does not arise from any feeling connected with the love of their ancestors, nor a tradition of their free state; they do not appear to know that their ancestors had been slaves, much less would any knowledge be preserved of their anterior state. The Indian who has escaped from control scarcely ever plants for himself—if he does, he sells the growing crop for half its value, and removes to some other district; fishing and hunting are his favourite pursuits, and he is never stationary for any length of time, unless it be near a lake or a rivulet." The strangest and worst part of their character is their want of natural affection—an old charge against them, which Mr. Koster's unexceptionable testimony confirms. "They appear," he says, "to be less anxious for the life and welfare of their children than any other race of men who inhabit that country."

These observations present the most fertile field of speculation to the phrenologists. The cast of the Brazil Indian shows a deficiency in size compared with the European; and hence it corresponds with the fact, that these Indians are regarded and treated as children, that they are destitute of foresight, and of that degree of steadiness of purpose which pursues a remote advantage through numerous intervening obstacles. When an adult individual is treated as a child, this is not done by his parents or guardians out of perversity, but because his inferiority in intellectual power is perceived both by him and them, although this may not be stated in so many words as the reason of his being subjected to guidance. When strength of mind appears, we are constrained by the very laws of our constitution to treat the possessor with respect, however infantine in bodily stature, or limited in point of age. Were the Indians, therefore, equal in their natural energies to Europeans, they would soon, by dint of this mental power, acquire their knowledge and accomplishments, and, instead of being their slaves, would become their rivals.

These Indians, however, have derived some improvement from education, although it has not supplied the defect of native energy. "If education has hitherto done little in implanting good qualities, it has done much in eradicating evil ones. They were among the fiercest and most revengeful of the human race; they are now quiet and inoffensive, rarely committing murder, (in a country where murder is accounted venial, and generally obtains impunity, if not applause;) and even those who are dishonest confine themselves to pilfering."

Mr. Koster draws the following comparison between the negro and the Brazil Indian: "The negro character," says he, "is more decided; it is worse, but it is also better." "The Indian seems to be without energy or exertion, equally incapable great evil or of great good. Rich mulattoes and negroes are not uncommon; there is no instance of a wealthy Indian, nor did he ever see an Indian mechanic. The priesthood is open to them, but to little purpose. Mr. Koster heard of only two Indians who were ordained as priests, and both died of excessive drinking."

It would be interesting to know whether the native Mexican brain is better developed, for a rude form of society existed in Mexico before the European conquest.

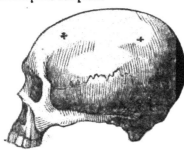

The skull of the NEGRO evidently rises in the scale of developement of the moral and intellectual organs: the forehead is higher, and the organs of the sentiments bear a larger proportion to those of the propensities, than in the New Hollander. The organs of Philoprogenitiveness and Concentrativeness are largely developed; the former of which produces the love of children, and the latter that concentration of mind which is favourable to settled and sedentary employments. The organs of Veneration and Hope also are considerable in size. The greatest deficiencies lie in Conscientiousness, Cautiousness, Ideality, and Reflection. The dimensions of this skull are given in the table.

Timothy Flint says, "The negro, easily excitable, in the highest degree susceptible of all the passions, is more especially so of the mild and gentle affections. To the Indian, stern, silent, moody, ruminating, existence seems a burden. To the negro, remove only pain and hunger, it is naturally a state of enjoyment. As soon as his toils are for a moment suspended, he sings, he seizes his fiddle, he dances."

The different tribes which inhabit Africa present very different appearances in point of civilization; but none of them have made so great a progress as the European nations. I have been informed by persons who have been long resident in the West India Islands, that great differences are observed in the natural talents of the negroes, according to the provinces from which they have been brought. Some parts of Africa yield persons capable of becoming excellent operative mechanics; others, clerks and accountants; and some mere labourers, incapable of any intellectual attainment. It would be extremely interesting to learn in what respect they differ in the forms of their heads.

Some nations of Africa greatly surpass others in energy of character and mechanical skill. "The Caffres are entirely black, but bear no trace of the negro features. In the form of their skull and face they differ little from the most perfect Europeans." This race is ingenious in several arts; but, on account of their constant wars, agriculture is in a depressed state. Although their coast is covered with excellent fish, they do not catch them, and indeed have no boats nor canoes Marriage is invariably conducted by sale. The Boshuans are represented as "gay, gentle, and

peaceable " in their manners ; yet they "carry on war as fiercely as all
other barbarians.   Mr. Campbell having, in the course of religious instruction, asked one of them, 'for what end was man made,' the answer
was, 'for plundering expeditions.' "*   Mr. Bowditch gives an account
of the Ashantees, by which it appears that they display great activity and
considerable ingenuity of mind ; but that they are debased by the most
ferocious dispositions and the grossest superstition.   The descriptions
given by a variety of travellers of Timbuctoo, and of the commerce carried
on upon the Niger by the natives of Africa, if they can be at all depended
upon, also indicate considerable scope of mind and some capacity for the
social state, and place the Africans decidedly above the native Americans.
all these facts coincide with the expectations which a phrenologist would
form, on examining their different skulls.

One feature is very general in descriptions of the African tribes ; they
are extremely superstitious.   They purchase *fetiches*, or charms, at a
high price, and believe them to be sure preservatives against all the evils
of life.   This character corresponds with the developement which we
observe in the negro skulls ; for they exhibit much Hope, Veneration, and
Wonder, with comparatively little reflecting power.   Their defective
Causality incapacitates them for tracing the relation of cause and effect,
and their great Veneration, Hope, and Wonder render them prone to
credulity, and to regard, with profound admiration and respect, any object
which is represented as possessing supernatural power.

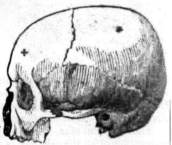

The heads of the SANDWICH
ISLANDERS are under, rather than
equal, to the average size of the European ; and the race certainly does not
indicate so high a natural character as
the European, although closely approaching to it.   The Phrenological
Society possesses five skulls of the
Sandwich Islanders.   They are characterized by the long form of the European—the Caucasian variety of Blumenbach ; and by a greater proportion lying
before than behind the external orifice of the ear.   This is remarkable
particularly in two of the skulls.   The coronal region is broad and tolerably well developed, but not equal in height above Cautiousness and
Causality to the European.   The anterior lobe, manifesting the intellect,
is pretty well developed, being decidedly larger than that of the negro,
American Indians, and New Hollanders.   All of them have a considerable portion of Eventuality, a faculty which Dr. Gall long ago denominated
Educability, and which must greatly expedite civilization.   Three of the
skulls are decidedly ancient, and, having been obtained from the older
Morais or burial-places, probably afford correct specimens of the heads
of the aboriginal inhabitants, before the islands were discovered by Captain Cook.   This navigator found this race very superior to most of the
other savage tribes which he visited.   Their advance toward civilization
is evinced by their respectful reception of the bodies of their king and
queen, who had died in London—by the appearance of their chiefs in English mourning—by their procession to the church, and the high improvement conspicuous in the whole community—circumstances which have
been noticed by the public papers, and are given more in detail in a narrative of the voyage of the Blonde Frigate to the Sandwich Islands, published in the year 1826.†

* Leyden and Murray's Historical Account of Discoveries and Travels in
Africa, vol. ii., pp. 332, 350.   † A more particular account of the
Sandwich Islanders will be found in the Phrenological Journal, vol. iii., p. 421.

SWISS SKULL.

The brains of the EUROPEAN NATIONS differ considerably from each other, but a common type characterizes them all, and distinguishes them from those now described. They are decidedly larger than the Hindoo, American Indian, and negro heads; and this indicates superior force of mental character. The portion before the ear, connected with the intellectual faculties, and the coronal region, or the organs of the moral sentiments, are more amply developed in proportion to the base and posterior inferior parts of the brain, or the organs of the animal propensities. In short, they indicate a higher natural power of reflection, and a greater natural tendency to justice, benevolence, veneration, and refinement, than the others. The organs in which the European brain in an especial degree excels are, Ideality, Conscientiousness, Causality, and Wit. The organs of these faculties are almost invariably small in barbarous and savage tribes. The European skull belongs to the Caucasian variety of Blumenbach, which he considers as the most beautiful and perfect of all the national crania in the world; and in this point he and the phrenologists agree. The cut represents a Swiss skull, which is very favourably developed in the region of the moral sentiments. If the space above the asterisks, Cautiousness and Causality, be compared with the same region in the New Zealander or New Hollander, a very marked inferiority in the latter will be observed.

The ANCIENT EGYPTIANS appear, from the stupendous monuments of arts and science left behind them, to have been a highly intelligent and civilized people: and it is a striking fact, that the skulls of ancient mummies almost invariably belong to the same class with those of modern Europeans. In the society's collection there are two skulls of mummies, five casts of the skulls of mummies, and I have seen or obtained accurate descriptions of the skulls of half a dozen more: full size, full developement of the anterior lobe, and broad coronal region characterize them all. The coronal region, however, is not high, and this is the point in which their inferiority to modern European skulls chiefly consists.

The society possesses also several skulls of ANCIENT GREEKS. They are large, and exhibit a favourable developement of the coronal region and intellect, combined with large organs of the propensities. In

ANCIENT GREEK.

particular, the organs of Constructiveness and Ideality are large, and in this respect they form as striking a contrast to the skulls of the New Hollanders, as the hovels of the latter do to the temples and works of art of the Greeks.

These facts appear to indicate that, when nations are independent, and left at liberty to follow the bent of their own judgments and dispositions, their institutions spring from the peculiar mental constitutions which they have respectively received from nature, and that this constitution is in accordance with the developement of their brains. Climate and other external causes modify, to some extent, the effects of natural endowment, but the distinguishing features of each people seem to bear a more direct and uniform relation to the size and form of their brain, than to those adventitious circumstances. When a people is subjugated by a foreign power, as the Greeks by the Turks, and the Italians by the Austrians, the national character has no adequate opportunity of unfolding its peculiarities ; and hence, if this circumstance be overlooked, the same race may seem to present different characteristics at different periods of their history. The modern Greeks, it was lately said, no more resemble their ancestors than the Hindoos the Europeans ; and this was urged as an insuperable objection against Phrenology. Now, however, when the Turkish yoke is loosened, so as to allow the native qualities to shoot, we see the same force of character, the same deliberate and determined heroism, the same capacity for stratagem in war, all the fickleness and proneness to dissension, and the same ascendency of passion which distinguished the Greeks in the days of Pericles, reappearing in their descendants. Many millions of Hindoos, Africans, and American Indians have been for ages independent of a foreign yoke, and never displayed qualities such as those exhibited by independent Europeans.

he effects of temperament are distinguishable in national skulls. The grain of the New Holland skulls is extremely rough and coarse ; that of the Hindoos fine, smooth, and compact, more closely resembling ivory ; the Swiss skulls are open and soft in the grain, while the Greek are close and finer. There would be a corresponding quality of brain in the individuals, which would influence the mental character.

The Phrenological Society have more specimens of national skulls than are there noticed. They afford interesting materials for philosophical reflection, but the great length to which this work has extended compels me to omit the notice of them.

	From Philoprogenitiveness to Individuality	From Concentrativeness to Comparison	From Ear to Philoprogenitiveness	From Ear to Individuality	From Ear to Firmness	From Ear to Benevolence	From Destructiveness to Destructiveness	From Secretiveness to Secretiveness	From Cautiousness to Cautiousness	From Ideality to Ideality
	Inch	Inch	Inch	Inch	Inch	Inch	Inch	Inch	Inch	Inch
Hindoo, ...	6¼	6¼	3¾	4	4¾	5¼	4¾	5	5¼	4
Charib, ...	7¼	5¼	4¼	4¼	5¼	4¼	5¼	5¼	5¼	4
New Hollander, . . .	7¼	5¼	5	4¼	5½	4¼	5	5	4¼	4
Negro, ...	7½	7	4¼	4½	5½	*	4¼	5	5¼	4
American Indian, . .	6¼	5	3¼	4½	5¼	5¼	4¼	5¼	5¼	4
Brazil Indian, . . .	6¾	5¼	3¾	4¼	4¼	4¼	4¼	4¼	5	4
Swiss, ...	6¾	6¼	4	4½	5¼	5¼	5¼	5¾	5¼	4
Ancient Greek, . . .	7	6¼	4¼	4¾	5¼	5¼	5¼	5¾	5¼	4
Sandwich Islander, . .	7	6¼	4	4½	5	4¼	5	5¼	5¼	4
Mummy, ...	7¼	6¾	4¼	4½	5¼	5¼	5¼	5¼	5¼	4

* Five and one-tenth.

The measurements in the foregoing table do not represent the size of any organs in particular, for the reasons stated on p. 94. They are intended to indicate whether the skulls are large or small. They do not, however, accomplish this object successfully, in consequence of the impossibility of measuring irregular spheres by diameters. They are, therefore, indications merely of the length of the particular lines stated in the different skulls ; from which a rough estimate of the relative dimensions of the skulls may be formed. A scientific mode of measurement is much wanted. These measurements are taken from individual skulls, and annot be given as an exact statement of the average of the different ational crania. They are, however, an approximation to truth, and are ufficient to show the interest of the investigation. The collection is still too limited to enable us to draw average results. The negro skull is a eay favourable specimen, and the Swiss is rather above an average.

The real characters of foreign nations will never be philosophically elineated, until travellers shall describe their temperaments, and the size nd combinations of their brains. Blumenbach's extensive work on National Crania is destitute of moral interest, owing to his omission of all notice of the characters of the nations whose heads he represents.

Dr. Vimont, in his *Traité de Phrenologie*,* has a valuable chapter on national heads, in which he describes, among others, the characteristic features of the German, French, and English heads and nations with great accuracy. He pronounces an eloquent eulogium on the Scotch character,[†] which derives a greater value from the unprejudiced and enlightened spirit in which he speaks of his own, the English, and other nations. He regrets that he is not informed concerning the Scotch and Irish developements of brain. In *The Phrenological Journal*, vol. ii., p. 169, some observations on the Irish head are recorded. We invite him to come to Scotland, and form his own judgment of our national heads. The SCOTCH lowland population, which has done everything by which Scotland is distinguished, excepting in the department of war, is a mixed race of Celts and Saxons. The long head of the Celts is combined with the large reflecting and moral organs which characterize the Germans. The following is an average specimen of the Scotch lowland head :

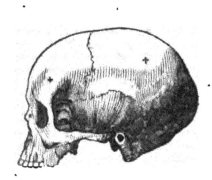
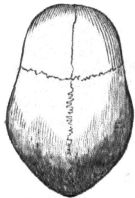

The SCOTCH lowland head is rather large ; and considerable variety of temperament exists among the people In the labouring classes the lymphatic and nervous, with an infusion of the bilious, temperament is very common ; the hair is of a sandy colour, the skin pale, the figure heavy, but the eyes are blue and clear. The individuals are capable of long enduring efforts. The organs of Amativeness are considerable, and Philoprogenitiveness and Adhesiveness large : and domestic attachment is a striking characteristic of the race. Combativeness and Destructiveness are generally large, and the people are irascible, fond of war, and addicted to the worst species of mischief, the wanton destruction of objects of utility and ornament. They are also not particularly merciful to the lower animals. The organs of Secretiveness, Cautiousness, and Firmness are generally large ; and the Scotch are remarkable for prudence, *savoir-faire*, and perseverance. Self-Esteem and Love of Approbation are large, and

* Tome ii., p. 470. † *Lib. Cit.*, vol. ii., p. 490.

relatively to each other equally developed ; the consequence of which is
that the Scotch stand in the middle line between the English and the
French in regard to these faculties. In the English Self-Esteem predominates, and their vices are pride and egotism. In the French the Love
of Approbation predominates, and they are prone to vanity, and show a
deficiency of dignity and self-respect. The Scotch, with equal Self-
Esteem with the English, temper its manifestations by Love of Appro-
tion, and present a mitigated egotism that is not offensive to foreigners.
With Love of Approbation equal to the French, but restrained by a large
Self-Esteem, Cautiousness, and Secretiveness, they present a more dignified and reserved politeness. The organs of Acquisitiveness are generally
large in the Scotch, and, taken in connexion with large Self-Esteem. the
result is a strong infusion of selfishness, or at least of attention to self-
interest. Aided by Cautiousness, Secretiveness, Firmness, and the moral
and intellectual organs, this combination leads them to general success.
when placed in competition with other nations, in the career of wealth.
and explains the extraordinary rapidity with which Scotland acquired capital when the markets of England and its colonies were opened to her industry. In the Scotch head the organs of Benevolence, Veneration. and
Wonder are generally largely developed : large Conscientiousness is
common, but not nearly so prevalent as these, and Hope in general is
only moderately developed. The combination of Adhesiveness, Benevolence, Conscientiousness, and Firmness gives the Scotch an attached,
faithful, and trust-worthy character. The combination of Veneration.
Wonder, and Conscientiousness renders them religious, but their great
Destructiveness, Cautiousness, and Firmness give a dark and stern character to their faith. They are sincere and ardent in their religious impressions, and cannot conceive the possibility of any form of belief being
acceptable to God except their own. They are, in consequence, regarded,
by the other European nations, as bigoted and intolerant ; but this character, in so far as justly attributable to them, is the result rather of an
undoubting sincerity in their own belief, than of feebleness of intellect or
deficiency of generous sentiment. The enlightenment of the understanding
of the people will correct these errors. The organs of Ideality and Imitation are only moderately developed in the Scotch, and they are not remarkable for quickness in adopting new modes, nor for refinement. They
are a homely people. The anterior lobe of the brain devoted to intellect is
generally well developed. The organs of Individuality, Form, and Constructiveness, however, are relatively deficient. Hence the Scotch do not
excel in precise knowledge of details, nor in the fine arts. The organs
of Time are larger than those of Tune, and the national music presents a combination of a few notes generally expressive of boldness,
affection, tenderness, or melancholy, formed into simple melodies strongly
marked by time. They have little genius for the pleasures of refined
harmony. The organs of Colouring are in general only moderately developed, and it is often remarked, that, in their selections of colours, in
furniture, dress, and ornaments, the Scotch are by no means successful.
Order and Number are tolerably large, and the national character is
orderly and calculating. The organs of Language are moderate in size :
Eventuality and Comparison are generally full, and Causality is frequently met with large. Causality is more frequently larger than Comparison
in the Scotch head than in those of the English and French : Concentrativeness is generally large. Wit is full, though not large. The combination of deficient Form and Individuality, with large Concentrativeness,
Comparison, and Causality, accounts for the Scotch intellect being speculative and analytic, rather than given to observation in philosophy. The
intellect of the Scotch appears in their music : their national melodies,

with much simplicity, display great completeness: every note hangs on another by necessary connexion, so that it could not be separated without deranging the whole. There is no incongruity. Each melody is a system. This combination of intellectual organs, joined with large moral organs, gives them that love of moral and metaphysical disquisition which distinguishes them; while it explains also their singular want of practical observation in their mental science. Reid, Stewart, and Brown knew enough of Bacon's rules of philosophizing to be aware of the necessity of facts, as the foundation of all science; but they were so little given to practical observation, that they looked only into their own minds, and not at the external world, for their data in regard to the qualities of human nature. They in consequence missed the facts which most forcibly strike a practical observer, viz., the existence of such propensities as Combativeness, Destructiveness, Acquisitiveness, and Cautiousness; and the immense differences between individuals in the strength of particular faculties in relation to the others. In the study of Phrenology this combination of intellectual faculties is conspicuous. How much of reasoning in proportion to accurately described facts do Scotch journals and works in general contain! The combination of full Wit with large Secretiveness accounts for the Scotch being famed for practical humour. Sir Walter Scott's works give many just representations of the national character, in this particular. The people are not destitute of Wit also, and, when placed in favourable circumstances, manifest it with considerable effect. When Dr. Spurzheim was in Scotland, he remarked, that the Scotch needed only a higher temperament to become one of the first nations in Europe.

I shall now present to the reader a few of Dr. Vimont's observations on national character. He describes the *German* head, of which Dr. Spurzheim's skull, represented on p. 401, is a correct, although favourable, specimen, in the following terms: "The regions of the reflective faculties, of Cautiousness, and of the moral sentiments are all largely developed, Veneration and Benevolence in particular are well marked. The perceptive faculties considered generally, with the exception of Tune, are moderately developed. The organs of Ideality, Constructiveness, and Gustativeness are often very prominent; Secretiveness and Self-Esteem are also very conspicuously large.

"The French head is smaller than the German. The region of the perceptive faculties is generally larger, while the organs of reflection are smaller, in the French than in the Germans. The organs of Tune and Number are larger in the Germans. The French are generally deficient in the organs of Cautiousness. The organs of Individuality, of Colour, and Form are generally large in the French, as also those of Comparison, Wit, Wonder, and Poetry. The organs of Constructiveness, Imitation, and of the sense of the beautiful in the arts are also large in them, particularly the last two. "The organ of Love of Approbation or vanity generally predominates. Benevolence is well developed; but Veneration, Self-Esteem, and Firmness are not so. The inhabitants of Normandy and Brittany form exceptions in regard to the last two named faculties. Born in Normandy, and having in consequence had occasion to examine a great number of the heads of the inhabitants of this province, I am convinced that Self-Esteem and Firmness are largely developed in them. Among the Bretons Firmness is often very large, but the head is in general not so high as in the Normans."

Dr. Vimont adds, "It is conceivable that, among a population exceeding thirty millions, and in a territory presenting upward of 26,000 square leagues, remarkable varieties of organization should be met with. It would be desirable that they were studied in the principal provinces of which

France is composed. Regarded in a philosophical and phrenological point of view, they could not fail to prove interesting to persons who occupy themselves with science, and to present results of incalculable value to those who are at the head of the government.

"I cannot avoid citing on this occasion some remarks of one of our most distinguished men, Baron Charles Dupin, because they relate directly to the subject in hand. Of all the provinces of France, those of the north are most remarkable, on account of their superior industry and intelligence. Almost all manufactured articles come from the north. The number of primary schools is more considerable in the north than in the south. Of 1933 pupils admitted into the Polytechnic school during thirteen consecutive years, 1233 were furnished by the departments of the north, while the departments of the south have given only 700. Of 65 members of the Academy of Sciences, 48 come from the departments of the north, and 17 from the departments of the south. Finally, of 2112 patents for inventions delivered from the 1st of July, 1791, to the 1st of July, 1825, 1699 have been delivered to the departments of the north, and only 413 to those of the south. Such great differences, founded on observations of indisputable authenticity, deserve every attention from phrenologists.

"Let us return to the relations which exist between the predominant organs of the French and the most striking features of their moral and intellectual character. The superior developement of the reflective faculties of the Germans becomes apparent in its results. , There is perhaps no country in the world where primary instruction is more widely diffused than in Germany ; where a taste for reading is more .decided ;' and in this respect the Germans are greatly superior to the French, among whom instruction has hitherto penetrated only into the great towns. Germany abounds in thinkers and philosophers of the first order ; but it is necessary to remark that their reflective faculties, so excellent in themselves, often give to their writings a character of tediousness and obscurity, which is not met with among French authors, whose thoughts, although they often present less depth than those of the Germans, infinitely surpass them in elegance, clearness, and precision. , ,

"The great difference which exists between the developement of Firmness and Cautiousness in these two nations explains that which is observable in the spirit of their actions. The French, under the influence of moderate reflective faculties and a small developement of Cautiousness and Firmness, are light, expansive, unreserved, and easily moved. The Germans, on the other hand, are grave, tenacious, reflective, and circumspect. The want of foresight frequently shows itself in the institutions of the French ; the contrary takes place among the Germans. Napoleon, in speaking of the French, said—' the nation, in its character and tastes, is provisional and lavish ; everything for the moment and caprice—nothing for endurance ! such are the motto and manners of France ! Every one passes his life in doing and undoing ; nothing ever remains. Is it not unbecoming that Paris has not even a French theatre, nothing worthy of her destinies! I have often resisted fêtes which the city of Paris wished to. give me. These were dinners, balls, fire-works, which would have cost 4, 6, or 800,000 franks ; the preparations for which obstructed the public for several days, and which cost subsequently as much to undo them as they had cost in their construction. I proved, that with these foolish expenses they might have erected durable and magnificent monuments.' —(Las Cases, Mémoires de Sainte-Helene.)

" Duclos, in his Considerations on Manners, has represented, with great fidelity, the character of the French. 'The great defect of the French character,' says he, ' is to be always young ; by which circumstance it is often amiable, but rarely steady. It has almost no ripe manhood, but passes from youth directly to old age. Our talents of every description appear early. We neglect them for a long time by dissipation, and scarcely do we commence to turn them to account before their time is past.'

"The extreme lightness of the French, arising in part from the small developement of Cautiousness, has been signalized by Jean Jacques Rousseau. 'The French,' says this great writer, 'have a manner of interesting themselves about you which deceives more than words. The fulsome compliments of the Swiss can impose only on blockheads: the manners of the French are more seductive, because they are more simple. One would believe that they do not tell you all that they would wish to do for you, in order to cause you the more agreeable surprise. I shall say more; they are not false in their demonstrations; they are naturally officious, humane, benevolent, and even, whatever may be said on the subject, more true than any other nation; but they are volatile and light: they really feel the sentiment which they express, but that sentiment goes as it came. In the act of speaking to you they are full of interest about you. When they see you no more—they forget you. Nothing is permanent in their affections: everything with them is the work of the moment.'—(Rousseau, *Confessions*.)

"The great developement of the sense for what is fine in the arts, combined with the faculties of Form, Imitation, Ideality, and the sense of construction in general, sufficiently conspicuous in the crania of the French, explain why they are the first people in Europe for the finish and exquisite taste of their manufactured articles. There is nothing comparable to the productions of manual labour in France. It is to the same faculties that we must attribute the high superiority of the French as painters and statuaries.

"Two faculties, the organs of which are largely developed in the French, Love of Approbation and Combativeness, coincide exactly with their character. The desire of being approved—of putting itself forward, is incontestibly the portion of our nation. If this desire be united to energetic reflecting faculties, it may give rise to great results, because it operates as a spur to the other powers. If not so combined, it produces only abuses. The man who possesses only vanity, seeks by all possible means to give himself the appearance of merit and of knowledge. This accounts for that excessive love of the French for titles, for *cordons*, and all those baubles which impose on nobody but blockheads and the most superficial of mankind. To the same cause must be ascribed all those plots, those cabals, and those miserable intrigues which, in France, reign in the bosoms of all learned societies. It is the unbridled desire to be spoken about which creates the coteries, and strikes with a mortal blow every kind of honourable emulation. It would be difficult to calculate how many faults the sentiment of vanity has produced in France, and with how many misfortunes it has inundated this fine nation, which would do well, as Napoleon remarked, to exchange its vanity for pride.

"Courage, the other distinctive faculty of the French, is too well known to be insisted on. The French have already afforded every proof of bravery which a nation can exhibit.

"I have said that the sentiment of Veneration, that is to say, the faculty which disposes us to respect men and things, is little developed in the French. It is to this deficiency of developement that the want of religion, nearly general in France, falls to be attributed. To the same cause must be ascribed the destruction and neglect of a multitude of monuments, for which other nations exhibit a kind of worship. In France, and particularly in Paris, a great number of extremely curious edifices exist, known to, and venerated by, foreigners, of which the inhabitants of this capital know nothing. Speaking generally, we may say, that everything that presents a character of antiquity is displeasing to the French. The low degree of veneration, united to the great developement of the talent of discrimination, or of combination, produces among the French that love of sarcasm and of raillery which attacks all without distinction of rank, merit, or fortune. This spirit generally manifests itself under the form of caricatures, which is easily to be conceived when we attend to the great developement of the organs of Constructiveness and Form in the French.

"The great difference which exists between the French and Germans in the organs of Alimentiveness accounts for the difference between the two nations in sobriety. After the Spaniards, no nation in Europe is more sober than the French, while the Germans are essentially great feeders. Among a pretty considerable number of German, Spanish, and French soldiers, who were in the same hospital at Caen, I have observed that a remarkable difference existed among them in regard to the faculty in question. A light soup, some fruit, or a little meat were sufficient for the Spaniards; the repast of the French consisted of three-fourths of the portion; while the Germans swallowed the whole allowance, and continually complained that they did not receive enough of meat and of potatoes. Every time I happened to pass the wards where the Germans were placed, I was certain to be assailed by the words *flesh, flesh, sir!*[*]

"The organs of Wonder and Imitation, largely developed in the French, contribute to distinguish them from other nations. This combination explains why all that is new strikes them, and also their eagerness to reproduce it. Who can calculate the varieties in the forms of French dress even within a single age. These changes frequently have relation to extraordinary personages or events. From the extreme developement of Imitation in the French, their marked gesticulations arise. Every class has its own, which is peculiar to it, and every one repeats it as one learns a form of politeness. Under the influence of Imitation, Love of Approbation, and the sense of the beautiful, the French are to some extent mannerists; but with taste and ease, and without awkwardness. Although the English attempt to ridicule our nation on this account, I am satisfied that they try to imitate us, although not very successfully. Although the reflecting organs are in general only moderately developed in the French, this is not a sufficient reason for believing that only a small number of individuals of the highest order of intellect appear among them. No nation in Europe has furnished so many men distinguished in the arts, sciences, and philosophy as France; and if we reflect that instruction is little diffused in this country, we may believe that the number of superior men would otherwise have been still more considerable." P. 487.

"During my stay in London, I went almost every Sunday to the churches. The result of my remarks may be shortly stated. Considered generally, the size of the heads of the inhabitants of London do not differ much from that of the Parisian heads :[†] in particular points the differences are very striking. In equal numbers, the reflective faculties are more developed in London than in Paris; and the same rule holds in regard to Cautiousness, Firmness, and Self-Esteem. The organ of Alimentiveness is larger in the English, and to this cause is to be ascribed their love of spirituous liquors. Drunkenness is the predominant vice of the English." Dr. Vimont quotes from Bulwer's "England and the English" the number of persons entering gin-shops within certain periods of time, and adds, "the Scotch, and particularly the Irish, appear to be greatly addicted to spirituous liquors. I have never spoken to an Irishman who has not

[*] The organ in question was little developed in the heads of five Spanish prisoners who died in France.

[†] According to my observation the London heads *are larger.*—G. C.

assured me that idleness, and particularly drunkenness, were the dominant vices of the mass of the Irish population."* P. 489.

"The organs of Number are larger, while the organs of Constructiveness, Form, and of beauty in the arts are smaller in the English than in the French." P. 490.

The Phrenological Journal, vol. viii., pp. 389 and 424, contains a valuable Essay, by Mr. Robert Cox, on the character of the Esquimaux, illustrated by figures of their skulls. In that work a variety of additional illustrations of the relation between national character and natural developement of brain will be found.

ON THE IMPORTANCE OF INCLUDING DEVELOPEMENT OF BRAIN AS AN ELEMENT IN STATISTICAL INQUIRIES INTO THE MANIFESTATIONS OF THE ANIMAL, MORAL, AND INTELLECTUAL FACULTIES OF MAN.

THE European public has recently taken a great and commendable interest in moral statistics; and in France several valuable works have been published on the subject. I have perused, with much interest, the "Essai sur la Statistique Morale de la France, par Mons. A. M. Guerry,"[†] and Mons. Quetelet's work "Sur L'Homme et le développement de ses facultés, ou Essai de Physique Sociale."[‡] The object of all works on moral statistics should be to bring to light the causes of human happiness and misery, with a view to enable mankind to increase the former and diminish the latter. Tables showing the average weight and strength of the body at different ages; the average weight of children of different ages employed in manufactures compared with that of children not so employed; the average strength of men and women at different ages; the number of beats of the heart and of inspirations of the lungs in a minute; and other similar facts, all founded on observations made on numerous individuals, and reduced to average results, are interesting and useful, because the facts brought to light may direct the efforts of society in devising circumstances calculated to promote the increase of valuable qualities, and to abate that of tendencies which are injurious. But great difficulties present themselves when an estimate is attempted to be made, in a similar way, of the moral and intellectual qualities of man, founded on mental manifestations alone, without reference to the cerebral developement of the individuals observed. Mons. Quetelet, for example, in pursuing his inquiries into the developement of the moral and intellectual qualities of man, presents tables of the number of plays of the first rank produced by authors of different ages in France and in England; tables of the numbers of insane facts in relation to the population in several countries of Europe; tables of the numbers of suicides; of men who have fallen in duels; and of criminals. He exhibits also in his tables the influence of Education, of Professions, of Seasons, of Climates, and of Sex on the tendency to crime; but a few remarks will suffice to show the insufficiency of this information to lead to practical results, when the laws of organization in relation to the brain are not taken into account.

* Idleness is the misfortune, not the fault, of the mass of the Irish people. The country is occupied by a dense population belonging to the lower ranks, reared on small patches of land, and it is nearly destitute of capital, of manufactures, and of middle and higher classes; the consequence of which is, that the great body of the Irish people cannot get work, although anxious to obtain it. They are idle of necessity, therefore, and not from inclination. When they come to England or Scotland, and obtain employment, they are extremely active and industrious labourers.—G. C.

† Paris, 1832.   ‡ Paris, 1835.

The following table, for example, represents the number of insane : relation to the whole population in several countries in Europe :

Countries.	Population.	Insane.	Numbers of the Population to each Insane.
Norway, ...	1,051,318	1,900	551
England, ...	12,700,000	16,222	783
Wales, ...	817,148	896	911
Scotland, (1825,)	2,093,454	3,652	573
New York, (1821,). . . .	1,606,458	2,240	721
France, (approximation,) . .	30,000,000	30,000	1,000

"In Norway," continues M. Quetelet, "the idiots constitute one-third of the total number of the insane, and one-half in Scotland and Wales It is the great number of idiots which renders the number of insane : Scotland so large compared with the number in England. It is genen : observed that in the mountains there are more idiots than in the plains and in plains devoted to agriculture there are more idiots than in cities In France and New York the number of idiots is inconsiderable."

The superabundance of idiots in Norway and Scotland may be sup posed to be owing to a variety of causes : 1st, To the coldness and damp ness of the climate. The remedy for this would be draining and improv ing the soil, building warmer houses, and providing better clothing for the people. Or, 2dly, To the imperfect nourishment of the people. To remove this cause, we should prescribe the introduction of capital and industry. Or, 3dly, To the intermarriages of near relations for success: generations, arising from a thin population scattered over a great extent of territory. To remedy this evil, instruction of the people in the functions and laws of health of the brain would be necessary, with the inculcation of the duty of their extending the sphere of their alliances Railroads and steam-boats, by extending the circle of social intercourse, may tend to remove this cause.

That this last, is probably one great cause of the evil may be inferred from the following facts : Mr. Brown, factor to the Duke of Hamilton who had charge, for a number of years, of several of the smaller isles lying on the west coast of Scotland, told me that he found, by a census that the number of idiots, in proportion to the total population, was greater in the islands than in the main land, which he attributed to intermarriage of near relations, resulting from their insular situation. Secondly, Among the royal, noble, and aristocratical families of Europe, who frequently marry near blood-relations, idiots are generally said to be more numerous in proportion to their total numbers than among persons in the humbler ranks of life. Thirdly, The inhabitants of cities have a wider range of choice, and in general are less given to marrying with blood-relations than the inhabitants of the country ; and the fact, that fewer idiots are produced among them, supports the principle here contended for. It is not enough therefore, for practical purposes, to know the proportion of idiots to the general population. We must discover the causes of idiocy before they can be abated ; and as the brain is the organ of the mind, every one of them will be found to affect directly or indirectly its size or its condition. These statistical tables, therefore, should embrace facts relative to the size and condition of the brain in the insane, and exhibit statements of causes, physical and moral, which are known to act injuriously on its developement and activity.

In making these remarks, I am far from undervaluing the importance of the facts brought to light in the foregoing table, even regarding them merely as facts apart from any opinions regarding their causes. To know the existence and magnitude of any evil is the first step toward the means

tigation and eventual removal of its causes; and the public is deeply indebted to statistical observers for presenting the phenomena of the moral world in tangible masses, measurable by figures, and capable of being generally understood. All I intend to say is, that the size, form, and laws of action of the brain form essential elements in any rational investigation into the causes of these phenomena, with a view to remove them; and that they should not be neglected as, through their ignorance and prejudices, they have hitherto been.

The Statistics of Crime have been treated in great detail by the authors before-named. Mons. Quetelet presents us with the following table relative to Crime in France:

Year.	Accused and brought personally before the Tribunals.	Condemned.	Number of Inhabitants for each person accused.	Number condemned out of each 100 accused.	Accused of crimes against the person.	Accused of crimes against property.	Proportion.
1826,	6988	4348	4457	62	1907	5081	2.7
1827,	6929	4236	4593	61	1911	5018	2.6
1828,	7396	4551	4307	61	1844	5552	3.0
1829,	7373	4475	4321	61	1791	5582	3.1
Total,	28,666	17,610	4463	61	7453	21,233	

"Thus," says Mons. Quetelet, "although we do not yet possess the statistical returns for 1830, it is highly probable that we shall find for that year also 1 person accused out of about every 4463 inhabitants, and 61 condemned out of each 100 accused. This probability becomes less for 1831, and less for the succeeding years. We are in the same condition for estimating, by the results of the past, the facts which we shall see realized in the future. This possibility of assigning beforehand the number of the accused and condemned which should occur in a country, is calculated to lead to serious reflections, since it involves the fate of seve-

Intellectual condition of the Accused.	1828 and 1829, Accused of crimes against the person.	1828 and 1829, Accused of crimes against property.	Number of crimes against property for one crime against the person.	1830 and 1831, Accused of crimes against the person.	1830 and 1831, Accused of crimes against property.	Number of crimes against property for one crime against the person.
Incapable of reading and writing,	2072	6617	3.2	2124	6735	3.1
Capable of reading or writing imperfectly,	1001	2804	2.8	1063	2840	2.8
Capable of reading and writing well,	400	1109	2.8	408	1047	2.6
Having received a superior education in this first degree,	80	206	2.6	135*	184	1.4
Total,	3553	10,736	3.0	3710	10,856	2.9

* The number of accused in this class is increased in consequence of political events, and of crimes against the state.

ral thousands of human beings, who are impelled, as it were, by an irresistible necessity, to the bars of the tribunals, and toward the sentence of condemnation which there await them. These conclusions flow directly from the principle already so often stated in this work, that effects are in proportion to their causes, and that the effects remain the same if the causes which have produced them do not vary."[*]

In the section entitled, "On the influence of Instruction, of Profession and of Climate on the tendency to Crime," Mons. Quetelet presents us preceding table.[†]

Tables are also given in the same form for each department of France and Belgium, and Mons. Quetelet sums up the results in the following words :[‡]

"1. The greatest number of crimes against persons and property take place in the departments which traverse or border on the Rhone, the Rhine, and the Seine, at least in their navigable portions.

"2. The smallest number of crimes against persons and property are committed in the central departments of France, in those which are situated in the west, toward the ocean, from the Lower Alps to the Charente, and those which traverse toward the north, the Somme, the Oise, and the Meuse.

"3. The shores of the Mediterranean and neighbouring departments show, other things being equal, a more marked tendency toward crimes against the person, and the northern part of France toward crimes against property.

"After having established these facts, if we seek to mount up to the causes which produce them, we are at once arrested by numerous obstacles. Indeed, the causes which influence crimes are so numerous and so various, that it becomes almost impossible to assign to each its due degree of importance. It frequently happens, also, that causes which appear highly influential, disappear before others, to which one scarcely dedicates a thought at first. I have particularly experienced this in actual researches. Perhaps I was too much preoccupied with the influence generally allowed to education as a means of extinguishing the propensity to crime. It appears to me that the common error on this subject arises from the expectation of finding less crime in a country because more children in it are sent to school, or because a greater proportion of the common people are capable of reading and writing. Account should rather be taken of the extent of moral instruction; because frequently the education which is received in schools affords only additional facilities for committing crime."[§] "Poverty also is generally regarded as leading to crime nevertheless, the department *de la Creuse*, one of the poorest in France, is that which presents, in every respect, the greatest morality. In like manner, in the Low Countries the most moral province is that of Luxembourg, where the greatest poverty reigns. It is necessary, however, to define what is meant by the word poverty—which is used here in a sense that may be regarded as improper. A province is not poor because it contains less wealth than another, if its inhabitants, like those in Luxembourg, are sober and active. If, by their labour, they succeed in providing securely for their wants and satisfying their taste, (which are the most moderate in respect that inequality of fortune is less common, and offers fewer temptations,) they may properly be regarded as enjoying a modest

---

* *Sur L'Homme*, &c., tome ii., p. 168.   † Lib. Cit., tome ii., p. 176.
‡ Lib. Cit., tome ii., p. 197.
† "Mons. Guerry has arrived almost at the same time with me at similar conclusions, in his Essay 'Sur la Statistique Morale de la France,' p. 5. and he has expressed them nearly in the same terms The results have been obtained also in England, in Germany, and in the United States."

competence. Poverty makes itself felt in provinces where great riches are amassed, as in Flanders, Holland, the department of the Seine, &c., and, above all, in manufacturing countries, where, by the least political commotion or obstruction in the usual outlets of commerce, thousands of individuals pass suddenly from a state of comfort to one of misery. The rapid transitions from one state to another give birth to crime ; especially if the individuals who suffer are surrounded by objects of temptation, and find themselves excited by the constant spectacle of luxury, and of an inequality of fortune, which drives them to despair."

"It appears to me that one of the first distinctions to be made in this study, is that of the *different races* of men who inhabit the country which we have under our consideration. It is, as we shall immediately see, of the highest importance, although it is not that which first presents itself to our observation." These are wise and profound remarks, and I commend Mons. Quetelet for having directed attention to them, which he does by quoting the following passages from Malte Brun's *Précis de la Géographie Universelle*, livre 159 ! "The population of France," says Malte Brun, "belongs to three principal races : the *Celtic*, which constitutes nearly three-fifths of its inhabitants ; the *Germanic*, which comprehends those of the ancient provinces of Flanders, of Alsace, and of a part of Lorraine ; and the *Pelasgian*, (named by Dr. Spurzheim the *Phenician*,) spread in the neighbourhood of the Mediterranean and in Corsica. Changes of manners and the progress of civilization may alter the character of a people, but may not change it entirely.". Mons. Quetelet proceeds to remark, that if we cast our eyes over the chart representing crimes against the person, this distinction of races makes itself felt in a very remarkable manner. "We see that the Pelasgian race, *spread on the borders of the Mediterranean and in Corsica*, is particularly addicted to crimes against the person. Among the German race, which extends over Alsace, the Duchy of the Lower Rhine, part of Lorraine, and of the Low Countries, where the dense population and abundance of property afford more opportunities for committing crime, and where the general use of intoxicating liquors more frequently occasions excesses, there are generally a great number of crimes against both property and person. The Batavians and the Frisons, who also belong to the German race, are addicted particularly to crimes against property. Finally, the Celtic race appears to be the most moral of the three which we have considered, especially in regard to crimes against the person. It occupies the greater part of France, and the Walloon portion of Belgium. It appears, moreover, that frontier countries, where the races are intermixed, where there is generally more agitation, and where lines of custom-house officers are established, are the most liable to demoralization."

These remarks are deficient in precision, arising probably from imperfect knowledge in the author of the mental qualities which distinguish the different races. In estimating these qualities independently of cerebral organization, we are exposed to the necessity of expressing mere general ideas in vague language, instead of stating positive facts with philosophical precision. Mental differences arise from differences in cerebral size and proportions, and the influence of the brain on the dispositions is fundamental ; that is to say, it determines the effect of external circumstances ; and the real operation of these on the mental manifestations cannot be understood until the developement of the brain of the individual exposed to them be comprehended. Individuals possessing a predominating developement of the moral and intellectual organs, like Melancthon, (p. 86,) or Eustache, (p. 87,) rise superior to circumstances. No condition could be more unfavourable to virtuous conduct than that of Eustache, when he was a slave, associated with slaves engaged in a war of extermination against their masters ; yet such was the preserving power of a high moral and intellectual organization, that he nobly discharged his duty to both belligerents, and triumphed over temptations which would have proved irresistible to a less favourably constituted brain. On the other hand, when the moral and intellectual organs are remarkably deficient, and those of the propensities predominate, no external circumstances short of physical restraint are sufficient to preserve the individual from vicious practices. The heads of Hare, p. 85, Gottfried, p. 86, and Pope Alexander VI., p. 181, are examples of this combination, and their lives show an appetite for atrocious crime, which sought its own gratification in circumstances the most dissimilar. It is only on brains in which the three regions of propensity, sentiment, and intellect are nearly equally balanced, (of which Maxwell's head, p. 412, is a specimen,) that external circumstances produce a powerful and decided influence. All inquiries into the developement of the animal, moral, and intellectual faculties of nations, therefore, in which the influence of the brain is omitted, must necessarily be defective ; and as this fact is one of great importance, I beg leave to support it by means of documents printed in the Appendix, No. IV, being Testimonials presented in 1836 by Sir G. S. Mackenzie to Lord Glenelg, Secretary of State for the Colonies, to induce his lordship to employ Phrenology in the classification of criminals.

At the time when I publish this edition no attention has been paid to that representation ; but the time must come when facts such as are here expounded cannot fail to influence the conduct of practical men.

❦ OBJECTIONS TO PHRENOLOGY CONSIDERED.

HAVING now considered the elements of Phrenology, I shall notice briefly some objections which have been urged against it. These shall be given, as nearly as possible, in the words of actual opponents, and an answer shall be subjoined.

Objection.—The idea of ascribing different faculties to different parts of the brain is not new. Many authors did so before Dr. Gall ; but their systems have fallen into disrepute, which proves that the doctrine is not true.

Answer.—Dr. Gall himself has called the attention of philosophers to the fact, that the idea alluded to is very ancient : he has given a history of previous opinions concerning the functions of the brain ; and shews that different functions have been attributed to different parts of it for centuries past, while he has assigned reasons for these ideas falling into oblivion. Dr. Spurzheim in his works does the same ; and, in the Phrenological Journal, No. vii., Art. 8, "An Historical Notice of early Opinions concerning the Brain" is given, accompanied with a plate of the head, showing it marked out into different organs in 1562 : it is copied on page 40 of this work. The difference, however, between the *mode of proceeding* of prior authors and that of Dr. Gall is so great, that the different results are accounted for. Former speculators assigned to certain mental faculties local situations in the brain, on account of the supposed aptitude of the place to the faculty. Common sense, for example, was placed in the forehead, because it was near the eyes and nose ; while memory was lodged in the cerebellum, because it lay like a store-house behind, to receive and accommodate all kinds of knowledge, till required to be brought forth for use. This was not philosophy. It was the human imagination constructing man, instead of the intellect observing how the Creator had constituted him. Dr. Gall acted on different principles. He did not assume any mental faculties, and neither did he assign them habitations in the brain according to his own fancy. On the contrary, he observed, *first*, the manifestations of mental talents and disposition ; and, *secondly*, the form of brain which accompanied each of these when strong and weak. He simply reported what Nature had done. There is the same difference between his method of proceeding and that of prior authors, as between those of Des Cartes and Newton; and hence it is equally intelligible, why he should be successful in discovering truth, while they invented only ingenious errors.

Objection.—It is admitted by phrenologists, that the functions of some parts of the brain are undiscovered; when these are found out, they may give a new view of the uses of the parts to which certain functions are now ascribed, and, therefore, no certain conclusion can be drawn on the subject in the present state of phrenological observations, even supposing them to be all correct.

Answer.—Each organ will always manifest its own faculty, whatever discoveries may be made in regard to other organs. The direction may be modified, but the function will remain unaltered. See page 405.

Objection.—It is ridiculous to suppose that the mind has thirty-five faculties; why not fifty-five? or a hundred and five? Besides, the phrenologists have been continually altering the number.

Answer.—As well it may be said to be absurd, that we should possess exactly five senses; why not ten, or fifteen? The phrenologists deny all responsibility for the number of the faculties. They admit neither fewer nor a greater number than they find manifested in nature. Besides, authors on mental philosophy admit as many, and some more, faculties than the phrenologists. Lord Kames, for example, admits twenty of the phrenological faculties; while Mr. Dugald Stewart, in his system, ascribes more faculties to the mind than are enumerated in the phrenological works.[*] The increase of the number of the phrenological faculties is easily accounted for. It has invariably been stated, that the functions of certain portions of the brain remain to be discovered; and, in proportion as this discovery proceeds, the list of mental powers will necessarily be augmented.

Objection.—"On opening the skull, and examining the brain toward the surface, where the organs are said to be situated, it seems to require no small share of creative fancy to see anything more than a number of almost similar convolutions, all composed of cineritious and medullary substance, very nearly in the same proportions, and all exhibiting as little difference in their form and structure as the convolutions of the intestine." "No phrenologist has ever yet observed the supposed line of distinction between them; and no phrenologist, therefore, has ventured, in the course of his dissections, to divide a hemisphere of the brain accurately into any such number of well-marked and specific organs."

This objection was urged by the late Dr. John Barclay, and is answered at full length by Dr. A. Combe, in the Phrenological Transactions. A summary only of his observations can be introduced here. *First*, Although the objection were literally true, it is not relevant; because it is an admitted principle of physiology, that the form and structure of an organ are not sufficient to convey an idea of its functions; no man who saw an eye, an ear, or a nostril, for the first time, (supposing it were possible for a man to be so situated,) could, merely by looking at it, infer its uses. The most expert anatomist had looked frequently and long upon a bundle of nervous fibres, enclosed in a common sheath, without discovering that one set of them was the organ of voluntary motion, and another that of feeling; on the contrary, from their similarity of appearance, these nerves had, for ages, been regarded as possessing similar functions. Nevertheless, Sir C. Bell and Magendie have demonstrated, by experiment, that they possess the distinct functions of feeling and motion. Sir C. Bell

[*] See answer to Mr. Jeffrey in *Phrenological Journal*, vol. iv., p. 30,

has, more recently, proved, that another nerve, the use of which nobody had conjectured from its structure, serves to convey to the brain intimation of the state of the muscles, so that there is now evidence of the muscular system being supplied with three distinct sets of nerves having separate functions, which was never conjectured from appearances. These discoveries are discussed on p. 56. It may, therefore, competently be proved, by observation, that different parts of the brain have distinct functions, although it were true that no difference of structure could be perceived.

But, 2dly, it is not the fact that difference of appearance is not discoverable. It is easy to distinguish the anterior, the middle, and posterior lobes of the human brain from each other; and, were they shown separately to a skilful phrenological anatomist, he would never take one for the other. The mental manifestations are so different, according as one or other of these lobes predominates in size, that there is, even in this case, ample room for establishing the fundamental proposition, that different faculties are connected with different parts of the brain. Farther, many of the organs differ so decidedly in appearance, that they could be pointed out by it alone. Dr. Spurzheim says, that he "should never confound the organ of *Amativeness* with that of *Philoprogenitiveness*; nor *Philoprogenitiveness* with that of *Secretiveness*; nor the organ of the *desire to acquire* with that of *Benevolence* or *Veneration*;" and after having seen Dr. Spurzheim's dissections of the brain, I bear my humble testimony to the truth of this assertion. Even an ordinary observer, who takes a few good casts of the brain in his hand, may satisfy himself that the anterior lobe, for example, uniformly presents convolutions different in appearance, direction, and size from those of the middle lobe; while the latter, toward the coronal surface, uniformly presents convolutions differing in appearance and direction from those of the posterior lobe; and, above all, the cerebellum, or organ of *Amativeness*, is not only widely different in structure, but is separated by a strong membrane from all other organs, and can never be mistaken for any of them. Difference of appearance, therefore, being absolutely demonstrable, there is much better reason on the side of the phrenologists for presuming difference of function, than on that of the opponents for maintaining unity.

3dly, It is admitted that the organs are not perceived to be separated in the brain by strong lines of demarcation; but those persons who have either seen Dr. Spurzheim dissect a brain, or have attended minutely to its impressions on the skull, will support me in testifying, that the *form* of the organs are distinguishable, and that the mapping out is founded in nature. To bring this to the test, the student has only to observe the appearance of any particular organ in a state of large developement, the surrounding organs being small; the *form* will then be distinctly visible. This subject is discussed at more length on pp. 91 and 92.

Objection.—All parts of the brain have been injured or destroyed without the mental faculties being affected.

Answer.—The assertion is denied: there is no philosophical evidence for it. The subject is discussed at length by Dr. A. Combe, in the Phrenological Transactions, and in a subsequent part of this work. The objection is now generally abandoned by persons who have considered the cases, with the answers to them.

Objection.—*Post-mortem* examinations do not show diseased structure in the brain from Insanity.

Answer.—They frequently do so; and when they do not, our ignorance of the appearances in health, and our want of power of discriminating minute changes of the structure, are the causes of our perceiving nothing different from health. Professor Christison observes, that "some poisons operate by irritating, destroying, or corroding the organ; while others neither corrode nor irritate, but make a peculiar impression on the sentient extremities of the nerves, unaccompanied by any *visible* change of structure." Similar observations may be applied to the appearances of the brain in Insanity. If the disease has been merely *functional*, no *structural* change may be discernible.

Objection.—" The most extravagant departure from all the legitimate modes of reasoning, although still under the colour of anatomical investigation, is the system of Dr. Gall. It is sufficient to say, that, without comprehending the grand divisions of the nervous system, without a notion of the distinct properties of the individual nerves, or having made any distinction of the columns of the spinal marrow, without even having ascertained the difference of cerebrum and cerebellum, Gall proceeded to describe the brain as composed of many particular and independent organs, and to assign to each the residence of some special faculty." These are the words of Sir Charles Bell, in his treatise *" on the Nervous Circle, which connects the voluntary muscles with the brain,"* reprinted from the Philosophical Transactions, p. 187, 1836.

Answer.—*First,* This objection itself is " an extravagant departure from all legitimate modes of reasoning;" because the most intimate acquaintance with the structure of the brain does not serve to unfold its functions. This subject is fully discussed on p. 56. The soundness of this principle admits of a demonstration which Sir Charles Bell will not easily overturn. He himself, of course, is intimately acquainted with all the anatomical knowledge of which he affirms that Dr. Gall was ignorant, yet does not pretend, even at this day, to have discovered the functions of the different parts of the brain! *Secondly,* Although Dr. Gall did not accomplish what was impossible, namely, the discovery of the functions of the different parts of the brain by means of dissection, yet it is a gross misrepresentation to say that he continued in ignorance of the anatomy of the nervous system. It is known to every physiologist of reputation in Europe, Sir Charles Bell excepted, that both Drs. Gall and Spurzheim were intimately acquainted with the anatomy of the brain and nervous system.* The brain never was dissected in a rational manner, nor the representation of its structure brought into harmony with its functions, until this was accomplished by them.

Their printed volumes and plates render such an assertion as that now combated injurious only to him who states it. Dr. Bailly, of Blois, in reply to what he calls " an inconceivable accusation " made by M. Leuret, that Dr. Gall neglected the anatomy of the convolutions, refers to Gall's large work, and " to some thousands of physicians of different countries, who, for upward of twenty years, learned, from the lectures of the founder of Phrenology, the most accurate and rational anatomy of the cerebral

---

* Dr. Spurzheim answered this attack of Sir C. Bell in his *Appendix to the Anatomy of the Brain.* Treuttel, Würtz, and Richter. London. 1830. He there says, " In our Memoir presented to the French Institute in 1808, and in our large work above mentioned, we make four principal divisions of the nervous system, and treat of them in four separate sections. In my work, 'The physiognomical System of Drs. Gall and Spurzheim,' there is a chapter on the Anatomy of the nervous system. In the second edition, 1815, p. 13, I say : 'We are of opinion that the nervous system must be divided and subdivided, and that each part of these divisions and subdivisions has its peculiar origin.' I speak of the common division of the nervous system into four portions. P. 23 : ' I admit a difference between the nerves of motion and those of feeling.' I treat of anatomical, physiological, and pathological proofs in favour of my opinion. I positively state that ' the same nervous fibres do not go to the muscles and to the skin ;' and conclude (p. 25) that ' the spinal marrow consists of nerves of motion and of feeling, and that the greater number of the pretended cerebral nerves belong to the nerves of motion or of feeling.' "

convolutions yet known." "I affirm," says he, "without fear of contradiction, that no anatomist before Gall had the slightest idea of the structure of the convolutions. This has been acknowledged by Cuvier himself, whom no one will accuse of too much partiality toward the works of Gall."*

Objection.—Sir Charles Bell proceeds, ": When the popularity of these doctrines is considered, it may easily be conceived how difficult it has been, during their successive importations, to keep my pupils to the examples of our own great countrymen. Surely it is time that the schools of this kingdom should be distinguished from those of other countries. Let us continue to build that structure which has been commenced in the labours of the Monros and Hunters, and which the undeserved popularity of the continental system has interrupted."

Answers.—*First,* I allow that it must indeed have been difficult for Sir Charles "to keep his pupils to the examples of his own great countrymen" on this subject, in the face of these successive continental "importations;" for the simplest of all reasons—because he was endeavouring to distinguish the noon-tide blaze of truth by the lustre of mere human authority. If the principles laid down in the introduction to this work be sound, neither the Monros nor the Hunters, any more than Sir Charles himself, could possibly discover the functions of the brain by the methods of investigation which they and he, with equal want of success, pursued. *Secondly,* It is *not* "time that the schools" (of anatomy and physiology) "of this kingdom should be distinguished from those of other countries;" because the structure and functions of the human body are the same in all countries, and in proportion as inquirers approximate to truth, the harmony of their doctrines must increase. This sentence, when analyzed, resolves itself simply into an appeal to national vanity to resist truth, because it has been discovered by foreigners. *Thirdly,* The structure which was commenced in the labours of the Monros and the Hunters, in so far as it had a basis in nature, has stood firm and continues to be respected in every country of Europe; in so far as it was founded in error, it has fallen, and cannot again be reared up; and in so far as it was utterly defective, without even the outline of the foundations being traced, (as was the case in regard to that department of it which should have included the functions of the brain,) it will be completed by men to whom God has given the necessary genius and industry to accomplish the work, without reference to the country in which they may chance to have been born. Sir Charles has showed no authority for the notion implied in this appeal—that the exclusive privilege of discovering the physiology of the brain has been conferred by Providence on the natives of the British Islands. For the benefit of my younger readers, I conclude in Sir Charles's own words, used by him in reference to the late Mr. Abernethy, "you may learn from this that it is dangerous to give a new idea to an old gentleman—even to one who, in his earlier life, was foremost in the pursuit of novelty—and that *it is better to keep to old theories when you go to the College of Surgeons.*"†

Objection.—The world has gone on well enough with the philosophy of mind it already possesses, which, besides, is consecrated by great and venerable names, while Phrenology has neither symmetry of structure, beauty of arrangement, nor the suffrages of the learned to recommend it. Its votaries are all third-rate men—persons without scientific or philosophical reputations. They are not entitled, therefore, to challenge the regard of those who have higher studies to occupy their attention. They complain that only ridicule and abuse are directed against them, and that

---

* *Journal de la Société Phrénologique de Paris,* April, 1835.
† On the Paralysis of the Portio Dura, No. xxv.

no one ventures to challenge their principles or refute their facts; but they do not yet stand high enough in public esteem to give them a right to expect any other treatment.

Answer.—The world has *not* gone on well enough without Phrenology. A fierce and general conflict of opinions is maintained on many important subjects connected with mind, which cannot be satisfactorily settled till the true philosophy of man shall be discovered and understood. Education and social institutions also rest, in many respects, on imperfect foundations; and at the present moment mankind need nothing so much as a sound, practical, and rational system of mental philosophy. Moreover, Phrenology being a new science, it follows that men who possess reputation in physiology or mental philosophy would appear to lose rather than gain renown, were they to confess their ignorance of the functions of the brain and the philosophy of mind, which is a necessary prelude to their adoption of Phrenology; and the subject does not lie directly in the department of other scientific men. In this manner it happens, oddly enough, that those who are most directly called upon by their situation to examine the science, are precisely those to whom its triumph would prove most humiliating. Locke humorously observes, on a similar occasion, "Would it not be an insufferable thing for a learned professor, and that which his scarlet would blush at, to have his authority of forty-years standing, wrought out of hard rock, Greek and Latin, with no small expense of time and candle, and confirmed by general tradition and a reverend beard, in an instant overturned by an upstart novelist? Can any one expect that he should be made to confess, that what he taught his scholars thirty years ago was all error and mistake, and that he sold them hard words and ignorance at a very dear rate? What probabilities, I say, are sufficient to prevail in such a case? And who ever, by the most cogent arguments, will be prevailed with to disrobe himself at once of all his old opinions and pretences to knowledge and learning, which with hard study he hath all his time been labouring for, and turn himself out stark-naked in quest afresh of new notions? All the arguments that can be used will be as little able to prevail, as the wind did with the traveller to part with his cloak, which he held only the faster."[*] Human nature is the same now as in the days of Locke.

There is, however, another answer to the present objection. Some individuals are born princes, dukes, or even field-marshals; but I am not aware that it has yet been announced that any lady was delivered of a child of genius, or an infant of established reputation. These titles must be gained by the display of qualities which merit them; but if an individual quit the beaten track pursued by the philosophers of the day, and introduce any discovery, although equally stupendous and new, his reputation is necessarily involved in its merits. Harvey was not a great man *before* he discovered the circulation of the blood, but became such in consequence of having done so. What was Shakspeare before the magnificence of his genius was justly appreciated? The author of Kenilworth represents him attending as an humble and comparatively obscure suitor at the court of Queen Elizabeth, and receiving a mark of favour in an "Ah! Will Shakspeare, are you there?" And he most appropriately remarks, that here the immortal paid homage to the mortal. Who would now exchange the greatness of Shakspeare for the splendour of the proudest lord that bowed before the Maiden Queen? Or let us imagine Galileo, such as he was in reality, a feeble old man, humble in rank, destitute of political influence, unprotected by the countenance or alliance of the great, poor, in short, in everything except the splendid gifts of a profound, original, and comprehensive genius—and conceive him placed

[*] Book iv., ch. xx., sect. 11.

at the bar of the Roman pontiff and the seven cardinals, men terrible in power, invested with authority to torture and kill in this world, and, as was then believed, to damn through eternity ; men magnificent in state, and arrogant in the imaginary possession of all the wisdom of their age—and let us say who was *then* great in reputation—Galileo or his judges' But who is *now* the idol of posterity—the old man or his persecutors! The case will be the same with Gall. If his discoveries of the functions of the brain, and of the philosophy of the mind, stand the test of examination, and prove to be a correct interpretation of nature, they will surpass, in substantial importance to mankind, the discoveries even of Harvey, Newton, and Galileo ; and this age will in consequence be rendered more illustrious by the introduction of Phrenology than by the victories of Bonaparte or of Wellington. .Finally, the assertion, that no men of note have embraced Phrenology, is not supported by fact. Professor Uccell, of Florence, sacrificed his academical chair for Phrenology. In "The Statistics of Phrenology, by Hewett C. Watson,"* the most irresistible evidence is produced that Phrenology is now embraced " by not only a large, but a highly talented and respectable body of adherents, of whom no cause need be ashamed." I earnestly recommend Mr. Watson's work to the perusal of all persons who desire to know the real state of the science. Besides, the writings of the phrenologists will bear a comparison in point of skill, extent of information, correctness of logic, and profundity of thought, with those of the most eminent of their opponents.

Objection.—All the disciples of Phrenology are persons ignorant of anatomy and physiology. They delude lawyers, divines, and merchants, who know nothing about the brain ; but all medical men, and especially teachers of anatomy, are so well aware of the fallacy of their doctrines, that no impression is made on them. They laugh at the discoveries as dreams.

Answer.—This objection, like many others, is remarkable more for boldness than truth. For my own part, before adopting Phrenology, I saw Dr. Barclay, and other anatomical professors, dissect the brain repeatedly, and heard them declare its functions to be an enigma, and acknowledge that their whole information concerning it consisted of " names without meaning." It is acknowledged, in an article on the Nervous System, in No. 94 of the *Edinburgh Review*, quoted on p. 49 of this work, that the functions of the brain are unknown to anatomists, and that their mode of dissecting it is absurd. This circumstance, therefore, puts the whole faculty, who have not studied phrenologically, completely out of the field as authorities. The *fact*, however, is the very reverse of what is stated in the foregoing objection. Drs. Gall and Spurzheim are now pretty generally admitted to have been admirable anatomists of the brain, even by those who disavow their physiology. Dr. Vimont's *Traité de Phrénologie* displays great anatomical attainments ; and in Mr. Watson's " Statistics " ample evidence is presented that Phrenology is embraced by a large number of medical men all over the British Islands. The leading medical journals also have adopted Phrenology as true.

Objection.—"It is inconceivable, that, after the discovery was made, there should be *anybody* who could pretend to doubt of its reality. The means of verifying it, one would think, must have been such as not to leave a pretext for the slightest hesitation ; and the fact, that, after twenty years preaching in its favour, it is far more generally rejected than believed, might seem to afford pretty conclusive evidence against the possibility of its truth."

This objection has been answered in the Introduction, p. 25, where it is shewn that all important discoveries have been equally despised and rejected at their first announcement.

* Longman & Co., London. 12mo., pp. 242. 1836.

The observations there quoted from Playfair and Locke are completely applicable to the case of Phrenology. The discovery is new, important, and widely at variance with the prevailing opinions of the present generation ; and its reception and progress have been precisely such as any sensible person, acquainted with the history of science, would have anticipated. "The discoverer of the circulation of the blood," says the *Edinburgh Review*[*]—" a discovery which, if measured by its consequences on physiology and medicine, was the greatest ever made since physic was cultivated, suffers no diminution of his reputation in our day, from the incredulity with which his doctrine was received by some, the effrontery with which it was claimed by others, or the knavery with which it was attributed to former physiologists by those who could not deny and would not praise it. The very names of these envious and dishonest enemies of Harvey are scarcely remembered ; and the honour of this great discovery now rests, beyond all dispute, with the great philosopher who made it." Posterity will pass a similar judgment on Dr. Gall and his opponents.

II. MATERIALISM.

There are two great questions connected with materialism, very different in themselves, which are often confounded. The one is—On what is the mind dependent *for existence?* The other—On what is it dependent for its power of *manifesting itself in this life?* Phrenologists declare themselves unable to decide upon the first ; but maintain, that facts demonstrate the second to depend on the condition of the organization. When, therefore, a phrenologist says that "the mental qualities and capacities are *dependent* upon the bodily constitution," the sentence should be completed, "not for *existence,* but for *the power of acting* in this material world." This explanation has been frequently stated in the phrenological books ; and it should be remembered, as its repetition would be tedious.

The objection, however, that Phrenology leads to materialism, has been so frequently urged against the science, that it demands some consideration. A few observations will suffice, for it appears singularly unphilosophical, even upon the most superficial consideration. Phrenology, viewed as the assertion of certain physical facts, cannot, if unfounded, logically lead to any result, except the disgrace and mortification of its supporters. On such a supposition, it cannot overturn religion, nor any other *truth ;* because, by the constitution of the human intellect, error constantly tends to resolve itself into nothing, and to sink into oblivion ; while truth, having a real existence, remains permanent and impregnable. In this view, then, the objection, that Phrenology leads to materialism, is absurd. If, on the other hand, the science is held to be a *true interpretation of nature,* and if it be urged, that, nevertheless, it leads fairly and logically to materialism, then the folly of the objection is equally glaring ; for it resolves itself into this—that materialism is the constitution of nature, and that Phrenology is dangerous, because it makes this constitution known.

The charge assumes a still more awkward appearance in one shape in which it is frequently brought forward. The objector admits that the mind uses the body as an instrument of communication with external nature, and maintains that this fact does not necessarily lead to materialism. In this I agree with him ; but I cannot perceive how it should lead nearer to this result, to hold that each faculty manifests itself by a particular organ,

* No. xciv., p. 76. The article quoted in the text is "On the Nervous System ;" and the names of Drs. Gall and Spurzheim are not mentioned in it from beginning to end. The author, however, in the above remarks, affords them just grounds of consolation, although he exemplifies the injustice he so eloquently condemns.

than to believe that the whole mind acts on external objects by means of
the whole body or the whole brain. In short, in whatever point of view
the system is regarded, whether as true or false, the objection of materialism is futile and unphilosophical; and one must regret that it should have
been brought forward in the name of religion, because every imbecile and
unfounded attack against philosophy, made in this sacred name, tends to
diminish the respect with which it ought always to be invested.

In entering on this subject, it is proper to take a view of the nature and
extent of the point in dispute, and of the real effect of our decision upon
it. The question, then, is, Whether the *substance* of which the thinking
principle is composed be matter or spirit? And the effect of our decision,
let it be observed, is not to *alter the nature of that substance*, whatever
it be, but merely to adopt an opinion consonant with, or adverse to, a fact
in nature over which we have no control. Mind, with all its faculties and
functions, has existed since the creation, and will exist till the human race
becomes extinct, and no opinion of man, concerning the cause of its
phenomena, can have the least influence over that cause itself. The
mind is invested by nature with all its properties and essences, and these
it will possess, and manifest, and maintain, let men think, and speak, and
write what they will concerning its substance. If the Author of Nature
has invested the mind with the quality of endless existence, it will, to a
certainty, flourish in immortal youth in spite of every appearance of premature decay. If, on the other hand, He has limited its existence to this
passing scene, and decreed that it shall perish for ever when the animating
principle passes from the body, then all our conjectures, arguments, discussions, and assertions respecting its immortality will not add one day
to its existence. The opinions of man, therefore, concerning the substance of the mind, can have no influence whatever in changing or modifying that substance itself; and if so, as little can these opinions under-
mine the constitution of the mind, or its relations to time and eternity,
on which, as their foundations, morality and religion must, and do, rest as
on an immutable basis. According to Phrenology, morality and natural
religion originate in, and emanate from, the primitive constitution of the
mental powers themselves. Innumerable observations have proved that
faculties and organs of Benevolence, Hope, Veneration, Justice, and Reflection exist. Now, our believing that the mind will die with the body
will not pluck these sentiments and powers from the soul; nor will our
believing the mind to be immortal implant a single one more of them in
our constitution. They would all remain the same in functions and constitution, and render virtue amiable and vice odious, although we should
believe the mind to be made of dust, just as they would do were we to
believe the mind to be a more immediate emanation from the Deity himself.

In short, therefore, this question of materialism is one of the most vain,
trivial, and uninteresting that ever engaged the human intellect; and
nothing can be more unphilosophical and more truly detrimental to the
interests of morality and religion, than the unfounded clamour, or cant,
shall I call it, which has been poured forth from the periodical journals
about the dangers attending it. A manly intellect, instead of bowing
before prejudice, would dissipate it, by showing that the question is altogether an illusion, and that, adopt what opinion we will concerning the
substance of the mind, every attribute belonging to it must remain unaltered and unimpaired.

But not to stop in our investigation till we have reached the goal, we
may inquire whether it be possible to discover the substance of which the
mind is composed, and whether it be material or immaterial? Previously
doing so, however, we ought to endeavour to ascertain what means we
possess of arriving at a knowledge of the essence of the mind. All our

knowledge must be derived from either consciousness or observation. Now, by reflecting on consciousness or on what we feel, we discover nothing concerning the nature or essence of the thinking being. We do not feel a spiritual substance stirring about within us, and elaborating sentiment and thought; and neither do we feel a *material substance* producing these effects. We are conscious only of feelings and emotions, of friendships and attachments, of high conceptions and glorious thoughts; but whether these originate from matter or spirit; whether the first embryo substance of reflection dwelt lowly in the dust, or soared a pure ethereal essence amid the regions of boundless space, before it was constituted a part of us; whether God, in creating man, was pleased to invest his material organs with the property of thought, or to infuse into him a portion of immaterial fire : on all these points consciousness gives us no information. A great deal of popular delusion has been kept alive on this point, by the fact being overlooked, that we are not conscious of the operations of the brain. Men in general, because they are sensible only of thought and feeling, and not of the movements of any material organ performing these acts of the mind, imagine that it is necessarily an immaterial substance which is thinking and feeling within them; but they are equally unconscious of the contraction and relaxation of the muscles, and they might as well imagine that their arms and legs are moved, not by material organs, but by the direct impulse of spirit, as entertain the supposition in question. In short, the truly philosophical conclusion is, that, by means of consciousness, we are unable to discover of what substance the thinking principle is composed.

Does observation, then, throw a stronger and steadier light upon this long agitated question? The mental organs, while in health, and in the natural state in which their functions are most perfectly performed, are completely hid from inspection. No eye can penetrate the integuments of the head; the tables of the skull, the *dura mater*, and the *pia mater*, to obtain a view of the operations performed in the brain while the thoughts run high and the sentiments swell with emotion : and when external injury or disease removes these coverings, the mind does not disport in all the vigour of its healthy action. Even when all these external obstacles to inspection are removed, it is only the surface of the convolutions which is perceived, and the soul may be enthroned in the long fibres which extend from the surface to the *medulla oblongata*, or thought may be elaborated there; yet, as the eye cannot *see* nor the hand *feel* thought, it may evade detection. It may be said, however, that death will solve the question, and allow the whole secrets of the soul to be disclosed; but, alas! when the pulse has ceased to beat, and the lungs no longer play, the brain presents nothing to our contemplation but an inert mass, of a soft and fibrous texture, in which no thought can be discerned and no sentiment perceived, and in which also no spirit nor immaterial substance can be traced; so that, from inspecting it, even imagination receives no food for conjecture, as to the presence or absence of an immaterial guest while life and health yet animated its folds.

Observation, therefore, reveals as little in regard to the substance of the mind, as does reflection on consciousness; and as no other modes of arriving at certain knowledge are open to man, the solution of the question appears to be placed completely beyond his reach. In short, to use an observation of Dr. Spurzheim, Nature has given man faculties fitted to observe phenomena as they at present exist, and the relations existing between them; but has denied to him powers fitted to discover, as a matter of direct perception, either the beginning, or the end, or the essence or anything under the sun; we may amuse our observation with conjectures, but shall never arrive at truth when we stray into these interdicted regions.*

Lord Brougham maintains that in this life "the mind is different from, and *independent of, matter altogether;*" (*Discourse of Natural Theology,* p. 107;) but this objection has been adverted to on pages 34 and 35.

The solution of this question, therefore, is not only unimportant, but impossible; and this leads me to observe, that no idea can be more erroneous than that which supposes the dignity and future destiny of man, as an immortal being, to depend, of necessity, on the substance of which he is made.

Let us allow to the materialist, for the sake of argument, that the brain is the mind, and that medullary matter thinks—What then? If, in fact, it does so, it must be the best possible substance for thinking, just because the Creator selected it for the purpose, and endowed it with this property. In this argument the religious constantly forget that the same Omnipotent hand made the brain which created the mind and the universe itself, and that, in the dedication of every cerebral convolution to its objects, be they thinking or any other process, the Divine Wisdom is as certainly exercised as in impressing motion on the planets, or infusing light and heat into the sun. If, therefore, *de facto*, God has made the brain to think, we may rest assured that it is exquisitely and perfectly adapted for this purpose, and that His objects in creating man will not be defeated on account of His having chosen a *wrong substance*, out of which to constitute the thinking principle. But what are his objects in creating man? This brings us to the jet of the question at once. Mr. Lawrence, it is said, founds no moral doctrine on his opinions regarding the essence of the

---

* The argument maintained in the text is very ably stated, in a different form, by the author of "Remarks suggested by the reading of Mr. Taylor's letter to the Lord Provost, &c., of Edinburgh, offering himself as a candidate for the Logic Chair," 1836. "Philosophers," says he, are now beginning to discover a glimpse of the truth, that MIND and MATTER, which have all along assumed to be real existences, are only the NAMES, and nothing more than the NAMES, of certain classifications of human ideas; there being within the scope of man's knowledge no such thing as Matter, independently of the different material objects of human perception, or of the individual elementary particles that compose them; and there being, on the other hand, no such thing as Mind, independently of the different individual beings that feel, think, and will. To compare, therefore, together Mind and Matter, *in the abstract*, as antagonist principles, having no common property, as philosophers and theologians have always done, is really, it appears to me, with all deference to the opinions of the great men who have wasted their energies upon it, one of the most futile operations in which the mind of man can be engaged, for it is a comparison of non-entities. There are no such things as extension, solidity, and resistance, form, size, colour, sound, or smell, different or separate from the material objects that exhibit them; and all that can be legitimately predicated of them is, that they are attributes, qualities, or properties, not of the abstract essence, or substance, called matter, but simply of the particular stock, stone, pigment, earth, metal, or gas that is the immediate object of thought." P. 10. "Thought and feeling are, equally with extension and solidity, qualities of *concrete* beings, and mankind have no knowledge of any other than concrete beings that possess such powers. Reflection, indeed, upon consciousness, has brought thinking men to the conclusion, that their powers of thinking, feeling, and willing are the attributes, not of their whole being indiscriminately, but of their brain exclusively; but beyond this their means of inquiry cannot carry them. It is the concrete being lodged within the skull (the *concrete* being, and not the abstraction called Mind) that feels, thinks, and wills; but what are the elements that compose that concrete? and what is the principle or mainspring of its activity? are questions that no man can answer." P. 14.

mind ; but other materialists, who make these opinions the foundation of
atheism, wish us to believe that the best evidence of the Divine intention
in creating the human soul, is to be found by discovering the *substance* of
which it is made ; and they insinuate that, if it be constituted of a very
refined and dignified material, the conclusion necessarily follows, that it
is intended for magnificent destinies, while, if it be composed of a rude
and vulgar stuff, it must be intended only to crawl on this filthy world.
Here, however, sense and logic equally fail them ; for no principle in
philosophy is more certain than that *we cannot infer*, from a knowledge of
the mere substance of anything, for what ends it is fitted. Exhibit to a
human being every variety of imaginable essence, and if you allow him
to know no more of its properties than he can discover from examining
its constituent parts, he will be utterly incapable of telling whether it
is calculated to endure for a day or last to eternity. The materialist,
therefore, is not entitled, even from the supposed admission that medullary matter thinks, to conclude that the human being is not immortal
and responsible. The true way of discovering for what end man has
been created is, to look to the *qualities* with which he has been endowed,
trusting that the substance of which he is composed is perfectly suited
to the objects of his creation. Now, when we inquire into his qualities,
we find the thinking principle in him to differ, not only in *degree*, but in
kind, from that of the lower animals. The latter have no faculty of
justice to indicate to them that the unrestrained manifestation of Destructiveness or Acquisitiveness is wrong ; they have no sentiment of
Veneration to prompt them to seek a God whom they may adore ; they
have no faculty of Hope, pointing out futurity as an object of ceaseless
anxiety and contemplation, and leading them to expect a life beyond the
grave ; and, indeed, several of the convolutions of the brain, which in
man form the organs of these sentiments, appear not to exist in the lower
animals. Those organs also, which in man serve to manifest the faculties of Reflection, are, in the lower animals, eminently deficient, and their
understanding, in exact correspondence with this fact, is so limited as to
be satisfied with little knowledge, and to be insensible to the comprehensive design and glories of creation. Man, then, being endowed with
qualities which are denied to the lower creatures, we are entitled, by a
legitimate exercise of *reflection*, the subject being beyond the region of
the external senses, to conclude, on principles truly philosophic, that he is
designed for another and a higher destiny than is to be allotted to them,
whatever be the *essence* of his mind.

These principles enable us to dispose of an objection which was long
ago stated by Dr. Barclay, and has since been repeated by many other
opponents, and yet is in itself very absurd. Dr. Barclay's hypothesis is,
that the mind fashions the organs. If it is impossible to discover the
substance of which the mind is composed, it is equally impracticable to
tell whether the faculties determine the size of the organs, or the organs
limit the power of the faculties. Some of the difficulties with which Dr.
Barclay's notions are beset are the following : If the immaterial mind
fashions the organs, then God bestows idiotic minds, insane minds, stupid
minds, and viciously disposed minds on different individuals ; and these
make bad organs : a doctrine which appears fully more objectionable than
the theory, that the mind itself, in all individuals, is perfect ; but that
the manifestations of its dispositions and powers, in this life, are affected
by the state of the organs with which it is connected. On the former
supposition, human efforts can do nothing to meliorate the condition of
the mind ; for the immaterial principle is beyond our reach, and, until we
modify it, no change in the organs can take place. On the latter hypothesis, we are encouraged with hopes of success to do our best ; for it

assumes that the mind in all individuals is sound, and that the imperfec
tions lie in the organs, which are subject to modification by means of
propagation and exercise. According to this view, also, insanity is not a
disease of the immaterial principle, but an affection of the organs, which
may be cured by medicine. See *Phrenological Journal*, vol. ii., p. 14.

III. ON THE EFFECTS OF INJURIES OF THE BRAIN ON THE MANIFESTATIONS OF THE MIND.

(BY DR. A. COMBE.)

Of all the arguments advanced for the subversion of Phrenology, no
one has been more frequently or more confidently urged, than that which
rests on the alleged fact of the brain having, in various instances, been
wounded or destroyed in whole or in part, without in any degree im-
peding the usual operations of mind. When narrowly examined, however,
this objection proves at variance with the views of those who maintain it,
and completely demonstrative of their ignorance of the principles of the
science against which it is directed. "The system of Gall and Spur-
heim," it is said, "however ingenious or amusing in theory it may be, is
annihilated by the commonest reference to fact. Experience has shown
us that a man may live in the *full enjoyment of his intellectual faculties*,
although a part of his brain is destroyed by disease. Portions of the
brain, various in situation and size, have been found to have been entirely
disorganized, yet no single power of the mind was *impaired*, even to the
very day of the patient's death. It would be difficult to find any one
portion of the brain that has not, in some case or another, been deranged
in its structure, without injury to the mind. Certainly, of the parts
specified by Gall and Spurzheim, every one has, in its turn, been found
wanting, without any deficiency in that *intellectual* faculty which they
would represent it either to produce or sustain."* Such are the *ipsissi-
ma verba* of a learned and respectable, though prejudiced, opponent; and,
although others might be quoted who go still farther than he does, I am
ready to admit that, if the statements here recorded were as clearly substantiated as they were sweepingly made, neither the system of philosophy
which we advocate, nor any other which acknowledges the necessity of
the intervention of a material instrument for the manifestation of the
mind, could possibly survive for a day.

At first sight the foregoing objection appears to be highly plausible and
relevant; and, coming as it generally does, directly or indirectly, from the
members of the medical profession, who, naturally enough, are supposed
to be best qualified to judge, it is received by many with implicit confidence, and thus operates upon them with all the force of truth; and, in
fact, to those who are alike ignorant of Anatomy and of Phrenology, and
who, therefore, have no means of forming an accurate estimate of its
force, it does present a very formidable aspect. As, however, to those
who are acquainted with both these sciences, and who are consequently better qualified to judge correctly, the very facts upon which the objections are
grounded seem, instead of invalidating the fundamental principles of the
new philosophy, to be clearly and unequivocally demonstrative of their
truth; it may be useful to state such an abstract of the evidence itself as
shall enable even the unprofessional reader to determine how far it authorizes the inferences which have been deduced from it by our opponents.
With this intention I shall first make some observations on the testimony
offered of the alleged integrity of all the mental faculties in cases of
xtensive injury of the brain; and then examine anatomically how far the

* Rennel On *Skepticism*, p. 100.

extent, situation, and nature of the injuries sustained in the cases alluded to authorize us to infer the partial or total destruction of any individual phrenological organ ; and, lastly, I shall offer a few remarks on the possibility of discovering the functions of the brain from noticing the effects of its injuries—a mode of proceeding lately recommended from high authority.

In proceeding to this inquiry, it must first be observed, that, without a single exception, all the cases alluded to are related by surgical authors for purely professional purposes, without the remotest idea of their being afterward founded on, to prove that entire preservation of the mental faculties may coexist with extensive disorganization of the organ of mind ; consequently, in all of them, as will be seen by a reference to Dr. Ferriar's paper, in the 4th volume of the Manchester Memoirs, and to the 48th number of the Edinburgh Review, the state of the mind is mentioned merely incidentally, and in very vague and general terms, as it was, in reality, scarcely attended to. For instance, it is stated in one case that " the senses were retained to the last ;" in another, that " there was no loss of sensibility ;" in a third, that there was " no alienation of mind ;" and, in a fourth, that " the patient remained quite well." The want of precision, indeed, and the utter inadequacy of the statements to establish the important conclusions deduced from them, are so palpably conspicuous, that even the reviewer already alluded to, hostile as he is to the doctrines of Phrenology, expresses a " wish to see cases more minute in all their details, and *observed with a view specially to this physiological inquiry*, substituted for those we at present possess,"* before he ventures to pronounce an irrevocable decree; and if *he* hesitates, it would surely be too much to expect *us* to pronounce, upon testimony rejected by *him*, a verdict against ourselves.

But, even supposing that these cases had been observed *with a view specially to this physiological inquiry* ; still this testimony, to be of the slightest value in establishing the point contended for, necessarily supposes two conditions or requisites in those by whom they are narrated, which were manifestly not possessed, viz., 1st, *A perfect knowledge of the number and nature of the primitive* faculties of the human mind ; and, 2dly, A previous knowledge of their relative degrees of endowment and energy, during health, in the individual cases under consideration.

Now, as to the first of these, it is well known that scarcely any two metaphysicians who make the philosophy of mind their particular study, are agreed either upon the number or nature of the primitive mental powers. Much less, then, can we expect the surgeon, engaged in the hurry of general practice, to be better informed. " Certain crude ideas," says the Edinburgh Reviewer, in his notice of Sir E. Hume's paper on the Functions of the Brain, " are attached to the words Intellectual Faculties ; *a vague conjecture arises as to the seat and nature of these faculties.*"† How, then, I would ask, can any one certify, even after the most scrupulous attention, that all the powers of the mind are retained, when he is ignorant what these powers are? when he is ignorant, for instance, whether the propensities of Destructiveness, Acquisitiveness, or Secretiveness exist, and whether the sentiments of Veneration, Hope, or Conscientiousness are primitive emotions. The state of these, and other feelings and propensities, proved by Phrenology to be primitive, is never once alluded to in the history of injuries of the brain ; and, consequently, for anything we are told to the contrary, they, along with their respective organs, might have been entirely wanting in every one of the cases which are advanced as instances of the entire possession of the faculties. The opponents never speak of any except *intellectual* faculties ; and in expecting

* *Edinburgh Review*, No. 48, p. 448. † Ib., p. 439.

lesion of these powers, when, for instance, it is only the cerebellum or posterior lobes of the brain that are diseased, they display at once their own ignorance of the nature and number of the primitive faculties, and their most profound ignorance of the doctrines which they impugn. If any injury occurs in that portion of the brain lying under the most prominent part of the parietal bone, which the phrenologist states to be the organ of Cautiousness, and if we be in doubt as to the accuracy of the function assigned to it, and wish to have our observations confirmed or refuted by the phenomena attending such a case, one would naturally suppose that as the organs are all double, we would begin by observing whether the corresponding portion of brain on the opposite side partook in the disorganisation or not; and that we would then proceed to investigate the state of that particular faculty, of which these parts constitute the organs, and thus ascertain whether the feeling of Cautiousness ever remained undiminished, when, from the extent of the disease, it ought, according to the natural laws of the animal economy, to have been either impaired or entirely awanting.

This mode of proceeding, plain and simple as it appears, is not that pursued by the opponents of Phrenology. The opponent does not care, and does not inquire, whether it is one side only, or both sides, which are diseased: he makes no inquiry about the presence or absence of the manifestations of the sentiment of Cautiousness; he proceeds at once to the state of the *intellectual* powers, with which, as Phrenology most distinctly teaches, that part of the brain has no direct connexion; and finding none of the faculties which he calls Attention, Perception, Memory, or Imagination, at all impaired, he, with great confidence, concludes that the part in question *cannot* be the organ of *Cautiousness*; and so satisfied is he with his own reasoning, that he thinks himself entitled to ridicule those who do not see its cogency as clearly as he does himself. On any other subject this mode of reasoning would be looked upon as proceeding from a very blameable and lamentable degree of ignorance; but such was once the state of the public mind, that, when directed against Phrenology, it was hailed almost universally as highly philosophical and satisfactory.

Even supposing, however, that the number of primitive faculties was known, still no dependence can be placed upon cases not observed with a view "specially to this physiological inquiry;" for daily experience proves that, whenever a patient is able to return a rational answer to any simple question about his health, the surgeon and attendants, whose attention is not directed to the point, invariably speak of him as in full possession of all his faculties, although he is as unable to think or reason on any serious subject with his accustomed energy and facility, as a gouty or rheumatic patient is to walk with his accustomed vigour. In one sense, no doubt, the former may be said to be in possession of all his faculties, just as the latter, merely because he can drag himself across a room, may be said to possess the power of muscular motion; but then the power of exercising the faculties may be, and is, as much diminished in the one case, as that of using the muscles in the other. Even take a convalescent from any acute disease, in which there has been no particular affection of the brain, and introduce a subject which requires a train of thinking and concentration of mind to which, in health, he is fully equal—so far from retaining his powers undiminished, he will soon be reminded of his enfeebled state, by painful confusion in the head and other disagreeable symptoms. But confine his attention to anything which requires no effort on his part, and you benefit rather than harm him by such exercise, for it is then suited to the diminished vigour of his mind. Now, this is precisely the kind of discourse which the judicious surgeon permits to his tient, and from it alone he forms his own opinion of the state of the mind ; and, therefore, a person in such a state is uniformly said " to retain his faculties," &c. In like manner, the convalescent, gouty, or rheumatic patient, if gently exercised by strolling about his room, reaps benefit and strength ; but suppose you force him to an effort beyond what his muscular energy is calculated to support, the same bad effect is produced as in the case of the mind ; and as well might this person be said to retain his power of voluntary motion undiminished, as the other all his force of intellect unimpaired.

That the evidence as to the state of the mind, after wounds or alteration of the cerebral mass, is really so vague and unsatisfactory, may easily be shown from Dr. Ferriar's paper, and from the Edinburgh Review, the text books of the opponents. Besides the objection of extreme latitude in such expressions, as " no loss of sensibility," " no loss of voluntary motion," &c., &c., when used to indicate the condition of *all* the mental faculties, it may be remarked, that Dr. Ferriar speaks of one man as retaining all his faculties entire, who, it appears, had laboured under hypochondriasis for ten years ; a disease the very existence of which implies a morbid activity of some of the mental feelings, and which, consequently, ranks in the list of insanities ; and of a girl who, with evident symptoms of oppressed brain, is also said to have retained her faculties : and that the reviewer speaks of a lady who, " the day before her death, was capable *of being roused from her stupor*, and was then in possession of all her senses." But the idiot from birth, when roused from his natural stupor by the exaltation of a fever, appears sometimes to gain a considerable share of intellectual power, only to be lost upon recovery. Will he, too, then, be said to be in full possession of every faculty, because thus shown to be susceptible of excitation from stimuli ? The inference in the one case is certainly as logical as it is in the other.

But, even allowing also that, from a previous acquaintance with the number and functions of *all* the mental powers, we were qualified to judge of their *presence* or *absence*, it seems still to be a self-evident proposition, that, before we can affirm that a man possesses them all *unimpaired* under disease, we must have had some previous knowledge of the relative degrees of endowment and energy in which he possessed them when in health. The differences of intellectual vigour, of temper, and of moral dispositions, between man and man, are exceedingly great. The scale extends from the lowest pitch of idiocy up to the highest endowment of genius ; and the history of diseases informs us that a man, whose faculties have suffered a great diminution of energy, may still be able to return a rational answer to a question, although his mind is unable to fathom the depths it penetrated before. If, then, our first acquaintance with a patient suffering from an injury of the brain is formed by the side of his sick-bed *after* the accident has occurred, what means do we possess of knowing how far his mental powers in general, or any one in particular, have been injured or impaired ? Even under the most favourable circumstances the difficulty is by no means easily surmountable ; and, when we consider that injuries of the head are by far more frequent in hospital than in private practice, and that, in the former, the surgeon has seldom seen the patient before, it will be obvious, that, even supposing the testimony as to the actual state of the faculties to be as specific and precise as it is generally and vague, still, in a great majority of instances, the surgeon is unfavourably situated for speaking of the comparative force of any of them, seeing that this does not form the direct or usual object of his inquiries, and that, although it did, he must necessarily be ignorant of the degree in which they were manifested before the injury was sustained.

Having now shown that the observers quoted by the opponent were evidently neither acquainted with the number and functions of the mental faculties, nor in possession of any means of judging of the actual existence or comparative diminution of any individual faculty, in cases of disease or wounds of the cerebral mass, I proceed to point out an anatomical requisite, which, although as essential as the other two, seems not to have been possessed in any perceptible degree by any of those to whom the cases occurred, or by whom they are quoted. I allude to knowledge of of the *situation, form,* and *direction* of fibre of the several organs of which the phrenologists state the brain to be a congeries. Without this knowledge, any observations must manifestly be imperfect: how, for instance, is a man to ascertain that the organ of Cautiousness has been wounded or destroyed, if he knows neither its local situation nor the direction in which its constituent fibres run? And yet this is precisely the state of the mind of those upon whose authority the objection we are now refuting is so strenuously urged: nine-tenths of the cases occurred long before the organs were discovered, and the remaining tenth were, I believe, observed in ignorance of the discovery, so that all come under one class. If any one, indeed, could prove that he has found *both* the organs of Cautiousness destroyed, while the corresponding feeling was manifested as powerfully as before, then he would prove the operation of that sentiment to have been erroneously ascribed to that particular part of the brain. But, unless he knows accurately the situation of that organ toward the surface, and the direction of its fibres toward the interior, whether they are horizontal, vertical, or oblique, and unless he ascertains the condition of the organs of both sides, How can he venture to affirm that they were destroyed either in whole or in part? We are told, it is true, by Mr. Rennel, and other opponents, that every individual part specified by Gall and Spurzheim has in its turn been destroyed, without injury to the faculty of which they call it the organ; but if we examine the foundations upon which such assertions rest, the same want of precision, the same inconclusive vagueness, will be found to prevail, as in the evidence of the state of the mind. Not a single case in point can be produced; and it is evident that Mr. Rennel, as well as the other opponents, supposes the organs to be confined to the surface of the brain, instead of extending to its very base, to the medulla oblongata. They also, by what rules of logic I know not, appear to think injury of one organ sufficient to destroy the function of both, although they may see the reverse exemplified in individuals who hear or see well with one ear or one eye after that of the opposite side has been destroyed.

The brain has been considered by many physiologists, and particularly by those of them who are hostile to Phrenology, to be a single organ, every part of which concurs in executing a single function, viz., that of manifesting the mind; but so far from supporting their own conclusions, the cases referred to, if true, are directly subversive of them, and leave no choice, except between the phrenological doctrine of a plurality of cerebral organs, and the notion that the brain, the most delicate, the best protected, and apparently the most important organ of the body, is, after all, a mere useless encumbrance, or at most a mere mass fitted into a case, and placed at the top of the neck, more for the sake of ornament, or of preserving equilibrium, than for any more rational purpose: a conclusion which, however logically deducible from their own premises, they would, I am satisfied, be fully more averse to admit than the truth of Phrenology itself. The phrenological doctrine is, indeed, the only one by which these facts, so far as they are true, are at all explicable; for the moment we can prove, not only that the brain consists of two halves or hemispheres, but that each half is a congeries of parts performing distinct functions, difficulty disappears, and the phenomena become consistent with the ordinary laws of nature. We then see how one side or one part may be wounded or diseased, without involving the functions of the opposite side or of the other parts, just as one eye may be put out without destroying the function of the other, and the organ of one sense, sight for example, be injured or destroyed, while the organs of all the others remain sound.

Upon the same principle, it will be evident that, before we can expect complete loss of any one faculty, the entire organ of *both* sides must be destroyed—a fact which has been altogether overlooked by the objectors. For it will be seen, upon an attentive examination of the cases quoted, that not a *single instance is recorded in which this destruction of both organs has occurred, while the alleged manifestations existed.* In almost all the cases the injury or disease is expressly said to be on one side only ; and where it is on both, the parts affected implicate different organs. But this will be better understood by an abstract of the cases themselves as they are recorded in the Manchester Memoirs and in the Edinburgh Review. In perusing them, I beg the reader's attention to the vagueness of the information which they offer in regard to the integrity of the mental faculties, and also to the extent and nature of the cerebral injuries.

Mr. Earle relates the case of a man *whose sensibility* remained unaffected till within a few hours of his death, although an abscess occupied nearly one-third of the *right* hemisphere. Mr. Abernethy saw a gentleman who lived for two years in the full possession of every faculty, notwithstanding a cavity two inches broad by one long in the *right* hemisphere. Another was perfectly sensible with an abscess in the *left* hemisphere. Sir John Pringle[*] found an abscess in the *right* hemisphere, as large as an egg, in a patient " *who had never been delirious, nor altogether insensible ;*" and, in another, " *who had never been so insensible as not to answer reasonably when spoken to,*" he found an abscess in the *cerebellum* as large as a pigeon's egg. Dr. Ferriar says, that Dr. Hunter found the whole of the *right* hemisphere destroyed by suppuration in a man who retained his faculties to the last. One of Wepfer's patients manifested no *loss of sensibility,* although a cyst was found in the *right* hemisphere of the brain as large as a hen's egg. Diemerbroek saw a young man who received a thrust from a sword, which entered at the eye, and passed upward through the *right* ventricle, as far as the sagittal suture. During ten days he " *remained quite well,*" with no loss of sensibility, of voluntary motion, or of judgment, " cum sociis convenienter, et bono cum judicio quacunque de re disserens ;" after which he was cut off by a fever. Petit[†] saw a soldier, shot through the *left* lobe of the cerebellum and *left* posterior lobe of the brain, live forty-three hours, whose faculties were perfect to the last. Another man, mentioned by Quesnai as seen by Bagieu, received a musket-shot from below upward through the *right* anterior lobe, who had *no bad symptom* till the twelfth day, and ultimately recovered. Next are mentioned three cases ; in the first of which a ball, in the second the end of a stiletto, in the third a part of a knife, remained in the brain *without inconvenience* for some years. Genga tells us of a man who, from a blow on the *left* parietal and occipital bones, lost a portion of brain as large as a pigeon's egg, and *yet recovered.* Petit saw a man with a corpus striatum converted into a matter like dregs of wine, with no *loss of sensibility,* although one side was paralyzed. Valsalva saw an old man who was *not insensible,* with an abscess of the *right* thalamus opticus extending to the surface of the brain. Then come some cases of diseased pineal gland and cerebellum, without loss of sensibility. The reviewer then speaks of a lady who complained for a fortnight of an affection of the head, became comatose, and died. " The day before her death she was capable of being roused from her stupor, *and was then in full possession of all her senses.*" The *left* hemisphere of the cerebel-

[*] *Diseases of the Army,* p. 259.   [†] *Mémoires de l'Acad.,* 1748.

lum was converted into pus. Next follows a case from La Peyronie,
nearly similar, without *loss of sensibility*. Drelincurtius* saw a steato-
matous tumour as large as the fist between the cerebrum and cerebellum,
produce first blindness, then deafness, and at last the abolition " omnium
sensuum et functionum animalium, et necem ipsam." Dr. Tyson† mentions a case where the *left* hemisphere of the cerebellum was found
sphacelated, and the testis of that side enlarged and stony. The patient
had been ill two months, and for the most part rational. In the *Mémoires
de l'Acad. Royale*, 1703, Duverney relates a case of extensive injury,
without loss of sensibility. The Chevalier Colbert received a blow from
a stone upon the temple, which drove in the bones forming the back part
of the orbit, as well as the sella turcica. The inferior portion of the middle lobe of the brain, as far as the cerebellum, was found broken down,
and partly in a suppurating state. He lived seven days, "retained his
judgment perfectly, continued to perform all his functions, and exhibited
a surprising tranquillity of mind till his death." Ferriar attaches little
importance to this case, as confused. One of the most remarkable cases
is that quoted by the reviewer from Planque, and by Dr. Ferriar from
La Peyronie, as having occurred to Billot.‡ A boy of six years received
a pistol-shot in the middle of the brow, which passed through to the occiput. He survived eighteen days, and lost a portion of brain as large
as a nutmeg daily, and yet *remained quite well* until within a few hours
of his death. The portion of brain found remaining in the skull *did not
exceed the size of a small egg*.

The reviewer then quotes three cases of hydrocephalus internus, or
water in the head, which convince him that *sensibility* may remain after
the whole brain has been destroyed.

Many of the reviewer's cases are taken from Dr. Ferriar's paper in the
Manchester Memoirs. I shall, therefore, select the most interesting of
those which he has omitted. Diemerbroek§ quotes a case from Lindanus,
of a patient receiving a wound in one of the lateral ventricles, who went
about as usual for fourteen days, and then died. His surgeon thrust a
probe into the ventricle every day, without exciting any sensation. He
says‖ he saw a woman who lost a portion of brain as large as the fist,
from a fracture of the *right* side. She lived thirty-six days without alienation of the mind, although paralytic on the opposite side. In the appendix
to Wepfer's *Hist. Apoplect.*, Dr. Brunner mentions a case of a drunken
blacksmith, aged sixty-four, who died of apoplexy, whose faculties were
rather excited than impaired, although he observed, after death, " piam
matrem aqua turgidissimam. Ablata dura màtre, serum perpetim exsu-
davit et effluxit limpidum. Uterque ventriculus aquá scatebat turbida,
quin omnes recessus et cerebri cavitates hac inundatæ et repletæ fuerunt.
Cerebellum minime flaccidum, sed sicut reliquæ cerebri partes firmum
apparuit," &c. He was rather acute in his intellect toward the end. La
Peyronie mentions a case of a man who had been troubled with hypochondriacal symptoms for ten years, whose faculties were never affected,
although the fourth ventricle and *cerebellum* were found diseased. A girl
died in the fourth month of an arthritic complaint, with *evident symptoms
of oppressed brain*, but in perfect possession of her intellectual powers,
although the brain was soft and water effused. Bonnet saw a case,
where, after eleven days' illness, and, only toward the end, occasional
alienation of mind, " tota fere basis cerebri, imprimis cerebellum, et ea
pars medullæ spinalis quæ primis vertebris excipitur, sphacelo inventa
sunt correptæ."

Dr. Ferriar concludes by quoting from Ambrose Paré what he considers

* Adden. ad Wepfer, *Hist. Apop. Obs.*, 83. † *Phil. Trans.*, No. 228.
‡ *Mém. de l'Acad*, 1741. § *Anat.* lib. iii., p. 637. ‖ Pages 580-1.

a most extraordinary case; but Paré's authority being very great, he thinks it merits confidence. It is that of the Duc de Guise, " who was wounded in the head by the thrust of a lance, which entered *under* the right eye near the nose, and came out at the neck, between the ear and the vertebræ. The steel remained *in the brain*, was extracted with great difficulty, and the patient recovered." Such are the principal cases.

The farther removed an account is from what we are accustomed to observe in ordinary circumstances, the stronger is the evidence required before we can believe it, and inversely. So, in the present instance, when we find almost all the cases mentioned consisting of very partial injury of *one* side only of the brain, with no striking disturbance of *intellect*, we are not disposed to be scrupulous in admitting them to be true. We see such things occur in our own day, and they are, in themselves, sufficiently probable; seeing that the organs are double, and that one may be affected without the other participating in the injury; and that the organs of the intellectual faculties constitute so small a portion of the brain, as to leave nearly. wo-thirds of the whole mass to be destroyed on *both* sides, without necessarily interfering with the intellect. But when we come to such cases as that of the boy, who is said to have lost all his brain excepting " *about the bulk of an egg*," and yet " *remained quite well* " till within a few hours of his death, we are compelled to pause, and ask for stronger evidence than that afforded by a quotation at third hand of a single case. Neither the reviewer nor Dr. Ferriar appears to have seen Billot's own account of it, since each has quoted from a different source; and not having been able to procure the original work, I know not whether it is correctly quoted by either. But if *one* such case could be made out by incontestible evidence, it would not only lay prostrate the whole fabric of Phrenology, but would save us a great deal of time and useless labour at present spent in trying to find out the functions of a part which, according to this account, could not possibly have any; and, therefore, when we see the whole body of physiologists persevering in their endeavours to discover the uses of the brain with as much zeal and earnestness as if no such case had ever been heard of, the only conclusion which we can legitimately draw is, that they, hostile as most of them are to Phrenology, have just as little faith in the accuracy of the details as the phrenologists themselves; and if they disregard the story as unworthy of credit, we have surely, at least, an *equal* right to pursue a similar course, and to withhold our belief. In like manner, when we are told, as in the three cases alluded to by the reviewer, of the faculties remaining entire after the complete destruction of the brain by water, we are entitled to require evidence of no ordinary force before giving credit to them; more especially since the late discoveries by Gall and Spurzheim of the structure of brain show the fallacy of the appearances commented upon as indicating the absence of that organ.

Out of the twenty-nine cases here quoted from different authors, *eighteen* expressly refer to injury of *one side only*. These require no remarks; for, granting that none of the faculties were lost, there still remained the sound organs of the opposite side to execute the functions. *Five* more expressly refer to injury or disease of the *cerebellum* and *fourth ventricle*, parts which have no immediate connexion with the exercise of the *intellectual* faculties, which alone are mentioned. In two the side is not mentioned. In three more the *whole* brain was extant, but altered in appearance; and, lastly, comes the case *par excellence*, in which the brain had almost disappeared, and which, if admitted, would undoubtedly bury Phrenology and its opponents in one common ruin. Some of these demand a few observations.

In Dr. Brunner's case of the drunken blacksmith, who died apoplectic, the whole of the brain was still extant at his death; but a quantity of water was found effused upon it; notwithstanding which, he not only retained his faculties, but was even more acute. "Cerebellum minime flaccidum, sed sicut reliquæ cerebri partes firmum, apparuit." This is the consequence of a certain degree of inflammation, which, in the case of the brain, as well as in that of other organs, often *exalts* instead of diminishes the function. Hence it proves nothing against us. The effusion appears to have been the cause of the apoplexy and of death.

In the hypochondriacal patient, already referred to, even supposing all the faculties to have been unimpaired, the visible seat of the disease was confined to the *cerebellum* and fourth ventricle, and did not extend to the organs of the *intellectual* powers. In Bonnet's case of eleven days' illness, with occasional alienation toward the end, where the cerebellum, part of the base of the brain, and a portion of the medulla spinalis were mortified, "sphacelo inventæ sunt correptæ," the part of the base of the brain is not mentioned; and, therefore, no conclusion can be drawn in favour of any of the organs of the intellectual faculties having been partially destroyed: besides, there is every reason to believe the sphacelus not to have existed for any length of time, but to have been the immediate forerunner of death.

Lastly, Although what Dr. Ferriar calls the very extraordinary case of the Duc de Guise be included in the eighteen cases of injury on one side only, it is deserving of particular attention. The lance entered *under* the right eye, near the nose, and came out at the neck between the ear and vertebræ. The steel, it is said, remained *in the brain*, was extracted with difficulty, and recovery followed. The state of the faculties is not even mentioned. In this case, he says, the base of the *brain* must have been extensively injured. I humbly apprehend, however, that the brain was not and could not be touched. Let any one examine on the living or on the dead subject the direction of such a wound, and he will instantly agree with me in opinion, and will then be at no loss to account for the difficulty of extracting the steel. Having seen it stated in Boyer's *Traité des Maladies Chirurgicales*, that the spear entered *above* the eye, I procured the original work of Ambrose Paré, and found that Dr. Ferriar was right in saying that it entered *under* the eye. *But Paré never once mentions either brain or faculty.* He says, "The head of the lance stuck so fast as to require a pair of smith's pincers for its extraction. Although the violence of the blow was so great, that it could not be without *fracture of the bones, a tearing and breaking of the nerves, veins, and arteries, and other parts,* yet the generous prince, by the favour of God, recovered." P. 235, lib. x. Although the state of the faculties is not mentioned by Dr. Ferriar, I remember to have read in some French historical author that the duke bore the extraction with great fortitude, and retained his faculties apparently undiminished, and the above quotation accounts perfectly for the fact; for it shows that the brain was not in the least affected, the wound being altogether below it. In the case of the Chevalier Colbert also Dr. Ferriar says, the eye was crushed to pieces, and the orbit knocked in; which misapprehension must have arisen from the confused account given by the original author, Duverney; for, in point of fact, the stone struck the *temple*, and not the front of the eye.

Little confidence can, at any time, be placed in the history of dissections made only to discover the cause of death, when afterward applied to physiological purposes. The surgeon who has been in the habit of seeing numerous dissections, and particularly in hospital practice, made with this object alone in view, knows well how *very general* the examination of the diseased parts frequently is, even when seated in organs whose structure d functions are both known; and this observation naturally applies with double force to parts so little known as those contained in the cavity of the cranium. The Edinburgh Reviewer himself, in speaking of some parts (such as the corpus callosum, fornix, &c.,) which have *not been expressly mentioned* as destroyed, says, p. 446, "We believe, indeed, that several, if not the whole of them, were actually destroyed in the cases we have quoted ; but that they were omitted in the detail of the dissection, either from a fear of being tedious, or because the authors did not conceive *minuteness of description to be an object either of practical or physiological importance.* As it is, however, instances are still wanting in which the parts we have enumerated are *expressly stated to have been destroyed ;* and we beg leave to call the attention of the physiologists to his circumstance," &c. The phrenologists, in like manner, beg leave to call the attention *of the public to this circumstance,* that instances are still wanting in which any of their organs is expressly stated to have been destroyed, and the function to have remained unimpaired.

To such an extent, indeed, have anatomical structure and minuteness of detail been neglected in the history of the diseases and injuries of the cerebrum and cerebellum, *in so far as they are connected with the mind,* that in almost every instance, the palpable fact of the organs being double has been overlooked : and not only has no attention been paid to the situation of the individual organs in examining the effects of their injuries in relation to Phrenology, but it never has once been taken notice of by the opponents, that, while they confine their attention to the state of the *intellectual faculties alone* in all cases of wounded brain, the organs of these faculties, in the new system, constitute not more than one-third of the whole cerebral mass, and that the other two-thirds constitute the organs of the sentiments and propensities, which are never inquired into, as not being conceived to have anything to do with the brain.

As it appears, then, notwithstanding the affirmation of the opponents, to be quite consistent with the principles of Phrenology, that injuries of the brain may occur, without necessarily affecting the *intellectual* faculties, I might, perhaps, here safely drop the subject. Before quitting it, however, we may shortly inquire how far the cases referred to coincide, or are compatible, with the doctrines which the opponents themselves profess. Many of them teach, for example, that the whole brain is the organ of mind, and that every part of it is engaged in every act of thought. Now, it seems to me, that their own cases are fatal to any such theory ; for, as the brain is subject to all the ordinary laws of animal organization, were any part of that general organ injured, the function, even according to their own account, ought always to be impaired in proportion. Instead of which, they tell us that the function which they believe it to execute does not suffer with *almost total* destruction of the organ ! No other part of the human body is known to retain its functions unimpaired, amid total or partial change, or destruction of its structure ; and, therefore, had they not been blinded by preconceived opinions, they must have perceived that the very circumstance of the brain being partially injured, without any considerable derangement of intellect, was sufficient to prove that every part of that organ was *not* necessary to every individual act of mind, and that the brain was not the single organ they believed it to be.

Phrenology, or the doctrine of a plurality of organs and faculties, alone satisfactorily explains the apparent contradiction, by showing that the state of one organ, or part of the brain, does not necessarily affect the condition and functions of the others ; and thus the phrenologist, who considers particular parts of the brain to be the organs of distinct mental faculties, may be quite consistent in believing that one of these organs, and the faculty with which it is connected, may be wounded and impaired without necessarily inducing any diminution or alteration in the functions of the others; and as he thinks it proved, that two-thirds of the brain constitute the organs of the propensities and sentiments, he may still be quite consistent in believing that large portions of these two-thirds, even on both sides, may be injured without necessarily disturbing, in any high degree, the *intellectual* operations carried on by the remaining sound third, which he has previously ascertained to constitute the organs of the *intellectual* faculties. But the opponent, who believes in the *unity* of the brain, is very differently circumstanced, and can no more account for the intellect continuing unimpaired, after the destruction of *any* part, than he could for sight remaining unaffected by disease or destruction of the eye. What, then, are we to think of the consistency of those philosophers who, like Dr. Ferriar, in one page gravely doubt whether the brain has not been altogether destroyed, without loss of mental faculties; and yet in another declare that they consider, as he does, "these medical facts as almost demonstrating that the brain is the *instrument*, not the cause, of the reasoning powers?" We, too, consider the brain as the instrument of the mental faculties; but we are not so inconsistent as to suppose that it is a matter of indifference to the manifestations of these faculties, whether that instrument be a whole or a broken one, or have even altogether ceased to exist. We farther consider that Phrenology, so far from having anything to fear from these "medical facts" derives additional confirmation from them; since it is upon phrenological principles alone that they are either explicable or consistent with any of the known laws of nature. It is in such circumstances that the new science rises so far superior to any theory of the mind hitherto invented; and it can only be from its being founded on the solid basis of truth, that it is ever so beautifully and simply consistent with the observed phenomena of mind, alike in a state of health and of disease.

I proceed, before concluding the subject, (being in some measure connected with the present essay,) to make a few observations on a mode of investigating the functions of the individual parts of the brain, proposed by that excellent surgeon, Sir E. Home,* and differing widely from that in use among the phrenologists. "The various attempts," says he, "which have been made to procure accurate information respecting the functions that belong to individual portions of the human brain having been attended with very little success, it has occurred to me that, were anatomical surgeons to collect, in one view, all the appearances they had met with in cases of injury of that organ, and of the effects that such injuries produced upon its functions, a body of evidence might be formed, that would materially advance this highly important investigation."

As this mode of inquiry is still looked upon by many as the most promising and philosophical that has yet been tried, and as such is recommended by the Edinburgh Review, it may be worth while to see what it is really able to effect. To me it appears to be totally inadequate to the purposes of original discovery, although it may be usefully employed to procure additional information, *after* the functions of the different parts of the brain have been ascertained by other means.

The defects of this mode of investigation are, 1*st*, That, so long as we remain unacquainted with the situation and limits of the different cerebral organs, it is impossible for us to pronounce whether, in any given case, one only, or several, are implicated; and also, whether the destruction of any organ is partial or complete.

2*dly*, That, so long as we remain ignorant of the number and functions of the mental faculties, and of the effects of their various combinations with each other, we are necessarily unable to decide, in any case, what particular faculty or quality of mind has been impaired or destroyed. Some

* *Philosophical Transactions* for 1814, p. 469.

faculties, for instance, require the presence of such external objects for their operation as are not to be found in the chambers of the sick or in the wards of an hospital ; and, therefore, it is possible that the power may be altogether destroyed, and yet its absence may not even be suspected by the surgeon or his attendants, who never were aware of its existence as an independent faculty, even when the brain was entire.

3dly, That the complex and delicate structure of the brain makes it exceedingly difficult, if not impossible, to injure or destroy one part, without the neighbouring parts, and the functions which they perform, participating in a greater or less degree. Thus, Professor Rolando, of Turin, who has devoted much of his time to the study of the anatomy and functions of the brain, in speaking of mutilations which he had performed with a view to discover the functions of a particular part of that organ in the lower animals, complains of this as an almost unsurmountable obstacle. " I have made," says he, "innumerable experiments to discover the results of injuries done to the bigeminal tubercles, and the parts in the neighbourhood of the optic thalami, *but I have rarely obtained consistent results ;* which is not surprising, if we consider the peculiar interlacing of the numerous medullary fibres which meet in these parts ; for, as it is extremely difficult to know what bundles of fibres have been affected in these operations, we cannot draw clear and precise conclusions where there is a difference in the result." If this holds true with regard to mutilations performed with every precaution to avoid wounding other parts, and under every advantage which an acquaintance with anatomy can afford, it certainly applies with tenfold force to injuries, the results of accidental and unguided violence.

Lastly, That, from the mere aspect of the wound, we are never certain of the precise extent of the injury done to the brain ; and, consequently, can never positively refer the phenomena to an affection of any particular part, and of it alone. One injury, for instance, apparently of the very slightest nature, often produces the most serious constitutional symptoms, and disturbance of the whole mind ; while another, in appearance much more severe, is productive of little inconvenience. In the former the effects of the violence seem to extend either immediately or from sympathy over the whole brain, or, at least, much farther than its external or visible seat ; while in the latter the affection is more strictly of a local nature ; and thus the results obtained in one case are often entirely negatived by those obtained in another.

In accordance with, and in corroboration of, the opinion which I have here ventured to express, as to the total inadequacy of this mode of investigation for the purposes of original discovery, I would ask no better authority than Sir E. Home himself. For although, for the sake of greater accuracy, he confines himself to cases which have come under his own immediate notice, and although these must have been observed with a view specially to this inquiry, yet his own essay on this subject affords the most convincing proof and apposite illustration of all the defects of the mode which it is written to recommend. The first things, for example, that strike the reader on referring to it are, 1st, That, out of the *ten* classes into which the cases are purposely divided by Sir Everard, no less than *seven* (1. Undue pressure of water on the brain, 2. Concussion of the brain, 3. Preternaturally dilated or diseased bloodvessels of the brain, 4. Extravasated blood, 5. Formation of pus, 6. Depression or thickening of parts of the skull, 7. Pressure from tumours) resolve themselves into affections, in which the *totality* of the brain is, in some way or another, concerned ; 2d, That in one (viz., 8. Injury of the medulla spinalis) *the entire brain is unaffected ;* and, 3dly, That *in two only* (9. Injury to the substance of the brain ; and, 10. Alternation of structure) is the affection generally confined to *individual* portions of that organ ; although in very many instances, even in these two classes, it extends over the whole brain. From his own statement, then, the reader would naturally anticipate *a priori*, that the effects resulting from most of these injuries would be such as are known to indicate derangement, not of one, or of several, but of all the parts of the brain ; and, consequently, that they could not, by any possibility, lead to the discovery wished for, of the functions of its *individual* portions. Accordingly, Sir Everard himself informs us that the effects produced were, *delirium, convulsions, coma, apoplexy, sickness, watching*, and the like, and not lesion of any particular faculty or of any individual function. In one or two instances, indeed, the state of the memory and of the external senses is mentioned, but without being connected in any way with specific injury. The reviewer himself, with every wish to be pleased with Sir Everard's method, is constrained to say, that the results obtained in this manner are so vague and contradictory, that they " serve only to confirm what had already perhaps been sufficiently made out by the authors we have named ; to wit, that there is no sort of uniformity either in the kind or degree of the symptoms which accompany diseases of the brain." And in this sentiment I cordially concur with him, in so far as regards violent injuries.

To render the results obtained, either from observing the effects of cerebral injuries in man, or from the performance of mutilations upon the brains of animals, at all valuable in illustrating the cerebral physiology, a previous knowledge of the seats of the organs, and of the nature of the faculties which they subserve, has been already shown to be an indispensable requisite ; and if we suppose these to have been accurately ascertained by other means, then the facility of making interesting and precise physiological and pathological observations is so greatly increased, that much valuable information may be obtained, especially in some individual cases, in the last-mentioned two classes of Sir E. Home. But without this preliminary knowledge to guide us in our observations, it is obvious that nothing precise or practical can be got at.

If an injury of the cerebellum, for example, or of part of the posterior lobes of the brain, occurs to a philosopher, who is firmly satisfied in his own mind " that the whole brain is engaged in every act of thought," and that no part of it is appropriated to the manifestations of any of the propensities or sentiments, what inference can he draw as to the function, upon finding no intellectual faculty with which he is acquainted impaired or wanting ? He cannot consistently investigate the state of the propensities, and refer any irregularities among them to the injury sustained; because these are not intellectual faculties, and, according to him, have no connexion with the brain. He remains of necessity as much in the dark as ever. But let such a case occur to a phrenologist, or to him who has ascertained, by previous observation, the uses of the part, it is evident that, although he could not, any more than the philosopher, infer the function from a consideration of the symptoms alone, yet, having discovered it by other means, he comes to the injury fully competent to judge whether his former observations are confirmed or refuted by the phenomena now before him. It is only when in possession of this previous qualification that we can derive any advantage from such cases in increasing our knowledge of mind.

That the philosopher, with such views, could never have been led to the discovery of the connexion between certain parts of the brain and the propensities and sentiments, by the mere observation of their injuries, is proved by wounds of these parts having been actually attended with symptoms corresponding to their phrenological functions, and neither him nor the anatomical surgeon having drawn any such inference. Wounds and diseases of the cerebellum, for instance, have forced themselves upon their notice, where the sexual propensity was extinguished by loss of substance, or preternaturally excited by the subsequent inflammatory action; and yet no one drew the inference that the cerebellum was the organ of Amativeness.* The temper and moral sentiments have also been entirely changed, in consequence of certain injuries of the brain, while the intellect remained unimpaired; and no one drew the conclusion that the parts affected were the organs of these sentiments. Nor would they have been warranted in doing so, because instances of injury confined so entirely to one part as to affect its function, without having any influence upon those of the neighbouring parts, are so rare, in comparison to those of an opposite kind, that no just inferences can be drawn from them alone; although, combined with other evidence, they are highly important.

CONCLUSION

(TO THE SECOND EDITION.)

In the Introduction to this work it is observed, that, "in surveying the philosophy of man as at present exhibited to us in the writings of philosophers, we perceive, *first*, That no account is given of the influence of the material organs on the manifestations of the mental powers; that the progress of the mind from youth to age, and the phenomena of sleep, dreaming, idiocy, and insanity, are left unexplained or unaccounted for; *secondly*, That the existence and functions of some of the most important primitive faculties are still in dispute; and, *thirdly*, That no light whatever has been thrown on the nature and effects of combinations of the primitive powers in different degrees of relative proportion. It is, with great truth, therefore, that Monsieur De Bonald, quoted by Mr. Stewart, observes, that "diversity of doctrine has increased, from age to age, with the number of masters and with the progress of knowledge; and Europe, which at present possesses libraries filled with philosophical works, and which reckons up almost as many philosophers as writers; poor in the midst of so much riches, and uncertain, with the aid of all its guides, which road it should follow; Europe, the centre and focus of all the lights of the world, has yet its *philosophy* only in expectation."

May I hope that Phrenology will now appear to the attentive reader calculated to supply the deficiency here pointed out, and to furnish Europe, at last, with the Philosophy so long in expectation?

Hitherto the writings of Dr. Gall have been little known to the British public, except through the medium of hostile reviews; and the most unmeasured ridicule and abuse have been poured out against them, as if they were a disgrace to the century in which they were produced: his fellow-labourer, Dr. Spurzheim, has sustained an equal share of this unmerited storm. In preparing the present volume for the press, I have drawn largely from the works of both of these founders of the science; in many instances I have compared their statements of fact with nature, sifted their arguments, and weighed deliberately their conclusions; and I now feel it an imperative duty to state, that the present generation has, in my humble judgment, reacted, in their cases, the scenes which have attached so deep a stigma to the ages of Galileo and Harvey. The discoveries of

* Wepferus's *Historia Apoplecticorum*, edit. 1724, p. 487. Magendie's. *Journal de Physiologie* for April and August, 1822; also *Medical Repository*. vol. xviii., pp. 268–358.— Larrey's *Memoires de Chirurgie Militaire et Campagnes*, vol. ii., p. 150; vol. iii., p. 262.

the revelation of the globe and the circulation of the blood were splendid displays of genius, interesting and beneficial to mankind ; but their results, compared with the consequences which must inevitably follow from Dr. Gall's discovery of the functions of the brain, (embracing, as it does, the true theory of the animal, moral, and intellectual constitution of man,) sink into relative insignificance. Looking forward to the time when the real nature and ultimate effects of Dr. Gall's discovery shall be fully recognised, I cannot entertain a doubt that posterity will manifest as eager a desire to render honour to his memory, as his contemporaries have shown to treat himself with indignity and contempt. If the present work shall tend in any degree to rouse the public attention to his merits, and to excite the philosophers of England to do him justice ere he die, it will accomplish one great end of its publication. Let them at last lay aside the prejudice which has so long kept them back from looking with their own eyes into his works, and from appealing, with the lights which he affords, to Nature, as the standard by which to try the merits of his pretensions. If they will examine, they will find that a fortunate thought opened up to him a vast region of discovery, and that he has displayed gigantic powers in prosecuting it to its results ; that, instead of being an ignorant pretender to knowledge, he is a man of profound and solid erudition ; that, so far from being a reckless theorist, he is the most stubborn adherent to fact that has perhaps ever appeared in the annals of inductive philosophy ; and that, instead of being characterized by a weak understanding and bewildered imagination, he manifests an intellect at once profound, regulated, and comprehensive.

Dr. Spurzheim's works and lectures have rendered him better known in this country, and the force of truth has for some years been operating in his favour. No reviewer would now reckon it creditable to use the terms so unceremoniously applied to him in 1815 ; but a great debt of respect and gratitude remains to be paid by Britain and the world to Dr. Spurzheim. He is second in fortune rather than in merit to Dr. Gall. The great discovery of Phrenology unquestionably belongs to the latter ; but to Dr. Spurzheim is due the praise of early appreciating its importance, and of fearlessly dedicating his life to the enlargement of its boundaries and the dissemination of its principles, at a time when neither honour nor emolument, but on the contrary obloquy and censure, were bestowed on its adherents. In admiring the science as it now appears, it becomes us to recollect, that we owe much of its excellence and interest to this gifted individual. He has enriched it with the most valuable anatomical discoveries, ascertained the functions of several highly important organs, shed over it the lights of a refined analytic philosophy, and pointed out the most important fields of its application. With profound gratitude and respect, therefore, I acknowledge myself indebted to him for the greatest gift which it was possible for one individual to confer on another—a knowledge of the true Philosophy of Man.

To my excellent friends, also, the Reverend David Welsh, Mr. Scott, Mr. Simpson, Mr. Lyon, and Dr. Andrew Combe, fellow-labourers with me in Phrenology, I owe many obligations. In availing myself freely of the lights which they have struck out, it has been my constant wish to acknowledge the source of my information ; but if, amid the habitual interchange of ideas with which they have honoured me, their discoveries have, in any instance, been amalgamated with my own thoughts, and their authors forgotten, I solicit their forgiveness, assuring them that inadvertency alone has been the cause of any such mistakes.

EDINBURGH, *October*, 1825.

POSTSCRIPT TO THE THIRD EDITION.

SINCE the foregoing observations were written, Dr. Gall has been numbered with the dead. Like many other benefactors of mankind, he has died without his merits being acknowledged, or his discoveries rewarded, by the "great in literature and science" of his own age; but he possessed the consciousness of having presented to the world one of the most valuable discoveries that ever graced the annals of philosophy, and enjoyed the delight of having opened up to mankind a career of improvement, physical, moral, and intellectual, to which the boldest imagination can at present prescribe no limits. This appears to be the reward which Providence assigns to men eminently gifted with intellectual superiority; and we may presume that it is wisely suited to their nature. A great duty remains for posterity to perform to the memory of Dr. Gall, and I cannot entertain a doubt that in due time it will be amply discharged.

It gives me the greatest satisfaction to renew, after five years' additional experience, the acknowledgment of my highest gratitude and esteem for Dr. Spurzheim; and to express my earnest wish that Britain may, by suitable encouragement, retain him permanently to herself.

EDINBURGH, *October*, 1830.

POSTSCRIPT TO THE FOURTH EDITION.

IT is painful in no ordinary degree now to speak of Dr. Spurzheim in the past tense; but, since the third edition of this work was printed, he too has been numbered with the dead. He died at Boston, U. S., on the 10th of November, 1832, while zealously engaged in communicating the invaluable truths of Phrenology to a people in every respect worthy of the doctrine, and of the man who came among them to teach it. The citizens of Boston, and of the United States generally, justly appreciated the talents and moral worth of this most excellent philosopher. They honoured him while alive, gave him a public funeral, and erected a beautifully appropriate monument to his memory in Auburn Cemetery. In expressing my heartfelt sorrow for his loss, I render a sincere tribute of respect and gratitude to them for the kindness with which they received him, and the honour with which they enshrined his mortal remains.

EDINBURGH, 31st *October*, 1836.

APPENDIX.

No. I.

Text, page 33.

The Brain the Organ of the Mind.

A VERY striking argument in favour of the doctrine that the brain is the organ of the mind, is found in the numerous cases in which changes of character have been produced by injuries inflicted on the head. In this way the action of the brain is sometimes so much altered, that high-talents are subsequently displayed where mediocrity, or even extreme dulness, existed before; in other instances the temper from being mild and amiable becomes irritable and contentious; while in others, again, it occasionally happens, in consequence of the effect of the injury being to depress instead of exalt the tone of the brain, that talents formerly enjoyed are obscured or lost. Dr. Gall refers to a case reported by Hildanus, of a boy ten years old, a portion of whose skull was accidentally driven in; nothing was done to remedy the injury, and the boy, who had previously given promise of excellent parts, became altogether stupid, and in that condition died at the age of forty. He adds a similar case of a lad whose intellectual vivacity was destroyed by cerebral disease accompanied with fever.*—The aëronaut Blanchard had the misfortune to fall upon his head, and thenceforward his mental powers were evidently feeble; after death Dr. Gall found his brain diseased.†—A lady of distinguished talent fell and wounded the back of her head; from this time she was subject to periodical fits of madness, and gradually lost her intellectual brilliancy.—A man whom Dr. Gall saw at Pforzheim, in the Grand Duchy of Baden, had his frontal bone fractured at the age of six years, and in consequence became liable to periodical fits of fury.—In another, residing at Weil, near Stuttgard, a portion of the skull was depressed by a blow from a stone; before this accident he bore the reputation of a peaceful citizen, but after recovery his friends were surprised to find his character entirely changed; though formerly so mild and good-natured, he was now a troublesome brawler. Dr. Gall preserved his skull, which is thick and very dense, thus showing how much the brain had been affected.‡—Father Mabillon had a very limited capacity in early youth, insomuch that, at the age of eighteen, he could neither read nor write, and hardly even speak. In consequence of a fall, it became necessary to trepan his skull: during his convalescence a copy of Euclid fell into his hands, and he made rapid progress in the study of mathematics.§—Dr. Gall mentions also the case of a lad who, up to his thirteenth year, was incorrigibly dull; having fallen from a staircase and wounded his head, he afterward, when cured, pursued his studies with distinguished success.—Another young man, when at the age of fourteen or fifteen, was equally unpromising, but fell from a stair in Copenhagen, and subsequently manifested great vigour of the intellectual faculties. Nor was this the full extent of the change. Before the accident his moral character was unexceptionable; but latterly it became so bad, as to deprive him of an important situation, and ultimately to consign him to prison.—Gretry tells of himself in his memoirs, that he was indebted for his musical genius to a violent blow inflicted on his head by a falling beam of wood.—Haller speaks of an idiot who, having been seriously wounded on the head, manifested intelligence while the injury was unhealed, but relapsed into imbecility as soon as the cure was complete.‖—Dr. Caldwell mentions the case of a mechanic, near Lexington, Kentucky, whose intellectual powers were greatly augmented by "an inflammatory action of the brain resulting from a mechanical injury." A similar change, he adds, "took place in one of the sons of the late Dr. Priestley. A fracture of the skull, produced by a fall from a two-story window, improved not a little the character of his intellect. For a knowledge of this fact I am indebted to the doctor himself."¶—

* Ib., ii., 172. † Ib., p. 173.
§ Ib., p. 176. ‖ Ib., i., 215, 216; v., 120.
ments of Phrenology, 2d edit., pp. 92, 93.

A young man who had received a considerable wound near the temporal bone was trepanned by Acrel. When cured, he felt an irresistible propensity to steal, although formerly no such disposition had existed : Acrel procured his liberation from prison by attributing this troublesome inclination to the effects of the wound.*—There is in Dr. Gall's collection a cast of the head of a relative of his own, whose brain was injured by the fall of a tile : before the accident this person was good-natured, pacific, and regular in his habits, but afterward became eccentric, quarrelsome, and apt to fly into a passion at the slightest contradiction.†—Mr. Hood, of Kilmarnock, has published similar cases. A man was waylaid and struck severely on the head with a pair of tongs, which penetrated to a considerable depth into his brain at the situation of the left organ of Cautiousness ; subsequently to this he manifested an unusual degree of timidity. Another individual had his skull fractured by falling from a stage-coach, the injury extending over the organs of Destructiveness and Combativeness ; and his temper in consequence became more irritable than before.‡ Little is yet known concerning the manner in which the injuries produced these effects.

No. II.
Text, pages 106, 180, and 238.

Objections to Dr. Spurzheim's Classification of the Mental Faculties. By. Robert Cox.—Abridged from the Phrenological Journal, vol. x., p. 154.

Every mental faculty is capable of acting in various forms ; in other words, it may exist in different states, each*giving rise to a distinct variety of consciousness—a distinct affection of the mind.§ The sense of feeling, for example, is one of the fundamental faculties, but the consciousness resulting from its activity is modified according to the particular state in which its organs happen to be, from the influence of some external or internal cause. Thus, when we hold our fingers near the fire, the sensation of heat arises, and this is one affection or mode of action of the faculty. If we prick the skin with a needle, the affection is that of pain : tickle the soles of the feet, and the sensation of itching follows : dip the hands into melting snow, and the sensation of cold is experienced. All these affections, it will be observed, are referrible to one faculty alone ; they are modes of action of a single power.

The affections or modes of action of the fundamental powers are divided by Dr. Spurzheim into *qualitive* and *quantitive* affections ; that is to say, first, those which differ in kind, as the sensation of heat differs from the sensations of pain, cold, and itching ; and, secondly, those which differ in intensity or power. The sense of taste, for example, is, like that of feeling, subject to modifications, giving rise to different affections or states of consciousness. According to the nature of the substances taken into the mouth, the affection is that of sweetness, bitterness, sourness, acritude, and so on. These are *qualitive* affections of a single faculty—affections different in kind, and not merely in degree. The sense of smell, in like manner, is modified when stimu lated by different odoriferous substances ; and that of hearing is variously affected by different sounds, as shrill, grave, creaking, and whistling. So also the sentiments of pride and contempt are two qualitive affections of the single faculty of Self-Esteem.

The *quantitive* affections are no other than the qualitive existing at different points in the scale of intensity, quantity, or power ; a single qualitive affection often receiving different names, according to its degree of force. Thus, one general qualitive affection receives at various points in the scale of intensity the names of velleity, desire, longing, and passion ; one general qualitive affection of Acquisitiveness or Love of Approbation is called at a certain point pleasure, at another joy, and at a third ecstasy ; while another general

---

* Gall, i., 450 † *Phren. Journ.,* vii., 33. ‡ Ib., ii., 75, *et seq.*

§ I employ the word *affection* as it is used by Dr. Spurzheim, " solely according to its etymology, to indicate the different states of being affected of the fundamental powers." See his *Philosophical Principles of Phrenology,* p. 43. In this article the last (American) editions of Dr. Spurzheim's works are quoted.

qualitive affection of the same faculties is termed on one occasion pain, on another grief, and on a third wretchedness or misery. The special qualitive affection of Cautiousness called *fear* includes the quantitive affections of wariness, apprehension, anxiety, terror, and panic.

It happens with many of the faculties that their affections are of two kinds: 1st, an *inclination* or propensity to act in a particular way ; and, 2dly, certain *emotions* or sentiments which accompany, but are easily distinguishable from, propensity. Thus, one affection of Acquisitiveness is an inclination to take possession of property and to hoard it up, while another is the sentiment of greed. Self-Esteem is the source of an inclination to wield authority, and at the same time of the emotion which its name denotes, including the various quantitive affections of self-satisfaction, self-reliance, self-importance, pride, and overweening arrogance. Contempt, which is a qualitive affection of the same faculty, falls, like the emotion named self-esteem, within the second or sentimental class of affections. Upon the existence of these two kinds of affections Dr. Spurzheim has founded an important part of his classification.

Gall and Spurzheim agree in dividing the mental faculties into two great orders, the first comprehending what are termed the dispositions, and the second the powers of the understanding. This division has been recognised, from the remotest antiquity, under the names of soul and spirit, (*l'âme et l'esprit*,) will and understanding, the moral and intellectual faculties, heart and head. Dr. Spurzheim calls the former the *feelings* or *affective faculties;*[*] of which, says he, " the essential nature is to feel emotions ;"[†] and the latter the *intellectual faculties,* whose " essential nature is to procure knowledge."[‡] To the designation *intellectual faculties* it appears impossible to object ; but as it is by no means evident that emotions are peculiar to the faculties called affective, the use of that term, as defined by Dr. Spurzheim, seems to be improper. In fact, many general emotions are modes of action of the intellectual as well as of the affective powers. Every faculty, without exception, desires ; and what is desire but an emotion ? Every faculty experiences pleasure and pain, and are not these emotions ? Take the sense of taste as an example. This, being an intellectual faculty, experiences, according to Dr. Spurzheim, no emotion ; but, as Dr. Hoppe, of Copenhagen, has already inquired, " when we sit down, delighting in the dainties of a well-stored table, is not then the working of the sense wholly affective ?"[§] I propose, therefore, to define the affective faculties as those of which the essential nature is to feel emotions, or inclinations, or both, but which do not procure knowledge.

Dr. Spurzheim's classification, however, does not stop here. " Both orders of the cerebral functions," says he, " may be subdivided into several genera, and each genus into several species. Some affective powers produce only desires, inclinations, or instincts ; I denominate them by the general title *propensities.* The name *propensities,* then, is only applied to indicate internal impulses which invite to certain actions. They correspond with the instincts or instinctive powers of animals. There are other affective faculties," he continues, " which are not confined to inclination alone, but have something superadded that may be styled *sentiment.* Self-Esteem, for instance, produces a certain propensity to act ; but, at the same time, feels another emotion or affection which is not merely propensity."[||] The affective faculties named by Dr. Spurzheim *propensities,* are Amativeness, Philoprogenitiveness, Inhabitiveness, Adhesiveness, Combativeness, Destructiveness, Secretiveness, Acquisitiveness, and Constructiveness ; those which he calls *sentiments* are Self-Esteem, Love of Approbation, Cautiousness, Benevolence, Veneration, Firmness, Conscientiousness, Hope, Marvellousness, Ideality, Mirthfulness or Gayness, and Imitation.

To Dr. Spurzheim's division of the affective faculties into propensities, or mere tendencies to certain modes of action—and sentiments, which are propensities with emotions superadded—I offer no objection except that, as will be shown in the sequel, a third genus ought to be introduced. But when the claims of the individual faculties to be ranked in one or other of the subdivisions are narrowly scrutinized, I fear that much inaccuracy becomes apparent.

Judging from the present state of our knowledge of the fundamental powers of the mind, the whole of the affective faculties, with the exception of only

[*] *Phrenology,* p. 131.   [†] *Phil. Prin. of Phren.,* p. 48.   [‡] Ibid., p. 52.
[§] *Phren. Journ.,* iv., 308.   [||] *Phrenology,* p. 131.

five, seem entitled to be called *sentiments*, taking that word as it is defined by Dr. Spurzheim. These five exceptions I conceive to be—*1st*, Constructiveness, which is understood to be a mere inclination or tendency to fashion or configurate, without, so far as I can see, any special emotion superadded to it ; *2dly*, Imitation, which is in exactly the same predicament, though classed as a sentiment by Dr. Spurzheim ; and, finally, Love of Approbation, Hope, and Ideality, which appear to be mere special emotions, superadded to no propensity whatever. Except these five, I repeat, the whole affective faculties seem to be propensities, tendencies, or inclinations, having emotions annexed to them. This position it will be proper to demonstrate in detail. In taking a survey of the faculties, I shall notice, first, the sort of actions to which they give a tendency ; and, secondly, the simple affections or emotions by which that tendency is accompanied.

Amativeness includes both a tendency to act in a particular way and a concomitant emotion. The former is the tendency to propagate, and inclination to acts of dalliance in general ; while the latter is the emotion of sexual love. This faculty, therefore, falls within Dr. Spurzheim's definition of a sentiment.

Of Philoprogenitiveness the same is true. The tendency is an inclination to associate with children, and the emotion is love of young.

Adhesiveness is a tendency to associate with our fellow-creatures generally, and the corresponding emotion is love or attachment between friends. This emotion never exists except in combination with a desire to be in the society of the person beloved.

The next faculty is usually named Combativeness ; but, for reasons elsewhere published,[*] I conceive that Oppositiveness is a more accurate term. The propensity is not in all cases a tendency to fight, but a general inclination to oppose. The emotion of which the mind is conscious when this tendency acts, is boldness or courage.

Destructiveness is a tendency to injure. The superadded emotion has no name that I am aware of, except when high in the scale of quantitive affections. Ferocity is then the appellation which it receives. The emotion is an ingredient in various compound affections, such as anger, jealousy, malice, and envy.

Alimentiveness may be regarded as a propensity to eat and drink. Hunger and thirst are not usually referred to this organ ; but these seem to be merely the sentimental affections which accompany the desire to feed.

Secretiveness is an inclination to conceal. The emotion, like that of Destructiveness, receives a name only when it is strong. Slyness and suspicion are emotions of this faculty in a state of vigorous action.

Acquisitiveness is a tendency to acquire and hoard property. Cupidity or greed is the emotion when it is very powerful.

Constructiveness is a tendency to fashion. As already observed, no special emotion accompanies its activity ; so that it is entitled to be called a propensity in Dr. Spurzheim's sense of that word.

Self-Esteem is the name of the emotion arising from the organ No. 10. Self-complacency is almost synonymous with it ; and pride is the emotion higher in the scale of quantitive affections of the faculty. The corresponding propensity is a tendency to take the lead, to exercise authority, to attend to self-interest and self-gratification, to prefer one's self to other people.

Love of Approbation is an emotion which assumes the name of vanity when in excess. It seems doubtful whether any propensity accompanies it. Shame is an affection of this power.

Cautiousness is the emotion of wariness, and, when powerful, of fear. The propensity is to take precautions against danger.

Benevolence is surely not less a propensity than Destructiveness, and no reason appears why they should be classified differently. It is a tendency to increase the enjoyment and diminish the misery of sentient beings. The emotions accompanying this tendency are good will and compassion.

Veneration is a propensity to act with deference, submission, or respect toward our fellow-men—to obey those in authority, and to worship the Supreme Being. The emotion is well expressed by the words *veneration* and *deference*, and, when in great vigour, is called *devotion*.

* See *Phrenological Journal*, vol. ix., p. 147.

Firmness I consider to be a tendency to persist in conduct, opinion, and purpose. Resolution is the name which its emotion receives.

Conscientiousness seems to be a propensity to give every man his due. The emotion is the sentiment of justice ; and the actions prompted by it are honest, candid, just.

Hope is a mere emotion, unaccompanied by any propensity. It can hardly be said to give rise, except indirectly, to a tendency to act in a speculative manner. Acquisitiveness, modified by the emotion of Hope, appears to do this. With Ideality no propensity appears to be connected. There is only the lively emotion of the beautiful and sublime.

Wonder is clearly an emotion, but whether no inclination is associated with it may perhaps be doubted. Is it not, for example, a propensity to exaggerate? The emotion of the ludicrous is accompanied by a propensity to act comically. Imitation is a mere propensity, without any special emotion whatever.

This concludes the list of the affective faculties. If we take the guidance of the principle by which Dr. Spurzheim was led, they ought, I think, to be divided into three genera instead of two—the first. including those faculties which give rise to tendencies as well as emotions ; the second, those which are tendencies without emotions ; and the third, those which are emotions without tendencies. In the first genus, therefore, we ought to rank Amativeness, Philoprogenitiveness, Adhesiveness, Oppositeness, Destructiveness, Secretiveness, Acquisitiveness, Self-Esteem, Cautiousness, Benevolence, Veneration, Firmness, Conscientiousness, Wonder, and Mirthfulness or the sentiment of the ludicrous. In the second genus—that of tendencies without emotions—I would place Constructiveness and Imitation ; and in the third, comprehending mere emotions, the faculties of Hope and Ideality, and perhaps also Love of Approbation. Such appears to be the classification of the affective faculties, on Dr. Spurzheim's principle, warranted by the present state of phrenological science.

No subdivision of the intellectual powers, or those which procure knowledge, was made by Dr. Gall ; but Dr. Spurzheim has minutely classified them. "They may be subdivided," says he, "into four genera. The first includes the functions of the external senses and of voluntary motion ; the second, those faculties which make man and animals acquainted with external objects and their physical qualities ; and the third, the functions connected with the knowledge of relation between objects or their qualities—these three genera I name *perceptive faculties :* the fourth genus comprises the faculties which act on all the other sensations and notions, and these I style *reflective* faculties."* Respecting the first and last of these genera I offer no remarks. The second includes Individuality, Form, Size, Weight, and Colouring, all of which, except Individuality, seem rightly classified. The exception of Individuality is here made on the ground that nothing but the qualities of external objects is perceptible, and that by these alone the existence of an object is revealed to us ; so that Individuality, which takes cognizance of no quality, cannot be said to "perceive" at all. Its essential nature appears to be, as Dr. Spurzheim expresses it, "to produce the *conception* of being or existence, and to know *objects* in their individual capacities."† In describing it, Dr. Spurzheim studiously avoids the use of the word *perception ;* he speaks only of conception, knowledge, and cognition.

Under the third genus of intellectual faculties—those " which perceive the relations of external objects "—Dr. Spurzheim ranges Locality, Order, Number, Eventuality, Time, Tune, and Language. In some respects he is here in error. Neither Eventuality, Time, nor Language is cognizant of relations of external objects ; Tune perceives only relations of *sounds ;* and, according to the best of our present knowledge, Order is merely (what Dr. Spurzheim calls it) a "disposition to arrange," and desire to see everything in its proper place.

In his *Philosophical Principles,* and *Outlines of Phrenology,* Dr. Spurzheim inconsistently comprehends the second and third genera of the intellectual faculties in one, which is described as embracing the "internal senses or perceptive faculties which procure knowledge of external objects, their physical qualities, and various relations."

* *Phrenology,* p. 131.   † *Manual of Phrenology,* p. 59.

No. III.

Text, page 106.

Names and Order of the Mental Faculties adopted by Dr. Gall.

NO.	FRENCH.	GERMAN.	ENGLISH Names given by DR. SPURZHEIM.
1.	Instinct de la generation.	Zeugungstrieb.	Amativeness.
2.	Amour de la progéniture.	Jungenliebe, Kinderliebe.	Philoprogenitiveness.
3.	Attachement, amitié.		Adhesiveness.
4.	Instinct de la défense de soi-même ét de sa propriété.	Muth, Raufsinn.	Combativeness.
5.	Instinct carnassier.	Wurgsinn.	Destructiveness.
6.	Ruse, finesse, savoir-faire.	List, Schlauheit, Klugheit.	Secretiveness.
7.	Sentiment de la propriété.	Eigenthumsinn.	Acquisitiveness.
8.	Orgueil, fierté, hauteur.	Stolz, Hochmuth, Herschsucht.	Self-Esteem.
9.	Vanité, ambition, amour de la gloire.	Eitelkeit, Ruhmsucht, Ehrgeitz.	Love of Approbation.
10.	Circonspection, prévoyance.	Behutsamkeit, Vorsicht, Vorsichtigkeit.	Cautiousness.
11.	Mémoire des choses, mémoire des faits, sens des choses, éducabilité, perfectibilité.	Sachgedœchtniss, Erziehungs-Fœhigkeit.	Eventuality and Individuality.
12.	Sens des localités, sens des rapports de l'espace.	Ortsinn, Raumsinn.	Locality.
13.	Mémoire des personnes, sens des personnes.	Personen-sian.	Form.
14.	Sens des mots, sens des noms, mémoire des mots, mémoire verbale.	Wort-Gedœchtniss.	Language.
15.	Sens du langage de parole, talent de la philologie, &c.	Sprach-Forchungs-sinn.	Held by Dr. Spurzheim to be included in the last organ.
16.	Sens des rapports des couleurs, talent de la peinture.	Farben-sinn.	Colouring.
17.	Sens des rapports des tons, talent de la musique.	Ton-sinn.	Tune.
18.	Sens des rapports des nombres.		Number.
19.	Sens de méchanique, sens de construction, talent de l'architecture.	Kunst-sinn, Bau-sinn.	Constructiveness.
20.	Sagacité comparative.	Vergleichenderscharfsinn.	Comparison.
21.	Esprit metaphysique, profondeur d'esprit.	Metaphysischer-Tief-sinn.	Causality.
22.	Esprit caustique, esprit de saillie.	Witz.	Wit.
23	Talent poétique.	Dichter-Geist.	Ideality.
24.	Bonte, bienveillance, douceur, compassion, &c.	Gutmœthigkeit, Mitleiden, &c.	Benevolence.
25.	Faculté d'imiter, mimique.		Imitation.
26.	Sentiment religieux.		Veneration.
27.	Fermeté, constance, persévérance.		Firmness.

NAMES AND ORDER OF THE ORGANS,

ACCORDING TO THE CLASSIFICATION IN THE FIRST AND SECOND EDITIONS OF THIS WORK.

ORDER I.—FEELINGS.

Genus I.—PROPENSITIES.

1. Amativeness.
2. Philoprogenitiveness,
3. Concentrativeness.
4. Adhesiveness.
5. Combativeness:

6. Destructiveness.
   Appetite for Food
7. Constructiveness.
8. Acquisitiveness.
9. Secretiveness.

Genus II.—SENTIMENTS.

1. Sentiments common to Man and Lower Animals.

10. Self-Esteem.
11. Love of Approbation.

12. Cautiousness.
13. Benevolence.

2. Sentiments proper to Man.

14. Veneration.
15. Hope.
16. Ideality.

Wonder.
17. Conscientiousness.
18. Firmness.

ORDER II.—INTELLECTUAL FACULTIES.

Genus I.—EXTERNAL SENSES.

Feeling or Touch.
Taste.
Smell.

Hearing.
Sight.

Genus II.—INTELLECTUAL FACULTIES WHICH PERCEIVE EXISTENCE.

19. Individuality.
    Upper Individuality.
    Lower Individuality.
20. Form.

21. Size.
22. Weight.
23. Colouring.

Genus III.—INTELLECTUAL FACULTIES WHICH PERCEIVE THE RELATIONS OF EXTERNAL OBJECTS.

24. Locality.
25. Order.
26. Time.

27. Number.
28. Tune.
29. Language.

Genus IV.—REFLECTING FACULTIES.

30. Comparison.
31. Causality.

32. Wit.
33. Imitation.

No. IV.

Text, page 448.

DOCUMENTS laid before the Right Honourable Lord Glenelg, Secretary for the Colonies.

REPRESENTATION sent by SIR GEORGE S. MACKENZIE, Bart., to the Right Honourable LORD GLENELG, Secretary for the Colonies—in reference to convicts sent to New South Wales. February, 1836.

THE recent atrocities that have occurred in New South Wales are proofs that there is mismanagement somewhere, and that caution is indispensable for the future. But the manner in which that caution is to be exercised involves questions of much importance, perhaps of difficulty. It is, however, obvious that caution must, in the first place, be directed to the convicts. At present they are shipped off, and distributed to the settlers, without the least regard to their character or history. A man or a woman, found guilty of an offence. is deemed an object of punishment, whether the individual have spent previous life in crime, or has been driven by hard necessity unwillingly to commit it. To bring back a person condemned by the law to a course of industrious and honest habits, by means suited to the natural character and dispositions, is a thing never thought of. Punishment is most ignorantly deemed a universal panacea for criminal propensities, and degradation is esteemed the fitting means to restore a human being to self-respect, and to inspire an inclination toward good conduct. Such ideas, though they lead to practice that has for ages been condemned by its results, arise out of ignorance of the human constitution; and until that ignorance shall have been dispelled from the minds of rulers, and its place filled up by an extended view of the actual constitution of man, error must continue to direct their measures in the highway to evil. To be able to legislate for man implies a knowledge of man. But in the case which is now specially adverted to, that knowledge is entirely absent. In a short address, as this must be, it is impossible to point out the means of acquiring a knowledge of the true mental constitution of man. It can only be stated that it has been discovered, has been neglected, but still is making rapid progress in enlightening the British people.

It is, therefore, submitted,

1st, That when the importance of the colony of New South Wales is considered, convicts should not be sent out indiscriminately. Their individual history and characters should be inquired into, and the best selected for the colony, and the worst kept for discipline at home. But, with every exertion, the selection cannot be accurately made without the assistance of some one acquainted with the true Philosophy of Man.

2d, It is conceived that the management of convicts should be a special department of Colonial government, to which attention ought to be given. At home the convicts are not under the superintendence of the Colonial Secretary; but when they are to be sent abroad, he ought to have the power to select such as are the fittest for the purposes of his department, and in which there ought to be an officer qualified to investigate the history of convicts, and to select them on phrenological principles.

That such principles are the only secure grounds on which the treatment of convicts can be founded, proof may be demanded, and it is ready for production. I now unhesitatingly offer to your lordship the following public test of their truth and efficacy, your acceptance of which, whatever may be your notions of what the result will be, will at all events do you honour. It is this:

Let your lordship direct inquiry to be made into the circumstances which brought a given number of convicts to trial and punishment, and, if possible, let so much of their previous history as can be got at, be stated. Suppose the number be fifty. Let these be numbered, and their history, trial, and crimes inserted in a catalogue—of course I trust that this shall be as correctly done as possible, and in strict good faith. Let this catalogue be laid aside. On being informed that this has been done, I will go to London and take with me an experienced phrenologist. Let the convicts be brought to us one by one, and we will make a catalogue of our own in the same order, and in it we will enter what we deem the characters of the individuals to be, and what were the crimes they probably had committed; and likewise, we will state, in particular cases, what employment, or at least the nature of the employment, they had probably been engaged in, and that in which they are likely to be useful. The only information we will desire is, whether the individual has or has not been educated. We will examine the individuals in the presence of whom your lordship pleases. When our catalogue shall be completed, we will then request a meeting with your lordship and such friends as you may wish to be present, and that the catalogues shall be publicly compared; reserving only this, that, if any discrepancy of importance shall appear, we shall be permitted to question the subject, and to make inquiry into the case ourselves, attended by those who made the previous inquiry.

The result of such an experiment as this will, I venture to perdict, satisfy your lordship that means do exist for the selection of convicts for the colonies, and for their classification for treatment. I refer your lordship to the fact of my friend Mr. Combe having actually done what is here proposed at Newcastle, in October, 1835, as narrated in the Phrenological Journal, No. 46, page 624, of which a copy accompanies this communication. If I can prevail on you to make this experiment, I shall ever feel deeply grateful, and your lordship will gain the gratitude of all truly wise patriots, and lay the foundation of a benefit to your country such as no ruler has yet conferred either for effect or extent.

LETTER—Sir George Mackenzie.

To the Right Honourable Lord Glenelg, Secretary of State for the Colonial Department.

My Dear Lord,

I now put into your hands a number of certificates from eminent men, confirming my former assertion, that it is possible to classify convicts destined for our penal settlements, so that the colonists may be freed from the risk of having atrocious and incorrigible characters allotted to them, and the Colonial public from the evils arising out of the escape of such characters. Allow me to take this opportunity to state, that, unless punishment shall be awarded, not only proportionally to the crime committed, but to the actual moral character and degree of enlightenment of the culprit, it cannot have the effect expected from it, and may even render criminals more wicked. The power to punish ought to be in the hands of those who have charge of convicted persons, not to be positively inflicted under an imperative law, but to be used in the business of reform only when, to a sound and philosophical judgment, it may appear necessary. The experience of penal settlements teaches us that, while all criminals condemned to transportation are regarded as equally deserving of punishment, however various their degrees of guilt, they are not by any means equally prone to continue in a course of crime; for we find that some, with the certainty of the severest punishment before them, do continue to manifest propensity to crime, and do commit it whenever opportunity offers; while others become, of their own accord, sensible of their errors, (though condemned as equally guilty with the others,) exert themselves to overcome their evil tendencies, and arrive at the station of peaceable, industrious, and respectable members of the community. These facts, though perfectly and long notorious, have not attracted the notice of either the Colonial government or the government at home; but they prove incontestibly, that there is a very great difference in the moral constitution of criminals condemned to transportation, a fact of which philosophy may make the most important use. The horrid slaughter of the people on my sons' property would not have happened, I am bold enough to say, had the government been in possession of means to classify the convicts, and to keep the most atrocious in restraint at home, sending to New South Wales only the better disposed among them.

Such means I am now the instrument of placing in the hands of a liberal government, whether it shall be regarded or not; and your lordship, I trust, will not think me tedious, while I very briefly set before you the general facts which have brought men of philosophical understanding and habits of investigation to perceive that a discovery of the true mental constitution of man has been made, and that it furnishes us with an all-powerful means to improve our race—and that the more rapidly, if those in whose hands the government of our country is placed will only listen to facts, look at their verification, and attend to philosophical induction from them.

Your lordship must be aware of the fact, that, independently of rank, education, or wealth, men differ from each other very widely in the amount and kind of their intellectual power, in moral-feeling, and in their tendencies to indulge their propensities. It is too well known that titled, intelligent, wealthy blackguards exist, guilty of the grossest violation of moral law, while they contrive to escape the penalties of statutes, which, however, occasionally reach their enormities. That such are rather encouraged by what is called high society is notorious; and surely a titled gambler, or cheat, or seducer, cannot be reckoned less guilty than a poor, ignorant wretch, who steals perhaps to sustain life, and not from a depraved propensity. It is, however, to the fact of difference of character and talent among men of all stations of society to which I anxiously desire your lordship's attention. This difference must clearly be the effect of something. There have been philosophers who taught that man is a tabula rasa, on which we may stamp what talent and what character we please. This, however, has long been demonstrated, by thousands of facts of daily occurrence, to be a mere delusion. Differences in talent, intelligence, and moral character are now ascertained to be the effects of differences in organization. The brain has been long regarded by physiologists as the organ by which the mind is connected with the body, and by means of which the mental faculties are manifested. To this conclusion the result of a vast amount of observation and experiment has conducted them. After this fact had been universally admitted, a similar amount of observation and experiment led to the demonstration, by the celebrated Gall, of different portions of the brain being allotted to the power of manifesting different mental faculties. In those who exhibit the manifestation of any particular faculty strongly, the organ in the brain is proportionally large The differences of organization are, as the certificates which accompany this show, sufficient to indicate *externally* general dispositions, as they are proportioned among one another. Hence, we have the means of estimating, with something like precision, the actual natural characters of convicts, (as of all human beings,) so that we may at once determine the means best adapted for their reformation, or discover their incapacity of improvement, and their being proper subjects of continued restraint, in order to prevent their farther injuring society. It is this that, for the sake of the future prosperity of the Australian colonies, and the security and peace of the settlers, and also for the sake of exalting them in the scale of morality, I wish your lordship to put to the test of experiment for your own satisfaction. With however little merit it may have been acquired, I have some credit which is at stake with the result of the proposed experiment, and which your lordship, it is hoped, will not think I risk rashly in this matter. But it is not only my own philosophical credit, but that of those who have written these certificates, and of many thousands besides in every quarter of the globe. With such support on all sides of me, your lordship cannot wonder at the confidence with which I urge you toward fame of the most enduring kind—that of being a benefactor to your country. Attacks are still made on the science of Phrenology; but it is a science which its enemies have never, in a single instance, been found to have studied; and I freely confess the fact that, when I myself derided it, I knew nothing of it. Gross misrepresentations of fact, as well as wild unfounded assertion, have been brought to bear against it again and again, and have again and again been exposed. It is spreading its light far and wide, and reduced, in many instances, to most beneficial practice; and it will be a proud day for our country when the same government that has provided vigorously to reform our institutions, shall proceed in the true path to moral reform. There is a near prospect of education being conducted on the true principles of man's nature under national sanction; and I hope the time is not far distant when their influence on criminal legislation will be apparent. I cannot help calling your lordship's notice to the fact, that many among the most able and zealous propagators of the new philosophy were at one time scoffers against it, until brought to attend to it by a display of most striking facts, exhibited to them by the amiable and lamented Spurzheim.

I need not detain your lordship longer. To save you as much trouble as possible amid your important and onerous duties, I have had the certificates and this address printed; and, if your lordship will permit me to do so, I should be glad to publish them, that phrenologists may know that one of the earliest converts to their science in Great Britain has not lost an opportunity, at the end of twenty years, to exert himself in attempting to spread its benefits in a direction in which they will, if not now, at a future period certainly, be duly felt and appreciated; and also that the world may know, I fondly hope, that your lordship has been the first member of a liberal government who has had sufficient moral courage to do that which alone can satisfy a liberal man of the truth or falsehood of what is pressed on his notice by the best possible motives. And if, as thousands of the most talented men in Europe and America confidently anticipate, experience shall convince you, your lordship will at once perceive a source from which prosperity and happiness will flow in abundance over all our possessions. In the hands of enlightened governors, Phrenology will be an engine of unlimited improving power in perfecting human institutions, and bringing about universal good order, peace, prosperity and happiness.

Believe me, my dear lord, very truly yours,

G. S. MACKENZIE.

CERTIFICATES.

I. From Dr. WILLIAM WEIR, Lecturer on the Practice of Medicine, formerly Surgeon to the Royal Infirmary of Glasgow, and joint Editor of the Glasgow Medical Journal.

To the Right Hon. LORD GLENELG.

BUCHANAN-STREET, GLASGOW,
March 14, 1836.

MY LORD,

At the request of Sir. Geo. S. Mackenzie, Bart., and in reference to a correspondence which has passed between your lordship and that gentleman, concerning the evils which the colony of New South Wales suffers from desperate characters being sent out as convicts, and let to the settlers as servants, I beg leave to make the following statement :

I have paid much attention during the last twenty years, to human physiology in general, and to the science of Phrenology in particular, and have had many opportunities of comparing the form and size of the head in living individuals with their talents and mental character. I have also been in the constant practice of examining the skulls and casts from the heads of deceased persons, and comparing these with their known mental characters and their actions exhibited during life ; and I have found a constant and uniform connexion between the talents and natural dispositions, and the form and size of the head.

I have no hesitation, therefore, in stating it as my firm conviction, drawn from these sources, and from long study and observation, that the natural dispositions of man are indicated by the form and size of the brain, to such an extent as to render it quite possible for persons who have had practice in such manipulations, to distinguish during life men of desperate and dangerous tendencies from those of good dispositions.

I have the honour to be, my lord, your lordship's most obedient servant,

WILLIAM WEIR, M.D.

II. From ALEXANDER HOOD, Esq., Surgeon, Kilmarnock.

To the Right Hon. LORD GLENELG.

KILMARNOCK,
March 14, 1836

MY LORD,

I take the liberty of addressing your lordship in consequence of having received a letter on the part of Sir George S. Mackenzie, Bart., whose sons are settled in the colony of New South Wales, respecting the great evils which the colonists there sustain from desperate characters being sent out as convicts, and let out to the settlers as servants. Sir George suggests that Phrenology might be beneficially applied in pointing out the natural dispositions of convicts, and employed as a means of draughting from among them the most desperate and incorrigible characters, previous to transportation.

Having for many years devoted a considerable time to the study of Phrenology, and tested the truth of its principles by the most severe and conclusive experiments, the result has been a gradual, but thorough, belief in the truth of the doctrines which it promulgates, and that it is susceptible of being applied with much advantage to the community in the manner suggested by Sir George Mackenzie. My daily observation as a medical man confirms me in this belief, and I conceive that a skilful phrenologist is capable, by an examination of the human head, of detecting any defective or predominant intellectual faculty, moral feeling, or animal propensity, nearly with as much accuracy as a physician can discover the healthy or diseased condition of the heart, lungs, liver, or spine.

I have the honour to be, my lord, your lordship's most obedient humble servant,

ALEX. HOOD, Surgeon.

III. From RICHARD CARMICHAEL, Esq., M. R. I. A., Corresponding Member Royal Academy of Medicine of France, Honorary Member of several Medical Societies ; Consulting Surgeon of the Richmond Surgical Hospital, and Author of several works on Surgery.

To the Right Hon. LORD GLENELG,
Secretary for the Colonies, &c.; &c., &c.

RUTLAND-SQUARE, DUBLIN,
March 15, 1836.

MY LORD,

Having received a letter at the instance of Sir George Mackenzie, desiring to know whether it is my opinion and belief that "the natural dispositions are indicated by the form and size of the brain to such an extent as to render it quite possible, during life, to distinguish men of desperate and dangerous tendencies from those of good dispositions," and to lay such opinion before your lordship:

I have no hesitation in certifying that such is my belief, and that I consider this mode of discriminating persons of good from those of bad dispositions, may be most usefully employed for various purposes advantageous to society.

I have the honour to be your lordship's very obedient servant,

RICHARD CARMICHAEL.

IV. From EDWARD BARLOW, M.D., of the University of Edinburgh ; Member of the Royal College of Surgeons of Ireland ; Senior Physician to the Bath Hospital, and the Bath United Hospital ; Fellow of the Royal Medical and Chirurgical Society of London, &c., &c.

To the Right Hon. LORD GLENELG,
  Secretary to the Colonies, &c., &c., &c.

BATH, SYDNEY PLACE,
MY LORD, March 15, 1836.

At the desire of Sir George Mackenzie, I willingly offer my testimony in favour of the application of Phrenology to the examination of convicts, which he has suggested to your lordship. Deeply interested in the science, from a thorough conviction of its truth, I have, for upward of twenty years, watched its progress ; and I have no hesitation in expressing my firm belief, that all mental functions are dependent for the manifestations on the conformation of the brain ; and that the natural dispositions are indicated by its form and size to such an extent, as to render it quite possible, during life, to distinguish men of desperate and dangerous tendencies from those of good dispositions.

In early life, my lord, I, through ignorance and inconsiderateness, joined in the doubts respecting Phrenology that then prevailed ; and mine was afterward no sudden conversion resulting from raised imagination, but the clear conviction produced by calm and patient inquiry. The grounds of my present faith it would be out of place here to display ; but I may remark, that the application of Phrenology which Sir George Mackenzie now advocates, was actually and most successfully made ten years ago, in the examination, by Mr. De Ville, of London, of one hundred and forty-eight convicts, transported in the ship England to New South Wales, and that the safe completion of the voyage was owing to the information respecting individual character that Mr. De Ville had supplied. The facts here referred to are matter of public record, as they were reported officially to Dr. Burnett, by Mr. G. Thomson, the surgeon of the ship. The history of the voyage, as detailed by Mr. Thomson, is deposited in the Victualling-office.

I consider the truths of Phrenology to be as well established as are those of any other branch of natural science ; being throughout, not fanciful nor hypothetical assumptions, but rigid inductions from numerous and accurately observed facts. By such course of observation and reasoning alone can natural truths ever be developed ; by it has the philosophy of matter attained its present advancement ; and to it are we indebted for the only sound and rational philosophy of mind that has yet been produced, namely, that which Phrenology teaches. The applications of this science to the affairs of human life are sure to extend as its principles become known and appreciated ; and eventually they cannot fail to prove of the very highest importance to the welfare and happiness of the human race. The application of it which Sir George Mackenzie has proposed to your lordship, has my cordial approval, and the full sanction of my unbiassed judgment.

I have the honour to be, my lord, your lordship's faithful and obedient servant, E. BARLOW, M.D.

V. From Messrs ALEXANDER HOOD, JOHN CROOKS, and JOHN MILLER, Surgeons, and DR. ROBERT WALKER, Kilmarnock.

The Right Hon. LORD GLENELG.
MY LORD, KILMARNOCK, 16th March, 1836.

Our attention having been directed to Sir G. S. Mackenzie's communication to your lordship, respecting the applicability of Phrenology to the discri mination of the character of convicts transported to the British Colonies, we whose names are subscribed, beg, with all submission, to offer our united and unqualified testimony in corroboration of his opinion.

We are led to do so, my lord, from a decided conviction that Phrenology is the *true* science of the mind—that the natural dispositions are so accurately indicated by the form and size of the brain, as to render it perfectly practicable for properly qualified persons to distinguish, by examination of the head, individuals possessing such as are dangerous to the peace and safety of society from those who are differently constituted ; and farther, that the bringing the doctrines of Phrenology to bear, not only upon the matter in question, but our social institutions in general—upon education, and other means of *preventing* crime, as well as upon the *punishment* of it, and the proper disposal of the perpetrators—would, besides its being an important advance in philosophy be attended with great *practical* advantage to the community.

With the highest esteem for your lordship's public and private character we have the honour to be, my lord, your lordship's obedient humble servants,

ALEX. HOOD, Surgeon.
JOHN CROOKS, Surgeon.
JOHN MILLER, Surgeon.
ROBERT WALKER, M.D

VI. From ROBERT FERGUSON, Esq., M.P. for Haddingtonshire.
To GEORGE COMBE, Esq., Edinburgh.

18 PORTMAN-SQUARE
17th March, 1836.
MY DEAR SIR,
I have no hesitation in declaring it as my belief, that the science of Phrenology enables those who have made themselves master of it to decide on any prominent and marked mental faculty or propensity of an individual. And in more directly answering your circular, I think it would be attended with the greatest advantage to society, if the heads of such convicts who have been guilty of the crimes of murder and such atrocious acts, should be examined.

For it is certain, and can be proved from innumerable examples, that such an investigation, by practical persons, could easily pronounce whether they were likely to be incurable in their propensities, or whether other dispositions in their intellectual constitution might, if properly cultivated, restore them to the rank of respectable citizens.

The first should be prevented from having any intercourse with society, or hope of future freedom whatever.

I see many difficulties yet in having a Board for this important investigation ; but means might be fallen upon to be enabled to come to such conclusions as might guide to the necessary character of the punishment, for the future safety of society.

I remain very truly yours,   ROBERT FERGUSON.

VII. From JOHN FIFE, Esq., one of his Majesty's Justices of the Peace for the Borough of Newcastle-upon-Tyne, Member of the Royal College of Surgeons of London, Member of the Medico-Chirurgical Society of Manchester, and of the Royal Medical Society of Edinburgh, Lecturer on Surgery in the Newcastle School of Medicine, &c., &c., &c.

To the Right Honourable LORD GLENELG,
Secretary for the Colonies.

NEWCASTLE-UPON-TYNE
March 19th, 1836.
MY LORD,
Having received a communication from Mr. Combe, at the request of Sir George S. Mackenzie, Bart., stating your lordship's disinclination to select convicts for New South Wales by phrenological signs, and requesting me to express my opinion upon the proposal, accompanying the statement of such opinion by an account of my claims to moral influence and to some share of your lordship's attention, I hereby assert my conviction that the natural dispositions are indicated by the form and size of the brain to such an extent as to render it quite possible, during life, to distinguish men of desperate and dangerous tendencies from those of good dispositions.

With reference to my position as a professional man, I beg to refer your lordship to the representatives in Parliament of this town or of the adjacent counties.

I have the honour to be, my lord, your most obedient servant,

JOHN FIFE.

VIII. From Dr. W. C. ENGLEDUE, late President of the Royal Medical Society of Edinburgh, and Secretary to the Phrenological Society of Portsmouth.

To the Right Honourable LORD GLENELG,
Secretary for the Colonies, &c., &c., &c.

PORTSMOUTH, 24 SANDPORT TERRACE,
March 23d, 1836.

MY LORD,

Having been requested to state to your lordship my opinion regarding the subject of Sir George Mackenzie's communication, I do so with considerable pleasure, being convinced both of its benefit and *applicability*. On the latter point I can speak with some degree of certainty, having numerous opportunities of testing the truth and application of the science in that division of the Convict Establishment situated at Portsmouth. It would be impossible, in the present instance, either to enter into minutiæ or bring forward proofs; but I can assure your lordship that, as far as my experience extends, I unhesitatingly assert, that phrenologists can detect and choose from a body of criminals those of decidedly bad character, whom it would be almost impossible to retrieve, and those who, perhaps for some trivial offence, are doomed to associate with the former, and who could not only be retrieved, but, by care and better example, become valuable members of society.

This is a fact which has almost entirely escaped the observation of those legislating upon this important subject. Convicts are now almost indiscriminately embarked for the colonies, without any regard to natural dispositions, or the effects which examples produce. They are huddled together, good, bad, and indifferent; and, after disembarcation, portioned out to the settlers, too often, as incontrovertible evidence proves, to have recourse to, if not exceed, their former depredations.

Viewing these colonies as young communities, where it is desirable to assemble individuals of the best character, it cannot be right to inundate them with the worst of beings—those which a country, protected by the justice and vigour of its laws, found it impossible to control.

I could enlarge upon the ulterior effects likely to ensue upon a continuation of the present system, but the limits of a certificate forbid it.

After the preceding, I need hardly repeat that Sir G. Mackenzie's memorial meets with my most cordial approbation; and feeling assured that your lordship will bestow on it your serious consideration,

I have the honour to remain your lordship's most obedient servant,

(Signed)   W. C. ENGLEDUE, M.D.

IX. From Dr. JAMES INGLIS, M.R.C.S.E., and Soc. Ed. Med. Reg. Soc. Ed.; SAMUEL M'KEUR, Esq., Surgeon, Castle Douglas; the Rev. WILLIAM GLOVER, A.M., Minister of Crossmichael; Dr. JOHN COLVIN, Bengal Establishment, M.R.C.S., Lond. and Mem. Med. and Phys. Soc., Calcutta.

To the Right Honourable LORD GLENELG,
Secretary for the Colonies.

CASTLE DOUGLAS, KIRKCUDBRIGHT,
March 22d, 1836.

MY LORD,

If to the truth of Phrenology as a science based on observation, and borne out by facts, our testimony can be of any use, either regarding its propagation, or, through it, the furtherance of the common good of mankind, and the lessening of human crime and misery; we unhesitatingly give it as our opinion, that the *tendencies* of the mind as it exists in this world, to cause actions either virtuous or vicious, can be discovered by the cranial developement—and that, while this holds in *every* case, it does so with much more *evident* certainty in the man of a desperate and dangerous character—who, uneducated and unrestrained, has allowed for a length of time the lower feelings to reign over the higher faculties of his mind. Believing this, we consider that Sir George Mackenzie's proposition regarding the practical application of Phrenology in discriminating the natural dispositions of convicts, may become of the highest possible advantage to the proprietors and cultivators in the Australian colonies.

We have the honour to be, my lord, your obedient servants,

JAMES INGLIS,   SAMUEL McKEUR,
WILLIAM GLOVER,   JOHN COLVIN.

X. From S. HARE, Esq., Proprietor and Medical Attendant of the Retreat
for the Insane in Leeds.

To the Right Honourable LORD GLENELG,
     Secretary for the Colonies.

MY LORD,   LEEDS, 23d March, 1836.
Having received a communication to the purport that Sir G. S. Mackenzie had lately presented a memorial to your lordship, representing that " Phrenology might be beneficially applied in discriminating the natural dispositions of convicts before being chosen for transportation," and requesting my opinion on the subject, I gladly avail myself of the opportunity of stating to your lordship, that I have repeatedly ascertained the characters of individuals through the medium of the principles of Phrenology, and believe that very great advantages will result to the nation from a proper application of those principles in the classification of convicts, and the improvement of prison discipline generally.

Having occasion to employ a number of servants, I beg to be permitted to state, that I prefer choosing them by their temperaments and phrenological developements, to taking them on the characters given with them.

Ardently hoping that these views will ere long be made available, as regards the enactment of laws for the prevention and punishment of crime, both in our own and other countries, I have the honour to subscribe myself, my lord, your lordship's most obedient servant,   S. HARE.

XI. From DR. JAMES STEWART, (A,) Surgeon, Royal Navy, and Physician
Extraordinary to His Royal Highness the DUKE of SUSSEX.

The Right Honourable LORD GLENELG, &c., &c.

MY LORD,   PORTSMOUTH, 22d March, 1836.
For some years past I have paid much attention to the science of Phrenology, and I am firmly of opinion that the natural dispositions are indicated by the form and size of the brain to such an extent as to render it quite possible, during life, to distinguish men of desperate and dangerous tendencies from those of good dispositions.   JAS. STEWART, M.D.

XII. From DR. JAMES SCOTT, LL. B., Surgeon and Lecturer to the Royal
Hospital at Haslar; Licentiate of the Royal College of Physicians of London; Surgeon and Medical Superintendent of the Royal Naval Lunatic Asylum; President of the Hampshire Phrenological Society, &c., &c.

The Right Honourable LORD GLENELG, Principal Secretary
of State for his Majesty's Colonial Department, &c., &c., &c.

                                   ROYAL HOSPITAL AT HASLAR,
MY LORD,   22d March, 1836.
I have just received a circular letter from Mr. Combe, of Edinburgh, in consequence of a communication made to your lordship by Sir George Mackenzie respecting the allotment of convict servants to settlers in Van Diemen's Land, in which communication Sir George recommended to your lordship that convicts should be phrenologically examined previously to their being sent out of this country; and, as it appears that your lordship does not believe in the truth of Phrenology, Mr. Combe is desirous of laying before you as many certificates as he can procure from medical men regarding their opinion of the science, requesting me to state in what estimation I hold it.

I therefore beg to say, that, after having for many years viewed it unfavourably by the false light of prejudice, chiefly from having read a most illogical and witty, but virulent, attack on the system, published in the Edinburgh Review, now well known as the production of the late Dr. John Gordon, who assailed it anonymously with all the shafts of ridicule, my attention was powerfully arrested by attending a course of lectures on the subject by the late amiable and highly gifted Dr. Spurzheim, at Paris, and by another course of lectures delivered by Mr. Combe, in Edinburgh; and after some more years spent in careful study and observation, I became a sincere convert to the doctrines of Gall and Spurzheim.

I beg to assure your lordship that my conversion is the result of an honest and careful examination; and as I have been for nearly ten years the medical attendant of the lunatic asylum in this great hospital, my opportunities, at least of observing, have been great indeed; and a daily intercourse with the unfortunate individuals intrusted to my care and management (whose number has never been less than one hundred and thirty persons, and often many more) has firmly, because experimentally, convinced me that mental disorder and moral dilinquency can be rationally combated *only* by the application of Phrenology; and that the man who treats them on any other system will much oftener be disappointed, than he who studies the manifestations of mind, and traces effects to their secondary causes, by the almost infallible beacon of Phrenology.

On this subject I could add much; but, at present, I have rather to apologize to your lordship for having so long occupied your truly valuable time.

I have not yet published anything, except an Inaugural Dissertation on Pneumonia, and some medical and surgical cases in various periodical journals —which I mention only in compliance with a request made in Mr. Combe's circular above referred to; but I have a mass of facts and observations bearing upon practical points.

Permit me, my lord, to conclude, by assuring your lordship that, viewing you as a statesman whose acknowledged political talents and consistency shed an additional lustre over those virtues by which you are distinguished in private life, I have the honour to be, with profound respect, your lordship's most obedient humble servant, JAMES SCOTT.

XIII. From HEWETT COTTRELL WATSON, Esq., F.L.S., late President of the Royal Medical Society of Edinburgh; Author of the " Geography of British Plants," and other works.

To the Right Hon. LORD GLENELG,
Secretary for the Colonies.

THAMES DITTON, SURREY,
March 18*th*, 1836.

MY LORD,

At the request of Sir George Mackenzie, I have the honour to offer to your lordship my humble testimony in support of the science of Phrenology; being convinced, after several years of careful attention to the subject, that it is quite possible to determine the dispositions of men, by an inspection of their heads, with so much precision as to render a knowledge of Phrenology of the utmost importance to persons whose duties involve the care and management of criminals.

I have the honour to subscribe myself your lordship's most obedient and humble servant, HEWETT COTTRELL WATSON.

XIV. From SIR WILLIAM C. ELLIS, M.D., Superintendent of the Lunatic Asylum for the County of Middlesex, at Hanwell.

To the Right Hon. LORD GLENELG,
Secretary for the Colonies.

LUNATIC ASYLUM FOR THE
COUNTY OF MIDDLESEX,
19*th March*, 1836.

MY LORD,

I am requested by Mr. George Combe to address a letter to your lordship on the utility of Phrenology. I cannot for one moment hesitate to comply with his request, and to give my strongest testimonial that, after many years' experience, I am fully convinced the dispositions of man are indicated by the form and size of the brain, and to such an extent as to render it quite possible to distinguish men of desperate and dangerous tendencies from those of good dispositions. I have been the resident physician in this establishment, where we have upward of six hundred patients, for five years, and for thirteen years previous held a similar situation in Yorkshire, where we had two hundred and fifty. If it was necessary, I could mention a great variety of cases in the treatment of which I have found the little knowledge I possess of this interesting science of the greatest utility; and I am fully persuaded that, when it is more known, and acted upon, very great advantages will result to society

have the honour to be, my lord, your lordship's very obedient and humble
servant,   WM. C. ELLIS.

Note by Sir W. C. Ellis to Mr. Combe.—"Sir William is quite convinced
that it is unnecessary for him to inform Mr. Combe himself, that, residing
amid 600 lunatics, no day passes over in which the truth of Phrenology is
not exemplified."

XV. From DR. DISNEY ALEXANDER, late one of the Physicians to the Wakefield Dispensary and the Pauper Lunatic Asylum, Lecturer on Phrenology,
Author of an Essay on the best Means of preserving Health, of a Treatise
on the Croup, and of Lectures on the Internal Evidences of Christianity.

LUPSET COTTAGE, WAKEFIELD,
March 30th, 1836.

I hereby certify, that I consider it as proved beyond all reasonable contradiction, that "the natural dispositions are indicated by the form and size of the
brain, to such an extent as to render it quite possible, during life, to distinguish men of desperate and dangerous tendencies from those of good dispositions ;" and that Phrenology might be beneficially applied in discriminating
the natural dispositions of convicts before their being chosen for transportation.

DISNEY ALEXANDER, M.D.

XVI. From GEORGE MARTELL, Esq., Member of the College of Surgeons,
London, Surgeon to the Jail of Portsmouth, and Senior Surgeon to the Dispensary, &c., &c.

To the Right Hon. LORD GLENELG,
    Secretary for the Colonies, &c., &c., &c.

MY LORD,   PORTSMOUTH, *March 24th*, 1836.
Having had frequent opportunities of seeing the examination of individuals
phrenologically, I am of opinion that their dispositions may be fully known by
external configuration, size, &c.; and that such examinations would greatly
facilitate the classification of prisoners.

I remain your lordship's most obedient servant,

GEORGE MARTELL.

XVII. From JAMES SIMPSON, Esq., Advocate, City Assessor of Edinburgh,
and Author of " Necessity of Popular Education as a National Object."

The Right Hon. LORD GLENELG
MY LORD,   EDINBURGH, 25th *March*, 1836.
Referring to the experiment on phrenological principles proposed by Sir
George Mackenzie, for ascertaining the distinctive characters of a number of
convicts, I respectfully beg to offer to your lordship my humble opinion, founded on fifteen years' experience, that the test will be entirely satisfactory, and
show that character may be ascertained from cerebral developement, as indicated externally on the head.

I have the honour to be, my lord, your obedient servant,

JAMES SIMPSON.

XVIII. From HENRY WITHAM, Esq., of Lartington, Yorkshire, Member of the
Geological Society of London, and Royal Society of Edinburgh, &c., &c.;
and Author of a work on " The Internal Structure of Fossil Vegetables."

The Right Hon. LORD GLENELG.
MY LORD,   LARTINGTON Co., YORK, 27th *March*, 1836.
With reference to Sir George Mackenzie's suggestion, that the heads of convicts should be examined, with a view to ascertaining their natural dispositions
before transporting them to New South Wales, I beg leave to certify, that, from
having studied the science of Phrenology during several years of my residence
in Edinburgh, I am convinced of the practicability of accomplishing, by means
of Phrenology, the object in view. The differences in point of form between
the brains of men of naturally good and men of naturally bad dispositions, are
so palpable, even during life, that a moderate share of attention is sufficient to
discover them.

I have the honour to be, my lord, your obedient humble servant,

HENRY THORNTON MAIRE WITHAM

XIX. From DR. FRANCIS FARQUHARSON, Fellow of the Royal College of Surgeons of Edinburgh, and Vice-President of the Phrenological Society.

The Right Hon. LORD GLENELG.

MY LORD, EDINBURGH, 28*th March*, 1836.

In consequence of a communication from Sir G. S. Mackenzie, Bart., regarding the phrenological experiment proposed by him in a memorial to your lordship, I beg to state my firm conviction that it would completely answer the object in view. This belief does not rest upon theoretical grounds, but is the result of an extensive experience during the last ten or twelve years.

I have the honour to be, my lord, your faithful and obedient servant,

FRAs. FARQUHARSON, M.D.

XX. From DR. S. E. HIRSCHFELD, Bremen.

To the Right Hon. LORD GLENELG, &c., &c.

BREMEN, 22*d March*, 1836.

I hereby certify, that I consider it practicable to distinguish between men of desperately bad dispositions and men of good dispositions, by examining their heads during life ; and that such knowledge may be successfully employed in discriminating dangerous criminals from those who are not destructive or blood-thirsty.

I state this opinion from my own experience.

S. ED. HIRSCHFELD, M.D.

XXI. From the SURGEONS to the NEWCASTLE INFIRMARY, and Fifteen other Gentlemen of that Town.

To the Right Hon. LORD GLENELG, Secretary for the Colonies.

NEWCASTLE-ON-TYNE, 17*th March*, 1836.

We, the undersigned, take the liberty of addressing this communication to your lordship, for the purpose of explaining that we are of opinion that the natural dispositions are indicated by the form and size of the brain, to such an extent as to render it possible, during life, to distinguish men of desperate and dangerous tendencies from those of ordinary dispositions : That, if this opinion be correct, it would be highly beneficial to use this means of discriminating the natural dispositions of convicts sent out to the colonies, and many of whom are let to the cultivators as servants : That, with the view of ascertaining the possibility of employing these means with advantage, it would be very desirable that a given number of convicts of marked characters be selected, and their dispositions put down in writing by the governor and chaplain of one or two of the public penitentiaries or prisons ; that their heads be submitted to the inspection of two or three experienced phrenologists, who should write down inferences concerning their mental qualities ; and that, in presence of competent judges, the two written accounts should be compared : That, if the result should be found to accord with the opinion we have taken the liberty of laying before your lordship, we conceive a valuable service might be conferred on the colonists, by paying attention to this means of regulating the selection of servants.

JOHN BAIRD, Senior Surgeon to the Newcastle Infirmary.

T. M. GREENHOW, Surgeon to the Newcastle Infirmary, &c.

WM. HUTTON, F.G.S., Member of the Geological Society of France, &c., &c., and Secretary of the Natural History Society of Northumberland, Durham, and Newcastle-on-Tyne.

JNo. BUDDLE, V.P. of the Natural History Society of Newcastle-upon-Tyne, F.G S., &c.

ROBt. WM. SWAN.

J. CARGILL, M.D.

WILLIAM MORRISON, Member of the Royal College of Surgeons of London, &c.

ANTHy. NICHOL.

WILLIAM NEIHAM, Member of the Royal College of Surgeons, London, of the Royal Medical Society, Edinburgh, &c., &c., &c.

JOHN THOMSON, C.M., Member of the University of Glasgow.

D. MACKINTOSH, Surgeon to the Newcastle Lunatic Asylum, &c.

J. C. BRUCE, A.M.

ROBERT CURRIE.
JOHN FENWICK, Alderman of Newcastle-upon-Tyne.
R. B. BOWMAN.
M. H. RANKIN, Solicitor, Newcastle, Author of " Present State of
Representation in England and Wales."
WM. CARGILL.

XXII. From W. A. F. BROWNE, Esq., Medical Superintendent of Montrose
Lunatic Asylum.

MONTROSE, *March* 15th, 1836.

I hereby certify, on soul and conscience, that I have been acquainted with
the principles of Phrenology for upward of ten years ; that, from proofs based
upon physiology and observation, I believe these to be a true exposition of the
laws and phenomena of the human mind ; that, during the whole of the period
mentioned, I have acted on these principles, applied them practically in the
ordinary concerns of life, in determining and analysing the characters of all
individuals with whom I became acquainted or connected, and that I have
derived the greatest benefit from the assistance thus obtained. But, although
the utility of the science be most apparent in the discrimination of the good
from the bad, those of virtuous and intellectual capabilities from the brutal and
imbecile, it is not confined to this. In the exercise of my profession I have
been enabled, by the aid of Phrenology, to be of essential service in directing
the education of the young as a protection against nervous disease, and in removing or alleviating the various forms assumed by insanity in the mature.
For several years I have devoted myself to the study of mental diseases and
the care of the insane. During my studies at Salpétrière, Charenton, &c , in
Paris, I was able to derive great additional information from my previous
knowledge of Phrenology ; and now that I have been intrusted with a large
asylum, I am inclined to attribute any little success that may have attended
my efforts to meliorate the condition of those confided to my charge, to the
same cause. I may add, that I was *converted* from a confidence in the accuracy of the philosophy of the schools to a belief in Phrenology ; that I did not
adopt its doctrines on the authority of my teachers, but tested their truth by
repeated experiment ; that I have since taught them to large bodies of my
countrymen, and feel fully convinced that, until they be recognised and acted
upon generally, no just conclusion can be drawn as to human character, nor
as to the administration of punishments for the improvement or rewards for the
encouragement of mankind.   W. A. F. BROWNE, Surgeon.

XXIII. From DR. C. OTTO, Professor of Materia Medica and Forensic
Medicine in the University of Copenhagen ; Physician to the Civil Penitentiary ; Member of the Royal Board of Health, the Royal Medical Society
at Copenhagen, and thirteen other Medical Societies abroad ; Editor of the
Danish medical journal " Bibliothek for Lieger," &c., &c.

To the Right Hon. LORD GLENELG,
Secretary for the Colonies, &c., &c.

COPENHAGEN, *March* 25th, 1836.

I hereby certify, that, from my own observation and experience, I consider
it quite possible to distinguish men of strong animal propensities, who, when
left uncontrolled by authority, or when excited by intoxication, would be dangerous to society, from men of mild dispositions, by examining their heads
during life. I farther certify, that I have practically applied this method of
distinguishing the natural dispositions of men, and found it uniformly successful.   C. OTTO, M.D.

Dr. Otto adds, in a letter to Mr. Combe, inclosing the above : " As a physician to the penitentiary, nobody can be more convinced than I of the truth
of the certificate. In fact, I reap the greatest advantage from Phrenology in
treating the criminals in my hospital, as I vary my moral treatment of them
according to the form of their heads--some ones necessarily requiring severity,
others mildness ; and I have often, without any failure, told the inspector beforehand which criminal was to be considered as dangerous, and which one
might be trusted as quiet and benevolent. The examination of the organs of
Secretiveness and Conscientiousness aids me extremely much in detecting
simulations of diseases."

XXIV. From the Honourable Douglas Gordon Hallyburton, M.P. for Forfarshire, to George Combe, Esq.

My Dear Sir,   London, *March 26th*, 1830.

You will, I know, excuse my not having, four or five days ago, sent an acknowledgment of the favour of your letter of the 14th instant, covering a copy of your printed circular of the 10th, on the subject of Sir George Mackenzie's communications to Lord Glenelg respecting *Australian convicts*, and his lordship's remarks on the same,

I am afraid that, in asking *my* testimony on this phrenological question, yourself and Sir George attribute an importance to it, which it can scarcely deserve, as adding sensibility to the weight of phrenological authority, of which your circular must long since have put you in possession. However, if the attention which I have given to this most important and interesting science, during a period now of twenty years—the personal acquaintance I had with Drs. Gall and Spurzheim on the continent—the friendship with which our latter departed friend was pleased to honour me—and my having let slip no opportunity, whether in Paris, London, Edinburgh, or Glasgow, to derive pleasure and instruction from his writings, lectures, and private conversation —and, lastly, let me add, with no intention whatever to flatter, the instruction and improvement I have derived from your own writings, lectures, and conversation, combined with those of your brother, Dr. Andrew Combe—if these circumstances, all well known to you, should lead yourself or Sir George Mackenzie to believe that my authority upon this subject ought at least to carry some weight with it, then my testimony, such as it may be, is entirely at your service.

The point, I think, in your circular letter, upon which you desire the opinion of competent judges, is this—" Whether the natural dispositions are indicated by the form and size of the brain to such an extent as to render it quite possible, during life, to distinguish men of desperate and dangerous tendencies from those of good dispositions."

Before I give *my* answer to this question, allow me, dear sir, to prefix a few remarks. It is well known, I am sure, to us, that the skill of the well-instructed and *practised* phrenologist might safely be put to a much more severe test than any that is implied in the above question. Instead of taking the *extremes* of human character, he might be required to read and to discriminate among that intermediate class which makes up the great bulk of mankind in civilized life ; where the qualities of the *animal man* and the *moral and religious man* are mixed up together, in all sorts of proportions—the combination in nineteen cases out of twenty in civilized life (and in various *grades* of society) being such as to give rise to those *apparent* contradictions in men's characters which are perpetually obtruding themselves upon every one's notice ; so that it is no exaggeration to say, that the great mass of society whom one meets at every turn, including *all ranks*, spend their whole lives in a sort of *rotation* (palpable or more covert) of sinning and repenting—now obeying all or any of their propensities—the animal man—now listening to—checked—brought up, by their moral and religious nature. *We* know how all this can be most satisfactorily explained by the demonstrated truths and doctrines of Phrenology. But, in truth, they are the same phenomena which are pointed at by moral and religious writers and preachers, (the latter too often in language unnecessarily quaint, and a misplaced adoption of Scriptural terms,) when they talk of men " walking after the flesh, or after the spirit,"—that " the *natural* man cannot please God," &c., &c., &c. All this, I take it, merely means that the lower part of man's nature, the animal, (which God and religion intended, and I doubt not have provided for the ultimate fulfilment of the intention,) should serve and obey the higher, the moral and spiritual part—takes the lead, and, instead of *serving*, presumes to dictate and domineer ; thus producing all the confusion and much of the misery of a true *servile war*. Now, I would ask you the question, Can the skilful phrenologist, in such *mixed* cases as I have described, point out, from an inspection of the brain, as indicated by the exterior head, the *character* of the individual ? I think you will answer *that he can*. At least he can enumerate the *forces* which are enlisted on either side, though, being no charlatan, and not pretending that he is a *prophet*, he will not venture to perdict what specific *action*, or *course of action* for a time, will result, under certain circumstances, from the antagonist motives which the man carries within him. In illustration of what I have hurriedly above been intending to say, I would ask you again, whether there are not *scores* of examples in all the *phrenological capitals* of Europe, where (let us take one example) parents have hesitatingly, tremblingly, half believing, half afraid, taken their children to be examined (for their characters, &c., &c., &c.) by the most reputed phrenologist they could hear of—submitting the heads of the little creatures to the eyes and fingers—the *wand* of the *conjurer*. If he be really an expert and well-instructed *conjurer*, he immediately detects the general outline of the children's (not infants') characters. But he goes much farther than this—he examines and *weighs*, he balances the *forces* of the different qualities, intellectual, moral, and animal; and in almost every instance (supposing him always to be a *good conjurer*) he fairly and fully delineates the *character*. So the poor parents *stand aghast*; propensities, sentiments, passions, virtues, and vices, which they vainly imagined could be known only to themselves or the immediate inmates of the house or the nursery, are brought to the surface under the wicked scrutiny of the phrenological *doctor*. The sequel of this proceeding very commonly is, that he is consulted by the anxious parents respecting the education, the general management, and ultimately the choice of *professions*, for the several children; and undoubtedly it would be well for the family if the counsels of a really *judicious* phrenological adviser, regarding the above-mentioned points, were attended to and acted upon. If the statements I have been making, and the opinion I have given respecting those classes (far removed from the two *extremes*) which make up the great mass of human society, be true, there can be no doubt how I must answer the query transcribed above from your circular letter. I consider it as proved to demonstration, that "the natural dispositions are indicated by the form and size of the brain to such an extent as to render it quite possible, during life, to distinguish men of desperate and dangerous tendencies from those of good dispositions."

I shall conclude this letter with a few observations, naturally arising out of the subject. We know that phrenological knowledge and skill have, in very many instances, been rendered most useful in the business of education, as respects both private families and public schools, where happily the masters or directors could avail themselves of such assistances, in conducting the moral and intellectual discipline of the pupils. We know farther, that medical science and art have been much indebted to Phrenology, in the case more especially of several institutions for the reception and treatment of patients labouring under various forms and degrees of mental alienation Of the latter, the instances of the Lancastrian Asylum, and that for the reception of paupers of the County of Middlesex, near the metropolis, at present occur to me, and I believe there are many similar examples both in England and Scotland. Can it be doubted, then, that Phrenology is capable of furnishing resources of equal magnitude, and to an extent not easily appreciated, in the classification of those unhappy persons whose crimes, in various degrees, have brought them under the dominion of criminal jurisprudence?

I might, my dear sir, have answered your letter much more laconically than I have done, and possibly an apology is due from me for having been too *diffuse*; but the subject is one in which I take a great interest, and I trust I shall be forgiven.

I remain, with much respect, yours faithfully,
                    D. G. HALLYBURTON, M.P.

XXV. From Dr. PATRICK NEILL, F.R.S.E. & F.L.S., London.

Right Hon. LORD GLENELG.

                              CANONMILLS COTTAGE,
MY LORD,   31st March, 1836.
In consequence of a suggestion by Sir George Mackenzie, I beg leave to mention to your lordship that, even before the first visit of Dr. Spurzheim to Edinburgh, I was satisfied that the leading doctrines of Gall were founded in truth, because the conviction was forced upon me by my own observations made before that visit: I mean that certain convolutions or portions of the brain are peculiarly the organs of certain faculties and propensities; that size is generally indicative of vigour; and that, in many cases, the relative use of the organs can be distinguished by external examination.

Knowing the powerful influence of surrounding society in encouraging or restraining, I have never given an opinion as to the probable actions of an educated individual, and indeed have uniformly declined examining heads among my friends, even when pressed to do so. But I have, on various occasions, been influenced by my private observations of developement, and can most conscientiously say that I have constantly seen more and more reason to trust, with confidence, to such observations. My abstaining from any public practice of Phrenology ought not, therefore, to lessen the weight of my testimony.

The organs of some faculties and propensities are much more easily recognised externally than those of others; and when they are *strongly* marked, no phrenologist (I would say no one who has ever attended to the subject, although no adept) can possibly be mistaken in drawing useful conclusions. In the case of convicts ordered for transportation, for example, he could undoubtedly point out the probably treacherous and the probably mischievous; so that, during the voyage, these might be more strictly guarded, and separated as much as possible from those who were likely to prove conscientious and benevolent; and, on arrival at their place of destination, that the former might be kept at work under public surveillance, and only the latter hired out to settlers.

To show that I ought not to be entirely unqualified for giving an opinion, your lordship will excuse me for mentioning that in my youth I studied for three years with a view to the medical profession; that I attended especially to Anatomy, and saw the human brain *dissected* by Monro secundus, and *developed* by Spurzheim, (for the latter scarcely used the scalpel;) that I have for upward of twenty years been Secretary to the Wernerian Natural History Society; and that I have, all my life, been attached to the study of natural history.

I am, my lord, your lordship's very obedient servant,   PAT. NEILL.

***

XXVI. From Dr. John Elliotson, F.R.S., President of the Royal Medical and Chirurgical, and of the London Phrenological Societies; Professor of the Principles and Practice of Medicine and of Clinical Medicine, and Dean of Faculty, in the University of London; Senior Physician of the North London Hospital; Fellow of the Royal College of Physicians of London, formerly Physician to St. Thomas's Hospital, and President of the Royal Medical Society of Edinburgh, &c., &c., &c.

Conduit-street, London,
To the Right Hon. Lord Glenelg.   April 7th, 1836.

Dr. Elliotson presents his compliments to Lord Glenelg, and begs to say that, at the desire of Sir George Mackenzie, he takes the liberty of communicating to his lordship his thorough conviction of the truth of Phrenology. He has not passed a day for the last twenty years, without bestowing at least some thought upon it; and the vast number of facts which he has witnessed, without any certain exception as to any of the chief points, convince him that it is as real a science as Astronomy or Chemistry. Nor does he know any branch of science more important, as it is interwoven with morals, religion, government, education, and, in short, with everything that regards human or brute nature.

***

XXVII. From Dr. John Scott, Fellow of the Royal College of Surgeons, Edinburgh.

To Sir George Mackenzie, Bart.   Edinburgh,
                                    31 Northumberland-street,
Dear Sir George,   10th April, 1836.

Having been informed by Mr. Combe of the nature of your correspondence with Lord Glenelg, relative to the proposed experiment as to a number of convicts to be sent to New South Wales, I have much satisfaction in stating my conviction of the very important advantages to be derived from it, in showing the practical usefulness of the science of Phrenology; of the truth of which I have been fully satisfied, from the period in which I studied it under Dr. Spurzheim in Paris, fifteen years since.

With sincere hopes that Lord Glenelg may be induced to accede to your benevolent wishes, I remain your obedient servant, JOHN SCOTT, M.D.

XXVIII. From JOSEPH VIMONT, M.D., of the Faculty of Paris, Honorary Member of the Phrenological Societies of Paris, London, Edinburgh, Boston, &c.

To the Right Hon. LORD GLENELG,
    Secretary for the Colonies.
MY LORD,   PARIS, 30th March, 1836.
    Sir G. S. Mackenzie, Bart., in applying to your lordship for permission to examine the heads of a number of convicts, in order to appreciate their mental faculties, might have dispensed with having recourse to the testimony of foreign physiologists. In the case proposed by the honourable baronet, the experiment cannot fail of being crowned with success, if made (as I do not doubt it will be) by phrenologists deeply versed in the theory and practice of Phrenology. The observations made by the founder of the science, Dr. Gall, in the prisons of Berlin and Spandau, those which have been repeated in all the civilized world, to which I may add those which I have made in three of the principal prisons of France, viz., Caen in Normandy, Bicêtre near Paris, and Melun twelve leagues from Paris, have convinced me that it is not only possible to appreciate the relation existing between the volume of the head and the energy of the mental faculties, but that one may still, by their examination, be able to establish among the convicts several classes, the discrimination of which would be very advantageous to society and for the convicts themselves. The work of Dr. Gall, the Phrenological Journal of Edinburgh, the large work which I have lately published, finally, the phrenological museums, abound with incontestible facts proving that the mental faculties of men may be appreciated in a healthy state by the examination of their heads. To deny the truth of those facts, is to put in doubt the existence of the best established phenomena.
    I have, my lord, the honour to be your humble servant,

                                                    J. VIMONT.

_____

XXIX. From DR. WILLIAM GREGORY, F.R.S.E., Fellow of the Royal College of Physicians of Edinburgh, Member, and formerly President, of the Royal Medical Society, Corresponding Member of the Société de Pharmacie and of the Phrenological Society of Paris, and Secretary to the Phrenological Society of Edinburgh.

To the Right Honourable
    LORD GLENELG, &c., &c., &c.
MY LORD,   EDINBURGH, 11th April, 1836.
    Having been requested to state my opinion of the proposition made to your lordship by Sir G. S. Mackenzie, Bart., in reference to a phrenological examination of convicts about to be transported, with a view to their classification according to their natural dispositions, so as to avoid many inconveniences to which their masters in the penal settlements are now liable, I beg to state to your lordship that, for some years past, I have studied the science of Phrenology, and have the firm conviction that, in the hands of properly qualified observers, this science affords the means of ascertaining with certainty the natural dispositions and talents of such individuals as possess healthy brains.
    My conviction is founded on a careful study of the works of the most distinguished phrenologists, confirmed by the repeated examination of several extensive collections, in which are deposited the heads of very numerous criminals of all shades of character. I have also had very frequent opportunities of witnessing the facility and certainty with which character is discriminated by practised phrenologists in the case of living persons. It would be superfluous to point out the advantage of such a power, especially in the case of convicts.
    Your lordship's official avocations have probably prevented you from devoting your attention to the subject of Phrenology; but I may be permitted to express my belief that your lordship could not examine it carefully without being satisfied of its importance to mankind, as being the only consistent and practical philosophy of mind yet offered to the world.
    And when those who have carefully studied Phrenology, and become convinced of its truth, offer, as Sir G. S. Mackenzie has done, to put it to a practical test, which may be highly advantageous, and cannot possibly be

hurtful, it is the duty of your lordship, and of all those who have-it in their power to authorize the experiment, not to pass by or neglect a proposition so important, merely for want of that faith in the truth of Phrenology which no one can reasonably expect to possess, unless he have made himself acquainted with the science, and the evidence on which it is supported.

I have the honour to be, my lord, your lordship's most obedient servant,

WILLIAM GREGORY.

XXX. From Dr. ROBERT HUNTER, Professor of Anatomy, &c., in the Andersonian University, Glasgow.

To the Right Hon. LORD GLENELG.

MY LORD, GLASGOW, 11th April, 1836.

At the request of Mr. Combe, I have taken the liberty of addressing your lordship on the subject of Phrenology. For more than thirteen years I have paid some attention to the subject, and I beg to state, that the more deeply I investigate it, the more I am convinced in the truth of the science. I have examined it in connexion with the anatomy of the brain, and find it beautifully to harmonize. I have tested the truth of it on numerous individuals, whose characters it unfolded with accuracy and precision. For the last ten years I have taught Phrenology publicly in connexion with Anatomy and Physiology, and have no hesitation in stating that, in my opinion, it is a science founded on truth, and capable of being applied to many practical and useful purposes.

I have the honour to be, my lord, your lordship's very obedient servant,

ROBERT HUNTER, M.D.

XXXI. From ROBERT MACNISH, Esq., Member of the Faculty of Physicians and Surgeons of Glasgow, and Author of " The Philosophy of Sleep," &c.

To the Right Hon. LORD GLENELG.

MY LORD, GLASGOW, 11th April, 1836.

Having been applied to by Sir George Mackenzie, to state my opinion with respect to the possibility of detecting the characters of convicts by an examination of their heads on phrenological principles, I have no hesitation in declaring my perfect conviction that, in very many cases, the dispositions of these individuals may, by such a process, be discriminated with remarkable accuracy.

The form of head possessed by all dangerous and inveterate criminals is peculiar. There is an enormous mass of brain behind the ear, and a comparatively small portion in the frontal and coronal regions. Such a conformation always characterizes the worst class of malefactors; and wherever it exists we find an excessive tendency to crime. This fact I have had ample opportunities of verifying; and, indeed, no person who compares criminal heads with those of persons whose natural dispositions are toward virtue, can entertain the slightest doubt upon the subject.

I have the honour to be, my lord, your lordship's most obedient servant,

R. MACNISH.

XXXII. From RICHARD POOLE, M.D., Fellow and Joint Librarian of the Royal College of Physicians of Edinburgh; Author of various Articles in Periodical Journals and the Encyclopædia Edinensis—as Language, Philology, Mathematics, Mind, Philosophy, and Education, the last of which has been republished separately.

EDINBURGH, 12th April, 1836.

During several years, actively employed, I have found the principles of Phrenology available in very important duties—more especially in the treatment of Insanity, to which, as a professional man, my attention has been greatly directed; and I feel warranted, by long study and observation, in maintaining the opinion, that it is practicable to distinguish individuals having naturally very low and dangerous characters from others who are naturally well constituted and disposed—by examining and comparing their heads during -life, according to the principles of Phrenology.

RICHD. POOLE.

XXXIII. From CHARLES MACLAREN, Esq., Editor of the *Scotsman.*

To the Right Honourable LORD GLENELG,
   Secretary for the Colonies, &c.   EDINBURGH, 9th April, 1836

In reference to a correspondence between your lordship and Sir George Mackenzie, on the propriety of subjecting convicts to a phrenological examination, I beg leave to state, that I have paid some attention to Phrenology during the last seven years—that I believe its principles to be substantially true, and am convinced that the natural dispositions are indicated by the form and size of the brain to such an extent as to render it quite possible, during life, to distinguish men of desperate and dangerous tendencies from those of good dispositions.

Perhaps I may be allowed to add, that my first impressions in favour of Phrenology were produced by the explanation which its doctrines afford of the phenomena of mind, and the relations of man to the external world—an explanation more clear, consistent, and satisfactory, in my opinion, than can be derived from any system of philosophy now taught in this country.

I have the honour to be, my lord, your lordship's most obedient servant,
                 CHARLES MACLAREN,
               Editor of the Scotsman Newspaper.

XXXIV. From WILLIAM WILDSMITH, Esq., Member of the Royal College of Surgeons, London, and of the Council of the Leeds Philosophical and Literary Society; and Author of "An Inquiry concerning the relative Connexion which subsists between the Mind and the Brain."

To the Right Honourable LORD GLENELG.
MY LORD,   LEEDS, April 16th, 1836.

Having been informed that Sir G. S. Mackenzie, Bart., has made proposals for applying the tests afforded by Phrenology for the discrimination of individual character in convicts subject to transportation, with a view to their better classification, I beg most sincerely to add my humble testimony in approval of the plan suggested, with the confident assurance that the result will prove highly valuable to the parties most interested, and prove to the entire satisfaction of any who may doubt it, the practical application of Phrenology to the common affairs of life. Nothing, I am convinced, can be easier than the discrimination of the naturally and the casually vicious by the aid of Phrenology; and, in the case in question, I doubt not of its complete success if a trial be permitted.

I have the honour to remain, your lordship's most obedient servant,
                       WM. WILDSMITH.

XXXV. From Mr. WILLIAM BREBNER, Governor of the County and City
                Bridewell, Glasgow.

To GEORGE COMBE, Esq.

                     COUNTY AND CITY BRIDEWELL,
DEAR SIR,   Glasgow, 18th April, 1836.

About two thousand persons pass through this establishment yearly, and I have had the charge for upward of twenty-five years. During that period, and long before I heard anything of Phrenology, I was often struck with the extraordinary shape of the heads of most of the criminals. When Dr. Spurzheim visited this city I attended his lectures; and although I do not yet pretend to have anything like phrenological knowledge, I have no hesitation in saying, that the most notoriously bad characters have a conformation of head very different from those of the common run of mankind.

I may be allowed to add, that Dr. Spurzheim, yourself, and many others, professing and believing in the science, who have visited this prison, have described the character, and told the leading propensities of the inmates, in a very remarkable manner. I am, &c.,
                 WILLIAM BREBNER, Governor.

XXXVI. From H. A. GALBRAITH, Esq., Surgeon to the Glasgow Royal Lunatic Asylum.

                GLASGOW ROYAL LUNATIC ASYLUM,
MY DEAR SIR,   19th April, 1836.

Situated as I am in the midst of a wide field for observation, more particularly in regard to disordered mental manifestations, I have been for several years past led to compare these with the phrenological developement of the individuals in whom they appeared; and from the result of numerous and well-marked instances, which have not only been known to me during a state of morbid activity, but from authentic accounts of the previous mental indications, I have not the least hesitation in declaring my firm belief in the general doctrines of Phrenology.

It gives me much pleasure on this occasion, and is but an act of justice, to add, that, when Dr. Spurzheim was in this city some years ago, he visited this institution, and examined several of the most remarkable heads of the then inmates; and, had I been more careless and skeptical than I really was, the correctness and facility with which his inductions were made from cerebral developement must have arrested my attention, and convinced me of the reality of the science he professed. It is also no small confirmation of the doctrine as well as proof of its utility, that exactly the same conclusions were drawn from the same heads, when submitted to you a few days ago at your visit here. It therefore can be no chance or random opinion, but one evidently founded on a common principle, that enables the experienced phrenologist, at the distance of years, not only correctly to delineate the character and conduct of individuals, but strictly to coincide with that formerly given. Although I have as yet no pretension to the name of an experienced phrenologist, yet be assured my faith in the verity of Phrenology is such as to induce me to cultivate it with more care than I have hitherto done, and it will be no small gratification if I can add with benefit to those under my charge. I am, my dear sir, yours very faithfully, H. A. GALBRAITH.

GEORGE COMBE, Esq.

XXXVII. From GEORGE SALMOND, Esq., Procurator-Fiscal of Lanarkshire; WALTER MOIR, Esq., Sheriff Substitute of Lanarkshire; and MR. D. M'COLL, Governor of Glasgow Jail.

To GEORGE COMBE, Esq.

SHERIFF'S CHAMBERS,
DEAR SIR, GLASGOW, 22d April, 1836.

A few days ago Sheriff Moir having told me of your intention to examine phrenologically some of the criminals in Glasgow jail, I expressed a wish to be present, in order that I might have a practical test of the system, and ascertain whether your inferences of character should accord with what was privately and officially known of them by myself; and Mr. Moir having kindly honoured me with an introduction to you, I had the gratification of attending your examination of a number of these persons, and of hearing with sincere interest the accurate conclusions you arrived at on each of them.

Never before having witnessed any such operation, and expecting that, after a tedious process of examination, taking notes, and comparing and calculating results, something of an oracular generality of character should be announced, I was very much pleased to observe that, while your examination of each did not average a minute, you instantly, and without hesitation, stated the character, not generally, but with specialties of feelings and propensities, surprisingly justified by what I knew of them; and being aware that you had no access to them, nor means of knowing them previously, as they were taken at the moment promiscuously from numbers of the other criminals, I was at once led to a conviction of the truth of the science, and to see eminent advantages of such knowledge to society, and more immediately in regard to criminal jurisprudence and practice.

Of the instances of your observation, suffer me to mention a few, which at the time occurred to me as peculiarly convincing.

The first man you examined you pronounced " a thief, reckless and dangerous, who, for instance, if under the influence of liquor, would not hesitate to murder or destroy all around him." Now this fellow has for years travelled about the country with a horse and cart, selling salt and trifling articles, and has acquired the character of a masterful thief, and just now stands indicted with a cruel assault on, and highway robbery of, a poor labourer, of all his hard earnings last harvest.

Another, you observed, had "a fine intellect, and was likely to have been guilty of swindling ;" and the accuracy of this observation on *a painter*, who is indicted for *falsehood, fraud, and wilful imposition, or swindling*, is self-evident.

A third, whom you pronounced " a cunning, *daring,* and decided thief," is an incorrigible thief, who for years has, in the most concealed and adroit manner, headed a gang of housebreakers, and is at present indicted for high-way robbery, committed by his savagely knocking down with a heavy stob a poor man, who was almost killed on the spot. Private information leads me to understand that he has been party to another crime, of a nature equally, if not more, *daring* and *cruel.*

A fourth you described to be " a depraved and most dangerous man." He is a crony of the man last noticed ; has long been a thief, and one of the most noted corpse-lifters while subjects were bought by the medical schools ; and he is said to have been concerned with the man last mentioned in the atrocious crime alluded to at the close of the observations as to him.

A fifth, whom you judged to be " a sly thief, who, with a meek and specious aspect, possessed daring even to cruelty," is a fellow who is by trade a thief, adroit and cunning, and who has often attacked and escaped from the officers of justice. He lately stole, in broad daylight, on the streets of Glasgow, a handkerchief from a gentleman's pocket, and ran off. Being promptly pursued, he, as a decoy, threw from him the napkin. Being after a race overtaken, he leaped into a dung-pit, whither the gentleman could not think of following him, but stood watching him till the police he sent for arrived. On this the fellow, in the most fawning manner, craved sympathy; and finding this did not move the gentleman's purpose, he suddenly sprung out, and, on being seized, made a desperate struggle, bit severely the gentleman's hand, and, by his force and violence, might soon have got off had not the police arrived.

The accuracy of your conclusions has deeply impressed me with the benefit which would accrue to society from the application of such investigations toward the better classification of criminals confined before and after trial, to the selection and treatment of convicts, and even to the more certain identification of such criminals as might effect their escape from justice or confinement.

With much regard, believe me to be, dear sir, yours most faithfully,

GEO. SALMOND,
Pror.-Fiscal of Lanarkshire.

We were present on the occasion of Mr. Combe's visit to the jail of Glasgow, and testify to the perfect accuracy of Mr. Salmond's representation of what happened. Mr. Combe's inferences of the characters of such prisoners as he then examined were most accurate, and never could have been the result of chance.

WALTER MOIR,
Sheriff Subst. of Lanarkshire.
D. M'COLL,
Governor of Glasgow Jail.

XXXVIII. Account of Mr. Combe's Phrenological Examination of Heads of Criminals in the Jail of Newcastle-on-Tyne, October, 1835. Extracted from the Phrenological Journal, vol. ix., p. 524.

On Wednesday, 28th October, Mr. Combe, accompanied by the following gentleman, visited the jail : viz., Dr. George Fife, assistant surgeon to the jail, (who is not a phrenologist ;) Benjamin Sorsbie, Esq., alderman ; Dr. D. B. White ; Mr. T. M. Greenhow, surgeon ; Mr. John Baird, surgeon ; Mr. George C. Atkinson ; Mr. Edward Richardson ; Mr. Thomas Richardson ; Mr. Wm. Hutton, and Captain Hooke.

Mr. Combe mentioned, that his chief object was to show to such of the gentlemen present as had attended his lectures in Newcastle, the reality of the fact which he had frequently stated, that there is a marked difference between the developement of the brain in men of virtuous dispositions, and its developement in decidedly vicious characters, such as criminals usually are ; and that the moral organs generally are larger, in proportion to the organs of the animal propensities, in the former than in the latter : and he requested that a few striking cases of crime might be presented, and that the heads of the criminals should be compared with those of any of the gentlemen present indiscriminately.

This was done; and Dr. Fife suggested that it would be farther desirable that Mr. Combe should write down his own remarks on the cases, before any account of them was given, while he himself should, at the other side of the table, write down an account of their characters according to his knowledge of them; and that the two statements should then be compared. Mr. Combe agreed to this request; and the following individuals were examined:

P. S., aged about 20.—*Mr. Combe* wrote as follows: Anterior lobe well developed; intellectual powers are considerable. The organ of Imitation is large, also Secretiveness; Acquisitiveness is rather large. The most defective organ is Conscientiousness. Benevolence and Veneration are large. The lower animal organs are not inordinate. My inference is, that this boy is not accused of violence; his dispositions are not ferocious, nor cruel, nor violent: he has a talent for deception, and a desire for property not regulated by justice. His desire may have appeared in swindling or theft. It is most probable that he has swindled: he has the combination which contributes to the talents of an actor.—*Dr. Fife's Remarks*: A confirmed thief; he has been twice convicted of theft. He has never shown brutality; but he has no sense of honesty. He has frequently attempted to impose on Dr. Fife; he has considerable talent; he attended school, and is quick and apt; he has a talent for imitation.

T. S., aged 18.—*Mr. Combe* wrote: Destructiveness is very large; Combativeness, Secretiveness, and Acquisitiveness are large; intellectual organs fairly developed; Amativeness is large; Conscientiousness rather moderate; Benevolence is full, and Veneration rather large. This boy is considerably different from the last. He is more violent in his dispositions; he has probably been committed for assault connected with women. He has also large Secretiveness and Acquisitiveness, and may have stolen, although I think this less probable. He has fair intellectual talents, and is an improveable subject.—*Dr. Fife's Remarks*: Crime, rape * * * *. No striking features in his general character; mild disposition; has never shown actual vice.

J. W., aged 73.—*Mr. Combe's Observations*: The coronal region is very defective; Veneration and Firmness are the best developed; but all are deficient. Cautiousness is enormously large; the organ of Combativeness is considerable, and Amativeness is large; there are no other leading organs of the propensities inordinate in developement; the intellect is very moderate. I would have expected to find this case in a lunatic asylum rather than in a jail; and I cannot fix upon any particular feature of crime. His moral dispositions generally are very defective; but he has much caution. Except in connexion with his Amativeness and Combativeness, I cannot specify the precise crime of which he has been convicted. Great deficiency in the moral organs is the characteristic feature, which leaves the lower propensities to act without control.—*Dr. Fife's Remarks*: A thief; void of every principle of honesty; obstinate; insolent; ungrateful for any kindness. In short, one of the most depraved characters with which I have been acquainted.—*Note by Mr. Combe*: I have long maintained, that where the moral organs are extremely deficient, as in this case, the individual is a moral lunatic, and ought to be treated as such. Individuals in whom one organ is so large as Cautiousness is in this old man, and in whom the regulating organs of the moral sentiments are so deficient, are liable to fall into insanity, if strongly excited, owing to the disproportion in the cerebral organs. It is common to meet with such cases in lunatic asylums; and as the criminal law has gone on punishing this individual during a long life, (for he has been twice transported,) and met with no success in reclaiming him, but left him in jail, under sentence for theft, at seventy years of age, I consider these facts a strong confirmation of my opinion that he ought to have been treated as a moral patient from the first.

XXXIX. From Dr. John Mackintosh, Surgeon to the Ordnance Department in North Britain; Lecturer on the Principles of Pathology and Practice of Physic; Fellow of the Royal College of Surgeons of Edinburgh; Member of the Medico-Chirurgical and Wernerian Natural History Societies of Edinburgh, Montreal, Heidelberg, and Brussels.

To George Combe, Esq.

My Dear Sir,   Edinburgh, *27th April*, 1836.
In reply to your letter of the 16th March, requesting me to state whether the

---

* The particular observations are not proper for publication.

natural dispositions are indicated by the size and form of the brain, so as to render it possible, during life, to distinguish men of desperate and dangerous tendencies from those of good dispositions, I have much pleasure in being able to offer my unqualified testimony as to the fact.

I was formerly not only an unbeliever in Phrenology, but a determined scoffer, and my conversion was slowly produced by the occurrence of individual cases that were accidentally brought before me; and I would now risk all I possess upon the general results drawn from the examination of the heads of one hundred convicts, by qualified persons I could name.

It would be well for society in the countries to which convicts are sent, if the plan proposed by Sir George Mackenzie, to the Right Honourable Lord Glenelg, were adopted. If any expense be occasioned by the investigation, I shall willingly contribute a share, because the interests of science will be advanced, and a great service will be rendered to the unfortunate convicts themselves.

I may add, that a great revolution has taken place within these few years, not only in this country, but also on the continent, in favour of phrenological doctrines; the number of opponents has diminished, and the disciples have increased in a remarkable manner; so much so, that in Paris there is scarcely an illustrious name connected with Medicine, or any of the sciences, that is not found enrolled in the list of Members of the Phrenological Society. You may make whatever use you please of this letter; and with much respect toward you, for the great share you have had in advancing our knowledge of the true science of mind, and placing it on a wider and more substantial basis,

I am, my dear sir, yours very faithfully,

JOHN MACKINTOSH, M.D.

XL. Certificate from HENRY MARSH, Esq., M B., M.I.R.A., one of the Physicians to Steven's Hospital, Consulting Physician to the Dublin General Hospital, St. Vincent's Hospital, and the Institution for the Diseases of Children; ROBERT HARRISON, Esq., M.D., M.R.I.A., Professor of Anatomy and Physiology, Royal College of Surgeons in Ireland; RICHARD TONSON EVANSON, Esq., M.D., M.R.I.A., Professor of the Practice of Physic, Royal College of Surgeons in Ireland; JAMES ARMSTRONG, D.D., M.R.I.A.; FRANCIS WHITE, Esq., President of the Royal College of Surgeons in Ireland; W. F. MONTGOMERY, Esq., M.D., Professor of Midwifery to the King and Queen's College of Physicians in Ireland; WM. W. CAMPBELL, Esq., M.R.I.A., Demonstrator of Anatomy to the College of Surgeons in Ireland, Resident Assistant Physician to the Dublin Lying-in Hospital; ANDREW BOURNE, Esq., Barrister; THOMAS EDWARD BEATTY, Esq., M.D., late Professor of Medical Jurisprudence; Royal College of Surgeons in Ireland; ARTHUR EDWARD GAYER, Esq., LL.D., Barrister; ANDREW CARMICHAEL, Esq., M.R.I.A.; JOHN HOUSTON, Esq., M.D., Curator of the Museum, Royal College of Surgeons, Ireland, Surgeon to the City Dublin Hospital, Surgeon to the Charter Schools of Ireland, and to the Deaf and Dumb Institution for Ireland; H. MAUNSELL, Esq., M.D., Professor of Midwifery to the Royal College of Surgeons in Ireland, and Member of the Medical Society of Leipzic.

DUBLIN, *March* 25*th*, 1836.

We, the undersigned, declare our belief, from what we know or have seen of the science of Phrenology, "that the natural dispositions are indicated by the size and form of the brain to such an extent as to render it quite possible, during life, to distinguish men of desperate tendencies from those of good dispositions; and we feel no hesitation in recommending, that trial should be made of the experiment proposed by Sir George Mackenzie, to prove the possibility of this application of Phrenology.

We conceive that, in affording this opportunity for putting publicly to the test the degree of accuracy to which Phrenology has been brought, as a scientific method of determining character, and so discriminating between the natural dispositions of criminals, the secretary for the colonies will but act the part an enlightened statesman, willing to keep pace with the advance of knowledge, to do justice to science, and afford the government opportunity for availing itself of all aid to be derived from the lights of philosophy, in fulfilling the arduous and responsible duties connected with criminal legislation.

HENRY MARSH.	ANDREW BOURNE.
ROBERT HARRISON.	THOMAS EDWd. BEATTY.
RICHARD TONSON EVANSON.	ARTHUR EDWd. GAYER.
JAMES ARMSTRONG.	ANDREW CARMICHAEL.
FRANCIS WHITE.	JOHN HOUSTON.
W. F. MONTGOMERY.	H. MAUNSELL.
WM. W. CAMPBELL.	

XLI. From his grace the ARCHBISHOP of DUBLIN.

I am fully convinced that the proposed phrenological experiment of Sir G. Mackenzie, Bart., is amply entitled to a fair trial.

RD. DUBLIN.

LII. From the PROVOST of TRINITY COLLEGE,

PROVOST HOUSE, *April 18th*, 1836.

I am decidedly of opinion that the experiment proposed by Sir Geo. Mackenzie should be made, especially when I consider that it can be made without difficulty or expense.

BAR. LLOYD, Provost T.C.D.

XLIII. From H. LLOYD, Esq., F.T.C.D., Professor of Natural Philosophy, Dublin.

TRINITY COLLEGE, *April 8th*, 1836.

Having seen a paper signed by Mr. Combe, relating to a phrenological experiment proposed by Sir George Mackenzie, I am of opinion that such experiment is deserving of a trial. H. LLOYD.

XLIV. From MOUNTIFORT LONGFIELD. Esq., F.T.C.D., Whayleaw, Professor of Political Economy.

I have been informed of the experiment proposed by Sir G. Mackenzie, and am of opinion that very important results may be obtained, if the state will, in that manner, lend its assistance to make the science of Phrenology available for purposes of public utility. I am altogether unacquainted with the details of phrenological practice; but, from what I have read upon the subject, I am convinced that the science is founded on true principles, and that to the writers on Phrenology we owe much of the light that has been thrown upon the philosophy of the human mind. Their metaphysics appear to me in general correct, with as small a proportion of error as could be expected on works written upon a subject which has not yet been made a branch of public education, nor converted into a source of profit to individuals.
MOUNTIFORT LONGFIELD.

XLV. From PHILIP CRAMPTON, Esq., Surgeon-General, Dublin.

DUBLIN, *April 12th*, 1836.

I am of opinion that the experiment proposed by Sir Geo. Mackenzie, with a view to ascertain whether or not "the natural dispositions are indicated by the form and size of the brain," is worthy of a trial.
PHILIP CRAMPTON.

XLVI. From AR. JACOB, Esq., M.D., Professor of Anatomy, Royal College of Surgeons, Dublin.

DUBLIN, *April 27th*, 1836.

I have not paid sufficient attention to the study of Phrenology to justify me in giving a decided opinion respecting its value, or the importance of its results; but I cannot hesitate to say, that such a case has been made out, (to prove "that the natural dispositions are indicated by the from and size of the brain to such an extent as to render it quite possible, during life, to distinguish men of desperate and dangerous tendencies from those of good disposition,") as warrants the experiment proposed by Sir G. Mackenzie.
AR. JACOB.

43

INDEX.

ABERNETHY, Mr., quoted on the connexion of the mind with the brain, 30.

Absolute size of a cerebral organ no criterion of the predominance of the faculty attached to it, 95.

Abuses of the faculties, what, 350.

Acquisitiveness, organ of, its situation, 165. History of its discovery, 167. Large in thieves, 167. Its disease, 172.

—— a primitive propensity, 166. Not treated of by the metaphysicians generally, ib. Admitted by Lord Kames, ib. Gives rise to avarice, 167. Not in itself base or sordid, 169. Its uses, ib. Its existence disputed by Mr. Owen, ib. Its effects modified by Self-Esteem, 170. Gives rise to a tendency to steal, 171. Manifested by the lower animals, 173. Remarks on, 480.

Acrel, case of diseased Acquisitiveness from, 172, 477.

Actions, why they cannot be predicted by the aid of Phrenology, 415.

Activity of mind distinguished from power, 98, 403. Influenced by temperament, 100, 351. Combination of faculties favourable to, 100.

Actors have large organs of Secretiveness and Imitation, 162, 261. Walks in which they are most successful, dependent on the combination of their faculties, 262. Ideality necessary to tragic actors, 244.

Adaptation of parts of the creation proves the existence of God, 348. Adaptation of the external world to the intellectual faculties of man, 349.

Addison, nature of his genius, 402.

Adhesiveness, one of the propensities, 130. Situation and discovery of its organ, ib. Its effects on the character, ib. Generally stronger in women than in men, 131. Distinguishable from Benevolence, 132. Gives rise to society, ib. Very strong in the dog and other animals, ib. Its disease, ib. Its natural language, 133. Remarks on, 479.

Admiration, love of, 189.

Affections, 477.

Affective faculties, 105 Modes of their action, 350. Are not the exclusive sources of emotions, 478.

Africans, character of the, 421. Their superstition, 434. Their sentiment of truth weak, 224.

Aikin, Dr., on love of life, 156.

Ainslie, Sir Whitelaw, case of a

large organ of Number reported by, 304.

Akenside's description of the sentiment of Wonder, 235.

Albert the Great, his division of the head into regions, 40.

Alderson, Dr., of Hull, his cases of spectral illusion, 358.

Alexander, Dr. Disney, his testimony in favour of Phrenology, 492.

Alexander VI., Pope, his head, 181, 215, 406.

Algebra, talent for, 304.

Alimentiveness, or organ of the appetite for food, 151. Views entertained respecting it, by Dr. Hoppe, ib., Dr. Crook, 153, and Dr. Spurzheim, ib. Cases of its disease, 154. Views of MM. Ombros and Theodore Pentelithe, 155. Appears to be the seat of hunger and thirst, 155, 272, 479, Its comparative developement in the French, Germans, and Spaniards, 442.

Allan, Mr. Thomas, mineralogist, his large organ of Form, 282.

Allegorical style, 336.

Almsgiving not the only manifestation of Benevolence, 202.

Amativeness, 107, 479. History of the discovery of its organ, 108. Gives rise to the sexual feeling, ib. Its influence in society, 110. Its abuses, 111. Its effects in combination, 406.

American Indians, their Secretiveness, Love of Approbation, and Firmness large, 164, 190, 216. Their sense of truth weak, 224. Their unimprovable nature, 421, 430. Character and skulls of the North American Indians, 429. Engraving of the skull of one, ib.

Analogies, perception of, 335.

Anatomists, objection that they universally disbelieve Phrenology answered, 454.

Anatomy does not reveal vital functions of organs dissected, 56. Anatomy of the brain, 72; of the skull, 79. Anatomical researches of Dr. Gall, 62, 451.

Angelo, Michael, his large Constructiveness, &c., 177, 341. Engraving of his head, 277.

Anger, a manifestation of Destructiveness, 146.

Animal magnetism, 371.

Animals, the lower, brains of, 42, 47, 97. Relation between their intelligence, and the depth and number of their cerebral convolutions, 77. Accurate comparison of their brains can

tained, 85. Its effects on the manifestation of the faculty, 399.

—— one of the perceptive faculties, 284.

Skull, never supposed to be the cause of different talents, 61. Accommodates itself to the size and form of the brain, 79. Its plates not parallel in heads of some animals, 206. Effects of temperament on its texture, 436.

S. L., Miss, curious case of spectral illusions, 287, 359.

Socrates, his great forehead, 346. His demon, 230. Believed in the existence of God, 342.

Speech, faculty of, not the result of the sense of hearing, 273. Fluency of, increased by practice, 395.

Spurzheim, Dr. J. G., birth and death of, 62, 475. Quoted on idiocy, 45. Engraving of his skull, 51. Warmth of his temper, 95. His classification of the faculties, 105, 477. His visit to Mr. Milne's workshop in Edinburgh, 176. On the perception of resemblance and difference, 253. On the cause of *single* impressions being communicated to the mind by *double* organs of senses, 270. On the anatomy of the nervous system, 451, *note*. His merits and discoveries, 474.

Stewart, Mr. Dugald, on the unimportance of determining the nature and essence of the mind with reference to the study of its phenomena, 70. Admits a moral sense, 219. Does not treat of wonder, 237. His theory of the origin of the pleasure derived from tragedy, 351. On the production of new principles of action by the association of ideas, 382. On the difference of the talents and dispositions of nations, 420. Admits more faculties than the phrenologists, 449.

Satures of the skull, 80.

Sympathy, analysis of, 390,

Tacitus, his style characterized by Concentrativeness, 126.

Tardy, murderer, 143, 144, 163.

Tasso believed that he saw and conversed with spirits, 230.

Temperaments indicate to a certain extent the constitutional qualities of the brain, 48. Modify the effects of Ideality, 244. Their effects on the activity of the faculties, 351. Nervous and sanguine, conduce to refinement, 380.

Time, one of the intellectual faculties, 313.

Tragedy, origin of the pleasure of from, 351.

Tune, one of the intellectual faculties, 316.

Uncle Toby, character of, 135.

Veneration, sentiment of, 208. Its effects in combination, 407. Weak in the French, 441. Remarks on, 497.

Vimont, Dr., his testimony in favour of Phrenology, 498.

Virtue, different theories of, given by the metaphysicians, 218.

Visions, sources of belief in, and liability to see, 230, 237, 358.

Vitellius, head of, 89, 143, 406.

Voltaire, an infidel, though his Veneration was large, 207. Believed in the existence of God, 343.

Washington, 407.

Watson, Mr. Hewett, on the writings of Sheridan and Pope, 310, *note*. His work on the Statistics of Phrenology, 454. His testimony in favour of Phrenology, 491.

Weight, a perceptive faculty, 285. Necessary to harp-playing, 317.

Welsh, Rev. David, on the singleness of the mind, 103. His views of the faculty of Concentrativeness, 121.

Wilson, James, a blind man, his organs of Colouring small, 297.

Wit, difficulty of its definition, 249. Case of its morbid excitement, 363.

Wonder, organ of, its situation, 230.

Wordsworth strongly manifests Philoprogenitiveness, 113. Errors of taste in his poetry, 397.

THE END.

Lightning Source UK Ltd.
Milton Keynes UK
UKHW052257191118
332599UK00025B/1261/P